BOTTOM LINE YEAR BOOK

1998

BY THE EDITORS OF

Bottom Line
PERSONAL

Copyright © 1998 by Boardroom® Inc.

10   9   8   7   6   5   4   3   2   1

All rights reserved. No part of this book may be reproduced in any form or by any means without written permission from the publisher.

Boardroom® Classics publishes the advice of expert authorities in many fields. The use of a book is not a substitute for legal, accounting or other professional services. Consult a competent professional for answers to your specific questions.

Library of Congress Cataloging in Publication Data
Main entry under title:

Bottom Line Yearbook 1998

   1. Life skills—United States.   I. Bottom line personal.
ISBN 0-88723-161-6

Boardroom® Classics is a registered trademark of Boardroom®, Inc.
55 Railroad Avenue, Greenwich, CT 06830

Printed in the United States of America

Contents

5 • INSURANCE SAVVY

6 • TAX SMARTS

7 • YOUR BUSINESS AND CAREER MOVES

8 • THE WINNING EDGE

9 • INVESTMENT SAVVY

14 • NUTRITION, FITNESS AND EXERCISE

15 • VERY, VERY SMART EDUCATION

16 • CONSUMER SAVVY

17 • YOUR CAR

18 • SELF-DEFENSE

19 • TECHNOLOGY 1998

20 • NATURAL HEALING BASICS

1

Your Health and Your Well-Being

Dr. Dean Ornish's Program for Reversing Heart Disease

Dean Ornish, MD
Preventive Medicine Research Institute

Bypass surgery, angioplasty and drugs may be lifesaving in a crisis but do not address the underlying *causes* of heart disease. It's like mopping up the floor around an overflowing sink without also turning off the faucet.

You can often make yourself feel better both physically and emotionally while opening the arteries in your heart.

People don't have to develop heart disease: In countries like China, where the diet is composed primarily of vegetables, heart disease is almost as rare as malaria is here in the US. If we implement what we know about diet and lifestyle, we can prevent 95% of the cases of heart disease that occur in this country.

In a study conducted in the early 1990s, we divided 48 patients with severe coronary heart disease into two groups, with one group making comprehensive lifestyle changes that affected diet, activity levels, relationships and spirituality.

The other group's patients made only moderate changes in their diet and activity levels. After one year, 82% of the patients who made the comprehensive lifestyle changes demonstrated some reversal of their coronary artery blockages.

After four years: There was even more reversal. And most people felt better, too… more energetic, more positive and less stressed.

In contrast, the patients in the "moderate change" group got worse and worse on average over time.

Lesson: Moderate changes in diet and activity alone are not usually enough to stop even the progression of heart disease, whereas more comprehensive changes often can begin to *reverse* it.

Good news: "Am I going to live longer or is it just going to seem longer?" You can make

1

comprehensive lifestyle changes to increase your joy of living, not out of fear of dying…

●**Big changes are often easier to make than small ones.** Because you usually feel so much better, so quickly, the choices become clearer.

●**Health information is important but not always sufficient** to motivate lasting changes in behavior. You need to work at a deeper level.

●**Learn how to rediscover inner sources of peace and well-being.**

Working with your doctor, try introducing the following components of what I call the "Opening Your Heart" program into your life…

YOGA AND MEDITATION

Peace—and stress—begin in your mind. Although we tend to think of some situations as being inherently stressful, emotional stress is more a function of how you *react* to it. How you react, in turn, is a function of your perception. For example, the father driving a car may say, "Darn, we have to wait for the train to go by!" Yet the son may say, "Oh, boy, we get to watch a train!"

The Opening Your Heart program includes a series of yoga-based stretches, meditation, breathing exercises and visualization techniques that can help lengthen your fuse. Also these techniques can help quiet down your mind and body, allowing you to experience an inner sense of peace, which will help you to achieve healing within and greater intimacy in your relationships.

How to begin: Deep breathing is a simple, effective stress management technique you can do anytime, anyplace. And, by focusing on your breathing, you can get yourself into a meditative state.

First, exhale completely through your nose. Then, place your right hand on your chest and your left hand on your abdomen and begin a progressive inhalation that begins in your abdomen.

Fill your abdominal area with air, then fill your lower chest with air and continue inhaling until you feel your collarbone rising. To exhale, slowly repeat the same process in reverse, from top to bottom, taking a bit longer to exhale.

If you get dizzy, return your breathing to normal.

SHARING AND OPENNESS

Altruism, compassion and forgiveness—opening your heart to others—can be powerful ways of healing the isolation that often leads to stress, suffering and illness. When we share ourselves with others, we feel freer.

Getting started: Create or join a support group that feels safe enough for you to let down your emotional walls and show your true self. Find a way to help others in ways that are comfortable for you. Learn to express yourself sincerely with people you love, using nonjudgmental "I feel" statements.

THE REVERSAL DIET

Reducing dietary fat to 30% is not enough to stop even the progression of heart disease in the majority of people, whereas a 10% fat diet may help to *reverse* it. Also, rates of breast cancer, colon cancer, lymphoma, osteoporosis, diabetes, hypertension and obesity are substantially higher in people who eat a meat-based diet than in vegetarians.

So, even if you don't have a heart problem, you may still want to follow the Reversal Diet, which is a low-fat, vegetarian diet that…

●Has less than 10% of its calories from fat.

●Excludes all oils and animal products except nonfat milk, yogurt and egg whites.

●Excludes other foods high in saturated fat such as nuts and seeds.

●Is high in fiber.

●Allows—but does not encourage—less than two ounces of alcohol per day.

●Excludes caffeine and other stimulants.

●Allows moderate use of salt and sugar.

●Is not restricted in calories.

QUIT SMOKING

Quitting smoking has long-term health benefits, like reducing your risk of lung disease and cancer. But quitting is also very good for your heart. It has been estimated that 30% of deaths from heart disease are attributable to smoking. If you already have heart disease, quitting smoking decreases for most smokers the frequency and severity of chest pain almost immediately.

EXERCISE

In our research, we chose walking as the preferred exercise, since it provides the most health benefits for the lowest risk of injury or sudden cardiac death.

Walking 30 minutes each day or an hour every other day is the *minimum* amount of exercise recommended in the Opening Your Heart program.

If your doctor agrees, you can do more, but remember—consistency is more important than intensity.

Dean Ornish, MD, president and director of the non-profit Preventive Medicine Research Institute in Sausalito, CA. Dr. Ornish is a professor of medicine at the School of Medicine, University of California, San Francisco, and an attending physician at California Pacific Medical Center. He is the author of four best-selling books, including his most recent, *Everyday Cooking with Dr. Dean Ornish.* HarperCollins.

It's Never Too Late To Start Taking Care Of Your Heart

Harvey B. Simon, MD
Massachusetts General Hospital

Some people mistakenly believe that if they've had bad health habits all their lives, it won't help to change now. But you can prevent—and in some cases even *reverse*—damage to your heart…no matter how old you are. And since heart disease is the number-one killer in America, it makes sense to do what you can to prevent it.

THE BIG FOUR OF HEART HEALTH

Lifestyle changes in four major areas can make an enormous difference in preventing heart disease.

●**Stop smoking.** Smoking is the greatest risk factor for coronary artery disease. It increases the chance of heart attack by 250%.

Even if you've smoked for years, stopping will improve your health. Heart rate and blood pressure will return to normal, and risk of heart attack will fall until it matches that of people who never smoked.

●**Reduce blood cholesterol.** The most effective way to do this is by watching your diet. It isn't just cholesterol in food that raises

levels in blood, it's the saturated fat—which stimulates the body to produce its *own* harmful cholesterol.

The average American gets 37% of daily calories from fat. A much healthier level would be 30% or 15%.

Helpful: New food labeling regulations make it easier to estimate the fat content of the foods you eat.

Cholesterol reduction diet: Cut back on desserts and animal products—eggs, meat, cheese and other whole dairy products. Increase your intake of vegetables, dried beans and whole grains. Switch from using butter or margarine in cooking to small amounts of olive oil, which appears to reduce "bad" LDL cholesterol but not "good" HDL cholesterol.

●**Exercise.** Exercise benefits the cardiovascular system by strengthening the heart muscle, improving circulation, raising HDL and lowering LDL cholesterol, reducing stress on arteries and fighting the formation of blood clots.

The best kind of exercise for the heart is aerobic—the kind that uses large muscle groups for prolonged periods of time.

Examples: Biking, swimming, fast walking, running, stair climbing, rowing, racquet sports.

You're exerting yourself at the right level if you work up a sweat but don't feel out of breath. Any amount of exercise is helpful—even an hour a week. But you'll reap greater benefits if you work up to a total of at least three to four hours a week.

●**Lower your blood pressure.** One-fourth of American adults—and half of those over age 60—have high blood pressure, also known as hypertension. High blood pressure strains the heart muscle and damages the arterial wall, making people with hypertension more than twice as likely as others to have heart attacks.

The best way to lower blood pressure is to get the correct amount of minerals in your diet…

●**Reduce sodium.** Aim for less than 1,500 milligrams of sodium per day. Check food labels for sodium content. Sodium comes in many guises—the familiar table salt, as well as baking powder, baking soda, monosodium glutamate and soy sauce. Snack foods and processed foods tend to be especially high in sodium.

●**Increase potassium and calcium.** Many fresh fruits and vegetables are rich in potassium, including bananas, dates, oranges, cantaloupe, apples, raisins, potatoes, winter squash, lima beans, beets and broccoli. Healthful calcium-rich foods include skim milk, broccoli, spinach, fish and soybean products—particularly tofu.

OTHER WAYS TO HELP YOUR HEART

In addition to these four basic lifestyle changes for heart health, research suggests several other behaviors that may help to prevent heart disease…

●**Take aspirin.** Aspirin reduces blood clotting and has been shown to lower risk of a second heart attack. It's possible that aspirin may help to prevent a first heart attack as well.

Recommended dose: One baby aspirin a day, or one adult aspirin tablet every other day.

Caution: Check with your doctor before taking aspirin regularly. People who have ulcers, excessive bleeding or who are on other medications may need to avoid aspirin.

●**Eat fiber.** Numerous studies suggest that water-soluble fiber—the kind found in oat bran and also barley, prunes, beans and other legumes—reduces LDL cholesterol in the blood.

●**Eat fish.** Two to three servings of fish per week can reduce heart disease risk by about 40%. *Exception:* Avoid shellfish, which is high in cholesterol.

Fish contains omega-3 fatty acids, which lower LDL and raise HDL, and may also reduce blood clotting and inflammation in the arterial walls.

●**Avoid secondhand cigarette smoke.** "Passive" smoking is thought to cause up to 35,000 deaths from heart attack in the US each year. At highest risk are people who live with someone who smokes or who work in smoke-filled environments. Try to reduce exposure as much as possible—ask smokers to consider *your* safety…or even leave the room when someone is smoking, if you must.

●**Take antioxidant vitamins.** There's some evidence that vitamins C, E and beta-carotene —which seem to fight the dangerous effects of unstable molecules in the body called free radicals—lower the risk of heart disease.

If you take supplements, stick to moderate doses—1,000 milligrams of vitamin C, 400 international units of vitamin E and 10,000 international units of beta-carotene.

Caution: One study found that smokers who took beta-carotene supplements had a higher rate of death from lung cancer—so until further research is done, smokers should probably avoid these supplements.

●**Learn to cope with stress.** The link between emotional strain and heart disease is difficult to prove. But if you're prone to anxiety or depression, learn more about stress-fighters—yoga, meditation, deep breathing or psychotherapy. You will be helping your heart —and you'll certainly enjoy life more.

Harvey B. Simon, MD, practices internal medicine and preventive cardiology at Massachusetts General Hospital in Boston. He is on the faculties of Harvard Medical School and the Massachusetts Institute of Technology and is a founding member of the Harvard Cardiovascular Health Center. He is also author of Conquering Heart Disease. Little, Brown.

Heart Attack Prevention

Heart patients who took a daily vitamin E supplement that contained natural *alphatocopherol* suffered 75% fewer heart attacks than those who took a placebo.

Morris Brown, MD, professor of medicine, University of Cambridge, Cambridge, England. His three-year study of 2,002 heart patients was published in The Lancet, 42 Bedford Square, London WC1B 35L, England.

Saving Your Heart Without Bypass Surgery…without Angioplasty

John A. McDougall, MD
St. Helena Hospital

For anyone with heart disease—even for anyone *at risk* for heart disease—it may seem as if time is running out.

But having treated thousands of heart patients in my clinic over the past 10 years, I know that there *is* time to recover cardiovascular health in nine out of 10 cases. This can usually be accomplished *without* angioplasty or bypass surgery.

Anyone eager to prevent or cure heart disease must learn to avoid fatty foods and other dietary "poisons."

I'm often asked, "How often can I eat steak and eggs without hurting my heart?" I reply, "How often can you smoke without any ill effects on your body?"

The only honest answer to both questions is *never.*

DRAMATIC CHANGES ARE POSSIBLE

Most of the people who participate in my two-week program are seriously ill. Many have already had a heart attack. Others are taking medication for chest pain (angina) or high blood pressure.

By the time they leave our clinic, most have significantly lowered their cholesterol and blood pressure…and stopped taking medicine. The vast majority go on to live full lives.

This remarkable transformation involves three simple steps…

● **Eliminate *all* excess fat from your diet.** That means substituting fruits, vegetables and grains for red meat, chicken, dairy products, eggs, oils, cakes and candies and refined and processed foods.

● **Get daily aerobic exercise.** Patients in my program are required to walk for at least 30 minutes a day.

● **Learn to manage psychological stress**— without resorting to overeating or other self-destructive behavior. Massage, meditation and group discussion are all effective ways to do this.

THE SKINNY ON FAT

The typical American gets a whopping 40% of his daily calories in the form of fat. It's this fat that clogs the coronary arteries with the fatty streaks (plaques) that cause heart attack.

Dietary fat endangers your heart by…

…*causing red blood cells to clump.* That slows circulation, reduces oxygen in the blood and raises blood pressure.

…*creating new plaques and making them prone to rupture.*

…*causing existing plaques to grow.*

…*causing abnormally rapid clotting of the blood.* That can lead to arterial occlusion if a new plaque bursts.

…*causing release of hormone-like compounds.* Called *prostaglandins*, these compounds boost the clumping effect.

To keep plaques from forming, the American Heart Association (AHA) suggests limiting daily fat intake to 30% of calories. Yet recent studies show that even at this level of fat intake, new plaques *continue* to form. Amazingly, the AHA stands by its misguided recommendation.

HOW HEART ATTACKS OCCUR

Many people think that a heart attack occurs when an *old* plaque grows so big that it occludes a coronary artery.

Actually, most heart attacks occur following the rupture of a *newly formed* plaque—which contains liquid fat and cholesterol.

This rupture leaves a wound on the artery wall—which is quickly capped with a blood clot. This clot can grow quickly, becoming so large that it occludes the artery and stops blood flow to the heart.

The implication? Heart attacks can occur even when the coronary arteries are relatively plaque-free. As I tell my patients, you play Russian roulette *each time you eat a fatty meal.*

THE MCDOUGALL PROGRAM

My diet separates foods into three categories…

● **Eat all you want:**

● **Brown rice**, wheat, corn, oatmeal and other whole grains.

● **Whole-grain products**, including noodles, breads, pancakes and waffles. Make sure they contain no fats or oils.

● **Potatoes and yams.**

● **Squash.**

● **Peas**, lentils, lima beans and string beans.

● **Green and yellow vegetables.**

● **Cucumbers**, onions, peppers and tomatoes.

● **Beets**, carrots, turnips and other root vegetables.

5

- **Mild spices and herbs.**
- **Eat in moderation:**
- **Fruit**, fruit juice and dried fruit (up to three servings a day).
- **Sugar and artificial sweeteners.**
- **Salt.**
- **Alcohol.**
- **Fatty plant foods**, including nuts, peanut butter and tofu.
- **Avoid:**
- **Red meat**, poultry, fish, seafood, eggs, milk and milk products like butter, cheese, yogurt and sour cream. Even *nonfat* dairy products should be avoided. They contain proteins that can trigger an artery-damaging immune response.

I allow fatty foods *only* on special occasions —eggs on Easter…turkey on Thanksgiving… cake on your birthday.

- **Cooking oil.** Instead, use a nonstick pan or wok. Sauté with water, soy sauce, wine, tomato juice, lemon or lime juice or Worcestershire sauce.

When baking, replace the oil in the recipe with half the amount of applesauce, mashed bananas or soy yogurt.

- **Sulfites.** These preservatives, used in wines and in salad bars, can cause an allergic reaction.

When buying packaged food, read labels carefully. Avoid products containing fats and oils, including monoglycerides, diglycerides and/or hydrogenated or partially hydrogenated fats or oils.

Before making long-term dietary changes, discuss your nutritional needs with a doctor or dietician.

ONE MAN'S STORY

Charles Schaefer of Santa Rosa, California, suffered his heart attack at age 46.

After undergoing balloon angioplasty, he was told he would probably need bypass surgery. At the time, his cholesterol was 220— average for Americans. His weight and blood pressure were normal, too.

After leaving the hospital, he went on my diet. His cholesterol immediately fell to 180. He then visited my office, and I put him on a cholesterol-lowering drug that brought his level down to 150.

He also began walking or bicycling several times a week.

Four years later, treadmill stress tests show that his coronary arteries are wide open. His heart is healthy, and he feels in better shape than ever.

"If I had stayed on the rich American diet," says Mr. Schaefer, "I would not be alive today."

John A. McDougall, MD, director of the McDougall Program for controlling heart disease at St. Helena Hospital in Santa Rosa, CA. He hosts the nationally syndicated television program McDougall, *and is author of* The McDougall Program for a Healthy Heart. *Dutton.*

Heart Bypass or Angioplasty— How to Choose

Deciding between the two major medical procedures for blocked coronary arteries is very complicated. Because five-year survival rates are about the same for both procedures, the decision depends on the patient's unique situation—including his/her disease severity, symptoms and preferences. Patients in their 40s or 50s often opt for the less drastic procedure —angioplasty—to defer invasive surgery as long as they can. Older people may prefer bypass because there's much less chance they'll have to go through a second procedure.

Bottom line: Discuss your options—and the trade-offs you'll have to make—with your cardiologist.

James Jollis, MD, a cardiologist and assistant professor of medicine at Duke University Medical Center, Durham, NC.

Aspirin and Heart Attack

Taking an aspirin during—or very soon after —a heart attack reduces the risk of death significantly. A study of more than 17,000 patients worldwide found that those who took aspirin within 24 hours of the first symptoms were 23% less likely to die from a heart attack than those who did not. When aspirin was taken along with the clot-dissolving drug *strep-tokinase*, the death rate dropped by 42%. It is believed that aspirin prevents production of prostaglandins, substances that encourage blood to clot and block blood vessels that carry vital oxygen to the damaged heart.

Charles Hennekens, MD, chief of preventive medicine at Brigham and Women's Hospital, Boston.

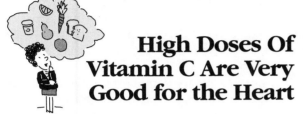

High Doses Of Vitamin C Are Very Good for the Heart

A study of 26 people with severely blocked arteries found that high doses of vitamin C helped their arteries open normally within two hours. Blocked arteries limit blood flow to the heart, causing angina and heart attacks.

Researchers theorize that vitamin C helps by suppressing superoxide, a substance that interferes with the body's natural way of opening arteries. Enough research has not yet been done to know how useful vitamin C supplements are as a treatment for artery problems.

Joseph A. Vita, MD, associate professor of medicine at Boston University School of Medicine, Boston.

Heart Palpitations

O ccasional heart palpitations are usually not serious.

Common causes: Fear or anxiety…stress…caffeine and other stimulants…alcohol…physical activity…thyroid disorders…mitral valve prolapse, a condition that occurs when the valve between the upper and lower chambers of the left side of the heart bulges or balloons. See your doctor if palpitations last more than a few moments or occur frequently.

Harold Karpman, MD, clinical professor of medicine and cardiologist at the University of California at Los Angeles School of Medicine. He is author of *Preventing Silent Heart Disease*. Henry Holt.

Milk Cuts Strokes

M en who drink milk have strokes much less often than those who do not.

A 22-year Hawaiian study of more than 3,000 men in their 50s and 60s found that those who drank two or more glasses of milk daily had fewer than half as many strokes as those who drank little or no milk.

Researchers found no link to total calcium consumption and do not understand where the protective effect comes from. The finding may simply reflect the fact that men who drink milk are likely to practice a healthier lifestyle.

Robert Abbott, PhD, professor of biostatistics at the University of Virginia School of Medicine, Charlottesville.

Cellular Phones Affect Pacemakers

A digital cellular phone can temporarily turn off a pacemaker or cause it to push the heart too quickly.

Self-defense: People who have pacemakers should use ordinary cellular phones—known as analog phones—which rarely cause interference. *Also:* When the phone is turned on, never hold it in a pocket near your pacemaker.

Study of 975 pacemaker users, led by David Hayes, MD, director of pacemaker services, Mayo Clinic, Rochester, MN.

Cancer Self-Defense

T he biggest cancer threats are eating too much fat…and too many calories…and drinking too much alcohol—far greater cancer threats than consuming "cancer-causing" foods.

Reason: Most carcinogens, whether natural or synthetic, are present at levels so low that they pose insignificant cancer risk.

Self-defense: Eat a varied and balanced diet that includes plenty of fruits and vegetables. This type of diet is not only better for your body but also helps protect against natural carcinogens. And, of course, don't smoke.

Ronald Estabrook, PhD, O'Hara professor of biochemistry, University of Texas Southwestern Medical Center, Dallas, who led a study of more than 200 cancer-causing substances found in the diet.

There's No Reason to Die From Colon Cancer: Self-Defense Essentials

Peter McNally, DO
Eisenhower Army Medical Center

Colon cancer kills more people than any other malignancy except lung cancer. Each year 140,000 Americans are diagnosed with colon cancer…and 55,000 die. One American in 20 will develop colon cancer in his/her lifetime—usually after age 50.

Tragically, 90% of colorectal cancer could be avoided through early detection.

DETECTION MEANS PREVENTION

Colon cancer doesn't just come out of nowhere. Most cases develop from a *polyp*, a premalignant growth on the lining of the colon.

Periodic screening offers a way to spot tumors early…and to find and remove polyps while they're still benign. It takes five to 10 years for a polyp to turn cancerous.

Here's what to do…

●**Age 40 to age 50.** Have an annual *digital rectal exam* (DRE). The doctor inserts a gloved finger into the rectum and feels for suspicious growths.

●**After age 50.** Each year, have a DRE and a *fecal occult blood test*. In this test, you'll be asked to put a smear of stool on a specially treated card on three successive days, while following a special diet.

If the test shows blood—or if you're at high risk for colon cancer—the doctor will examine the full length of your colon with a long, flexible viewing scope (colonoscope). Any polyp that is found is removed during the procedure.

Because colonoscopy can cause discomfort, you will probably be given an intravenous sedative like Demerol or Valium.

Undergo *flexible sigmoidoscopy* every three years. Using a short, flexible tube inserted into the rectum, the doctor inspects the lower one-fourth of the colon. That's where most tumors develop.

The procedure causes only mild discomfort, so it's usually done without sedation.

WHO IS AT HIGH RISK

Colon cancer runs in families. Your risk is above average if one or more first-degree relatives (parents or siblings) has had the disease.

In such cases, it's prudent to have a flexible sigmoidoscopy every three to five years, starting at age 35.

A rare hereditary condition known as *familial adenomatous polyposis* dramatically raises your risk of colon cancer. If genetic tests reveal that you have this condition—in which hundreds of polyps form in the colon—screening should begin in adolescence.

If you've had one polyp removed, you're likely to develop more. Have a colonoscopy every three years.

Ulcerative colitis and Crohn's disease are also associated with an elevated risk. Anyone who has either condition for 10 years or more should have an annual colonoscopy.

REDUCING RISK WITH DIET

Colon cancer is rare in regions where vegetables and grains make up the bulk of the diet. It's common in the US and other Western nations where the diet is largely based on meat.

Implication: A diet rich in fruits, vegetables, beans and whole grains prevents colon cancer. The American Cancer Society recommends at least five servings of these foods each day.

While it's hard to determine exactly which components of this healthy diet are protective, research has zeroed in on several candidates…

●**Low fat.** There is a clear link between dietary fat and colon cancer. Fats boost the body's production of bile acids, which promote rapid cell growth.

●**High fiber.** The indigestible part of plant-based foods, fiber moves food through the bowel quickly—reducing its contact with carcinogens and bile acids.

Wheat bran is more protective than fruit and vegetable fiber. Oat bran has little impact on colon cancer risk, though it does reduce cholesterol levels.

Get at least 25 g of dietary fiber per day—from whole grain cereals and breads and vegetables, fruits and beans.

●**Calcium.** Some studies suggest that calcium protects the colon by neutralizing bile acids and fatty acids.

Consume at least 1,000 mg of calcium each day—ideally through diet, not supplements.

●**Antioxidants.** Low blood levels of vitamins C and E and beta-carotene seem to confer an increased risk of colon cancer.

Eat lots of citrus fruits and dark-green and yellow vegetables—these are the best sources of antioxidants.

WHAT ELSE MAY HELP

●**Exercise.** A sedentary lifestyle increases the risk of colon cancer. Like fiber, physical activity reduces the risk by hastening the passage of waste through the body. It also stimulates blood flow to the colon.

Walk briskly or do some other exercise at least 30 minutes, three days a week.

●**Nonsteroidal anti-inflammatory drugs** (NSAIDs). As several recent studies have shown, individuals who take aspirin or ibuprofen regularly for years face a reduced risk of colon cancer.

Unfortunately, there is not enough evidence to justify taking aspirin or NSAIDs strictly for cancer prevention.

●**Estrogen.** Preliminary studies suggest that postmenopausal women who take estrogen are less likely to develop colon cancer than similar women who don't take estrogen.

WATCH OUT FOR SYMPTOMS

See a doctor at once if you experience changes in bowel habits…blood in the stool …rectal pain…and/or recurrent abdominal cramps.

The earlier cancer is detected, the better the chance for cure.

Peter McNally, DO, chief of gastroenterology at Eisenhower Army Medical Center in Augusta, GA, and a spokesperson for the American College of Gastroenterology, 4900 B South 31 St., Arlington, VA 22206. He is author of the medical textbook GI/Liver Secrets. *Hanley & Belfus.*

Drinking Water May Reduce Risk Of Colon Cancer

Researchers found that middle-aged women who drank more than five glasses of water a day developed colon cancer about half as often as those who drank less than two glasses a day. It is speculated that water may speed food through the digestive system, reducing exposure of the colon to carcinogens. There is no theory as to why the protective effect in men was less pronounced.

Jackilen Shannon, PhD, a postdoctoral fellow at the Fred Hutchinson Cancer Research Center, Seattle.

What to Avoid Before a Prostate Cancer Test

Prior to a prostate cancer test, men should avoid ejaculation for 48 hours.

Reason: Ejaculation raises levels of prostate-specific antigen (PSA) in the blood by as much as 40%. High levels of PSA are associated with prostate cancer—so an artificially high reading could lead to needless worry and more tests.

Other factors affecting PSA: Prostate infection (prostatitis)…and a prostate "massage," done by a doctor. Have the PSA test done at a different time.

Prostate screening schedule: Annually from ages 50 to 75 for all men…and for men with family histories from either parent and for African-Americans—from age 40.

Joseph E. Oesterling, MD, professor, urologist-in-chief and director of the Michigan Prostate Institute, University of Michigan Medical Center, Ann Arbor.

Most Breast Lumps Are Normal

Human breast tissue is naturally very lumpy. But 20% of women who are between the ages of 25 and 50 have fibrocystic changes that produce unwanted, often painful lumps. These lumps are usually benign...but they can mask early detection of breast cancer.

Self-defense: Wear a supportive bra to minimize your discomfort...cut your salt intake to reduce swelling from water retention...perform breast self-examinations monthly...and see a doctor to make sure a lump is normal and not potentially troublesome.

Christiane Northrup, MD, assistant clinical professor of obstetrics and gynecology, University of Vermont College of Medicine, through a teaching program at Maine Medical Center, Portland.

How to Stop Free Radicals

James W. Anderson, MD
Kentucky Veterans Affairs Medical Center

We hear more and more about free radicals—molecular fragments believed to play a key role in many health problems...but what are they? Why are they dangerous and how we can limit their destructive effects?

A free radical is an oxygen molecule destabilized by the loss of an electron. To regain stability, the molecule replaces the missing electron by "stealing" one from a neighbor.

This sets off a chain reaction in which each newly destabilized molecule steals an electron from a neighboring one.

Free radicals are continuously created during oxidation, the process by which the oxygen we breathe reacts with other compounds in the body to release energy.

But free radicals harm the body in several ways. They...

...*speed oxidation of "bad" low-density lipoprotein (LDL) cholesterol.* This causes cholesterol to accumulate along artery walls—a process that leads to heart attack or stroke.

...*damage DNA.* This leads to uncontrolled cell growth—in other words, cancer.

...*promote diabetes.* They do so by damaging insulin-producing "beta cells" in the pancreas.

...*damage brain cells.* This leads to Alzheimer's, Parkinson's and other degenerative neurological diseases.

Good news: The body makes its own free radical neutralizing compounds called *antioxidants.* It also uses plant antioxidants called *phytochemicals* to repair cells damaged by free radicals.

FRUITS AND VEGETABLES

A diet rich in fruits and vegetables—especially those containing the phytochemicals beta-carotene and vitamins C and E—lowers the risk of heart disease, cancer and other deadly ailments caused by free radical damage.

Pills are no substitute for a healthful diet—at least five servings of fruits and/or vegetables a day. Emphasize fruits and veggies containing more than 50% of the daily recommended allowance for beta-carotene and vitamin C.

Honor-roll veggies: Carrots...red peppers ...spinach...sweet potatoes...cruciferous vegetables like broccoli, cabbage and cauliflower ...and allium vegetables like garlic, onions and scallions.

Honor-roll fruits: Apricots, cantaloupe, oranges, grapefruit and kiwi.

VITAMIN SUPPLEMENTS

Since few people *consistently* get enough antioxidants from their diets, supplements are a good idea. Several studies suggest that vitamin C protects against cancer. The research on vitamin E is especially dramatic...

• Studies suggest that vitamin E supplements protect against hardening of the arteries.

• A Harvard study of nurses found that those who took vitamin E supplements for two years cut their heart attack risk by 50%.

Most researchers believe that moderate amounts of beta-carotene lower risk of cancer and heart attack. But two years ago, in a Finnish study of male smokers, those who took beta-carotene had an 18% *higher* lung cancer rate than those on a placebo.

Last year, a study of US doctors, including many smokers, failed to show significant positive or negative effects from beta-carotene.

But these studies involved large doses—50 mg every other day in the US study, and 20 mg a day in the Finnish study. It's possible that *smokers* may be at risk from high doses of beta-carotene...but there is no evidence that it harms nonsmokers.

Daily dosages: Betacarotene, 10,000 IU... vitamin C, 500 mg (250 mg twice a day)...vitamin E, 400 IU.

To enhance absorption, take these vitamins at mealtime.

Also helpful: Selenium, 60 micrograms daily. In a Chinese study, death rates fell by 9% over five years for people taking beta-carotene, vitamin E and selenium.

SOYBEANS, GRAPES AND TEA

Soybeans are a unique source of a potent phytochemical called *genistein*. This antioxidant guards against breast cancer...and may combat prostate cancer as well.

Eat a one-ounce serving of tofu or another soy food each day. You can stir soy powder into orange juice...or add soy-based textured vegetable protein (TVP) to spaghetti or taco sauce.

Red wine, grape juice and purple grapes are rich in *polyphenols*, antioxidants that reduce risk of heart disease.

Helpful: Six ounces of red wine or grape juice (or 20 grapes) daily.

Another source of polyphenols is green tea. Drinking two to three cups a day lowers high blood pressure and cuts the risk of cancer.

MELATONIN AND MORE

Melatonin does appear to have antioxidant effects. But more research is needed to support the effectiveness and safety of this hormone.

Pycnogenol—a product sold in capsule form in health-food stores—contains *proanthocyanidins* (PACs). This family of phytochemicals is thought to slow the aging process, prevent cancer and protect against heart attack. But further research is needed before it can be recommended.

An antioxidant called *coenzyme Q* is produced by the body and in high levels helps protect against oxidation of LDL cholesterol. Further research is needed before coenzyme Q supplements can be recommended.

EXERCISE

Moderate exercise protects against damage from free radicals. It does so by diverting oxygen and free radicals to the muscles, thus protecting blood vessels and other more vulnerable tissues.

Best approach: Walk 14 miles a week (or the equivalent).

James W. Anderson, MD, professor of medicine and clinical nutrition at the University of Kentucky, and section chief at the Kentucky Veterans Affairs Medical Center, both in Lexington. He is author of *Dr. Anderson's Antioxidant, Antiaging Health Program*. Carroll & Graf.

Antiperspirant Risk

Antiperspirants may interfere with mammography. They contain aluminum and/or other metals that can be mistaken for suspicious calcium deposits. Deodorants don't interfere—because they contain no metal.

Other substances that interfere with mammography: Lotions, oils, powders and zinc oxide.

Daniel Kopans, MD, director of the Breast Imaging Division of Massachusetts General Hospital, and associate professor of radiology at Harvard Medical School.

Aspirin vs. Breast Cancer

Women who took aspirin or ibuprofen at least three times weekly for five years were 33% less likely to develop breast cancer than other women, a recent survey found. More research is needed to determine whether women should start taking aspirin or ibuprofen to prevent cancer.

Randall E. Harris, MD, PhD, epidemiologist at Ohio State School of Public Health, Columbus. His survey of 511 breast cancer patients and 1,534 healthy women was published in *Epidemiology*, 1 Newton Executive Park, Newton Lower Falls, MA 02162-1450.

Black Tea and Cancer

Drinking regular black tea reduces risk of cancer. A study of over 35,000 postmenopausal women showed that those who drank two or more cups of tea a day were 60% less likely to develop cancers of the urinary tract, including those of the kidney and bladder, and

30% less likely to develop cancers of the digestive tract, including those of the esophagus, stomach and colon. Researchers theorize that the cancer-fighting effect comes from compounds in tea called *polyphenols*. The study found that the cancer risk decreased even more for women who drank four or more cups of tea a day. Drinking tea at too hot a temperature may reduce the anti-cancer effect.

Wei Zheng, MD, PhD, assistant professor of epidemiology at the University of Minnesota, Minneapolis.

Cellular Phones and Cancer

Cellular phone users do *not* have an elevated death rate—despite recent reports suggesting a link between microwave radiation emitted by the phones and brain cancer. In a recent study of 250,000 cellular phone users, there was no increase in overall mortality. The study included "flip phones," which have antennas that must be held close to the head. It did *not* specifically address the question of whether these phones cause cancer.

Kenneth J. Rothman, DrPH, senior scientist at Epidemiology Resources, an epidemiology research and education company in Newton, MA.

Mouth Cancer Risk Aid

Blue-green algae reduce risk of mouth cancer. After one year of consuming a daily dose of the blue-green alga *spirulina*, 45% of those with whitish precancerous patches in the mouth (oral leukoplakia) experienced total regression. Spirulina, a low-cost source of beta-carotene and related carotenoids, is sold in health-food stores.

Padmanabhan P. Nair, PhD, research scientist at the Human Nutrition Center of the US Department of Agriculture, Beltsville, MD. His study was reported in Food & Nutrition Research Briefs, 6303 Ivy Lane, 4th Floor, Greenbelt, MD 20770.

What I Learned About Doctors and Hospitals On My Way to Recovery

Evan Handler

By the time I was 24 years old, I had already played leading roles in five Broadway productions and three major movies. Then in 1985, just as I was up for a part in a film with Dustin Hoffman and Warren Beatty, I was diagnosed with leukemia...and told that my chances for survival were slim.

For the next five years, I learned a great deal about hospitals and doctors. I was in and out of four hospitals, and I saw more than 100 doctors as I underwent repeated courses of chemotherapy and a bone-marrow transplant.

Now I'm 35 years old and have been considered cured of the disease for more than seven years. I like to believe that part of the reason for my medical success was my intense curiosity and assertiveness during my treatment.

Here's what I learned about the medical system—and what anyone can do to ensure the best possible care for any serious illness...

●**Fight medical mediocrity and carelessness.** Someone dealing with a health crisis hopes to have a kindly doctor, like the ones shown on TV. But reality rarely lives up to that expectation.

Hospitals are large bureaucracies that are set up to care efficiently for many patients. Unfortunately, most are not designed to help individual patients flourish. The result is that any departure from conformity is often discouraged by administrators, doctors and staff—even when the standard procedure could *put your health at risk.*

Example: During my hospitalization, I had serious adverse reactions to several drugs routinely prescribed, including medications to combat the dangerous side effects of chemotherapy. So my doctors prescribed other drugs. Though this fact appeared on my bedside medical chart, it was *overlooked.* When nurses brought the standard medications to my room, I would have to remind them to check my chart—and request one of the alternative drugs that I could tolerate.

This meant delays while a doctor was summoned to write a new order...the pharmacy filled the prescription...and new tests were run. More than once, I was yelled at by nurses for the "trouble" I was causing—by insisting on medication that wouldn't make me sicker.

Don't be intimidated. It isn't easy to stand up for yourself when you're sick, vulnerable and dependent on others, so get support wherever you can.

When I was too weak to challenge the nurses' errors, my girlfriend did it for me. My refusal to conform may have made me unpopular—but it helped me survive.

● **If you have the time, it pays to shop for a doctor and a hospital.** My treatment began at one of the country's most renowned cancer centers. Yet I encountered conditions there that appalled me—ranging from a chronic shortage of bed linens to repeated examples of staff arrogance and insensitivity toward patients. There were even technicians who overlooked safe hygiene practices, such as properly sterilizing the catheters inserted into my body.

It doesn't have to be this way, as I realized only after visiting other, equally respected cancer centers. Many hospitals discourage comparison shopping—yet it's your right as a medical consumer to compare institutions and choose one you believe is right for you.

Self-defense: Get lists of medical centers and doctors from hotlines that specialize in your illness. Seek recommendations from everyone you know, especially people who work in the health care field. Call and visit medical centers. Interview doctors—dozens if necessary.

Consider not only the reputation of the person or facility, but the attitude with which you are treated as a potential patient. Are calls returned promptly? Are doctors and staff reluctant to answer questions...or are they generous with information?

Example: Be wary of any doctor or administrator who implies that, *Our facility is the only appropriate one for you. You would be foolish to accept any other. We are your only hope.*

Knowing what I now know, I would say to any doctor I was considering, *I want to work with someone who is willing to let me be a partner in the treatment. I don't want to be told what procedures may be "planned for" me. I want to know about the range of possible treatments, hear your recommendations and make my own decisions. I don't want interns and residents showing up every day to administer procedures and tests that I haven't been informed about.*

Look for the doctor who responds, *Of course —I wouldn't dream of anything else*—rather than the one who sputters...won't look you in the eye...or replies defensively, *Look, do you want to get well or not?*

● **Get the information you need about your illness and treatment.** The more you know about your condition and the treatment options, the easier it is to stand up for your rights.

While having faith in your doctor is important, you must always assume that there are other effective ways of dealing with your problem. You must be assertive.

Since accessibility to information about your illness is rare to nonexistent at most hospitals, it's up to you to do the research.

Strategy: Look for alternative treatments and medications by calling hotlines that specialize in your illness. Visit medical libraries and read journal articles yourself—or have a family member or friend do it for you. Call or visit a number of major medical centers known to treat your condition. You never know when you might discover information with which your doctor is not yet familiar.

There are also many medical professionals out there who would be willing to discuss options with you—even though they aren't personally treating you. Keep calling until you find them.

● **Choose your words carefully at hospitals.** Midway through my treatment at the hospital, I decided to "fire" the cancer specialist with whom I had been working—and request another doctor. I didn't feel he was treating me with the respect and consideration I needed or allowing me to adequately participate in decision making. I also found his brusque manner and pessimistic outlook to be frightening and depressing.

Many patients don't realize that they have the right to change doctors—even when they're already in the hospital. The usual procedure is to make an appointment for a consultation with another doctor and explain to the new doctor that you are considering changing physicians. Then continue this approach while interviewing doctors until you find one with whom you feel most comfortable.

Important: When making the request, avoid specific criticisms about your first doctor. Instead, stick to the message, *We have trouble communicating.* Otherwise, you run the risk of creating a "political" mess that could affect your care, since most doctors are highly collegial and easily offended in this situation.

●**Explore alternative treatments.** I wouldn't recommend that people force themselves to try methods with which they're uncomfortable. But I'm glad I explored a variety of nontraditional therapies, from visualization and meditation to hypnotherapy and psychic healing.

I entered into this investigation in a receptive frame of mind—coupled with a healthy dose of skepticism. I viewed these techniques as tools to maximize my potential to heal, not as rigid formulas that guaranteed certain results.

To the rescue: With the help of family and friends, I sought out stories of unexpected healings. I read news accounts and books about alternative therapies, talked to people who had successful recoveries, attended a week-long retreat on guided imagery and other ways of coping with illness. I even had friends of friends recommend psychic healers.

I'm still a skeptic about many of these alternative therapies, but I believe that stimulating my emotions helped me cope with stress, which in turn affected my vulnerability to illness...and my ability to heal.

Evan Handler, actor and writer in New York. He is author of *Time on Fire: My Comedy of Terrors*, a memoir of his diagnosis and recovery from leukemia. Little, Brown & Co.

Do You Need A Second Opinion? A Third?

Timothy McCall, MD

When a doctor recommends surgery or another involved treatment, it's only natural to wonder if that treatment is really needed. Perhaps you'd like to get a second opinion—but worry about offending your doctor.

Don't worry. Get the second opinion.

These days, it's routine for patients to get a second opinion before elective surgery. Surgeons expect second opinions, and almost all insurance companies pay for them.

Don't think of second opinions only when surgery is recommended. If your doctor proposes *any* major intervention—including a potentially risky diagnostic test or a drug with serious side effects—consider getting another point of view. In fact, any time you have doubts about the way your medical care is being managed, consider getting a second opinion. If you think your doctor may be missing something, you may be right.

Here are my suggestions for making the most of a second opinion:

●**Be honest with your primary-care doctor.** Even though it may be difficult, it's best to inform your doctor of your desire for a second opinion. That way, copies of all relevant medical records and test results can be forwarded to the second doctor. Even if your doctor doesn't agree with the need for a second opinion, he or she should respect your wish for more information and cooperate with the process. If your doctor throws up roadblocks, you've got to ask yourself whether it's time to find a new one.

●**Get the second opinion from a doctor unaffiliated with the first.** Preferably, this will be one practicing at another institution. Since doctors with close ties may share biases, you may simply end up hearing the same opinion twice.

●**If you're seeking a second opinion regarding surgery**, see a nonsurgeon. Surgeons tend to be more convinced than other doctors of the power of the scalpel, particularly of *their* scalpel. For back surgery, for example, I recommend you consult a neurologist. For heart surgery, try a cardiologist. These nonsurgeons will have a more balanced view of the effectiveness of surgery.

● **Consider the financial incentives.** In sorting out a doctor's recommendations, it pays to know where the financial incentives lie. If you have traditional medical insurance, a surgeon may stand to make thousands of dollars if you have the operation he or she recommends.

In health maintenance organizations (HMOs) and other managed-care plans, a doctor's income is often directly proportional to how *little* he/she does. As a result, he or she may be more likely to advise against costly interventions that might benefit you. In HMOs, it's often a good idea to get an opinion from a doctor *outside* of the plan. Some plans will pay for this. Others require you to pay—but it may be worth the extra expense.

Under some HMO "gag rules," doctors risk being fired if they advise you of viable alternative treatments that the plan doesn't want to pay for.

What if the opinions of two physicians differ greatly? In such cases, it's reasonable to get a *third* opinion—or even a *fourth*. Ultimately, your preferences should guide your decision.

Medicine is an inexact science. Given the lack of proof of the effectiveness of many interventions, different doctors of equal competence may look at the same information and come to different conclusions. In many cases, more than one approach will work. On the other hand, just because two doctors agree does *not* mean they're right (or that what they recommend is right for *you*).

In the 1960s most doctors felt that routine tonsillectomy was a good idea. Now we know better.

Timothy McCall, MD, an internist practicing in the Boston area, and author of *Examining Your Doctor: A Patient's Guide to Avoiding Harmful Medical Care.* Citadel Press. Dr. McCall hosts the *Examining Your Doctor Forum* on America Online, featuring weekly columns and regular online chats. *Keyword:* dr.mccall.

Charles Inlander Tells How to Survive A Hospital Stay

Charles B. Inlander
People's Medical Society

S ome US hospitals are among the best in the world. Others are very, very good. But that doesn't mean that they are risk-free.

Better ways: You can greatly reduce the chance that something will go wrong in a hospital. To get special attention from doctors and nurses, take a few straightforward precautions and make use of inside information about the way hospitals operate. *Survival tactics…*

INFECTION SAFEGUARD

Ten percent of hospital patients contract an infection after being admitted, adding $4,000 to $10,000 to a typical bill.

Examples: About 300,000 patients a year contract pneumonia in US hospitals. Other common hospital infections attack the urinary and respiratory systems. Staph infections are also a big problem.

Chief reason: Hospitals house a high percentage of infected people, many of whom have weakened immune systems. *Precautions:*

● **Make sure that all hospital staff members wash their hands before they touch you.** Don't be afraid to ask. It's your right.

● **Also ask personnel to put on a fresh pair of gloves before touching you.**

● **If you have a catheter**, insist that hospital personnel monitor it at least three or four times a day. A faulty catheter is an open door to infection.

THE TEAM APPROACH

Since you probably won't be at your most alert during a hospital stay, ask friends to help you monitor the treatment you receive.

Best: Ask three or more friends to stay with you in around-the-clock shifts.

Their very presence will help keep doctors and nurses on their toes, increasing chances that you'll receive above-average attention.

Myth: Guests are allowed to see you only during visiting hours.

Reality: Hospitals *hope* patients believe this, but visitors are *legally* allowed to see you at any time of day as long as they don't interfere with your treatment or that of any other patient in the room.

If your hospital stay is for more than a couple of days, consider making it more pleasant by decorating your room with some pictures from home or other familiar objects.

Leave valuables home. Many people have access to your room, so there's high risk of theft.

ATTENTION TO MEDICATION

With hundreds of patients receiving multiple medications each day, there's a great likelihood of a mistake in the type of medication you're given, in its dosage or in the frequency that it's administered.

The average error rate is 2% to 3%, meaning that in a 300-bed hospital there can be six medication errors an hour. *Precautions:*

• **Each time you receive medicine**, check to see if it's the same type you got on the last occasion. If it isn't, insist that hospital personnel check and double-check their instructions.

• **Similarly**, ask staff members to justify any change in the frequency of medication that you might notice.

• **Ask your doctor if the food you're served will have an adverse effect on your medication.** If it will, have him/her arrange for the appropriate diet.

REJECT THE UNKNOWN

If you don't understand a procedure or treatment, don't permit it until you *do*. Most hospitals will send in senior staff members to give you a proper explanation.

Myth: The release form you sign on entering a hospital means that you give up virtually all your rights.

Reality: You give up no rights whatsoever. You can accept or reject any type of treatment as well as any doctor who's assigned to you.

Exception: In life-or-death emergencies, hospitals are obligated to give you the appropriate treatment.

Above all, if you suspect that a doctor, nurse or other staff member is incompetent or negli-

gent, call it to the attention of appropriate hospital authorities.

If hospital administrators don't correct the situation, ask for advice from an attorney who specializes in malpractice. If necessary, change doctors or even hospitals.

Many patients don't realize that they have the right to fire their doctor at any time and to leave the hospital whenever they wish.

SURGICAL SAFEGUARDS:

If in the hospital for surgery…

• **Make sure that everyone involved in your surgery knows precisely what it's all about.** If you're having a cataract removed from your right eye, for instance, remind nurses, attendants, the anesthesiologist and the surgeon exactly which eye is to be operated on.

Some patients even use a marker to highlight the correct body part with an arrow or a circle. The measure might sound extreme, but it doesn't hurt to play it safe.

• **Choose a surgeon who frequently performs the operation.**

Rule of thumb: About 100 coronary bypasses a year and a higher frequency for more common operations, such as appendectomies. This is no guarantee of getting a competent surgeon, but it's an easy way to weed out those who lack experience.

• **Meet with your anesthesiologist before the operation.** The meeting alone can help you get better treatment because it makes you stand out as a real person. You'll no longer be the "gall bladder in room 305" but a person whom the anesthesiologist knows by name.

At the meeting, ask the anesthesiologist how many times he has performed your type of procedure. If he is inexperienced, ask for another anesthesiologist. Also tell him about all your medical conditions, including allergies—they can have an effect on anesthesia.

PURSUING DISPUTES

Not every mistake in a hospital is reason for a lawsuit. But if the error causes serious damage and you suspect negligence or (in rare cases) intent, check with an attorney.

Retain a lawyer who does nothing but malpractice work. Ask for recommendations from your regular attorney, the local bar association or from the Association of Trial Lawyers of America (202-965-3500).

Reputable malpractice attorneys can assess your chances of a successful lawsuit.

Charles B. Inlander, coauthor of *Take This Book to the Hospital With You: A Consumer's Guide to Surviving Your Hospital Stay.* People's Medical Society. Mr. Inlander is also president of the People's Medical Society, a consumer health advocacy organization, 462 Walnut St., Allentown, PA 18102.

Common Surgery Danger

A common surgical procedure may be unsafe. Called *pulmonary artery catheterization*, the procedure is used to diagnose and treat heart failure and other critical illnesses. It involves threading a catheter through a vein in the neck and into the heart.

Recent finding: Patients who underwent the procedure had a higher death rate and longer hospital stays than those who didn't receive it.

Self-defense: Before undergoing the procedure, patients should discuss its pros and cons with a doctor.

Alfred F. Connors, Jr., MD, director of Health Services Research and Outcomes Evaluation at the University of Virginia School of Medicine, Charlottesville. His study of 5,700 critically ill patients was published in *The Journal of the American Medical Association*, 515 N. State St., Chicago 60610.

 Transfusion Trap

Patients who donate blood for their own use during surgery—a process called *autologous donation*—don't always get to use it.

Self-defense: Your doctor should notify the hospital's transfusion service upon your admission to the hospital. Just prior to transfusion, a recheck of the patient's blood type is necessary.

Karen Shoos Lipton, JD, CEO of the American Association of Blood Banks, 8101 Glenbrook Rd., Bethesda, MD 20814.

Shrewder Hospital Stays

Keep a detailed log of treatments, drugs, services and supplies so you can later compare it with your itemized bill to ensure you're not being overcharged. If you're unable to maintain the log, ask a friend or family member to do it. *Also:* The log lets the staff know that you intend to keep informed of your situation.

Common mistakes found on hospital bills: Same supplies billed by more than one department, unrequested personal supplies—such as toothpaste—and charges for services not rendered, such as hours of physical therapy.

An Insider's Guide to Understanding Your Hospital Bill by Nancy Collins, RN, and Jan Sedoris, RN, hospital bill auditors. Eggman Publishing.

Check Bills Closely

An astounding 90% of hospital bills contain errors. Less surprising perhaps, is that 75% of them are in favor of the hospital. *To prevent billing mistakes:*

•**Ask for *daily* bills**. Some hospitals may balk, but all can provide them if you insist. The request alone is often effective because it tells the billing clerks that you're looking over their shoulders.

•**With the help of your support team, keep track of all major treatments and procedures.** Watch out for duplications and unauthorized treatments.

•**If you're not satisfied with the answers**, phone your insurance company. But instead of talking with the claims department, ask for the fraud division.

Charles B. Inlander, coauthor of *Take This Book to the Hospital With You: A Consumer's Guide to Surviving Your Hospital Stay.* People's Medical Society. Mr. Inlander is also president of the People's Medical Society, a consumer health advocacy organization, 462 Walnut St., Allentown, PA 18102.

Outpatient Surgery... Self-Defense

Pack for a one-night hospital stay. Even patients scheduled merely for ambulatory surgery must sometimes stay overnight because of complications during surgery.

Common procedures that generally don't require overnight stays: Cataract removal, breast biopsy, inguinal hernia repair, dilation and curettage (D&C), repair of deviated septum.

Hospital Smarts by Theodore Tyberg, MD, internist/cardiologist, New York Hospital, New York. Hearst Books.

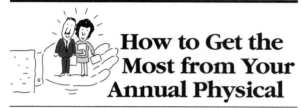

How to Get the Most from Your Annual Physical

Richard Podell, MD
Robert Wood Johnson Medical School

While studies have shown that physical exams aren't absolutely necessary each year for most healthy men under age 40 and women under age 50, they're worthwhile if your HMO or insurance carrier offers free or low-cost regular checkups.

Even when you're feeling fine, a physical exam is an excellent opportunity to clarify your short- and long-term health needs with your doctor. It also helps to be reminded by your doctor of the importance of a healthy lifestyle.

Here's how to make the most of your physical—whether you're visiting your longtime doctor or switching to a new one...

REVIEWING YOUR HEALTH

The most important part of an annual checkup is the exchange of information between you and your doctor.

• **Before your appointment**, send your doctor a memo. Fax or mail a one- or two-page memo that clearly outlines your recent health problems. Be concise. Type or print neatly. Include any new symptoms...what time of day the symptoms occur...and how long they last.

Even if your condition is ongoing and not new to your doctor, describing it and any changes will help your doctor when you arrive. *Also include in the memo...*

• **Information about your family's medical history.** Don't assume that your doctor remembers it or will have reviewed it before your appointment.

• **A list of all prescription and over-the-counter medications and supplements you're taking—or have taken in the past year.** When making a diagnosis, your doctor needs to know what other doctors have prescribed. It's also important that he/she have this information in case one drug interacts with another you're taking.

• **Before your appointment, call your doctor's assistant** to request that your exam be preceded and followed by a chat with your doctor in his office to discuss your memo and other related health issues.

• **Discuss your lifestyle.** Too often, doctors forget to ask patients about lifestyle factors that affect their health. These include diet, exercise, weight gain or loss, unusual stress or emotional upsets, disrupted sleep patterns, consumption of alcohol or tobacco, etc.

Too many patients, however, either minimize the impact of lifestyle on their health...or are hesitant to discuss such things as emotional problems, addictions and diet with their doctors.

A PHYSICAL EXAM CHECKLIST

Even though physical exams are standard, I find that most patients aren't aware of the tests—and don't know the benchmarks of good health. *Here's a physical exam checklist to help you ask your physician better questions...*

• **Blood pressure.** Any reading over 140/90 is cause for concern.

• **Cholesterol.** A blood test result that is over 200 mg/dl should lead to a more detailed evaluation of your LDL, HDL and triglyceride blood levels.

• **Skin-cancer screening exam** is for men and women of all ages. The doctor examines every area of your body, including your scalp, genital area, bottoms of feet, fingers and toenails for suspicious lesions and/or changes in existing moles.

• **Electrocardiogram (EKG) exam.** Sensors placed on key parts of your body produce data about the rhythm of your heart. It is useful to have a baseline EKG done at age 40 for men…age 50 for women. Changes in EKG readings offer clues in the diagnosis of heart disease.

●**Fecal occult blood test** checks for colorectal cancer. This test is recommended starting at age 50—or if there is family history of the disease. Sigmoidoscopy should be considered after age 50…and earlier if there is a family history.

●**Height/weight.** Ask your doctor whether he feels you have a weight problem and how serious it is.

●**Urine analysis** screens for diabetes and kidney-function problems.

●*Additional tests for women:*

●**Pap smear.** Women of all ages should have a pap smear each year to check for cervical cancer.

●**Pelvis and breasts.** Women should have a breast exam once or twice a year…and a pelvic exam once a year. Breasts should be examined in sitting and lying positions. Starting at age 50, women should have annual mammograms. Some experts would start earlier—especially if there's a family history of breast cancer.

Reproductive organs are checked for changes in size and evidence of ovarian cysts and fibroid tumors. Women with family histories of ovarian cancer should request a CA-125 blood test and ultrasound of the ovaries.

●*Additional tests for men:*

●**Testicles.** Men should have them examined once a year for testicular tumors. While they're not common, they are deadly—and can almost always be cured if detected early. Men should ask their doctors to show them how to do this exam themselves.

●**Prostate.** Men over age 50 should have annual rectal exams to screen for prostate cancer—*especially* if they have a family history of the disease. They should also have annual Prostate-Specific Antigen (PSA) blood tests.

Note: You may prefer to have the blood test before the rectal exam, since the rectal exam can affect PSA levels. However, recent studies suggest that in most cases the rise in PSA is insignificant.

IMMUNIZATION

People over age 65 and those with chronic conditions such as cardiac disease, cancer or diabetes should have annual flu vaccinations. Older people and those with chronic illnesses who contract the flu are at higher risk of death from complications—particularly pneumonia.

Younger adults who work with children—such as teachers and day-care workers—as well as health care professionals should consider annual flu shots.

Important: I advise people over age 65 and those with chronic conditions to be vaccinated against pneumococcal pneumonia.

Every adult should have a tetanus booster every 10 years…and anyone who is sexually active and has more than one sexual partner should be vaccinated against hepatitis B. A series of three shots will protect you for many years.

MULTIPLE APPOINTMENTS

The goal of an annual physical exam is to review your general health. If you have a major chronic health problem, such as diabetes or cardiovascular disease, it is better to schedule a series of appointments rather than expecting the doctor to cover everything in one visit.

AFTER THE EXAM

Here are questions to ask your doctor in his office when the exam is over…

●**Do you view me as being at an increased risk for any disease or health problems?** If so, what kind of lifestyle changes should I make to protect myself—and what type of early detection schedule do you recommend?

●*If diagnosed with a condition:* Do you feel the condition is under control—or should we map out a long-term treatment plan?

At the end of your exam, you and your doctor should be in agreement about testing and treatment strategies.

Richard Podell, MD, clinical professor of family medicine at the University of Medicine and Dentistry of New Jersey–Robert Wood Johnson Medical School in New Brunswick, NJ. He is author of Patient Power. Fireside.

Better Medical Tests... Better Treatment... Better Health

Timothy McCall, MD

Seeing your doctor for routine exams is an important way to assess and monitor your health. But many doctors are so rushed these days that they may not fully explain the best way to prepare for those tests.

The result could be a mistaken diagnosis... the hassle and expense of repeating tests...and unnecessary anxiety or worse. *Here's what to do—and not to do—before taking a major medical test...*

CHOLESTEROL

No special preparation is required before blood is taken for the simple measurement of total cholesterol.

But most cholesterol tests today include a more sophisticated analysis that is run on the blood sample to determine your HDL—or "good" cholesterol—level. This test is more subject to error than the simpler test.

Action: To get an accurate result, eat nothing after midnight or in the morning before the blood is drawn. *Also:* If you are currently under great stress, you may want to delay your test. Your reading may be higher than usual.

THROAT CULTURE

A common mistake many patients make is to take leftover antibiotics when they feel a sore throat coming on. Old antibiotics usually aren't helpful, and they can even be problematic. They can interfere with the correct diagnosis of strep throat or other bacterial infections...and can reduce the effectiveness of antibiotics diagnosed for you in the future.

URINE TESTS

If a urine sample is too dilute, abnormalities are less likely to be detected.

Best: If possible, go to the doctor or clinic early in the morning so that your urine sample is concentrated. Otherwise, try not to urinate for three hours before giving the sample.

STOOL TESTS

For three days before going to the doctor—or while completing the tests at home—avoid eating rare red meat, high doses of Vitamin C, iron supplements and uncooked broccoli, cauliflower or turnips.

If possible, avoid aspirin or other nonsteroidal anti-inflammatory drugs (NSAIDs), such as ibuprofen (Motrin, Advil, etc.) and naproxen (Naprosyn, Aleve, etc.). All can cause stomach bleeding that will turn the test positive.

PAP SMEARS

Any foreign substance, such as blood, semen, lubricants and contraceptive gel, that is present within three days of a test can interfere with interpreting a Pap smear. Condoms should be used during intercourse for the three days before the test. Plan to take a Pap test at least three days after a menstrual cycle is completed. And don't douche within three days of a Pap smear because you could rinse out the cells that need to be examined.

Timothy McCall, MD, an internist practicing in the Boston area, and author of *Examining Your Doctor: A Patient's Guide to Avoiding Harmful Medical Care.* Citadel Press. Dr. McCall hosts the *Examining Your Doctor Forum* on America Online, featuring weekly columns and regular online chats. *Keyword:* dr.mccall.

Dangerous Drug Interactions Are Very Easy to Avoid

Joe Graedon and Teresa Graedon, PhD

No doubt you know that the body's response to medication can be affected—sometimes lethally—by taking other drugs or eating certain foods at the same time.

What you may *not* realize is that doctors aren't always very good about warning their patients about these drug-drug and food-drug interactions.

Self-defense: Have all your prescriptions filled by *one* pharmacist—so he/she will better be able to alert you to potential problems. Prior to taking any prescription or over-the-counter

(OTC) medication—especially for the first time —*triple* check for any precautions you should heed...

• **Ask your *doctor*** if there are any foods or drugs you should avoid while taking the drug.

• **Ask your *pharmacist*** the same question.

• **Reconfirm what the doctor and pharmacist have said** by reading a comprehensive drug interaction guide.

If you notice unusual symptoms while taking a drug—fatigue, rash, diarrhea, etc.—contact your doctor and pharmacist at once. Do *not* stop taking a prescription drug without a doctor's permission.

Common interactions you should be alert for...

• ***Acetaminophen and...***

...alcohol. Taking Tylenol or another *acetaminophen* formulation in large doses for long periods of time while drinking may cause severe liver damage.

• ***Antacids and...***

...broad-spectrum antibiotics. Rolaids, Tums and other OTC antacids interfere with the body's absorption of *tetracycline* and certain other broad-spectrum antibiotics.

• ***Warfarin and...***

...aspirin. Both *warfarin* (Coumadin) and aspirin thin the blood. Taking them together can lead to uncontrolled bleeding.

...anti-inflammatory drugs. *Ibuprofen* (Advil, Nuprin, Motrin IB), *naproxen* (Aleve), *ketoprofen* (Orudis) and other nonsteroidal anti-inflammatory drugs (NSAIDs) can irritate the stomach lining. Taking them with warfarin may lead to a bleeding ulcer.

• ***Seldane or Hismanal and...***

...ketoconazole (Nizoral) or macrolide antibiotics. Ketoconazole or erythromycin (or another macrolide antibiotic) taken in combination with Seldane or Hismanal can cause *torsade de pointes*, a potentially fatal heart rhythm disturbance.

• ***Anti-inflammatory drugs and...***

...beta-blockers. Ibuprofen, naproxen, *indomethacin* (Indocin) and other NSAIDs reduce the effectiveness of *propranolol* (Inderal) and other beta-blockers, which are prescribed to lower elevated blood pressure. This reduced potency might lead to difficulty controlling hypertension.

...alcohol. The NSAID-alcohol combination can cause stomach irritation or bleeding.

• ***Calcium and...***

...antibiotics. Dairy products and calcium pills block absorption of *ciprofloxacin* (Cipro), tetracycline and other tetracycline-like formulations. Avoid milk products and calcium pills for two hours before and after taking tetracycline.

• ***Dietary fiber and...***

...digoxin (Lanoxin). High-fiber cereal, oatmeal and bran muffins contain enough fiber to affect absorption of this heart drug—which makes it less effective.

...tricyclic antidepressants. Fiber can actually interfere with absorption of *desipramine* (Norpramin) and other tricyclics. Avoid high-fiber foods for two hours before and after taking a tricyclic.

• ***Grapefruit juice and...***

...terfenadine (Seldane) or astemizole (Hismanal). Grapefruit contains compounds that interfere with liver enzymes that break down these drugs—thereby boosting blood levels of these medications. High levels can cause *torsade de pointes*, a heart rhythm disturbance.

...Plendil, Procardia or Adalat. Grapefruit can increase blood levels of these blood pressure drugs, causing headaches, flushing and light-headedness.

...cyclosporine (Sandimmune). Increased blood levels of this drug—prescribed for transplant patients and rheumatoid arthritis sufferers—can cause kidney problems, high blood pressure and muscle tremors.

...warfarin. Research suggests that grapefruit may elevate blood levels of warfarin, increasing the risk of bleeding.

• ***Iron and...***

...thyroid supplements. The typical multivitamin/mineral supplement contains enough iron to reduce the effectiveness of *levothyroxine* (Synthroid) by up to one-third.

Safer: Iron-free supplements.

• ***Licorice and...***

...digoxin. Candy, cough drops, tablets or tea that contain licorice deplete the body of potassium. That can lead to irregular heart rhythms.

Safer: Artificial licorice flavoring made from anise.

...diuretics (potassium-wasting) or corticosteroids. Taken with licorice, these drugs cause a dangerous drop in potassium levels. That can lead to muscle pain or weakness—or irregular heart rhythms.

•MAO inhibitors and...

...foods rich in tyramine. This protein building block—found in aged cheese, ripe avocados, fava beans, Chianti wine, yeast concentrate and salted, smoked or pickled fish—can send blood pressure levels skyrocketing in individuals taking Nardil, Parnate or another monoamine oxidase (MAO) inhibitor.

...serotonin-reuptake inhibitors (SRIs). Taking an MAO inhibitor along with *fluoxetine* (Prozac) or another SRI can cause shivering, agitation, confusion, blood pressure changes—even coma or death.

Wait at least five weeks after going off Prozac before starting an MAO inhibitor. If you're switching in the other direction, wait at least two weeks after stopping an MAO inhibitor before taking an SRI.

Joe Graedon and Teresa Graedon, PhD, husband-and-wife coauthors of The People's Guide to Deadly Drug Interactions. *St. Martin's Press. The Graedons host the nationally syndicated weekly radio program* The People's Pharmacy.

Prescription Danger

When writing prescriptions, few doctors take into account the patient's weight.

Trap: Most of the standard dosages are calibrated for a 155-pound person.

Example: A 130-pound person needs 10% to 15% less medication. Taking too much can cause nausea, drowsiness—or worse.

Self-defense: If you weigh less—or more—than 155 pounds, talk to your doctor to make sure he/she is prescribing the proper dosage.

Daniel Albrant, PharmD, president of Pharmacy Dynamics, a health care consulting company in Arlington, VA.

Medication Self-Defense

Urge your doctor to write on the prescription what it is for, so the pharmacist can give you better information. This also ensures that the pharmacist is reading the doctor's handwriting properly.

Make sure the dosage instructions on the bottle are the same as the ones the doctor told you to follow...and ask for the package insert that comes with every drug.

Reminders: Inform your doctors and pharmacists of all the prescriptions and over-the-counter drugs that you use, so they can be alert for possible interactions...and use only one pharmacy so that all your medication records are in one place.

Timothy McCall, MD, an internist practicing in the Boston area, and author of Examining Your Doctor: A Patient's Guide to Avoiding Harmful Medical Care. *Citadel Press. Dr. McCall hosts the* Examining Your Doctor Forum *on America Online, featuring weekly columns and regular online chats.* Keyword: *dr.mccall.*

How to Harness the Amazing Power of Your Immune System

Henry Dreher

The single best way to stay healthy is to strengthen your immune system. A strong immune system aggressively fights diseases ranging from common colds to arthritis and cancer. It can even *prevent* a wide range of ailments—particularly heart disease and cancer.

As the number of antibiotic-resistant bacteria increases, a strong immune system is your best defense against illness.

THE BODY'S POLICE FORCE

To help you understand your immune system, think of it as a police force of cells that conducts surveillance missions throughout the body. There are cells of different rank, and each has a different job to do.

Like any good militia, all of the immune cells cooperate with each other to identify and arrest "invaders"—bacteria, viruses, cancer cells, etc. They also rush to each other's aid when necessary.

The cells' marching orders originate in the brain and certain organs, such as the thymus, a gland located behind the breast bone. The thymus acts as a "training school" for immature white blood cells.

Enemy viruses are captured by "field officers"—immune cells—including T-cells, B-cells and protein molecules called *antibodies.*

These immune "officers" communicate by spewing various "messenger" molecules that travel to other "troops" moving throughout your body.

When we don't have enough immune cells to conquer invading infections, we become ill. We can also become sick when our cells don't receive the proper messages because the different levels in the cell hierarchy fail to communicate with each other.

In the case of arthritis and other autoimmune diseases, our immune cells mistakenly attack our own cells, causing inflammation and crippling pain. Put differently, the police attack suspects who are really innocent.

SIZING UP YOUR IMMUNE SYSTEM

How can you tell if your immune system is dangerously weak?

Although there are numerous expensive tests that are used to diagnose immune deficiency, such specific conditions are rare. Most people have suboptimal immune function because they are run down.

An easier, more affordable way to assist your immune system's strength is to ask yourself a series of questions:

●**Am I constantly fighting bouts of colds, the flu or bronchitis** that last for two or more weeks at a time?

●**Am I fatigued throughout the day**...or on a regular basis?

●**Do I suffer from chronic conditions** such as allergies, asthma or arthritis?

If you answered *yes* to any of these questions, your immune system is probably flagging.

Consult your doctor—but also consider taking several immune-boosting steps.

STRENGTHENING YOUR IMMUNITY

●**Improve the quality of your diet.** High-fat diets and a lack of vital nutrients compromise your immune system. That's because excessive intake of animal fats, such as red meats and whole-fat dairy products, trigger *free radicals* —unstable molecules that can harm immune cells.

Eating polyunsaturated vegetable oils, which are found in many snack foods, sauces, margarine and salad dressings, also produces free radicals.

●**To lower fat, cut back on red meats.** Instead, eat skinless chicken, fish and beans, which are excellent sources of protein.

●**Use moderate amounts of the safest oils—** olive and canola—instead of butter and other vegetable oils.

●**Eat more vegetables and fruits.** Nearly all are fat-free and contain immune-system-boosting nutrients such as vitamins A and C as well as *phytochemicals.* These compounds are found in plants and can fight disease.

Helpful: To get the proper amount of vitamins in your food each day, doctors advise that you eat a steamed vegetable side dish and a salad that includes dark leafy lettuce, peppers, bean sprouts, radishes and carrots at lunch and dinner. They also suggest you eat two to three pieces of fresh fruit each day.

●**Consider a vitamin/mineral supplement.** In a recent study of 96 people at the Memorial University of Newfoundland, some of the participants received a supplement with 18 nutrients while the other group received a pill with only calcium and magnesium in it. Those who received the larger supplement had fewer infections and half the number of sick days compared with others in the study. And... blood tests proved they had stronger immune responses to viruses.

Essential: Be sure any multivitamin and mineral supplement contains vitamins A, C, D and E...the B vitamins...beta-carotene...and the minerals zinc and selenium. Each nutrient plays a role in strengthening your immune system. Consult your doctor or nutritionist for doses.

Important: Avoid megadoses of specific vitamin supplements. Such doses can be dangerous—and won't boost your immune system any more than if you had taken the recommended amount.

● **Get into the habit of exercising daily.** Regular exercise has been shown to strengthen a particular group of immune cells that kills viruses and cancer cells. Researchers at the Harvard School of Public Health have shown that regular exercise can even prevent breast and gynecologic cancers among women.

Contrary to popular opinion, however, excessive exercise is not necessarily better for you. One recent study showed that excessive exercise—several hours a day of strenuous activity for five or more days a week—may actually dampen immunity, making you more susceptible to various ailments.

Better: About 30 minutes of aerobic exercise, such as walking, bicycling or swimming— three to five times per week. If that isn't possible, try a comfortable walking routine for 15 minutes a day.

● **Learn to reduce stress—and control your emotional health.** In a famous 1991 study published in *The New England Journal of Medicine*, scientists at Carnegie-Mellon University injected cold viruses into people and studied their stress levels. The researchers discovered that the chance of catching a cold was directly proportional to the amount of stress the volunteers had experienced.

Though most busy people can't avoid stress entirely, they can protect themselves from becoming consumed by it and learn to manage anxiety and pressure more efficiently. *Strategies…*

● **Write about your anxiety.** Holding in negative emotions has been shown to worsen stress levels and weaken immune cells. James Pennebaker, PhD, of Southern Methodist University, has shown that one can bolster immunity and prevent illness by jotting down thoughts of fear, grief and anger about stressful events—both past and present. Dr. Pennebaker suggests writing about such events for 20 minutes a day without stopping or censoring yourself.

By keeping a stress journal for three or four days, you will train yourself to identify toxic thoughts and unhealthy stress levels. You will develop a private way to release them and avoid letting them build up and aggravate and harm you.

● **Teach yourself to be more assertive.** Studies show that the patients who beat the odds against cancer and other serious illnesses are often assertive types who stand up for themselves and take charge of their own well-being. *Strategies for becoming more assertive…*

● **Use quiet contemplation or meditation** to develop an awareness of your needs and rights versus those of everyone else.

● **Engage in assertive communication** in which you clearly state your needs.

● **Learn to say *no*.** Conquer the habit of saying *yes* to every request or obligation when your energy is at stake. Remind yourself that your health comes first and taking on too much can risk your immune system.

● **Practice relaxation.** A study at Ohio State University showed that people who practiced relaxation techniques had stronger immune system cells. Two relaxation techniques that are easy to practice any time of day are *meditation* and *deep breathing.*

Useful exercise: Sit in a quiet room. Close your eyes and breathe deeply. Say the word *om* in your mind as you breathe in…and say the word *sah* as you exhale.

If your mind wanders, gently bring your attention back to your breathing. Allow each exhale to be an opportunity to let go of tensions in your body and mind. Practice this at least once a day for 20 minutes or whenever you feel that stress and tension have risen to an uncomfortable level.

Henry Dreher, a medical and science writer who specializes in complementary medicine. He is author of four books, including *The Immune Power Personality: Seven Traits You Can Develop to Stay Healthy* (Plume) and co-author with Alice Domar, PhD, of *Healing Mind, Healthy Woman* (Henry Holt).

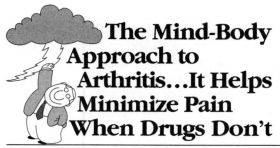

The Mind-Body Approach to Arthritis...It Helps Minimize Pain When Drugs Don't

Margaret A. Caudill, MD, PhD
Arnold Pain Center, Deaconess Hospital

If you suffer from arthritis, you probably already know that medication provides only partial relief.

Fortunately, arthritis—as well as headaches, back pain and most other forms of chronic pain—can be managed via a set of mind-body techniques. These techniques cost nothing and can be self-administered. They are effective whether your pain is caused by a clearly identifiable disease or is of mysterious origin.

ACUTE VS. CHRONIC PAIN

Acute pain is the body's way of warning us that something is wrong. When we get this "warning signal," we take immediate action to protect ourselves.

Example: We drop a plate that's too hot to hold. Doing so helps us avoid additional injury and gives the injury time to heal.

With *chronic* pain, there is no hot plate to drop. With no obvious way to protect ourselves, we respond emotionally. We slip into depression...become unable to work...experience trouble with our relationships, etc.

The key to coping with chronic pain is to live well *despite* the pain.

KEEP A PAIN DIARY

Keeping a pain diary will help you look at your pain objectively.

What to do: Three times a day, rate the intensity of your pain, from zero (no pain) to 10 (the worst pain ever). Also—describe the sensation. Is it an ache? Burning sensation? Tightness?

Note what you are doing when pain strikes. Rate your distress—the frustration, anger, anxiety or sadness you feel in response to the pain.

Record what you did to alleviate the pain— took an aspirin, went for a walk, applied heat or cold, etc.

Your diary will help you pinpoint things that ease or exacerbate your pain...and clearly show the difference between the pain itself and your emotional response to it.

USE THE RELAXATION RESPONSE

In many cases, the psychological stress caused by pain is worse than the pain itself.

Stress causes muscular tension that can lead to new ills—headache or upset stomach, for instance. Stress also aggravates the fatigue that often comes with chronic pain.

By eliciting your natural "Relaxation Response," you can alleviate this emotional stress.

Technique: Pick a time when your pain is relatively mild, and find a peaceful place where you won't be disturbed. Sit comfortably or lie down. Use a heating pad, ice pack or pillows to make yourself comfortable, if necessary.

Focus on your breathing. With each exhalation, silently repeat a word or phrase of your own choosing. This can be something neutral, like "one"...or something uplifting, such as "God."

Or, count each inhalation and exhalation, starting over when you reach 10. When your mind wanders, gently bring it back to your focus word or phrase. Elicit the Relaxation Response for at least 20 minutes a day.

If you like, elicit the Relaxation Response while exercising. Just make sure your breathing and thoughts are synchronized with your movements.

PERFORM SELF-HYPNOSIS

Once you have mastered the Relaxation Response, add self-hypnosis. While deeply relaxed, close your eyes and imagine that your right hand is becoming pleasantly warm and heavy. Each time you exhale, imagine the pleasant sensation intensifying.

Now imagine a pleasant numbness that begins in your thumb, then moves to each finger with each exhalation. Feel it spread to your palm and the back of your hand, stopping at the wrist.

Place that numb hand on the painful area of your body, or imagine the numbness moving to that spot. When all the numbness has been "absorbed" by the painful area, return to your focus word.

End each session by returning the numbness to your right hand. Feel the normal sensations return to that hand, breath by breath.

PACE YOURSELF

Some chronic pain sufferers try to ignore their bodies—pushing on until the pain becomes unbearable. Others simply shut down, withdrawing from social and/or professional activities.

Better: Pace yourself. Learn to complete your daily activities and live as normally as possible.

To do this, you must…

…tune in to your body. Use your pain diary and the Relaxation Response to become aware of subtle sensations that signal a flare-up.

…switch to a less demanding activity when you feel pain building. If you're washing dishes when your pain worsens, sit down and use the time to pay bills. Go back to the dishes later.

CHANGE YOUR SELF-TALK

The meaning you ascribe to your pain makes an enormous difference in its effect on your life and your mood.

What does your pain mean to you? To find out, listen to your *self-talk.* That's the voice in your head that continually comments on and interprets your pain.

In individuals with chronic pain, self-talk is quite distorted. They tend to *catastrophize*—making a bad situation worse by engaging in exaggerated self-talk.

Example I: Instead of telling yourself you can bear a flare-up, you think, "This pain is unbearable."

Example II: Instead of acknowledging the many things you can still do despite your pain, you say, "My whole life is ruined."

Don't give in to such negative self-talk. Make a conscious choice to change it. Say your pain is too severe to keep a lunch date. You think, "My whole day is ruined."

Substitute a realistic interpretation. "This is unfortunate, but I can make other arrangements. I'll invite my friend to come here, and we'll send out for pizza."

PLAN FOR FLARE-UPS

No matter how well you manage your pain, there will be times when it becomes intense. To be ready for these episodes, keep a written list of strategies that make you feel better—things you can do to reduce the pain *and* ease your emotional distress.

Examples: Lying down…applying heat or ice…performing self-hypnosis…calling a friend… or distracting yourself with a funny video.

HIGH-TECH HELP

Though medication can't stop chronic pain entirely, it can make your self-help program more effective. Four drugs are especially effective…

●*Gabapentin* (Neurontin). It seems effective for nerve pain caused by diabetes and post-herpetic neuropathy.

●*Mexiletine* (Mexitil). This is an oral form of the anesthetic lidocaine.

●*Fentanyl* (Duragesic). A new skin patch system delivers this potent painkiller continuously for three days.

●*Morphine* (Duramorph). The *intrathecal pump* constantly delivers morphine to the area around the spinal cord.

Margaret A. Caudill, MD, PhD, codirector of the Arnold Pain Center at Deaconess Hospital in Boston, and pain management director of the Lahey Hitchcock Clinic in Nashua, NH. She is author of *Managing Pain Before It Manages You.* Guilford Press.

Diet Pill Danger

Diet pills can cause a rare but often fatal lung disease called *primary pulmonary hypertension* (PPH). In a study of 450 people, those who took an appetite suppressant for more than three months faced a 23-fold increase in their risk of PPH, in which blood pressure in the lungs becomes elevated. Appetite suppressants studied include dexfenfluramine, fenfluramine, diethylpropion, phenmetrazine, fenproporex and mazindol.

Lucien Abenhaim, MD, director of the Centre for Clinical Epidemiology and Community Studies at Jewish General Hospital, Montreal.

Ginseng vs. Diabetes

Perilously high blood glucose levels fell to safe levels when individuals with non-insulin-dependent diabetes took 100 mg to 200 mg a day of ginseng. The diabetics also felt happier and more vigorous.

Caution: Diabetics should take ginseng only under a doctor's supervision.

Eero A. Sotaniemi, MD, PhD, associate professor of internal medicine at the University of Oulu, Oulu, Finland. His study was published in *Diabetes Care*, Children's Hospital, Rangos Research Center, 3705 Fifth Ave., Pittsburgh 15213.

Magnets Help Relieve Depression

Four of six patients felt better after undergoing an experimental procedure called *transcranial magnetic stimulation* (TMS).

What's involved: A handheld electromagnet is moved along the outside of the head. The magnetic field stimulates the "thinking" portion of the brain (*prefrontal cortex*)...and reactivates other areas of the brain shut down by depression. A larger clinical study of the treatment is under way.

Caution: TMS should be performed only by a physician. Trying it yourself could trigger a seizure.

Mark S. George, MD, associate professor of psychiatry, radiology and neurology at the Medical University of South Carolina, Charleston.

The Medical Gender Gap: Why Female Patients Are So Often Misdiagnosed... And What to Do about It

Susan Swedo, MD
National Institute of Mental Health

When a particular ailment causes psychological as well as physical symptoms, it may be mistaken for a purely psychological problem. Such misdiagnoses are especially common when the patient is a woman.

What explains this "medical gender gap?" There are three primary reasons...

● **Depression, anxiety and other emotional problems are more prevalent among women.** Because doctors are trained to think first of the most common illnesses when making a diagnosis, they may overlook other possible causes of psychological symptoms.

● **Doctors tend to dismiss women's complaints as exaggerated or imagined.** That goes for psychiatrists, gynecologists and other specialists, as well as general practitioners.

Most doctors do take patients' complaints seriously. But some are quick to attribute women's symptoms to hysteria. That's the name Freud gave to the theoretical condition in which women unconsciously create physical symptoms as a means of coping with inner conflict.

● **Women are more tentative than men in describing their symptoms.** In addition, they often fixate on an ailment's psychological manifestations.

Here are six common medical problems that are frequently misdiagnosed in women—even by competent doctors.

HYPOTHYROIDISM

Insufficient secretion of thyroid hormone (hypothyroidism) has been linked to fatigue and depression, including that occurring in the aftermath of childbirth (postpartum depression).*

Physical symptoms include loss of appetite, weight gain, muscular aches and/or dry skin.

Women with hypothyroidism are often assumed to be experiencing depression—and given a prescription for an antidepressant. But if underlying hypothyroidism goes untreated, levels of thyroid hormone will continue to fall...and the antidepressant's side effects may only exacerbate the physical symptoms.

Hypothyroidism can be detected via a physical examination and a blood test...and treated with thyroid-replacement medication. But the doctor has to do the test first—and not all do.

*Pregnancy places extreme stress on the thyroid. Up to 10% of women diagnosed with postpartum depression actually have a thyroid disorder.

*Hyper*thyroidism—a condition marked by *excess* thyroid secretion—is less common but potentially fatal.

It causes *physical* symptoms such as heat sensitivity…weight loss and hair loss…and *psychological* symptoms like anxiety, and—in extreme cases—confusion. Like hypothyroidism, hyperthyroidism is usually diagnosed by a blood test.

HEART ATTACK

Each year, many women with heart disease are sent home from emergency rooms after having been told by a doctor that they had suffered only a panic attack.

Doctors are especially likely to misdiagnose heart attack in women who have a history of anxiety.

Panic attacks often *do* mimic heart attacks. Both cause tightness in the chest, racing pulse and shortness of breath.

But since prompt treatment for heart attack can spell the difference between life and death, doctors should always err on the side of safety—for example, by keeping the patient in the hospital for observation. That doesn't always happen.

Any woman who has had panic attacks in the past should seek immediate medical attention if her symptoms feel any different from earlier episodes—or if they last longer.

AUTOIMMUNE DISORDER

Lupus, rheumatoid arthritis and other autoimmune disorders—more common among women than men—are often accompanied by changes in mood and/or mental function. Symptoms include fatigue, irritability, memory lapses, mental fuzziness and depression.

In part because these symptoms are so vague, autoimmune disorders are notoriously difficult to diagnose. The doctor must consider the patient's medical history and the results of physical exams and lab tests.

Once diagnosed, these conditions can often be controlled with immunosuppressive drugs such as prednisone.

ANEMIA

Several kinds of anemia affect women. The most common, iron-deficiency anemia, occurs when iron loss exceeds iron gained from the diet. In women, losses may be greater due to menstruation or the greater demand for iron due to pregnancy.

Anemia can also be caused by a lack of vitamins B-6 and B-12. This is usually caused by an intestinal disorder that prevents absorption of these essential vitamins.

Vitamin B-6 and B-12 anemia can also affect vegetarians and women taking oral contraceptives.

Psychological symptoms of anemia include depression, apathy and trouble concentrating. Physical symptoms can include poor appetite, weight loss, weakness, constipation and diarrhea.

B-vitamin deficiency can be controlled with a daily B-complex pill…or in shot form for patients who can't absorb B-12.

LYME DISEASE

In addition to fever and the characteristic bull's-eye rash, this tick-borne disease can cause a host of psychological symptoms, including irritability and personality changes.

The blood test for Lyme is not 100% accurate, and delaying antibiotic treatment can lead to chronic problems. Consequently, doctors in regions where Lyme is endemic often prescribe antibiotics solely on the basis of suspicious symptoms.

MEDICATION SIDE EFFECTS

Almost any prescription or over-the-counter drug *can* affect mental health. *Worst offenders:*

●*Oral contraceptives* can cause or aggravate depression.

●*Steroids* can cause anxiety, depression, mood swings and hallucinations.

●*Sleeping pills* can cause memory loss, confusion and difficulty concentrating.

●*Decongestants* and *appetite suppressants* can cause anxiety.

●*Ulcer drugs* can cause depression.

GETTING THE RIGHT DIAGNOSIS

Each time you see the doctor, bring a list describing your symptoms, what appears to trigger them and when they first appeared. Use the list to give the doctor specific, concise and *complete* information.

Also: Bring a list of all prescription and over-the-counter drugs (including nutritional supplements) you take.

If your symptoms are complicated, ask for the last appointment of the day. The doctor may be more focused if he/she doesn't have to rush off to the next appointment.

If the doctor seems unable to decipher your problem during the initial appointment, schedule a longer follow-up.

If your doctor fails to take your complaints seriously, find one who does.

Susan Swedo, MD, acting scientific director of the National Institute of Mental Health, Bethesda, MD. She is coauthor of *It's NOT All in Your Head.* Harper San Francisco.

Women Must Be More Aggressive about Their Own Health Care

Studies show that some *male* doctors are not as attentive to the needs of their female patients as they are to the needs of their male patients. This does not mean that women should only see female doctors.

Vital for women: Come to your appointments prepared with questions…fill out the health questionnaire thoroughly…make notes of the doctor's answers to your questions as well as any advice…and be sure the doctor explores all the options for treating a particular problem.

Helpful: If a doctor has taken a course on *women's* health.

Lila Wallis, MD, clinical professor of medicine at Cornell University Medical College and a former president of the American Medical Women's Association, Alexandria, VA.

Stop Muscle Pain In 90 Seconds

Dale Anderson, MD
University of Minnesota Medical School

Using a simple "fold-and-hold" technique, it's possible to stop most muscular aches in less time than it takes to make a doctor's appointment.

Fold-and-hold involves no drugs, dietary supplements or special instruments—just four simple steps…

1. Find the tender spot.

2. Move your body into a position that minimizes the pain. This usually involves "folding" one part of the body over another to reduce tension on the underlying muscle.

3. Hold the folded position for 90 seconds. Then slowly return to the original position.

4. Gently stretch in the opposite direction.

FOLD-AND-HOLD IS ESPECIALLY USEFUL FOR…

•**Bunions.** Twist the big toe under the foot and push toward the center of the foot. Do this yourself—or with the help of another person. Hold and release.

•**Heel spurs** (plantar fasciitis). Fold the bottom of your foot by pushing the heel and toes together. Although it's easier to get someone to do this for you as you lie on your stomach, you can do it yourself by pushing the top of your foot against the seat of a chair. Hold and release.

If fold-and-hold doesn't work after three tries, see a doctor. If fold-and-hold worsens your pain, stop immediately.

Dale Anderson, MD, clinical assistant professor at the University of Minnesota Medical School, Minneapolis. He is author of *Muscle Pain Relief in 90 Seconds.* Chronimed.

Vitamin E Benefits

Vitamin E can reduce muscle soreness and damage from vigorous exercise. Studies found the benefit when people took large

29

doses of vitamin E during the 24 hours before —and after—they engaged in vigorous exercise.

Recommended dosage: 400 IU daily for adults. Physicians believe this effect comes from the ability of vitamin E to combat DNA-damaging free radicals released by exercise. Other researchers are studying the relationship between exercise and other vitamins, including riboflavin (vitamin B2) and vitamin C.

Kenneth Cooper, MD, MPH, the inventor of aerobics and founder of the Cooper Clinic in Dallas. His most recent book is *Advanced Nutritional Therapies.* Thomas Nelson Publishers.

All You Ever Really Wanted to Know… Almost…About Vitamins & Minerals

Jeffrey Blumberg, PhD
Tufts University

Given the many conflicting vitamin studies that have recently emerged, it's easy to see why so many people are confused about which supplements to take and, of course, which ones to avoid.

•***Does beta-carotene prevent cancer…or cause it?*** The body converts beta-carotene into vitamin A. But beta-carotene is also an antioxidant—which neutralizes "free radicals" in your blood. Left unchecked, these highly reactive compounds can damage tissues and cells and possibly lead to diseases such as cancer.

More than 200 studies suggest that beta-carotene does indeed play a role in *preventing* cancer. A Chinese study of 30,000 people showed a significant decrease in the incidence of cancer and mortality in those who took a combination of beta-carotene, vitamin E and selenium.

Conflict arose with the release of three major studies that contradicted established results…

•***Two widely reported studies*** found that taking supplements of beta-carotene in the 30-to-50-milligram (mg) range may increase the risk of lung cancer. What wasn't mentioned in detail

by the media was that those who developed cancer were heavy smokers, heavy drinkers and/or asbestos workers.

•***The other major trial*** tracked 22,000 doctors and found that those taking 50 mg of beta-carotene every other day for 12 years had no increased risk of cancer—but no decrease either.

However, this study tracked men in the highest socioeconomic group in the US—physicians who had full access to health care and were more likely than the average person to have healthy lifestyles. Evidence suggests a potentially modest effect of beta-carotene, which is unlikely to be readily found in a low-risk group.

Strategy: Because we are not certain whether large doses of beta-carotene increase the risk of lung cancer in smokers or heavy drinkers (those who have more than two drinks per day), people who smoke and/or drink heavily should avoid beta-carotene supplements. But nonsmokers who do not drink heavily can take between 10 mg and 20 mg of beta-carotene daily to reduce their risk of cancer.

•***Do iron supplements cause heart attacks?*** One Finnish study showed a correlation between iron intake and increased risk of cardiovascular disease in older adults.

Reality: Several subsequent studies—most of which were conducted in the US—found absolutely no link between iron intake and heart disease.

Strategy: People age 50 or older who take a vitamin/mineral supplement containing the Recommended Daily Allowance (RDA) of iron —10 mg—need not worry that this minimal amount will trigger a heart attack.

Because people over age 50 do not need large amounts of iron anyway, it is best to steer clear of high-dose iron supplements—such as those containing more than 25 mg, which are wrongly promoted as "energizers" for the 50-plus crowd.

Women who are premenopausal should take 15 mg of iron per day…adult men should take 10 mg of iron per day.

•***Is folic acid only a must for pregnant women?*** When taken during the weeks before conception and the first two months of pregnancy, folic acid helps prevent neural tube problems and other birth defects.

But folic acid is an important supplement for everyone. A major study recently suggested that folic acid might prevent more than 50,000 deaths from cardiovascular disease each year in adults.

Folic acid lowers blood levels of a toxic amino acid called *homocysteine*, which is produced in the normal course of cell metabolism. High levels of homocysteine significantly raise the risk of heart attack and stroke.

Folic acid may also protect against colon cancer.

Strategy: All adults need to consume 400 micrograms (mcg) of folic acid daily. Spinach and dark leafy lettuces, such as romaine, are good sources...but you would have to eat about two cups of spinach a day to get your 400 mcg.

Alternative: A multivitamin supplement containing 400 mcg of folic acid.

●*Does vitamin E prevent serious diseases?* Probably not at the current US RDA level—which is 30 international units (IU).

Numerous studies link considerably higher doses of vitamin E to a decreased risk of cardiovascular disease...some forms of cancer... and cataracts and macular degeneration.

Preliminary research also indicates that vitamin E may slow the progression of neurological diseases, such as Parkinson's and Alzheimer's.

A recent British study of 2,000 people who had suffered heart attacks found that those who took 400 IU or 800 IU of vitamin E daily for a two-year period had a 77% reduction in the incidence of a second attack.

Strategy: There is little risk in taking vitamin E—and there is much evidence that it prevents disease. Supplements between 100 IU and 400 IU daily are advisable.

Why supplements? It's almost impossible to get enough vitamin E from a low-fat diet. The richest dietary sources are vegetable oils and nuts.

●*Is it true that calcium is the most important dietary factor in preventing osteoporosis?* Almost every major health organization recommends that people get their RDAs of cal-

cium. This mineral helps prevent osteoporosis and may reduce the risk of colon cancer and hypertension.

The problem is that calcium absorption depends on adequate levels of vitamin D in the body. The body manufactures vitamin D when it is exposed to sunlight. Vitamin D is also found in fortified milk and multivitamins.

As you age, your body becomes less able to manufacture vitamin D. About 80% of women over age 60—and almost as many older men— get less than two-thirds of the RDA of this nutrient.

Strategy: Make sure you get your daily dietary requirement of calcium—1,200 mg to 1,500 mg per day.

For those age 60 or older, a 400-IU vitamin D supplement daily is advisable.

●*Does vitamin C prevent colds?* While there is no sound evidence that vitamin C *prevents* colds, some studies show that daily 1,000-mg to 2,000-mg supplements can *lessen* the severity and duration of colds. That's because vitamin C has an antihistamine effect.

In addition, numerous studies link a lower daily intake of vitamin C to a decreased risk of some forms of cancer and heart and eye disease.

Strategy: A National Institutes of Health study suggests the current RDA of 60 mg of vitamin C is far too low—and that doses of 200 mg may be closer to our actual daily requirement for optimal health.

To lower your risk of serious diseases, consume between 250 mg and 1,000 mg daily in food or supplement form.

●*Do chromium supplements aid in weight loss?* Health food manufacturers claim that this trace mineral helps body-builders bulk up and the overweight shed pounds. The evidence for both claims, however, is weak.

Emerging research suggests that chromium may be an important player in the prevention of one of this nation's top killers—adult-onset, or Type II, diabetes—since chromium helps regulate glucose (sugar) levels.

Strategy: For people who are at risk for adult-onset diabetes because it runs in their families, studies suggest a 200-mcg chromium supplement daily. The average adult consumes only

25 mcg to 30 mcg a day, which may not be enough to ward off diabetes if you're at risk.

Important: Taking nutritional supplements can have health benefits, but too much of any nutrient can be dangerous to your health. Be sure not to exceed suggested dosages and to discuss any supplements with your doctor.

Jeffrey Blumberg, PhD, professor and chief of the Antioxidants Research Laboratory at Tufts University, Boston, one of the country's most prestigious schools for the study of health and nutrition. Dr. Blumberg is a leading vitamin supplement expert and has served on several national health advisory committees.

Medication for Headaches May Cause Headaches

Daily use of aspirin, acetaminophen, ibuprofen or other analgesics can create a rebound effect called *daily headache syndrome.*

Alternatives: Ice packs, heat massage, relaxation therapy or other nondrug means. Use medications sparingly for more troublesome headaches.

Robert Sheeler, MD, staff physician at the Mayo Clinic, Rochester, MN.

Magnesium Poisoning

Magnesium poisoning from antacids can occur in people who take large doses for a long time. Magnesium is also found in many laxatives and some pain relievers.

People most at risk: Those with improperly functioning kidneys...older people, since kidney function generally declines with age...people who have had intestinal surgery...those taking medicines that slow intestinal transit...anyone with longtime diabetes.

Self-defense: Use only the recommended amount of medicines that contain magnesium. If those doses do not help, do not increase them—see your doctor.

Bruce Yaffe, MD, an internist and gastroenterologist in private practice, 121 E. 84 St., New York 10028.

Heartburn Relief

Chewing gum helps control heartburn. In a recent study of 78 women, those who chewed gum after meals experienced much less heartburn than those who did not chew gum. They needed an average of only two antacid tablets a day, down from four a day before they began chewing gum.

Theory: Gum chewing stimulates production of saliva, which helps clear the esophagus of stomach acid.

Robert D. Marks, MD, assistant professor of medicine at the University of Alabama School of Medicine, Birmingham.

 # Back Pain Relief

Back pain can often be relieved by stretching the hamstrings (the muscles that run up the backs of the thighs). Tight hamstrings flatten the normal curvature of the lower back and "lock" the pelvis, increasing pressure on spinal disks.

How to stretch: Lie on your back with your left leg straight and your right knee drawn to your chest. Loop a belt around the sole of your right foot. Straighten the right leg, pushing the foot toward the ceiling. Use the belt to gently pull the outstretched leg upward, toward your head. Hold for a minute. Repeat three times, then switch legs.

Edward Laskowski, MD, codirector of the Sports Medicine Center of the Mayo Clinic, Rochester, MN.

Beating Back Pain

Glenn S. Rothfeld, MD
Spectrum Medical Arts

If you suffer from recurrent back pain, you've got lots of company. Eighty percent of Americans get back pain at some point during their lives...and each year billions of dollars are spent on surgery and pain pills to correct the problem.

Despite this investment, it's increasingly clear that conventional modern medicine is relatively ineffective against chronic back pain.

According to recent studies—including one published in the *New England Journal of Medicine*—most surgery to repair a herniated spinal disk is useless. In fact, the study found no correlation whatever between back pain and disk abnormalities.

Of course, if you have chronic back pain, it's prudent to have a doctor check you for tumors, infections, osteoporosis or other treatable conditions. Once these causes have been ruled out, look into alternative treatments...

STRETCHING/STRENGTHENING

Just a few years ago, doctors thought bed rest was the thing to do for back pain. Now we know that exercise is the single most important thing you can do to prevent and cure back pain.

Stretching and strengthening tight, weak muscles improves posture and helps prevent the leading causes of back pain—muscle fatigue and spasm.

Three days each week, get at least 20 minutes of aerobic exercise (walking, swimming, cycling, etc.). This boosts your metabolism and helps keep excess weight off. Obesity exacerbates back pain.

In addition, do the following three exercises daily...

●**Pelvic tilt.** Lie on your back, with knees bent. Suck in your stomach and tighten your buttocks. Keeping your feet and lower back flat on the floor, raise your hips. Hold this position for 10 seconds. Release slowly, then repeat.

●**Lower back stretch.** Lie on your back, legs straight in front of you. Clasp your hands behind your right knee and slowly pull it toward your chin, making sure to keep your left leg straight. Hold for 10 seconds, then repeat with your left knee.

●**Abdominal curl.** Lie on the floor with your knees bent. Tuck your chin into your chest, and place your hands across your chest. Tighten your abdominal muscles until your shoulders lift off the floor. Hold for three seconds, then slowly release. Repeat 20 times.

BIOFEEDBACK/MEDITATION

Many doctors—myself included—are now convinced that psychological stress plays a key role in most cases of back pain. Some—including John Sarno, MD, a professor at New York University and author of *Healing Back Pain* (Warner Books)—believe that the culprit is stress-induced clenching of the muscles in the lower back.

That's why it is of vital importance to take time each day to sit down and *consciously* relax —no matter how busy you are.

Problem: Some people have been under so much stress for so long that they've forgotten *how* to relax. If that describes you, consider biofeedback. Using electronic equipment, a practitioner can teach you to "switch off" your anxiety.

For more information and to find a biofeedback practitioner in your area, send a self-addressed, stamped, business-sized envelope to the Association for Applied Psychophysiology and Biofeedback, 10200 W. 44 Ave., Ste. 304, Wheat Ridge, Colorado 80033-2840.

Meditation offers another way to control stress. Once or twice a day, retire to a quiet place. Sit on the floor or in a straight-backed chair with your hands resting on your legs and eyes almost shut.

Take a deep breath and let it out slowly. Then start counting your breaths—inhale one, exhale two, inhale three, etc. Once you reach 10, start over.

For the first few weeks, limit each meditation session to five minutes. Once you get the hang of it, shoot for 15 to 30 minutes.

For more on meditation, see Jon Kabat-Zinn's *Full Catastrophe Living* (Dell).

PROGRESSIVE RELAXATION

Relaxation exercises are a good adjunct to meditation. *What to do:* Lie on your back with the small of your back flat against the floor and your knees bent. Take a deep breath and clench your toes. Then relax your toes and exhale, saying to yourself, "I feel relaxed."

Repeat this tension-relaxation cycle with your calves, thighs, stomach, chest, arms, shoulders, back, neck and face. When you've finished, lie with your eyes closed for five minutes.

THERAPEUTIC MASSAGE

I prescribe massage for almost all of my patients suffering from back pain. Massage soothes cramped muscles, increases blood flow and helps bring bones and muscles into proper alignment.

Especially effective: Therapeutic massage, myotherapy, Rolfing, Trager therapy and acupuncture.

Or, try acupressure. Stand with your knees slightly bent. Use the flat part of your thumb to stroke up and down along your spine several times, from tailbone to upper back, or as far as you can reach.

Next, stroke down with your thumb from the base of your neck to the middle of your back. Repeat on both sides.

CHIROPRACTIC

Recent studies suggest that chiropractic manipulation—having your spine "adjusted"—is just as effective as drugs or surgery...and far less costly.

If your doctor cannot recommend a chiropractor in your area, contact the American Chiropractic Association at 800-986-4636.

DIETARY INTERVENTION

Consumption of white flour, caffeine and especially sugar causes the body to produce high levels of insulin, which drives your blood sugar down.

Perceiving this subtle change in blood chemistry as a threat to the body's well-being, the brain activates the "fight-or-flight" response. That causes back muscles to tighten and even spasm.

Self-defense: Make fruits, vegetables and protein sources like lean meat the mainstays of your diet.

And—ask your doctor about taking a daily supplement containing magnesium, calcium, boron, the B-vitamins and vitamin K...as well as daily flax oil or fish oil capsules containing essential fatty acids.

YOGA

Yoga helps stop back pain by keeping the muscles and tendons of your back lithe and supple. Enroll in a yoga class at your local Y or experiment on your own. The following pose is especially effective...

Cobra pose. Lie face down with your legs together. Place your hands on the floor directly under your shoulders, fingers pointing forward. Breathe in deeply. At the same time, press down with your hands and lift your chest off the floor until your arms are fully extended. Hold, then slowly release while exhaling. Repeat three times.

CONTROLLING BACK PAIN

If you stress your back by exercising too vigorously, lifting a heavy object, etc., a cold pack applied to the injured area is often enough to ease the pain.

If you're still sore the following day, replace the ice pack with a hot water bottle wrapped in a moist towel.

If pain persists, ask your doctor about using a prescription muscle relaxant such as *cyclobenzaprine* (Flexeril) or *diazepam* (Valium)...or an anti-inflammatory like aspirin or ibuprofen.

Natural remedies for back pain include valerian tea, lotions containing willow and the homeopathic remedy *arnica*. These are available at health-food stores.

Glenn S. Rothfeld, MD, founder and medical director of Spectrum Medical Arts, an Arlington, MA, primary care center that blends conventional and complementary medical care. He is author of Natural Medicine for Back Pain: The Best Alternative Methods for Banishing Backache. Rodale.

Irritable Bowel?

Peppermint has long been a folk remedy for flatulence. But it's also effective for irritable bowel syndrome (IBS), a chronic disease marked by abdominal pain and altered bowel habits.

Theory: Menthol, peppermint oil's major constituent, blocks contraction of muscles lining the gut.

Peppermint can be taken in capsule form... or as a tea.

Jamison Starbuck, ND, a naturopathic physician in private practice in Missoula, MT.

The Truth About Dietary Iron: Too Much Can Be as Bad as Too Little

Herbert L. Bonkovsky, MD
University of Massachusetts Medical Center

Like many Americans, you may worry about not getting enough iron in your diet.

Yet there's growing evidence that most of us get all the iron we need from the food we eat …and that for some people, too much iron can be deadly.

●*How much iron does the average adult need?* About 10 mg a day. If you get less than that, and your body may be unable to transport oxygen and other nutrients to tissues…generate energy…and carry out other essential functions.

But iron deficiency is a public health problem primarily in emerging countries—because of their poor nutrition and the high prevalence of parasitic infection.

●*What's dangerous about consuming too much iron?* Beyond the tiny amount of iron excreted each day as cells die, the body has no way to get rid of excess iron.

Excess iron leads to increased production of *free radicals*, renegade molecules thought to play a role in causing heart disease and cancer.

Ironically, vitamin C supplements boost iron absorption. If someone with the iron-metabolism disorder *hemochromatosis* takes vitamin C supplements, this could lead even more quickly to dangerously increased levels of iron in the body.

If you want to boost your intake of antioxidants, it's safer to eat more fruits and vegetables …or to take supplemental vitamin E. It doesn't affect iron absorption.

●*Exactly what is hemochromatosis?* It's a condition in which the body absorbs too much iron from food. Since the body can't excrete it, the excess iron is deposited in the organs, where it causes inflammation and scarring.

Over time, iron-induced organ damage can cause serious health problems. The most common of these problems is cirrhosis of the liver. That's because the liver is the major storage site for excess iron.

Iron overload can also lead to heart failure (if iron is deposited in the heart)…diabetes (pancreas)…impotence or sterility (pituitary) …and arthritis (membranes lining the joints).

Since these effects are the culmination of years of iron deposition, they usually show up in people over 40. But there have been cases of fatal iron-related organ damage even in teenagers.

●*What causes hemochromatosis?* The usual cause is a defective gene. Though few people have heard of this condition, it's the most common heritable disease among whites in the US.

One out of every 10 whites carries a copy of the defective gene, which can be passed on to children. One out of 400 has two copies (one from each parent) and is therefore predisposed to develop hemochromatosis.

Iron overload is rare among Asians and African-Americans.

●*Does hemochromatosis have any non-hereditary causes?* Yes. A few cases are caused by multiple blood transfusions, such as those required in serious cases of anemia.

Anemia is a shortage of red blood cells—*not* a shortage of iron, as many people mistakenly think. Since red blood cells contain iron, repeated transfusions can lead to huge amounts of iron being stored in the body.

●*How is iron overload diagnosed?* Via a simple blood test, for serum iron and iron-binding capacity. Ideally, blood for this test should be drawn in the morning, eight hours after the most recent meal.

The results are expressed as *percent saturation*. Iron levels in excess of 60% suggest hemochromatosis.

A related blood test, called *serum ferritin*, measures the body's total iron stores. Any reading above 150 nanograms per milliliter (ng/ml) for women, and 250 ng/ml for men, is considered abnormal.

For an accurate diagnosis, *both* tests should be given—and repeated if levels are elevated.

•*Who should be tested?* Any white person age 21 or older. If the results are normal, the tests should be repeated every five years until age 45. An abnormal result calls for further testing.

Since hemochromatosis isn't the only condition that can cause an abnormally high iron saturation level, doctors often confirm a preliminary diagnosis of hemochromatosis with a liver biopsy.

•*How is hemochromatosis treated?* Most cases are treated via phlebotomy, a process similar to voluntary blood donation in which blood is drawn, usually 500 milliliters at a time.

Done once or twice a week, phlebotomy signals the bone marrow to use up excess iron to make more red blood cells—which are removed at the next bloodletting.

Rather than feeling fatigued from the blood loss, most hemochromatosis patients begin to feel *better* after several weeks of treatment, as the body rids itself of toxic levels of iron.

Treatment continues until the patient becomes *mildly* anemic. That can take from several months to a year or more.

Once iron stores have been depleted, patients generally continue giving blood indefinitely every two or three months to prevent reaccumulation of excess iron.

•*Can donating blood regularly keep people healthy?* I think it's a good idea for most people to donate blood regularly.

Blood banks don't accept blood from hemochromatosis patients. This is unfortunate, since hemochromatosis is not contagious and the blood is perfectly usable.

I hope the US will follow the lead of Canada and many European countries so that phlebotomy blood need not go to waste.

Herbert L. Bonkovsky, MD, professor of medicine, biochemistry and molecular biology, and director of the Center for the Study of Disorders of Iron and Porphyrin Metabolism, at the University of Massachusetts Medical Center in Worcester.

Relaxation Can Control Seizures

An epileptic who practices deep diaphragmatic breathing daily in meditation may be able to stop a seizure from taking control.

Helpful: A partner can focus the epileptic on the relaxation techniques. If someone reminds him/her to relax and breathe deeply, the epileptic can switch into the relaxation technique and minimize the seizure's effects.

Epilepsy: A New Approach by Adrienne Richard, an epileptic who uses mind/body techniques instead of anticonvulsants, and Joel Reiter, MD, a neurologist in Santa Rosa, CA. Walker & Co.

CFS Relief

Chronic fatigue syndrome (CFS) can often be helped by *cognitive behavior therapy*. In a recent study, two-thirds of CFS patients given this form of psychotherapy got better... compared with 27% who received only reassurance from the doctor.

Michael Sharpe, MD, tutor in psychiatry at the University of Oxford, England. His 12-month study of 60 CFS patients was published in the *British Medical Journal*, Tavistock Square, London WCIH 9JR, England.

Microwave Danger

Make sure there's an air space between the food and plastic wrap, or the food can become dangerously tainted with dyes and adhesives from the wrap.

Alternative: Use a dish made of heat-treated glass or porcelain...or a *microwave-safe* plastic (PETE or PP). While it's safe to microwave food on a paper plate or wrapped in a napkin or paper towel, cook only for a short time. Heat can release harmful dyes, coatings and/or additives.

Timothy Begley, research chemist at the Indirect Additives Branch of the Food and Drug Administration, Washington, DC.

Baldness Myths

Frequent shampooing increases hair loss… massaging the scalp stimulates hair growth …wearing a tight hat causes hair loss by reducing circulation and preventing the scalp from "breathing"…shaving makes hair grow thicker…a better diet or vitamin supplements will boost growth.

Reality: None of these factors affect hair growth.

Neal Schultz, MD, a dermatologist in private practice, 1040 Park Ave., New York 10028.

All About Hair Thickeners

For people with straight hair who want increased volume: Thickening shampoos and conditioners force *panthenol* into the hair to make each strand expand. Results last about two days.

For those with curly or layered hair: Thickening gels and mousses coat the hair with polymers and contain panthenol. They offer some control and soften curls.

For those with very wispy hair or who want to spot-treat one area: Thickening sprays coat the hair with polymers and help hair strands repel each other.

Mary Ellen Brademas, MD, assistant clinical professor of dermatology at New York University Medical Center, New York.

Wrinkle Relief

Some wrinkle-removing creams do work. Prescription products containing glycolic acid and others based on tretinoin (Retin-A) can remove fine wrinkles in the skin…not the deeper ones. Treatment, under a physician's supervision, takes several months to produce satisfactory results and must be continued to maintain results.

Warning: These substances may irritate the skin. Retin-A can make the skin very sensitive to the sun. It should not be used during pregnancy. Over-the-counter products containing alpha-hydroxy acids can improve skin texture and color but do not remove wrinkles.

Neal Schultz, MD, a dermatologist in private practice, 1040 Park Ave., New York 10028.

Estrogen May Delay Wrinkles

Estrogen treatment may slow wrinkling in postmenopausal women. Belgian researchers who tested postmenopausal women found that those who took estrogen hormone replacement therapy had skin that was almost as taut as that of premenopausal women. Scientists theorize that estrogen increases collagen levels and/or strengthens elastic fibers in the skin.

Brian Walsh, MD, director of the menopause clinic at Brigham and Women's Hospital, Boston.

Massage Promotes Good Health

Massage promotes general good health, not just relaxation. Massage also strengthens the immune system by increasing the number of natural killer cells in the body.

Study: HIV patients who received regular massage showed reduced stress and improved immune function. Massage may soon be considered as basic a component of good health as diet and exercise.

Tiffany Field, PhD, director of the University of Miami's Touch Research Institute, Dept. of Pediatrics, Box 016820 (D-820), 1601 NW 12 Ave., Miami 33101.

How Tuberculosis Can Be Spread

Tuberculosis can spread through social contacts. But the risk of developing the infection from a single exposure in a public place is extremely low because it generally takes many hours of exposure to a person who has TB in its active phase for any infection to occur.

Contagious case: A man with active TB infected 45 patrons of a bar. All of them—and the TB carrier himself—were regular customers.

Kenneth Castro, MD, director of the Division of Tuberculosis Elimination of the Centers for Disease Control and Prevention, Atlanta.

Permanent Hearing Loss

Permanent hearing loss can occur after only 30 minutes at a loud (120-decibel) concert. Rifle ranges, power tools, industrial noise, discos and personal stereo headsets can also cause damage.

Self-defense: Wear earplugs, sold at drugstores or hardware stores, if noise becomes bothersome or painful. They won't block out noise completely, but they will soften it. *If you don't have earplugs:* Insert cotton in your ears. But it is always best to remove yourself from the noise.

Christopher Linstrom, MD, chief of neuro-otology at the New York Eye and Ear Infirmary, New York.

Grief Helplines

If you'd like emotional support following the death of a loved one, here are five helplines...

- **Widowed Persons Service** (202-434-2260).
- **Compassionate Friends** (630-990-0010).
- **Grief Recovery Helpline** (800-445-4808).
- **Hospice Link** (800-331-1620).
- **National Self-Help Clearinghouse** (212-354-8525).

Petroleum Jelly Aid

Prevent chafed skin due to friction from clothes—or from skin rubbing against skin —during exercise by applying petroleum jelly to the problem areas on the skin.

Bruce Katz, MD, director of the Laser and Skin Aesthetics Center, and associate clinical professor of dermatology at Columbia College of Physicians and Surgeons, New York.

Painless Adhesive Bandage Removal

Soak a cotton ball in baby oil and wipe it around the sides of the bandage. In about 10 minutes, the adhesive will be softened—making bandage removal easy and painless.

Kathryn Marion, editor of *The Reality Check Gazette*, 8667 Sudley Rd., Manassas, VA 22110.

Mouth Piercing Dangers

Piercing the tissues of the mouth can cause permanent damage. Rings, small metal barbells and other objects can fracture teeth... damage cheek tissue...cause permanent numbness or loss of taste or movement...inflame or enlarge the lips.

Howard S. Glazer, DDS, FAGD, president of the Academy of General Dentistry, Chicago, and in private practice in Fort Lee, NJ.

Better Dandruff Shampoo Use

Apply shampoo twice. Leave the first application on your hair for one to two minutes, then rinse and relather. Leave the second application on your hair for three to five minutes. That is how long the medication needs to work.

For serious dandruff problems: Ask your doctor about *Nizoral,* a potent antidandruff shampoo available only by prescription.

Richard Berger, MD, clinical professor of medicine at the University of Medicine and Dentistry of New Jersey, Robert Wood Johnson Medical School, New Brunswick, NJ.

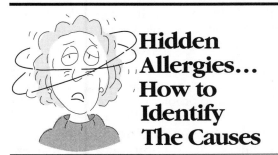

Hidden Allergies... How to Identify The Causes

Janice M. Joneja, PhD
Vancouver Hospital and Health Sciences Centre

Ever had a rash, stomach problem or respiratory ailment that defied diagnosis? You might have been suffering from a hidden food reaction.

Up to 1% of adults and 7% of children under age five have at least one food *allergy*—an abnormal immune system response triggered by exposure to "foreign" proteins.

Food allergies can produce severe symptoms. Severe cases can lead to anaphylactic shock.*

Leading causes of food allergy: Fish (including shellfish)...cow's milk...eggs...wheat (including bread and pasta)...peanuts...tomatoes...spinach...strawberries...raspberries... oranges...mangoes.

It's estimated that 5% to 50% of all adults suffer from a related problem called food *intolerance.* This adverse reaction does *not* involve the immune system—but it produces similar symptoms.

Many cases of food intolerance are caused by a lack of one or more digestive enzymes. This deficiency impairs the body's ability to break down certain proteins in food.

Leading causes of food intolerance: Lactose...sulfites...artificial colors...food additives

*A potentially deadly condition marked by a drop in blood pressure, anxiety, reddening and swelling of the face, sometimes hives, tightness in chest and throat, difficulty breathing. Anyone experiencing these symptoms needs immediate medical attention.

like *monosodium glutamate...histamines* (compounds in fermented foods like cheese, sauerkraut, alcoholic beverages and vinegar) ...*tyramine* (an amino acid in aged cheeses, yeast extract, wine, beer, raspberries and bananas)...and food preservatives like *benzoic acid* and *sodium benzoate.*

PINPOINTING FOOD REACTION

Food allergies and intolerances manifest themselves differently in different people. A food that might give one person a rash might give another stomach pain.

Predictably, doctors often have a hard time pinpointing the trouble. Misdiagnoses are very common.

If you suspect certain foods are making you ill, ask your doctor to refer you to a food-allergy specialist—someone experienced in the use of the "elimination and challenge diet."

This diet—the only surefire way to pinpoint food reactions—has two phases. During the four-week *elimination* phase, all suspect foods are off limits. Symptoms often begin to clear up during this phase.

During the ensuing *challenge* phase, lasting a few weeks to a few months, suspect foods are reintroduced one at a time. The patient watches carefully to see if symptoms return.

Here are four case histories illustrating the most common—and commonly overlooked— food allergies and intolerances...

CASE HISTORY #1

Jack, a 48-year-old salesman, had a long history of headaches, bloating, gas and abdominal pain. His symptoms usually began an hour or so after breakfast and lasted all day. He also complained of constant fatigue and was having difficulty concentrating.

Jack exhibited no signs of gastrointestinal disease and had regular bowel movements. He went on a diet that excluded wheat, rye, oats, barley, corn and milk products. (He took an 800-mg calcium supplement to make up for the lost calcium.) In addition, he ate no raw fruit or vegetables—only cooked or canned were permitted—and no whole nuts or seeds.

After four weeks, Jack was "challenged" with each of the above foods. It turned out he was allergic to wheat, raw fruits and vegetables and highly fermented foods (cheese, wines, beer).

Now that Jack avoids these foods, his symptoms have abated. His energy has increased threefold, he says.

CASE HISTORY #2

Mary, a 50-year-old nurse, was troubled by constipation, mood swings and leg cramps. She was also concerned about the poor condition of her nails and teeth.

She was taking a variety of medications—including herbal supplements and an antidepressant. Nothing seemed to help.

Mary's symptoms suggested an intolerance or allergy to several *different* foods. Indeed, an elimination diet revealed allergies to food additives, wheat and dairy products.

After giving up these foods for three months, her physical and emotional health improved. Within six months Mary was no longer constipated. She felt better than she had in 10 years.

CASE HISTORY #3

A 62-year-old telephone company employee named Virginia had a history of asthma and hay fever dating back to childhood. She was also bothered by stomach upset, flaky skin on her hands and feet...and a dangerously elevated cholesterol level.

Though she had been on a restricted diet, Virginia couldn't shake her symptoms. Then a series of elimination and challenge tests revealed sensitivity to certain nuts and seeds, wheat and and dairy products.

Within months of giving up these foods, Virginia's symptoms had disappeared, and her cholesterol level had fallen to normal.

CASE HISTORY #4

Rita, a 56-year-old computer worker, was plagued by diarrhea, gas and abdominal pain. She'd had these problems since childhood, but they had intensified over the past year.

When a thorough exam revealed no underlying illness, Rita was put on a diet that excluded grains, starches and sugar.

In the next four weeks, she reported only two episodes of diarrhea—and each occurred after she cheated on her diet. Subsequent challenges showed that she was affected adversely by foods containing refined sugar.

Having given up these foods permanently, Rita is now completely free of symptoms.

Janice M. Joneja, PhD, director of the allergy nutrition program at Vancouver Hospital and Health Sciences Centre, British Columbia. She is author of the medical textbook *Managing Food Allergy & Intolerance: A Practical Guide* (McQuaid), and coauthor of *Understanding Allergy, Sensitivity and Immunity* (Rutgers).

2

The Savvy Traveler

Lessons in Traveling Smarter and Cheaper

Richard Reeves and Catherine O'Neill

Travel is nothing new to us. Through our careers in journalism and charity work, we've traveled all over the world.

But taking our five kids—ages 10 to 35, and a five-week-old grandchild—around the world in just 34 days for only $29,700 taught us a great deal about saving money and avoiding hassles. *Here are the most important things we learned on our trip...*

• **Research the cost of complicated flights on your own.** Turning the job over to a travel agent might save you some time, but it's likely to cost you more than it should for a trip like this. Quite a few airlines offer round-the-world tickets, and no two plans are exactly the same. There also might be differences between the total number of miles or stops you're allowed

...or the time period in which you must complete the trip. Some tickets are good for six months...others for 12.

In our case, selecting round-the-world tickets required considerable compromise. When we planned the trip, we had pins all over our map indicating places we hoped to visit. In the end, we had to skip many of these places because our planes didn't stop there.

There were so many variables involved in selecting tickets that a travel agent would have had no way of knowing where best to compromise.

Example: I spent a few months gathering brochures on the plans offered by various airlines. Then we picked the one that came the closest to our goal at the lowest possible price. It turned out to be a combination ticket offered by Delta, Swissair and Singapore Airlines for $2,628 each—with one-third off for our 10-year-old daughter. Unfortunately, these tickets couldn't get us to some of the destinations that we had hoped to visit. We decided to pay extra to have other carriers take us to Indonesian and Pakistani cities we especially wanted to visit.

41

Once we had the whole thing worked out, I called our travel agent. I told her that we would be willing to list her as the travel agent —even though we did all the work—if she would throw in half of her 10% commission. So…we saved an extra 5%.

●**Buy a few business-class tickets—they're worth it.** We upgraded two of our tickets to business class but left our children in coach. That seems a bit undemocratic—and business- or first-class tickets sometimes cost about 50% more than coach tickets—but in the end it was one of the best moves we made.

As parents, we felt we deserved the extra comfort. It also let our family settle in two different sections, so we could separate the kids if they started to get on each others' nerves.

As business-class travelers, we got to use the "priority" check-in lines and special customs booths. With the number of flights we were taking, this saved us a tremendous amount of airport time and stress.

Moreover, we found that as long as one person in the group had a business-class ticket, our whole group could use the airline's VIP lounge. We saved money by eating meals there, and occasionally we even used the lounges to get some sleep between flights.

●**Never pay full price for lodgings.** Unless you know the areas you're visiting well, it's best to start by calling worldwide hotel chains before you depart. Find out which ones offer discounts.

If nothing turns up, call the country's national tourist office. Explain that you're looking for affordable lodging, and they might be able to send you some promotional materials.

Example: The Japanese National Tourist Office sent us some "Budget Tokyo" brochures that were a great help. The train from the airport was a lot cheaper than the hundreds of dollars it would have cost for cabs.

Whenever you contact any hotel or hotel chain, see if you can work out a better deal. Mention AAA, AARP or any other organization to which you belong. You never know what's going to work best. Some people are too proud to ask for a senior citizen's discount… but it can reduce hotel bills by as much as half.

●**Each person needs only one bag.** We've always tried to limit the amount of luggage we take on family vacations—and we have had limited success.

An extended trip required us to take the one-bag rule seriously. We couldn't just drop our bags at a hotel and be done with them. We had to lug them from country to country. *Strategies…*

●**Copy key pages from travel guides,** instead of lugging books for every country you visit.

●**Cut back on the fancy clothes.** Unless you're heading to locations where you know formal clothes are expected, bring a single set of decent clothes—and nothing you would feel bad about if it were ruined. Travel is hard on clothes.

●**Dress nicely enough so that you can respect local customs.** It is especially important not to let teens talk you out of taking appropriate clothes for them or yourself.

Example: Richard missed out on seeing the inside of a historic mosque because he was wearing Bermuda shorts, which wasn't appropriate garb.

●**Look presentable when deplaning at airports.** We adults always sailed through customs. But our boys—who were unshaven and in T-shirts—were strip-searched in Tel Aviv.

●**Consider mailing all of your large purchases home** and carrying your small, light souvenirs with you.

WHAT YOU SHOULD TAKE WITH YOU

●**Bags of dried fruit and nuts.** These came in handy where we didn't trust that the food was safe. They also were a good idea for traveling with young children, who didn't always appreciate the local cuisine. In fact, we wish we had brought enough for the entire European leg of the trip so that we could have avoided eating at expensive restaurants three times a day.

●**Bag of medicines.** During an earlier trip, one of our sons had become very sick after drinking the water in India. We didn't want to be running around desperately looking for medication if something similar happened this time, so we packed Imodium. Especially important were alcohol swabs for cleaning things, ibuprofen, anti-mosquito lotion and sunscreen.

• **Binoculars.** They're the one thing people often forget. You can see so much more with them.

BOTTOM LINE

• **Don't wait for the perfect opportunity for a dream trip.** Perfect opportunities never arrive. Because of our schedules, we had to complete our trip around the world in 34 days. That's not a lot of time to travel the globe, but it was the best we could do…and it was great for us—and the kids.

Richard Reeves, a nationally syndicated columnist and former chief political correspondent for *The New York Times*, and his wife, Catherine O'Neill, founder of the Women's Commission for Refugee Women and Children. Mr. Reeves is author of several books, including *Family Travels: Around the World in 30 (or So) Days*. Andrews and McMeel.

For Cheaper Travel And More Comfort… Planning Pays

Ed Perkins

When I travel, I like to have an enjoyable, comfortable trip without spending a lot of money on higher levels of luxury.

The secret of being pampered and saving big is a little advance planning.

AIRLINE UPGRADES

Before I travel on vacation, I amass as many frequent-flier miles as I can on the leading carrier that serves my destination.

My goal isn't to fly free, but to get upgrades as inexpensively as possible. I hate coach and would rather stay home than travel cattle-car style. *Strategies…*

• **Make sure you fly enough on one airline to reach at least the first level of frequent-flier status.** Each airline has a different name for this status.

Examples: "Continental Elite," "Delta Medallion" and "United Premier."

The minimum requirement is 25,000 to 30,000 actual air miles per year. When you're a "very frequent flier," you are allowed to buy upgrades to business or first class for relatively small amounts. Cost of an upgrade to business is often $40 for each 1,000 miles you'll be flying. If the airplane has no business class, you fly first class.

Example: Upgrading from coach to business on a San Francisco to New York trip would cost about $120.

Improve the odds of getting what you want by making your reservation on a plane that has a lot of business-class or first-class seating. Shop for the best flight—ask the airline how many business-class seats different flights have.

Additional savings: When traveling in the US, I purchase one-way senior discount tickets—$598 for a book of four coach tickets. Then I upgrade those seats. Any travel agent or airline ticket office sells books of tickets.

On international flights, I use frequent-flier miles instead of cash to upgrade my seat. It's a better deal, since business class on foreign flights can cost from two to 10 times what coach does.

HOTELS

When booking hotel rooms in the US, I usually save $50 to $150 per room per night by using a hotel broker.

Generally, hotel brokers can get you great deals in the top 25 metropolitan areas on hotels that are mid-priced or above.

Examples: You should expect to get 20% to 60% off the standard rate by using a broker. Two that handle many different cities are Hotel Reservations Network (800-964-6835) and Quikbook (800-789-9887).

RESTAURANTS

I use an airline dining card that gives me 10 frequent-flier miles for each dollar I spend at a restaurant.

I also have a separate dining card which gives me a 25% rebate when I dine in designated restaurants.

Though I don't plan my entire trip around restaurants that accept these cards, I do check to see which places that I'd like are listed as restaurants that accept the card.

CAR RENTALS

I never assume that any car rental company has the cheapest rates, no matter where I am. So—I call four or five rental companies in advance to see who has the best deal when I need to rent a car.

When traveling to Europe, I always reserve the car before I leave. That usually guarantees me a lower rate.

Be sure to ask your travel agent about promotional rates for American travelers.

Size counts: Don't ever rent a car that is too small for your needs. I've learned the hard way that when you're doing a lot of driving, and someone has to sit in the backseat, it is essential that you have enough leg room. In such cases, getting a compact car is never worth the money you save.

SHOPPING

Before shopping abroad, know exactly what a similar item costs in the US. That way, you'll buy less, and you'll avoid bad buys.

Ed Perkins, editor of *Consumer Reports Travel Letter*, which specializes in travel savings strategies and lists current deals on hotels and cruises, 101 Truman Ave., Yonkers, NY 10703.

Airfare "Sales" May Not Be Bargains

Sale prices may be higher than standard prices for advance-purchase tickets.

Example: One airline heavily advertised a Chicago-to-Denver fare of $287 as a 40% saving over its regular fare of $478. But it had been offering a $268 advance-purchase fare for some time.

Helpful: Buy tickets as far in advance as possible. The farther in advance you buy, the lower the price usually is. But—since this is not always the case—it is best to book through a knowledgeable travel agent, not directly with the airline.

Tom Parsons, editor of *Best Fares Discount Travel*, 1301 S. Bowen Rd., Arlington, TX 76013.

Big Airfare Moneysaver: Red-Eye Flights

These overnight flights can cost 20% to 50% less than daytime flights to the same desti-

nations. Many do not require advance purchase or a Saturday night stay to get the low fares. Some offer even deeper discounts if you do buy tickets in advance.

Caution: Overnight flights tend to be crowded because of their low fares. And many are not nonstop, making trips longer.

Randy Petersen, editor of *Inside Flyer*, 4715-C Town Center Dr., Colorado Springs 80916.

You and Your Frequent-Flier Miles

Get more value for your frequent-flier miles by *not* using them for airline tickets.

Find out the number of miles needed for a ticket—and the price if you paid cash. Divide the miles into the cash price to find the value per mile.

Example: If it takes 25,000 miles to get a ticket worth $306, each point is worth 1.22 cents.

Compare that with the point value if you take a free night in a hotel or a discounted shopping spree. The value of each mile is likely to be twice as great when not used for a ticket.

Randy Petersen, editor of *Inside Flyer*, 4715-C Town Center Dr., Colorado Springs 80916.

Better Airporting

Get seat assignments and boarding passes in advance. Airline and travel agents cannot issue the passes more than 30 days before a flight—so if you purchase your ticket earlier, have your travel agent arrange for the boarding pass to be sent to you when available. If tickets are purchased directly from the airline, boarding passes can be obtained only at the airport or city ticket offices.

Geoff Collins, director of public relations for the International Airline Passengers Association, Dallas.

Your Seating Can Be Dangerous to Your Health

Too-tight airline seats can lead to "economy-class syndrome"—a circulatory condition that can result in potentially fatal blood clots. On long flights, when you have little opportunity to move around, clots may develop in your legs. They usually dissolve once you get off the plane—but in very rare instances, they can travel to the lungs or brain, causing an embolism.

Self-defense: During long flights, get up and stretch every 45 minutes…massage your legs and feet while seated…don't wear tight socks or shoes while flying.

Stanley R. Mohler, MD, director of aerospace medicine at Wright State University School of Medicine, Dayton, OH.

Need More Room?

To get three seats for two people on an airplane, book the window seat and aisle seat in a three-seat row. Agents usually book the middle seat last, so if your flight isn't full, you are likely to get an empty seat between you. And if the middle seat *is* taken by someone, that person probably will be happy to "swap" into a window or aisle seat, enabling you and your companion to sit together.

Herbert J. Teison, publisher of *Travel Smart*, 40 Beechdale Rd., Dobbs Ferry, NY 10522.

More Comfortable Airline Seating

Don't just ask for an airline seat on the aisle —ask to have the aisle on the side that your writing arm is on. If you plan to work on the flight, your "working arm" will have more room. And you'll feel more comfortable even if you just plan to relax.

Merrill Douglass, president of Time Management Center, Atlanta, quoted in *Industry Week*, 1100 Superior Ave., Cleveland 44114.

All Flights Booked?

Get to the top of the waiting list by asking for a full-coach or first-class ticket. Airlines don't talk about it, but they give priority to full-fare standbys—pushing discount-ticket holders to the bottom of the list.

Nancy Dunnan, managing editor of *Travel Smart*, 40 Beechdale Rd., Dobbs Ferry, NY 10522.

On-Time Performance

Ask about a flight's on-time performance rating before booking it. Every airline flight is rated from one to 10. One means it arrives on schedule 10% of the time…10 means a 100% on-time record. Before booking, ask your travel agent for the flight's rating —especially if making connections or traveling to a meeting for which you cannot afford to be late.

Herbert J. Teison, publisher of *Travel Smart*, 40 Beechdale Rd., Dobbs Ferry, NY 10522.

How Much Time to Allow Between Flights

When you must make an airline connection, allow at least an hour between flights. When taking a flight that makes stops, look for one that stops at small airports—their lighter air traffic makes delays less likely.

Wing Tips: How to Deal with Airline Delays, Cursed Cancellations, Lamentably Lost Luggage and Any Unexpected Adversity and Still Keep Smiling by Allen Klein, a speaker on using humor in stressful situations. Wings Books.

Connecting Flight Trap

Never book the last connecting flight of the day. If your incoming flight arrives late or the connecting flight is canceled, you may be stranded and forced to spend the night in the hub city.

Consumer Reports Travel Letter, 101 Truman Ave., Yonkers, NY 10703.

Lost Airline Ticket

Losing an airline ticket can be costly as well as inconvenient. Airlines have varying requirements for replacement. You may have to buy a new ticket—often at current rates, which could be much higher than what you originally paid—and then file a lost-ticket application. It can take up to 18 months for reimbursement. You may also have to sign a form stating that if someone uses the ticket you lost, you agree to pay the cost of your replacement ticket and that you will *not* be refunded for the lost ticket.

Helpful: Photocopy your tickets and store them separately while traveling—for documentation in case of a loss.

Condé Nast Traveler, 360 Madison Ave., New York 10017.

Ask Airline for Refund

If airfares drop *after* you buy your ticket, ask for a refund of the difference. Airlines will give it if your trip meets the restrictions of the new fare.

Example: If the new fare requires two-week advance purchase, you must change your ticket two weeks before your flight. And—there must still be seats available at the new fare for the airline to change your ticket. You may be charged a ticket-changing fee.

Wendy Perrin's Secrets Every Smart Traveler Should Know by Wendy Perrin, consumer travel writer. Fodor's Travel Publications.

No More Earaches When Flying

Take one decongestant tablet containing pseudoephedrine at least 30 minutes before your flight leaves. A recent study found that following this regimen relieved discomfort in 68% of travelers with recurrent ear pain, compared with only 38% of those who took a placebo. One pill works all day, so there's no need to take more if your flight is delayed.

Important: Check with your doctor before trying this regimen to ensure that the pseudoephedrine does not conflict with other medications or health conditions.

Jeffrey Jones, MD, director of the department of emergency medicine at Butterworth Hospital, Grand Rapids, MI. His study of 190 fliers with recurrent ear pain was reported in *Annals of Emergency Medicine.*

Air Pressure Change Relief

Nasal decongestants work faster than oral decongestants and can be helpful on airplane trips to ease painful blockages triggered by changes in pressure.

What to do: Shortly before takeoff, spray each nostril with a nasal decongestant such as Afrin. Before landing, start chewing gum as the plane begins its descent.

Also: Hold your nostrils closed, and gently try to blow through your nose. This can keep your ears open.

Jack B. Anon, MD, associate clinical professor of otolaryngology at the University of Pittsburgh, Erie, PA.

Use Earplugs when Flying

This cuts noise that contributes to fatigue and jet lag.

For added comfort: If you did not get enough to eat or did not like your meal, ask for something else. Airlines usually have extra food on board, which they throw away at the end of the flight.

Old trick used by flight attendants to relieve earaches: Moisten a tissue in hot water, put it into a disposable cup and hold it over the ear until pain disappears, usually five to 10 minutes.

Herbert J. Teison, publisher of *Travel Smart*, 40 Beechdale Rd., Dobbs Ferry, NY 10522.

Ordering Special Meals

When booking a flight, ask your travel agent to order a special meal even if you *don't* need one for medical purposes.

Why: You'll eat better. Special meals are prepared to order, so they are fresher than standard meals.

Herbert J. Teison, publisher of *Travel Smart*, 40 Beechdale Rd., Dobbs Ferry, NY 10522.

Always Carry Photo ID

Always have photo identification when traveling by air—airlines now require it for security purposes. Make sure the name on the ticket is the same as on your photo ID. Women who use their maiden names in business, but have their married names on their identification, have been turned away by airlines. Avoid using nicknames or initials on tickets unless they also appear on a photo ID.

Caution: Do not try to use someone else's ticket. Previously it was possible for family members to trade tickets. This is no longer possible with increased security. *Also:* Children under age two should have birth certificates or immunization records to prove age.

Jim Langley, owner of The Travel Agency, Chiefland, FL.

Less Back Pain on Plane

If cramped airline seats make your back hurt, ask the cabin attendant for a small pillow… double it over…place it in the middle of your lower back. This helps maintain your spine's natural curve and will make the flight more comfortable.

Glenn Rothfeld, MD, founder and medical director of Spectrum Medical Arts, Arlington, MA.

Help for Dry Cabin Air

The dry cabin air on any long airline flight can lead to eye irritation, itchiness and scratchiness.

Helpful: Moisten travel-induced dry eyes with artificial tears containing *carboxymethylcellulose (CMC)* in a preservative-free solution such as Refresh Plus™ from Allergan.

Caution: Do not treat the condition as *red eye* and use vasoconstrictors—which eliminate redness only temporarily and will not restore needed moisture.

Alan Shabo, MD, clinical professor of ophthalmology at UCLA's Jules Stein Eye Institute, Los Angeles.

In-Air Contact Lens Care

Soft contact lenses, especially disposables, are more likely to dry out in the zero-humidity environment of airplane cabins.

Self-defense: Travel with eyedrops and a lens case. Use drops regularly on short flights. Remove lenses during long flights.

Melvin Schrier, OD, retired optometrist who was in private practice for more than 45 years.

Electronic Airline-Ticketing Traps

Electronic tickets—which replace paper tickets with confirmation numbers—won't speed up check-in, even if you have only carry-on luggage. You still need a paper boarding pass. They are not transferable to other carriers if you end up switching flights. And their receipts may not be accepted for business reimbursement since the receipts do not prove you actually flew.

Ed Perkins, editor of *Consumer Reports Travel Letter*, which specializes in travel savings strategies and lists current deals on hotels and cruises, 101 Truman Ave., Yonkers, NY 10703.

Free Flight Insurance Is Offered by Many Credit Cards

Many cardholders and their beneficiaries do not realize that they must make a claim in case of an accident or death. A card issuer will pay out only when a beneficiary makes a claim and proves with a receipt that the ticket was bought with a credit card.

Ruth Susswein, executive director of Bankcard Holders of America, 524 Branch Dr., Salem, VA 24153.

Hotel Savvy

Check hotel rates carefully when planning a trip. On trips lasting more than a few days, savings on accommodations can be far more important than lower airfares. But many travelers focus on finding the lowest airfares and spend too little time researching hotels.

Jens Jurgen, editor of *Travel Companions*, Box 833, Amityville, NY 11701.

Little-Known Hotel Discounts

Ask for the *shareholder rate* if you own stock in the company that owns or manages the hotel. A *frequent-flier rate* may be available if you fly on an airline with which the hotel has a partnership. *Emergency-situation rates* are given to people traveling because of family illness or stranded by natural disasters. *Family package rates*, often available at resorts, include breakfast or recreational discounts. *Corporate rates* are often available if you have a business card, even if you are not traveling on business.

The Beardstown Ladies' Guide to Smart Spending for Big Savings by The Beardstown Ladies' Investment Club, Beardstown, IL. Hyperion.

Specify Hotel Room Requirements when Making Reservations

Hotels may not be able to honor specific requests—for instance, for nonsmoking rooms—at the time of arrival.

Useful: Call the hotel directly, not the toll-free reservations number. Call at a slow time—usually around lunchtime, local time. Then make specific requests.

Examples: A room away from the ice machine and elevators...a room on a different floor from the one a convention will be using during your stay. Restate requests on arrival. Do not hesitate to ask to see a room before accepting it.

Roundup of travel experts reported in *The New York Times.*

Questions to Ask Before Booking a Room

Can I cancel my reservation—or check out a day early—without penalty? How late can I arrive without having paid for my room in full? Is there room service—and if so, during what hours? Some hotels have reduced the hours for room service or cut it out entirely. Does the quoted rate include tax and service charges... breakfast...parking?

Travel Companions, Box 833, Amityville, NY 11701.

Watch Your Bags During Hotel Check-In

A thief can make off with something while you are dealing with room reservations. Be equally careful when checking out—do not be distracted while you are focusing on the bill.

Helpful: Choose a small hotel instead of a large, bustling one. Smaller hotels do not attract many thieves, because people who do not belong there are more conspicuous.

Protecting Your Assets: How to Safeguard and Maintain Your Personal Wealth by Andrew Westhem, chairman of Wealth Transfer Planning, Inc., La Jolla, CA. Carol Publishing.

Early Checkout Penalties

Ask about early checkout penalties—if you're booking at a hotel for more than one night. Most charge only for the nights you actually stay. But some charge a penalty for early departure—claiming they could have turned away reservations because they expected your room to be occupied. If you tend to change your itinerary while traveling, avoid hotels that charge penalties.

Ed Perkins, editor of *Consumer Reports Travel Letter*, which specializes in travel savings strategies and lists current deals on hotels and cruises, 101 Truman Ave., Yonkers, NY 10703.

Great Villa Vacations

Rent a villa abroad to truly experience a different locale. *Example:* Four-bedroom villa on a Greek isle...seasonal rates $250 to $350 per day. Contact Villa Helios, Box 158, Montreal, Canada H3Z 2T2. Illustrated. Free details.

Best Kind of Traveler's Checks

Two-signature traveler's checks are more convenient than the one-signature kind. Two people buy and sign them together—and either person can cash them. A couple need not decide before a trip how many checks each person will need. American Express charges more for two-signature checks than for the one-signature type. For Visa checks, individual member banks set their own retail pricing.

Alternative to traveler's checks: Bill as much as possible to charge cards—and/or use ATMs for cash when traveling overseas.

If You Must Cancel a Trip...

You can recover many costs by canceling *early* enough—even if you do not have trip insurance.

●**Most *hotels* allow same-day cancellations,** though more and more require three days' notice.

●**Most *beach house* owners who rent do not make refunds,** or they charge steeply if they do.

●**Most *cruise lines* will refund much of your money** if you cancel early enough for them to resell your cabin. Expect a full refund if you cancel at least 60 days before the start of the cruise.

●**Tours have policies similar to those of cruises.**

●**Planes usually charge $25 to $50 for re-booking tickets** if you do not use them as scheduled.

●**Amtrak charges $20 on long-distance rides** and usually nothing on short trips.

Nancy Dunnan, managing editor of *Travel Smart*, 40 Beechdale Rd., Dobbs Ferry, NY 10522.

Shrewder Organizing for Traveling Executives

Stephanie Winston
The Organizing Principle

An organized approach to business travel can make trips more productive and comfortable...and minimize paper pile-up when you return.

BEFORE YOU GO

●**Designate a separate briefcase as your "office-to-go."** Keep it stocked with basic supplies—pens and pencils, calculator, portable tape recorder, stapler, paper clips and overnight express mailing labels addressed to your office. A hard-sided briefcase can also serve as a writing surface.

During the week before your trip, keep this briefcase beside your desk. As trip-related materials come across your desk, drop them into the briefcase.

Some managers prefer briefcases with compartments for multi-city trips. Each compartment can hold materials needed at a given destination or to be worked on during a particular flight.

●**Prepare a written itinerary.** Distribute it to your spouse, assistant and close colleagues. Keep a copy for yourself. *Include…*

●**Flight numbers**, dates and times.

●**Hotel names**, addresses, phone numbers and dates of stay.

●**Time and location of appointments**, together with contact names and phone numbers for each.

ON THE ROAD

●**Keep up with work back at the office** by setting aside one hour each day for "office hours." Call your assistant—or a colleague who has agreed to handle this chore—to review incoming correspondence…and give instructions on how to respond in your absence.

●**Send work generated on your trip back to the office.** Do it via fax or overnight mail so that your staff can continue working on it while you're away.

Examples: Conference tapes to be transcribed…documents that need multiple signatures.

●**Put all receipts in one designated place** —such as a compartment in your wallet or briefcase—to simplify expense record-keeping.

Helpful: One frequent traveler takes his company's expense account form along with him and jots down expenses as he incurs them.

●**Save time and energy by hiring a car and driver** for the day instead of renting a car—if your budget allows. You won't have to worry about getting lost in a strange city…and you can use passenger time to catch up on work and review notes.

ON YOUR RETURN

●**Have a routine task waiting on your desk** —to be tackled first in order to ease your re-entry.

●**Avoid coming back to the office in the middle of the day**, when the transition from travel mode to office mode tends to be most abrupt.

Better: Schedule your return for late afternoon/early evening, when you'll be winding down anyway…or early morning, so you can feel as though you're starting fresh.

●**Try to refrain from making major decisions on your first day back**—especially if you've been gone for more than a week. At one brokerage firm, analysts noted that their colleagues showed less-than-optimal judgment for the first few days after an extended trip.

Stephanie Winston, president of The Organizing Principle, a time-management consulting firm, 230 E. 15 St., New York 10003. She is author of Stephanie Winston's Best Organizing Tips. *Fireside.*

Luggage Basics… A Review

Use an ID tag with your name and *business* address and phone number—not your home address, which could alert potential thieves to an empty house. Check in well in advance, so the airline has plenty of time to get your luggage aboard. If using curbside check-in, watch to make sure your bags go into the terminal. Watch the person checking the bags to make sure he/she puts the right destination tags on them. Mark luggage with colored tape or ribbon to make bags easy to find when you arrive.

Glamour, 360 Madison Ave., New York 10017.

How to Pack Clothes So They Won't Wrinkle

Judith Gilford

If you are in constant need of an iron when traveling, try the "bundle method" of packing. This method nearly guarantees wrinkle-free results and can be applied to any 22- or 24-inch suitcase that opens like a book. *It accommodates both tailored and casual clothing...*

• **Lay your suitcase on the bed and open it wide so that it lies flat.** Start by packing your largest, heaviest and longest item of clothing—excluding slacks.

• **For a straight dress,** place the shoulders in the corners of the bag, centering the collar at the hinge end. Drape the bottom of the dress over the top end, where the handle is. Drape sleeves over the side walls.

• **For a suit jacket,** button it and lay it facedown with the collar centered at the hinge end and the bottom draped over the handle end. Cross sleeves down the back of the jacket.

• **Then lay slacks lengthwise on top** of the jacket or dress, with the waistband touching the side of the suitcase. Drape the bottom of the slacks over the other side of the suitcase. For a full skirt, tri-fold vertically and pack as you would slacks.

• **For straight skirts,** lay the waistband along the handle edge of the suitcase, with the hem draped over the hinged end.

• **Add long-sleeved shirts or blouses.** Lay shirts or blouses facedown as you did the first jacket, starting with the collar centered at the hinge end. Drape the sleeves and bottoms over the sides of the bag or cross down the back.

• **Short-sleeved shirts come next.** Place in the same way you placed long-sleeved shirts.

• **Pack sweaters over the short-sleeved shirts.** Drape the sleeves and bottoms over the sides.

• **Pack shorts.** Long shorts can be packed vertically with bottoms draped over one end of the suitcase. Shorter shorts can be packed horizontally and added last.

• **Create a core "pouch"** in the center for your swimsuit and undergarments. The "pouch" should take up an 11" x 16" space, with about two inches of space left all around it. The fuller the edges of the core, the less wrinkling.

Examples: Two products that work great are the Carry-rite Mini-organizer ($22.95) and the Deluxe Core Pouch ($15.95). Both are available from Easy Going Travel Shop and Bookstore in Berkeley, California, 800-675-5500.

FOLDING IT ALL UP

• **Place the core pouch in the center of the draped clothing.** Take the last item packed and fold over the core and so on until all are folded.

• **Fold the hem of the garment up over the top of the core.** Then fold one sleeve across the core, wrapping extra material around the curve of the core. Repeat for the other sleeve. Continue down through the layers. Pack as tightly as possible.

• **Pack remaining items,** such as toiletries in plastic or nylon bags, and shoes, belts, etc., around the edges or in the suitcase's other compartments.

Judith Gilford, a packing specialist who holds seminars nationwide for business travelers. She is author of The Packing Book: Secrets of the Carry-on Traveler. *Ten Speed Press.*

Flight-Crew Bags

Flight-crew bags hold three days' worth of clothes and are easy to handle.

To buy the right one: Make sure it fits in a 9" x 14" x 18" space—the maximum available under a coach seat. The retractable handle should be fastened with Velcro or lock in place. Make sure parts like wheels and handles are replaceable.

Cost: About $200—and up.

Travel Holiday, 1633 Broadway, New York 10019.

Use Address Labels

Put address labels inside bags when traveling —for checked luggage and carry-ons. If the *outside* tag comes off, there is a chance you will get back a lost bag. *Also:* Pin each child's name and the address of where you are staying inside the child's clothing—to make it easier for someone to help the child find you if he/she wanders off.

Cynthia Butz, editor of *Common Cents Newsletter*, 13611 Tamiami Trail, Box 7075, North Port, FL 34287.

Beat Travel Illness

Do not limit yourself to only required immunizations. Get recommended shots, too.

• **Find out about any health issues** at your destination to anticipate problems.

• **Get physically fit** so you can better handle airports, luggage lifting and walking tours.

• **Take *twice* your normal medicine supply** with you—half on your person and half in your luggage.

• **Watch the water supply.** Use only bottled, boiled or purified water.

• **Eat only well-done, hot food.** Avoid street vendors.

• **Find out about local pollution areas.** Swim only in truly safe areas.

Michele Barry, MD, professor of medicine and co-director of the Tropical Medicine and International Travelers Clinic at Yale University, New Haven, CT.

Beware: Medication Mishaps When Traveling Across Time Zones

Just as your body must adjust to jet lag, you must adjust your medication schedule to be sure your body gets what it needs, when it needs it.

Self-defense: Take along a second wristwatch, set it on home time and use it to tell you when to take medications. If a time-zone change would require several doses at inconvenient hours, have your doctor adapt your medication schedule.

Donald Sullivan, RPh, MS, travel and medicine expert and author of *A Senior's Guide to Healthy Travel.* Career Press.

How to Get Discounts On Cruises

To get deep discounts on cruises, be flexible about when you travel—early or late booking often saves money. Check local Sunday newspaper ads in travel sections for the names of cruise discounters. Their advertisements are usually small.

Comparison shop: Contact several discounters and ask for their best deals on the same cruise and category—prices will vary. After booking, ask for a free upgrade—the request will be entered in the cruise line's computer and honored if there is space available. Ask for a discount if you are a senior citizen, AARP or travel-club member or repeat customer.

Herbert J. Teison, publisher of *Travel Smart*, 40 Beechdale Rd., Dobbs Ferry, NY 10522.

Almost-Free Cruises

Cruise lines recruit volunteer single men to dance with women traveling solo, sightsee and participate in social shipboard activities. *The Gentlemen Host™ Program* recruits men who are single, at least 45 years old, skilled dancers and good minglers. *Cost:* $25 per day, but cruise lines generally provide accommodations, meals, entertainment, reception, some shore excursions, gratuities and even airfare for longer periods of time.

More information: The Gentlemen Host™ Program, c/o Laurette Blake, The Working Vacation, Inc., 610 Pine Grove Ct., New Lenox, IL 60451.

Bigger Cruise Ships... Better Buys

The size of cruise ships is increasing. A 1,300-passenger ship is now on the smaller side. New ships carry from 1,800 to 2,600 passengers. But the number of people taking cruises is not increasing so rapidly. *Result:* Bargains aboard many larger liners—two-for-one offers, early booking specials, free upgrades, frequent-flier points and more.

Travel Holiday, 1633 Broadway, New York 10019.

International Travel

Roger Axtell

Here's what to watch for when traveling to some of the world's major cities. Much of the advice is good throughout the country in which the city is located.

FRANKFURT

• **Don't automatically use a person's first name.** Stick with titles, such as *Herr* (Mr.), *Frau* (Mrs.) and *Fräulein* (Miss), until you're invited to be more familiar.

• **Don't chew gum.** Germans find it distasteful and a sign of laziness.

• **Don't fold your hands in your lap at the dinner table.** In the past, hiding your hands implied that you were holding a weapon. Instead, rest your wrists lightly on the edge of the table.

• **Do arrive on time for appointments.** Germans are extremely punctual and expect the same of everyone.

LONDON

• **Don't ignore protocol.** You can't be too formal or too polite in London.

Example: People form orderly lines—called *queues*—for everything. Breaking in or moving to the front when a bus arrives, for instance, can cause a major stir.

• **Don't boast or use words like *biggest* and *best*.**

Example: When asked if you play tennis, play down any awards or tournament championships. The proof, as the British like to say, is in the pudding.

• **Don't use the word *English* when referring to anything that is British.** Use *British* instead. English refers only to England and ignores Wales and Scotland.

PARIS

• **Don't try out your high school French.** Parisians are very defensive about their language, and they hate to hear it butchered. Unless you're fluent in French, stick to English, which is a language that many Parisians know well.

• **Don't eat with your fingers.** Even a sandwich should be eaten with a knife and a fork. Parisians pride themselves on being among the world's top food experts and take table manners very seriously.

Exceptions: French bread and rolls.

• **Do shake hands with everyone in the room when you enter a meeting**—even if that means more than a dozen greetings.

SÃO PAULO

• **Don't make the *OK* hand gesture.** In Brazil, this gesture is likely to be misinterpreted as a rude sexual reference.

• **Do expect to be served small cups of very strong coffee at all hours of the day.** Try to pace yourself if you're not used to that much caffeine, or decline politely.

TOKYO

• **Don't expect *yes* to mean yes.** A Japanese citizen speaking English might say yes almost continually throughout a conversation. But that doesn't mean that he/she agrees. In fact, *yes* in Japan only implies, *Yes, I hear you.*

• **Don't expect to hear *no*.** The Japanese believe that saying *no* disrupts the harmony of a relationship. Instead, a phrase such as *That would be very difficult* should usually be taken as a rejection.

• **Don't expect direct eye contact, even while speaking to someone.** The Japanese consider eye contact rude, although most citizens know to expect it from Westerners.

•**Don't be embarrassed by periods of silence in conversations.** In Japan, they're considered perfectly natural. A Japanese listening to an American speak nonstop is prone to wonder if we ever pause to think.

Roger Axtell, a former marketing executive at a major international corporation who has traveled extensively around the world. He is author of six books on foreign customs and etiquette, including *Dos and Taboos Around the World.* John Wiley & Sons.

Better Visits to Europe

Since flights from the US usually arrive early in the morning, try to get a guaranteed early hotel check-in so you can rest and freshen up. When eating out, expect more cigarette smoke than in the US—if you want smoke-free dining, call in advance to find out if the restaurant has a no-smoking section…and reserve a table in it.

Nancy Novogrod, editor of *Travel & Leisure*, 1120 Avenue of the Americas, New York 10036.

Where to Stay for Less On the Expensive French Riviera

Doris Lehman

The Hotel Carlton is located in Beaulieu-Sur-Mer, along the train line between Nice and Monte Carlo. The town has mountains coming out of the sea and offers excellent restaurants. The hotel itself has 35 rooms—all are equipped with air-conditioning—as well as an outdoor pool. It is just a few blocks from the beach and harbor on the Mediterranean. $160 to $170.* 011-33-4-93-01-14-70.

*All rates are based on per night/double occupancy and are subject to change.

CANNES

•*Hotel le Mas Candille* is actually in Mougins, a hill town located just five miles from Cannes. The hotel has 23 rooms and recently was renovated to include modern private bathrooms. There are beautiful views from every room—either of the hills or the Mediterranean …a swimming pool…and an excellent restaurant. There are also golf courses…tennis courts …and horseback-riding stables nearby. Mougins has narrow streets that are full of bistros, shops and galleries. $200 to $495. 011-33-4-93-90-00-85.

•*Hotel les Muscadins* is also found in Mougins. The hotel has eight rooms and a superb restaurant. It is located in town—making it an ideal spot for people who don't have a car. $150 to $220. 011-33-4-93-90-00-43.

MONTE CARLO

•*The Beach Plaza* has its own private beach. There are 313 rooms, three swimming pools and two restaurants. The Monte Carlo sights, such as the Prince's Palace with the changing of the guard, are within walking distance. Technically not in France, but in Monaco, this hotel is first class in every way—yet offers many packages at lower rates. $160 to $340. 011-37-7-93-30-98-80.

•*Hotel Balmoral* is situated in a hill town that is above the Monte Carlo harbor. There are beautiful views of the harbor from all five suites—but not from all of the rooms. $120 to $270. 011-37-7-93-50-62-37.

NICE

•*La Perouse* is located across from the beach and near the entrance to the Old City of Nice. The hotel has 64 rooms…and each is equipped with a shower or a bath. There is a swimming pool…a restaurant…and a garden. Also, nearby are the Chagall and Matisse museums. Nice is ideal for people who are traveling without a car, since buses, taxis and trains are accessible. $140 to $180. 011-33-4-93-62-34-63.

ST. PAUL DE VENCE

•*Hotel le Saint Paul* is situated on the main street of this medieval village, approximately five miles from the sea. Nearby can be found some of the Riviera's best museums, including the Maeght Foundation, which offers a spectacular sculpture garden. Seven of the hotel's 18 rooms overlook the valley, while the others overlook the quaint narrow streets. Superb restaurant. $140 to $420. 011-33-4-93-32-65-25.

Doris Lehman, a travel agent in Livingston, NJ, who vacations frequently on the French Riviera. She is author of *The Riviera: Off-Season and On*. St. Martin's Griffin.

Criminal Cabbies In Mexico

Cabdrivers have abducted, assaulted and robbed passengers. The incidents involved cabs hailed on the street.

Self-defense: Use hotel cars, found in front of most hotels or cabs operating from taxi stands that can be contacted by telephone. It is important to discuss the fare to your destination before you get in the cab—to avoid a misunderstanding at the time of payment. Pay the driver *inside* the cab with the doors shut so passers-by cannot grab your money. It is also smart to ask the hotel concierge for an estimate of cost.

Kevin Coffey, police detective and president of Corporate Travel Safety Inc., 20756 Skouras Dr., Canoga Park, CA 91306.

Foreign Taxi Alert

Taxis in many foreign countries overcharge —and are frequently unsafe due to reckless drivers.

Self-defense: Ask your travel agent for information about airport-to-hotel transfers. Before leaving the US, find out what transportation your hotel provides or recommends. Consider public transportation—in Tokyo, taxi fares from Narita Airport can be $200 or more...but the Narita Express train costs as little as $31. If you must take a cab, always agree on a price before getting in.

Ron Salk, publisher of *Salk International's Airport Transit Guide*. Salk International Travel Premiums, Inc.

Better Car Rental In Europe

Book through a US firm that you know and trust...through an experienced travel agent...or through Auto Europe or Rail Europe —two respected firms specializing in European rentals. It is hard to compare car-rental rates in Europe on your own. Basic rates and the value-added tax (VAT) vary...car models are likely to be unfamiliar...and there may be unexpected restrictions on rentals.

Examples: Automatic-transmission cars are scarce and expensive...many models may not be driven into Italy or Eastern Europe.

Information: Auto Europe, 800-223-5555 ...Rail Europe, 800-438-7245.

Travel Companions, Box 833, Amityville, NY 11701.

Tune In to Traffic

Ask about local traffic reports when renting a car. Car-rental personnel should be able to tell you which radio stations carry the reports regularly. Also ask an agent or rental-company mechanic how to adjust the radio's push buttons to pick up traffic-reporting stations. Radio controls vary widely. It is best to figure out the radio and adjust to stations you want before leaving the car-rental lot.

Ed Perkins, editor of *Consumer Reports Travel Letter*, which specializes in travel savings strategies and lists current deals on hotels and cruises, 101 Truman Ave., Yonkers, NY 10703.

Randy Petersen's Favorite Travel Web Sites

Randy Petersen

Of the thousands of sites on the Internet offering information to travelers, only a handful offer real value. *Among my favorites...*

55

ARRIVALS/DEPARTURES

Trip.com (www.thetrip.com). Browsers can track flights to determine whether or not they're on time.

In fact, the site actually tells you where the flight is in the sky at the time of your request by direct contact with the FAA Air Traffic Control. This site is ideal for people who are due to meet an arriving flight and want to know if it's on time.

FLIGHT RESERVATIONS

I have several favorite sites in this category. Each allows you to place reservations and order tickets, which can be picked up at the airport.

Strategy: To get the best price, I type in the flight I want at all three sites and choose the least expensive. Each site uses a different reservation system, which accounts for the differences in pricing.

Three top discount ticket-booking sites...

Expedia (www.expedia.com). Also offers news and weather reports from around the world...a currency converter...and advice from travel experts.

Instant Air (www.got.com). Also offers a question/answer service via E-mail.

Travelocity (www.travelocity.com). Also has great leisure travel information, as well as a fare-watcher service that notifies you when fares go on sale to a destination you indicate.

FREQUENT FLIER MILES

WebFlyer (www.webflyer.com) has more frequent-flier information than any other site. Here you can access most major airlines sites, where you can call up your frequent-flier statement by inserting your frequent-flier number...browse an on-line magazine that offers strategies to earn more miles...and access "@deal Watch," which highlights frequent-flier awards offered by a variety of airlines. Simply type in the first letters of the city you want to fly from, and all the deals are listed.

VACATION PLANNING

Three Perfect Days (www.ual.com/tips/perfect.asp) is sponsored by United Airlines and provides suggestions on what to do... where to go...what to see...where to stay... and self-guided tours in 19 cities around the world. Ideal for planning trips.

Randy Petersen, editor of *InsideFlyer*, 4715-C Town Center Dr., Colorado Springs 80916.

3

Your Family and Your Home

How to Get Kids Off TV... And What to Do with Them Once the TV Is Off

Blakely Bundy, MEd
The Winnetka Alliance for Early Childhood

Television can be entertaining and instructive...but if its use is left unchecked, it can be destructive and debilitating.

Problem: The average child sits passively in front of a TV screen for 28.5 hours each week.

In many households, TV has become a "babysitter," allowing parents to not pay attention to their kids. After a while, parents even forget that the TV is on. The result is that their children learn negative lessons from programs that do not meet with their parents' approval.

Though banning TV completely may be impractical—it can be an excellent source of popular culture and educational programming —most parents want their kids' TV time reduced.

Here's how to reduce the amount of TV viewing in your home...and some examples of more productive activities.

TUNING OUT TV

●**Leave the TV off for one week.** Make a seven-day commitment to live without television—adults included—and see the wonderful changes it can make in your family life.

After an initial struggle, once the TV is off, your children will find many alternatives—discovering old toys, playing dress-up, playing outdoors and reading more. When the family returns to TV the following week, everyone will be ready to make more thoughtful choices.

Tune out the TV periodically (for one week each month, season or year) for continued benefit.

●**Attach a list of rules to your TV.** *Best:* Have the kids make the list. If necessary, make it yourself. If you have limited TV watching to certain days of the week or a certain number of hours, post the rules above the TV screen so everyone will be reminded.

During a tune-out week, your child can tape a drawing of a favorite activity over the TV screen as a reminder of the wonderful world beyond television.

During other weeks, ask children to use the TV listings in the Sunday paper to determine which programs they want to watch. Everyone in the family can make thoughtful choices regarding TV.

● **Watch TV with your children.** Watching TV together helps you monitor the content of the programs. If you don't watch with them, you may be unaware of the topics and situations to which your children are being exposed.

During an ad or after a program, click off the sound and talk about what you all have seen. Remind the children that these are actors working from a script. When you add your comments and observations, TV becomes a social activity.

● **Have your kids talk with someone who grew up before there was TV.** Have your child ask a grandparent about what his/her life was like before TV. What kinds of things did he do for fun when he was your child's age? Have him teach how to play games from his childhood.

TV-FREE ACTIVITIES

Once the TV is off, what do you do? Replacement activities need not be fancy. Simple, old-fashioned ideas work best. Your house may become a little messier than it was before you cut back on TV time, but your family will be happier—and much better—for it. ·

● **Leave a jigsaw puzzle out for a few days.** Children and adults can work on it at their leisure.

● **Buy a book with seven or more chapters in it.** Read one chapter each night.

● **Listen to books on tape, or read aloud, which stimulates everyone's imagination.** Ask your children what they think the characters look like.

● **Ask children to help you prepare dinner by measuring, stirring or washing.** If your child is too young for this task, have a special toy or art box that comes out only while you are preparing dinner and can be used only in the kitchen.

● **Have a family sing-a-long.**

● **Work on an art project.**

Example: Make a food face. Cut out pictures of food from magazines, and use them to create a funny face.

● **Listen to music,** a pleasure that is fast being forgotten in today's world of electronic visual diversions.

Blakely Bundy, MEd, executive director of The Winnetka Alliance for Early Childhood, an organization that promotes the healthy growth and development of children from birth to age eight, 1235 Oak St., Winnetka, IL 60093. The group recently succeeded in organizing a community TV tune-out in which 3,500 children participated for one week. They also publish an information packet on organizing similar events.

Boosting Your Child's Reading Skills

Talking at the dinner table boosts children's *reading* skills. Kids who were exposed to interesting dinner-table conversation as preschoolers do better on vocabulary and reading tests in elementary school than those who were not.

Note: Talking to kids about adult topics at any time increases their vocabulary and reading skills...but because of the pace of modern life, dinnertime is often the only opportunity parents have to talk at length with their children.

Catherine Snow, PhD, professor of education at Harvard Graduate School of Education, who led a study of 55 children.

 # Boys' Intelligence Comes From Their Mothers

Several genes for intelligence are located on the X chromosome. Boys receive an X from their mothers and a Y from their fathers—so only their mothers contribute these intelligence genes. Girls receive an X from each parent, so their intelligence genes come from both.

Australian geneticist Gillian Turner, writing in The Lancet, *the preeminent British medical journal.*

Repeating a Grade Doesn't Help

Repeating a grade usually does not help children. It hurts their self-esteem—too often causing social and emotional problems.

Alternatives to discuss with your child's school: Creating a "readiness" class for children who are not quite prepared to advance to the next grade…moving children to new classes during the year, as they catch up academically…allowing children to repeat a single semester instead of a whole year.

If the school wants your child to repeat a grade, talk to your child's pediatrician, another teacher or a psychologist about possible results and alternatives.

Caring for Your School-Age Child, Ages 5–12 by Edward Schor, MD, medical director of the division of family and community health at the Iowa Department of Public Health, Des Moines. Bantam Books.

Children's Self-Esteem

Have a success-sharing time at dinner or in the evening for each member of the family to discuss one great thing he/she did that day.

Encourage your child to keep a scrapbook of things he is proud of.

Suggest he make a tape discussing things he likes about himself and things he does well—so he can replay it when he is feeling down.

The Myth of the ADD Child by Thomas Armstrong, PhD, former special-education teacher in Sonoma County, CA. Dutton.

Worst Parent-Child Arguments…and How to Defuse Them

Anthony Wolf, PhD

Trying to be reasonable with kids usually prolongs arguments and raises the levels of passion and tension on both sides.

I have found that listening to counter-arguments and trying to reason during the heat of battle with kids do not produce children who grow up to feel appreciated or reasonable. Such reactions produce children who are skilled at arguing.

Instead, the key to defusing parent–child arguments is learning to end debates quickly. You can do this by stating your position firmly …repeating it if necessary…and then disengaging from the discussion.

Reason: Children need to know that once you've made up your mind, no amount of whining will change your decision.

Here are the most common parent–child battles and the strategies to help you resolve them…

NEGOTIATING WITH PICKY EATERS

Children who are choosy about what they eat often will do anything to eat less of what they don't like. Unfortunately, in most cases, the foods they don't like are essential to a proper diet.

Example: Your child may say, "I know you said I could have dessert if I ate eight more green beans, but how about six?"

Wrong response: "How about seven?" or, "Come on, honey, you know you liked the green beans last time."

The problem with such replies—and the reason they rarely work effectively—is that you're still negotiating with the child. You've left the issue open for discussion.

Better: Put your offer on the table, close the subject and your child will understand the deal. *Alternatives:* "OK, six is enough" (it's all right to give in if you really don't care)—or "I said eight" (it's also all right to stick to your guns). *End of discussion.*

YOU'RE ACCUSED OF BEING UNFAIR

One of the most potent weapons kids have in their arsenal is the charge, "It's not fair!" Then they proceed to tell you why—which makes good parents feel guilty and rethink their request.

Example: You've asked your daughter to put away her toys. "It's not fair!" she wails. "Some of them belong to Josh! He should have to put his own toys away!"

Wrong response: "Everybody in this family pitches in to keep the house clean. Josh put away your toys yesterday."

This type of comment only invites an emotionally charged, drawn-out conversation. You're also shifting the argument from what she must do to why she must do it. Kids don't see themselves as interchangeable—even when they're brother and sister.

Unfortunately, it's *impossible* to be totally fair in every situation—and it isn't always important. As long as you know that you try to be fair, trust yourself enough to make a quick decision. If your decision turns out to be less than perfect, you can apologize later.

Helpful: Try either, "Please put away your toys," or, "I didn't think of it that way. OK?"

YOU'RE BUSY, BUT YOUR KIDS ARE BORED

When children start to complain that there's nothing to do and that they're bored, busy parents are often pestered to entertain them. That's fine, unless, of course, you've just spent time with them and now you're busy.

Wrong response: "Have you thought about coloring?" or…"What about reading that book you just got from the library?"

While it doesn't hurt to offer a few practical suggestions, they often are not very effective.

Parents must realize that it's important for kids to learn to *find* things to occupy their time. Left to their own devices, kids almost always come up with something.

Better: "Gee, sounds like you have a problem on your hands. I'm busy right now. I guess you'll have to find something to do yourself."

FIGHTS BETWEEN SIBLINGS

The truth about sibling fights, whether they are over the TV or toys, is that you have two choices. You can either train them to work it out for themselves—or train them to rely on a parent to work it out for them.

Unless there is a real risk of the kids getting physically hurt in a battle, do not intervene on one side or the other—ever. And don't judge disagreements either.

When kids disagree, it's best to get them to stop, sit down and talk it out.

If you begin to get irritated by the squabbling, you can end the situation in a way that both children lose. This way your children will also learn the limits of how far they can push each other without incurring your wrath.

Example: "If you can't watch TV without arguing, then nobody watches TV."

YOUR CHILD SAYS, "I HATE YOU"

In the heat of battle, your child may utter words guaranteed to drive a stake into your heart. Try not to take it personally. We've raised our kids to be outspoken, and children of the 1990s often say things that we would never have dared say to our own parents.

Wrong response: "How can you say such a thing…after all I do for you?"

Children must feel that their anger toward their parents is not dangerous, that their attachment to their parents is so secure that nothing bad will result.

This reinforces that they—and their anger—are part of the little world of childhood and cannot seriously threaten the big adults.

If you are truly offended or hurt by your children's angry words, you can say so—at a later time, when you're not arguing.

Better: "I'm sorry that you feel that way, but you still have to do what I told you to do."

OTHER POINTS TO KEEP IN MIND

● **There may be times when you can't make a quick decision.** If you really need more time to think about something, make it clear that you will take time to think about the problem—and that you will not listen to further arguments at this time.

● **If an issue comes up during an argument that needs to be discussed at greater length,** save it for a neutral time when your children have nothing to gain or lose by discussing it with you.

Example: "I'd like to discuss this with you after dinner."

Don't be surprised if the issue no longer matters very much to them.

●**Take heart.** Your children are probably much better behaved in the outside world than they are with you. What you see at home is their most childish selves…and what better, safer place is there for them to express it?

As long as we can remain adults and allow our children to be children—complete with occasionally rude or obnoxious behavior—they are not likely to grow up to be wild or disrespectful or to take advantage of others. On the contrary, they will become giving, caring people.

Anthony Wolf, PhD, a child and adolescent psychologist in private practice in Longmeadow, MA. He is author of It's Not Fair: Jeremy Spencer's Parents Let Him Stay up All Night! A Guide to the Tougher Parts of Parenting. *The Noonday Press.*

When Your Kids Fight

Avoid the worst three words—*Who started it?* It is safer to assume both are guilty—don't focus on who is to blame. Instead, help them work out a solution with which they can both live.

Nancy Samalin, founder and director of Parent Guidance Workshops, 180 Riverside Dr., New York 10024. She is author of Loving Each One Best: A Caring and Practical Approach to Raising Siblings. *Bantam.*

Learning from Failure

Help kids build on failure, not just success. See your kids doing things well, and praise them. But also notice their failures. Help them rebuild their feelings by reminding them that there will always be another chance…and that you will love them, no matter what. Tying self-esteem to success is a recipe for *unhappiness* later in life. The anchor of a caring family is at least as important to self-esteem as any string of successes.

Finish Strong by Richard Capen, Jr., former media executive and US government official. HarperSanFrancisco.

Life Lessons for Kids From Sports

Competing with someone better than you can help you improve—and being on the same team with better players can inspire you to be better, too. Rules need to be internalized—playing within them ensures that everyone starts on the same basis. Resourcefulness within the rules can make the difference between victory and defeat. Morale is both an individual and a team experience—anyone can push a team to better performance by getting people to believe in themselves. The game is never over—there will be another game or more competition elsewhere in life.

Boys! by William Beausay II, consultant for the American Academy of Sports Psychology, Maumee, OH. Thomas Nelson Publishers.

Kids and Change

Help kids handle change by keeping them informed…involving them in decisions to give them a sense of control…encouraging them to express feelings…maintaining as many family routines as possible.

Also: Let the family pet be a source of security…encourage children to reach out to new friends…give children lots of love and attention while they readjust.

The Four-Footed Therapist: How Your Pet Can Help You Solve Your Problems by Janet Ruckert, EdD, psychotherapist in Los Angeles. Ten Speed Press.

Talking to Children About Sex

This should not be a one-time talk—and not strictly anatomical. The topic will come up as a child grows older. When a child asks a straightforward question, answer directly and honestly in an age-appropriate way, using the correct names for body parts. Then respond to any follow-up questions.

Bottom line: Be glad your children come to you with questions—otherwise, they will go elsewhere to learn about sex. If you do not answer perfectly the first time, you can always restate your answer later.

Jan Faull, a child development and behavior specialist in Seattle, writing online in *Family Planet*, http://family.starwave.com.

No More Troublesome Ear Infections

Children with ear infections often don't need antibiotics.

While antibiotics have been the primary treatment for kids' middle-ear infections, researchers have established that more than 80% would get better within 10 days without treatment.

Antibiotics raise the cure rate somewhat—and reduce risk of developmental gaps from hearing problems—but they may cause resistance to antibiotics in the future.

In light of this, physicians are being urged not to prescribe antibiotics right away for children over age one with fluid in the ear unless they show other symptoms of infection.

One strategy common in Europe: Observe the patient for up to four days. If there is no improvement or symptoms worsen, treat with antibiotics.

Robert Baltimore, MD, a professor and faculty member of the pediatric infectious diseases program at Yale University School of Medicine, New Haven, CT.

Backpack Safety

A child's backpack should not weigh more than 20% of his/her total body weight. Overloaded backpacks can cause shoulder or lower back pain or posture distortion. Straps should be well-padded, and children should use both straps. Carrying packs on one shoulder can lead to neck or muscle spasms.

Researchers at Johns Hopkins Children's Center, Baltimore.

Calm Fussy Babies

Calm babies who are inexplicably soothed by the "white noise" of a vacuum cleaner or a hair dryer by making an audiotape of the noise. You can then take the tape with you and play it anywhere, anytime. It will usually calm the child just as well as the real thing.

Parents, 685 Third Ave., New York 10017.

Steps to Reduce Risk of SIDS

Get good prenatal care so your baby's heart, brain and lungs develop properly. *Do not smoke or use the nicotine patch during pregnancy*—smoking or exposure to nicotine may double your baby's risk of Sudden Infant Death Syndrome. *Use firm, flat bedding*—the fluffier the surface, the greater the risk. Especially when the baby is ill, *do not overheat your baby or his/her surroundings*—keep the household temperature at 68°F to 70°F, and dress your baby in the same type of nightclothes you sleep in. *Put your baby to sleep on his back or side*—if he falls asleep on his stomach, gently turn him onto his back after he is asleep.

Phipps Cohe, public affairs director at the SIDS Alliance, Baltimore.

Better Baby "Talk"

Sign language for babies can help them make their needs known before they can speak—reducing frustration, enriching parent-child interactions and helping babies develop verbal language faster than babies who were not encouraged to sign.

The movements need not be from a formal sign language. Parents can use any gesture they choose to represent the things their baby needs to "talk" about.

Examples: A thumb to the lips for *drink* or *bottle*...index fingers tapped together for *more* ...arm flapping for *bird*...a petting gesture for *kitty*.

Babies in this study learned up to 60 signs.

Linda Acredolo, PhD, professor of psychology at the University of California at Davis, who conducted the study with Susan Goodwyn, PhD, of California State University at Stanislaus. They are coauthors of *Baby Signs: How to Talk with Your Baby Before Your Baby Can Talk.* Contemporary Books.

Security Blankets Are OK

Let kids have security blankets as long as they feel they need them. A blanket or other familiar, comfortable object can help children adjust to a new environment, new sleeping arrangements, even the arrival of a new sibling. The need for security objects changes over time but never really goes away. Even adults eat certain foods or sit in a favorite chair when feeling anxious.

Lawrence Kutner, PhD, clinical psychologist in Lafayette, CA, and author of *Your School-Age Child.* William Morrow & Co.

Check Caregiver References Carefully

When hiring a caregiver for your child or elderly parent, check at least two references—plus the references of any agency you are using. Call the caregiver's references yourself. Watch out for fake references. You can deliberately make mistakes in his/her history to see if the reference corrects them. When checking the agency, ask how it screens applicants' references and reviews public records... and ask to be referred to other people who have recently

hired caregivers from the agency. You may want to consider hiring a private investigator to check an applicant's background thoroughly.

Cost: Less than $100. After hiring a caregiver, monitor him closely—including making unannounced visits during the day.

Ellen Galinsky, president of Families and Work Institute, 330 Seventh Ave., New York 10001.

Look for Long-Term-Care Facility Early

Start looking for a long-term-care facility for an elderly relative at least a year—preferably two—before you think you'll need it. *Reason:* The best homes have waiting lists of up to two years.

Joseph A. James, MD, head of the Yarmon Division of Geriatric Medicine at Beth Israel Medical Center, New York.

Best Ways to Talk to Aging Parents

Ease into conversations about money, moving, illness, wills, funerals and other difficult subjects. Present only one idea at a time.

•**Ask for advice**—say you are making your will and want advice based on how they made their wills.

•**Keep conversations focused on the well-being of the whole family**, not that of the parents alone.

•**Support every bit of independence aging parents have.**

•**If talk gets tense, take a deep breath, nod your head and just listen.** Realize that parents may not want to discuss some things with their children—so seek help from other family members, friends, doctors or other trusted professionals.

The Complete Elder Care Planner by Joy Loverde, national speaker and elder care adviser for numerous major organizations. Silvercare Productions.

When to Walk Away From a House You Want to Buy

Robert Irwin

Problem: An underground oil or gas tank on the property.

What to look for: Check the home owner's disclosure statement. This document details anything that's wrong with the house and property. *Also:* Check the ground around the house for a telltale fuel-fill cap.

Why walk away: Danger of leaks…tanks are considered an environmental hazard. Tanks —and much of the surrounding soil—must be removed. Removal costs can reach tens of thousands of dollars.

Problem: Little or no wall insulation.

What to look for: Turn off the electricity and remove an interior wall switch plate. Using a narrow screwdriver, poke around in the space between the drywall and the outside of the socket box. You should be able to feel if there's insulation, or even snag a small piece. If there's no insulation, try another socket or two, just to be sure.

Why walk away: Insulation is vital in very hot or cold climates. Retrofitting insulation in walls is either very expensive or yields uncertain results. Without proper insulation it's virtually impossible to control monthly energy costs.

Problem: A "floating" in-ground pool.

What to look for: Rather than being flush with the ground's surface, the edge of the pool is raised from several inches to two feet high. Surrounding soil is wet enough that the empty pool "floated" up out of the ground.

Why walk away: Returning a pool to its original position is virtually impossible. The only remedy is to put in a new one.

Problem: A house built on a "cut-and-fill" lot.

What to look for: Half the building site will seem to be dug into a hillside, and half will appear to jut out into space. Check for any shifting of the house by placing a marble on a bare floor to see if it rolls toward one side of the room.

Why walk away: Stabilizing such a house could involve driving pilings deep into the ground. If the ground has begun to shift, the house may develop irreparable cracks in the foundation and walls.

Problem: A shared driveway.

What to look for: Two or more homes that —either because of location (cul-de-sac) or home siting—share all or most of a single driveway.

Why walk away: Even if you and your neighbor start out as the best of friends, disagreements about parked cars, clearing leaves or snow and how the driveway is used may eventually cause problems.

Robert Irwin, a real estate broker and investor based in Los Angeles. He is author of *The Home Inspection Troubleshooter* and *Buy Right, Sell High*. Dearborn Financial.

FISBO Sales

People selling homes on their own usually overprice—and negotiating with them can be difficult because of their emotional attachment to the home.

Helpful: Find a buyer's agent who will represent you in such situations. Many sellers are willing to pay a buyer's agent 50% of the usual commission.

Alternative: Have a real estate attorney draw up a purchase contract to protect you. *Or:* Be patient. Most self-sellers give up within 60 days and list their homes with agents.

Robert Bruss, nationally syndicated real estate columnist, writing in *The Washington Post*.

Faster Home-Sale Strategy

Renovate areas of the house that are popular with buyers now.

Fix-ups that turn lookers into buyers: A dramatic foyer that is suited to the house's architectural style…a modern-looking and neat home office/computer room whose equipment can be concealed when not in use…a well-designed media/entertainment room with space for a big-screen TV.

Additions that are not appreciated: A new fireplace, unless you live in a cool/cold climate…a glass-enclosed solarium, which is perceived to cause more leakage trouble than it is worth.

Donald Jacobs, chairman of the American Institute of Architects' housing committee and president of JBZ Dorius Architecture & Planning, 2415 Campus Dr., Irvine, CA 92715.

Beware: No-Points, No-Fees Mortgages

Beware of no-points, no-fees offers when shopping for a mortgage. If the loan is at a much higher interest rate than one with points, you might be better off paying the points.

Example: A mortgage with no points and an 8% interest rate is not as good a deal as a mortgage with one point and a 7.75% interest rate.

Self-defense: Have your financial adviser compare available mortgage offers to find the least expensive one.

Keith Gumbinger, vice president and analyst of HSH Associates, a fee-based mortgage data service, 1200 Rte. 23, Butler, NJ 07405.

Beware of 40-Year Mortgages

Beware: 40-year mortgages are being promoted to let buyers acquire more expensive houses at affordable monthly payments. But these adjustable-rate loans make sense only for people who plan to keep a house for just a few years and have plenty of cash. There is little equity buildup in the early years—and if loan rates rise, even less of each payment goes to principal.

Bottom line: Most people should avoid 40-year mortgages.

Keith Gumbinger, vice president and analyst of HSH Associates, a fee-based mortgage data service, 1200 Rte. 23, Butler, NJ 07405.

When to Replace a Major Appliance

Replace a major appliance if the repair bill is more than 40% to 50% of the cost of a new unit.

Helpful: Take into account the average life of common appliances…and how long the appliance is likely to last if you have it repaired. A range usually lasts about 17 years…refrigerator, 15 years…clothes washer, 13 years…clothes dryer, 14 years…dishwasher, nine years.

Good Housekeeping, 959 Eighth Ave., New York 10019.

No More Home-Repair Headaches

Kevin Brenner and Kate Kelly

Even if you have hired the best contractor or workers in the world to renovate, repair or paint your home, it's important to keep an eye on a project while it's in progress.

By correctly monitoring the work and materials, you'll not only minimize surprises—you'll also motivate workers to take extra care with what they're doing for you.

BETTER JOB-MANAGEMENT BASICS

●**Draw up a contract that specifies what materials will be used.** By including everything from the type of wood to be used in the project to the color and brand of paint, you will ensure that you and your contractor are thinking alike from the beginning.

It also pays to have the contractor detail in the contract what *won't* be included—such as painting, polishing, staining, etc. This eliminates false expectations.

Important: Have the contract include a warranty period of at least one year for all work done by the contractor. The contract should also state who is responsible for getting the work permit. Make sure the permit is displayed before work starts.

●**Provide an incentive to get work done at a reasonable pace.** Some renovation delays are unavoidable—you can't control the weather, illness, etc.

Most delays can be averted by including a date of *substantial completion* in the contract. That's when 90% of the job is expected to be completed.

Some people add a penalty for failure to meet the deadline—but a *bonus* for on-time completion is often a better idea.

Bonuses are negotiable and range from a few hundred dollars to a few thousand dollars, depending on the job. A penalty can create an adversarial relationship, which could result in shoddy work done just to meet the deadline. The contractor may even abandon your project before it's done if the penalties mount up.

●**Check to be sure the correct materials are used.** While it is impossible to verify every detail, you can double-check the major parts.

Have the contractor notify you when each stage of your renovation—such as framing, electrical, plumbing and ductwork—is complete. Then check materials as each tradesperson completes the "rough-in" stage—the point at which installation of materials is complete, but the walls are not yet sealed.

The ideal time to make your visits is in the evenings, after the workers have gone for the day. That way, you won't disturb their schedules or offend anyone by checking up on their work. *What to do...*

●**Check the model names and numbers of materials against those listed in your contract.**

Example: Make sure a subcontractor didn't install a $100 toilet instead of the $500 toilet that was specified.

●**Bring along blueprints and a tape measure when you conduct your check.** Make sure everything seems to be the correct size— and in the right place.

If the insulation is not yet installed, check with the contractor about when it will be. If the insulation is in place, check that it is of the quality specified in the contract. Also, be sure any pipes in exterior walls are insulated. Frozen pipes could lead to another costly renovation down the road.

●**Communicate with the contractor throughout the job.** It's not unreasonable to speak every day. But if you expect this level of involvement, make it clear to the contractor when you first discuss the job.

Helpful: Arrange a regularly scheduled time for the meetings. The best time is at the beginning or end of the day. Don't waste too much time socializing. Most contractors prefer to get right down to business.

If you're uncomfortable talking on the phone or in person, a note may work just as well, provided you start with a face-to-face meeting and let the contractor know you prefer the notepad approach.

OTHER COMMUNICATION ISSUES

●**Speak up immediately** when some aspect of the project isn't to your liking. Your contractor will likely be able to help you find a better solution if you catch the problem early enough.

●**Discuss problems directly with the contractor**—not the workers.

●**Be prepared to take a final walk through the site.** Rather than waiting to be shown what has been done, it's important to carefully tour the nearly completed project on your own in the evening.

●**Details...details.** Make a list of things you think require additional attention. Generally, these are small items such as dents, scratches, leaky faucets and missing handles that the contractor can assign a worker to repair. *Don't forget to...*

●**Have the contractor arrange to remove any debris from the renovation site.**

●**Check that the water and power have been reconnected and restored throughout your home.**

●**Have the contractor test-run all new appliances.** Installing appliances such as dishwashers and washing machines generally is done by a subcontractor. Because the water main is often shut off while the project is under way, the work might not have been properly checked.

●**At the end of the job, be certain to get a "Certificate of Occupancy."** This certificate is issued by the local building-codes enforcement office after all the building requirements have been met.

In most cases, your contractor would obtain this for you—but not always. Discuss the appropriate steps with your contractor.

This document is your guarantee that the work has been fully inspected and approved.

Without it, you can't legally live in the renovated structure, and you could have trouble if you ever try to sell the house.

Kevin Brenner, president of Brenner Builders, a home building and remodeling firm in New Rochelle, NY… and Kate Kelly, a homeowner who has undertaken a number of renovations. They are coauthors of *Renovating with a Contractor.* Taylor Publishing Co.

Holding Down Costs on Home Renovations

To ensure that renovations end on budget, tell the contractor that you're setting aside 15% for changes, problems and cost overruns.

Imply that the total is every dollar you have to spend. Cost overruns inevitably crop up, but if you tell the contractor that the money you have will dry up at a certain point, he will make every effort to stay within your budget for fear of not being able to collect final payment.

John Rusk, owner of Rusk Renovations, Inc., New York, and author of *On Time and On Budget: A Home Renovation Survival Guide.* Doubleday.

You and Your Dog

Give a dog extra attention first thing in the morning and when you first come home at night. Greeting rituals are very important in dogs' lives. Take time to pet and praise the dog when you first see it each day and return from work. This will lower its anxiety level and keep it more relaxed when you are home.

Betty Fisher, bull dog breeder and professional trainer, quoted in *Dog Fancy,* Box 6050, Mission Viejo, CA 92690.

Dogs Reduce Stress

People who were facing stressful situations had the lowest heart rates and blood pressure if they were with their dogs—even lower than those of people who were with their spouses.

Possible reason: Dogs are perceived as completely nonjudgmental.

Karen Allen, PhD, research scientist at the University of Buffalo School of Medicine, Buffalo, NY, and leader of a study of 480 people under stressful conditions.

Picking a Puppy

When choosing a puppy, it's best to pick one with a droopy tail. It shows that the dog acknowledges you as the leader—making for a smooth relationship and easier training.

If picking from a litter: Avoid the boldest puppy, which may be hard to train…and the runt, which may be sickly.

Useful test: Hold a dog on its back. It should struggle briefly, then submit. An aggressive dog will fight to change position.

The Expert's Book of Practical Secrets, edited by Edward Claflin. Rodale Press.

Natural Animal Repellent

You can keep deer and rabbits out of your garden with homemade repellent.

Mix: Two tablespoons of hot pepper sauce —such as Tabasco…one gallon of water…a tablespoon of non-detergent dish soap, such as Ivory. Spray the solution directly onto flowers, fruits and vegetables. *Also:* Dust plants with red or black pepper or chili powder.

Important: Reapply repellent after every rainfall and as new leaves appear.

Bonnie Wodin, owner of Golden Yarrow Landscaping & Design, a garden consulting firm, Box 61, Heath, MA 01346.

Test for Termites

Poke a screwdriver or an awl into exposed wood near areas where termites might enter—especially where wood is near soil. If you can poke into the wood easily, termites may be present.

Self-defense: Contact a licensed pest-control expert for an inspection.

New type of treatment: Termite baiting systems—monitoring stations in the soil around the house, containing wood as termite bait. The stations are monitored until termites appear—then replaced with a slow-acting poison.

Cost: Approximately $1,100 to $1,600.

Greg Baumann, president, National Pest Control Association, 8100 Oak St., Dunn Loring, VA 22027.

Houseplants that Thrive on Neglect... Yes, Neglect

Bonnie Wodin
Golden Yarrow Landscape Design

Everyone has a love-hate relationship with houseplants. While they raise our spirits in the winter, many require so much care that busy people tend to do without plants for fear of killing them.

Fortunately, there are plants that need only minimal watering and light. *Among my favorites...*

•**Aspidistra** is known as the "cast-iron plant" because of its tolerance for neglect. The plant has tall, dark green, arching leaves that are four inches wide and grow up to two and a half feet long. Its striking brownish-purple flowers hide near the bottoms of the leaves.

Care: Water only when the soil begins to dry out. Place in a window with a northern or eastern exposure, since it has low light requirements.

•**Dracaena** is ideal for hot, dry homes, apartments or offices. Sword-like leaves—sometimes marked with red or creamy white stripes—arch gracefully out of a strong central stem. Some may grow five feet high.

Care: Keep dracaena in a warm spot with strong light. Water it weekly—or when the soil starts to feel dry to the touch.

•**Philodendron** is a vine that is native to the West Indies, and can be grown as a hanging plant. While it will thrive in medium light and even moisture, it can tolerate both dryness and poor light. Leaves are poisonous if ingested.

Care: The plant grows best when its roots are cramped—a boon for those who cringe at the thought of repotting.

•**India Rubber Plant** will survive anywhere, although it will grow more rapidly if it has light.

Care: Keep evenly moist and away from drafts. Weekly misting is advised.

•**Spider Plant** is a hanging plant that needs little care. The long, skinny green-and-white grasslike leaves grow in small clusters or plantlets on long thin stems. It prefers bright but indirect light and even temperatures.

Care: Grow in potting soil that is kept moist but not wet. If leaves turn brown, feed it a teaspoon of lime.

Bonnie Wodin, owner of Golden Yarrow Landscape Design, a garden consulting firm, Box 61, Heath, MA 01346.

4

Money Savvy

Andrew Tobias Answers the Big Financial Questions

Andrew Tobias

How can I save more money? Spend less. That may sound like a smart aleck answer, but consider this: Taking into account federal, state and local taxes, you're probably paying close to 40% or more of every dollar you earn in taxes. You're earning less than you think.

Whom can I trust for financial advice? No one. The fact is that most of the people and institutions trying to sell you investments are in it for the money. Much as they want to see you prosper, that's not their first priority.

That doesn't mean you can't rely on experts. But you have to be the person in charge of your finances.

What's the best way to make money in the stock market? Buy—and don't sell. If you can afford to wait long enough—10 to 15 years—you're almost sure to make more money in stocks than you will in less volatile investments. Don't try to time your stock market investments. That's why most people should buy their stocks through no-load, low-expense mutual funds.

How much life insurance should I buy? Enough to pay for things like funeral expenses that you'll incur when you die, as well as to replace the income your family will lose as a result of your death.

Remember that you only need to replace your *net* income minus the Social Security benefits your family would receive in your absence.

Then figure out how long your family will need that income, depending on your children's ages and how long you think it will be before your spouse can support him/herself.

Next, add a lump sum for things such as debts or family illnesses that might come up.

69

That amount should equal at least half a year's salary.

Last step: Subtract money you have amassed in savings, and subtract some more if you have group life insurance at work or can depend upon a wealthy parent to help out in a jam. Round up to the nearest $50,000 or so, and that's your number.

Andrew Tobias, author of several personal finance books, including *The Only Investment Guide You'll Ever Need*. Harcourt Brace.

Commonsense Rules of Financial Well-Being

Alexandra Armstrong
Armstrong, Welch & MacIntyre Inc.

If you want to become wealthy—or at least financially secure—you have to spend a few hours once a month thinking about it.

People who put off financial planning or ignore its importance because they don't have the time or assume they're not good with money are making a costly mistake. Money isn't hard to understand—once you know the simple steps to gaining control of your financial universe...and it doesn't take that much time.

RULES FOR SUCCESS

●**Know where you stand.** Before you plan ahead, you must find out how much you're worth now.

Many people avoid doing this exercise because they don't know how to do it...they're too lazy...or they just don't want to face the reality of their financial situations. All are big mistakes. Your net worth is like the gas gauge in your car, and no driver would ever ignore that.

The calculation is easy—and most people who do it are surprised to learn they are worth more than they thought.

You can determine your net worth simply by making a list of your assets...and another list of what you owe.

Don't forget to include in assets the market value of your home, retirement savings or other investments and the cash value of your life insurance policy.

Do not include the market value of cars, furniture or personal possessions. They're never worth as much as you expect, and you're unlikely to sell them.

Debts include your mortgage, home-equity or car loans, and any credit card debt. Subtract your total debt from your total assets. The result is your net worth. Keep track of it over six-month periods. You'll be able to see how your wealth is growing—or shrinking.

If your net worth isn't growing as fast as you would like, an item in the debt column may be increasing faster than your assets. It's time to evaluate where you're spending your money and determine the cause.

●**Keep track of how you spend your money.** If you aren't sure where all of your money goes each month, you can't develop a smart plan for saving and investing.

It's easy to account for a fixed expense that arrives in a single bill, such as a mortgage or a car payment. But keeping track of discretionary expenses—gifts, entertainment and dining out—is just as important.

Helpful: For the next three months, keep a record of your purchases in a pocket-sized notebook. It also may help to go through old checkbook registers and credit card statements to get an idea of where your cash is going.

If you have a computer at home, personal finance software programs such as *Quicken* are an efficient and user-friendly way to track cash flow. They can keep your checkbook organized and current, track expenses by category and compare year-to-year information.

●**Think about tomorrow.** Most people recoil when I mention the importance of planning goals because they say they hardly know what they'll be doing next weekend—let alone in five years. *Relax,* I tell them. What I mean by goals is simply two or three *major* expenses you're going to have to deal with over time. These could include college tuition, a vacation home, early retirement...and any big costs that will be needed to help you realize your dreams.

Once you determine what you want out of life and the level of quality that is important to you, you can begin to calculate how much you're going to need. You may also have to prioritize your goals, since many tend to overlap.

Example: The cost of your children's college educations may coincide with when you planned to retire. You might have to postpone your retirement until all of your children have completed college.

● **Slash those credit card balances.** While you hear this often, I can't say it enough. If you want to be financially comfortable and reduce emotional stress, you must reduce debt.

The typical credit card rate—17% to 18%—is exorbitant. If your debt is draining your income, consider taking out a home-equity loan at a lower interest rate to pay off your credit card balances. Interest payments on that loan are tax deductible. Interest payments on your credit card debt are not.

● **Take your retirement plan seriously.** Most people who say they can't contribute the maximums to their 401(k) plans or IRAs usually say it's because they need the money to live on.

If you fall into this category, you need to find a way to live on less so that you can take advantage of what is probably the best investment you'll ever make.

Your 401(k) contribution is deducted automatically from your paycheck before taxes, and earnings that accumulate in the plan and your IRA grow tax-deferred.

You should contribute as much of your salary as the 401(k) plan allows—usually around 10% to 15% (up to $9,500 in 1997)…and also try to deposit the $2,000 maximum a year in your IRA. Even if it is nondeductible, the earnings accumulate tax-free until they are withdrawn.

● **Get smart about investing.** Saving and investing are the only sure ways to amass great wealth. If you hope to achieve financial independence, time and compound interest are strong allies. Don't waste time agonizing over which mutual funds to buy—there are hundreds of good funds out there. Simply pick funds with good 10-year records that suit your financial objectives.

In the years before retirement, invest up to 80% of your assets in stocks or stock mutual funds. Over the long term—10 years or longer —these investments have delivered much greater rates of return than bonds.

With a longer time horizon, there is much less risk since you will be able to weather even major corrections in the market.

After retirement, you may want to invest a larger percentage in fixed bonds and mutual funds that invest in them. Keep the rest in good-quality stocks or stock funds.

Diversify your investments. Many people put all their money into one or two stocks because they think those stocks will make them rich. It's important, however, to spread your money among investments such as individual stocks and bonds and mutual funds that invest in both, so your savings won't be wiped out if one investment hits hard times. I recommend 10% to 20% be invested in international stocks.

● **Review your financial plan regularly.** Once you have organized your finances and outlined your goals, you've done a lot of the work. Don't stop there. Review every aspect of your plan for a few hours once a month.

Reviewing your saving and investing patterns forces you to be responsible about your own financial future.

Alexandra Armstrong, chairman of Armstrong, Welch & MacIntyre Inc., a fee-based financial-planning firm, 1155 Connecticut Ave. NW, Ste. 250, Washington, DC 20036. She is coauthor of On Your Own: A Widow's Passage to Emotional and Financial Well-Being. *Dearborn.*

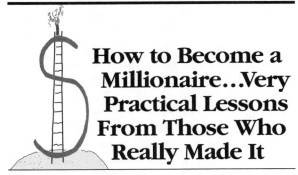

How to Become a Millionaire…Very Practical Lessons From Those Who Really Made It

Thomas Stanley, PhD
Affluent Market Institute

During the past 20 years, my colleague Bill Danko and I have interviewed thousands of wealthy people to find out what sets them apart from everyone else.

We discovered something surprising. Many people who live in expensive homes and drive luxury cars don't actually have much real wealth.

By contrast, we also found that many people who have great wealth do not live in upscale neighborhoods.

Wealth isn't the same as income. If you make good money each year and spend it all, you're not getting wealthier—you're just living high. Wealth is what you accumulate, not what you spend.

APPRECIATING MONEY

If you want to become financially independent, you need to make the necessary trade-offs among time, wealth, energy and consumption habits.

Contrary to popular opinion, most rich people did not inherit their wealth. About 80% of America's millionaires are first-generation rich.

Meaning: They made their money themselves. And it is rarely luck, advanced degrees or intelligence that enabled these people to amass their fortunes.

Wealth is more often the result of a lifestyle built on hard work, perseverance, planning, saving and, most of all, self-discipline. In our research, we found some common denominators among those people who successfully build wealth. We called these people PAWs *(Prodigious Accumulators of Wealth)* as opposed to UAWs *(Under Accumulators of Wealth)*.

BECOMING A MILLIONAIRE

●**Live well below your means.** Wealthy people know that financial independence is far more important than displaying high status.

The millionaires with whom we spoke have an average household net worth of $3.7 million but live in homes that are currently valued at about $320,000. About half have occupied the same homes for more than 20 years.

They are similarly frugal in other ways. Most never spent more than $400 on a suit…half never spent more than $29,000 on a car…and half never spent more than $235 for a wristwatch.

They aren't misers. And they don't deprive themselves, either. They're just not into trendy consumerism, which is the worst kind of consumption because it costs the most money.

●**Spend the necessary time managing your money.** Those who are wealthy devote nearly twice the number of hours a month to evaluating their budgets and planning financial investments as those who are not wealthy. This amounts to about eight-and-a-half hours a month. *Examples…*

●**Millionaires keep close tabs on how much their families spend each year** on food, clothing and shelter…and they have clearly defined sets of daily, weekly, monthly, annual and lifetime goals. But they go beyond stating them. They ask themselves *why* these goals are important. In most cases, the answer is greater control and financial independence.

●**UAWs are nearly twice as likely to hold at least 20% of their total wealth in cash** or near cash, such as CDs and money market funds.

●**People we found to be PAWs invest more wisely than UAWs.** PAWs are great believers in the financial markets, and they invest in stocks that usually appreciate in value but don't produce realized income. They are calculated risk-takers but not active stock market traders. They are buy-and-hold investors, viewing the stock market as a place to preserve wealth rather than make a killing. About 40% of the millionaires we interviewed had made *no* trades in their stock portfolios during the year prior to our interview.

STAYING RICH

●**Raise children who are economically self-sufficient.** When parents teach their children the value of money, they raise kids who successfully manage their own finances at early ages and do not become financial burdens to their parents later in life.

The affluent parents of successful adult children shared with us some of the guidelines they felt were important to raising self-supporting children…

●**Never tell your kids that they are wealthy.** Wealthy and successful children whose parents were millionaires told us time and again, "I never knew my parents were wealthy until I became the executor of their estate. They never looked or acted rich."

●**Never tell your children you have money** until after they have established their own mature, disciplined and adult lifestyles and professions. Some of the millionaires we studied set up for their children trusts that don't distribute any money until the children are age 40 or older. They said, "This way my money will have little effect on their way of life. They will have already adopted their own lifestyles."

●**Explain your expenses.** Instead of simply buying their kids $18,000 cars, many millionaires explain how they came up with the money. They tell how they invested $6,000 years ago and how that money grew to be $18,000.

●**Don't try to compete with your children.** Never start a conversation with, "When I was your age, I had already…" Instead, emphasize your children's achievements—no matter how small—rather than placing emphasis on your symbols of success. This will teach them to achieve, not consume.

●**Teach your children that there are a lot of things more valuable than money.** Good health, longevity, happiness, a loving family, a good reputation, integrity, respect and a history of achievements are all goals toward which they should strive.

●**Don't hand over money to adult children too quickly.** In our research, we found that giving money freely to your adult children can drain your assets and won't help them in the long run. We found that the more money adult children received from their parents, the less they accumulated themselves. Those children who were given fewer dollars tended to accumulate more.

Reasons: Money given by parents to adult children tends to encourage unrealistically high-spending lifestyles. We also found that gift-receivers tended to be more dependent on credit than others and invested less money than non-receivers.

Better: Some forms of economic help can have a strong positive influence on the productivity of recipients. Such assistance often includes subsidizing children's educations and earmarking gifts so that children can start or enhance a business.

Thomas Stanley, PhD, chairman of the Affluent Market Institute, a research firm in Atlanta. He is coauthor, with William Danko, PhD, chairman of marketing at the State University of New York at Albany, of *The Millionaire Next Door: The Surprising Secrets of America's Wealthy.* Long Street Press.

Budget Basics

Track small expenses if you make them *regularly.* It usually does not pay to try to keep track of anything costing less than one dollar. But if you buy bottled water from the office machine every day—paying around 75 cents—and work about 200 days a year, you can save $150 a year by simply bringing water from home.

Bottom line: Track expenses to identify areas that take a disproportionate amount of your income. These will usually be big expenses like dining out. Even small expenses can add up.

Wealth in a Decade by Brett Machtig, senior portfolio manager at D.E. Frey, an investment firm in Minneapolis. Irwin Professional Publishing.

Where to Look for Money That You Didn't Know You Had

David W. Folsom

As a guest on *The Oprah Winfrey Show*, I fielded a call from a woman whose husband was a railroad employee at the time of his death in 1977. With very little effort, we found a $6,000 insurance policy that had remained uncollected for nearly two decades.

Thousands of people die every day with assets that their heirs never know about. And 95% of unclaimed assets have no statute of limitations.

If you think you might be an heir—you can track down these hidden assets on your own.

Where the assets are: Bank accounts, pension funds, insurance policies, property (e.g., cars, boats and condos), retirement plans and brokerage accounts, safe-deposit boxes, health insurance policies and closely held corporations that the deceased controlled.

FAMILY TREES

Often a person wills his/her estate to someone who doesn't even know he is an heir. If the heir dies before the estate can track him down, then *that* person's heirs may have a claim against the original estate.

About 60% of people die without a will. Check your family tree, especially for relatives who died before reaching age 65. Above that age, people usually have wills executed.

Also look for older relatives who lived alone before they died and for divorced relatives who may have died before realizing that they were in line to inherit part of a former spouse's estate.

STEPS TO A SUCCESSFUL SEARCH

●**Check death records.** Deaths are first recorded by the county where the person died and then by the state's office of vital statistics within 12 months of the death.

●**Check probate records.** They are public record in all states. Ask for a list of the deceased person's estate inventory. The list may contain information about stocks or privately held companies through which he owned other assets.

●**Establish heirship.** That's necessary for access to many types of personal data, including bank accounts and other financial records. Later, you need proof of heirship to make a claim to an estate.

To prove heirship: You need certified records, not photocopies, that link you with the deceased relative. Usually only the original issuing agencies can provide certified records.

Examples: Birth and death certificates, marriage licenses and military identification documents.

●**Track down the relative's Social Security number.** The number is usually found on death certificates, and it's the key to locating nearly all assets because the IRS requires banks and other institutions to list the Social Security number on all accounts. Since most states put Social Security numbers on driver's licenses, the easiest way to learn the number is simply to find the relative's license.

Inside maneuver: If you have trouble finding a person's Social Security number, add his name to your own automobile insurance policy. The insurance agent will quickly get the Social Security number through his company's computer database that it uses to check on driving records.

If the agent discovers that the second driver has died, tell him you made a mistake, but ask him to tell you the Social Security number.

●**Look through bank records.** When you produce proof of heirship, banks generally let you go through the deceased relative's canceled checks. They can be especially useful clues to other assets such as insurance policies, brokerage accounts and out-of-state property.

●**Find out whether your relative controlled a corporation that might have owned assets.** In some states, you can get this information by contacting the state's Secretary of State. Then, use your proof of heirship to get copies of personal and/or corporate income tax returns. If they're accurate, the returns will list assets. But all states do not make this information available to the public.

●**Contact your relative's employers to see if he had a life insurance policy or retirement plan (lump sum benefits).** Both can be sources of assets, especially for professions with strong unions.

Income tax records are a good source of employer information. If the deceased belonged to a professional organization, also check there to see if it had a group policy. Make inquiries of the Veterans Administration if your relative served in the armed forces.

●**Check the state's unclaimed property office.** If your claim is uncontested and your proof of heirship is in order, most offices will turn the assets over to you within 30 to 45 days.

To claim other property, go to the probate court in the jurisdiction where your relative died. Here the procedure usually takes three to four months.

Since most probate court clerks will help you fill out the appropriate forms, you probably won't need an attorney.

But, if the estate is complex, it may be wise to consult a lawyer at this point. If you do retain an attorney, most states limit lawyer's fees to 10% of the estate's value.

During your search, don't be overly concerned if you discover other legitimate claimants. At worst, you may have to share the estate with them.

David W. Folsom, author of *Assets Unknown*. Two Dot Press.

Practical Emergency-Fund Strategy

Set up a home-equity line of credit while you're healthy and employed.

Reason: If you need medical treatment that is not covered by your health plan or money to pay bills, you will have access to cash at a low interest rate. Apply for the biggest line of credit you can.

Important: Do not draw on the account until it is necessary.

Martin Shenkman, CPA, an attorney specializing in estate, tax and financial planning, who practices in New York and Teaneck, NJ.

How Much Money Should You Put in an Emergency Fund?

Two months' take-home pay in a savings or money market account is an adequate emergency fund.

Reason: People have easier access to cash these days—including home-equity loans... cash advances on low-interest credit cards... loans against 401(k)s.

Exception: Keep more money in your emergency fund if you have poor credit or if your spouse doesn't work and your paycheck is the family's only source of income.

Jonathan Pond, president of Financial Planning Information Inc., 9 Galen St., Watertown, MA 02172, and author of *Four Easy Steps to Successful Investing*. Avon.

Personal Cash Crunch Self-Defense

For those who have been laid off or are experiencing an unexpected financial emergency...

•**Prioritize all payments.** Mortgage or rent, insurance and credit card bills should be at the top of your list. These organizations report delinquencies to credit bureaus. (Utility companies do not report to credit bureaus and usually wait several months before acting on delinquencies.)

•**Stretch out payments when possible**, either by formally contacting creditors or by taking advantage of built-in options.

•**Consider all possible money sources**, including relatives, checking overdraft privileges and life insurance with cash value. Use savings-account money instead of charging on credit cards at high interest rates. Before selling investments, compare potential returns and selling fees with interest payments on alternative sources.

Jocelyn R. Kaplan, CFP, president of Advisors Financial Inc., Falls Church, VA.

Credit Card Dirty Tricks, Traps...and Self-Defense

Gerri Detweiler
National Council of Individual Investors

It's becoming difficult to find a truly good deal on a credit card. Rising penalties, reduced grace periods and disappearing benefits make it much harder for cardholders to evaluate tricky credit card offers.

To make the search even more challenging, the laws regulating what credit card issuers can and can't do keep changing.

What's happening now in credit cards—and how to defend yourself against issuer traps...

Trend #1: **Rising penalty fees.** A recent Supreme Court decision allows card issuers to charge high fees when user payments are late …or credit limits are exceeded. Expect fees possibly as high as $25 to $30 if your check is just one day late…or if you exceed your credit limit. Some credit card issuers are also boosting interest rates to around 22% if you're late a few times.

Self-defense: It's now more important than ever to keep track of when your credit card bill is due, since your check must arrive at the credit card company by the due date. An envelope that is *postmarked* on the due date doesn't count.

Helpful: On the front of each bill's envelope, write the date when the bill must be mailed so that it arrives by the due date. Then arrange envelopes in the order of when the bills are due.

Even easier solution: Reduce your paperwork by canceling all but two of your credit cards. Transfer the other balances to lower-rate cards.

If you slip up once and are penalized for missing a deadline after having paid your bills on time consistently, you may be able to get the issuer to drop the penalty. If you have a good record and the issuer won't waive the fee, consider finding an issuer with a more reasonable policy.*

Trend #2: **Making life harder on debt-free customers.** Credit card issuers are putting the squeeze on "convenience users"—customers who don't carry balances and avoid paying interest charges. People who use credit cards only occasionally and charge less than $3,000 to $5,000 a year may be hit with annual fees for low usage.

The issuer may also eliminate the grace period—the amount of time users are given to pay their bills in full to avoid being charged interest on the purchase. Or a card may be canceled if a balance isn't boosted. Revoking cards is becoming more common and is completely legal.

Strategy: Before you sign up for a new credit card, request a copy of the cardholder agreement, which spells out the terms. This agreement is usually sent *after* you apply, when you get the credit card. Don't rely on the card application for this information. Applications only contain bare-bones data about rates and fees. If you don't carry a balance and use your card infrequently, consider switching to a MasterCard or Visa *debit* card, which offers the convenience of plastic while deducting purchases directly from your bank account.

Trend #3: **No warning that your introductory rate has expired.** If you signed up earlier this year for a card with a super-low six-month introductory rate, check your statement. The low rate may be about to expire—or it may have already risen five percentage points or more.

If your rate has skyrocketed during the last month or two, call your credit card issuer and ask that your old rate be continued for another six months. If you have paid all your bills on time and carry a balance, you're a terrific customer and the bank will want to keep you.

If the credit card issuer agrees to continue the lower rate, mark your calendar so you'll remember to call and haggle again before the rate goes up. If your issuer won't at least compromise and offer a better deal—13% or less—switch to another card with a lower rate. *My current favorite low-rate cards:*

●**Federal Savings Bank** offers 9.35% interest with a $33 annual fee. 800-285-9090.

●**Pulaski Bank and Trust** offers 9.45% interest with a $35 annual fee. 800-217-7715.

Important: When you switch cards, close out the old ones. You are more likely to use accounts that are left open in the future—defeating the purpose of switching cards.

Also, too many open credit card accounts may cause lenders and other card issuers to reject you, thinking you are risky because you have too much available credit.

Write to the credit card issuer and ask it to report to the three major credit bureaus that your old account has been closed at your request. *The credit bureaus are:*

●**Equifax**, 800-685-1111.

●**Trans Union**, 316-636-6100.

●**TRW**, 800-682-7654.

Trend #4: **Vanishing perks.** The free perks that issuers used to lavish on cardholders in

---

*A complete list of low-rate cards is available from *CardTrak*, Box 1700, Frederick, MD 21702.

the early 1990s are now all being scaled back as cost-conscious card issuers become more frugal.

Examples: Chase Manhattan and Citibank dropped free extended manufacturer warranties from their standard cards.

And almost all frequent-flier programs have raised the number of miles they require for a free round-trip domestic ticket from 20,000 to 25,000 miles. Since you generally earn one mile for every dollar charged on an airline program card, you'll have to charge $5,000 more to get a free ticket.

Helpful: Call new card issuers and ask them to read you a list of perks. Think about whether you need what you'll be receiving. If a particular benefit is missing but important to you, chances are you can still find it elsewhere.

Example I: Free purchase insurance is still offered on all gold MasterCards and American Express cards.

Example II: If you want frequent-flier miles, the Old Kent Bank's CardMiles (800-245-5353) is one of the most flexible programs. There is a fee plus a relatively competitive interest rate. Cardholders earn one mile for every one dollar charged on this MasterCard or Visa and can either cash in 5,000 miles for a certificate worth $100 off a round-trip ticket on any airline or accumulate 20,000 miles for a free round-trip domestic ticket on any airline.

A guide to frequent-flier/rebate cards is available for $5 from BankCard Holders of America, 524 Branch Dr., Salem, Virginia 24153.

Trend #5: Lower credit limits for new card-holders. Many issuers are now targeting potential customers with mail that says they are preapproved for cards with attractive interest rates.

Trap: After you sign up and the new card arrives, you may discover that your credit limit is for only a few hundred dollars. This common tactic is used by card issuers that send out mass mailings, then wait until later to fully evaluate applicants' credit ratings.

Self-defense: If this happens, demand an immediate increase in your credit limit. If the issuer won't budge, politely say that the card is of no use to you and therefore you must send it back.

Alternative solution: If the issuer won't budge and the card is terrific, consider offering to transfer a large balance from another card—but only if the issuer will raise your credit limit.

Gerri Detweiler, a consumer-credit consultant in Woodbridge, VA, and head of public policy for the National Council of Individual Investors, 1900 L St. NW, Ste. 610, Washington, DC 20036. She is author of *The Ultimate Credit Handbook.* Plume.

Troublesome Credit Card Trend

More major issuers are not disclosing the interest rate you will receive until after you are approved for the card. "Personalized" rates are based on your credit reports...number of credit card switches...number of cards owned...and level of outstanding debt.

Strategy: When considering a new card, first call the issuer and ask what your rate will be. Avoid issuers that won't tell you up front.

Gerri Detweiler, a consumer-credit consultant in Woodbridge, VA, and head of public policy for the National Council of Individual Investors, 1900 L St. NW, Ste. 610, Washington, DC 20036. She is author of *The Ultimate Credit Handbook.* Plume.

Credit Card Trap

Late-payment fees are rising for credit card users—and grace periods are falling. Late fees are often as high as $20, up from about $15. The period before the late fee kicks in, which was five to 15 days, is being eliminated—companies are cutting it to one day.

Self-defense: Mail payments for credit card bills on time. *Helpful:* Mail each bill at least one week before it is due—to give your check plenty of time to reach the card issuer.

Ruth Susswein, executive director of Bankcard Holders of America, 524 Branch Dr., Salem, VA 24153.

Credit Cards, College Students... And Less Trouble

Robert McKinley
CardTrak

My 18-year-old daughter is going to college this fall. As a credit card industry insider, I know how easy it is for college-bound kids to get into financial trouble with their credit cards.

So here are the steps I recommend you take to ensure your child has the convenience of a card and all of the safeguards...

HAVE A CREDIT CARD TALK

Many young people do not take credit cards seriously. Eventually, of course, they do learn —often the hard way—that plastic is every bit as real as cash.

Helpful: Explain how easy it is to get into debt and how hard it would be for your child to pay it off.

WEIGH THE OPTIONS

There are three different types of credit cards for students who are heading off to college...

• **Card that is an extension of the parents' account.** The benefits of adding another card to an existing account is that it will likely not have an annual fee and the interest rate will be lower than what your child could get on his/her own. In addition, you can monitor precisely how your child is using the card.

Drawbacks: Because your child shares your account, he also shares your high spending limit, which from a student's perspective is unlimited. In addition, your child won't be building credit in his own name, which can make it tougher for him to get good credit deals—or needed loans—after graduation.

• **Card in the child's name.** This option allows your child to build up his/her own credit history while providing a sense of financial independence.

Drawbacks: Interest rates on these credit cards tend to be high. You also cannot supervise your child's spending—unless you ask him to show you the monthly credit statements.

• **Secured card in the child's name.** A secured credit card is backed by cash deposited either by you or your child into a savings account set up by the issuer. So—a child can't spend/borrow more than the amount on deposit.

This forces the child to be conscientious about his spending habits. The card also helps the child build an individual credit history.

Drawback: A secured card that is backed by a small deposit may be inadequate for big-ticket emergency spending.

I believe in secured cards for students because it's impossible for temptation to cause excess spending and debt.

If a major purchase is needed quickly, I can always deposit additional funds for things like expensive airline tickets.

Robert McKinley, publisher of *CardTrak*, a consumer guide to the best credit card deals in the US, Box 1700, Frederick, MD 21702.

If You Cannot Repay Your Student Loan

Contact your lender. Do not simply skip payments—which can ruin your credit rating. Lenders will often consider a deferral or forbearance for a period of time if you are out of work, in graduate school or temporarily disabled. Under a deferment, students are not liable for any interest that accrues during a period of nonpayment. Under a forbearance, interest accrues but collection activity ceases during the agreed nonpayment period. You might also consider asking for a graduated repayment plan, in which payments rise over time as you presumably earn more money.

Suzanne Boas, president of the Consumer Credit Counseling Service, 100 Edgewood Ave., Ste. 1500, Atlanta 30303.

Beware of the New Bank Services

Banks can now sell life, health, auto and home owner's insurance—thanks to a recent Supreme Court decision. But that doesn't necessarily make their policies a good buy.

Self-defense: Shop around before buying a bank's policy—check with several insurance agents and with low-cost direct sellers like Geico (800-841-3000).

Caution: Don't be fooled into thinking there is federal government guarantee or backing for bank-sold insurance, as there is for bank savings accounts. There is not. And—do not let a bank say you must buy its insurance in order to get a loan or other services. Such "bundling" is illegal.

Robert Hunter, insurance director of the Consumer Federation of America, 1424 16 St. NW, Washington, DC 20036.

Instant Check Protection

Write *for deposit only* on checks *before* taking checks to the bank or ATM. Sign below the words, then write your account number below the signature. If the check is lost or stolen, it can be deposited only to your account—it cannot be cashed or deposited to someone else's account.

Edward F. Mrkvicka, Jr., president of Reliance Enterprises Inc., financial consultants, 22115 O'Connell Rd., Marengo, IL 60152. He is author of several books, including *Your Bank Is Ripping You Off*. St. Martin's Press.

Beware: "Free" Checking

So-called "free" checking is on the rise again as bank competition heats up. But these accounts often come with strings attached—they may have a time limit on the free offer, after which they charge monthly fees…pay no interest…or have high charges for bounced checks or ATM use.

Self-defense: Ask for details on any checking account that is supposedly free. Before switching, find out if your current bank will give you a better deal.

Edward F. Mrkvicka, Jr., president of Reliance Enterprises Inc., financial consultants, 22115 O'Connell Rd., Marengo, IL 60152. He is author of several books, including *Your Bank Is Ripping You Off*. St. Martin's Press.

Shrewder Banking

Look for accounts that charge the least in *fees*, rather than those that pay the most in interest.

A noninterest-bearing account may be a better value if the bank's interest-bearing account comes with numerous fees that cost substantially more than the interest earned.

If you maintain low balances: Choose a checking account with a "no minimum balance" requirement. This account won't pay interest, but you won't be socked with extra charges.

Edward F. Mrkvicka, Jr., president of Reliance Enterprises Inc., financial consultants, 22115 O'Connell Rd., Marengo, IL 60152. He is author of several books, including *Your Bank Is Ripping You Off*. St. Martin's Press.

New Bank Trap

If your bank has recently been taken over and its fees raised, it's time to do some comparison shopping. Most banks have special fee structures for retirees or senior citizens, but they don't advertise them. You have to ask. If it's too embarrassing in person, do it by phone.

Try several banks, savings and loans and credit unions (which generally have the lowest fees and loan rates, as well as paying higher interest on savings). To locate a credit union you might be eligible to join, call 800-358-5710 to find the phone number of your state's credit union league.

Edward F. Mrkvicka, Jr., president of Reliance Enterprises Inc., financial consultants, 22115 O'Connell Rd., Marengo, IL 60152. He is author of several books, including *Your Bank Is Ripping You Off*. St. Martin's Press.

Credit Unions vs. Banks

Edward F. Mrkvicka, Jr.
Reliance Enterprises Inc.

I encourage people who are fed up with paying high bank fees to consider taking their business to a credit union. By switching, you can reduce your charges...receive better interest rates...and save about $300 a year in fees.

But—people have questions...

What exactly is a credit union? Credit unions were authorized by the Federal Credit Union Act of 1934 as a low-cost way to serve the financial needs of their members. By contrast, banks exist only to earn a profit for the owners.

Unlike a bank, which accepts deposits from anyone who wants to open an account, you must qualify to join a credit union, which is a private institution.

Do credit unions provide the same services as banks? Yes. Services include everything from checking accounts and credit cards to auto loans and mortgages. Credit unions generally impose fewer and lower fees than banks...have lower balance requirements... pay better interest on savings...and charge lower interest rates on loans.

Example: Bank checking account fees typically amount to $100 to $120 a year for customers who have low balances. Credit union fees for a similar account average half that amount.

And...credit unions offer greater flexibility than other lenders. They're more likely than banks to approve a borrower who can't afford the standard down payment on a mortgage.

Are deposits insured, as they are at a bank? Credit unions are insured by the National Credit Union Administration—not the Federal Deposit Insurance Corp., the group that protects customer deposits at banks. Both agencies insure accounts up to $100,000 with the full faith and credit of the US government.

Are there any drawbacks to a credit union? Not many. It might take a bit of time to find the right credit union because some don't offer a full range of services. And you might not qualify for membership at your first choice. Also, the credit union you select may not be as conveniently located as your neighborhood bank, but some offer ATM cards.

Some small credit unions won't be able to make loans as large as banks. But unless you want to borrow millions of dollars, this isn't likely to affect you.

How can I find a credit union? Call the Credit Union National Association (800-358-5710) for assistance locating credit unions in your area.

Call approximately five credit unions to find out if you qualify for membership. While some are restricted to narrow groups, such as the employees of a specific company, others may require only that you live in the region. Virtually everyone will qualify for at least one or two local credit unions.

Next, determine if these provide the services you need—and compare their rates and fees. Ask for copies of their brochures for details of their programs.

If you don't find a credit union in your region that meets your needs, consider doing business with one in another part of the country. If you do your banking by mail, the distance won't matter. Banking through the mail may slow down your transactions by a few days, but that is a small price to pay for lower costs and better service.

Edward F. Mrkvicka, Jr., president of Reliance Enterprises Inc., financial consultants, 22115 O'Connell Rd., Marengo, IL 60152. He is author of several books, including Your Bank Is Ripping You Off. *St. Martin's Press.*

On-Line Banking... The Fee Trap

When shopping for an on-line banking service, there are two types of fees you need to be concerned with...

● **The fee you are charged for accessing the Internet**—it is usually one set figure a month.

● **How the bank charges you for the privilege of doing business transactions with**

them on-line—which is similar to the fees that a bank charges each time you use an ATM. While many banks are currently waiving these fees, they probably won't for long.

Self-defense: Find out exactly what the charges are per transaction before you sign on for the service.

James Lowell, finance expert and editor of *America Online's Mutual Fund Resource Center* and author of *Investing from Scratch: A Handbook for the Young Investor.* Penguin Books.

Tax-Free Municipal Bond Funds Trap

Tax-free municipal bond funds are not completely tax free. Dividends from municipal bond funds may be subject to state or local income taxes. A part of each dividend may represent taxable income or capital gains that the fund realized. If you sell shares in the fund at a profit, your capital gain is taxable.

David S. Rhine, CPA, partner and national director of family wealth planning, BDO Seidman, LLP, 330 Madison Ave., New York 10017.

Best Type of Money Market Offered Through Banks

One that pays interest from day of deposit to day of withdrawal.

Avoid: Daily-collected-balance accounts, which pay interest only after checks that you deposit clear the banks on which they are drawn ...and low-balance compounding, which pays only on the lowest balance during the time period.

The Complete Idiot's Guide to Making Money on Wall Street by Christy Heady, syndicated financial journalist. Alpha Books.

Top-Yielding Money-Market Funds May Lose Rankings

Many top-yielding money-market funds quickly lose their top rankings. *Reason:* Their high yields come from waiving some—or even all—of the fund's expenses. When high yields bring in enough money so the fund reaches its desired size, it starts to phase in expense payments—and yields drop.

Self-defense: Check your money-market fund yield regularly. Compare it with yields of other funds—and consider switching if your yield starts to slip. Selling money-market fund shares is not a taxable event, since the net asset value of each share is constant at one dollar.

Walter Frank, chief investment officer at *Moneyletter,* which tracks mutual funds, 1217 St. Paul St., Baltimore 21202.

Beware: Brokerage Account Forms

Brokerage account forms provide information about you that can be used against you if you ever face some sort of dispute. Many forms required to open a brokerage account ask for information on your investment goals, finances and personal background. If you lose money and believe you were unfairly treated, the brokerage can and will use whatever you said on the forms to prepare its case against you.

Self-defense: Read the forms very carefully. Be sure you understand them. Decline to respond to questions you do not wish to answer. Write a letter to your broker confirming your understanding of your investment goals.

John McKeegan, partner with Shockman & McKeegan, a law firm in Scottsdale, AZ, that represents investors in brokerage disputes.

When to Pay Off a Mortgage Early

Paying off a mortgage early can be a smart move if you plan to live in your home for many years, until well after the mortgage is paid off.

Benefits: After paying off the mortgage your monthly expenses will drop, giving you extra funds to support a child in college or to live on in retirement…you get a guaranteed return on your payments equal to the mortgage interest rate—other investments that can pay as much are unlikely to be guaranteed…the equity you build up in your home can be tapped through a home-equity loan to obtain *tax-free* cash at any time.

Jonathan Pond, president of Financial Planning Information Inc., 9 Galen St., Watertown, MA 02172, and author of *Four Easy Steps to Successful Investing*. Avon.

Mortgage Prepayment Trap

Avoid biweekly mortgage plans that charge fees—sometimes $300 or more—as a one-time charge plus an annual renewal fee.

How they work: A mortgage holder makes half of his/her mortgage payment every two weeks to a mortgage-payment firm—instead of to the lender. Then the firm pays the lender at the end of the month.

Best: Pay down your mortgage principal more quickly by doing it yourself at no additional cost. Simply send a prepayment of principal with your regular monthly mortgage check—clearly indicating that the second check should be applied to principal. Then watch your mortgage statement to be sure that the prepayments are credited correctly.

Important: Make sure that your mortgage agreement does not have a prepayment penalty.

Keith Gumbinger, vice president and analyst at HSH Associates, a fee-based mortgage consulting firm, 1200 Rte. 23, Butler, NJ 07405.

Better Mortgages for Fixer-Uppers

Buyers of houses that need substantial work can now get one long-term, market-rate loan—instead of separate loans for the house purchase and the repairs. To qualify for this 203(k) program—from the Federal Housing Administration—the home must need repairs that are not completely cosmetic and have an estimated cost of at least $5,000. *More information:* Contact your local HUD office.

Home Mortgage Audits

A home mortgage "audit" can uncover errors that cost home owners significant sums of money over the life of a mortgage. Mistakes are more common in adjustable-rate mortgages (ARMs) than in fixed-rate ones. Consider a home mortgage audit if your mortgage has been sold or transferred to another institution …if you have had an ARM for a number of years…or if your interest rates are going down, but your monthly payments are going up. *Cost of an audit:* From $95 to $350.

Greg Bibas, operations manager at Mortgage Monitor, a national mortgage auditing firm based in Stamford, CT.

Home-Equity Loan or Line of Credit?

Choosing whether to take a home-equity *loan* or home-equity *line of credit* depends on the timing of your need for money. To cover one large expense—like a major home improvement or a one-time debt consolidation—take a loan. If you expect major expenses over a period of time—like several home projects or years of college tuition—a credit line is best. Shop around to find the best rate…then push the lender to waive any fees. Some small local lenders offer better rates than the megabanks that advertise widely.

Warning: Equity lines have adjustable interest rates. Find out the cost of the loan over the total repayment period. Don't just look at the introductory rate.

Keith Gumbinger, vice president and analyst at HSH Associates, a fee-based mortgage consulting firm, 1200 Rte. 23, Butler, NJ 07405.

When a Friend Asks for a Loan...

If a friend asks for a loan, decide whether you can afford to lose the money. If you can, think of it as a *gift*. Consider it a bonus if he/she pays you back. If you do not have the money, help your friend think of resources—but be wary of going into debt to help him. If you have the money but do not want to lend it, refuse gently by telling him the friendship is too important to risk in case of possible repayment difficulties.

Herbert Freudenberger, PhD, a clinical psychologist in private practice in New York.

Give Kids Salaries... Not Allowances

While the word "allowance" carries with it the feeling of entitlement, "salary" connotes money earned for performing certain chores that will be used to pay living expenses.

Example: A sixth-grader who is paid a salary of $50 per month might be required to save 10%, give 10% to charity and use the remaining 80%—$40—for expenses such as video games, gifts for birthday parties and school lunches.

Benefits: Giving kids accountability for how they earn and spend their money—even when they spend it stupidly—gives them a sense of responsibility and maturity.

Mary Hunt, publisher of *The Cheapskate Monthly* newsletter, Box 2135, Paramount, CA 90723. She is author of *The Best of The Cheapskate Monthly: Simple Tips for Living Lean in the '90s.* St. Martin's Press.

Teach Children Money Management

The concept of relative value is the key to teaching children responsible financial management. An item's relative value is the price of that item in relation to what you personally have to do to pay for it. Understanding the "real cost" of an item can make purchasing decisions clearer.

Example: If your child had to mow 10 lawns to pay for a model airplane he saw on TV, he may decide he doesn't need the airplane after all.

Neale Godfrey, a children's financial counselor in Mountain Lakes, NJ, and author of *Money Doesn't Grow on Trees: A Parent's Guide to Raising Financially Responsible Children.* Fireside.

Dangerous: Cosigning Your Child's Credit Application

If you cosign your child's credit card application and he/she does not make payments, the credit card issuer has no obligation to notify you—but will probably record the account's troubled history on your credit report as well as your child's. *Result:* You end up with credit damage before you even know there's a problem.

Alternative: Give your child a card on your account. It won't help him/her build a credit history, but it can teach him to use credit wisely.

Kristin Davis, a Washington, DC-based financial writer and author of *Financing College.* Kiplinger Books.

Very Useful Money-Saving Web Sites

Hy Bender

Shareware.com is a software library that lets you copy thousands of business programs, games, picture files, audio and video clips, etc., at no charge (www.shareware.com).

FREE PHONE NUMBERS

•**Four11** is a free national telephone directory that lets you find virtually anyone's telephone number—or e-mail address—without having to pay for directory assistance (www.four11.com).

LOW AIRFARES

•**Travelocity** provides free access to the schedules of more than 700 airlines…and to a program that identifies the lowest available fare. Includes airplane seating diagrams, a 15,000-destination travel guide, ticket-ordering services and more (www.travelocity.com).

TRAVEL BARGAINS

•**Shoestring Travel** has free information about reduced-rate hotels, inexpensive auto rentals, discount travel clubs and other bargains around the globe (www.stratpub.com/shoe1.html).

DISCOUNT BROKERAGE

•**The Net Investor** is an online brokerage house that provides free 20-minute delayed stock quotes, up to 50% off investment commissions and other useful services for investors (pawws.com/tni).

INEXPENSIVE BOOKS

•**Amazon.com** is a book superstore that offers more than a million titles at 10% to 30% off list prices. Books are ordered on-screen and paid for by credit card. Expect delivery for most books within three days (www.amazon.com).

DISCOUNT ENTERTAINMENT

•**CDworld** is a music superstore that offers more than 170,000 CDs and tapes—as well as thousands of movies, music videos and video games at 10% to 30% off prices found at stores. Expect delivery within two weeks (www.cdworld.com).

LOW-COST PERSONAL FINANCE

•**ConsumerWorld** lists more than 1,200 consumer resources to help you obtain a low-interest credit card, find discount eyeglasses, buy a house or get virtually any other consumer product inexpensively (www.consumerworld.org).

CHEAP HOME-OFFICE SUPPLIES

•**Industry.Net** sells thousands of business-related products. Items range from staplers to factory robots (www.industry.net).

Hy Bender, author of eight books on computers and the Internet. He is coauthor, with Margaret Young, of *Dummies 101: The Internet for Windows 95*. IDG Books. Information about additional discounts can be found on the Internet by accessing net.dummies. com/internet101.

5

Insurance Savvy

How Not to Lose the New HMO Game

Timothy McCall, MD

I am an internist who is *not* part of a Health Maintenance Organization (HMO)—but many of my colleagues are HMO doctors. During the past six months, I've listened to them and patients talk about the problems they and their friends are facing with HMOs.

HMOs push to keep their expenses down. In an ideal world, they would accomplish this by preventing illness and detecting problems early, while treatment is still easy and cost-effective.

Reality: Many HMOs hold down expenses by denying medical services that might be important to you.

Knowledge and the willingness to be assertive go a long way to helping your case. *Here's what you can do...*

•**Find the loopholes before you need them.** To keep down the number of services they provide, HMOs set up roadblocks to limit people from obtaining care, such as requiring preauthorization for emergency services and approval for expensive therapies.

Key: Understand how to get over these obstacles now, before you're faced with a medical problem or an emergency. Carefully read your membership booklet, your contract and any newsletters that contain benefit information. If you follow the rules every step of the way, the HMO will have a harder time denying payment to you.

•**Get in good with your doctor.** Because your primary care doctor is the person who will treat you for routine illnesses and decide whether or not the HMO will cover visits to specialists, a very good relationship with your doctor is valuable.

What you can do now: Get to know your doctor well. Determine whether this is someone primarily concerned with the bottom line—or whether he/she will go to bat for you when the HMO takes a hard line, like trying to deny an extra day in the hospital or an expen-

85

sive test. HMOs sometimes fire doctors who appeal too much on behalf of their patients. If your doctor is willing to do so anyway, it is a good sign.

Guide: Keep track of how much time your doctor devotes to you…and how often he recommends expensive services, such as specialist referrals and high-tech tests. If you get the impression the doctor is primarily interested in making money—and not so concerned about your health—switch to another doctor before a health problem occurs.

The better your relationship with your doctor and his staff, the better service you're likely to receive. Come prepared for visits with lists of symptoms and questions…but be reasonable. Time is limited.

How to negotiate with doctors: Although it pays to be assertive, remember the old saying, *You catch more flies with honey than with vinegar.* Rather than arrogantly demanding tests and specialist referrals, try striking deals with your doctor.

Examples: Ask whether he will refer you to an orthopedist if your knee is still bothering you in three months. Ask whether he will schedule an MRI scan if one month of medicine and physical therapy don't help your lower back pain.

Pick your battles. If the doctor perceives you as a rational and reasonable patient, you're more likely to get the service you need.

• **Uncover what is motivating your doctor.** Many HMOs pay doctors bonuses for keeping down the expensive services they provide, such as days in the hospital or referrals to specialists.

A common system—known as *capitation*—pays doctors a fixed monthly fee per patient. Doctors have an incentive to sign up lots of patients and see as many as possible in one day.

In addition, the costs of tests and other services may come out of a doctor's capitation checks, thus encouraging him to order as few services as possible.

Warning sign: When your doctor's recommendations always seem to be in accordance with the financial incentives of the HMO. People who tend to be healthy and rarely require special care can ask coworkers and others in the plan of their experiences.

Example: You doctor is quick to say you don't need to see a specialist, have an MRI scan or undergo an operation. It's the *pattern* of denials, not one, that is most telling.

Doctors who are paid salaries by the HMO have no incentive to deny services…or recommend ones you don't need, as happens with traditional insurance.

To know how your doctor is paid: Ask the benefits coordinator where you're employed. If that fails, try speaking with your doctor. Tell him that you've read about HMO doctors' financial incentives and that you would be more comfortable if you knew.

Bad sign: If your doctor says that his HMO contract forbids him from publicly revealing how he's paid. In this case, consider switching plans next year.

• **Know what ails you.** Learn as much as possible about your medical conditions. Patients who are well-informed can ask better questions and will know if what their doctor and HMO are recommending is the best treatment—or just the most economical.

Good resources: The National Health Information Center (800-336-4797), a government-run service, refers callers to some 1,200 organizations. If you have Internet access (available at many public libraries), try searching your topic on AltaVista (http://altavista.digital.com) or Yahoo! (http://www.yahoo.com).

If the results of your research suggest a treatment option that your doctor hasn't suggested, mail or fax him the article a week before your appointment with a note asking him to review it.

Research about your condition may include seeking the opinion of a doctor outside of your plan—even though you'll have to pay. That's because many HMOs actually forbid their doctors from informing you of treatment options the plans *won't* cover. Ask your benefits manager at work or your doctor if the plan has such a "gag rule."

Helpful: Some managed-care plans have a *point-of-service (POS)* option that allows you—for a higher copayment—to consult the doctor of your choice. If you later need to appeal to your plan for a service that was denied, the opinion of this doctor could prove useful.

●**When all else fails, complain creatively.**
All HMOs have grievance procedures, though
they don't always advertise that fact. If the information is not covered well in the membership
booklet, call and ask explicitly what the appeal
procedure is. HMOs respond best to those who
know how to ask for what they need.

***First try to get satisfaction from your
doctor.*** Ask whether it is his decision or
whether plan administrators decide. If necessary, appeal to the administrators informally.

Try a formal appeal if you are still denied
approval. You should get an answer within 30
to 60 days—sooner for more urgent problems.

If your appeal within the plan is still unsuccessful, try to interest a local paper, radio or TV
reporter in your case. Write a well-organized,
one- or two-page description of your situation
that emphasizes your HMO's uncaring behavior. The media may be interested in publiciz-
ing your story.

Aim: An HMO might be much happier paying for an expensive service than seeing you talk
about your plight on the news. If necessary,
consider enlisting the services of an attorney
who specializes in this area.

Timothy McCall, MD, an internist practicing in the
Boston area. He is author of *Examining Your Doctor: A
Patient's Guide to Avoiding Harmful Medical Care.*
Citadel Press. He hosts the *Examining Your Doctor
Forum* on America Online, featuring weekly columns
and regular online chats. *Keyword:* dr.mccall.

Questions to Ask an HMO Before Joining

Jane Howell
American College of Emergency Physicians

B efore joining a Health Maintenance
Organization (HMO), ask how it covers
emergency care. *Key questions…*

●**What defines an emergency?** The best
answer is that a covered emergency exists
when severe symptoms cause you to believe
an emergency exists. If coverage instead
depends on the final diagnosis, you may be
denied coverage for a "false alarm"—no matter
how costly it is.

●**What hospital may I use?** Managed care
plans often cover only member hospitals—so
find out what hospital you should go to and
how to get care when traveling.

●**Whom do I call for approval?** Most
HMOs require notification within a specific
time period after receiving any emergency
procedures, and advance approval of any continuing treatment. Be sure you know the rules.

●**How do I get after-hours care?** Know
procedures for getting care and any required
permissions from the HMO after normal work
hours or on holidays.

Jane Howell, director of public relations at the American
College of Emergency Physicians, 1111 19 St. NW, Ste. 650,
Washington, DC 20036.

Gaining Access to Specialists

H MO members can protect their access to
specialists by naming one as their primary
care physician (PCP). In fact, a number of
states require HMOs to allow members to
choose a specialist—rather than a family
physician—as a PCP under some conditions.
Women, the disabled and the chronically ill
may need to see specialists regularly and could
benefit from having one as a PCP. If your state
doesn't require HMOs to allow this—and your
HMO refuses to make the arrangement—you
may be able to obtain a fixed number of preau-
thorized specialist referrals from your doctor.

Cathy Hurwit, a Washington, DC–based legislative
director for Citizen Action, a national consumer watchdog organization.

Another HMO Trap

A n HMO's list of doctors may be inaccurate
or out of date. Doctors may have died,
quit the plan after the list was printed or been
dismissed right after the sign-up period for
new members.

Self-defense: Don't assume that a doctor is
in an HMO just because his/her name appears

in the plan's list. Call the doctor directly and ask if he is in the plan—and is accepting new plan patients.

If you need a specialist's care, call doctors on the specialist list.

Vincent Riccardi, MD, head of American Medical Consumers, a for-profit patients' rights group, 5415 Briggs Ave., La Crescenta, CA 91214.

Question HMO Surveys

Be skeptical about HMO satisfaction surveys. *Reasons:* Polling techniques vary widely among HMOs, so results are not comparable. And some techniques can be used to improve an HMO's scores.

Examples: Phone surveys yield more positive results than mail surveys...surveys with lower response rates often show happier respondents...surveys do not include members who have recently quit HMOs.

Michael Hays, president of National Research Corp., a market research company in Lincoln, NE.

HMO Checkup

To find out how your HMO compares with others, contact the National Committee for Quality Assurance (NCQA). This nonprofit watchdog organization has accredited more than 240 managed care plans and has detailed "report cards" on 87 of them.

For a free report, call the NCQA at 800-839-6487...or http://www.ncqa.org.

Health Emergencies... Travel...and Your HMO

Gregory Henry, MD
American College of Emergency Physicians

When preparing to leave on a trip, people who belong to health maintenance organizations (HMOs) often forget to check whether they are covered for emergency medical care on the road.

Here's what to do if you need a doctor or an emergency room while you are traveling on vacation or business...

BEFORE YOU GO

●**Examine your policy** to see what steps your HMO requires when you're traveling. Most plans will cover out-of-area emergency care for "acute" conditions. Others require that a condition be life-threatening.

An HMO may later refuse to pay the bill, but —if in doubt—you should be examined by a doctor and work out the payment problems later.

●**Pack a list of the steps the HMO requires**, such as when to call the HMO to alert it to your condition.

Some HMOs have special toll-free numbers for travelers requesting information or confirmation that a condition is covered.

●**Call your plan to see whether it has reciprocal arrangements** with any hospitals or doctors at your destinations. Make a list of where the HMO wants you to go in emergencies.

●**Take some blank claim forms** to ensure their speedy submission after you have been treated.

IN AN EMERGENCY ON THE ROAD

●**If it is a major emergency, forget about the HMO.** If you face a major crisis—such as a stroke, heart attack, broken bones, fainting spells, etc.—seek care immediately and worry about the HMO later. Your health is much more important than whether or not your HMO covers such treatment.

If you are traveling alone, be sure that your family members at home have access to your HMO's phone numbers. In a crisis, call home as soon as you are able to and ask someone there to make all of the time-consuming, stressful calls for you.

If you are traveling with others, each person should have everyone else's HMO data.

●**When calling your HMO**, be very specific about your symptoms and why you must seek care. And be absolutely clear about why you're seeking care now rather than waiting until you return home.

Note: HMOs usually have health care professionals available 24 hours a day, but some HMOs are better than others when responding to emergencies.

Example: Don't say you've been having chest pains for two weeks. Instead, say you've had a sudden onset of pain—or that it just got much worse.

● **Get copies of all bills** and, if possible, letters from doctors who treated you explaining why you needed treatment immediately. Ask them to mail your medical chart to you. The information on the chart should give the HMO everything it needs.

Gregory Henry, MD, president of the American College of Emergency Physicians, Box 619911, Dallas 75261. He is chief of the department of emergency medicine at Oakwood Hospital Beyer Center, Ypsilanti, MI.

How Ordinary People Fought Health Insurers... And Won

William Shernoff
Shernoff, Bidart & Darras

In recent months, our law firm has taken on 10 new cases a week involving people who want to sue their insurance companies or health maintenance organizations (HMOs) for refusing to pay their medical claims.

That's a big jump over a year ago, when we saw only *two* new cases a week.

The reason for the jump is that many more health insurance providers are coming up with a wider variety of ways to evade their legal responsibilities—and reduce costs. HMOs are particularly troublesome because they aggressively limit patient care.

Here are three cases we recently settled involving patients who took on their health insurers—and won.

CASE #1—ENLISTING THE MEDIA

Three years ago, a health insurance company decided to halt coverage of specialized at-home care for a seven-year-old boy.

He was born with a rare heart and lung ailment that can cause dangerous health complications while he sleeps. As a result, he requires constant overnight monitoring at home by machines and a nurse.

By day, he is an honor student, plays baseball and takes acting classes—none of which affects his condition.

The cost of his at-home care is nearly $150,000 a year. It had been covered by insurance ever since his illness was diagnosed when he was six weeks old.

But problems began when his father's employer switched medical plans. The new insurer determined that the at-home care was no longer medically necessary.

One month later, payment for the overnight care stopped. His mother appealed to the insurer, but the doctors who reviewed the case for the insurer maintained that the special care was not needed to keep the boy alive. That was when we filed a lawsuit against the father's health insurance company—and the company that reviewed medical claims for the insurance company.

The parents' next move: His mother also wrote to local politicians, local newspapers and went on national talk shows. She was persistent and media savvy. Over and over, she told the story of her son and her complaints that the insurer was disregarding the recommendations of her son's personal doctor—a pediatric pulmonologist who had cared for him since birth.

Four months later, a court ordered the insurer to pay for the home health care until the lawsuit was settled.

When preparing for trial, we found that the doctors retained by the new insurance company were unqualified to review a case as complicated as this one. None of them had expertise with pediatric heart and lung disease, and one of the doctors was a 73-year-old internist who had never even practiced pediatric medicine.

We also found that the contract with the insurer had a "savings clause" that created an incentive for doctors to deny treatment.

Result: The case was settled out of court—two-and-a-half years after we filed suit. Not only has the insurer agreed to pay the cost of the boy's $150,000-a-year home nursing care as long as he needs it, the company will also pay more than $1 million in emotional distress damages to the mother and son.

Lesson: A major factor in our victory was the aggressive and indefatigable media campaign the mother waged on behalf of her son. She was tireless in talking about his predicament and used every opportunity to share their story with someone who might be able to help.

CASE #2—GAINING DOCTOR'S SUPPORT

About two years ago, a 68-year-old man signed up with an HMO. Under the contract, he agreed to assign his Medicare benefits to the HMO in return for coverage to match or exceed minimum Medicare benefits. Among the promised benefits were 100% payment of comprehensive inpatient and outpatient rehabilitation services.

Six months after he enrolled in the HMO, the man broke his hip in a fall. After surgery, he suffered serious complications, including two major heart attacks, pneumonia and a large blood clot in his leg. When he was finally moved out of the intensive care unit two months later, he was still unable to walk or stand.

The man needed extensive rehabilitation, so he was transferred by the hospital to a rehabilitation facility, where he began a physical therapy program.

But the HMO questioned whether the patient had the medical ability and stamina to participate in the program. Instead, the HMO mandated that he be admitted to a nursing home—which was less expensive but had no rehabilitation program.

His physicians maintained that, after the physical therapy, the man could get back to work. Therefore, a nursing home was not appropriate. The HMO refused to pay for his inpatient and out-patient physical therapy on the grounds that it was not medically necessary.

We initiated legal action against the HMO as soon as it began to oppose his physical therapy. Fortunately, while waiting for the lawsuit to be settled, he was able to continue getting physical therapy with the help of a charitable foundation and eventually made a full recovery.

Three years after filing suit, the patient received a multimillion-dollar settlement from the HMO.

Key to his victory: The unanimous support of all three of his doctors—his personal physician, his hospital physician and his hospital psychiatrist. The physical therapy services they recommended were clearly within Medicare guidelines. But their decisions had been overruled by HMO representatives who were not as professionally qualified and who were getting paid to say *no.*

CASE #3—LOOK FOR VIOLATIONS

A 61-year-old high school teacher was diagnosed with advanced breast cancer after being continuously covered by the same health insurance plan for more than 30 years.

Originally she was insured under her husband's group policy at work, but later her own policy provided primary coverage and her husband's policy provided secondary coverage.

The double coverage meant that her husband's policy would cover part of whatever her policy did not.

Once her cancer was diagnosed, the woman underwent chemotherapy. Then her doctors determined that her only hope for a cure was to undergo a bone-marrow transplant.

When her physician sought authorization for the procedure, both her and her husband's insurance companies denied her coverage. They said the treatment was not medically necessary...and it was "experimental in nature."

Since time was running out, she had the bone-marrow transplant—despite the denial of her claim. Part of the more than $200,000 total cost was raised by donations. Fortunately, the transplant hospital agreed to accept her as a patient with a partial payment.

Result: Eventually, after three years of legal wrangling, we settled this case for $1.5 million.

Lesson: Several issues helped our case. Bone-marrow transplants are considered a routine treatment for advanced breast cancer, not experimental in nature. The weight of medical opinion and court cases supports this treatment approach. In addition, some years earlier, both the woman's policy and her husband's had been changed to reduce coverage for certain benefits, including bone-marrow transplants. But no notices of these reductions were ever provided to the woman or her husband. We argued that this was a violation of the law in her state.

BOTTOM LINE

Keep careful records, and never be afraid to fight back against your insurer. Your chances of success are always better if you can document your case, enlist your doctors' support, take your story to the media and find alternative ways to pay the bills until your case can be heard.

William Shernoff, partner at Shernoff, Bidart & Darras, a California law firm specializing in insurance issues, and author of *How to Make Insurance Companies Pay Your Claims: And What to Do If They Don't.* Hastings House.

Challenge a Bad Insurance Rating

Make a written request for negative information in your health insurance file. Bad ratings—which bring higher rates—usually result from health problems found during medical exams or evidence of a lifestyle problem, such as drug or alcohol abuse. You must refute the underwriting records to challenge the rating successfully.

So—after learning what the problem supposedly is, use doctors, other professionals and your insurance agent to establish the truth.

Example: If you were 30 pounds overweight when you applied for insurance, offer proof you have lost the weight.

William Shernoff, partner at Shernoff, Bidart & Darras, a California law firm specializing in insurance issues, and author of *How to Make Insurance Companies Pay Your Claims: And What to Do If They Don't.* Hastings House.

Medical Claims— How to Get Paid... Faster...Easier

Janet Bamford

When you've suffered an illness or have been in an accident, you should be focused on making a full recov-ery—and not distracted by a struggle with your health insurer to get your claims paid.

But filing a claim is so complex that it provides many opportunities for errors and misunderstandings. When mistakes occur, insurers, already under pressure to hold down costs, are more likely to question, deny or reduce the amount you're claiming.

In response, a new type of service has emerged to help people file claims and battle insurers.

Known as *claims assistance professionals,* many of them formerly worked for insurance companies as claims administrators. They charge anywhere from $25 to $90 per hour, and with their help, an estimated 50% of the claims that are challenged end up being paid by insurers.*

Here are the effective strategies of claims assistance professionals...

●**Avoid clerical errors.** A significant number of claims are rejected because of clerical errors. When you send in your claims, clerks may have to keyboard them into computer systems, raising the risk of error. Even electronic claims can be problematic. Insurance group or Social Security numbers can be transposed.

Example: I once had a claim for my son—who has a different last name than I do—denied because it had been submitted with my last name, instead of my husband's.

These days, every diagnosis and procedure performed by a doctor is given a code number. Insurers look to the codes to decide if the doctor overcharged or used an inappropriate treatment—so if the numbers are wrong, claims will be thrown out.

Your insurer should tell you why a claim is denied or reimbursed at a lower level—so that you can correct any claim error. If the insurer says that treatment was not related to the diagnosis or was inappropriate, it could be a sign that the codes are wrong.

●**A letter carries more weight than a phone call.** When challenging your claim, do it in writing and keep careful records of all

*To find a claims assistance professional near you, write to the National Association of Claims Assistance Professionals, 5329 S. Main St., Ste. 102, Downers Grove, IL 60515. Enclose your request and a $1 fee to cover postage and handling costs.

contacts with your health insurers. Don't be intimidated by having to write letters. You're not writing a legal brief.

Example: A simple note stating, *In reference to my claim for Dr. Smith's services on May 5, I disagree with your denial for the following reasons*...is sufficient.

Send copies to your doctor or hospital and the insurance company—and keep a copy for yourself.

Keep notes about any telephone conversations you've had with the insurer detailing with whom you spoke, when you had the conversation and what was said, in case you need to refer to those conversations at a later date.

●**Enlist your doctor's help if your insurer won't pay what your doctor is charging.** An insurer may feel the charges are more than the *usual, customary and reasonable* fees.

Example: If your doctor charges $400 for a medical procedure—but the insurer says that $200 is reasonable compensation, ask your physician for the names of insurance companies that pay the full amount or a sum closer to his/her fee. Then write a letter to your insurer showing that such a charge is not so out of line.

It's in your doctor's best interest to prove that his tab isn't out of line, and he should be willing to send a letter to your insurance company detailing the facts.

In other cases, the doctor may need to submit a more detailed explanation of treatment and services. The procedure may be more complicated than the insurance company realizes.

●**Provide more information about the symptoms** if your insurer says the treatment wasn't medically necessary. Additional details may explain why you needed the treatment.

Example I: If you're in physical therapy while a broken ankle is mending and you slip on the ice and reinjure it, explain that to the insurer, which may not understand why you need prolonged treatment.

Example II: If you go to the emergency room with chest pains that turn out to be diagnosed as indigestion, explain your other symptoms. Perhaps you were cold and clammy...or the ambulance medics thought you might be going into shock.

If your insurer protests that your treatment was experimental and not eligible, have your physician write a letter—or if you write it, have your doctor add to it—citing medical studies or discussing how commonly used the treatment is.

●**Take the matter to a higher authority** if you're not satisfied with what the customer service representative tells you. That person has a supervisor who may be able to help you.

If you feel you are being denied care by an HMO, ask for a medical director...a customer relations vice president...or someone whose job it is to oversee such problems. Most HMOs are required by law to have an appeals process.

If your medical insurance is provided by your employer, complain to your company's employee benefits people. Since they're the ones that choose and pay for the health insurance coverage, they may have more clout with the company than an individual employee does. Insurance company executives should be notified if employees are getting poor service.

If you still can't get satisfaction, try your state insurance commissioner's office. Most require that any claim can be challenged as long as it is done in writing.

Just threatening to contact the state insurance commissioner's office will likely cause your insurer to review your claim.

●**Keep careful track of policy changes** and of what you've spent that qualifies against your deductible. Carefully read those memos and booklets from your employee benefits department or your health insurer.

Coverage for expenditures like mental health care, prescription drugs, vision care or hearing tests may be added to or dropped from your plan, causing you to miss out on getting reimbursed or to unknowingly incur expenses that you can no longer recover.

Janet Bamford, a specialist in insurance and personal finance. She is author of *Smarter Insurance Solutions* (Bloomberg Press), and coauthor of *The Consumer Reports Money Book* (Consumer Reports).

Your Medicare Rights

Medicare patients have a legal right to an immediate review if denied acutely needed medical services from an HMO in which they are enrolled. This ruling by a federal judge came in response to a lawsuit filed against the Health Care Financing Administration—the government Medicare agency—by Medicare beneficiaries whose HMOs had denied them services their physicians had recommended as medically necessary. The services included emergency care, home health care and physical therapy.

Sally Hart Wilson, an attorney with the Center for Medicare Advocacy in Tucson, AZ.

How to Fight a Medicare Decision

When you appeal a decision made by Medicare, the burden of proof is on you. *Once a claim is denied...*

...ask the Medicare carrier that handled the claim to review it. You must do this within six months of a denial.

...if you are not satisfied with the review and the dispute involves at least $100, ask for a hearing before a carrier hearing officer.

...if you are still dissatisfied, and the amount in dispute is at least $500, you have 60 days to request a hearing before an administrative law judge.

Helpful: If you belong to an HMO, find out about its appeals process in case it—not Medicare—makes a decision against you.

Ken Stern, president of Asset Planning Solutions, a full-service estate planning firm, and author of *The Comprehensive Guide to Social Security and Medicare.* Career Press Inc.

Document All Medicare Treatments

When receiving Medicare treatments, keep a log of all your medical visits and any procedures done. This will help you know if you are billed incorrectly...and make it easier if you have to file an appeal for additional payment. Review every bill carefully. Medicare bills from hospitals and doctors often contain errors. *Also:* It usually takes 35 to 45 days for Medicare to pay a claim. If you do not get an explanation of Medicare payments within 45 days, contact the Medicare carrier in your region. *Caution:* Before traveling outside the US, find out what Medicare will cover.

Ken Stern, president of Asset Planning Solutions, a full-service estate planning firm, and author of *The Comprehensive Guide to Social Security and Medicare.* Career Press Inc.

How to Prevent Financial Disaster

Don't let your financial nest egg be wiped out for lack of adequate insurance. *The facts of life:* Individuals are seven times more likely to become *disabled* before they retire than to die.

Safety net: Workers ideally should have disability coverage equal to 60% to 70% of their current gross salary. Social Security and worker's compensation alone aren't adequate salary replacements. Even if your company provides some disability coverage, you may need more.

Umbrella coverage: At least $1 million worth of "umbrella" liability coverage is also a must in these litigious times. This addition to your homeowner's policy protects you against such damage suits as physical injury, libel, slander, mental anguish, sickness or disease and wrongful entry or eviction. *Cost:* About $200 a year.

Professional liability: Most professions that provide services (doctors, lawyers, accountants, architects, real estate agents, engineers, veterinarians, teachers, clergy) also involve a degree of risk that requires protection through professional liability insurance. Except for doctors' and lawyers' policies, there is very little standardization in this field, so you will have to shop around. Check with your trade association for advice and possible price breaks.

Professional liability insurance is also available—and often needed—for those serving as trustees, guardians, executors or in other fiduciary positions.

Jonathan Pond, CPA, president of Financial Planning Information, Inc., 9 Galen St. Watertown, MA 02172. He publishes *Jonathan Pond's Quarterly Investment Review.*

What Isn't Covered by Workers' Compensation

Some on-the-job injuries are not covered by workers' compensation. *Among them:* Injuries incurred during activities for your own benefit —or for the benefit of someone other than the employer…injuries suffered in an activity that is forbidden by the employer.

The Court TV Cradle-to-Grave Legal Survival Guide by the editors of "Court TV" and *The American Lawyer.* Little, Brown & Co.

The New Traps In Disability Insurance

Frank N. Darras
Shernoff, Bidart & Darras

It has become tougher to find a generous disability policy these days. Many insurance companies added all sorts of bells and whistles to policies in the 1980s and have been swamped with sharply higher claims.

Now they're redesigning these policies. Among other things, insurers are limiting the amount of benefits they'll pay on new policies if you can't return to work at your present job or won't work at a job they deem comparable. Some insurers are no longer offering policies that promise never to raise your premium.

NEW REALITIES

●**Don't assume that you have adequate coverage through work.** Most people who have group coverage at work for long-term disabilities are complacent and think they don't need to purchase individual policies.

The problem with most employer-sponsored policies is they have provisions that reduce benefits if you are eligible to receive benefits from Social Security, worker's compensation and other state programs.

Even though it is difficult to *qualify* for government benefits, most company policies say the insurer can offset these benefits as long as you are *eligible* for them, not just if you actually *receive* them.

Result: Workers who make between $1,500 and $3,500 a month may find that their long-term disability benefits from their company plans are only $50 a month. This can be devastating.

●**You can protect only about half your income with a policy you buy on your own.** It used to be that you could buy policies that would pay 60% to 70% of your former income. As the number of claims increased, that figure dropped…and dropped.

Now, the best policy you can buy will replace up to about half of the income you had before you were disabled.

Helpful: Look for a policy that covers loss of income from your "own occupation." These policies will pay benefits if you can't work at your specific occupation, even if you are capable of holding another lower-paying job.

Expect to pay extra for this protection— about 15% to 20% more than other types of policies. But it is protection well worth the extra cost, especially if you are a high-paid professional with a lucrative specialty.

Important: Ask for a policy with "own occupation" coverage until you reach age 65. If the insurance company turns you down, ask for such coverage for the first five years of disability. If you are denied again, ask for such coverage for at least the first two years of disability.

●**Avoid buying "loss of income" policies if possible.** These policies are being touted as the successors to "own occupation" policies.

Theoretically, they are supposed to provide benefits that will bring you up to your old income level if you become disabled and can't do your old job—or must take a job that pays less than your old job.

Problem: After paying you your lost earnings for the first 24 months, the insurer may then argue that you must return to work at any reasonable job for which you are trained, educated or suited and which can pay you at least 50% of your former earnings. But you may not want or be able to take such a job…and there may not be that kind of work in your area of expertise. If you didn't choose to return to work at "any reasonable occupation," you would get only 50% of your benefit.

● **Look for a noncancelable and guaranteed-renewable policy.** A noncancelable policy is one that the insurance company can't cancel unless you die or fail to pay your premium on time. This type of policy has fixed premiums throughout the life of the contract.

A guaranteed-renewable individual policy means the company cannot cancel or change the terms of the policy even if you change occupations or your health history changes. But the insurer can raise your premium if it does so for *all* policies in a certain class.

In addition, the insurer cannot drop you if you develop health problems. It will be hard to find a policy with both provisions.

Important: If you own a noncancelable guaranteed-renewable policy that pays if you are disabled from your own occupation to age 65 or for life, don't trade it in or let it lapse after you have trouble getting a claim paid.

By failing to pay your premiums when you are disabled and trying to collect a claim, you will give up a very valuable policy that you probably won't be able to replace. To safeguard your rights in this situation, pay the premium on time and write on the check: *Contested premium, should be on waiver*—so that the insurance company cannot say you agreed that you were not disabled.

● **Compromise on the waiting period.** This is the period you must wait before you can start collecting benefits. The longer the waiting period, the cheaper the premium.

The typical waiting period is 90 days. But if you have the resources to support yourself for a longer period, the premium can be dramatically lower.

Example: Extending the waiting period to 180 days will cut the premium by 20% to 25%.

● **Be thorough and accurate when you apply.** When an insurance company representative takes your medical history, list all the physicians you have visited and the ailments for which you have been treated. Take the application…read the medical questions yourself…and respond fully.

Otherwise, the company may be able to rescind or cancel your policy—alleging you lied on the application—if you become disabled within a certain period after applying for coverage. It can rescind your coverage for any fraudulent misstatement, even if the information has no bearing on your disability.

Example: You have a slipped disk and can no longer sit at a desk. If you failed to state that you broke your ankle in the third grade, you might lose coverage.

If you have had serious health problems, ask your insurance agent whether these problems will adversely affect your chances of obtaining coverage. If the answer is yes, submit a trial application—which is reviewed by the agent/broker with the company underwriters to see whether or not a policy might be written.

Beware: You don't ever want to be declined for disability insurance because that will make it harder and more expensive for you to obtain other types of coverage, such as life insurance.

Frank N. Darras, one of the country's top disability insurance experts. He is a partner with Shernoff, Bidart & Darras, a California law firm specializing in insurance issues.

Life Insurance…How to Get Much More Out of Your Current Policy

Glenn Daily

When life insurance premiums become difficult to pay, many people consider giving up the policies entirely or replacing them with cheaper ones.

But giving up an existing life insurance policy isn't cheap. When you give up a cash-value insurance policy, there are often surrender charges—which are sometimes very steep—so you'll likely walk away with less than you might think.

Here's how to make your current policy cheaper to own—and earn more on your savings…

●**Pay your premium annually**—not monthly or quarterly—no matter what type of policy you own.

Insurance premiums are always lowest when you pay in one lump sum, once a year, rather than spreading out the payments.

If you can pay the single premium, you will save between 6% and 20%, depending on the interest rate your insurer charges for the luxury of paying in installments.

●**Drop unnecessary riders.** Nearly every life insurance policy (including term policies and whole life policies) offers riders—extras that push up the cost of owning the policy—for which you may have signed up and aren't aware you own.

Call your insurer or agent for a list of the riders in your policy and an explanation of each one. Then determine which to keep and which to eliminate. *Two examples of riders that have little value and can be eliminated…*

●**Waiver of premium for disability.** If you're already receiving disability coverage at work or through a policy you bought on your own, coverage through your life insurance policy may be unnecessary.

Even if you don't have any type of disability coverage, you're better off eliminating this rider and using the extra money to help pay for a *high-quality* disability plan with better features.

Important: Be sure you qualify for a new personal disability policy *before* canceling the life insurance policy rider.

●**Accidental death coverage.** This rider doubles the amount of coverage a family receives if the policyholder's death comes as a result of an accident. Your family's protection needs don't depend on how you die, so this rider is for gambling, not for financial planning.

●**Get higher policy dividends** by switching to a variable interest rate on policy loans. If you own a cash-value policy, your insurer pays annual dividends on the cash portion you have invested.

If you bought your insurance policy in the 1970s or early 1980s, you probably are receiving a low dividend in exchange for the ability to borrow money from the insurer at a low fixed interest rate of 5% to 8%.

Helpful: If you own such an insurance policy, you may be able to make a one-time switch from a fixed rate to a variable rate, which will boost your dividends. Call your insurer or agent to determine if such a switch is possible and to ask about the benefits and the drawbacks.

Important: Avoid this strategy if you borrow regularly from your policy and prefer the low fixed rate…or expect to do so.

●**Reduce your policy's face value** to improve performance. Most people don't realize this option exists. *Here's when it makes sense…*

You now have a cash-value policy that pays you an attractive interest rate—but its internal costs are no longer competitive.

You can make the policy more attractive by reducing the face amount—and, therefore, the internal charges—and continue to enjoy the high interest rate. You may also want to reduce the face amount in order to cut the premium you need to pay.

●**Convert existing policies to other types.** You may need some help with this one from an independent insurance consultant or a financial planner. *Here's the basic premise…*

An existing insurance policy is too costly to keep and impossible to alter using one of the strategies already mentioned.

By converting from one type of policy to another, you can still salvage some of the policy's underlying value.

Example: Let's say you own a universal life insurance policy and have paid $50,000 so far in premiums. A universal policy has a flexible premium, and your savings earn a rate of return that changes periodically. Let's assume that if you gave up the policy, you would only be left with about $10,000 after paying the surrender charge.

Strategy: Exchange the insurance policy for a variable annuity, which lets you invest your savings in a family of mutual funds.

You preserve the $50,000 you've invested in premiums by using it as a deduction against future earnings generated by the annuity.

Even though your annuity's cash value starts at $10,000, your cost basis for tax purposes will be $50,000.

So—if you wait until the value of your annuity grows to $50,000, you'll be able to withdraw the entire sum without paying income taxes on it.

Result: You've been able to salvage real value—in the form of a tax shelter—from an existing policy that you believed was nearly worthless. Just be sure the annuity company follows proper procedures to make certain the exchange qualifies for tax-free treatment.

Glenn Daily, an independent, fee-only insurance consultant, 234 E. 84 St., New York 10028, and author of *Life Insurance Sense and Nonsense*, which is available from the author.

Life Insurance Trap

Don't let inflation fears trick you into thinking of adding a *cost-of-living-adjustment (COLA)* to your policy. COLAs are offered by insurers to policyholders when annual premiums are due. By paying a slightly higher premium, total coverage is increased to keep up with inflation. *Reality:* Inflation and how much insurance coverage you need have little to do with each other. *When a COLA makes sense:* When your financial needs change and you require more coverage…or when your poor health means buying extra coverage would be prohibitively expensive.

Glenn Daily, an independent, fee-only insurance consultant, 234 E. 84 St., New York 10028, and author of *Life Insurance Sense and Nonsense*, which is available from the author.

Credit Life Insurance Trap

Beware: Credit life insurance is a poor deal in most states, even though the prices are capped in every state. Banks and other lenders push it because it is lucrative for them—not for borrowers.

Trap: When purchased with big-ticket items—a new car, for example—it can cost several times the price of basic term life insurance. *Exception:* Rates do not vary by age, so older buyers—especially those over age 50—may find it reasonably priced. *Also:* Younger individuals who smoke or have health problems may find it helpful, too.

James Hunt, life insurance actuary for the Consumer Federation of America, 1424 16 St. NW, Washington, DC 20036.

Higher Life Insurance Premiums for Smokers

Cigar and pipe smokers are being hit with higher life insurance premiums when they shop for new policies. In the past, only cigarette smoking meant higher fees. Now, more insurers define smokers as those who test positive for the regular use of any form of tobacco—including chewing tobacco.

Example: One major insurer allows someone who smokes an average of one cigar per month to qualify as a nonsmoker. Its $500,000 10-year term policy issued to a 40-year-old healthy man costs $574 a year for a nonsmoker…and $1,529 for a smoker.

Glenn Daily, an independent, fee-only insurance consultant, 234 E. 84 St., New York 10028, and author of *Life Insurance Sense and Nonsense*, which is available from the author.

Lower Home Insurance

Ask for a discount if you have had your homeowners' insurance with the same company for at least three years.

Many companies reduce premiums by 5% for policyholders who have been with them for three to five years…and 10% for people with them for six years or more.

More savings: Review your policy annually to be sure you're not paying for coverage you no longer need.

Jeanne Salvatore, with the Insurance Information Institute, 110 William St., New York 10038.

Surprising Insurance Discounts

When shopping for homeowners' insurance, ask about discounts for certain activities that are perceived as lowering the risk of claims.

Examples: Discounts for people who live in communities that enforce building codes or who have taken classes in home safety. *Also:* Ask about discounts for home improvements such as fire-retardant shingles…or roof clips that minimize hurricane damage.

Trap: Some firms offering discounts start with high rates—so watch the bottom line.

Robert Hunter, director of insurance for the Consumer Federation of America, 1424 16 St. NW, Washington, DC 20036.

Asset Safety

Once a year, document your belongings for insurance purposes by videotaping the contents of your entire house.

Do a walking tour—narrating a description of what you have in each room. Then store the tape in a safe-deposit box or in a location away from the house. If during the course of the year you make a major purchase, you can add documentation of it at the end of the videotape.

Steve Goldstein, vice president of the Insurance Information Institute, 110 William St., New York 10038.

Drop Private Mortgage Insurance (PMI) As Soon as You Can

Lenders usually require PMI when someone buys a house with less than 20% down. PMI protects the lender in case the buyer can't pay the mortgage. Once your loan drops to 80% of the house's value—because you pay down the principal or your home increases in value— PMI is no longer required. Call or write your loan servicer and the PMI company to ask how to drop it.

More savings: Switch your homeowners' insurance to a less-expensive company—shop around by phone, or ask your state insurance department if it surveys costs. Consider a higher deductible to reduce costs further.

David Schechner, real estate attorney with Schechner & Targan, 80 Main St., West Orange, NJ 07052.

Winter Mishap Lawsuit Trap

Shoveled walkways and driveways are hazards if they aren't de-iced daily. *Reason:* An injured person has a stronger case if icy areas looked dry. *Limit the odds of a wrongful suit* by asking anyone who falls if he/she is all right …getting the names of people who witnessed the encounter…photographing the area and the person walking away. *Self-defense:* A $5 million umbrella policy.

William E. Bailey, an insurance law attorney and homeowners' policy specialist in private practice in Boston.

Some Cars Cost Much More to Insure

Kim Hazelbaker
Insurance Institute for Highway Safety

When purchasing a car, most people forget to factor in the cost of insuring it. How expensive—or inexpensive—the policy is depends partially on how often the car model has been in an accident or stolen.

- **Most costly to insure for…***

COLLISION

- **BMW 8 Series 2-door**
- **Mitsubishi 3000 GT 4WD**

*Collision results are based on 1994–1996 model year passenger cars. Theft results are based on 1993–1995 model year passenger cars.

- **Dodge Viper convertible**
- **Porsche 911 Targa/Coupe**
- **Toyota Supra**

THEFT

- **Acura Legend 2-door**
- **BMW 3 Series convertible**
- **Acura Legend 4-door**
- **Mercedes S Class**
- **Mercedes SL Class convertible**

- **Least costly to insure for…**

COLLISION

- **Chevrolet Astro Van**
- **GMC Safari Van**
- **Eagle Summit wagon**
- **Mercury Sable wagon**
- **Oldsmobile Cutlass Ciera station wagon**

THEFT

- **Buick Park Avenue 4-door**
- **Chevrolet Lumina 4-door**
- **Buick Skylark 4-door**
- **Saab 900 4-door**
- **Saturn SW wagon**

Kim Hazelbaker, senior vice president of the Insurance Institute for Highway Safety, Highway Loss Data Institute, 1005 N. Glebe Rd., Arlington, VA 22201. Data are based on claims filed with insurance companies from 1994–1996.

Big Mistakes Consumers Make with Auto Insurance

Robert Hunter
Consumer Federation of America

It's easy to avoid the most common mistakes people make when buying auto insurance…

Mistake: Paying too much attention to discounts—and not looking at the bottom-line cost. Some companies with big discounts have high costs.

It is also a mistake not to use all the discounts to which you are entitled. You can save hundreds of dollars by claiming all of the appropriate discounts. *Examples…*

- **You can receive about 20% off the cost of insuring two or more cars** if you buy coverage from one insurance company.

- **Good drivers**—ones who haven't had an accident or moving violation in the last three to five years—often qualify for insurers' lowest preferred rates.

- **Teenage drivers can get discounts of as much as 20%** if they take drivers' education classes.

- **A car alarm can still shave the cost of your theft coverage by about 20%.**

- **Air bags can produce large discounts for bodily injury coverage.**

Mistake: **Buying the wrong car.** If you're in the market for a new car, find out what the cost of insuring it will be *before* you purchase it. Some less glamorous models can be costly to insure if they're stolen frequently for parts.

Expensive cars with safety features, such as antilock brakes and air bags, that have done well in crash tests often are less expensive to insure for collision than cheaper cars that do not have such features.

Mistake: **Buying coverage you *don't* need**—and skimping on coverage you do need. The most important coverage is *bodily injury liability.* It pays for another person's medical care, rehabilitation or funeral costs when you're found at fault in an accident. At the very least, you need coverage of $100,000 per person and $300,000 for any single accident. The most affordable way to protect against a successful liability claim is with an umbrella policy from your auto or homeowner's insurance company. It pays for losses above and beyond what's covered by an auto or homeowner's policy.

Where to cut back: Most drivers have too much collision and comprehensive insurance.

Collision pays for the cost to repair or replace your car if it is in an accident, regardless of who is at fault.

Comprehensive provides similar coverage if your car is stolen or damaged by fire, flood or wind. If your car is old—seven years or more—the cost of collision and comprehensive may not be worth it.

Rule of thumb: When collision and comprehensive coverage costs more than 10% of the car's market value, drop it.

Mistake: **Setting your deductibles too low.** While low deductibles may be appealing, they're usually not a good idea. You pay a lot for protection that is often unnecessary, since you can afford to pay the amount yourself. Insurance is to protect you against financial catastrophe.

Examples: Raising your deductibles from $100 to $250 can save about 15% on your collision and comprehensive premiums. Raising them to $500 can save about 25%. Raising them to $1,000 can save about 33%.

Robert Hunter, director of insurance for the Consumer Federation of America, 1424 16 St. NW, Washington, DC 20036.

When You Should Buy Rental Car Insurance

Rental car company insurance only makes sense if you don't already have insurance coverage. Most people are covered while they drive a rented vehicle by their personal auto insurance policy…the credit card they use to pay for the rental car…or both. There is no point in spending extra for coverage that you already have, especially at the inflated price of rental company insurance. And if you have an accident while you are driving the rented car, it won't prevent a rate increase on your personal auto insurance because the accident will still be reported.

Andrew Tobias, Miami-based consumer advocate and author of *The Only Investment Guide You'll Ever Need.* Harcourt Brace.

Business Insurance Basics: How to Cut the Cost Without Raising Risk

Gary Applebaum
DMAS

Business insurance is an easy expense to cut—since it doesn't directly contribute to the bottom line like merchandise or raw materials. But cutting insurance can become a costly blunder when a major catastrophe occurs and the business is not adequately insured.

Good news: Nearly every business in America can cut its insurance costs by 10%… 15%…or sometimes even more—*without* putting itself into undue jeopardy.

The secret: Become a super-shrewd insurance buyer and the sort of customer insurance companies love to insure.

Here's what I tell my clients to help them get the coverage they need for the lowest possible cost…

• **Stick with insurers that are familiar with the business you're in.** Most insurance companies are perfectly willing—even eager—to insure just about any type of business that comes their way. But certain insurance companies have an appetite and aptitude for certain types of business.

Example: You own a corner drugstore. The ABC Insurance Co. has been happily writing a policy for your business even though drugstores are not their area of expertise. On the other hand, XYZ Insurance Co. has extensive experience with corner drugstores. Their marketing and pricing, and the specifics of their policies all are aimed at insuring every corner drugstore in America.

By going with an insurer that is familiar with your company's type of business, it should be possible to obtain coverage for 10% or 15% less. And the coverage should be *better* than what the business now has.

Guideline: Any insurance agent worth dealing with should have a good idea of which insurance companies specialize in which types of business. If your company's present agent can't steer you to the right company, shop for an agent who represents the kind of company that is experienced in your kind of business.

Helpful: A trade association should know which insurers specialize in your line of business. The association may even have given its approval to one or more companies to write coverage for businesses in your industry.

●**Choose the best possible policy.** Agents typically will offer either a multiple-peril package or a business owners' policy. Picking the best form of insurance for the business can save thousands of dollars a year. *Examples:*

●*Multiple-peril package:* This form of insurance tends to charge individually for each area of coverage. You might be charged separately for the building...separately for the contents...separately for liability...separately for glass exposure. The company buys what it needs for its unique situation.

●*Business owners' policy:* The commercial equivalent of homeowners' insurance, you pay one premium for all of the different types of coverage.

Strategy: Normally, it pays to take the business owners' policy. I've seen cases where someone was paying $10,000 a year on a multiple-peril package and reduced that to $6,000 a year by switching to a business owners' policy.

Caution: Because each business is different, don't automatically assume yours will save with a business owners' policy. The rate on a business owners' policy is based on coverage for the property. But if the company has an inordinate amount of inventory stored in cheap warehouse space, it might get a better deal with a package of multiple-peril coverages.

Before signing, ask the agent, "Is this the best policy we can be on?" Insist that the agent work it out both ways to make sure you're getting the best coverage for the business's exact needs—at the right price.

●**Be a customer that an insurance company would love.** The only way an insurance company makes money is if companies are profitable for it. If your company is profitable for it, the insurer will be willing to pass along a portion of that savings. And the best way to be profitable is to set up your business so it never has a loss.

Strategy: Make risk management and loss avoidance the cornerstones of the business. Do more rigorous screening of job applicants before hiring them—to prevent careless and inexperienced people from jeopardizing themselves or the company.

Example: You may not think of a delivery person as a key employee. But if he/she hits a school bus with the company's van, it will trigger potentially costly liability problems.

Make sure any driver you hire has all the proper licenses. Have the company's insurance agent run a motor vehicle check on the individual to make sure he doesn't have speeding tickets or accidents on his record.

Similarly, when hiring someone to handle cash, check out the person's background as carefully as possible. Insist on getting references before offering a job.

Important: Once people are hired, provide all the training the business can afford so they know how to do their jobs without getting hurt or putting the company at risk.

The mindset shouldn't be, "We have insurance and if anything happens, we're covered." Instead, it should be, "We don't want anything to happen because that would cost the insurance company money and everything the insurance company does is predicated on minimizing claims."

●**Look at your business through an insurance company's eyes.** I don't advise customers to avoid filing insurance claims just because the insurance company won't like it. I *do* advise customers to be very astute before filing an insurance claim.

Reason: People don't realize that insurance companies don't worry about the severity of a claim. They're much more concerned about the frequency of claims.

Insurance companies know that the occasional severe incident is going to happen, and that they're going to have to pay out a considerable sum of money. They expect it as part of doing business—even for their best customers.

What they don't like is the guy who hits them with one small claim after another. They know from actuarial data that these clients are not just costing small outlays fairly frequently, but that they will also come in with a major claim someday.

Cost-cutting strategy: Self-insure the company against routine cost-of-doing-business losses. Remember that what you have is an insurance policy—not a maintenance policy. So, plan to cover losses up to $1,000 out of the company's own pocket, and negotiate insurance coverage with a deductible of no less than $1,000 per incident.

At the least, that $1,000 deductible will cut the annual premium by 10% or more compared to having a lower deductible. And by absorbing the small claims, the company has taken another step toward becoming the sort of customer insurance companies love. If the company does have a big claim, settling it should go much more smoothly than it would if you filed a small claim every month or two.

●**Avoid insuring every risk.** Taking on a bigger deductible is one great way to cut the cost of insurance. Another is to analyze your business step by step and consider what abso-lutely must be covered and where there might be another way of protecting against risks.

Example: If the company is paying too much for burglary insurance, consider getting an alarm system instead. It might cost a little more in the first year, but by the second year you're ahead. After that, the saving on burglary insurance is pure savings for the business.

Important: If there is no alternative to reducing coverage, at least protect against the losses that can shut the business down.

Example: If the business has $25,000 in inventory, that is its maximum exposure even if the whole inventory is stolen or destroyed. That would be a major loss, but it probably wouldn't kill the business.

But if the company van hits a bus, liability claims could run into the millions. That could kill the business.

Gary Applebaum, vice president of DMAS, an independent insurance agency, 1132 Forest Ave., Staten Island, NY 10310. He is a former board member of the Independent Insurance Agents Association of New York.

6

Tax Smarts

How Everyone Can Pay Less Taxes and Keep More Money

Laurence I. Foster
KPMG Peat Marwick LLP

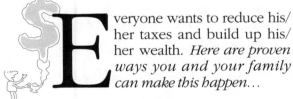

Everyone wants to reduce his/her taxes and build up his/her wealth. *Here are proven ways you and your family can make this happen...*

SAVING IDEAS

•**Make IRA gifts to children.** If a child earns at least $2,000 during the year, the child can make a contribution to an IRA. Or, you can make a gift of $2,000 to the child who can then make the IRA contribution. If the child does not have enough income to benefit from a $2,000 deduction, the IRA contribution can be labeled as nondeductible.

But even more important, the child can receive a *tremendous* financial benefit from the tax-deferred compound investment returns that can be earned on an early-in-life IRA contribution.

Example: Let's say that from age 18 until age 27, your child puts $2,000 annually in an IRA that earns 9%. If the child never saves another dime, the IRA will be worth close to *$1 million* at age 67.

•**Make interest-free loans.** By making an interest-free loan to a family member, you can move funds *out* of an investment account that is taxed at your tax rate.

The loan recipient can then invest the money in an asset that generates deductions, such as a new home...or a start-up business that produces business deductions.

Important: The Tax Code restricts interest-free loans, but "safe harbor" provisions let you make a loan with no adverse tax consequences if the loan amount is...

•**Up to $10,000,** and not used to produce investment income.

•**Up to $100,000,** and the recipient has no more than $1,000 of investment income.

● **Take big-ticket deductions.** You can deduct home improvements and purchases of equipment that are made for bona fide medical reasons.

Example: Air conditioners and humidifiers installed to alleviate respiratory conditions, if prescribed by a doctor.

The amount of a home improvement that is deductible is its cost *minus* any resulting increase in your home's value.

If you buy deductible equipment, you can also deduct the cost of operating and maintaining it.

● **Start a sideline business.** A sideline business can be a source of extra deductions as well as extra income.

Self-employed persons aren't subject to any deduction limit on business expenses—so by setting up a sideline business you may be able to deduct business costs (for supplies, phone bills, etc.) that you can't deduct as an employee. *Note:* Costs must be directly related to your business.

Self-employed people also can make deductible Keogh plan retirement contributions based on income from their sideline businesses.

And if you set up a qualified home office, you may become able to deduct a portion of household expenses that you cannot deduct now.

Examples: Depreciation or rent, utilities, insurance, repair costs and similar expenses allocable to your office.

If you employ a child in your business, you can deduct a reasonable salary paid to the child—cutting the family's tax bill by moving income from your high bracket to the child's lower one. *Note:* This must be legitimate—the child must have a job description and actually work.

No Social Security tax is owed on salaries paid to a child under 18 by a parent's proprietorship.

Opportunities: Consider setting yourself up as an *independent consultant* in your current line of work.

Or, if you have a serious hobby, qualify it as a business by operating it with a "for profit" objective. Register it as a business, keep good books and records and have a business diary in which you record your business plans and objectives.

Your business does not actually have to make a profit to qualify as "for profit." If it does qualify, any losses it incurs will be deductible. An activity is presumed to not be a hobby if you have made a profit at least three out of five consecutive years starting in the first year of business.

● **Use spousal IRAs.** If you qualify to make a $2,000 deductible IRA contribution and have a spouse who is not earning a taxable income, you can contribute an extra $2,000 to a spousal IRA.

Laurence I. Foster, tax partner in personal financial planning practice at KPMG Peat Marwick LLP, 345 Park Ave., New York 10154.

Deductions without Proof

When John Jorman's employer transferred him to a new job in a different city, he deducted his moving expenses. But because his records were inadequate, the IRS disallowed his deductions entirely.

Tax Court: Although Jorman lacked the records he needed to prove the deductions he claimed, it was clear that he had relocated for work and must have incurred moving expenses. The court estimated these expenses at $1,500 and allowed a deduction of that amount.

Point: Although Jorman got a deduction, if he had kept records he would probably have gotten a larger one—and avoided the cost of the court fight.

John K. Jorman, Jr., TC Memo 1996-297.

Beware of Your Accountant

Your accountant is the person you should fear the most if you ever become the subject of an IRS criminal investigation.

Did you know that…there is no such thing as accountant-client privilege? He/she is one of the best witnesses the IRS can have to help it make its case that you committed a tax crime. If the accountant doesn't cooperate, he will be subpoenaed. IRS special agents regularly obtain testimony from a taxpayer's accountant to refute the defense "I don't know anything about income taxes—my accountant told me to do it that way."

Strategy: Arrange for your criminal defense attorney to obtain separate counsel for your accountant. Even though this tactic will not prevent your accountant from testifying against you, it will enable your attorney to learn, first-hand, of the accountant's potentially damaging testimony.

Ms. X, a former IRS agent who is still well connected.

Tax-Free Cash

If you own a business that is organized as a regular corporation (not an S corporation), you can withdraw cash from it on a tax-free basis by borrowing from the company, instead of taking taxable salary or dividends.

Key: You must document the fact that your withdrawal is a legitimate loan to keep the IRS from asserting that it is a disguised taxable dividend.

How: Execute a note that carries a market rate of interest and specifies repayment terms …record the company's approval of the loan in the corporate minutes…have the company carry the loan on its books…follow the terms of the loan.

Irving Blackman, CPA, partner at Blackman Kallick Bartelstein, LLP, 300 S. Riverside Plaza, Chicago 60606.

How to Keep All of Your Next Raise

When you get a salary increase, you owe income and employment taxes on it. But you may be able to get extra money from your employer tax free by asking for an expense reimbursement account instead of a normal pay hike.

Key: Most employees incur out-of-pocket business expenses that their employers will not reimburse.

Snag: You may not be able to deduct these expenses on your own return, either because you don't itemize or because of the deduction "floor" on employee business expenses. They're counted among miscellaneous expenses, which are deductible only to the extent that they exceed 2% of your Adjusted Gross Income.

Expense reimbursements are tax free, so if you take your money through an expense account instead of as salary, you'll keep more after taxes. Your employer will come out ahead too because it won't owe employment taxes on the expense payments either.

Favorite benefit: Up to $170 per month of employer-paid parking in 1997.

Murray Alter, tax partner at Coopers & Lybrand, LLP, 1301 Avenue of the Americas, New York 10019.

Make the Kiddie Tax Work for You

Investment income received by a child younger than age 14 is taxed at the tax rate of the child's parents.

However, in 1997 each child can receive $650 per year of tax-free income, plus another $650 that is taxed at the child's own tax rate of 15%—for a total of $1,300 of tax-favored income.

Example: When funds are in a CD that pays 6% taxable interest, each child can have about $21,000 in savings to earn $1,300 of tax-favored interest.

The Kiddie Tax can be avoided on additional savings held in the child's name by investing them in tax-exempt bonds or appreciating assets—such as growth stocks, shares in a real estate partnership or Series EE savings bonds.

Strategy: Have the child hold the appreciating assets until after reaching age 14 and then cash them in. The child will owe tax on them at his/her own low tax rate—likely 15%—instead of the 20% capital gains rate you would probably pay.

Edward Mendlowitz, CPA, partner at Mendlowitz Weitsen, LLP, CPAs, 2 Pennsylvania Plaza, New York 10121. He is the author of several books on taxes, including *New Tax Traps/New Opportunities* (Boardroom Classics) and *New Business Kit and Tax Compliance Guide*, New Jersey edition (Practical Programs, Inc.).

Shrewd Ways to Avoid Capital Gains...Big Time

Robert Willens
Lehman Brothers Inc.

Investors like capital gains, but they don't like paying taxes on those gains. *Problem:* If you hold onto appreciated positions you run the risk that the value of your holdings will plummet.

Ideally, you'd like to cut your risk of future losses, cash in unrealized gains, or both. Wall Street has come up with some inventive "equity-linked derivatives" designed to accomplish these objectives.

These strategies are mainly for investors with seven-figure positions in appreciated stock. However, competition among financial firms is increasing. If you are an important client, your broker or financial adviser may be able to help you use some of these techniques on a smaller scale.

● **Zero-cost collar.** One approach would be to buy a two-year put option on XYZ, Inc., allowing you to sell your shares at the current trading price of $140 per share.

Such an option would be expensive. To raise the money, you might sell a two-year call option on your shares. Suppose the striking price on the call is $150 per share. This limits your future upside to a further $10 per share, in return for eliminating ongoing risk in the stock.

Strategy: If XYZ, Inc. goes over $150, your shares would be called away and your capital gain triggered. Before this happens, you could buy back your $150 call at a loss and sell another one at, say, $160.

● **Equity swap.** In this recent innovation, you'd enter into a contract with a bank or brokerage firm. While you retain your ownership of XYZ, the financial firm assumes all risk of loss and all upside potential in those shares for the next several years.

In return, you assume the same risks/rewards for a basket of stocks, perhaps the S&P 500. At the end of the period, whichever party has done better collects from the other.

Advantage: Equity swaps allow you to diversify your stock market exposure without selling one greatly appreciated position.

● **Swap fund.** The idea here is that you contribute your XYZ shares to a partnership, Jack contributes his UVW, Inc. shares, Jill contributes her RST, Inc. shares, etc. After a certain time period, the partnership terminates and distributes its assets.

Result: Instead of a huge position in XYZ, you wind up with smaller holdings of RST, UVW, XYZ and dozens of other stocks. Gains will be triggered, pro rata, as you sell these shares.

For swap funds to deliver tax-free exchanges, at least 21% of the partnership's assets must consist of *illiquid* holdings. Some major Wall Street firms have filled out these partnerships with venture capital pools. Although many of these pools have done well lately, their presence increases the risk.

Caution: The IRS has the authority to decide whether these transactions fall under the new *Constructive Sale Rule.* If this occurs, investors will lose not only the tax break, but also transaction costs.

Robert Willens, CPA, managing director at Lehman Brothers Inc., 3 World Financial Center, New York 10285.

Make Property Profits Vanish from the IRS

Jeffrey M. Boyle
Gary Iskowitz & Co., LLP

Real estate investors face a tax quandary. When they sell a property, they'll owe tax not only on any appreciation but also on the amount they've depreciated. *Worst case:* All the sale proceeds will be taxed.

One solution: A tax-deferred exchange. Such exchanges of property will let you defer the tax indefinitely, until it disappears altogether. Tax-deferred exchanges, also called like-kind exchanges, are increasingly popular. In some areas of the US, more than half of all investment property transactions are exchanges rather than sales.

Example: You live in Michigan, but you want to retire and move to California. Years ago, you bought a local apartment building as an investment. After you move, you do not intend to be a long-distance landlord. You have fully depreciated the building so you have zero tax cost (basis). If you sell the building for its current value of $500,000, you'd owe at least $140,000 in taxes. Instead, you enter into a tax-deferred exchange for a small shopping center in California, near your future retirement home. *Your tax bill on the trade:* Zero.

Tax-deferred real estate exchanges are specifically covered in Section 1031 of the Internal Revenue Code.

● **They must involve business or investment properties** (not personal residences).

● **The properties need not be perfect pairs.** Your office building doesn't have to be exchanged for another office building—it may be swapped for a warehouse or any type of business or real property investment.

Tax help for your heirs: If you hold on to the replacement property (or another property acquired in a subsequent exchange) until your death, your heirs will inherit the property at its current market value on the date of your death. They can sell the property and owe no income tax on any prior appreciation. *Downside:* The property will be included in your taxable estate.

MULTIPARTY EXCHANGES

To exchange properties, you don't have to make a direct swap. That is, you don't have to find a property owner in California who wants to trade for your Michigan office building. Instead, most swaps today are multiparty deferred exchanges, often involving the services of a qualified intermediary, known as an accommodator.

How a deal might work: You find a buyer for your property and close the sale. The proceeds go to the accommodator, who puts the money into an escrow account.

Caution: Your relatives and business associates can't serve as accommodators.

To protect your funds: Insist that the accommodator provide a third-party guarantee, such as a bank letter of credit. The contract between you and the accommodator should state that this property transfer is one step in a planned exchange. After you transfer your property, you have 45 days to identify potential replacement properties, in writing, to the accommodator. You must find a replacement property within that time. (You don't have to sign any agreement with the owner, you just have to identify it as a possible replacement property.) Several properties may be identified, so you're covered in case an intended acquisition falls through:

● **You can name up to three properties** of any value, or

● **You can name any number of properties** with an aggregate value no more than 200% of the price you received for your property.

You have 180 days from the time you relinquish your property to actually close a deal for replacement property. In case you transfer your property after October 15 of any calendar year, the second deadline is actually April 15 of the next year, when your personal income tax return is due.

But you can get the full 180 days by requesting an automatic extension of time to file your personal income tax return. The maximum time you have to close a deal is 180 days regardless of any tax extensions you received.

After you have finalized the replacement purchase, the accommodator uses the money held in escrow to buy the replacement property.

Tax impact: You've disposed of one property and acquired another, but you've never touched any cash so capital gains taxes are deferred.

OTHER PATHS

Tax-deferred exchanges can take a variety of forms.

Other exchanges may be very complex, involving multiple parties. In all cases, though, certain criteria must be met for all taxes to be deferred...

● **The amount you pay for the replacement** property must be at least as much as the price you receive for the property you relinquish.

● **All cash received by the accommodator** must be reinvested in the new property.

● **Any debt relief*** must be replaced by a combination of assumption of new debt and additional cash put into the deal.

The way the math works, if you meet the first two requirements, you'll meet the third one as well.

If you wind up with net cash or a lower mortgage, the difference is considered income. You'll owe tax on that income, which is known as *boot.*

Example: You transfer your Michigan property for $500,000, after all related costs. After paying off a $100,000 mortgage, you net $400,000 in cash. You buy the California property for $525,000, using the $400,000 as a down payment and taking out a $125,000 mortgage. Because you have received no cash and have a larger mortgage, you meet all the requirements for a tax-free exchange. On the other hand, if you buy the property for $475,000, with $400,000 in cash and a $75,000 mortgage, you would have a $25,000 taxable gain because of boot, in the form of a reduced mortgage.

Tax-free exchanges are not cost-free. You'll likely have to work with a tax professional as well as an accommodator, who'll receive either a flat fee (perhaps $1,000 or more) or a percentage of the transaction.

Key: You must weigh all the costs versus the value of the tax deferral.

Big payoff: The more heavily mortgaged your property, the more attractive a deferred exchange may be. That is because a large portion of the sale proceeds would go to debt repayment, leaving you with less cash to pay the IRS.

Net gains: In the example above, you might enter into an exchange because you're moving from one area to another. In other cases, you

*Debt relief means debt on the property relinquished that is paid off or assumed in the exchange.

may be tired of actively managing investment property. If you exchange for property that is net leased, the tenant assumes all the operating responsibility and you won't have to do much besides collect monthly checks.

Bottom line: There are many ways to avoid tax on real estate gains through tax-deferred exchanges. Be sure you work with experienced real estate and tax professionals.

Jeffrey M. Boyle, CPA, partner specializing in real estate and estate and trust taxation with the accounting firm Gary Iskowitz & Co., LLP, 1801 Century Park E., Los Angeles 90067.

Toolshed and Garage Tax Loopholes

The rules that limit deductions available for home offices do not apply to *freestanding structures* that are located on your property.

Examples: An office in a converted freestanding garage, toolshed or gardener's house, or a specially built small office structure.

You can also claim deductions for depreciation and expenses for such freestanding structures under normal business-deduction rules, even if it's not the primary place where your business is conducted and it's not a place where you meet clients, patients or customers regularly.

Laurence I. Foster, tax partner in personal financial planning practice at KPMG Peat Marwick LLP, 345 Park Ave., New York 10154.

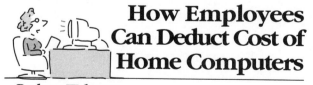 # How Employees Can Deduct Cost of Home Computers

Barbara Weltman

It is commonplace for an employee to take work home and complete it on a home computer. Or an employee may use a laptop to work on a plane, a train or while vacationing. *But is the cost of the computer deductible?*

PRECEDENT

An employee of Pacific Bell who was the manager of telemarketing sales bought a used computer and printer for her home.

She used the computer exclusively for business to write various reports and other documents required by Pacific Bell, and to keep up with the volume of work.

She could not use the computer in the office after hours since only higher-level management was permitted access to the building after hours. Still, she was required to complete her work.

Decision: In spite of IRS objections, the Tax Court allowed her to claim a first-year expense deduction for the cost of the computer and the printer. (*Case: Sherri A. Mulne*, TC Memo 1996–320.)

Reason for allowing the deduction: The taxpayer met all requirements for claiming a first-year expense deduction by an employee.

EXPENSING REQUIREMENTS

A first-year expense deduction (instead of depreciation) can be claimed for equipment acquired for use in the active conduct of a business (including the business of being an employee). The deduction is limited in 1997 to the cost of equipment up to $18,000. This deduction will increase further in annual steps over the next six years. An employee may not claim a first-year expense deduction for "listed property" (which includes a computer) unless use is for the "convenience of the employer" and required as a "condition of employment." These two requirements are identical. Satisfy one and you've satisfied the other.

●**Condition of employment.** To satisfy this test, the use of the property must be required for the employee to perform the duties of his/her employment properly. Whether use is required depends on the facts and circumstances of the particular case.

An employer need not specifically require that the employee use the property. On the other hand, a statement by the employer that the use of the property is a condition of employment is not sufficient to show that use is required. Even an interest-free loan by an employer to allow an employee to buy a home computer does not implicitly or explicitly establish that the computer was required for the job. (*Case: Robert L. Bryant*, CA-3, unpublished opinion 9/15/94 aff'g TC Memo 1993-597). Where, as in the new case, there is no alternative for an employee but to use a home computer to finish work required on the job, use of the property will be treated as a condition of employment.

But where the purchase of a computer is primarily for the employee's convenience, as was the case with a teacher who chose not to use school computers but her own to prepare report cards and student evaluations, the test is not met.

●**More than 50% business use.** Listed property must be used more than 50% for business to be eligible for expensing. Then, of course, only the cost of the business portion of the property can be expensed.

Where a computer is used exclusively for business, record keeping is simple. But where the computer is used partly for business and partly for personal purposes, record keeping is critical because of the 50% rule. Use a log or diary to note the computer time spent on business use and personal use. Failure to keep this record can result in loss of the deduction.

Expensing allows a full write-off for property in the year it is placed in service (bought and put into use). If not for expensing, the cost would be recoverable over a number of years using depreciation. Expensing is an option that must be elected on the tax return. Since the amount of the expense deduction cannot exceed taxable income from the business in which the equipment is used (such as compensation in the case of employment), it may not be wise to make the election in a year with little or no income.

Under depreciation, the cost of a computer can be recovered over a period of six years. Use of depreciation will provide write-offs in future years. When deciding to buy a new computer or other equipment, keep in mind that as long as it is placed in service by December 31, a full expensing deduction is allowed. You do not have to prorate the deduction for the portion of the year that the equipment was in use.

Caution: In a year when the computer or other equipment is no longer used predominantly for business, a portion of the expense deduction may have to be "recaptured" (reported as income).

Barbara Weltman, attorney and author of *J.K. Lasser's Tax Deductions for Small Business*. Macmillan.

Loopholes for Taxpayers With Sideline Income

Edward Mendlowitz
Mendlowitz Weitsen, LLP, CPAs

More and more people moonlight, consult...and have set up sideline businesses. The tax advantages of having a business of your own, even if it's only a sideline, are significant. *Opportunities:*

●**Report income and expenses on Schedule C of Form 1040.** There's an advantage to doing this. Business expenses, such as transportation costs, are deductible in *full* on Schedule C. They are not subject to the 2%-of-Adjusted-Gross-Income limitation that applies when the same expenses are taken on Schedule A of the 1040.

Loophole: If you get a commission, report it on Schedule C, even if you have no business expenses to write off against it. *Reason:* If the income qualifies as self-employment income, you can use some of it to set up a Keogh plan.

●**Have bigger pension plans.** The amount of money employees can put into tax-favored retirement plans is relatively modest. If they qualify, they can only put $2,000 a year into Individual Retirement Accounts (IRAs) and deduct it...or up to $9,500 a year into 401(k) plans, if their companies have such plans.

But people who have sideline businesses can build bigger retirement nest eggs. They can open Keogh plans and Simplified Employee Pension plans (SEPs), which have more generous contribution and deduction limits. You can put up to $30,000 a year into a Keogh or $24,000 into a SEP in 1997.

Super Keoghs: There's a kind of Keogh called a *defined benefit Keogh*, where contri-

butions are determined actuarially. You can contribute to—and deduct from—this kind of Keogh an amount that will provide you with a retirement benefit of up to $125,000 a year.

Loophole: Contributions to IRAs must be made by April 15 to be deductible on the prior year's return. But contributions to Keoghs and SEPs can be made after April 15, until the extended due date of your return. However, in the case of a Keogh, the plan must have been set up by December 31.

●**Depreciate business equipment.** Depreciation deductions on equipment, such as an office computer, shelter some of your income from tax. Instead of taking depreciation deductions, you may, under Section 179 of the Tax Code, write off up to $18,000 worth of business equipment in the year of purchase for 1997. This write-off amount will increase over the next six years.

●**Hire your children.** A child who works in his/her parent's sideline business can earn up to $4,150 in 1997 without owing any federal income tax. The salary is deductible by the business. An additional $2,000 of the child's salary would escape tax if it were put into an IRA.

Loophole: If your business is unincorporated, you don't have to pay FICA (Social Security and Medicare taxes) on wages paid to a child who is under age 18.

●**Deduct advertising expenses.** These are deductible along with all other ordinary and necessary business expenses.

Example: A freelance computer consultant is drumming up business among his neighbors. He decides to sponsor the Little League team his child plays on. The cost of his sponsorship is a deductible business expense—it's advertising.

●**Deduct home office expenses.** If you work out of your home and it is the main place of business for your sideline business, you can deduct a portion of your expenses—insurance, utilities, rent, etc.—as home office expenses.

●**Maximize your interest deductions.** When you borrow money to put into an unincorporated business, the interest you pay is fully deductible as business interest on Schedule C. If you borrow money on your credit card to put into the business, the interest is business interest—not personal interest—and is fully deductible.

Compare: If you borrow money to invest in an incorporated business, the interest is deductible only as investment interest, subject to investment-interest limitations. These limit your interest deductions to the amount of investment income you have for the year.

● **Hire independent contractors.** When you hire people who are self-employed, as you are in your capacity as the owner of a sideline business, they may be considered "independent contractors," rather than employees, for withholding tax purposes.

Benefit: You don't have to withhold income tax or pay the employer's portion of FICA for independent contractors.

The key test for determining whether someone who performs services for you is an employee or independent contractor is this—do you control what will be done and how it will be done? If you do, the person is an employee. If you don't exercise control over the methodology of services, the person is an independent contractor.

● **Minimize Social Security taxes.** When both spouses work in the business, and one has a full-time, high-paying job, that spouse should be listed as the sole owner of the business. Business income paid to that spouse will not be subject to self-employment tax if the spouse pays the maximum Social Security tax on his salary from his job. (For 1997, the maximum amount of salary that Social Security tax is taken from is $65,400. However, the 1.45% Medicare tax is figured on unlimited earnings.)

Compare: If the business was in the name of the spouse who did not have a full-time job, that spouse would have to pay self-employment tax on up to $65,400 of business income.

● **Write off your losses.** If your deductions for the year are more than your income, your net loss can be used to offset other income.

Caution: Certain deductions can't be used to create a loss. These include home office deductions and the expensing deduction under Section 179.

● **Minimize estimated tax payments.** If you have sideline income, you're required to make quarterly estimated tax payments to the government. You'll be penalized by the IRS if your payments fall short in any quarter.

Loophole 1: You can avoid making estimated payments on your sideline income by increasing the amount of tax that is withheld from your salary. You do not have to make estimated tax payments if your withholding for the year equals 90% of the total tax shown on this year's return, or 100% of the tax you paid last year, or 110% of last year's tax if your AGI was more than $150,000.

Loophole 2: If you receive most of your income late in the year, use what is called the annualized income installment method to figure your quarterly estimated payments. This will allow you to pay the bulk of your estimated tax after you've received the bulk of your income. To calculate your payments, use the annualized income installment worksheet in Form 2210, *Underpayment of Estimated Tax by Individuals, Estates and Trusts.*

Edward Mendlowitz, CPA, partner at Mendlowitz Weitsen, LLP, CPAs, 2 Pennsylvania Plaza, New York 10121. He is the author of several books on taxes, including New Tax Traps/New Opportunities *(Boardroom Classics) and* New Business Kit and Tax Compliance Guide, *New Jersey edition (Practical Programs, Inc.).*

Tax-Free Fringe Benefits

Sidney Kess

Fringe benefits offered by many businesses benefit usually both the employers and employees…

● **They serve to attract and retain valuable employees.**

● **Their costs are deductible by employers.**

● **In giving these fringe benefits**, employers avoid employment taxes that would be due if they simply gave employees additional salary to pay for the benefit directly.

● **Employees can enjoy personal benefits at little or no tax cost.** If the benefits weren't tax free, employees would have to earn more money to cover their cost.

NEW FRINGES FOR 1997

●**Medical Savings Accounts (MSAs).** Companies that have no more than 50 employees and *high-deductible* medical plans can contribute to employees' MSAs.

The employees are not taxed on the contributions.

The funds in the accounts, including earnings on contributions, can be used by the employee to pay medical expenses that are not covered by insurance. Funds that remain in the account when the employee turns 65 can be withdrawn penalty free and used for any purpose.

Caution: Withdrawals for nonmedical purposes are subject to income tax and, if made before age 65, a penalty as well.

High-deductible plans are health insurance policies with deductibles and out-of-pocket limits over set dollar amounts (e.g., a maximum deductible of $4,500 for family coverage). Contributions to MSAs are limited to 65% of the deductible for single employees and 75% for families.

Overall limit: The contributions can't exceed the employee's compensation.

Caution: Employers who choose to make contributions to MSAs can't discriminate between employees. They must make the same contribution for each employee or use the same percentage-of-deductible formulas to calculate contributions. Violation of this rule can result in a 35% penalty.

●**Adoption aid.** Companies can help defray the expenses an employee incurs when adopting children. Employees receiving such assistance are relieved from paying tax on up to $5,000 of adoption expenses per child ($6,000 for a child with special needs who is adopted in the US).

For the assistance to be tax free to the employee, the company's adoption-aid program must be in writing and it must provide aid on a nondiscriminatory basis.

Caution: An adoption assistance plan may not be suitable for small companies. *Reason:* Not more than 5% of the amounts paid under the plan can be provided to "owners." That means those owning more than 5% of the company's stock or more than 5% of the capital or profits in the company.

●**Long-term-care insurance.** Companies of any size can pay for the cost of long-term-care insurance for employees, their spouses and dependents. Employees can exclude from income up to $175 a day in 1997 on per diem contracts. The amount the company pays in premiums is tax free to the employee.

Note: Long-term-care insurance need not be offered to terminated employees through COBRA, a federal law that requires companies to permit such employees to continue health insurance coverage for a period of time.

MORE FRINGES

●**Child- and dependent-care assistance.** Companies can help employees pay for child or dependent care. Up to $5,000 of such benefit does not have to be included in income by the employee.

●**Medical insurance.** There is no dollar limit on the amount of medical insurance a company can provide employees on a tax-free basis.

Companies may also set up medical reimbursement plans in order to pay for expenses not covered by insurance. For those who are self-employed (and for the more-than-2% S corporation owners), personal medical coverage is not a deductible business expense. But they can deduct 40% of their health insurance coverage from gross income on their personal tax returns. This is up from 30% in 1996 and will increase further over the next several years.

Opportunity: A self-employed person whose spouse is on the payroll can make medical expenses *fully* deductible by providing coverage for employees and their families (which includes the self-employed person as spouse of his/her spouse-employee).

●**Group life insurance.** Companies can provide up to $50,000 of coverage on a tax-free basis ($2,000 of coverage for spouses and dependents is also excludable from employees' pay).

Coverage in excess of this amount is taxed to employees using favorable IRS tables that impute income (which is less than would result using the actual cost of coverage).

●**Transportation benefits.** Up to $65 of the cost of monthly transit passes for public transportation or van pooling is excludable in 1997. Company-paid parking is also excludable in 1997 up to $170 per month.

●**Retirement plans.** Perhaps the most important employee benefit a company can offer is a retirement plan. Employer contributions are deductible.

Employees are not taxed on contributions or earnings until they make withdrawals. But recently employers have shied away from offering retirement plans because of the complication and cost.

On January 1, 1997, *SIMPLE* plans *(Savings Incentive Match Plans for Employees)* went into effect. Employers can offer a retirement plan with little or no reporting requirements and modest cost.

Companies with 100 employees or fewer (as well as self-employed individuals) can use these new retirement plans.

●**Employees can contribute up to $6,000 via salary reduction.**

●**Employers *must* match employee contributions** (up to 3% of compensation)…or contribute up to 2% of compensation (without regard to employee contributions).

Caution: Employee contributions are still treated as wages for employment tax purposes (both employers and employees must pay Social Security and Medicare tax on employee contributions).

●**Employer contributions are not treated as wages.**

Sidney Kess, attorney and CPA, 630 Fifth Ave., New York 10111. Mr. Kess has lectured to more than 500,000 tax professionals on taxation. He is coauthor of 1040 Preparation 1997 Edition. *CCH Inc.*

Gambling Losses Are Deductible

Gambling losses are deductible from winnings—but only up to the total amount won. Gambling losses cannot be deducted from *other* forms of ordinary income. Lottery winnings of $5,000 or more are subject to withholding of 28%. Keno, bingo and slot machines are exempt from withholding if a tax identification number (usually a Social Security number) is given—but not exempt from reporting requirements.

Edward Mendlowitz, CPA, partner at Mendlowitz Weitsen, LLP, CPAs, 2 Pennsylvania Plaza, New York 10121. He is the author of several books on taxes, including New Tax Traps/New Opportunities *(Boardroom Classics) and* New Business Kit and Tax Compliance Guide, *New Jersey edition (Practical Programs, Inc.).*

How to Keep Lottery Winnings from the IRS

Elizabeth Winkler and her children bought lottery tickets regularly at a gas station, with whoever had a $1 bill buying the ticket. Mrs. Winkler won $6.5 million. Afterward, Mrs. Winkler set up a family partnership and said it owned the ticket. Each child received a share of the winnings taxed at his/her own low tax rate instead of at Mrs. Winkler's top rate. But the IRS objected that the partnership was a sham.

Tax Court: For the family. They had acted like a partnership by sharing ticket-buying duties regularly.

Estate of Emerson Winkler, TC Memo 1997-4.

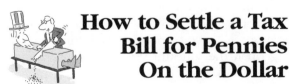

How to Settle a Tax Bill for Pennies On the Dollar

Arnold S. Goldstein, JD, LLM, PhD
Arnold S. Goldstein & Associates, PA

Few things in life cause as much dread as a big tax bill you can't pay. *But there's good news:* It is now easier to reach a compromise settlement with the IRS—sometimes for as little as *five cents* on the dollar. In recent years, the IRS has begun encouraging delinquent taxpayers to settle their back tax bills through *Offers in Compromise (OICs)*… and tens of thousands of taxpayers have successfully done so.

WAYS TO PAY LESS

Before going for an OIC, first consider alternative ways to reduce your tax bill that may be simpler or more appropriate.

•**Abatement.** If you owe penalties and/or interest on a tax liability, but have a good excuse for incurring the liability, you can ask the IRS to cancel the penalties and interest through an abatement.

Reasonable excuses that the IRS may accept include...

•**An illness left you unable to attend to tax affairs.**

•**Family problems, such as the death of a close family member.**

•**The loss of tax records due to factors beyond your control.**

•**Incorrect advice received from a tax professional.**

Limits: An abatement applies only to penalties and interest that are added to a tax bill, not to the underlying tax itself.

Request an abatement by filing IRS Form 843, *Claim for Refund and Request for Abatement.*

You have a good chance of success—penalties are abated in about 40% of all cases. Interest is abated less frequently.

•**Installment payments.** If you can afford to pay the IRS over a period of time, but not right away, you can get extra time to pay through an installment arrangement.

File IRS Form 9465, *Installment Agreement Request*, with your income tax return, indicating on it the amount you can afford to pay each month.

If the tax that is due is less than $10,000, the IRS will not ask for any further financial information, but simply will inform you of whether your proposed payment plan is acceptable.

If you owe less than $10,000 and propose to pay it off within one year, there is a very good chance the IRS will accept your proposal.

If you owe more than $10,000, the IRS will ask for more information concerning your personal finances, to be sure that you are paying all you can afford up front.

•**Borrowing.** If you ask the IRS for more than one year to pay off your tax debt, you can expect it to pressure you to borrow money or sell assets to pay your taxes more quickly.

You may want to borrow money to pay off the tax debt since a lender probably will charge less in interest than the IRS will charge in interest and penalties on what is owed.

•**Declare bankruptcy.** This can provide two benefits:

•**It stops the IRS from taking any further collection action against you.** So if the IRS is about to seize vital assets—such as a business bank account—you can stop it from doing so by filing for bankruptcy. You might even be able to force the IRS to return assets that it has already seized.

•**The bankruptcy court may provide you easier terms to pay off your tax bill than you would obtain from the IRS.**

TYPES OF BANKRUPTCY

•**Chapter 7 liquidation.** All your assets (except exempt assets) are sold to pay off your debts. Any remaining unpaid debts generally are erased. Exempt assets are determined by state law, but many states include an amount of equity in your home and other specified personal assets.

Check with a local bankruptcy expert.

•**Chapter 11 reorganization.** The court approves a plan to pay off your creditors while giving you a chance to reorganize your affairs. This often is used by businesses, but sometimes by individuals as well.

•**Chapter 13 "wage-earner plan."** The court approves a plan that allows you to pay off your creditors through earnings.

Bottom line: Tax debts more than three years old may be erased in a Chapter 7 bankruptcy—provided you did not understate your income or make other false tax claims on your returns.

If you file under Chapter 11 or Chapter 13, you'll probably pay the IRS the full tax you owe, but may be given extra time to do so—usually three to five years in a Chapter 13 plan and up to six years in Chapter 11.

THE ULTIMATE DEFENSE

•**Be "judgment proof."** If you have negligible assets and no income beyond what you need to live, the IRS simply may be unable to get any money from you.

In that case, it will categorize your case as uncollectible and move on. You'll still owe the tax, and interest will continue to accrue on it, but the IRS will cease collection action. You can expect, however, the IRS to review your case periodically to see if your financial situation has improved.

The IRS has 10 years to collect a tax assessment, after which the assessment lapses. So if you don't expect your situation to improve within that time range, remaining uncollectible may be a viable option.

●**Offers in Compromise.** If you can afford to pay a portion of your tax bill but not all (even if you get extra time), don't wish to declare bankruptcy or become uncollectible, and do wish to reach a settlement with the IRS that will put your tax problems behind you, then an OIC is the option to pursue.

Key: In the past few years, the IRS has become much more willing to accept compromise settlements, realizing that it collects more revenue from reasonable settlements than it does from pursuing taxpayers for larger amounts that it won't ever be able to collect.

To make an OIC, file IRS Form 656, *Offer in Compromise*, and IRS Form 433-A (for individuals) or 433-B (for business), *Collection Information Statement*. You must make a small deposit with your offer, which will be refunded if the IRS rejects your offer.

You must propose settlement terms to the IRS. It will either accept or reject them. To get the IRS to accept your offer, you must convince the IRS that this is the most you will be able to pay. If your OIC looks reasonable to the IRS, it probably will suspend further collection actions against you while the OIC is under review.

If the IRS rejects your OIC, it will send a letter explaining why. Then it will be up to you to make an amended offer. The IRS will not tell you what an acceptable offer would be, though your IRS agent may hint at it.

You have 30 days to appeal the IRS's rejection of an OIC. An appeal gives you the right to examine the notes of the agent who rejected your OIC, which may describe an offer that the IRS would have accepted.

Many OIC disputes are resolved on appeal, with the IRS appeals officer forging a compromise between the taxpayer and the IRS agent who rejected the offer.

If you lose, you retain the right to amend your OIC in light of the information you obtained during the appeals process, and try again.

Arnold S. Goldstein, JD, LLM, PhD, senior partner in the Florida and Massachusetts law firm of Arnold S. Goldstein & Associates, PA, and author of How to Settle with the IRS for Pennies on the Dollar. *Garrett Publishing Inc.*

What Happens to Cheaters?

What is the chance of a tax cheater getting caught and prosecuted by the IRS? During 1993, the criminal investigation division completed 5,992 investigations and secured 3,216 convictions. Even though the chances are statistically small that a cheater will get caught, the odds of the IRS successfully obtaining a conviction after making the catch are quite high.

Targets: High-profile business people and organized crime figures.

Best sources of IRS information: Informant allegations and court transcripts, especially in nasty divorce cases.

Ms. X, a former IRS agent who is still well connected.

IRS Audits: How to Beat The IRS at Its Own Game

Frederick W. Daily

Most taxpayers dread the prospect of an audit by the IRS—fearing that the IRS may use its vast resources to investigate every corner of their lives.

But the truth is different. In reality, the IRS is no more effective than any other government bureaucracy—and knowing its shortcomings can be a great help in planning how to limit what the IRS learns in an audit, and minimizing any tax that may result.

SURPRISING FACTS ABOUT THE IRS

● **Its technology is outdated.** Some of its computers date back to the 1960s—and efforts to upgrade technology have been criticized by Congressional overseers as being a costly fiasco.

● **Its information is not well coordinated.** It stores tax information in more than 200 databases that are not integrated—so it cannot pull up your whole file on a computer at any time, the way any credit card company can.

● **It operates under time pressures.** Its auditors are overworked and pressured to dispose of their case inventories quickly.

● **It has a hard time keeping good people.** Pay is low compared with the private sector, and top IRS officials have complained openly about the difficulty of retaining skilled workers at the agency's lower levels—where they deal directly with taxpayers.

When preparing to meet an IRS auditor, remember that...

● **The auditor does not have easy access to information about you**—he/she can't scan your file on a computer. The papers on his desk and those you bring with you are all he has to work with.

● **Auditors aren't rewarded for handling "tough cases."** Rather, they are evaluated by the number of cases that they close "agreed" with the taxpayer—meaning the taxpayer does not appeal.

This means an auditor will not want to spend a lot of time on your case if there's no good reason to do so—it will only delay the handling of the rest of his inventory.

DEALING WITH THE AUDITOR

The *golden rule* for dealing with an auditor is: Make the auditor earn all the information you provide.

Provide exactly the information needed to answer a legitimate inquiry by an auditor in a cooperative manner—and nothing more. Never give out anything extra. *Reasons...*

● **The auditor doesn't have easy access to information about you.** Any "fishing expedition" that the auditor conducts probably will

be through information you provide. So don't provide it unless you absolutely must.

● **Requests for extra information that are made by the auditor delay the audit.** You are entitled to ask for a reasonable amount of time to pull the information together, and then another meeting must be scheduled.

But the auditor won't want to delay the audit with such requests unless they will have a clear payoff—so by always providing the minimum amount of information you help contain the audit.

Important: You do not have to provide information to the IRS just because an auditor requests it. Legally, you are required to provide only information that relates to the year or years dated on the audit notice.

Example: An audit notice typically asks you to bring copies of the returns you filed for the years before and after the tax year being audited. You do not have to.

If the auditor asks you for the other years' returns, politely ask: "How do they relate to the year that is being examined?" If the auditor doesn't have a specific reason for asking for them, you'll have averted an IRS fishing expedition through other tax years.

Best: Every time an auditor asks for more information, politely ask how it relates to the taxes that are being examined.

● **You'll deter unjustified IRS fishing expeditions.**

● **If the auditor does have a reason you'll learn what it is,** see what he is targeting on your return, and be able to prepare a defense.

To contain an audit, it can sometimes pay to fail to produce even records the auditor is entitled to see—and then deal with the resulting tax assessment in Tax Court.

Example: Say that an auditor is questioning a few deductions on your return, but hasn't noticed a much larger "gray area" item. You're afraid that if you produce full records to support the deductions, they will point the auditor to the bigger potential trouble area.

Tactic: Don't provide the records for the deductions. The auditor then will most likely disallow them, and you'll get a "90-day letter" that gives you 90 days to file a case in Tax Court or pay the tax.

On receiving the 90-day letter you can either…

● **Pay the tax on the disallowed deductions to get the whole matter behind you,** or…

● **Fight the tax by producing the supporting records for the disallowed deductions in Tax Court.** *Key:* The IRS generally is barred from raising new issues for the first time in Tax Court—so filing a Tax Court case generally will not open other items on your return that the IRS may have overlooked to further examination.

KNOW ABOUT APPEALS

At the end of the audit, you'll be able to appeal the auditor's final report first within the IRS by going to the IRS Appeals Division in most cases, and then by filing a Tax Court petition.

If the tax and penalty at issue are less than $10,000 per tax year, the IRS offers simplified appeal procedures and you can go to the small case division of Tax Court, where legal rules are simplified and you don't need a lawyer.

Each filing gives you an extra chance to negotiate your tax bill with higher-level IRS personnel who, unlike the auditor, are authorized to reach a compromise settlement with you.

THE STATISTICS

Statistics show that the average appeal results in a 40% decrease in the amount of taxes, penalties and interest imposed by the auditor. Yet only one out of every 16 audited taxpayers goes to appeals—*many more should!*

Important: Knowing your appeal rights from the beginning can strengthen your position throughout the audit.

Psychologically, you'll be less intimidated if you know the audit isn't the end of the process, but just the beginning—and that you'll have an excellent chance of reducing any tax imposed by the auditor on appeal.

Tactically, you'll gain leverage with the auditor—whose performance is evaluated by the number of cases he closes "agreed."

Example: Say that an auditor is unsympathetic to your arguments and is putting you through a drawn-out process that you are sure will result in a big tax bill.

You may save yourself both time and aggravation by simply telling the auditor, "Look, just write me up and I'll resolve this when I'm in Appeals." *The benefits…*

● **You'll quickly get to a higher level of the IRS where your arguments may be better received,** and where you'll have a chance to negotiate.

● **Often, just saying these words will have a surprising impact on the auditor,** getting you a more sympathetic hearing. *Reason:* The auditor will realize that you know the rules of the game and won't be intimidated by the process—and he would rather you did not appeal.

Frederick W. Daily, a tax attorney based in San Francisco and author of *Stand Up to the IRS.* Nolo Press.

Mortgage Applicants, Beware

Do everything right. A new IRS audit program targets home-loan applicants who exaggerate their incomes—a criminal offense—to obtain loans.

Trap: The IRS can obtain from lenders copies of returns submitted with loan applications. If they don't match the filed returns, that person may be audited. If an audit confirms suspicions, the FBI may investigate further.

Frederick W. Daily, a tax attorney based in San Francisco and author of *Stand Up to the IRS.* Nolo Press.

How the Very Rich Avoid Estate Taxes… How You Can, Too

David S. Rhine
BDO Seidman, LLP

Wealthy people pay little or no taxes, even in death. Why? Because they get expert advice and plan carefully. They hire the best lawyers, accountants and estate planners, and they take advantage of every tax break the law allows. And—there's nothing illegal in that.

WHO'S WEALTHY

You may not think of yourself as wealthy, but you very well may be.

Add up the value of your house, retirement accounts, IRAs, life insurance, vacation home, mutual funds and other property.

You may be surprised to learn that the estate tax law considers you wealthy. Each dollar in your estate over $600,000 that you fail to protect will be taxed at rates starting at 37% and going up to 55%. The threshold will rise to $1 million by the year 2006.

You can avoid immediate estate tax by leaving everything to your spouse. Property left to a spouse passes tax free, of course, but without planning, that property will be taxed when your spouse dies. What can you do about that?

Wealthy people have the answers. *Here are some strategies they use to keep estate taxes down...*

MAKE MAXIMUM USE OF THE ANNUAL GIFT-TAX EXCLUSION

Each year you can give up to $10,000 to each of as many individuals as you choose ($20,000 a year if your spouse consents to split the gift). You won't owe any gift or estate tax on annual gifts if you keep them under these limits. These amounts may seem insignificant in relation to the fortune you have to protect.

But this kind of negative thinking ignores the cumulative power that annual gift giving has on your eventual taxable estate.

Example: A couple with more assets than they can ever use have five grandchildren. This couple can give away $100,000 every year to just the grandchildren ($20,000 split gifts times five grandchildren). If they do this for five years, they will have given away $500,000 completely tax free, or $1 million over 10 years. They've taken that money out of their taxable estates by giving it to their grandchildren. *Bonus:* Future interest on that money and any appreciation are also removed from their estates.

Caution: Even those with very large estates may not be sitting on enough cash to make these gifts. What they often do instead is use interests in *property* to make their annual tax-free gifts.

Example: Grandparents owning a $1 million building put it into a partnership. Instead of giving $20,000 cash a year to each grandchild, they give them partnership interests valued at $20,000.

Loophole: The grandchildren only get minority interests in the property—the grandparents retain control of it. So their gifts qualify for "minority interest discounts" for tax purposes. Because of the discount, the $20,000 annual gift-tax exclusion might cover $30,000 worth of property.

Impact: A 30% minority interest discount would mean that a $1 million building could be completely transferred to five grandchildren in seven instead of 10 years, free of gift and estate tax.

PAY A RELATIVE'S EDUCATION AND MEDICAL EXPENSES DIRECTLY

There is no annual dollar limit on gifts made by paying someone's education or medical expenses directly to the institution providing the service.

Example: A grandparent who writes a check to the university bursar for a grandchild's education pays no tax on the gift. In this way, grandparents could easily transfer more than $100,000 out of their estate to each grandchild— tax free.

The directly paid tuition exception is *in addition* to the annual gift-tax break. *Impact:* You can give $20,000 in cash each year gift-tax free, in addition to directly paying $25,000 (*or more*) of tuition expenses, also gift-tax free.

MAKE FULL USE OF YOUR $600,000 ESTATE- AND GIFT-TAX EXEMPTION—USE IT OR LOSE IT

The current $600,000 exemption can be used while you are alive or in your estate after your death.

Problem: Inflation erodes the value of the exemption, making it more valuable now rather than at your death.

At a 4% annual inflation rate the value of the exemption is cut in half in just 17½ years.

Planning for the exemption: As the exemption threshold increases, you can make additional tax-free gifts.

GIVE AWAY YOUR HOME FOR A FRACTION OF ITS VALUE WITHOUT MOVING OUT OF IT

A person who owns a home and plans to retire in five or 10 years and relocate to the Sun Belt is an ideal candidate for another gift strategy frequently used by the very rich.

How it works: A parent transfers the family home to a trust called a *Qualified Personal Residence Trust (QPRT)* for the benefit of his/her children.

The parent retains the right to live in the house for a fixed number of years. At the end of that time, the trust ends and distributes the house to the children who then own it outright. The tax cost of this gift is based on the value of the "remainder interest"—the home's value less the value of the parent's right to live in the house for those years.

Rule of thumb: The right to live in the house for five years cuts the taxable value of the gift to the children by one-third. A 13-year term cuts it by two-thirds (a gift of a $300,000 home would be valued at only $100,000 for gift-tax purposes.) Exact computations are necessary, of course. They vary based on the interest rate in effect for the month the gift is made and the age of the person putting the house in trust.

During the trust's term, the parent continues to pay the mortgage and taxes and claims itemized deductions for these expenses on his income tax returns.

Downside: If the parent dies during the term of the trust, the property is included in the parent's estate so no benefit will have been achieved. If the parent outlives the trust's term, the child takes over the parent's tax cost (basis) in the home so there is no step-up in basis for the house. This means that the child will pay capital gains tax on appreciation in value when he sells the house.

After the trust ends: If the parent wants to continue to live in the house at the end of the trust term, he must pay fair market rent to the child. As a practical matter, it may be a good idea to continue having the trust own the home. This allows the parent to pay rent to the trustee rather than the child. Setting things up in this way may avoid problems, should the parent have a falling out with the child.

SET UP A LIFE INSURANCE TRUST

Many wealthy people are cash poor but insurance rich. At little or no gift-tax cost, a large amount of insurance can be removed from the estate—tax free. What people do is set up a

trust to own the insurance policy and receive the proceeds on the insured's death.

Caution: If the insured dies within three years of the transfer of an existing policy to a trust, the insurance proceeds are included in his taxable estate.

To get around this: Set up a trust to buy a brand new insurance policy. When that's done, there is no three-year waiting period.

If the insured continues to pay premiums, this can eat away at the $600,000 exemption. But a special clause in the trust, called a *Crummey Power,* can give the trust beneficiary the right to withdraw annual sums. This right to withdraw makes the gifts to pay the premiums eligible for the annual $10,000/$20,000 exclusion.

Protecting your spouse: One drawback to an insurance trust is the limit on a spouse's authority over the proceeds. Had they been payable directly to the spouse, there would have been no limit. But with a trust, the spouse is subject to the trustee's discretion as to how funds are paid out.

Friendly trustee: Make the trustee "spouse-friendly" by naming as trustee someone who is sympathetic to the spouse's interests (e.g., your spouse's brother).

Withdrawal power: Ensure control over some portion of the proceeds by giving your spouse a "five and five" power. *Meaning:* Your spouse can withdraw 5% of the principal each year. If your spouse has other assets, your spouse should not draw from the trust since this will only build up your spouse's estate and create a tax.

Caution: Don't make distribution of income from the trust to the spouse mandatory since that, too, will put money back into the spouse's estate and create additional estate tax on the spouse's death.

 ### SET UP A GRANTOR RETAINED ANNUITY TRUST (GRAT)

Someone facing potential appreciation in assets—say a business that may be sold or go public or property where an upscale mall may be developed next to your property—may want to shift the appreciation in his property out of the estate by setting up a type of trust called a Grantor Retained Annuity Trust.

Example: Suppose the property is currently worth $1 million. If it is transferred to a GRAT in exchange for an annuity of $130,000 for 12 years, there is no gift (the value of the property equals the value of the annuity). This is called zeroing-out the gift. If the property appreciates as anticipated, the appreciation belongs entirely to the beneficiary of the GRAT, not to the person setting up the trust.

Caution: The trust needs cash to pay the annuity. Or it can give back property in kind (an interest in the property transferred to the trust).

David S. Rhine, partner and national director of family wealth planning at BDO Seidman, LLP, 330 Madison Ave., New York 10017.

Wisest Ways to Pass On Your Money

David Gerson and Charles Cangro
Ernst & Young, LLP

One of the easiest ways to cut your tax burden is to shift assets to younger family members. *By doing so you may:*

• **Reduce income taxes** by having family members in lower tax brackets hold income-producing assets.

• **Cut estate taxes** by removing appreciating assets from your taxable estate.

Asset shifting may also help you attain family goals, such as enabling a member of the younger generation to start a business, finance a home or meet tuition expenses.

GIFT-GIVING OPPORTUNITIES

The simplest way to shift assets is by giving gifts. *Strategies…*

• **The annual gift-tax exclusion** allows you to make gifts of up to $10,000 each to as many separate recipients as you wish, all free of gift tax. The limit per gift is $20,000 when gifts are made jointly by a married couple. When such gifts are made annually over a period of years, they can add up to a sizable amount, shifting family wealth to the younger generation in an orderly manner without utilizing any unified credit.

• **Education and medical expenses** can be paid without incurring gift tax, regardless of the amount involved. The beneficiary of the gift need not be a dependent or relative. However, the amount must be paid *directly* to the educational or medical institution. Gift tax applies if the amount is paid to an individual who then remits it to an institution.

• **The unified gift and estate tax credit** lets you transfer to your children, grandchildren or other heirs up to $600,000 of assets free of gift or estate taxes ($1 million by 2006). This is in addition to your right to make annual $10,000 tax-free gifts. When the credit is applied to a current gift, you reduce the amount of the credit that remains available to offset estate taxes when you die.

But you can come out ahead if the gift is an asset that will likely appreciate in value.

Example: Property that is worth $600,000 today is anticipated to appreciate before you die. When you apply the unified credit to a gift of the property that is made today to anyone other than a spouse, no gift tax will be due. You can spread the gift over time by making "fractional gifts" over a few years to take advantage of multiple annual gift tax exclusions. If you pass the property through your will, estate tax will be due upon your death.

Another reason to use the credit today is that the $600,000 amount loses value to inflation every year.

• **IRA gifts** are a low-cost way to give younger family members a head start on financial security. The key is that while a person must have earned income to make a deductible IRA contribution, the contribution does not have to be made with the earned income. Thus, a child who has $2,000 of income from a first job can receive a $2,000 gift to fund an IRA. The gift may reduce the child's tax bill.

How: In 1997, a child of working age may receive up to $4,150 of earned income tax-free because of the standard deduction. A child who earns $6,150 a year and receives a gift of $2,000 that is placed in an IRA account can actually receive a total of $8,150, through salary and gifts, totally tax free.

When $2,000 is invested annually in a growth investment or growth mutual fund for a child starting in the teen years, compounding tax-deferred earnings provides a start on financial security.

OTHER WAYS TO TRANSFER ASSETS

●**Interest-free loans.** By making an interest-free loan to a family member, you can move funds out of an investment account subject to a high tax bracket. This allows the recipient to invest in an asset—such as a home or business —that generates deductions and may cut the family's overall tax bill.

Although large interest-free loans are penalized by the Tax Code, "safe harbor" provisions let you make such a loan with no adverse tax consequences when the loan amount is...

●**Less than $10,000** and is not used by the recipient to produce investment income.

●**Less than $100,000** and the recipient has no more than $1,000 of investment income.

●**S corporations.** A family business can be structured as an S corporation, with shares gifted to low-tax-bracket family members. Its income is taxed to its shareholders on their personal tax returns, so gifts to persons in low tax brackets will reduce the family's income tax bill. Gifted shares also escape estate tax when the donor dies.

Point: The donor of shares can retain control over the business by making gifts of nonvoting shares.

●**Family limited partnership.** A family limited partnership can be used to hold a family's investments or income-producing real estate.

One family member acts as the general partner and manages the partnership's assets. Other members become limited partners who obtain share interests through gifts. Income is shifted to them in proportion to their holdings and is taxed at their personal rates.

Again, transferred interests will avoid estate tax when the donor dies. Also, substantial valuation discounts may be obtained for transfers of limited partnership interest even if the partnership contains marketable securities.

●**Grantor retained annuity trust.** This type of trust can be a big estate tax saver when a parent owns a business or assets that are expected to appreciate in value.

How it works: The parent places ownership of the assets in a trust that will pay a fixed annuity amount to the parent for a period of time and, when that term is up, distribute the assets to a beneficiary such as a child.

Key: The trust is set up so that the present value of the annual payments from the trust is almost equal to the current value of its assets. The IRS sets, on a monthly basis, the interest rate factor to be used in calculating the present value of the annuity payments. Thus, any trust property remaining in the trust is transferred to the beneficiary subject to a small initial amount of tax.

Next: If the trust property appreciates at an annual rate in excess of the interest rate factor, this excess appreciation will be transferred to the trust beneficiary at no additional gift tax cost. If the trust assets do not appreciate enough in value, the trust will be exhausted at the end of its term. However, if the trust assets grow in value—as a family business might—a substantial amount of appreciation may be passed to the beneficiary free of estate or gift tax.

MISTAKE TO AVOID

Don't put money in a child's name to help save for future college costs without thinking through the nontax consequences. This strategy can indeed save taxes if the child is in a lower tax bracket than the parent or grandparent who makes the gift. *But...*

●**It can cause the loss of future tuition assistance**, since a child's own wealth is the first thing a college financial aid officer looks at when determining how much aid a child is eligible to receive. The lost tuition aid may outweigh the saved taxes.

●**The child may decide to spend the money put in his name in a manner that is contrary to the donor's wishes.**

STEPS TO TAKE

Before transferring interest in a family business or family investments, ask yourself whether the sudden shift of wealth or control will produce undesirable results. Look for alternative possibilities that may better meet your goals.

Examples: A younger parent who can borrow from a 401(k) plan or retirement account may do well by making extra deductible contributions to the account over time, then borrowing from the account when the child goes to school.

When assets are put in trust for a child, a 2503(c) trust gives a parent or donor more control over the assets than does a Unified Gifts to Minors Act account. A 2503(c) trust stays in effect until the child reaches age 21 and may also provide the child with only a 30-day "window" to withdraw trust assets. After the window closes, assets in the trust remain subject to its terms for an indefinite or predetermined period.

Many other planning strategies can be custom-tailored to meet a family's needs, so consult with an estate planning expert about the possibilities.

David Gerson, tax partner and area director of estate planning, and Charles Cangro, senior tax manager at Ernst & Young, LLP, 787 Seventh Ave., New York 10019.

Mutual Fund Double-Tax Trap

Many people automatically reinvest their fund dividends or capital gains in additional fund shares. But taxes are owed in the year the dividends are paid, even though you receive no cash from the fund.

Careless investors pay taxes twice…once when dividends are paid and again when they sell their shares.

Self-defense: To avoid double taxation, keep records and add reinvested dividends and capital gains to your tax cost (basis) in your fund shares. Increasing the tax cost reduces your tax bill when you sell.

Reason: You pay capital gains tax on the difference between the selling price of the shares and your tax cost.

Robert Willens, CPA, managing director at Lehman Brothers Inc., 3 World Financial Center, New York 10285.

How to Audit-Proof Your Business… With Help from the IRS

Don Rocen
Coopers & Lybrand LLP

New opportunities exist now to "audit-proof" your business from a future IRS challenge. And surprisingly, the IRS will help you.

Why: The IRS thinks the most effective way to collect taxes is to have taxpayers pay them voluntarily—rather than after an audit or a costly court fight.

So under its *Compliance 2000* initiative, the IRS is following a two-pronged strategy to more effectively target its audit efforts…and to tell the public about its compliance expectations.

The IRS now even releases to the public the very same audit guides that its agents use when auditing a business.

IRS's idea: Taxpayers who know the areas the IRS will target will voluntarily comply in those areas—or voluntarily take steps to correct their past mistakes if they have not complied.

INDUSTRY EXPERTISE

How to learn what the IRS will look at when examining your business…

●**Audit guides.** The IRS is gaining detailed knowledge of midsized and smaller businesses through its *Market Segment Specialization Program (MSSP)*.

Under the MSSP, teams of agents in different IRS districts study the particular kinds of businesses concentrated in their districts to develop an expertise in them.

Once an MSSP team completes its study of an industry, it publishes an audit guide that explains how the business works and gives details of areas of noncompliance that are commonly encountered.

This guide is then made available to IRS auditors nationally to enable them to audit local businesses of the same kind more effectively.

Example: The MSSP guide for attorneys is more than 70 pages long and describes the various types of bank accounts maintained by attorneys as well as the ins and outs of partnership agreements, methods of compensation, fee structures, expense reimbursement patterns and so forth.

Obviously, having an IRS audit guide for your business can be an immense help in heading off future tax problems. It will reveal the issues the auditor is most likely to scrutinize when examining your firm's return—and alert you to the kinds of "economic reality" tests that may be used by an auditor to determine if the business has reported all its income.

The IRS audit guide for your business can help you organize its records to better withstand a tax examination, and alert you to any innocent tax-planning mistakes you may be making.

If you have a legitimate disagreement with the IRS on a tax issue, the audit guide can inform you of the approach you can expect the IRS to take on the issue and give you a better start on preparing your side of the argument.

● **Industry issue papers.** The IRS also develops and releases issue papers for specific industries. These are used to provide an auditor with guidance when examining a specific issue that is involved in a company's business.

Issue papers are drawn up as the direct result of the IRS's examination of large corporations through its *Industry Specialization Program (ISP)*—but issues that affect large corporations often appear on the tax returns of smaller businesses in the same industry. Thus, issue papers drawn up by the IRS during an examination of a major national retail company may be used as guidance by IRS auditors during the examination of local retail stores.

Again, the issue papers that are used by IRS tax examiners are available to the public. And once again, advance knowledge of the IRS's instructions to its own auditors can be invaluable in heading off audit problems.

To date, the ISP has produced 72 sets of coordinated issue papers. So it is very possible that IRS issue papers may exist for your business even if no audit guide has yet been released.

● **Independent contractors.** A hot issue for large and small businesses is the tax treatment of independent contractors…and the risk that the IRS may recategorize a business's contractors as employees, resulting in a big tax bill for back employment taxes.

Problem: When the IRS is determining whether a worker is a contractor or an employee, it looks at 20 factors (listed in IRS Publication 15A, *Employment Taxes*). But it weighs the factors differently in different situations, so businesses face a great deal of uncertainty about what the IRS may conclude in any one case.

Here, too, the IRS is conducting industry-specific studies and releasing the results to the public.

Through its *Market Segment Understanding (MSU)* program, the IRS examines the employment practices of particular kinds of businesses. It then releases MSUs for those businesses that explain in advance how the 20-factor test will be applied to them—giving the businesses advance notice of the steps they must take to preserve contractor status for their workers. The MSU program is newer than the MSSP and ISP. So far, MSUs have been released for the food-service industry, video and advertising producers, and agricultural workers who receive payment in kind.

However, other MSUs are under development, so be on the lookout for them.

PERSONALIZED SAFETY

● **Private rulings.** Every business faces unique tax problems. When a company wants assurance that a transaction won't have surprising adverse tax consequences, it can have its tax adviser ask the IRS for an advance private ruling on the subject.

To obtain a private ruling, the taxpayer writes a letter to the IRS detailing the facts of the situation, relevant law, and the ruling he/she seeks. A filing fee is required.

● **If the IRS provides the desired ruling**, the taxpayer is protected from future IRS challenges on the subject.

● **If the IRS has a problem with the ruling request**, it will inform the taxpayer, who can then amend the request to overcome the IRS objection or withdraw the request to avoid receiving a negative ruling—having been warned of a potential problem.

Don Rocen, partner in charge of the IRS practice and procedures group at Coopers & Lybrand LLP, 1900 K St. NW, Washington, DC 20006. Mr. Rocen formerly served as assistant to the IRS commissioner.

The Best New Tax-Saving Opportunities for Business Cars

James A. Cox
Ernst & Young LLP

Businesses rightly put great effort into getting the biggest deductions possible for the cars they own and the cost of business driving.

Challenge: IRS auto deduction rules are complex and require taxpayers to make numerous choices.

OWNERS' RULES

There are *two* ways to deduct the cost of a car that a company or individual *owns* and uses for business…

●**Actual expense method.** This method involves deducting the actual costs of owning the car.

Included: Depreciation, gas, oil, insurance, licenses, repairs, tires, garage rent, parking, tolls.

Under general rules, the full purchase price of the car can be deducted over six years through depreciation taken at the following rates…

Year 1: 20% of cost.

Year 2: 32%.

Year 3: 19.2%.

Years 4 & 5: 11.52%.

Year 6: 5.76%.

But there's a *catch.* The Tax Code limits the maximum deductions that can be taken for "luxury" cars.

For cars placed in service during 1997, the deduction limits are…

Year 1: $3,160.

Year 2: $5,000.

Year 3: $3,050.

Year 4 and later: $1,775.

Result: Deductions for cars costing more than $15,300 will be restricted. And if a car costs much more than this it may take many years to fully depreciate it.

Example: A new auto costing $35,000 is placed in service in 1997. It won't be fully depreciated for almost 17 years—until the year 2014.

Expensive cars also are hit with a 10% "luxury tax" at the time of purchase that applies to price to the extent that it exceeds $36,000 in 1997.

Loophole: Vehicles weighing more than 6,000 pounds aren't subject to these restrictions because they are considered to be trucks under the Tax Code.

Many popular sports-utility vehicles designed for passenger use exceed this weight limit—opening potential tax advantages for their owners.

Deductions for such a vehicle may be greatly accelerated compared to those for a car of the same price.

Example: A new sports-utility vehicle costing $35,000 purchased in 1997 can be *fully depreciated in six years*, compared with 17 years for a sedan costing the same amount. The first-year deduction will be $7,000, compared with only $3,160 for a car. And the sports-utility vehicle avoids the luxury tax, too.

Caution: Only business driving costs are deductible, so an individual who owns a car and uses it for personal and business purposes must keep records that separate out business costs.

Deductible: Actual costs incurred driving for business, plus a percentage of "ownership costs" that corresponds to the percentage of all driving that is business driving.

Example: A person uses a car 75% for business. He can deduct all tolls and parking fees incurred during business driving…plus 75% of the cost of auto insurance, license fees and depreciation.

The advantage of the actual expense method of deducting driving costs is that it can provide larger deductions for cars with high operating costs. The disadvantage is the extensive record-keeping that is involved in recording every driving cost.

●**Standard mileage rate.** This lets car owners deduct business driving at a flat rate of 31½¢ per mile in 1997. Tolls and parking are also deductible. But ownership costs such as depreciation, maintenance and insurance are not. They are included in the mileage rate. *Rules:*

●**If the driver wants to use the standard mileage rate,** it must be done in the first year a car is used for business purposes. But drivers can switch to the actual expense deduction method later if they want to.

When switching to the actual expense method, the driver must calculate the adjusted basis of the car and estimate its remaining useful life. The standard mileage rate includes a flat rate for depreciation (12¢ per mile in 1997), which reduces the original basis of the car. Going forward, the straight line depreciation method must then be used. If a driver uses the actual expense method in the first year of business use, he/she *cannot* switch to the standard mileage rate.

Tactic: Switch from the actual cost method to the standard rate by filing amended tax returns for *all* the years that the car has been used for business, switching to the standard rate on those returns. But drivers can file amended returns only three years back, so they must have begun to use the car for business purposes within that time.

●**Drivers cannot use the standard rate if they use *more than one* car for business *at the same time.***

It *is* legal to use the standard rate if an individual owns two cars and *alternates* their use for business. So a businessperson who owns two cars and is the *only* person who drives them for business, *can* use the standard rate for both since he/she doesn't drive both cars at the same time.

Individuals who drive one car themselves and let employees drive the other *cannot* use the standard mileage rate on either car.

Thus, the primary effect of this rule is to prevent companies from using the standard rate for two or more cars—but individuals who are business owners should be aware of the potential pitfall here, too.

The disadvantage of the standard rate is that it does not vary with a car's real cost. So the more expensive a car and the higher its operating costs, the less likely it is that the standard rate will fully cover operating costs.

Trade-in trap: Because of the luxury automobile depreciation limits imposed by the Tax Code, after a few years an expensive car's market value is likely to be much *lower* than its "depreciated basis"—the car's cost minus depreciation deductions. If you then sell the car, the difference between its market value and basis will be a *deductible loss*.

Individuals who trade in an old car toward the price of a new car end up with a *nontaxable exchange* and no loss deduction will result— the loss is deferred until the second car is sold.

This is true whether car costs are deducted using the actual expense method *or* standard rate. The standard rate includes a flat rate for depreciation (12¢ per mile in 1997).

BIGGEST DEDUCTIONS

Bigger deductions overall are available if a *business* owns cars and provides them to employees. *Reasons:*

●**A business can deduct interest and finance charges on auto loans,** while employees cannot.

●**Employee business expenses on a personal tax return are counted among miscellaneous expenses,** the total of which is deductible only to the extent it exceeds 2% of Adjusted Gross Income (AGI). So an employee with AGI of $60,000 gets no deduction for the first $1,200 of such expenses.

●**When AGI on most personal returns exceed $121,200 in 1997,** certain itemized deductions are reduced by 3% of the excess over that threshold.

These deduction limits do *not* apply to businesses that own autos.

PROVIDING THE CAR

When a business owns cars and provides them to employees, it gets a *100%* business use deduction for the cars. But employees must keep records accounting for both business and personal auto use.

The percentage of a car's value that corresponds to the percentage of personal use is taxable income to the employee and must be reported on the employee's W-2 form.

The car's value may be set at the actual cost that would be incurred to lease a similar vehicle. Or the company can refer to the IRS's published lease-rate table, which generally produces an annual value close to 25% of the car's purchase price plus $500.

The value of personal use can also be figured at 31½¢ per mile, but only if the car is driven at least 10,000 miles during the year, and has a market value of no more than $15,300 when first provided to the employee.

Simpler: The company can report the *entire* value of cars it provides to employees in their income, and have them deduct business use of the cars on their own returns. But while this simplifies the company's bookkeeping, employees will be subject to the deduction limits.

James A. Cox, partner in personal financial counseling at Ernst & Young LLP, 555 California St., San Francisco 94104.

How to Boost Auto Deductions Retroactively

If you initially deduct business driving expenses for a car you own and use for business using the actual expense method—then realize you could get a bigger deduction by claiming the standard mileage rate—you can file *amended tax returns* to claim the standard mileage rate for the car beginning in the year that you put it in service.

The mileage rate may provide a larger deduction when you drive a large number of miles, because depreciation deductions that can be claimed under the actual expense method are sharply limited by the Tax Code.

You also might choose the standard mileage rate because of the extensive record keeping required by using the actual expense method.

Rules: You can amend returns only three years back, so the car must have been acquired within that period. And you must use the standard mileage rate—and file amended returns—for all the years you've used the car.

Randy Bruce Blaustein, Esq., senior tax partner at Blaustein Greenberg & Co., 155 E. 31 St., New York 10016.

Get an Interest-Free Loan From the IRS

Randy Bruce Blaustein
Blaustein, Greenberg & Co.

Getting a big tax refund means you overpaid your taxes during the year, probably through too much wage withholding, making an interest-free loan to the IRS.

Opportunity: You can reverse the process by underpaying your estimated taxes during the year—then making up the shortfall with last-quarter, last-minute withholding—and have the IRS make an interest-free loan to you.

Key: The IRS treats wage withholding as taking place at an even rate throughout the year—even when in fact it is increased in the last part of the year. So by paying withholding tax at the normal rate, then boosting it in the last weeks of the year you can "repay" the IRS for any amount by which estimated taxes were underpaid earlier in the year—and avoid penalties.

This strategy is available if you and your spouse have both wage income *and* investment or self-employment income for which quarterly estimated taxes normally would be owed.

Critical: Be sure you can increase withholding by enough in the last quarter to cover the full year's tax liability.

Randy Bruce Blaustein, senior tax partner at Blaustein, Greenberg & Co., 155 E. 31 St., New York 10016.

When "Tax-Free" Isn't Really Tax-Free

Tax-free municipal bond funds are not completely tax free. Dividends from municipal bond funds may be subject to state or local income taxes. A part of each dividend may represent taxable income or capital gains that the fund realized. If you sell shares in the fund at a profit, your capital gain is taxable.

David S. Rhine, CPA, partner and national director of family wealth planning, BDO Seidman, LLP, 330 Madison Ave., New York 10017.

7

Your Business and Career Moves

How to Buy a Business With No Money Down

Edward Mendlowitz
Mendlowitz Weitsen, LLP, CPAs

Few people who work for small companies realize how easy it can be to buy the businesses that now employ them by using a leveraged buyout (LBO).

An LBO is the term the financial community uses to describe the sale of a company to a buyer—usually an executive or manager of the company—who puts up little or none of his own money. Instead, the buyer uses the company's assets as collateral for a loan. This borrowed money is then used to pay the seller.

The idea really isn't that much different from taking out a mortgage when you buy a house. In that case, a bank lends up to 90% of the value of the home.

In an LBO, the lender is paid back out of the company's after-tax profits. For that reason, the lender looks for a buyer in whom it has confidence to keep the company profitable.

ARE YOU A GOOD CANDIDATE?

Lenders look for people who know their businesses inside and out...professionals who can steer the company through critical periods of new management and heavy debt. If your track record shows that you can, lenders will look at your personal credit history and stability next.

Even if you are highly successful in your career, lenders may shy away from you if you have a history of changing jobs or getting into unmanageable debt.

You can score big points with lenders by showing them how the company, under your management, can generate bigger profits than it is currently making.

HOW TO START

Before looking for a lender, you must find a company that you're interested in buying. If you're a real pro in your field, you'll probably know whether the company you work for is for sale. If it is not, you may know of similar ones that are.

Once you find a company for sale that is of interest to you, carefully go over its financial statements to determine whether an LBO is possible. The effort will usually require the assistance of an accountant, preferably one who has solid experience in LBOs.

In general, lenders who finance LBOs let you borrow up to about 75% of the company's accounts receivable plus around 25% of the inventory. But paying the loan back at the current LBO rate of about 12% will put a huge burden on the company's cash flow.

For that reason, even though a company may have the collateral for a loan, it still may not be a good LBO candidate if it is going to need big capital expenditures in the near future.

Example: A printing business that is doing very well—but whose presses will soon have to be replaced.

That's where your expertise comes in. As a professional with a successful track record in your field, you'll be in a good position to forecast future business and project how the company can make it without big expenditures while the loan is being repaid.

Obviously, however, few people are experts in all areas of a business—production, marketing, finance, etc. So to prove to a lender that all these areas will be in competent hands, you need to assemble a strong team to help you steer the business through the critical period.

These people can come from the company's current management ranks, or you can bring in professionals from other companies.

Until the loan is repaid—generally within three to five years—the management by you and the other members of the team will be under constant scrutiny by lenders. The lenders usually insist on rigorous auditing requirements that will put an extra burden on management.

FINDING A LENDER

LBOs are typically financed by banks, venture capital groups, brokerage houses, commercial finance companies and factors (specialists who deal in accounts receivable).

It is often best to turn first to a banker who knows the company and you. If the bank isn't interested in an LBO, it can usually point you to venture capitalists or other groups who may be in the market for what you have to offer.

YOUR CONTRIBUTION

Though your contribution to an LBO deal is management skill, lenders will want you to put down some cash. That doesn't have to come out of your pocket because you may be able to borrow the additional amount in exchange for part interest in the company.

Recent case: A knowledgeable buyer with whom we worked was able to get $14.5 million in financing for a $15 million buyout, but the lenders wanted him to put up $500,000. To get the cash, we went to a group of venture capitalists, who agreed to a $500,000 loan in exchange for 50% of the company. He had to give up a big share in the business…but he bought it with none of his own money.

Edward Mendlowitz, CPA partner at Mendlowitz Weitsen, LLP, CPAs, 2 Pennsylvania Plaza, New York 10121. He is author of several books on taxes, including *New Tax Traps/New Opportunities* (Boardroom Classics) and *New Business Kit and Tax Compliance Guide*, New Jersey edition (Practical Programs, Inc.)

Top Sources of Money To Start a Business

Barbara Weltman

Running short of cash is one of the biggest reasons new businesses fail. You can try to get a commercial loan from a bank, but such loans are hard to come by for new entrepreneurs.

Here's where to turn when you need capital fast, in order of preference…

●**Home-equity loan.** You can usually borrow up to 75% or 80% of your home's equity—what you would pocket if you sold your home and paid off any existing mortgage.

Shop around for the best loan by checking out the fees for getting the loan, the repayment period and the interest you will pay.

Caution: A home-equity loan is secured by your home. If you fail to repay the loan, you could lose your home.

●**Life insurance loan.** If you own a life insurance policy that has built up cash value over the years, you can apply and be approved for a loan from your insurer within a few days.

The interest rate is low—often between 6% and 8%, but it varies depending on your contract—and you can repay the loan in any increments that you choose, whenever you have the money to do so.

Caution: If you don't repay the loan, your beneficiaries will receive less insurance protection than you had intended for them.

●**Retirement plan borrowing**—usually from a 401(k) or pension plan. The most you can borrow is 50% of your vested account balance—or $50,000, whichever is less. You are not taxed on borrowing the money if the loan meets tax-law requirements.

A loan used for a business must be repaid in equal payments within five years and bears a rate of interest that is comparable to the going rate.

Caution: You usually must repay the loan in full if you leave the employer. Also, you are reducing your retirement savings, since the funds withdrawn are not available for tax-deferred compounding. *Note:* One cannot borrow from IRAs or Keogh accounts.

●**Borrow from your brokerage** by setting up a margin account and putting your securities up as collateral.

The borrowing limits usually are 50% of the total value of stocks and corporate bonds… and 90% of government securities, such as Treasury bonds.

There is no set repayment schedule. Interest continues to accrue on the outstanding balance and on any interest you don't repay. The interest rate can adjust monthly.

Caution: If the value of your securities drops, you may be forced to sell them at low prices to raise enough cash to cover a "margin call"—to bring your loan balance within the 50%/90% limits.

Barbara Weltman, an attorney in Millwood, NY, who has written extensively on taxes and small business. She is author of *The Big Idea Book for New Business Owners.* Macmillan.

We Turned $30,000 into a $500,000/Year Business… You Can, Too

Edd and Charlotte Davies
Molly Maid

Five years ago, my job at a major telecommunications company was eliminated. I was in my late 40s and unable to find suitable work in New Jersey. So my wife and I sold our home and moved to northern Virginia.

Rather than take another job where I'd have to worry about being laid off again, my wife and I decided to explore buying a franchise. After researching the market, we invested $30,000 of our life's savings in a Molly Maid housecleaning franchise.

It was one of the best investments we ever made. Today, our business grosses nearly $500,000 a year, and we net about 20% of that. *Here's our advice to anyone considering buying a franchise—and how to make it a success…*

●**Decide what type of business you want to own.** We knew that people who start their own businesses have a high failure rate, and that franchising represented a much better chance of success over the long term.

We also chose franchising because neither of us had previous business experience. A good franchise company will teach you the business…and provide you with the proven systems of making it work.

Helpful: Attend a franchise show. We went to one in Washington, DC. We walked the entire show floor with an open mind. We talked at least briefly to many of the 500 exhibitors. We took the phone numbers of those we liked. Then we called and talked with them at length.

We saw the housecleaning field as a high-growth industry with tremendous potential. After living here for a few months, we decided our suburban Washington location was an ideal market for such a service. There are lots of two-income households here, with both spouses having no time to clean the house, but earning enough income to pay for help. It also looked like a fairly easy business to get into and learn.

●**Be prepared to make a sizable investment.** Depending on the franchise, you must have from a few thousand to more than $100,000 to invest.

But there is no relationship between the cost of the franchise and your ultimate success and happiness. You have to do your own research, and read up on franchising.*

Size up the management of the franchise company you're interested in by talking to other people who already have franchises from that company.

Example: We didn't make our final decision until after we had visited the Molly Maid headquarters in Ann Arbor, Michigan, and talked to all the managers and to several other franchisees. Only then were we ready to commit our money— and our lives.

The amount we had to pay initially for the franchise and start-up materials from Molly Maid was $17,500.

Molly Maid told us it would take six months before we would start taking out more money than we were putting in and that we would need enough capital to keep running for that long.

Between the franchise fee, start-up costs and operating expenses, we put up $30,000 of our own money. It came from the sale of our home in New Jersey. We had put that money in the bank and rented a home in Virginia.

Our franchise turned profitable in just four-and-a-half months, although we didn't take in any real money for a year. But we always had the rest of the money we banked from the sale of our house to fall back on.

●**Get the training you need.** You need help with everything when you start out in a franchise. If you don't have any previous business experience—and most franchisees don't—you will have to be led by the hand each step of the way.

You will need training not only in the franchise business itself, but in the business basics— bookkeeping, marketing, managing people, etc.

●**Know it all.** Once the training is over, you'll be open for business, so use your train-

*Our favorite book on franchising is *Franchise Opportunities: A Business of Your Own* by Robert Perry. Sterling Publishing Co.

ing time to ask every question you can think of, such as…

●**How do I recruit** and train people?

●**How do I find** my best customers?

●**What are the worst mistakes** most start-ups make, and how can I avoid them?

Molly Maid flew us to its headquarters and put us up for a week of intense training.

We needed both a business plan and a marketing plan to help us get the business started and to set goals of where we wanted to be over time.

Molly Maid helped us create our plans and formulate our goals, and provided us with a program to track our progress toward achieving those goals.

All the help we got during the training period gave us a sense of "Yes, we can do this. There are people out there who have done it before us, and we can do it, too."

●**Hire people who work hard**—and work hard to keep them. Finding great employees is still our toughest challenge.

All franchise owners go through a lot of people at first because it takes time to find people who are trainable, willing to listen and willing to do a good job.

Start by advertising for help in newspapers. As you grow, employees will start bringing in friends and relatives. Offer a bonus to those who bring in a friend who stays three months.

Once you find good employees, reward them for their efforts. Pay a bonus each month to employees who score high in customer satisfaction. Pay an annual bonus to employees who perform well over the year. Those who do a good job should be praised in front of their peers.

Edd and Charlotte Davies, owners of a Molly Maid housecleaning franchise, 1175 Herndon Pkwy., Ste. 200, Herndon, VA 20170. Molly Maid was established in 1979 in Canada and expanded into the US in 1984. Today, Molly Maid has more than 250 locally owned and operated franchises.

More Productive Workdays

To make workdays more productive: throughout the day, ask yourself if what you are doing is the best use of your time. *Focus on top priorities*...not necessarily projects you enjoy. Start working only after you clearly understand a task. Stay focused on one activity at a time—do not jump from project to project. Keep your desk clear of distractions—if you use an item only occasionally, move it to a space out of the main flow. Refuse to spend time mediating between feuding coworkers. Don't compare your productivity level with anyone else's—just do your best and work as hard as you can.

Everything's Organized by Lisa Kanarek, founder of Everything's Organized, a Dallas-based consulting firm specializing in office organization. Career Press.

No More Problems With Interruptions

Keep an interruption log for one week—to track the sources of your interruptions.

Write down list who interrupts you...when...for what reason...and for how long. Then figure out what you can do to reduce the interruptions.

Also: Stop interrupting *yourself*. Remove distractions from your work area. Keep needed supplies close at hand. Set small goals with scheduled breaks. Do not start a new project without finishing an old one. Resist temptations to slack off, such as drop-in visitors. Do not procrastinate.

The Overwhelmed Person's Guide to Time Management by Ronni Eisenberg, a time-management consultant in Westport, CT. Plume Books.

The Best Times to Return Phone Calls

Return phone calls during the first hours of the morning and the last two hours of the afternoon. *Reason:* Most people are in their offices then and reachable by phone.

George R. Walther, president of Speaking from Experience, Inc., Seattle, and author of *Power Talking: 50 Ways to Say What You Mean.* Berkley.

Better Business Writing

Keep paragraphs short to avoid a gray wall of type that discourages reading. *Always add a PS.* It's usually the first thing—and sometimes the only thing—that gets read. *Handwrite something*, such as the salutation or the PS. This makes the letter more personal. *Helpful:* Use the PS to reiterate the letter's main point or to highlight a premium or other special offer.

Ilise Benun, editor of *The Art of Self-Promotion*, Box 23, Hoboken, NJ 07030.

For Ads that Get Results

Be different—use black and white when everything else is in color, or place a small ad when all the others are large.

Compose ads visually to draw viewers to a specific point—do not confuse them with a lot of imagery.

Communicate your message quickly, clearly and without an over-complicated design. Use simple, easy-to-read copy. Use pictures to convey as much of your message as possible—people spend two-thirds of their time looking at images, not words.

Research by Perception Research Services, Fort Lee, NJ, and Cahners Advertising Research Report, New York, reported in *Home Office Computing*, 555 Broadway, New York 10012.

Temporary Employees: The Essential Steps To Make Them More Productive

Joseph Gibbons
Towers Perrin

Through creative hiring and thoughtful management, a company's temporary workers can be much more productive. *Temps are especially important today because...*

● **Temporary workers form a larger portion of the staff** in more and more businesses than ever before. And—companies that downsize usually wind up hiring temps to fill in unanticipated staffing gaps.

● **There is stiff competition for temps.** This is especially true for those who are highly qualified. Today, temporary workers often choose their employers—not the other way around.

● **Temps are being hired for increasingly senior positions.** These positions include chief accounting officers and heads of major functions such as accounts receivable or computer services.

HIRING AND TRAINING

Obvious, but not always a consideration—before recruiting temps, make sure they are being hired for the tasks for which they are most needed...at the times when they are most useful.

Example: An Ohio bank did a time-and-motion study of retail customers who used their branches. Not surprisingly, they discovered that peak hours were 11:30 am to 1:30 pm.

Using that information, the bank advertised for temps who wanted to work during those hours five days a week. Applicants who responded to the ads were some of the most qualified in the area, including housewives with PhDs and retirees with more experience than some of the bank's managers.

Many companies forget one of the best places to look for talented temporary workers—their state labor department. Thanks to the Job Training Partnership Act, most state agencies are aggressive in recruiting and placing temps.

Another valuable source of temps—local companies that are downsizing. Many of these businesses welcome a chance to help laid-off workers find temp jobs.

Caution: Office systems and technology are changing so fast that it is unrealistic to expect that most temps won't need some on-the-job training.

SHREWD MANAGING STRATEGIES

Companies that are able to hire temps without going through a recruiting agency have more leverage in managing and motivating them. That's because when temps are hired through an agency, the agency controls many employment terms—from compensation to hours to types of assignments. That can demoralize temps and undermine productivity.

But because the vast majority of temps *are* hired through agencies, it is important to look for ways around these motivational obstacles.

BEST WAYS TO MOTIVATE TEMPS

● **Before long-term temps are hired,** ask applicants why they are temping and what their expectations are. From the answers, the company can find ways to motivate them.

Examples: A student who's saving for college might be interested in little more than monetary compensation. A housewife who's just reentered the workforce, on the other hand, might want help in finding a permanent position.

In both cases, the company can attempt to help fulfill those expectations, but only in exchange for top performance.

● **Avoid giving temps inferior working conditions** simply because they are temps. Temps quickly learn which companies treat them best and give them adequate space and support for doing their jobs.

Companies that give temps outdated equipment or uncomfortable furniture quickly get a bad reputation. And unless there's a labor glut, those businesses will have a hard time attracting qualified temps.

● **When appropriate, tell temps they'll be considered for permanent jobs** if their performance warrants it. In fact, hiring temps for potential full-time positions can be especially effective because the company gets a unique chance to see exactly how they do their jobs *before* they're hired.

If you use an agency, expect to pay at least $5,000 to hire away one of its temps. Regardless, the fee is often far less than the company would pay to recruit and train a worker who had not been evaluated on the job.

●**When hiring temps, consider telling them they'll be eligible for raises** after an initial period of work. Of course, if temps come from an agency, raises may require an up-front agreement with the agency so that extra compensation will go directly to the workers.

●**Make temps a key part of the enterprise.** Put them on memo lists, invite them to company functions and share information.

Problem: Permanent employees often don't fully accept temps as equals, a reluctance that obviously undermines productivity.

Solution: Before temps arrive, explain to permanent workers that...

●**Temps are here to help** give the company a competitive edge by raising productivity.

●**They must be treated with the same courtesy** and professionalism extended to permanent employees.

●**Regular employees will be evaluated on how well they work with temps.**

●**Consider providing benefits to temps,** perhaps prorated to the length of time they're expected to be on the job. At the very least, give them the same paid holidays that permanent coworkers receive.

Example: The Friday after Thanksgiving. If you don't give temps the paid holiday, it is unrealistic to expect their productivity to be high during the following week.

●**Consider giving them bonuses and rewards.** This is one of the most cost-effective ways to motivate temps and attract highly qualified temps.

Productivity can be hard to measure since they're usually not on the job more than a few months. Instead, offer spot bonuses for outstanding work.

●**Offer to become part of the temps' networks.** Tell them the company will put them at the top of the list for future temp jobs and alert them to positions in other companies. In return, ask temps to give the company names of talented colleagues.

Joseph Gibbons, human resources consultant for Towers Perrin, 335 Madison Ave., New York 10017.

Build Confidence

Build the confidence of those who work for you and they will reward you by accomplishing more than even they thought they could.

Effective: Stress their past successes, their individual and team accomplishments and regularly review what made those victories possible. Publish a regular list of individual and team/department achievements every month. Make sure the list is posted in a visible area. It lets employees know you believe in them and encourages a healthy competitive desire in others to make the list.

William Hendricks, PhD, editor of *Coaching, Mentoring and Managing.* Career Press.

 **Wrongful Termination Lawsuits...
Self-Defense Strategies**

Peter M. Panken
Parker Chapin Flattau & Klimpl, LLP

It's a bit late in the game to start thinking about how to avoid a wrongful termination lawsuit once an employee has already been fired.

In fact, one of the most effective defense measures against wrongful discharge lawsuits is a short statement on the employment application form specifying that employment at the company is on an "at-will" basis, giving the company full discretion in terminating employment. The statement should end with a place for applicants to sign, indicating that they understand and accept the terms of the statement.

ADDITIONAL DEFENSIVE STEPS

For people already on the payroll, it is vital to have a set of work rules spelled out in an employment manual listing any specific actions that could result in immediate dismissal.

For less urgent problems, we advise enforcing a clear and consistent program of progressive discipline—such as documented warnings followed by more severe measures leading, finally, to termination.

But before terminating anyone, answer these questions...

●**Is the reason for termination fair?** In many states, employees have won suits based on allegations that they were fired for filing workers' compensation claims, serving on juries or refusing to participate in practices they considered unprofessional, unethical or illegal.

Ultimately, in any wrongful termination suit, the case will be tried before a jury. Juries like to hit hard at employers who they think are being unfair. Multimillion dollar verdicts are possible if an employee wins big, including back pay, damages for pain and suffering and, if the jury thinks the company acted willfully or maliciously, punitive damages.

●**Did the person receive fair warning?** A typical recipe for a disastrous wrongful discharge lawsuit involves a long-term employee who received pay increases every year and whose personnel file contains no written warnings...and then was abruptly fired. It is important not only to impress on managers the need for fair warning of substandard performance, but also for documentation that an employee was given a reasonable opportunity to improve.

●**Is there any chance that the person being terminated may have any grounds for claiming discrimination?** Or that the company has violated a "contract" based on something said orally or promised in its personnel manual?

Employees must establish a prima facie case by showing:

●**Membership in a protected class** (race, sex, age, etc.).

●**Termination or some other adverse employment** action by the company.

●**Someone not in the protected class** received better treatment.

The company will need to be able to articulate a nondiscriminatory business reason for its actions that can't be disproved by the employee plaintiff.

●**Are you very clear that the person is guilty of what is being charged?** Always try to get the employee's side of the story *in writing*, before he/she gets to a lawyer who may embroider the facts. Check with witnesses.

●**If you were sitting on the jury, how would this case sound to you?** If you aren't confident about your defense, maybe you should reconsider, cut your losses and offer the person his/her job back. That would avoid the risk of compensatory and punitive damages, which under the Civil Rights Act of 1991 can range from $50,000 to $300,000 for each defendant. And—there may be no cap for damages under state antidiscrimination laws.

ALTERNATIVE DISPUTE RESOLUTION

Because lawsuits are expensive, time consuming and bad for morale, the only way for a company to really win employee litigation is to avoid it.

The use of alternative dispute resolution (ADR)—or arbitration—is creating a whole new world in which employment disputes can be resolved short of court action.

ADR can be especially useful in convincing an intransigent employee to engage in more reasonable settlement negotiations.

Best: Have all employees sign an agreement to arbitrate any dispute concerning the application of law to his employment or the termination of employment. Require complaints be submitted through a grievance procedure and waive claims not submitted through that procedure.

Even if arbitration is not final and binding in your state, your company can still require an arbitration procedure as a first step.

Result: The arbitration becomes, in effect, a minitrial. If the arbitrators deny an employee's charge, it could encourage that person to settle instead of going ahead with a full-fledged lawsuit. The company has a chance to see how its side of the story holds up with the panel of arbitrators and to evaluate how much risk full-scale litigation in front of a judge and jury might entail. This also gives the company a chance to reconsider its options. But the employer should assume that it will be bound by the arbitrators' decision.

Peter M. Panken, chair of the labor and employment law department at Parker Chapin Flattau & Klimpl, LLP, 1211 Avenue of the Americas, New York 10036.

Tape-Record Your Own Phone Calls

Tape-record your own phone calls and play them back afterward. It's the best way to improve your telephone technique. Hearing yourself the way others hear you enables you to eliminate annoying telephone habits—such as repeatedly saying "umm" and "you know" —and take simple steps to improve your telephone speaking manner.

Art Sobczak, editor of *Art Sobczak's Telephone Selling Report,* 13254 Stevens St., Omaha 68137.

Save Big Money on Long-Distance Calling

Philip Ghali
White & Blackwell Inc.

Large companies can use their leverage to pressure the big long-distance carriers— AT&T, MCI and Sprint—to give them lower long-distance rates.

While smaller companies do not have the calling volume to get such concessions—they, too, have great opportunities to cut their long-distance rates significantly.

Key: Sign up with one of the hundreds of long-distance phone service resellers. These companies buy long-distance time in volume— and at deep discounts—from the Big Three carriers. They then resell the time to end-user companies at a profit, but at still greatly reduced prices for end users.

Big advantage: The rate applies to all long-distance calling—regardless of distance or time of day. For many resellers, that rate is as low as 13¢ per minute.

Most long-distance resellers do not require the company to sign a contract for a minimum number of long-distance minutes.

With some of the carriers, signing a one-year contract earns customers even deeper discounts—as low as 11.9¢ per minute. Avoid carriers that charge a monthly fee.

Three of the top long-distance resellers are...

●*LCI International,* McLean, Virginia, 800-524-4685.

●*Telegroup,* Fairfield, Iowa, 800-338-0225.

●*Unidial,* Louisville, Kentucky, 800-895-7474.

Helpful: Find a discount provider that bills in increments of six seconds—you won't get charged for a whole minute when a call goes over by a few seconds.

For additional guidance, contact a private telecommunications consulting firm or local business contacts with experience in using such services.

Philip Ghali, White & Blackwell Inc., independent telecommunications consultants, 8801 McNulty Dr., St. Louis 63114.

Motion Attracts Trade Show Visitors

Motion attracts visitors at trade shows. Sales increase up to 50% when motion is added to point-of-purchase displays. Trade show booths can also benefit from the use of motion. Use materials that attract light, like metallic foils and neon colors. Backlit graphics, bubbling water towers and revolving signage can also help attract visitors. If using video and slide presentations, keep total length to about one minute—and pace them the way TV commercials are paced.

Tom Letourneau, president of Customer Development Group, trade show consultants, 3447 S. Norfolk Way, Aurora, CO 80013.

You Oughta Be in Pictures

Anyone can be an extra in a Hollywood movie. To qualify, you must register with a casting company that hires nonmembers of the Screen Actors' Guild (SAG).

Union rules require that for *every* TV show or movie, a certain number of extras hired must work under the union agreement. Joining SAG is no cheap shortcut. Membership is about $1,100 plus annual dues of $85. That's what a non-union extra earns in 30 days of work.

When you register as a non-union extra, the casting company records a summary of your physical features, availability, talents and a video image for a minimal fee of about $20. Then you just wait for a suitable small part.

Carl Joy, senior vice president of Central Casting and Cenex, a casting company that hires non-SAG actors, Burbank, CA.

For the Over-50 Applicant

Job applicants over age 50 should emphasize the advantages mature workers bring to an employer—more experience and skills, reducing the need for training...greater pride in work...more productivity, thanks to a better work ethic...good attitude and judgment developed through years of experience...stability and reliability.

Better Résumés in Three Easy Steps by Ben Field, an advertising executive in Evansville, IN. F&W Publishing.

Great Web Sites for Job Seekers

John Edwards

Adams JobBank Online is from Adams Media Corp., which specializes in self-help books for those seeking jobs. This site includes leads to technical, management, computer and medical jobs as well as a wide range of other types of positions. It also pro-vides a career center that includes profiles of companies, strategies for students who are graduating and job-fair listings (http:// www. adamsonline.com).

● **America's Job Bank** contains information on approximately 250,000 jobs. The site provides listings from 1,800 state employment service offices. The job openings originate from all over the country and represent all types of work—from professional and technical to blue collar (http://www.ajb.dni.us).

● **CareerMosaic** offers thousands of job listings in virtually all occupations from employers worldwide. It also provides helpful job-hunting advice, employer profiles and direct links to major corporations that are currently hiring (http://www.careermosaic.com).

● **CareerPath** is an indispensable resource for anyone who is looking for employment in or near any major US city. This site includes the Sunday job listings from *The New York Times...The Washington Post...Chicago Tribune...Los Angeles Times...The Boston Globe* and several other big city daily newspapers (http://www.careerpath.com).

● **NationJob Network** offers job listings that are culled from newspapers, businesses and numerous other sources. The site's Personal Job Scout (P.J. Scout) searches for positions based on a user's preferences, background and qualifications and returns leads via E-mail (http://www.nationjob.com).

John Edwards, a computer industry analyst and writer on high-tech subjects, 3111 Rte. 38, 11 Larchmont Commons, Ste. 118, Mount Laurel, NJ 08054.

How to Get The Headhunters To Hunt You

Millington McCoy
Gould, McCoy & Chadick

In order to be hunted by an executive recruiter, you have to maintain a visible profile in your industry.

That includes writing articles for industry publications...staying active in professional associations...consulting outside your job... volunteering for interdepartmental projects at work...and staying in touch with former associates.

If you've done all of this, you probably won't need to contact a recruiter because one will already have found you. *But if you haven't been found yet...*

● **Consult one of the recruiter directories.** The top two are *Directory of Executive Recruiters* ...and *Hunt-Scanlon's Executive Recruiters of North America.* They are available at most libraries.

● **Get recommendations.** Talk to colleagues, friends and people in your industry's professional associations. Ask which recruiters they have worked with—and send your résumé with a cover letter to your top choices.

● **Attend career-development programs** sponsored by your professional associations. Follow up a recruiter's lecture with a note introducing yourself and commenting on his/her presentation.

● **Ask friends in your industry to refer you to recruiters** when they are "hunted."

WHEN A HEADHUNTER CALLS

During the initial conversation with the recruiter, be sure to ask about the specific job opening and the company. What is the level of responsibility? Salary? Corporate culture?

If none of these are right for you, tell the headhunter what *would* be right. If you can, suggest someone else who might be good for the position. Remember that you will be judged by the quality of your recommendation. Good people know good people.

HANDLING THE INTERVIEW

The recruiter is probably interviewing many other candidates. You must demonstrate that you are the best choice. *To do this...*

● **Be knowledgeable and enthusiastic about your field of expertise.** This is especially important if you are currently unemployed.

● **Prepare questions for your interview.** This shows that you are actively interested.

Issues to cover: Job responsibilities, insider's information about the company, potential pitfalls of the position, possible career opportunities, what happened to the person previously holding the job.

Declining a position won't damage your relationship with a recruiter as long as you are professional and honest throughout the process.

TO KEEP HEADHUNTERS INTERESTED IN YOU

● **Offer to be a source for future searches.** If you're helpful, the headhunter will think of you when other openings arise.

● **Stay in touch.** Follow a meeting with a thank-you note. Periodically drop a line about your latest accomplishment or promotion. Don't write too frequently—only when something is newsworthy...every few months is ideal.

Millington McCoy, cofounder and managing director of Gould, McCoy & Chadick, a top executive-search firm, 300 Park Ave., New York 10022. She has served as a board member of the Association of Executive Search Consultants.

 **Better Résumés**

The best length for a résumé depends on the job you are applying for. A recent survey of executives at the 1,000 largest US companies found that 64% prefer to receive two-page résumés from candidates for executive positions...73% said they preferred to receive one-page résumés from applicants for staff-level jobs.

Survey by Accountemps, reported in *Office Systems96*, 1111 Bethlehem Pike, Springhouse, PA 19477.

Interviewing... Last Can Be Best

Schedule yourself to be the last job applicant of the day.

Reason: You'll be more likely to be remembered by the interviewer, while those who came before become just a blur of faces.

And—try to arrange it so that you make the follow-up call after the interview. Tell the interviewer you're going to be in and out for the next several days and ask if you can call back later in the day or the next morning. Then you'll have the advantage and will get a second shot to stimulate interest in your candidacy.

Robert Mayer, a Los Angeles–based attorney who also runs negotiating workshops and seminars. He is author of Power Plays: How to Negotiate, Persuade and Finesse Your Way to Success in Any Situation. *Random House.*

Smart Interviewing Strategies

Don't mistake friendliness for enthusiasm during an employment interview. Good interviewers are friendly to get candidates to relax and reveal more about themselves. Be careful not to relax too much—especially near the end of the interview, when candidates frequently let down their guard. Keep all your thoughts and comments focused on the job and the excellent work you can do for the organization.

Get Hired! Winning Strategies to Ace the Interview by Paul Green, PhD, an industrial organization psychologist in Memphis. Bard Press.

Be Discriminate about Making Friends when Starting a New Job

Beware the new close friend at work who latches onto you when you start a new job. He/she is likely to be someone who spends a lot of time passing along gossip about fellow workers. People like this love to find out everything about new hires. And they usually reach out to new employees for companionship, since experienced workers avoid them.

Self-defense: Before you start to develop any significant business friendships, try to learn as much as possible about the company's office politics and the personalities of your fellow workers. Establish communication with your boss, subordinates and as many peers as you can as soon as you can.

VGM's Complete Guide to Career Etiquette by Mark Satterfield, a career counselor in Alpharetta, GA. VGM Career Horizons.

Secrets of Successful Selling on the Internet

Jill H. Ellsworth
Oak Ridge Research

As the Internet rapidly becomes a valuable business tool, companies have new opportunities for selling products and services on the "net." However, because of the newness of electronic commerce and the innate confusion of high-tech business for many marketers, learning how to sell via the Internet can be a daunting challenge.

To learn the practical steps to selling on the Internet, we spoke with Jill Ellsworth, one of the country's top experts in Internet marketing…

Thousands of businesses have tried to sell on the Internet over the last couple of years. What have they learned? First of all, they've learned that having a good product—and an attractive Web site—isn't enough. Many companies had the mistaken notion that customers would magically appear once they established Web sites.

These sites—presentations in graphics, text and even sound on the World Wide Web—not only display advertising and product information, but can also be used to take orders and give customers video demonstrations of how products work.

Web sites differ from most conventional marketing outlets because nothing is actually sent to customers to electronically tune them into a company. Instead, it is up to the prospective buyers themselves to learn about the sites and to access them.

As a result, Internet marketing requires that a business pay special attention to the medium and to the customers whom it attracts.

Then what else does it take to sell via the Internet? First, conduct basic market research. Through surveys and available demographic data, determine how many potential customers have computers as well as how many actually use the Internet.

There are no clear data yet on what percentage of a company's customer base must be on-line to justify launching an Internet sales campaign. But clearly a business with 15% of its customer base on-line shouldn't risk as much of an investment as one with 50% on-line.

What about the Web site itself? What separates winners from losers? Above all, a successful Web site must be user-friendly. Specifically, it should be designed so that browsers can find what they want on it with only a few clicks of the mouse.

The site should also be up to date. Most savvy Internet users visit sites several times before they make a purchase. Out-of-date sites quickly lose their appeal.

I advise updating a business site at least once a week and whenever there's new information such as a change in price or merchandise.

How much does it cost to design and maintain a Web site? An attractive, efficient Web site costs $3,000 to $5,000 to launch, but the price skyrockets with the addition of sophisticated video and audio effects.

Monthly maintenance fees run $400 to $1,000, depending on how many users access the site and how often it is updated.

Companies that design sites are known as Web-site providers. To find a provider, look in the Yellow Pages under computers, in the business sections of daily newspapers and in local business journals.

Providers can also be located through referrals from marketing and computer consultants and from computer user clubs.

For ideas on Web-site design, look at CNN's (http//www.cnn.com) at the top end of the price scale, and at Virtual Vineyards' site (http//www.virtualvin.com) in the lower price range.

Once a business sets up a site, how can it attract enough electronic prospects? To attract customers, a Web site must be supported by a wide mix of Internet catalog listings and popular search engines.

A search engine is a software system that helps Internet users find Web sites that interest them. Without a search engine listing, even a person interested in a particular product would probably have a hard time finding an Internet marketer who sells it. *Popular engines:* Alta Vista, InfoSeek, Lycos, Webcrawler and Yahoo.

Catalog listings are directories of sites on the World Wide Web. *Popular catalogs:* Galaxy, Commercial Sites Index and Yahoo.

Web-site providers and most computer consultants have lists of engines and catalog listings, which can also be found on the Internet itself at http://www.search.com.

When you set up a Web site, simply give companies that make the popular search engines your company's Internet address, known as a *Uniform Resource Locator (URL)*. The more search engines you list it with, the better the chances of attracting customers.

What else is essential to successful Internet selling? For maximum impact, use your Web site to give Internet users all possible avenues for reaching the company.

Example: The site should list an "800" number if the company has one, and an address to write or fax for promotional giveaways or for more information.

But—of course, use the site to try to answer any questions that customers might have. Because the Web is an *information-based* resource, customers who use it often are motivated by a need for knowledge that they cannot or prefer not to get via conventional shopping.

It was clear from the start that computer-related products would sell especially well on the Internet.

What other types of products and services have also done well? Consumer products and services are best suited to Internet selling today. One of my favorite success stories is Virtual Vineyards, a California-based marketer of wines. Its Web site has great appeal to wine-savvy customers because it presents in-depth information about a wide variety of vintages.

In this respect, Internet customers are like catalog shoppers. Consumers who buy from catalogs peruse them at their leisure and crave lots of information before they buy a product. *Other Internet successes include…*

●**Harley-Davidson** (http://www.hdstamford. com), which recently began marketing clothing, motorcycle memorabilia and accessories as well as motorcycle parts via the Web.

●**Tennis Server** (http://www.tennisserver. com). This company attracts customers by posting a rich body of information about tennis and tennis products on its site.

One of the advantages of the Internet is that while it would be difficult to include thousands of pictures in a print ad, that number poses no problem on a Web site.

Example: A faucet maker uses its Web site to enable contractors to browse through hundreds of pictures of faucets—a task that would be inconvenient and time-consuming if they had to visit a showroom.

The Internet is also an effective way to reach repeat customers. Companies that regularly re-stock basic office supplies are prime customers, as are men who purchase the same style of shirt every few months.

Unlike print catalogs, however, Web sites can be changed immediately—as stocks run out and new merchandise is acquired.

Other hot products on the Internet appeal to collectors, hobbyists and sports nuts. Many of them are so passionate about their pastimes that they would indulge them anywhere. The Internet makes that easier since it takes the place of hard-to-find specialty shops and mail-order catalogs.

Example: Golfers can access several Web sites within minutes to see and order the latest clubs and other equipment.

What are some examples of selling efforts that have failed on the Internet? Companies that try to sell several different types of products at one Web site haven't had much success. The reasons are not yet fully understood, but these so-called horizontal malls probably don't offer customers much more than real malls do.

Businesses should also think twice about selling on the Web if their product or service is difficult to describe, if new customers usually come by word of mouth or if buyers want to see the actual product.

How does a company transact sales via the Internet? Businesses can use the Internet to invite phone or mail orders or to invite inquiries, after which a company rep can phone back and close the sale. Alternatively, a company can ask buyers to transmit their orders and credit card numbers directly over the Internet.

Despite fears about security on the Internet, it is proving to be just as safe as most other means of paying with a credit card. And consumers in general are becoming more comfortable with using the Internet for credit card transactions.

Jill H. Ellsworth, senior partner at Oak Ridge Research, Internet marketing consultants, 101 High Rd., San Marcos, TX 78666. She is also coauthor of *Marketing on the Internet.* John Wiley & Sons.

8

The Winning Edge

Life Lessons from the Famous and Wealthy

Michael Levine
Levine Communications

While writing my book *Take It from Me*, I interviewed more than 300 of America's most prominent and successful people and asked them to share their advice for career success.

Again and again, they returned to the classic principles that are so often ignored or overlooked in our busy times.

Here are the strategies that they use to do well at work—and in life...

KNOW WHERE YOU'RE GOING

With all that has been written about planning and goal setting over the years, you would think goal-setting skills would be second nature to us.

Yet an astonishing number of people still fail to give much thought to what they want out of life and how to get it.

Plans are dreams with deadlines. They include both a strong vision and steps for making that vision real.

In today's rapidly changing environment, your plans need to be flexible. But there's a big difference between having a plan that can be adapted and passively letting other people and circumstances determine your goals.

A good way to focus is to write an imaginary article about yourself to celebrate your 100th birthday. What would you like to be celebrated?

Example: Although I enjoy and am proud of my career as a theatrical publicist, I realized some years ago that I didn't want to die with nothing but the words *He made TV game-show hostess Vanna White famous* written on my tombstone. I wanted to create something that would outlive me and make a difference in people's lives. So I decided to write a book, which gave me a deep sense of accomplishment and purpose.

Helpful: A way to determine your vision is to make a list of everyone you admire—famous or not—with a word or two beside each name describing what you respect about that person. The ideas that come up over and over will reflect what you value most.

THROW YOURSELF INTO WHATEVER YOU DO

The people I interviewed didn't simply show up at their jobs every day. They worked with intensity—as if their lives depended on it. Successful people aren't satisfied with *good enough*. They prize excellence the way most of us value survival. Every one of them found some way of saying that passion is basic to success.

Actress Meryl Streep told me, *Take your heart to work, and ask the most and best of everybody else.*

Helpful: One way to inspire better performance in yourself is to associate with companies and people that reward excellence.

If you don't have passion, at least act as though you do until you find it. Your feelings will be inspired by your actions.

TAKE THE INITIATIVE

Comedian Steve Allen tells a story that he read as a youth, about a dozen boys who showed up to answer a help-wanted ad. A broom was partially blocking the hallway, and each boy who went in to be interviewed stepped over the broom on his way to the boss's office. Finally, one boy picked up the broom and moved it out of the way. He got the job.

Too many people don't take the initiative to do what's needed. Afraid of making mistakes, they keep doing things the way they've always been done. They wait for instructions or permission. Success doesn't come from making the fewest mistakes…it comes from getting results. You don't get results without action.

There are times when patience is called for. Moving too fast while negotiating can ruin a deal. But as a rule, successful people don't *wait*. They *do*.

USE YOUR IMAGINATION

Unsuccessful people think simplistically—as though there's only one right way and one wrong way to do things.

Successful people are more creative. They envision alternative scenarios. They invent multiple ways of asking a question and defining a problem. They come up with more than one solution.

Successful people are curious. They love to explore the questions, *What if…?* and *Why?* They reach breakthroughs by pursuing the questions that others never bothered to ask.

Example: Barbra Streisand is intensely curious about everything she does. Whether it is directing movies, acting or singing, she wants to understand every detail so that she can improve her craft.

Helpful: A good way to encourage multidimensional thinking is to make a *five-ways* list. Whatever your project, think of at least five ways to approach it.

Examples: Five ways to launch a new product or *five ways to improve customer service.* Don't censor yourself—and don't stop until you've come up with at least five ideas.

BE PERSISTENT—BUT POLITE

The people I interviewed had determination. When confronted with obstacles, they looked for ways around them. They did not give up.

Being doggedly determined doesn't mean suspending the rules of decorum and courtesy. Following up may get you the job, but making yourself annoying won't. Successful people are aware of how their actions affect others.

Politeness is not wimpy—it is good business. You would be amazed at how many people overlook the basics—*Would you mind if…, Is this a good time?* and especially, *Thank you.*

One of the most powerful tools for success is using your courage to ask for what you need …and coupling that with the sensitivity to treat others as you would like to be treated.

Michael Levine, president of Levine Communications, a major entertainment public relations firm representing celebrities and corporations, 433 N. Camden Dr., Beverly Hills 90210. He is author of *Take It from Me: Practical and Inspiring Career Advice from the Celebrated and the Successful* (Perigee) and *Lessons at the Halfway Point* (Celestial Arts).

How Some People Meet Life's Challenges... Cope with Difficulties... Survive Setbacks... And Prosper

Al Siebert, PhD
Portland State University

What's the secret of their success? Were these people gifted at birth with rare abilities that others can only envy?

Not at all. Successful people have the same inborn capacities that all humans possess—but they have simply *learned to use them better*.

They have developed the life skills built into our genetic blueprint and honed to perfection the tools that allow them to thrive at work...in relationships...in life. With these skills, they turn adversity to opportunity, obstacles to strengths.

During my decades of work as a psychologist, I've identified the key skills that make up the *success personality*—skills that you, too, can learn to build.

THE NEED TO HAVE THINGS WORK

Men and women who are the best at survival and success are skilled troubleshooters.

Successful people *want* and *need* things to work smoothly and well—for themselves and for others. They've developed a "feel" for the natural flow of things and a sense of how to work with the flow, not against it.

I call it the "synergistic personality"—this ability to know what's needed and the drive to supply it. It's both selfish and unselfish...you make the world a better place for yourself by making it better for others.

While synergy seems instinctive, it can be nurtured and honed...

●**Look for creative solutions**...and ways to turn obstacles into opportunities.

●**Approach every new or difficult situation with a question:** *How can I act so that things work out well for everyone?*

●**Learn to tell the difference** between *allowing* things to work well and *forcing* them to happen.

Perhaps the most subtle talent of synergistic people is the ability to sit back and let things run themselves when no help is needed. In this way, they save their energy for crises and obstacles, expend less effort and achieve great results.

THE DRIVE TO LEARN

In the "school of life," you learn valuable lessons *after* you take the tests. One skill that distinguishes successful survivors is their ability to learn from their experiences.

Success doesn't come from sitting back and waiting for others to tell you what to do. It is an intensely active quest for knowledge, new skills and new information. The most successful people enjoy trying out different approaches. Their playful curiosity drives them to get better, learn more and solve problems.

They're constantly getting smarter...by asking questions, searching for answers, learning from their mistakes and the mistakes of others. *To build life-learning skills...*

●**If an unplanned event upsets you**, express your feelings by writing in a journal or talking to a friend. Then reflect on the experience... replay it in your mind as an observer.

●**Ask yourself what you can learn from the event.** Imagine how you would act more effectively the next time something similar occurs.

●**Practice acting the way you want.**

BECOMING MORE FLEXIBLE

It's often hard to describe successful people. They're serious and humorous...industrious and lazy...calm and emotional.

Instead of being locked into rigid patterns, they're flexible enough to respond to the shifting demands of every situation. Having a varied repertoire of responses is especially crucial in these times of rapidly changing conditions.

Example: Most companies value an optimistic outlook that puts a hopeful, positive spin on plans and problem solving. But truly valuable team members can become intensely pessimistic before taking action...to expose flaws, risks, possible weaknesses. They have the courage to speak up.

Becoming more flexible may not come easily. It demands acting in ways you've ridiculed or condemned in others...allowing yourself to get angry even if you were raised to stay calm and to be assertive even if it feels authoritarian.

Practice, patience and time are necessary to develop parts of yourself that you've long suppressed.

LEARNING EMPATHY

Successful people don't regard other people as obstacles to be steamrolled over. They have the ability to step out of themselves and into the shoes of others...to think the way other people think and feel as they feel. Because they see every situation from different angles, they learn more.

We all have the potential for empathy, and practice makes it stronger...

• **In every situation**, ask yourself, *What is this person thinking and feeling?*

• **Be curious enough to verify your impressions by inquiring directly:** *I get the impression you're upset over this plan...am I right?* Each time you do this, you improve your ability to act synergistically.

DEALING WITH DIFFICULT PEOPLE

The two questions businesspeople most often ask me are *How can I work with negative people?* and *How can I handle angry people?* Unless you master these skills, you'll let others drain your energy and effectiveness.

If constant complainers and criticizers wear you down and irritate your nerves, look to your *own* attitude. You're permitting this to happen by *your* negativity...toward them.

Helpful: Develop a more positive attitude toward negative people. Appreciate the contribution naysayers make (putting a brake on unrealistic optimism, for example)...but stay in control to neutralize the toxic effects of their negativity.

• **Withhold attention from the constant complainer**...just keep working.

• Say, *You may be right*—and then change the subject. Or ask them to be quiet—tactfully (*Your complaining is troublesome to me...can we keep our discussions more constructive?*).

• **Be playful and beat them at their own game.** After a string of complaints, say, *Things are worse than you know*, and suggest more to be upset about.

• **Reward them when they're quiet or positive.**

The best way to handle angry people is with curiosity and empathy. Instead of withdrawing or angrily defending yourself, act as you would with a good friend. Listen, try to feel the anger the other person is feeling, ask clarifying questions. Agree that the feeling is legitimate...and then make constructive suggestions.

Al Siebert, PhD, an ex-paratrooper who has taught management psychology for more than 25 years at Portland State University and through corporate consulting and workshops, Box 505, Portland, OR 97207. http://www.thrivenet.com. He is author of five books, including The Survivor Personality. Berkley Publishing.

How to Simplify Your Life And Enjoy It Even More

Karen Levine

A simpler life is truly a happier life—one that's filled not with junk but with the people and things that are important to you. To see if your life could use some simplifying, answer the following two questions...

• **Is your life a complicated mix** of paperwork, obligations and clutter?

• **Are your relationships with others**, your errands, your bills and the "stuff" you've accumulated over the years squeezing the joy out of living?

If you answer "yes," then it's time to simplify your life.

GETTING STARTED

Begin by uncovering the mystery of how you currently spend those 16 or so hours that you're awake each day. For one week, jot down details about your daily activities. Ask yourself these questions about each task or event...

• **What am I doing?**

• **How efficient am I?**

• **When am I doing it?**

• **How satisfying is it?**

• **In what role am I** (mother, grandmother, employee, boss, volunteer) when I'm doing it?

At the end of each day, examine how you spent your time...

• **What offered you the most pleasure?**

• **What would you most like to change?**

THE SEVEN GUIDING PRINCIPLES

You can identify the things in your life that eat up your time and clutter your home, office —and mind. *Simply follow these seven guiding principles...*

• **Relax your standards.** Why iron the whole shirt if the collar is the only part that will show? Why make elaborate, homemade holiday gifts for everyone on your list—even the next-door neighbor?

Why wash the grills on your barbecue when you can just burn off what's there and scrape the grills down with a wire brush?

If you're struggling to meet standards because you find the effort satisfying—then keep it up. If, however, meeting your standards leaves you with too little energy to enjoy other things, it's time to relax them.

• **Free yourself of stereotypical roles.** It makes no sense to use your time and energy doing tasks you're neither good at nor enjoy just because they are traditionally done by men or by women.

Some men are great cooks and some women are gifted when it comes to fixing plumbing. Think about all that needs to be done in a day and divide tasks based on preference rather than on stereotypical roles.

• **Take time to figure out what you find most satisfying.** A lot of what we do and how we do it is the result of habit.

For years, I stayed up every night to watch the 11 o'clock news. In the morning I'd be tired. In fact, I usually fell asleep during the broadcast!

At some point, I realized that I preferred the morning newspaper as a source of news and that bedtime was more pleasurable when I listened to music and read a good book. What's really best for you?

• **Create time for the activities you care about.** If you hate cooking and love reading,

why spend two hours on dinner preparation and save a mere 15 minutes before bed to read your beloved books? With a little thought and effort, you can shave time off the things that don't matter to you...

• **Instead of scrubbing aluminum pans,** boil in them water that has been mixed with a teaspoon of cream of tartar.

• **Instead of peeling carrots and other vegetables,** scrub the dirt off them with a scrub sponge or bristle brush.

• **Line your cat's litter box with a garbage bag** and fasten it around the rim with a rubber band. When it's time to empty the box, just remove the band, lift and twist-tie the bag shut.

• **Learn to enjoy what's in front of you.** There's skill involved in looking at what's in front of you and finding the gift in it. Live in the moment—truly finding the joy in where you are and what you're doing—and you'll cut away all kinds of mental and emotional clutter.

• **Learn to be flexible.** Allow yourself flexibility in all aspects of life—what you eat when, what you do when, how you typically react to a challenge or problem and how you might react, etc. *Examples...*

• **Eat a baked potato for breakfast** and pancakes for dinner.

• **Try hosting a pot-luck dinner party** and letting everyone just bring what they want.

• **Set your alarm a half hour early two or three times a week** and use that time to indulge yourself—to read, lie in bed, meditate or exercise.

• **Prioritize.** What activities, material possessions and relationships are you able to live without? What's important for you to preserve? What new activities or things would you like to incorporate into your life? We all have things that we must do and would rather not, but we'll have more time and energy to invest in the pleasures of life if we prioritize.

Exercise: As you begin to examine your life and keep track of your time, think of your activities in terms of...

• **The things that are important and that only you can do.**

• **The things that are important but can be put off or done by someone else.**

• **The things that aren't all that important and can easily be done by someone else.**

You have the ability to make choices—and to choose a simpler and more satisfying life!

Karen Levine, a writer of books, television shows and magazine articles. She is author of *Keeping Life Simple: 7 Guiding Principles, 500 Tips & Ideas.* Storey Publishing.

How to Have Much More Energy than You Do Now

Ronald Hoffman, MD
Hoffman Center

Accomplishing what you set out to do each day requires time *and* energy. Without energy, time is of little use.

Yet more people today focus all of their efforts on beating the clock rather than considering ways in which they can boost their energy levels.

Complaints about feeling tired account for about 500,000 doctor visits every year—second only to colds and flu.

WHY WE GET TIRED

The body is constantly striving to achieve a perfect, healthy harmony. It does this by channeling energy to the cells, where the energy is harnessed and converted into fuel.

The main source of energy in the human body is glucose. This body "fuel" can be *stored* —or put into action—depending on your body's needs. As long as your body has enough fuel, it can function properly.

However, when it is confronted by a constant stressor, such as anxiety or lack of sleep, your body loses its ability to adapt and rejuvenate. This often results in fatigue, sheer exhaustion—and even illness as your immune system weakens.

HOW TO BEAT FATIGUE

No two people have the same fatigue "factors" —he things that cause them to feel tired and worn out.

However, learning the general rules about limiting the biggest causes of fatigue is an important start to boosting your energy…

• **Get up off the couch.** Inactivity can actually make you *more* tired.

Studies have shown that exercise helps create a wave of energy in your body, allowing it to respond quickly to internal and external demands.

Exercise can also help increase your metabolism so you generate more oxygen and burn fuel more efficiently. And it raises the levels of your *endorphins*—the "feel good" chemicals in your brain that help reduce pain and make you more alert.

Examples: Skipping rope…walking fast… climbing stairs.

Caution: Overexertion can cause your muscles to produce a waste product called lactic acid, which not only causes pain, but means that your body is functioning without an adequate oxygen supply. Make sure you discuss your exercise plan with your doctor.

• **Get to sleep at the same time every night.** Sleep allows your body to replenish its energy. Moreover, the body has a natural rhythm that responds to light and darkness and tells it when to rest.

Disruptions to this rhythm, whether they're a result of staying out late, working the night shift or flying to another time zone, can cause irritability, illness and, of course, fatigue.

But getting *too* much sleep can cause a constant feeling of lethargy known as "sleep intoxication."

Recent data show that on average, people slept one hour less in 1996 than in 1940. Even though our basic physiological needs haven't changed, the dictates of modern society have.

Helpful: If you lose an hour or so of sleep one night, make it up gradually—catching an extra half hour to 45 minutes is usually enough to reset your clock.

If you're traveling to a different time zone, try to conform to the new schedule as quickly as possible. A walk outside in the early morning light will help reset your body clock.

• **Eat energy-boosting foods.** Food is one of the most overlooked sources of fatigue.

Example: Refined sugar—the type found in carbohydrates like cookies, doughnuts and many breads—can cause a sharp surge in blood sugar levels. That causes your metabolism to go awry, resulting in listlessness, irritability and exhaustion.

Additionally, some people are unaware that they have a food intolerance—a reaction to certain foods that causes stress to the body and leads to a constant state of low energy.

Common triggers: Dairy products, corn, nuts and wheat.

Helpful: Play diet detective for three or four days. Replace the foods you eat regularly with meals that focus on protein (fish, skinless poultry), complex carbohydrates (beans, legumes and unmilled whole grains like brown rice, barley, oats) and monounsaturated fats (olive and canola oil).

These foods are converted to energy slowly, allowing the body to maintain a metabolic balance. Avoid beef, pork, whole dairy products, white flour, refined sugar and stimulants such as caffeine, which actually deplete the body's energy resources.

If after this trial period you notice that you are beginning to feel more energized, it's a sure sign that your diet may be the culprit.

● **Manage your time more efficiently.** Many people believe that to be successful, they need to ride the crest of an energy high.

But, while a busy life can move you to excellence, it can also rob your body of much-needed rest and restoration.

Helpful: Create an oasis from the demands of your life. Allocate time to get your work done effectively and efficiently and then create a balance between sleep, structured exercise and unstructured time to relax and do something enjoyable.

● **Stop thinking and worrying only about yourself.** Have you ever noticed that *some* people seem to have endless reserves of energy? It's often because energy has a funny way of producing more energy.

People who put out a lot of energy are invigorated by their activity. Instead of focusing on their own worries and anxieties—negative energy—they shift their efforts to helping others. Positive energy creates more positive energy.

Example: Altruism is one of the best ways to achieve this. Helping people at work to do their jobs better or volunteering after work makes you feel better about yourself, which helps build your energy reserves, not to mention your self-esteem.

Ronald Hoffman, MD, director of the Hoffman Center, a nutritionally oriented medical practice, 40 W. 30 St., New York 10014. He is author of *Seven Weeks to a Settled Stomach* and *Tired All the Time: How to Regain Your Lost Energy.* Pocket Books.

Greetings from the 100+ Club

Walter M. Bortz II, MD
Stanford University Medical School

As we age, our bodies go through biological changes that alter how we look and feel. How rapidly we age is within our control.

Most people begin a gradual mental and physical shutdown years before death occurs —a shutdown that robs them of many healthy, fulfilling years.

Most scientists now agree that the maximum human life span approaches 120 years. Living 100 years or more is not a freak of nature. Right now, there are an estimated 50,000 Americans over 100 years old. By the year 2050, there will be *one million* over age 100.

To take that all-important first step and make the commitment to a long, productive life takes…

● **Smarts**—the ability to distinguish natural, normal signs of aging from the societal stereotypes that turn up in advertising and movies.

● **Guts**—having the resiliency to stay the course in the face of small setbacks or minor aches and pains that begin to show up more regularly after age 50.

DIET

Most of us are too sedentary, which puts us at dietary risk.

● **Stay active.** You should burn about 1,500 to 2,500 calories a day to maintain your weight. Activity clearly facilitates weight control and digestion.

● **Eat a varied diet.** Go easy on salt and animal fats, which are found in meat and dairy products. Instead, increase your intake of carbohydrates and fiber by eating fresh fruits and vegetables. Steer clear of foods that have undergone extensive chemical processing.

As important as knowing what to eat is knowing *when* to eat. We Americans tend to call a cup of coffee breakfast...a sandwich and a soda lunch...and then at dinnertime, we sit down to a big plate of food.

Better: Eat four or five smaller meals spaced evenly throughout the day. Studies show that eating behavior can lower cholesterol levels.

Very important: Don't let yourself dry up. Many experts recommend drinking at least six eight-ounce glasses of water per day. But most people don't come close to reaching that goal.

Older people whose sleep is disrupted by the need to urinate at night may cut back on fluids to about three glasses per day.

Helpful: Drink enough water early in the day, so that the bladder has an easier time at night.

ATTITUDE

Keeping your body healthy is critical for longevity. So is the right mental outlook. You must first believe that a long, fulfilling life is a realistic personal goal. Then other important attitude adjustments come into play.

●**Be an optimist.** Don't dwell on negative thoughts, and don't be discouraged by occasional setbacks.

●**Stay in control.** Self-sufficiency, autonomy and independence are critical to successful aging.

●**Maintain your creative spark.** You don't have to write a book. Stimulate your creativity by reading a book—preferably by an author or on a subject now unfamiliar to you. Or study a new language, take an art class, tend a garden, learn to play a musical instrument.

●**Train your brain.** Smart people live longer. Keep learning. It helps your memory and presents new opportunities for productive interaction with others.

●**Make yourself necessary.** Stay interested and involved with the world around you. Do volunteer work, care for a pet, work on a project with your grandchildren or the neighbor's kids.

An often-overlooked quality-of-life issue for older people: Recognize that sex is for life. Older people can and do engage in and enjoy sex, despite the many myths surrounding the idea of sexual behavior in those who have passed reproductive age.

Sexual problems among the elderly were believed to be mostly psychological, but new evidence points to many physical causes, including chronic illness and prescription drug use. Responsibility, trust and intimacy are the keys to better sex at any age. *Goal:* A robust sex life into the 90s and beyond.

●**Sleep.** First renew your body by getting enough sleep. Many older people experience disturbed sleep, which has been considered a natural consequence of the aging process.

However, the real culprit may be inactivity. It has been demonstrated that, after physical exercise, older people experience a decrease in the time it takes to fall asleep, and that, once asleep, they remain asleep longer.

A warm bath two hours before your desired sleep time may also be helpful. A bath helps you unwind and often eliminates stress that may keep you up.

●**Recharging your emotional and mental resources.** This may be achieved in a number of ways, but one of the most enjoyable and rewarding is travel. Instead of dashing from one place to another, take time to savor the journey as well as the destination.

EXERCISE

In any exercise program, the first step is the hardest. But even a small step is a good start. A walk around the block is better than spending the whole day in your favorite chair, and you can increase your distance in gradual increments that feel right for you. Optimal health value comes with three half-hour exercise sessions per week, at an intensity that increases your heart rate and makes you sweat but still allows you to carry on a conversation.

LIVING TO 100

Here are some useful strategies for achieving your Diet, Attitude, Renewal and Exercise (D.A.R.E.) goals...

●**It takes time.** Don't think you'll completely remake yourself tomorrow. Even small steps will set you in the right direction. Walk to the post office, take the stairs instead of the elevator, begin to reduce your cholesterol level, get involved with people and new projects.

●**Look for role models for later in life.** The news is full of stories of 80- and 90-year-old people who are earning college (or advanced) degrees, leading dance and theater groups or doing useful volunteer work.

●**Arm yourself with knowledge.** Your muscles and brain don't have to wither away as you age. Keep your mind active by reading, playing games, doing puzzles, etc.

●**Small failures should not become excuses to quit.** If you're sore after walking to the post office, know that some pain may be expected. If you're short of breath, slow your pace but keep going.

Walter M. Bortz II, MD, clinical associate professor of medicine at Stanford University Medical School and a practicing physician at the Palo Alto Medical Foundation. He is author of Dare to Be 100. *Fireside Books.*

How to Build Brain Power

Arthur Winter, MD, FICS
New Jersey Neurological Institute

Mental abilities don't have to decline with age. Cared for properly, the brain can be maintained in top condition even beyond age 100. *What researchers have found:*

●**The idea that a great many brain cells are lost as we age is a myth**—based on faulty research.

●**There is no significant difference in metabolism** between healthy older brains and healthy younger brains.

●**A stimulating environment** can produce new glial (supporting) cells in the brain at any age.

●**The abilities of the brain's neurons** (message-carrying cells) can also be enhanced at any age.

For your brain to thrive, however, it needs exercise, nourishment and protection from toxins. To keep your brain in top condition…

STRETCH YOUR SENSES

One of the brain's important functions is to process sensory input. "Exercising" your various senses on a regular basis increases the brain's metabolism and blood flow—and enhances your ability to receive and process sensory information.

●**Vision exercise:** Take a penlight or small flashlight and hold it over your head. Stare straight ahead, then look up at the penlight without moving your head for a count of five. Repeat with the penlight below your head, then five inches from your right ear and five inches from your left ear. Do it with both eyes open, then close each eye in turn, and repeat. These exercises stimulate the areas of the brain involved in light perception.

●**Hearing exercise:** Tune in to a news program or talk show on the radio and turn the volume all the way down. Use your dominant hand to slowly draw a pencil line on a piece of paper, while using your nondominant hand to slowly turn up the volume. As soon as you can make out what's being said, stop drawing. Repeat at least once a week, trying to make the line shorter each time.

●**Smelling exercise:** Your olfactory (smelling) nerves are connected directly to the brain's limbic system—which also deals with sex, hunger and thirst.

To stimulate this area, take six cotton swabs. Wet each swab in one of the following liquids—vanilla flavoring, ammonia cleaner, cooking oil, water, alcohol and vinegar. Put each swab into a separate envelope, with a slip of paper labeling the scent. Close your eyes, shuffle the envelopes, remove each swab in turn and sniff it, and write down what each scent is. (Allow a count of 60 between scents.)

EXERCISE YOUR CREATIVITY

Creative thought requires that the brain's normally dominant left hemisphere give up control to the more intuitive right hemisphere.

The following exercises will stimulate the "right brain" and encourage communication between hemispheres.

- **Name as many breeds of dogs** as you can think of.

- **Finish this sentence** as many different ways as you can: "Her/his eyes were as green as _____ ."

- **Make a row of circles.** Use each circle to draw a different object (e.g., a smiling face/a sun/a target). Then repeat the exercise using a row of squares.

- **In three minutes**, write as many different words beginning with "Y" as you can.

- **Study clouds** to discover what images you can see.

DO AEROBIC EXERCISE DAILY

Everyone knows that regular exercise is good for your heart *and* your waistline.

But a daily session of aerobic exercise is also very important for your brain. It increases blood and oxygen flow, boosts the brain's production of stress-relieving endorphins and prevents depression.

Useful activities: Walking, jogging, tai chi chuan, swimming, bicycling, square dancing, dancing to your favorite popular music.

CONTINUE TO LEARN

Education improves the health of the brain, especially as you age. Every time you learn, you create new connections between neurons.

Ideas: Take a college course in an area different from your expertise, do puzzles, learn to play chess or take up a challenging hobby. *Best of all:* Learn a new language or a musical instrument.

Turn off the television! Watching TV is a passive act, requiring minimal mental activity.

IMPROVE YOUR MEMORY

Short-term memory can be improved by:

- **Writing down what you want to remember**, then repeating it out loud. This stimulates both the right (visual) and left (verbal) parts of the brain.

- **Developing word-association skills.** *Example:* Take a word, then write down four related words.

To facilitate transfer of new information into long-term memory, review it 10 minutes later (when initial consolidation occurs). Further reviews should be one day, one week, one month and six months after your first study session.

Caution: If you experience a rapid, progressive decline in your memory, or chronic headaches or confusion, see a neurologist for a full neurological exam. The cause may be diabetes, concussion or early Parkinson's, all of which can be treated by a doctor.

Normal forgetfulness: Misplacing car keys …getting lost in an unfamiliar neighborhood.

When to worry: Holding your car keys in your hand, but not remembering why…driving your car, and suddenly forgetting where you are going.

EAT A HEALTHFUL DIET

A sound diet is essential for optimal brain function. Keep sugar intake down, and salt and fat to a minimum.

Recommended foods: Grains, beans, vegetables and fruit. *Other important nutrients for a healthful diet:*

- **The B vitamins** thiamine, niacin and especially B-12. I often prescribe monthly B-12 injections for patients over age 50. B-12 is also found in meat and dairy products.

- **The amino acids** tyrosine, tryptophan (found in milk and starchy foods) and acetylcholine (derived from meat, fish, dairy products and grains).

- **Ginkgo.** I prescribe this herbal supplement to improve blood flow in the brain.

AVOID TOBACCO AND ALCOHOL

Besides damaging your lungs, cigarette smoking also reduces oxygen flow to the brain.

Alcohol is worse: Alcohol actually destroys brain cells. The alcoholic's brain is softer than normal, and animal studies have found heavy alcohol intake causes changes in the way nerves are organized. *If you must drink:* Avoid distilled liquor. Drink wine or beer instead.

Arthur Winter, MD, FICS, a neurosurgeon at the New Jersey Neurological Institute, Livingston, NJ. He is coauthor of *Build Your Brain Power—The Latest Techniques to Preserve, Restore and Improve Your Brain's Potential.* St. Martin's Press.

Six Ways to Sharpen Your Memory

Get enough sleep—the brain uses sleep to restore itself.

- **Improve your aerobic fitness.**
- **Exercise your mind.**
- **Be nutritionally balanced.**
- **Discuss with your doctor medications you take.** Some—either individually or in combination—may affect the memory.
- **Keep a note card or small pad and pen to jot down what you need to remember.**

Barry Gordon, MD, PhD, author of *Memory: Remembering and Forgetting in Everyday Life*. MasterMedia Ltd.

No More Procrastination

Change procrastination into action by challenging yourself to get a task done in less than a half-hour…and then committing yourself to an even shorter time period for the next task.

Or…promise yourself that you will start working on a project for just 10 minutes and then quit if you get bored.

If you continue to have trouble getting started, figure out why. You may need clarification or help from someone else.

Reward yourself for completing parts of any project—perhaps by taking a walk…spending a few minutes reading an article that interests you…or taking another type of short break.

Lisa Kanarek, founder of Everything's Organized, a Dallas-based consulting firm specializing in office organization and author of *Everything's Organized*. Career Press.

Replacing Bad Habits

Bad habits don't really disappear—but they can be replaced. They exist for good psychological reasons, even if they are not effective at what they are supposed to do. *Example:* Eating to relax.

Self-defense: Replace a bad habit with one better for health and effective in filling basic needs.

Example: Instead of simply trying to keep away from fattening foods, concentrate on all the good things you can eat that are delicious …healthful…nurturing.

100 Ways to Motivate Yourself by Steve Chandler, a corporate trainer based in Gilbert, AZ. Career Press.

How to Tell when Someone Is Lying

Charles V. Ford, MD
University of Alabama at Birmingham School of Medicine

The secret to detecting lies is to focus on *how something is being told to you*, rather than on *what is being said*.

WHEN INTERVIEWING JOB CANDIDATES

It is common for job hunters to bend the truth about prior income, work history and reasons for leaving jobs. While big lies can be uncovered by checking out information on résumés, smaller ones require astute questioning.

Helpful: Listen for a lack of verbal and physical spontaneity. Applicants who are lying may sound wooden and automatic as they run through their rehearsed programs.

Interrupting their planned scripts with specific questions will throw them off guard and make it easier to glean the truth.

It also pays to watch for what I call *emblems of emotion*. These are largely unconscious body movements, such as shrugs, grimaces, nods or frowns, that reveal what a person really thinks. When an *emblem* conflicts with what's being said, it suggests that the speaker may not be saying what he/she really believes.

Examples: An initial head nod indicating *yes* may be a clue that the person's *no* response is a lie. Shrugging and then going on to state strong agreement may be a sign that the speaker is not so sure.

WHEN TALKING WITH TEENAGERS

While small children don't lie much, teenagers lie a lot. This is a time in life when they're naturally inclined to push limits. They lie to avoid punishment. They may even lie when they know there's no need to do so, just to establish a sense of independence.

Helpful: Recognize that lying is part of the normal developmental process. By allowing teens increasing autonomy and freedom, you can reduce their perceived need to lie.

At the same time, don't underestimate your teen's capacity for lying and the need for your direction. Some lies can be injurious to their well-being.

Spotting the signs: When lying, teens are more likely to display an increased number of *adapters*—nervous movements, such as scratching or playing with their hair. They will also overact, in an effort to cover up their nervousness.

If you suspect a teen is lying about things that could harm him, be direct. Instead of grilling him with questions, simply say, *I'm concerned that you're not telling me the truth. And if you're not, you're putting yourself at risk and we're going to have to work this out.*

WHEN DATING

Everyone tries to put his best foot forward when dating or meeting someone new. But there are some differences between the sexes in what they lie about and how they lie.

For cultural reasons, men tend to deceive about their occupations and incomes. Women tend to deceive about ages and personal histories.

While men's lies are more lies of commission, women's lies are more lies of omission. In other words, men typically will make direct statements to pump themselves up—whereas women will subtly try to weave impressions by leaving things out.

Helpful: As everyone knows, interrogation-like tactics do not go over well in romantic interactions. Instead, you want to detect deceit without letting the other person know that you're doing it.

When interacting with a man: Keep careful track of the statements he makes and come back to them later in the conversation by asking a question regarding each one.

This dance will put the man off guard and let you get more details in order to spot inconsistencies. After all, the more details someone has to come up with, the more he has to lie and the easier it is to detect.

When interacting with a woman: Pay special attention to what a woman *doesn't* say. If she describes a big trip to Europe but doesn't mention any companion, you might wonder with whom she went.

Closely observe body language while she's talking. If she seems stiff, tense and is leaning away from you rather than toward you, she may be holding back verbally as well. Watch also for facial and/or neck flushing in response to questions.

WHEN ON THE PHONE

Talking on the phone deprives us of visual lie-detection clues. But it frees us to tune in intently to language and voice clues and makes it easier to ask direct questions.

Remember that talking on the phone also makes the other person more confident. It's much easier for people to lie when they don't have to face you.

Helpful: Listen for signs of deceitful language, including an endless patter of irrelevant and extraneous information. People who are lying tend to create a lot of noise, talking more than they should in the hope that any lies will be lost.

The trick is to slow them down by frequently interjecting questions such as, *I'm sorry, would you repeat that?*

Once you get them slowed down, listen carefully to how they talk. When lying, they will hesitate, speak more slowly, use fewer words and may make more grammatical errors. And—the pitch of their voices is likely to rise.

Charles V. Ford, MD, professor of psychiatry and director of the Neuropsychiatry Clinic at the University of Alabama at Birmingham School of Medicine. He is author of *Lies! Lies!! Lies!!! The Psychology of Deceit.* American Psychiatric Press.

9

Investment Savvy

How to Build Your Fortune... Even if You Don't Have A Lot to Start With

Harold Evensky, CFP
Evensky, Brown, Katz & Levitt

You don't need a lot of money to make a lot of money. You just need to invest your money prudently...be willing to leave it invested for *at least* five to 10 years...and accept the ups and downs of the economy and the markets.

Bonds and bank accounts won't make you a millionaire. They barely keep pace with inflation.

Here, though, are investments with the potential for strong returns that are open to investors with as little as $2,000. *Ideally, you'll want to invest in at least two of these invest-* *ments to give your assets enough diversity and lower your risk...*

REIT MUTUAL FUNDS

REITs—or real estate investment trusts—are companies that invest in a range of properties.

I expect these companies will produce some great returns in the near future as local economies in many regions of the country continue to bounce back. In fact, I think REIT funds could outperform blue-chip stocks over the next three to five years, returning as much as 15%.

But the best reason to invest in REIT funds is that their success isn't as dependent on the same economy and business cycles as most other stocks.

So the smart strategy is to invest in REIT funds in addition to—not instead of—stock mutual funds. REITs will likely do well during a period when stock funds do poorly, since REITs don't often rise and fall with the stock market. *My current no-load favorite...*

●**Cohen & Steers Realty Shares.** This fund has a minimum initial investment of $2,000 if you purchase shares through a discount

153

broker like Charles Schwab (800-435-4000)… Fidelity Funds Network (800-544-9697)…or Price Waterhouse (800-934-4443). 800-437-9912.

SMALL-CAP DIVERSIFIED INTERNATIONAL FUNDS

These funds invest in small companies outside of the US—typically concentrating in mature markets such as those of Europe. Over the past five years, these funds have returned 16.2%. *My current no-load favorite…*

•**Barr Rosenberg International Small Cap Series.** The fund itself is brand new. However, the group that runs it has a great track record. There is a minimum initial investment of $2,500. 800-447-3332.

MICROCAP FUNDS

These funds invest in the market's smallest stocks—generally those with market capitalizations of less than $300 million or so.

I prefer microcap funds whose managers have a "value" style of investing—their managers select underpriced rather than growth stocks. Research shows that these stocks provide the best returns over time. Over the past five years, these funds have returned 15.7%.

Look for a fund that has less than $300 million in assets. Higher asset levels can hinder a microcap fund manager's performance. *My current no-load favorite…*

•**Royce Microcap Fund** has a $2,000 minimum—but you can invest with as little as $500 if you set up an automatic investment plan and commit an additional $50 or more per month. 800-841-1180.

EMERGING-MARKET FUNDS

These funds invest in companies in developing markets, such as Latin America, Africa, Eastern Europe and the Far East.

Choose a fund that spreads its investments among emerging markets around the world instead of concentrating in just one region, such as Latin America. That will remove some risk.

Warning: Emerging markets can produce some tremendous long-term returns, but also some of the world's greatest short-term volatility.

Example: The average emerging-markets fund fell nearly 15% in 1994, and many funds fell much further.

My current no-load favorite…

•**Montgomery Emerging Markets** has a minimum initial investment of $1,000. 800-572-3863.

DIVIDEND REINVESTMENT PLANS

DRIPs let individuals invest directly in select stocks. Because these investments are made through the company that issued the stock, not a broker, you save the commission, which could otherwise eat up the profits on small stock purchases.

As a result, this is an effective way for investors to buy individual stocks when they don't have a lot of money.

In my opinion, small investors are best served to stick with mutual funds and leave stock selection to professional money managers.

But if you already invest in individual stocks and are comfortable with them, here are some big-name DRIPs with low barriers to entry…

•**Exxon**/800-252-1800.

•**Home Depot**/800-774-4117.

•**McDonald's**/800-774-4117.

•**Procter & Gamble**/800-764-7483.

Harold Evensky, CFP, a principal of Evensky, Brown, Katz & Levitt, 241 Sevilla Ave., Coral Gables, FL 33134. He is author of *Wealth Management*, a book for financial planners and thoughtful investors. Irwin.

Good Starter Investment

Municipal bond funds are good starter investments for people with small amounts of money to invest—$40,000 or less—who want to generate tax-free income. Buy funds with low expenses to maximize yield.

Drawbacks of municipal bond funds: Yields may vary—they are not fixed, as in the case of individual muni bonds…funds buy medium-quality muni bonds…you must sell funds to get your money back and, therefore, have market risk. Look for funds that give tax-free income in your state.

James Lynch, editor of *Lynch Municipal Bond Advisory*, Box 20476, New York 10025.

To Find a Winning Stock Investment

To find a winning stock investment, look to see how much a company's CEO has invested in his own company's stock.

Recent study: Companies with above-average CEO stock ownership returned 11.4% to shareholders annually, compared with only 7.3% by companies with below-average CEO ownership. *Keys:* A large investment by a CEO in his/her own company indicates that he is motivated to make the company succeed, and that he is confident it will succeed.

Ira Kay, national practice director for executive compensation consulting at The Wyatt Company, 461 Fifth Ave., New York 10017.

The Best Time To Buy a Stock

The ideal time to buy a stock is right after brokerage analysts begin announcing new, upward earnings estimates for the company.

Reason: Analysts's estimates convey new information that is not yet reflected in stock prices.

Strategy: Ask your broker to call you as soon as top analysts announce positive forecasts for companies you're considering. *Companies with recent higher earnings estimates:* Intel (NASDAQ: INTC)…and Merck (NYSE: MRK).

Ben Zacks, executive vice president of Zacks Investment Research, which tracks analysts' earnings estimates.

When to Sell Your Stock

If you bought the stock for growth, hold it as long as the company's earnings continue to rise steadily. If profits slow, find out why—and sell unless you have good reason to believe profits will increase within a year.

If you bought the stock for income: Keep it as long as the company is financially solid and its earnings per share are rising more than

5% per year—and exceed the dividend by at least 10%. If earnings stagnate or the firm's creditworthiness is downgraded, seriously consider selling.

Also: Consider selling any stock that becomes overvalued or whose price suddenly drops 20% or more for no apparent reason.

Dun & Bradstreet Guide to Your Investments 1996 by Nancy Dunnan, a New York financial expert and author of over 30 books. HarperPerennial.

Shrewder Stock Selling

If you must sell investments during a market downturn, consider stocks you have been gifted but did not want to sell because of large capital gains since being received. Selling them with smaller gains reduces the tax bite.

If, at the same time, you also sell stocks that you've purchased that have lost value, you can offset gains against losses and cut taxes further.

Sell a stock versus selling a stock fund? It usually makes sense to sell the stock and retain the diversification of the fund.

Selling bonds before maturity? Sell the shortest maturities, whose returns tend to be low…or the longest, which are most vulnerable to inflation.

Lewis Altfest, president of L.J. Altfest & Co., fee-only financial planners based in New York.

Time-Tested Investment Advice from David Granger

David Granger
Ingalls & Snyder LLC

David Granger hadn't planned a career as a stock picker. But during the 1920s, his two older brothers worked for the family's Wall Street firm, Granger & Co., and their father wanted all his sons to work together.

So in 1925, David Granger joined the firm... and, for $125,000, a seat on the New York Stock Exchange was purchased in his name. Today, at age 93, he is the oldest member of that stock exchange.

Granger's first great investment was in 1930, when he bought IBM, a medium-sized maker of time clocks and tabulating equipment, for $165 per share. He added more shares over time and, about 25 years later, sold his whole IBM stake at a 500% profit.

David Granger is still an avid stock picker. He goes to work daily and tracks the market closely from the computer terminal on his desk.

Here is his meaningful investment advice after spending seven decades on Wall Street....

●**Many people believe in asset allocation** —but I don't. I keep hearing how allocating your assets among stocks, bonds and cash is the prudent method of successful investment.

I have never been an allocator, investing instead primarily in common stocks. I do purchase bonds for a few clients who want them for income. But again, I prefer stocks, which hold purchasing power. Bonds don't. Even if you think you need some bonds for protection, you should still weight your investments overwhelmingly in favor of common stocks.

●**You don't require great diversification either.** Many people say you should diversify by investing in many different industries, but I don't put much emphasis on this.

The people who have made the most money on Wall Street have concentrated their investments in just a few areas.

Sometimes I'll own a bunch of chemical stocks or auto stocks—without worrying about owning so many companies in the same industry.

Example: What difference does it make if Chrysler and General Motors are both in the same industry—if that industry is doing well?

Your portfolio should have no more than 30 stocks—you can't keep track of any more... and you can get a lot of diversification from just a half-dozen stocks.

●**Management matters most.** What you're really paying for when you buy a stock is the company's management.

Example: Look at the job that Jack Welch has done at General Electric. When you buy General Electric, you're buying his great skills as a manager.

Helpful: Before you buy a stock, read the company's annual report. What feel does it give you for the company? Do you find yourself getting excited about the company and its prospects? Are you impressed with how the chief executive comes across?

It's no different from going to the theater. You walk away with a sense of whether the play was good or not and whether the star was worthy of the part he/she played.

●**Buy companies with global products.** Demand throughout the world keeps growing and growing. The most successful companies are those that are capable of spreading out worldwide and whose products have global applications.

Examples: Coca-Cola sells its products in every corner of the world. General Electric makes products that can be sold in both Sweden and Thailand.

Important: Pick companies with a demonstrated ability to adapt to each new market. Coca-Cola does that. But many companies have gone abroad, tried to operate as they did in the US and ended up failures. Keep your eye on newspaper coverage and earnings reports.

●**Bet big on technology.** Everybody should own technology stocks. You don't have to know anything about technology to know that these are the stocks of the future.

I just bought some shares of Intel and Microsoft for my wife because they are powerhouses and two of the most profitable companies in the world. They will continue to stay in that position.

If you fail to invest in technology, you do so at your own peril.

●**Don't let a stock's high price scare you off.** Many people say, *Don't buy that stock. It's selling for 30 times earnings, and that's too expensive.*

Is any stock worth 30 or 40 times earnings? Maybe.

IBM sold at about 40 times earnings for approximately 20 years. Look at the stock's record. If the stock has consistently sold at a high price-to-earnings (P/E) ratio, there must be a good reason for it.

A high P/E doesn't necessarily mean a stock is high-priced. Maybe the high P/E is because of its management or earnings growth record. Or maybe over time, savvy investors have come to realize that the stock deserves to sell at a high multiple.

●**Trust your own instincts.** The key to investment success is your own intuition. Experience was my best teacher on Wall Street. It should be your best teacher, too.

Best approach: Read as much as you can to get a feel for the markets and the most interesting stocks.

I favor *The New York Times* because it tells you just enough about the markets and companies to be useful.

The *Wall Street Journal* is filled with lots of information, but it is more than the average investor can digest.

The more you read, the more you'll come across stocks that seem like ideal investments for you. When you do, don't be afraid to follow your intuition. You'll do better following your own instincts and emotions than listening to those whispers in your ear.

●**Never be bearish.** The overall trend in this country is growth. About 40 years ago, we only had 150 million people. Today, we have more than 250 million people.

Think of the purchasing power and demand of those people. Then add in global demand. How can the future offer anything but continued growth?

Growth makes for great investment opportunities…which is why the market is *20 times higher* than when I came to Wall Street. I don't expect that growth to slow anytime in the future. That's why I'm still bullish about stocks and why I insist bearishness never pays.

David Granger, a limited partner/director in the investment firm of Ingalls & Snyder LLC, 61 Broadway, New York 10006. He has served on the finance committees of several prominent New York City organizations and cultural institutions.

Money-Management Rules of Thumb

Nancy Dunnan

Financial planning isn't nearly as complicated as it seems. *Some of my simple rules…*

●**Reinvest.** All mutual funds let you automatically reinvest earned income in additional shares. Sign on. You can't spend what you don't get your hands on.

●**Enter credit card purchases in your checkbook.** This running tally of how much you're spending lets you know whether you really can afford that next purchase.

●**Buy stocks after they split.** A stock's price often rises on news of a split and falls right after the split. Wait and take advantage of the lower price.

●**Beware of very high stock dividend yields.** The higher the yield, the higher the risk. A high yield is designed to attract investors.

●**Beware of when a *no-load* fund has a load.** Although *no-load* funds don't charge you to buy or sell shares, some have annual 12b-1 fees to cover promotional costs. Switch out of a fund with a 12b-1 fee that is higher than 0.25% of assets, but beware of tax implications.

●**No-load index mutual funds make experts of us all.** These funds invest in a representative basket of stocks of an index—such as the Standard & Poor's 500 Index—and their returns mirror that index. It's a no-brainer way to at least keep pace with the market. Three-quarters of all professional money managers do not outperform the S&P 500 Index on a regular basis.

●**Limit the number of funds you own.** The average investor needs five funds at the most —a money market fund, a growth fund, a growth and income fund, a small-company fund and an international fund.

●**Don't choose bond funds for fixed income.** Contrary to what many people think, these funds do not hold onto bonds until they mature. A fund's yield varies continually as the manager buys and sells securities. *Better:* Individual A-rated (or better) corporate bonds or Treasuries held until maturity.

●**Keep municipal bonds out of your IRA, Keogh or SEP.** Because the income from these bonds is tax-exempt, yields are lower than on taxable bonds. Anything you put in your IRA is sheltered from taxes, so go for higher-yielding corporate bonds.

●**Check Social Security records every three years.** Compare your W-2 withholding with the Social Security Administration's printout, which you can obtain by calling 800-772-1213. An uncorrected mistake could reduce your lifetime benefits.

●**Have your kids take college courses in high school.** Eliminating one college course can save at least $600—if the college charges by the credit, not by the semester.

●**Double-check the check.** Always add up the restaurant tab. Miscalculations are usually in the restaurant's favor…not yours.

Nancy Dunnan, a New York financial expert and author of 30 books, including Never Call Your Broker on Monday …and 300 Other Financial Lessons You Can't Afford Not to Know. HarperPerennial.

10 Golden Rules for Financial Success

Gary Moore
Gary Moore & Co.

I have spent 15 years studying the life and work of the great investor and humanitarian Sir John Templeton. Both mentor and father figure, he's taught me the most important things I know about investing…things I've recently expanded upon in my book about his ideas.

Sir John is no longer actively involved in the management of the Templeton mutual funds, which he sold to Franklin in 1992. But I am still in regular contact with him as a member of the board of advisers for his John Templeton Foundation and in regard to a column we do for The New York Times Syndicate.

How was Sir John able to average nearly 15% a year on his investments over the past 40 years? I believe it was by following these 10 golden rules…

1. Be neither an optimist nor a pessimist —but a realist with a hopeful nature. On TV's popular *Wall Street Week with Louis Rukeyser* in June 1982, when the Dow Jones Industrial Average (DJIA) stood at 790, Sir John startled viewers by predicting that despite the prophets of doom, the DJIA would probably reach 3,000 within a few years. By 1990 it did, even as Ravi Batra's book *The Great Depression of 1990* became the new number-one *New York Times* best-seller.

In 1993, Sir John ventured another positive prediction, saying he thought there was at least an even chance that by the year 2000, the Dow would have reached 6,000—or more. By mid-1997, the average stood close to *8,000.*

2. Count your blessings. As Sir John told Louis Rukeyser on another occasion, "America is still the land of opportunity…but we are negative-minded. It's a pity. The truth is far better than the mood of the American people."

Example I: According to *The Economist,* the US has generated 38 million net new jobs in the past 20 years alone, while Western Europe created no net new jobs.

Example II: A large percentage of Americans believe the Japanese economy is larger than ours. Actually, Japan produces only about $2.5 trillion—less than 40% of our $7 trillion gross domestic product.

3. Debt, whether personal or collective, should not keep you from investing in your future. Sir John has always believed in living a debt-free lifestyle, and he wishes that more Americans would do so. But he is not paranoid about the federal debt. As he explained at a shareholders meeting in the 1980s, few governments ever totally pay off their debt. To do so might devastate their economies. While reducing annual deficits that keep adding to the already huge existing national debt is important, many economists warn that legally requiring a balanced budget, even in times of war or deep recession, could plunge the US economy into depression, as has happened several times in the past.

4. Invest in many different places—for safety. Sir John has always recommended diversification by company, by industry, by risk and by country. Such diversification is particularly important right now. Sir John and I are strict value investors and, with the exception of real estate investment trusts (REITs), the US market is not a value investor's market right now.

In fact, the Templeton funds have moved much of their money out of the US market and into the international arena, where the need for capital is now greater than it is in America and the values are more substantial.

5. Remain flexible and open-minded about types of investments. There is no one kind of investment that is always best. There are times to buy blue chip stocks, cyclical stocks, corporate bonds, convertible bonds, US Treasury investments and so on. And—there are times to sit on cash because cash enables you to take advantage of investment opportunities.

Sir John also believes that money should do more than simply make more money. By purchasing Ginnie Mae mutual funds, for example, you can get a return close to Treasury bonds and get a monthly income check from a government-guaranteed source, at the same time you're helping people to own homes.

6. Patience is a virtue. Sir John says, "Invest, don't speculate. The stock market is not a casino, but if you move in and out of stocks every time they move a point or two...or if you continually sell short...or deal only in options...or trade in futures...the market will be your casino. And, like most gamblers, you will lose eventually—or frequently."

Even with mutual funds, a Morningstar study has shown that low-turnover funds have made more money and assumed less risk than moderate-turnover funds, which in turn do better than high-turnover funds. Among other things, rapid trading is expensive for investors.

7. Investigate before you invest. If you can't do your own homework, hire a wise expert to help you. Besides Sir John's own dis-cipline, which always impressed investors, the reason the Templeton funds achieved such success from modest beginnings was that he has always surrounded himself with talented and dedicated people. Sir John recognizes the contributions that these individuals can make to refine his own sound thinking and successful investment instincts.

8. Invest for the good of mankind. Sir John believes that the secret of creating riches for oneself is to create them for others. Unlike Midas, whose wealth exerted a negative force, Sir John's attitude toward his worldly success has always involved a sense of stewardship—a belief that what you have is not actually yours, but is held in trust for the good of all humanity.

Over the years, countless shareholders and brokers have asked Sir John what he thought was the best investment.

His answer: Giving at least 10% of your income to churches and charities. In fact, Templeton doubles that, giving away 20% of his income and also devoting most of his time to helping the people he comes in contact with develop their minds and souls.

9. Looking out for Number One doesn't make you Number One. Sir John worries that today more people worship idols than God, and those idols are often the institutions and governments created by people.

Though glad that governments, with the lead of the United States, have taken some responsibility for the poor, he feels that it would be better spiritually if people gave individually through churches or other charitable organizations, or person to person. Sir John's reminder that giving is more important than getting will be needed more and more as the US government, now preoccupied with fiscal conservatism, shifts more responsibility for the needy back to churches and individuals.

10. Measure success with a single word —love. After 15 years of studying his life and work, I am convinced that the true secrets of Sir John's success are that he has held to a simple belief and has lived that simple faith.

Much as the apostle Paul used the commercial trade routes of his day to spread the gospel, Sir John Templeton has shown us by the example of his life that practicing ethics in money management can result in financial as well as spiritual success.

While many cynics point out that the so-called socially conscious mutual funds haven't done too well for investors, it's a little-known fact that five of the 50 top US mutual funds don't invest in tobacco, alcohol or gambling as a matter of policy.

These socially conscious funds just don't advertise the fact. They are: *American Mutual, Pioneer Funds, Templeton Foreign, Templeton Growth* and *Washington Mutual.*

Gary Moore, founder of Gary Moore & Co., Counsel to Ethical and Religious Investors, 7569 Seth Raynor Pl., Sarasota, FL 34240. He is author of *Ten Golden Rules for Financial Success: Riches I've Gathered From Legendary Mutual Fund Manager Sir John M. Templeton.* Zondervan Publishing House.

Meeting Your Investment Goals

You are more likely to achieve your investment goals if they are specific, not general.

Example: Instead of simply trying to do the *best possible,* choose an objective like paying off your mortgage within a specific number of years.

Calculate how much money you will need by a specific time…set your sights on that goal…promise to attain your goal…and manage your investments with that in mind.

Ari Kiev, MD, president and medical director of the Social Psychiatry Research Institute, New York, and author of *A Strategy for Daily Living.* The Free Press.

Better Investing

Read *three* annual reports before investing in a stock—the last two reports from the company whose stock you are considering buying…*plus* the most recent one from that company's largest competitor.

Theory: This allows you to discover similarities and differences between the two companies.

Eric Gelb, CPA, MBA, vice president of corporate finance for a major bank, and author of *10-Minute Guide to Annual Reports and Prospectuses.* Alpha Books.

Investing Strategy for Good Times… and Bad

James O'Shaughnessy
O'Shaughnessy Capital Management

No matter what the stock market is doing on any day, I have always followed one rule for successful investing: Base your decisions on a great *strategy,* not on great stories about stocks or companies.

As compelling as stock stories are, investing based on their advice isn't really the way to achieve long-term financial success.

STRATEGY POWER

If you're a *strategy investor,* you follow a plan that has proven to be successful and is not influenced by market fads. You will do well because consistency has been shown to pay off, while helter-skelter investing does not.

By using a great strategy, you remove the emotion factor from investing…and emotion is often the downfall of an investment portfolio.

Example: For one of our private clients, my firm uses an aggressive-growth strategy. Since March, the overall stock market has been up only about 4%—but that client's portfolio is up 18%.

That didn't happen because I'm a genius. It happened because we followed a strategy that suits this client's needs and historically has been highly effective, regardless of the overall stock market's ups and downs.

CHOOSING A STRATEGY

So what is the best strategy to follow for investment success? *Here are three of my favorite strategies that are easy for individuals to use…*

Strategy #1: **Dogs of the Dow.** You invest in the 10 Dow Jones Industrial Average stocks with the highest yields. These stocks are also among the top 30 Dow stocks that are beaten down and about to come back.

These stocks are easy to find. The "Money & Investing" section of *The Wall Street Journal* lists the 30 Dow industrials each day.

It takes only about five minutes to check the stock tables and get the yield for each stock. Adjust your portfolio once a year, so that you stay invested in the stocks that are about to rise.

If you followed this strategy over the past 10 years, you would have beaten the performance of 99% of all actively managed mutual funds. *Recent "dogs" of the Dow…*

- **AT&T.** NYSE:T.
- **Chevron.** NYSE:CHV.
- **DuPont.** NYSE:DD.
- **Exxon.** NYSE:XON.
- **General Motors.** NYSE:GM.
- **International Paper.** NYSE:IP.
- **JP Morgan.** NYSE:JPM.
- **Minnesota Mining & Manufacturing (3M).** NYSE:MMM.
- **Philip Morris.** NYSE:MO.
- **Texaco.** NYSE:TX.

Strategy #2: **Growth and value.** The goal here is to invest in good stocks that have been overlooked by the market and that are finally coming into favor.

You know that they have been overlooked because they sell at low price-to-sales (P/S) and price-to-earnings (P/E) ratios. You know they are coming into vogue because they recently have become strong performers in the market.

How to find them: A good broker can find such stocks with a computer program. Or you can check *The Wall Street Journal* for stocks selling at P/Es of less than 20 that also are trading at close to their 52-week highs.

The more stocks you hold, the better…but you should own a minimum of 10. Aggressive investors can rebalance their portfolios every six months…but rebalancing annually is best for most investors in order to obtain preferential tax treatment of earnings.

These are stocks about which market opinion is changing. You are buying value at a time when the stock is still cheaply priced but on its way back up. *Examples…*

- **Callaway Golf** is one of the dominant names in the golf-equipment industry. NYSE:ELY.
- **Champion Enterprises** produces and sells manufactured homes and buses. NYSE: CHB.
- **CompUSA** operates computer retail superstores. NYSE:CPU.

- **Dell Computer** has a strong position in the business computer market.NASDAQ:DELL.
- **Nortek** makes products for commercial and residential building. NYSE:NTK.
- **Ross Stores** is an apparel retailer. NASDAQ:ROST.
- **Safeguard Scientifics** is engaged in information technology, industrial services, commercial real estate and specialty services. NYSE:SFE.
- **Sun Microsystems** makes high-end computer workstations. NASDAQ: SUNW.
- **USAir Group** is one of the major US airline companies providing air transportation for passengers, property and mail. NYSE:U.
- **Western Digital** is a major manufacturer of computer hard drives. NYSE: WDC.

Strategy #3: **Industry leaders with high dividend yields, a cornerstone value approach.** If you want a portfolio that does extraordinarily well over *long* periods of time —and has virtually the same risk as the Standard & Poor's 500—concentrate on industry leaders with high dividend yields.

This strategy provides a stable portfolio with better returns than the S&P 500 but with almost the same risk.

Approach: You and/or your broker should look for stocks with sales that are 50% greater than those of the average company. They also should have greater market capitalizations, cash flows and shares outstanding than the average company as well as higher dividends.

Helpful: You can find the dividend yield of any stock in the stock market tables. For information about the industry position of a company, check the quarterly "Corporate Scoreboard" reports in *Business Week.* Generally, such companies are household names.

Since these companies tend to be leaders in their industries and dominate the stock market, they can be expected to do the same as the market on a capital appreciation basis. When you add in the boost from the high dividend, you end up doing about 3% better every year than the average holder of big stocks.

As with *Strategy #2, Strategy #3* requires you to have a minimum of 10 stocks, and investors should rebalance their portfolios annually. *Examples of industry leaders…*

●*Atlantic Richfield* is a large diversified oil company. NYSE:ARC.

●*Chrysler* is one of the Big Three automakers. NYSE:C.

●*Elf Aquitaine* is the French-based international oil company. NYSE:ELF.

●*Emerson Electric* is a manufacturer of electrical and electronic products. NYSE:EMR.

●*Genuine Parts* is a major distributor of aftermarket auto parts. NYSE:GPC.

●*International Flavors & Fragrances* develops and manufactures flavor and fragrance products. NYSE:IFF.

●*JC Penney* is a large retailer. NYSE:JCP.

●*Minnesota Mining & Manufacturing (3M)* is a highly diversified company that makes products ranging from Scotch tape to abrasives. NYSE:MMM.

●*Unilever* is the Dutch-British international food and consumer products giant. NYSE:UN.

●*US West* is a regional Bell operating company that serves the Rocky Mountain states and the Pacific Northwest. NYSE:USW.

James O'Shaughnessy, president of O'Shaughnessy Capital Management, an investment firm that advises individuals and five major brokerage houses, helping them manage more than $200 million in assets, 60 Arch St., Greenwich, CT 06830. *Minimum initial investment for private accounts:* $1 million. He is author of *What Works on Wall Street*. McGraw-Hill.

Best Stocks in Downturn

Best performances in stock market downturns come from the container (metal and glass) industry…electric utilities…nondurable household products. These industries are considered highly defensive.

Worst industries in a big market drop: Building materials…diversified machinery… and trucks and parts.

Sam Stovall, sector strategist for Standard & Poor's, writing in *The Outlook*, 25 Broadway, New York 10004.

Temporarily Depressed Stock Prices Are Buying Opportunities

Look for companies selling for significantly less than recent high prices. Favor solid companies that have fallen out of favor among Wall Street analysts. Find out from news reports or a firm's investor-relations department what sort of bad news has hit the company. If a large loss is caused by restructuring or downsizing or an earnings drop is caused by temporary factors, the stock may be a buy. But avoid firms facing significant lawsuits that could jeopardize major assets.

Donald Kalil, president of Compu-Val Investment Inc., 1702 Lovering Ave., Wilmington, DE 19806.

New Strategy for Picking Value Stocks

Look for companies with price/earnings ratios in the bottom 20% of their industries. Such stocks have outperformed the average of 1,500 stocks in the S&P over the past 25 years. Ask your broker for your favorite industries' average P/Es. Then ask for a list of stocks with the lowest P/Es in those industries.

Important: Diversify by buying low-P/E stocks in at least 10 different industries.

David Dreman, chairman of Dreman Value Advisors, 10 Exchange Place, Jersey City, NJ 07302.

Financial Services Stocks Hot and Getting Hotter

Christopher Davis and Ken Feinberg
Davis Financial Fund

Even though many financial stocks had big runups in price and then dropped, there's plenty of room for growth.

Financial stocks are now selling near 12 times 1997 earnings—compared with 17 times earnings for the overall stock market. That's about a 33% discount to the market.

These companies are now in a period of consolidation, and we expect that this sector will soon be widely recognized for having better growth characteristics than at any other time in the last 20 years.

REASONS FOR OUR OPTIMISM

• **Financial companies are now well positioned for the preretirement explosion.** Several of the major companies—such as American Express...Charles Schwab...SunAmerica...Travelers...and even Allstate—have already started to take advantage of the booming preretirement market.

The US is only now in the early phase of an explosion in savings and investing, as the front end of the baby-boom generation plans for retirement and begins to enter its peak saving years.

The transformation of this huge group from consumers and spenders to savers and investors implies a low-inflation and low interest rate environment, lasting at least through the end of this decade.

• **Global investment banking has emerged.** The spread of American-style capitalism around the world has coincided with the collapse of Japanese investment banks and the lack of competitiveness of the European investment banks.

Example: Five years ago, if a Brazilian power company was going public, you could expect the underwriters to include the Japanese bank Sumitomo, Germany's Deutsche Bank, maybe a British firm or perhaps the brokerages Merrill Lynch or Goldman Sachs. Now, major American banks are putting up the cash for such deals. When the Russian natural gas company recently went public, Morgan Stanley's name was on the cover of the prospectus.

• **Mergers are on the rise in the property-casualty insurance and banking industries.** Look at the proposed Dean Witter and Morgan Stanley merger or the acquisition of First Interstate by Wells Fargo. This move will make these companies stronger and their stocks more valuable.

The property-casualty industry also will be helped by the same favorable demographics that are boosting other sectors of the financial services market. The result will be a slower rate of growth in claims costs since cars are safer and people are driving more carefully.

Example: Baby boomers are having children and are turning to minivans, driving them at more conservative speeds and obeying the new, tougher drunk-driving laws.

WHERE TO LOOK FOR BARGAINS

When choosing stocks—regardless of whether they are in the financial industry or some other line of business—we always look for what's undervalued. *Our favorite financial stocks now...*

• *Donaldson Lufkin & Jenrette* is a preeminent investment bank with a long and distinguished history. It has top-notch analysts and is known as "the house that research built." But Wall Street loves to hate other Wall Street firms. NYSE:DLJ.

• *Morgan Stanley Group Inc.* This premier investment bank's stock can be volatile. There's no denying that investment banking is a tricky business in terms of earnings and growth rates. Morgan Stanley is 40% owned by insiders. NYSE:MS.

• *SunAmerica.* This financial services company concentrates on selling a wide range of retirement savings products and services. It is building a strong brand name, and the stock is up tenfold over the last five years. The company's chairman, Eli Broad, is a great entrepreneur who made a fortune in housing with his first company, Kaufman & Broad. NYSE:SAI.

• *Travelers Group* is probably the best-managed insurance company around. It is headed by Sandy Weill, a visionary entrepreneur who delivered on his promise that the company would double its earnings over the last five years. Weill says he wants to double earnings again over the next five years. The company is selling at 14 times this year's earnings and 12.2 times next year's estimated earnings. NYSE:TRV.

• *Wells Fargo & Co.* There's a saying about successful regional banks that they can either have great management or be in a great market. Wells Fargo has both. It has made a series of strong strategic acquisitions, including First Interstate. It is also a strong player in California, which is the fifth-largest economy in the world and bigger than France in size. Not only is California the center of our country's technology and entertainment industries, it is the gateway to the Pacific Rim. NYSE: WFC.

Christopher Davis and Ken Feinberg, comanagers of the Davis Financial Fund, which invests primarily in the stocks of banks, insurance companies and financial services companies.

Lessons from the Investor Whom Warren Buffett Admires Most... Philip Carret

Philip Carret
Carret & Co.

Philip Carret was born in 1896—the same year the Dow Jones Industrial Average was launched. When he was 32 years old, Mr. Carret started the Pioneer Fund, one of the first mutual funds in the US, and he managed it with great success for 55 years.

If you had invested $10,000 when the Pioneer Fund was founded in 1928, that $10,000 would have grown to more than $37 million, assuming the reinvestment of all dividends and capital gains.

In 1963, Mr. Carret started Carret & Co., a money management firm that today manages $600 million in assets. Though Mr. Carret has given up the day-to-day control of the company, he still remains an astute and active investor, inspiring Warren Buffett to state, *Philip Carret has the best truly long-term investment record of anyone I know.*

Here's his advice...

●**Don't be afraid of common stocks.** I'm for holding at least 60% of one's assets in common stocks—no matter what your age. That's in individual stocks or stock funds. And I say that even though I believe the stock market is currently overvalued and still poised for another correction.

The reason I favor stocks over bonds is inflation. If you view investing as I do—as a way to keep your money's value from being eroded by the rising cost of living—stocks outpace that foe. Bonds also outpace inflation, but at a much lower rate over time.

While we probably are never going to see the inflation that existed in Germany during the 1920s, when people walked around with wheelbarrows of money, inflation is always going to exist. The Federal Reserve can control the inflation rate to some degree, but inflation will never disappear.

●**Pick stocks for what they'll do in the coming *years*, not the coming *weeks*.** Only invest in stocks you think are going to be worth more in five years. Never mind what the stock is going to do next week or in the next few months.

If you buy stocks because of what you hope will happen next week, you are trying to be a market timer. I never knew anyone who could time the market consistently—so why even try?

How do you know if a stock will be worth more in five years? You don't. But the odds favor the stock being worth more in five years if it is from a company with a good track record, where the management owns a significant stake in the company and the balance sheet is strong.

I also look for a company that is a leader in its industry, preferably number one. Your broker can provide this information. In addition, I prefer the company to have $2 in current assets for each $1 of current liabilities. If it is an industrial company, I prefer it to have no long-term debt.

●**Growth potential means more than dividends.** Most people like to get dividend checks in the mail. But dividends are of minor importance when compared with whether the company reinvests its earnings for growth.

Even though Warren Buffett's Berkshire Hathaway has never paid a dividend, I bought the stock for less than $400 a share in the 1960s. Today, *each* share is worth around $30,000.

Management has only so much cash at its disposal. If it pays dividends, I see it as a confession of failure. The company is saying, *We don't know where to invest the money, so we'll give it to you, the stockholders.*

Important: Income from dividends is taxed at regular income tax rates, while capital gains are taxed at the 28% rate, which is lower for some individuals.

•**Be patient.** Knowing when to sell is as important as knowing when to buy. Don't sell simply because the price of a stock is going down. If a stock price's drop is in line with the market, ignore it.

But if the stock is declining when the rest of the market is increasing, take another look. Ask yourself whether you are wrong about the stock or whether the market is wrong. If you think you are wrong, you should consider selling.

How long should you hold a stock? As long as the good things that attracted you to the company are still there.

Example: One of my favorite stocks is Greif Bros. (NASDAQ:GBCOA). I bought my first shares in 1939. The company started in the 1870s making barrels. Today it makes fiber, steel and plastic drums and other industry packaging items. The company is well-managed and very strong financially, so I still own shares.

•**Never borrow money to buy stocks.** Investing on margin—using your stock as collateral for a brokerage loan so that you can buy more shares—skews your judgment. When you have a margin account, you worry. When you worry, your judgment is bad and you aren't a good investor.

•**For your best investment ideas, look around you.** I've been following this strategy for more than 70 years.

Example I: In the early 1920s, not all water was metered in New York City. That wasn't going to last forever because water is a scarce resource, and there was no incentive for people to conserve water. Sooner or later, they were going to have meters for everyone. So I bought stock in a company called Neptune Meter, and it turned out very well.

Example II: I came across Neutrogena soap in a hotel in Boston. I liked it, so I began buying its stock in 1979. Eventually Johnson & Johnson bought out the Neutrogena company. My cost per share, adjusted for splits, was $1. Johnson & Johnson paid me more than $33 a share when it acquired Neutrogena several years ago.

CURRENT FAVORITE STOCKS

•**American International Group** is the leader in the international market for property casualty insurance. NYSE:AIG.

•**Amoco.** Everyone should have an energy company in his/her portfolio. This one is the best of the bunch. NYSE:AN.

•**Berkshire Hathaway (Class B).** Everybody wants to own what Warren Buffett owns. Now they can, at an affordable price compared with $32,000 for a Class A share. NYSE:BRKB.

•**Gillette** has a solid earnings core and will keep on growing since the demand for its products is always increasing. NYSE:G.

•**Hawaiian Electric Industries** is not only a very good utility that is expanding into the Pacific Rim area, it also owns a savings and loan in Honolulu. NYSE:HE.

•**Hewlett-Packard** is a technology leader whose shares are attractively priced. NYSE:HWP.

•**Lucent Technologies** is the company spun off by AT&T. It includes Bell Labs. NYSE:LU.

•**MBIA's** specialty is insuring municipal bonds. It has a nearly perfect no-loss record. NYSE:MBI.

•**Norwest** is an excellent bank holding company. Eventually, we are going to have 500 banks in the US instead of 10,000. In the process, the strongest ones will make a lot of money. NYSE:NOB.

•**Property Capital Trust** is a Real Estate Investment Trust (REIT). Like Warren Buffett, I have a major position in it. ASE:PCT.

Philip Carret, founder and former chairman of Carret & Co., 40 E. 52 St., New York 10022. Minimum initial investment: $500,000. Mr. Carret is author of four books, including the investment classic The Art of Speculation (Fraser Publishing) and The Patient Investor (Fraser Publishing).

Aggressive-Growth Investing Doesn't Have to Be Very Risky

Gloria Santella and Eric Maddix
Stein Roe Capital Opportunities Fund

As aggressive-growth stock investors, we concentrate on the potential and performance of individual companies rather than trying to guess how the economy or entire industries will do in the future.

But unlike many of the other funds in our category, we don't buy and sell stocks rapidly to generate returns. Instead, we look for high-growth companies relatively early in their growth cycles and hold them for the long term.

WHAT WE LOOK FOR

We don't buy companies that are in the speculative stage of growth. The risk of a poor-earnings surprise is too great. The companies in which we're interested have their information systems and sales forces already in place. This gives them something to build on but still leaves plenty of room to grow.

Instead, our focus is on earnings growth. Not only does it drive the price of a stock—it also supports the stock in down markets. We want earnings growth to be both high and consistent.

Our *minimum* earnings-growth requirement to buy a stock is 15% per year. During the past five years, our portfolio of stocks has averaged 25% to 30% annual increases in earnings.

We also want earnings growth to be *sustainable*. We want companies that grow at higher rates, quarter after quarter, year after year. *To achieve that goal, we look for two main characteristics...*

•**Companies that target very large markets**—or rapidly growing markets. Otherwise, they will dominate their markets or run out of steam too quickly, and their growth rates will diminish.

•**Companies that go after big ideas and have the ability to exploit their opportunities.** We scrutinize their growth strategies, competitive positions and organizational infrastructures to see if they have the ability to meet financial targets.

SECRETS OF OUR SUCCESS

Our portfolio turnover is very low, reflecting our long-term approach. When we do sell, the primary reason is disappointing earnings. Of course, we'll look at the reason for the disappointment. Most of the time, it's a management error or a misguided strategy.

Currently, our major holdings are companies that dominate their niches in emerging-business sectors. Many are in the outsourcing business with clients that are reluctant to change providers.

This status gives them predictably high recurring revenues, which are very important if you prize consistency and stability of earnings as we do.

OUR CURRENT FAVORITES

•*Clear Channel Communications* is a broadcaster with 97 radio and 18 TV stations, mostly in small- and medium-sized markets. It is a consistent low-cost operator and a beneficiary of the recent telecommunications legislation, which has increased the number of stations a company can own. NYSE:CCU.

•*Gartner Group* is an independent provider of technology industry research and advisory services to corporate America. It is the leader in the field and at least twice as big as its biggest competitor. Services are sold on a subscription basis, so the company knows where 90% to 95% of its revenues will be coming from in a given year. NASDAQ:GART.

•*HBO & Co.* is the dominant provider of data-information services to hospitals, managed-care organizations and other health-related industries. The company has a large installed software database, which means that it has loyal customers who tend to buy add-on services provided by HBO & Co. There's also plenty of room for growth. Nationally, companies spend 8% of their revenues on information services, but in the health care sector, the average is only 2%. NASDAQ:HBOC.

•*Paychex, Inc.*, provides payroll processing and human resource products for small- and medium-sized businesses. Its average client has 14 employees and is run by one entrepreneur who needs to be freed from doing the business's books. Paychex stands nearly alone in its field. Its biggest competitor is the in-house bookkeeper or accountant. Once a client signs on with Paychex, it is reluctant to change—so 88% of the company's business is recurring, which means earnings growth is likely to be consistent. NASDAQ:PAYX.

•*PHYCOR, Inc.*, is a rapidly growing medical-clinic and Independent Practice Association of Physicians (IPA) operator. As HMOs have proliferated, physicians need more bargaining power to deal with them and gain more control over their professional lives. PHYCOR provides expertise on accepted business practices and tailors the advice to doctors. It hires nurses and receptionists, streamlines office procedures and improves bill collection, which ultimately boosts profit margins. NASDAQ:PHYC.

TECHNOLOGY

While the percentage of technology stocks in our portfolio is heavy relative to the S&P 500, it is light compared with other aggressive-growth funds.

Reason: We limit the portfolio to 25% in any single sector. This forces us to be selective about the technology stocks we buy.

Many of our stocks in this sector are in the telecommunications infrastructure business, which specializes in equipment to transmit information. These companies benefit from telephone deregulation. Best of all, the competition is less intense than in the computer software side of technology. *Our current favorites...*

●*Cascade Communications.* NASDAQ: CSCC.

●*Cisco Systems.* NASDAQ:CSCO.

●*Tellabs Operations.* NASDAQ:TLAB.

Gloria Santella and Eric Maddix, comanagers of the Stein Roe Capital Opportunities Fund.

Dollar-Cost Averaging

Dollar-cost averaging is particularly effective in volatile markets—because as stock prices drop, the same dollar amount buys more shares. When prices eventually rise, the investor owns more shares and benefits more from the price increase.

Helpful: Arrange a direct transfer of funds from your bank to a mutual fund every month. Most mutual funds have simple forms you can use to arrange this.

Study by Ibbotson Associates, a stock research firm based in Chicago, reported in *Investor's Business Daily*, 12655 Beatrice St., Los Angeles 90066.

Mutual Fund Mistake

Rushing to invest in funds that announce they are about to close to new investors can be a mistake.

Trap: Many investors assume that closing funds are hot, so they buy them regardless of whether or not the funds fit their asset allocations.

Reality: Of the 15 equity funds that closed last year, 10 underperformed their peer groups for the rest of the year. *Better:* Buy funds only if they meet your investment criteria.

Jim Raker, senior research analyst at *Morningstar Mutual Funds*, a publication that tracks fund performance.

Short-Term Mutual Fund Ratings Are Misleading

Short-term mutual fund ratings are a misleading basis for investment. So if your broker calls you touting such information—beware. While Morningstar just added short-term mutual fund ratings, they're really for *financial professionals* only.

Wisest strategy: Base investment decisions on returns of at least three years—preferably five or 10 years...how the fund's investment philosophy compares with your own...and the fund's management team.

Don Phillips, president of Morningstar, Inc., an independent rating service that evaluates and ranks mutual funds, 225 W. Wacker Dr., Chicago 60606.

How to Sell Mutual Fund Shares

Don't sell fund shares all at once if you are trying to raise a specific amount of cash by a particular time. Instead, use dollar cost averaging on the sell side. Rather than buying the same dollar amount of a fund every month or quarter, you sell the same dollar amount.

AdvantFage: You lock in profits even if the fund's performance deteriorates. And you know you'll have the money when you need it—for instance, for a down payment on a house.

Helpful: Move the money to a lower-risk stock fund or a money market fund, to keep generating income.

John Markese, president of the American Association of Individual Investors, 625 N. Michigan Ave., Ste. 1900, Chicago 60611.

Load Funds

Mutual funds with "B" shares are still *load* funds, no matter what your stockbroker tells you. Brokerages position B shares as no-load investments because no fees are charged if shares are held for at least five years. But B shares have high—too easily overlooked—12b-1 fees that can erode returns.

Strategy: Before investing, be sure the 12b-1 fee is no higher than 1%.

Better: If you really like the fund, invest in its *A shares*. The up-front load will likely be less than the B shares' 12b-1 fees over time.

Robert Veres, a respected observer of mutual funds and editor of *Inside Information*, which critiques the financial services profession, 2087 Shillingwood Dr., Kennesaw, GA 30152.

Beware: Brokerages Play the Float with Customers' Money

Many brokerage firms do not start to credit interest on customers' deposits until five business days after receiving a check. Interest-crediting policies vary by broker. Brokers will sometimes make exceptions to their policies for good customers—*but you have to ask.*

John Markese, president of the American Association of Individual Investors, 625 N. Michigan Ave., Ste. 1900, Chicago 60611.

Flat-Fee Brokerage Accounts

Flat-fee brokerage accounts are a poor deal for many investors. Investors are charged a percentage of their total assets each year in return for a set number of trades of any size without further commissions.

Example: 1% of assets between $50,000 and $99,000 for 10 trades.

Problem: Fees are set so that investors profit from the arrangement only if they make more than the average number of trades for accounts of their size each year. If you don't, the cost per trade is too much.

Trap: This encourages more frequent trading—the enemy of most successful investing, which involves holding stocks for the long term.

Alexandra Armstrong, chairman of a fee-based financial-planning firm. Washington, DC.

The Country's Top REIT Investor Tells How To Profit from REITs

Martin Cohen
Cohen & Steers Realty Shares

Whenever the future direction of the stock market and the economy becomes hazy—as is the case now—investment in Real Estate Investment Trusts (REITs) picks up.

REITs (rhymes with *beats*) are publicly traded trusts that pool investors' money to buy, develop and manage real estate properties. Investors favor REITs in tricky times because REITs have little correlation with the stock or bond markets.

INSULATED FROM THE ECONOMY

Because REITs invest in properties—not manufacturers or producers—they are more dependent on real estate values than on the economy as a whole. That's why REITs tend to rise or remain stable in volatile market environments.

Example: When the Standard & Poor's 500 Index slipped 4.4%, the Morgan Stanley REIT Index was up 0.2%. When the S&P recovered with a 2% gain, the REIT Index did twice as well, with a 4% rise.

REITs are frequently compared to bonds because of their healthy yields—the average REIT yield is 5.9%, compared with 6.4% for a 10-year Treasury note.

REITs, however, are not interest-sensitive the way bonds are. Their characteristics and behavior are so different from stocks and bonds that investors should consider them a separate asset class.

Example: In 1996, REITs had their best year since 1984. The Morgan Stanley REIT Index returned 35.9% versus the S&P 500's annual return of 23%. And if you compare the REIT Index's 35.9% return with the Lehman Bothers Government/Corporate Bond Index—which returned 2.9% last year—REITs had their best returns since 1979.

GOING WITH A REIT FUND

Unless you are fully knowledgeable about the country's different real estate markets, the best way to invest is through a REIT mutual fund.

Like individual stocks—or any other security, for that matter—picking REITs can be tricky. Investors are better served by a REIT fund manager who has a strong feel for the market.

How much of your money should be invested in a REIT fund? There is no one right number, since the answer depends upon many different factors, including your other assets and risk tolerance.

I can tell you that 75% of the money in our fund comes from professional financial advisers who suggest that their clients devote between 5% and 20% of their assets to a REIT fund.

LONG-TERM OUTLOOK

Long term, the real estate investment outlook is still very positive. In nearly every region of the country and almost every property sector, the real estate recovery is gathering momentum.

Building occupancy and rental rates are rising, and the amount of new construction is not keeping pace with demand.

I think it will take a long time before this country becomes overbuilt again, as it was in the 1980s.

REIT earnings are also rising. The weighted average of "funds from operations" (the standard measure of REIT earnings) should grow at around 10% this year. And dividends that REITs must pay out annually to investors should begin to accelerate as well.

OUR FAVORITE SECTORS

We like office properties and regional malls, each of which accounts for about 20% of our total portfolio.

We believe the office sector nationwide should benefit from increases in occupancy and rental rates. Also, there are several large, well-capitalized real estate companies in this category that should have good opportunities to acquire world-class properties at attractive prices compared with the properties' replacement cost and their stature, size and access to capital.

We also like regional malls throughout the country. They were among the best performers in 1996 and should repeat this feat this year.

The retail environment is vastly improved over its position several years ago, with many retailers reporting solid sales increases as consumer confidence and consumer spending rise.

As a result, we expect very few tenant bankruptcies and think that occupancy and rental rates in premier properties should show healthy increases. These increases will drive up the price of solid REITs.

Other attractive sectors: Apartments… community shopping centers, where people can satisfy their regular needs for groceries and prescription drugs…and industrial properties.

Our largest REIT holdings—in order of the number of shares we own…

• *Highwoods Properties, Inc.*, owns office buildings in the southeastern US. NYSE:HIW.

• *Vornado Realty Trust* owns mostly community shopping centers in the Northeast. They are typically anchored by a supermarket at one end of the property and a large drugstore at the other. NYSE:VNO.

• *The Rouse Co.* owns regional malls throughout the US. It also recently acquired a large piece of real estate outside Las Vegas that was formerly owned by Howard Hughes. Land sales, property operations and other development there have given a big boost to earnings. NYSE:RSE.

●**Spieker Properties** owns office and industrial properties on the West Coast, from San Diego to Seattle. NYSE:SPK.

●**Public Storage Inc.**, is one of the biggest public storage companies in the US. It rents trucks to customers so they can transport furniture to and from the storage centers. It also has stores on-site that sell various packing items. NYSE:PSA.

●**Taubman Centers Inc.** owns 21 of the most upscale malls in the country, and it is negotiating to purchase more. NYSE:TCO.

Martin Cohen, comanager of Cohen & Steers Realty Shares, the largest and one of the oldest mutual funds specializing in Real Estate Investment Trusts and other real estate securities.

Aggressive IPO Strategy

Consider investing in new stocks *four weeks after they begin trading.*

Reason: That's when the "cooling off" period is over and the company's financial data are released publicly. Strong earnings, income and sales signal potential for rapid double-digit growth. Ask your broker to fax the data to you.

John Fitzgibbon, editor of *IPO Aftermarket*, which tracks new-stock performance, 40 W. 57 St., New York 10019.

David Dreman's Shrewd Investment Strategies for Roller-Coaster Stock Market

David Dreman
Dreman Value Advisors

After climbing 80% in just over two years, the stock market has entered a highly volatile phase—up sharply one day and down sharply the next.

Some experts call this type of market a "trading range," implying that the stock market will stay pretty flat for quite a while, without going up or down dramatically.

Investment adviser David Dreman looked at where the market is headed and what investors should do now in light of the current trend.

MIXED SIGNALS

After such dramatic price gains in the past two years, it's easy to question whether most stock prices are too high. Dividend yields are down and price/earnings (P/E) ratios are up, which are usually signs that the market is skating on thin ice.

There still are great undervalued stocks out there, but the number of low-priced stocks is smaller than a year ago.

Could the stock market suffer a sharp downturn of 1,000 points? Sure. All it would take is a report on rising inflation…and some of the inflationary indicators now are worrisome.

Examples: Employment is rising, which is good for individuals but worrisome for the economy. More jobs mean companies are cranking up production. Wages may start to edge up, too, which would boost consumer spending. Both factors traditionally cause the economy to overheat and send prices higher.

On the other hand, this same argument for a correction was being made one year ago…two years ago…and six years ago. If we didn't get a correction when the Dow average was at 5,000 and 6,000, why should we get it at 7,000?

This is the most exuberant period in the stock market during this century. There is likely to be continued movement by investors into stocks until something shocks them. Such an event hasn't happened yet.

Not all the economic indicators point to inflation.

Example: Commodity prices—what companies pay for raw materials—have stayed pretty flat. Those prices are the ideal inflation advance-warning system, since higher commodity prices are usually passed along to consumers.

So…is it likely that the stock market will lurch higher? When all is said and done, probably not. That is why it is important now to look for stocks that are undervalued—no matter what the market or the economy is doing at any given time.

WHAT TO DO

Given all the uncertainties, what should you do? Don't do anything foolish, such as dumping your stocks because you think the bull market is over.

Market and economic fundamentals weren't all that much different at the start of 1995 than they are today. If you had bailed out of the market then, you would have missed the 80% run-up we've experienced since.

Better: If you are nervous about the outlook of the stock market, here are some suggestions for what you should do…

●**Reduce risk.** Sell high-risk stocks, particularly aggressive growth stocks and funds. The average aggressive growth stock did pretty poorly last year and is doing even worse this year. Even though aggressive growth stocks have been out of favor recently, in a large market drop they typically fall more than value stocks.

●**Buy value stocks.** Concentrate your investing on value stocks rather than growth stocks. If you're a fund investor, buy one of the Vanguard index funds (800-523-7731) that simply try to keep pace with the market.

If you invest in individual stocks, concentrate on big, blue-chip companies whose stocks are selling at below-market P/Es. You can get these figures in the financial pages or from your broker.

My favorite large-cap value stocks that make sense for today's volatile, uncertain market…

●*AT&T* is one of the great companies in America whose stock is selling at just 10 times earnings. The company's earnings are expected to be depressed over the short term, but they should rise over time. NYSE:T.

There are two major oil company stocks whose prices haven't risen substantially in years.

While oil prices have been down, oil supplies worldwide are tightening. Both stocks have above-average dividend yields and low P/Es. And both companies have among the largest domestic reserves of any major oil company.

●*Amoco Corp.* NYSE:AN.

●*Atlantic Richfield Co.* NYSE: ARC.

There are also several financial services companies and banks that are worth considering.

●*Federal Home Loan Mortgage Corp.* (Freddie Mac). NYSE:FRE.

●*Federal National Mortgage Association* (Fannie Mae). NYSE:FNM.

My favorite bank stocks now…

●*Barnett Banks.* NYSE:BBI.

●*Crestar Financial Corp.* NYSE:CF.

●*First Chicago Corp.* NYSE:FCN.

●*First Union Corp.* NYSE:FTU.

●*J.P. Morgan.* NYSE:JPM.

David Dreman, one of the country's foremost value investors and chairman of Dreman Value Advisors, an investment advisory firm in Red Bank, NJ. His firm's High Return Fund was ranked No. 1 by Lipper for the past one, three and five years. The fund's five-year annualized return, through December 31, 1996, was 18.23% compared with 15.89% for the S&P 500. *Minimum initial investment: $1,000. Load: 5.75%.*

How I Helped My 9-Year-Old Learn All about Investing

Adriane Berg

As a financial planner, I know how important it is to teach children about money. But while saving money is a relatively easy concept to explain, investing is another matter.

With saving, the coins and cash go into a jar, and when there's enough in there, your children can buy things they want. But it's a much harder job getting children to see the wonders of investing—sending money far away where, hopefully, it will grow…maybe.

LESSONS OVER LUNCH

When my son, Arthur, was six years old, I took him and a copy of the financial pages to a Chinese restaurant. While we ate, I pointed out companies he knew in the stock listings, like Disney and Mattel, and said that anyone could buy a little piece of those companies.

I also showed him the share prices and told him what the abbreviations meant.

By the time he was nine, Arthur was making his own investments. Now, at age 14, his investments have been so successful that he has turned a few thousand dollars into nearly enough to finance his entire college education.

TEACHING INVESTING

● **Explain the concept of interest.** When I first raised the subject of investing with my son, he didn't understand how his money could *earn* money.

I explained that there were two ways to make money with an investment...

● **You can lend your money to a company or government and get extra money for doing the favor.**

● **Or you can buy a little piece of a company and make money as the company gets bigger.**

Helpful: To illustrate the point, pay your children a small amount of interest at the end of each month on the money they have saved in their piggy banks or jars.

● **Explain equity.** The concept of part ownership in a company is difficult because kids aren't sure what exactly it is that they will own.

Example: To show my son, I took him to stores that he liked and asked, "Wouldn't it be nice to own part of this store?" I explained that anyone could become a part owner of a company like Toys 'R' Us or McDonald's.

To drive home my point, we watched the cashiers take in money. I explained that the money belongs to the people who own stock in the store.

● **Follow a favorite stock in the newspaper.** Let your children choose a company that interests them. Together, monitor the stock's progress every day in the newspaper.

Post a record of the stock's progress on your refrigerator door and have your children update its price daily. Keep an eye out for stories in the press that relate to the company, and then read them together.

● **Buy a few shares of real stock.** When your children show enough enthusiasm about the process, suggest the purchase of a few shares of real stock.

The commission for purchasing one or two shares can be high, since it's easier for brokers to buy and sell blocks of 100 shares. But it's not so expensive that the purchase isn't a worthwhile experience.

Example: One share of Disney (NYSE:DIS) or a share of Coca Cola (NYSE:KO) is a great start. More than 1,000 companies permit you to buy directly from them and will reinvest the dividends for your child in a fractional share of stock.

Buying real shares means your children will learn the mechanics of stock transactions, receive account statements and feel that there's something at stake.

If you already have an account with a broker, ask if he/she will give you a discount on the usual cost of trading a share or two as a favor.

Ask your broker for a *copy* of the company's stock certificate. It is a fun thing for children to hold. But today, most transactions are electronic. The biggest thrill is for children to get a monthly statement with their names on it—even though your name will also be on it, as custodian.

● **Make investing competitive.** Kids love games and challenges. One way to keep your children interested in investing is to have them select more than one stock, and follow the shares' progress.

Children can also lose interest in investing if the "game" drags on too long.

Helpful: A quick sale is a good idea if your investments are imaginary.

But there is another motivation to sell shares. If the stock has advanced, you want to show your children how to lock in their profits. In that way, your children will be able to experience the excitement of making money in the stock market.

Self-defense: If your children's shares have lost money, ask your broker for a report on the company, discuss holding on to the stock or even buying more at the lower price. If you do sell at a loss, discuss feelings about it and explain to your children that not all the money was lost. Stock investing is not gambling.

Adriane Berg, an attorney and editor of *Adriane G. Berg's Wealthbuilder* newsletter, 71 Valley St., Ste. 300, South Orange, NJ 07079. She is author of *The Totally Awesome Money Book for Kids and Their Parents*. Newmarket Press.

10

Retirement Planning

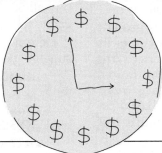

Bull Markets...
Bear Markets...
How to Retire Wealthier, Healthier, Happier

James O'Shaughnessy
O'Shaughnessy Capital Management

hile investors and money managers have been cheering the stock market's exciting rise, privately they have been growing uneasy about whether this wild bull market can continue much longer.

In the wake of this uncertainty, some nervous investors are considering selling retirement savings invested in stocks in anticipation of a market decline. More confident investors are planning to restructure retirement portfolios to capitalize on even bigger expected gains.

Both types of short-term responses often lead to big disappointment. My research shows that the way to a wealthy retirement is to invest in the right types of individual stocks and use a consistent strategy—year in and year out—no matter what the stock market is doing.

FUND TAX-DEFERRED PLANS

Before you begin to invest your retirement savings in individual stocks, invest the maximum in all tax-favored retirement accounts available to you...401(k)s...IRAs...and, if you are self-employed, Keoghs. Such accounts can grow rapidly, since they are not taxed until withdrawn.

But these accounts are limited by the amounts they permit you to contribute. You'll need to invest more in non-tax-deferred accounts if you want to live comfortably in retirement off the income from your assets.

SAVE OUTSIDE YOUR PLANS

To reach retirement goals, take some risk by investing in individual stocks. The amount of risk depends on when you'll ultimately need the money.

173

Examples: If you're in your 30s or 40s, 100% of your retirement savings should be in stocks...if you're in your 50s, 70% should be in stocks and 30% in bonds...and if you're within five years of retirement or retired, your mix should be 50% in stocks and 50% in bonds.

While stocks represent the best investment for gains over time, only the right mix of stocks and a consistent investment strategy will improve your chances of success.

THE POWER OF VALUE STOCK

By analyzing the performance of thousands of individual stocks from 1951 through 1994, I have found that the less time you have until retirement, the greater the number of *value stocks* you should have in your portfolio now.

Value stocks are less volatile than growth stocks and have been better performers in bear markets. Value stocks' share prices are cheap, according to various financial ratios. They also consistently outperform *growth stocks*, whose share prices are high, based on the expectation that prior good earnings will continue in the future.

But don't overlook growth stocks, since they tend to do best when the market as a whole is rising.

How much your portfolio should tilt toward value or growth stocks depends on your age. Here are suggestions for investors at different life stages. The older you are, the more value stocks you should have in your portfolio.

- **Age 25:** 20% *value*...80% *growth*
- **Age 35:** 40% *value*...60% *growth*
- **Age 45:** 50% *value*...50% *growth*
- **Age 55:** 80% *value*...20% *growth*
- **Age 60:** 90% *value*...10% *growth*
- **Age 65 and over:** 100% *value*

FINDING THE RIGHT VALUE STOCKS

Now that you know how important individual stocks are to your retirement portfolio, how much you should have in stocks, and why value stocks are critical to every retirement portfolio...the next step is to identify the right value stocks.

The strategy I suggest involves buying shares of at least 10 of the highest dividend-yielding stocks from the universe of what I call *market leaders* at the beginning of the year and rebalancing that portfolio once a year after that. Ideally, you want to own the top 50 value stocks with the highest dividend yields.

Over the decades, this strategy has beaten purchasing only large-company stocks in both bull and bear markets.

Example: If you had invested $10,000 in my portfolio of *value stocks* at the end of 1951, it would have grown to $5.3 million by the end of 1995, compared with only $1.4 million for an investment in the Standard & Poor's 500 Stock Index. This is an average annual return of 15.32%, compared with only 11.89% for the S&P 500 Index.

If you don't have the $100,000 needed to buy all 50, you can start by investing $2,000 in each of 10...and add gradually.

Here are 10 value stocks. To maximize this strategy, you need to buy them all...

- **Amway Japan Ltd.**, Japanese division of the household products distributor. NYSE:AJL.
- **Bankers Trust Co.**, a big money-center bank. NYSE:BT.
- **BAT Industries**, a British insurance conglomerate. AMEX:BTI.
- **British Telecommunications**, a long-distance provider that plans to acquire MCI. NYSE:BTY.
- **Chrysler Corp.** NYSE:C.
- **Ford Motor Co.** NYSE:F.
- **GTE Corp.**, a US telephone company. NYSE:GTE.
- **Reader's Digest Association**, a big international publisher. NYSE:RDA.
- **Shell Transport & Trading**, an oil company. NYSE:SC.
- **Stone Container Corp.**, manufacturer of packages and containers. NYSE:STO.

FINDING THE RIGHT GROWTH STOCKS

Younger investors can add growth stocks to their portfolios to enhance returns beyond the value approach. *My research suggests you should limit yourself to stocks that have...*

- **Market capitalizations of $150 million or more.**
- **Earnings that are higher than the previous year's.**
- **Price-to-sales ratios lower than 1.5.**

Ask your broker to screen for the stocks with the best 12-month price performances versus other stocks in the group. You may get stunning returns.

Example: If you had invested $10,000 at the start of 1955 and rebalanced at the start of each year, your money would have grown to nearly $9.5 million by the end of 1995, compared with $790,000 for all S&P stocks—a compound annual return of 18.2%, compared with 11.25% for all large-cap stocks.

A portfolio of 50 growth stocks is ideal. Here are 10 to start. *To maximize this strategy, you should buy them all...*

• *Allied Irish Banks*, an Irish bank. NYSE: AIB.

• *Bank of Boston*, a big money-center bank. NYSE:BKB.

• *Bush Industries*, a furniture maker. NYSE:BSH.

• *Coherent Inc.*, a manufacturer of laboratory analytical instruments. NASDAQ:COHR.

• *Columbia/HCA Healthcare Corp.*, operator of general and surgical hospitals. NYSE:COL.

• *Consolidated Stores Corp.*, a variety store holding company. NYSE:CNS.

• *Dollar General Corp.*, the owner of five-and-dime stores. NYSE:DG.

• *Goodyear Tire & Rubber Co.*, a tire manufacturer. NYSE:GT.

• *Oakwood Homes*, maker of mobile homes. NYSE:OH.

• *Rollins Truck Leasing Corp.*, which leases both trucks and autos. NYSE:RLC.

James O'Shaughnessy, president of O'Shaughnessy Capital Management, an investment advisory firm in Greenwich, CT. He also manages Cornerstone Value and Cornerstone Growth, two new no-load mutual funds that follow the strategy discussed in this article. *Minimum initial investment:* $5,000. He is author of *What Works on Wall Street*. McGraw-Hill.

Jonathan Pond's New Solutions to the New Retirement Saving Challenge

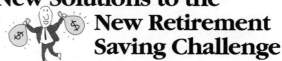

Jonathan Pond
Financial Planning Information Inc.

The astonishingly rapid rise of the stock market has shattered records...but it has also laid the foundation for a number of retirement savings problems.

Mistake: **Huge annual market gains mean that you don't have to sock away as much.** Many people have cut back on the amount they're *saving* for retirement. They believe that the rise in the stock market means their 401(k) contributions alone are adequate for a comfortable retirement.

Reality: The stock market has had an unbelievable two years. But the party could end at any time...or we could see the market trading in the same 500-point range for years, limiting annual returns.

Relying on just your 401(k) to provide you with the amount you'll need when you retire only makes sense if you began socking away 10% of your salary when you were in your 20s. The problem is that most people didn't start saving that early.

If you began making 401(k) plan contributions in your 30s, you need to boost your contributions to 15% to 20% of your income to amass enough for a financially sound retirement. Your annual contributions would have to be at least 25% if you waited until your 40s or 50s.

The only way to accumulate enough money so you can retire in the style you would like is to supplement your 401(k) plan with other types of savings. First fund IRAs...then deferred annuities...and then mutual funds and other investments in your taxable accounts.

Mistake: **Assuming that the stock market will return at least 10%.** After two years of strong stock market performance, many investors now assume that a worst-case scenario is an annual return of 10%—the historical average and a perfectly fine rate of return.

But there's another, more worrisome scenario. If you have the bad luck to retire and need your invested assets during a year—or a decade—of subpar stock market performance, you could face some mighty lean times.

Example: Let's say you were invested heavily in large-cap US stocks and retired soon after 1966, which ushered in a period of lackluster stock market performance and accelerating inflation, culminating in the bear market of 1973–1974. You would have had no net returns over 18 years, forcing you to use up your principal.

Strategy: Boost returns by diversifying your portfolio. Instead of limiting yourself to large stocks in the Standard & Poor's 500 Index and intermediate-term bonds, include in your portfolio some small-company stocks, foreign stocks and cash investments—money market funds and Treasury bills. The additional stocks will help to insulate you from down years, and the cash investments will protect your portfolio from interest rate risk.

Mistake: **Assuming you'll need almost the same annual income in retirement as you have now.** As confidence in the future grows, more people are willing to spend money. Many also cringe at the thought that they might not be able to live as well as they do while they're working. The rule of thumb has been that you'll need 75% of the income you have while you're employed.

Reality: This formula may be true if you're currently earning $50,000 to $80,000. But if you're earning $150,000 or $250,000, you will probably find it easy to scale back your living expenses considerably without crimping your style.

If you're mortgage-free and have put your children through college, it may turn out to be much easier than you expect. I think such high-income couples can get by with spending income of $40,000 to $60,000 a year (after taxes). Singles should be able to live comfortably on $30,000 to $40,000 a year.

The point is not to stop saving aggressively, but to think of ways to reduce your expenses before you retire so that your savings will last longer and provide you with the ideal quality of life.

Mistake: **Becoming much more conservative as you near retirement.** Conventional wisdom says you should shift your portfolio from stocks to bonds within five years of retirement.

Reality: Most people who retire today at age 65 will live at least another decade or two. Even with inflation running at a modest rate of 3%, someone whose annual living expenses are $60,000 today would see those expenses grow to almost $80,000 in 10 years and about $100,000 in 20 years.

There's no way that a portfolio of 100% bonds could appreciate enough in two decades to provide that kind of income. The only way that you can protect yourself against the risk of inflation eroding your future purchasing power is to keep a sizable portion of your investments—about 60%—in stocks or stock funds when you reach retirement.

Once you stop working, it's probably time to shift the nature of your equity holdings from aggressive stocks (or stock funds) to more conservative dividend-paying stocks or equity-income mutual funds.

These types of stocks or stock funds provide opportunities for future growth. And because they generate a steady stream of dividends, they are less speculative than momentum stocks that don't pay dividends but have high projected future earnings growth rates. *My current no-load favorites:*

•*Fidelity Equity Income II.* *Minimum initial investment:* $2,500. *Performance:* 16.59.* 800-544-8888.

•*T. Rowe Price Equity Income.* *Minimum initial investment:* $2,500. *Performance:* 17.34%. 800-638-5660.

*Performance figures are the funds' five-year annualized returns through February 28, 1997.

Jonathan Pond, president of Financial Planning Information Inc., 9 Galen St., Watertown, MA 02172, and host of public television's *Your Financial Future with Jonathan Pond.* His latest book is *Four Easy Steps to Successful Investing.* Avon.

Retirement Planning

Retirement can *increase* stress instead of lowering it. Financial planning is *not* enough.

If you're thinking about relocating, consider activities you want to participate in…and how much time you'll spend with your spouse.

Do not expect to travel constantly—the appeal wears thin quickly, and the expenses mount just as fast.

If you drink, beware of overusing alcohol—retirement can give people more opportunities to drink.

Important: Structure your retirement so you don't have long periods of hanging around with nothing to do.

Virginia Richardson, PhD, professor of social work at Ohio State University, Columbus, who led a study of 222 new retirees in central Ohio.

What to Look for In a 401(k) Plan

The opportunity to sign up as soon as you are hired…employer matching of at least 50% of your contributions…choice of at least six funds with different investment styles… easy access to account information through a toll-free number…freedom to make transfers at least quarterly…plan expenses of no more than 1% of assets…the ability to borrow against your account and make hardship withdrawals. Not all plans have all these features. But the more a plan has, the better it is.

Ted Benna, president of the 401(k) Association, which helps members maximize their plans, 201 Corporate Dr. E., Langhorne, PA 19047. Mr. Benna discovered a little-noticed tax-law provision that led to the creation of the 401(k) savings plan. He is author of *Escaping the Coming Retirement Crisis.* Piñon Press.

Check Your Retirement Plan

Check your business's retirement plan for defects before the IRS does. New IRS procedures make it possible for businesses that *voluntarily* report defects to correct them *without penalty.* But you can't use the no-penalty procedures after the company's tax return has been selected for audit.

Randy Bruce Blaustein, Esq., senior tax partner with Blaustein, Greenberg & Co., 155 E. 31 St., New York 10016. He is author of *How to Do Business with the IRS.* Prentice Hall.

Maximize Your Employer's 401(k) Contributions

You can maximize your employer's 401(k) contributions by allocating your own contributions. *Strategy:* At the beginning of the year, calculate the percentage of your salary represented by ($9,500—the maximum individual 401(k) contribution for 1997). Make your 401(k) deduction that percentage of your salary.

Result: The company will make matching contributions the whole year, instead of stopping earlier when your contributions might otherwise reach the maximum.

Note: The rules are complex—especially if you earn more than $160,000 in 1997 or expect a large year-end bonus. Speak with your tax adviser.

Ted Benna, president of the 401(k) Association, which helps members maximize their plans, 201 Corporate Dr. E., Langhorne, PA 19047. Mr. Benna discovered a little-noticed tax-law provision that led to the creation of the 401(k) savings plan. He is author of *Escaping the Coming Retirement Crisis.* Piñon Press.

When You Max Out Your 401(k)

Margaret Miller Welch
Armstrong, Welch & MacIntyre

Investors in 401(k) plans who have reached the $9,500 maximum—and who want to keep saving for retirement—often wonder where to invest next. *Here's what I am telling clients…*

●**Reduce your debt.** Before investing another penny toward your retirement, use the extra cash to eliminate or reduce any credit card debt. No other investment pays a guaranteed annual 18%—the average rate on a credit card.

●**Fund your IRA.** You can contribute up to $2,000 a year to an IRA. The money will compound tax free until you begin withdrawing it.

Helpful: One way to keep saving is to have the same amount you had withdrawn from your check for your 401(k) directly deposited to a money market account in your IRA. Or you can have your IRA withdraw it electronically from your checking account.

If you have more than 10 years until your retirement, your IRA should contain almost nothing but growth stock mutual funds. *Current favorites...*

●**American Funds New Perspective Fund.** *Minimum initial investment:* $250. The fund is available through financial advisers only.

●**Janus Fund.** *Minimum initial investment:* $2,500. *Load:* None. 800-525-8983.

If you are within 10 years of retirement, split your IRA between a growth mutual fund and a growth-and-income mutual fund. *Current favorite no-load growth-and-income fund...*

●**Vanguard Windsor II.** *Minimum initial investment:* $3,000. 800-523-7731.

●**If you own a variable or universal life insurance policy**, consider contributing to the cash-value portion of the policy. This strategy makes sense only if your insurance policy's investments are performing as well as those in your 401(k) plan and other holdings.

Caution: Be sure your policy is structured so additional cash builds investments, not buys more insurance.

●**Buy a tax-deferred variable annuity.** This can be bought through insurance companies, and the money is tax-sheltered. *To make this strategy work...*

...you must leave the money alone for at least 15 years after signing up.

...you should make periodic withdrawals instead of a lump sum when you need to use the money.

If you don't do both, the high expenses charged by most annuities make purchasing them unwise. *Variable annuities with relatively low expenses...*

●**American Skandia—ASAP II.** *Minimum initial investment:* $1,000. 800-752-6342.

●**Nationwide Best of America IV.** *Minimum initial investment:* $1,500. 800-848-6331.

●**Phoenix Home Life Big Edge Choice.** *Minimum initial investment:* $1,000. 800-843-8348.

●**Use a plain, old investment account.** Though there is no tax benefit to investing outside of a tax-deferred account, you're still saving for retirement, which is better than spending the money.

Helpful: You can lower your tax bite by buying a growth stock fund, which pays low dividends and generates substantial capital gains. Withdraw from these funds after you retire, when your income will have dropped and you'll be in a lower tax bracket.

Margaret Miller Welch, a certified financial planner and president of Armstrong, Welch & MacIntyre, a financial planning firm, 1155 Connecticut Ave. NW, Washington, DC 20036.

Helpful Advice from the Inventor of the 401(k)... Ted Benna

Ted Benna
The 401(k) Association

When considering making changes to your 401(k) plan here are three smart steps to take...

●**Reexamine the mix of stocks and bonds.** Every major study shows that your asset allocation—how your money is divided among stocks, bonds and money market funds—accounts for 90% of your long-term investment return.

Helpful: Don't determine your mix based on how close you are to retirement but instead on your *life expectancy.** Most healthy retirees live decades after age 65, which means you'll

*Internal Revenue Service publication No. 590, *Individual Retirement Arrangements (IRAs)*, provides an actuarial table showing life expectancy at different ages.

need growth investments to outpace those years of inflation. I suggest aggressive investors have 100% of their money in stocks…moderate investors, 60% in stocks and 40% in bonds…conservative investors, 20% in stocks, 60% in bonds and 20% in money market funds.

Formula: To determine how your money is allocated among stocks, bonds and cash now, divide your total account balance by the amounts in stock funds, bond funds and money market funds.

Say you decided a few years ago to divide your money evenly between stocks and bonds. The market performances of 1995 and 1996 have likely boosted your stock portion to 60% or 70%. Rebalance your mix by selling shares in your stock fund and investing in your bond fund.

● **Review your plan's investment choices.** More companies are adding investment choices to their plans, and it's not unusual to have six or more choices. There's nothing wrong with choices, provided you know exactly what each one does and how it relates to your goals.

Helpful: Most of your stock investment should be in a growth fund and a growth-and-income fund. These are core funds because they produce steady returns over time. Consider an S&P index fund for which the manager does not actively buy and sell stocks. Index funds have less volatility than actively managed accounts.

If you're more aggressive and provided with other choices, you could invest smaller amounts in a stock fund that invests in small companies and international stocks. These funds are more volatile, but the small amount you have in here won't jeopardize your overall portfolio—and should reduce your long-term risk due to broader diversification.

If possible, split your bond allocation between funds that invest in bonds of different maturities or types.

● **Decide on your asset allocation for this year's contributions—and leave it alone.** Changing your allocation to time the stock and bond markets is dangerous. You may catch it right once or twice, but "market timing" can become addictive, and you're bound to miss the call and lose returns. It's better to make your decisions and then leave your allocation alone.

Example: Let's say you've been aggressive in the past and put 100% of your money into stock funds. Now, with the market at an all-time high, you want to be more conservative, so you put 60% of your 1997 contribution into stocks and 40% into bonds.

But let's assume that a few months from now, the stock market starts dropping. Before you start changing your allocation to halt the purchase of stock shares, remember that the best time to buy stocks is when prices are low—not when they're at record highs. As a steady 401(k) investor, it's easy for you to do this because you're investing the same amounts at regular intervals.

Ted Benna, president of The 401(k) Association, which helps members maximize their plans, 201 Corporate Dr. E., Langhorne, PA 19047. Mr. Benna discovered a little-noticed tax-law provision that led to the creation of the 401(k) savings plan. He is author of *Escaping the Coming Retirement Crisis.* Piñon Press.

How to Crash-Proof Your 401(k)

Julie Jason
Jackson, Grant & Co.

If you're saving for retirement through a 401(k) plan that's heavily weighted toward stocks, and plan to retire within two years, your future could be savaged by a severe market correction, one that knocks hundreds (even thousands) of points off the Dow.

Worst case: A rerun of 1973–1974, when the market lost 50% of its value. *Never forget:* The word *crash* still appears in the dictionary.

Example: After a long bull market, you now have $500,000 in your 401(k), 100% invested in stocks. If the market makes a big correction before you retire in say, 1998 or 1999, your account may have shrunk to $400,000, perhaps $300,000. That's $100,000 or $200,000 you won't have available to spend in your retirement.

Trap: After you stop working you can't replenish your 401(k) with additional contributions.

Safety play: If you'll be retiring soon, lighten up on stocks and move some 401(k) money into fixed-income options (see below). That's especially important if a large portion of your 401(k) is tied up in your employer's stock. *Note:* There is no tax on profits you make on trading 401(k) assets.

Many 401(k) plans offer these fixed-income choices...

•**Money market funds.** Although your income fluctuates, you won't lose principal. Such funds now yield about 5%, on average.

•**Stable value accounts** made up of several insurers' Guaranteed Investment Contracts. Your principal stays intact while you lock in a fixed return for a year or longer. Such accounts now pay around 6%.

•**Bond funds.** Dividends will vary. Corporate bond funds pay more than government funds. You likely can earn 6% to 8% today from a mix of well-managed bond funds.

The more your 401(k) portfolio tilts toward stable-value accounts, the less your principal will be at risk. However, you don't want to move entirely out of stocks and sacrifice future growth potential.

Strategy: If you expect to retire soon and tap your 401(k) for income, you should plan to get that income from your fixed-income accounts. Use your stocks for growth.

Example: You'll need $20,000 per year before taxes from your 401(k), in addition to Social Security benefits, investment interest, etc. Assume a 6% return on your fixed-income accounts. At that interest rate, you'll need $335,000 of your 401(k) money in fixed-income investments to generate $20,000 a year, all of which will be taxable. The rest can be kept in stocks.

Note: This strategy is meant for those retiring within two years. If you have a longer time horizon, emphasize stocks, because long-term growth likely will override any near-term corrections. Indeed, before age 55, it makes sense to channel most of your 401(k) contributions into stock funds.

Julie Jason, a principal and cofounder of Jackson, Grant & Co., an investment firm in Stamford, CT. Ms. Jason is author of You and Your 401(k). *Simon & Schuster.*

Avoid Borrowing From Your 401(k)

Such borrowing is tempting because you get a low interest rate, don't have to deal with a bank loan officer and make repayments to yourself. It's so tempting that one in three have taken such loans, says the Government Accounting Office. But it may be much more costly than it seems.

Why: (1) You may sharply reduce your future retirement wealth. The real cost of the loan is not the interest rate you pay, but the tax-deferred investment returns that you *won't* earn on the borrowed-out money. (2) If you leave your employer for any reason, the entire loan becomes immediately due. (3) If you can't repay the loan, it becomes fully taxable to you, with a 10% penalty if you are under age 59½.

Avery E. Neumark, Esq., CPA, at Rosen Seymour Shapss Martin & Co., 757 Third Ave., New York 10017.

How to Earn the Most From Your IRA

Earn more by paying into your IRA as early as possible in the year—to give your money the benefit of tax-free accumulation for as long as possible. Over time, this strategy will make a big difference.

Example: Assume you contribute $2,000 per year and get an 8% return. If you contribute on January 1, 1998, instead of December 31, 1998, you will have $2,318 more after 10 years...$7,322 more after 20 years...$18,125 more after 30 years.

Investing on Your Own by Deborah Rankin, a financial writer in Portland, OR. St. Martin's Press.

No-Paperwork 401 (k) Loans

No-paperwork 401(k) loans have been approved by the IRS. Borrowing against

401(k) retirement accounts may be becoming easier than ever. Bankers Trust has announced it has received approval to offer 401(k) loans to customers with no paperwork at all. It's expected that this will lead to innovations such as 401(k) loans being taken out through ATM machines and touch-tone phone transactions.

Caution: It can be *too easy* to take out a 401(k) loan. You should carefully consider whether you really wish to lose tax-deferred compounding of your retirement savings by borrowing the money.

Avery E. Neumark, JD, LLM, CPA, Rosen Seymour Shapss Martin & Company, 757 Third Ave., New York 10017.

Inheriting IRA Assets

Those who inherit IRA assets from a deceased spouse will have these options: (1) Take a lump-sum payout of the IRA funds and pay tax on it…(2) Leave the money in the IRA and take annual distributions based on the deceased spouse's expectancy (can be done in the following year)…(3) Roll the inherited IRA into your own IRA to obtain all the rights of IRA ownership, including the right to name a new beneficiary.

Harold Evensky, an investment adviser in Coral Gables, FL.

Pension/Work Trap

Anyone vested in a pension plan can leave his/her job after the retirement age established in the plan, work for another employer and still receive his pension from the first employer. But under federal rules, if you return to the employer who is paying your pension, the employer may suspend part of your pension as long as you keep working there.

Self-defense: Before returning to the same employer—or another one covered by the same pension plan—find out if your pension will be affected.

Gloria Della, acting chief of public affairs for the Pension and Welfare Benefits Administration of the US Department of Labor, Washington, DC.

Miscalculations Can Cost You

Pension miscalculations may result in your receiving less money after retirement than you expect. Almost 10,000 lawsuits involving disputes over pensions and related company benefits were filed in a recent year. In some cases, companies have made errors calculating benefits…stated the incorrect amounts in writing…then later sent follow-up letters saying the pensions should have been lower—and docked retirees for company errors.

Self-defense: Request an Individual Benefit Statement from the plan. Ask how the amounts were calculated. Check the plan's information against your work records.

The Pension Book: What You Need to Know to Prepare for Retirement by Karen Ferguson, director of the Washington, DC–based Pension Rights Center, and Kate Blackwell, a freelance writer. Arcade.

Happier Retiring

Distributions from pension plans should be carefully arranged to minimize tax impact.

Usually, all distributions from qualified retirement plans must be included in gross income when they are received—potentially raising your tax bill significantly. But paying taxes on a distribution can be postponed by rolling it over into an IRA or other qualified retirement plan. Special five- and 10-year tax averaging is available to some retirees.

Consult your financial adviser about the best method for you.

Randy Bruce Blaustein, Esq., senior tax partner with Blaustein, Greenberg & Co., 155 E. 31 St., New York 10016. He is author of *How to Do Business with the IRS.* Prentice Hall.

Monthly Pension vs. One Lump Sum

If your company offers the choice of a traditional monthly pension—an annuity—or a single lump sum payment, the lump sum is usually better.

Reason: The pension is probably not as good as an annuity you could buy on your own, after some comparison shopping. If you are healthy when you retire, you could take the lump sum...move it into a rollover IRA...and invest for growth and income until you are in your 70s. At that point, take half the money and purchase an annuity from an insurance company. Leave the rest in the IRA, continuing to invest for future growth.

Jonathan Pond, president of Financial Planning Information Inc., 9 Galen St., Watertown, MA 02172, and host of public television's Your Financial Future with Jonathan Pond. *His latest book is* Four Easy Steps to Successful Investing. *Avon.*

Retirement and Health Benefits Alert

Retiree health benefits can usually be cut by companies. And—more firms are reducing them as cost-cutting pressures increase. Retirees age 65 and older can continue to rely on Medicare, but that does not cover spouses or children. Even companies that promise to provide retiree health benefits often include *reservation clauses* stating that they reserve the right to make benefits changes.

Self-defense: Before taking early retirement, check documents carefully. Consider negotiating guaranteed health coverage as part of your retirement package.

Alexandra Armstrong, chairman of Armstrong, Welch & MacIntyre, Inc., a financial planning firm, 1155 Connecticut Ave. NW, Washington, DC 20036.

Best States for Retirement...Tax-Wise

Harold F. Soshnick
KPMG Peat Marwick LLP

Many factors go into the decision about where to retire—cost of living, climate, proximity of family and friends.

Another important factor is taxes, which affect the income you have to spend and the money you have left over to leave to your heirs.

INCOME TAXES

While there is no escaping federal income tax, the state you're planning to retire to may or may not have a *state* income tax. The state tax may be high (such as in California, New York and Massachusetts) or not so high.

Nine states do not have any state income tax: Alaska, Florida, Nevada, New Hampshire, South Dakota, Tennessee, Texas, Washington and Wyoming.

But where there is no income tax, there will likely be other taxes to raise revenue.

Examples: Florida has an "intangibles tax" of 1% to 2% on stocks and bonds. New Hampshire and Tennessee have a tax on interest and dividends.

Many other states, with or without income tax, impose *sales tax*. Again, the sales tax rate varies considerably in different states.

Five states do not have any sales tax: Alaska, Delaware, Montana, New Hampshire and Oregon.

Pension relief: In the past, some states tried to tax pensions earned within their borders but paid to retirees living in other states. Congress has put a stop to this practice.

A law enacted in January 1996 prevents states from taxing retirement income payable after 1995 to nonresidents. Retirement income includes income derived from qualified retirement plans, IRAs, 401(k) plans, SEPs, 403(b) annuities and government deferred compensation plans.

Note: Even those states that do impose income tax may provide special exclusions for pensions. The state of New York, for example, does not tax the first $20,000 of pension income.

DEATH TAXES

There are two types of death taxes: Estate tax and inheritance tax.

Estate tax is imposed on a person's estate. Inheritance tax is imposed directly on the heirs.

A number of states impose only a "pick up" estate tax. This is the amount of the federal death tax credit used to reduce the federal estate tax. The rate of the credit is between 0.08% and 16% of the federal estate tax.

States with low death tax because they rely only on the pick up include: Alabama, Alaska, Arizona, Arkansas, California, Colorado, District of Columbia, Florida, Georgia, Hawaii, Idaho, Illinois, Maine, Minnesota, Missouri, Nevada, New Hampshire, New Mexico, North Dakota, Oregon, Rhode Island, South Carolina, Texas, Utah, Vermont, Virginia, Washington, West Virginia, Wisconsin, Wyoming.

Some states have high tax costs at death. New York's runs up to 21%.

OTHER TAXES

In addition to the taxes already discussed, there may be other taxes to examine in deciding where to retire.

Consider the rate on property taxes. Look not only at the current rate but also estimate future tax increases.

Gift taxes: Some states have a tax on gifts. Where there is such a tax, check the rate and what amounts are exempt.

MOVING STATE TO STATE

●**Income taxes.** States with income tax impose it on their residents. Residency in all states is determined by physical presence. Individuals who maintain homes in a state are treated as residents if they are physically present in the state for more than 183 days a year. If relocating, be sure to time a move to ensure residency in the lower-tax state.

When a person has homes in more than one state, care should be taken to time physical presence in the lower-tax state.

Example: George, a longtime New Yorker, buys a home in Florida while maintaining an apartment up north. He spends the colder months in Florida and the warmer months in New York. If he is in New York for more than 183 days, he is treated as a resident of that state. But if he remains in Florida for at least 184 days, then he is not a New York resident, provided he has changed his "domicile" to Florida (see below).

Caution: Even a nonresident can be subject to state income tax on "situs income" (income derived from the state). Thus, for example, even if George lived in Florida for eight months each year, he would still be taxed by New York on rental income from property located in New York.

●**Death taxes**. For individuals maintaining dual residency, the determination of which state will impose death taxes is based on "domicile." Unlike residency, which is based on physical presence, domicile is a matter of intention. It is the state that an individual calls home.

The subjective intent of domicile is evidenced by objective factors—voter registration, car registration, church/synagogue membership and other ties to the community.

It may be possible to file a declaration of domicile (or similar document) with the town or county.

Example: In Florida, a person can file a declaration of domicile and obtain "homestead" protection for a home against the claims of creditors.

Trap: Individuals maintaining dual residency could face the possibility of two states making a claim on an estate. Many years ago, the US Supreme Court allowed two states to levy estate taxes against one estate where each state could show the decedent had been domiciled there. Filing a declaration of domicile will avoid the cost and delay of an estate having to contest a tax claim by another state.

Harold F. Soshnick, partner at KPMG Peat Marwick LLP, 345 Park Ave., New York 10154.

Taxes and Retirement

Best and worst tax locations for retirees, based on nine hypothetical married couples with incomes from $24,281 to $68,098 and owning property valued at $50,000 to $250,000...

Among the best: Anchorage and Juneau, Alaska...Wilmington and Dover, Delaware... Honolulu and Kahului, Hawaii...Portland,

Eugene and Bend, Oregon...Las Vegas...Jackson and Cheyenne, Wyoming...Santa Fe and Carlsbad, New Mexico...Houston...Dallas...Baton Rouge.

Worst: Major Northeast and Midwest cities, including Pittsburgh...Philadelphia...Milwaukee ...Topeka...Des Moines...Minneapolis...Chicago ...New Haven.

R. Alan Fox and Eve Evans, authors of *Tax Heaven or Hell*. Vacation Publications.

How to Find the Home of Your Dreams

William Seavey
The Greener Pastures Institute

Nearly 80% of Americans live in urban areas, where there is more concrete than dirt. It's no wonder then that the retirement plans of many people include relocating to a smaller town.

Living in a small town can be all it's cracked up to be, if you pick the place with care and make the move with your eyes wide open. To decide if small-town life is for you and how to pick the right town:

●**Prepare for the realities of the move.** A Census Bureau report shows people moving to small towns at three times the pace of the 1980s. But any move, even just across town, is among the major stresses of life. Think of how traumatic it will be to move far away.

Major considerations: How far will your move put you from family and friends? Could your children afford the time and money to visit you on a regular basis? Will your retirement savings pay for as many trips home as you'd like?

Strategy: Don't make your move irreversible. Consider it a trial that can be canceled if things don't work out.

Example: Rent your home for the first few years after retirement instead of selling it. That way you'll have a place to return to if relocating proves a mistake.

●**Beware of weather extremes.** People often relocate to a warmer climate. Northern winters are bad enough when you're young. When you're a little older, even shoveling snow can be a health hazard.

Caution: Be sure you can handle the climate you are moving to. Baking heat may be great in January when you're on a brief break from bitter cold back home. But could you live with yearlong heat and high humidity? Will your budget let you run an air conditioner year-round? Would you enjoy a round of golf in the full heat of midsummer?

HOW TO INVESTIGATE

●**Pick a town that's the right size for you.** Size of population determines the prevailing lifestyle. The pace of life will be slower and living costs lower in a small town. But small towns may not offer the amenities you are used to.

Example: Many small towns have lost big sections of their downtown business districts. You may have to drive many miles to a shopping mall for anything beyond the basics. The mall might also be home to the nearest movie theater and restaurant. That presupposes you have a car and remain physically able to drive it.

Since few small towns offer public transportation, look for a town that offers shuttles to shopping areas, medical appointments, cultural events, etc.

Useful: If you own a home, the Vacation Exchange Club (800-638-3841) may be able to help you work out a swap that will let you explore the new area close-up. Someone from the area you're considering moving to spends a few weeks in your home...you get to spend a few weeks staying in their home.

●**Avoid budget-busting locales.** It is assumed that the cost of living will be less where you want to move than where you are right now. But living costs aren't likely to be cheaper if you have your heart set on a resort area.

Helpful: Cost-of-living comparisons for various cities are available through the American Chamber of Commerce Research Association (ACCRA, 4232 King St., Alexandria, Virginia 22302, 703-998-3540).

Critical: Don't forget taxes when you're calculating living costs. Government services have to be paid for somehow. You may be drawn to a state that boasts a low sales tax or no state income tax only to run into crushing property taxes.

●**Investigate local medical services.** A common concern is whether there is an HMO nearby. Many times there is not.

Reality: Managed care is here to stay and many retirees will be relying heavily on managed care facilities. You could be in trouble if the nearest HMO is 100 miles from your new home.

Warning: Many smaller towns are not home to a general practitioner, let alone a specialist. Small-town resort areas are apt to have the best medical facilities, but their costs can run very high.

Checking out the local medical facilities should be a top priority on your inspection tour...

●**Check the Yellow Pages** for a list of medical specialties.

●**Inspect local hospital and other health care facilities** for appearance, quality of care and cost.

●**Interview several local physicians** as a potential patient if you should decide to make the move.

Helpful: Discuss your own medical situation with the physician. Do you have some special condition, such as an allergy, that might prove troublesome or even risky in the new location? Are specialists available if your particular condition suddenly worsened?

●**Decide if you want to keep working.** Even if you don't plan to work after retirement, your financial situation could force you to do so, at least part-time.

Living costs may be higher in a resort area, but there may also be part-time work during the season. If you opt for a smaller town, pick one with a variety of industries. The more diverse the local economy, the greater the likelihood of work being available.

Helpful: The local Chamber of Commerce should be able to brief you on the job situation. Check out employment ads in the local newspaper for the types of jobs in the area.

●**Don't go where you won't fit in.** Wherever you move, you're an outsider with different interests, a different lifestyle and probably an accent that sets you apart. Depending on the town, it can take a long time to be accepted, or you may never be accepted. Do some research.

●**Spend all the time you can** on your inspection trip with year-round residents.

●**Have coffee in a local café** and chat with other patrons.

●**Talk to the local newspaper editor.**

●**Visit churches you might consider joining.**

●**Attend meetings of community groups** to get a sense of whether this is the type of place that wants you.

Example: You may learn that newcomers are taxing local facilities and that the hot topic at the community meeting is how to discourage more people from moving in.

Your best choice for relocation may be a college town. It is most apt to provide enjoyable activities. And residents of college towns tend to be more accepting of outsiders than residents of a town where newcomers are rare.

William Seavey, director of The Greener Pastures Institute, which specializes in helping people relocate to smaller towns, 6301 South Squaw Valley Rd., Ste. 1383, Pahrump, NV 89048. He is the author of *Moving to Small Town America: How to Find and Fund the Home of Your Dreams*. Real Estate Education Co.

Traps in Buying a Retirement Home

Jack P. Friedman, CPA

When you near retirement, your most important task is to find suitable housing. Instead of focusing on your family's needs, you can focus solely on your own. To make a suitable match in today's housing market, avoid these mistakes...

●*Mistake:* **Blindly putting your home up for sale.** When you stop working, it's natural to think of moving, too. But—people rarely move when they retire.

A recent survey conducted by the Harvard–MIT Joint Center for Housing Studies found that only 20% of people over age 55 had moved. Only 5% said they planned to move in the next five years, and that declined to 1% for people over age 65.

•*Mistake:* **Misjudging your space needs.** A popular misconception is that retirees want to sell their homes because they are too big for their needs.

Reality: More people move into larger homes when they retire than into smaller homes.

However, because large homes are more expensive, you should critically evaluate how much space you really need.

Most important: Usable space. Bedrooms should be convenient to bathrooms. Other rooms should be easily accessible.

And—realistically gauge your needs for outdoor space and guest rooms for visitors.

•*Mistake:* **Failing to consider your retirement lifestyle.** Your new home should fit the way you live, especially after retirement when you have more time to do what you want.

Examples: Space for hobbies and crafts, or a smaller home with minimal upkeep and good security if you want to spend time traveling.

•*Mistake:* **Buying a home in the wrong location.** Location is always critical, but more so in retirement homes. To assess locations, rank in order of importance the places you need and want to be near.

Factors to consider: Proximity to medical care, public transportation, family, shopping, recreation, religious and cultural institutions.

•*Mistake:* **Ignoring neighborhood safety.** Spend time checking out potential new neighborhoods. Look for areas where nearly all people are home owners. Look for such signs as good lawn and property maintenance. Streets and sidewalks should be in good repair. Check out other public services—police, sanitation, parks.

Caution: An overly conspicuous presence of police officers may indicate the area is dangerous.

•*Mistake:* **Buying a home with the wrong floor plan.** When you evaluate a new home, consider your daily activities and how easily they could be accomplished in the space.

Important: The kitchen and bath areas, where so much everyday routine occurs. If you need special aids to move around, make sure there is enough space in the hallways and doorways. Generally, a single-story home is preferable.

Access to areas for moderate exercise is also necessary.

Examples: A backyard lap pool, wooded areas for taking walks, nearby leisure sports.

Choose easy-to-maintain materials for the interior spaces of your home. It's easier to hire people to keep your lawn and grounds than to hire maid service.

•*Mistake:* **Failing to consider remodeling your existing home.** If you choose not to move, you can redo your home to make it more suitable. *Caution:* Some of these changes may not appeal to a prospective buyer when you are ready to sell, so you may not recoup your investment.

Example 1: If your home is too large, convert some of the space to a separate dwelling unit. Make sure local zoning ordinances permit the conversion. *Bonus:* You can supplement your retirement income with rental income and tax breaks for the rental unit.

Example 2: Change unused bedrooms into recreation areas. Remodel a kitchen or bath. Remodel to remove hazards or obstacles. Add handrails and replace steps with ramps.

Before you retain a contractor…obtain references. Contact your local Better Business Bureau and the Associated General Contractors of America (202-393-2040). *Best:* Use contractors who have been in business five years or longer—and get written estimates and guarantees.

•*Mistake:* **Failing to consider reverse equity mortgages.** When you *don't* want to sell your home, you can convert the equity you have built up over the years into cash with a *reverse equity mortgage.*

How it works: You own your home or have a substantial amount of equity. When you take out a reverse equity mortgage, you pledge your home as collateral. The lender pays you a specified sum, depending on the payout option you choose. All outstanding principal and interest earned by your lender accumulate in an account. The loan is repaid when you move or sell the home, or from your estate after your death.

Typical payout options: One lump sum cash payment at closing, a regular stream of cash over time, a line of credit that allows you to draw cash whenever needed.

Insured loans: When the loan is insured by the Federal Housing Administration, payments can be arranged to last as long as you live in the house.

Cost: One-time premium equal to 2% of the loan balance plus a monthly premium, which can be included in the amount you borrow.

•***Mistake:*** **Failing to consider a sale-leaseback arrangement.** Another way to tap the equity in your home without selling it is a sale-leaseback arrangement.

How it works: An investor buys your home for its appraised value. You receive a sizable amount of cash as a down payment. You finance the balance of the purchase price on a 10- or 15-year mortgage, which provides you with a regular income stream. You pay rent to the buyer, who takes the tax benefits connected with rental real estate.

Drawbacks: You relinquish equity and ownership rights in your home. Be sure to limit rent increases in your lease because your income from the mortgage payments is fixed. Because the income is for a fixed term, purchasing a deferred annuity is recommended. Arrange for insurance to protect you should the investor default on the mortgage.

Charitable donation: You can arrange a similar transaction by donating your home to charity with the stipulation that you live in it as long as you wish. When you arrange a so-called charitable remainder trust, the difference between your home's market value and the price you receive is a deductible donation.

Jack P. Friedman, CPA, 7815 Kilbride Lane, Dallas 75248. He is coauthor of Keys to Buying a Retirement Home. *Barron's Educational Series.*

When Relocating

Before relocating by choice—for retirement or a lifestyle change—contact the Chamber of Commerce in any community that interests you. Get cost-of-living figures and year-round weather information—so you will know what you are getting into financially and climatically. If the Chamber of Commerce does not have the information, call the town's public library and speak to someone at the reference desk.

The Complete Idiot's Guide to a Great Retirement by Carolyn Janik, author of more than 20 books on business, real estate and lifestyles, Guilford, CT. Alpha Books.

Social Security News... New Traps... New Opportunities... And a Brighter Future Than the Media Let On

J. Robert Treanor
William M. Mercer, Inc.

One of the biggest fears people have now is that after decades of paying into the Social Security system, they will not receive the benefits they had expected.

Many of these fears are excessive—and there are many little-known Social Security provisions that can help you.

Here's what everyone needs to know about Social Security—and the steps to take to make the most of your benefits...

DON'T WORRY

•**Social Security will be solvent for a long time, despite dire predictions.** The system faces major problems—mainly because people are living longer and the ratio of active workers to retirees will decline in the next century. But it is unthinkable that a program of this magnitude will be allowed to go bankrupt.

Besides, the system is in far better financial shape than many people realize. Even those in their late 30s can count on collecting retirement benefits.

Contrary to public opinion, which holds that most people will never collect a dime, the Social Security system will be in good condition until the year 2012. Until that time, it will be taking in more in payroll taxes than it pays out in benefits.

And from then until the year 2029, the system will be able to continue paying out benefits from a combination of payroll taxes, interest income and assets in the Social Security trust funds.

This projection is assuming benefits will be paid at current levels. It is almost certain that the program will undergo some changes, but these changes don't have to be huge to save billions of dollars. Because of the enormous number of retirees, even modest changes to account for longer life expectancies—such as slightly decreasing cost-of-living adjustments or gradually increasing the age at which workers qualify for full benefits—can cut costs.

EARN MORE…KEEP MORE

•**Retirees can earn more than they used to and still collect full benefits.** People ages 65 to 69 can earn as much as $13,500 a year in 1997—and still keep their entire benefit checks.

This may come as news to retirees who are working part-time and have postponed receiving benefits to avoid going over the threshold.

If you are between the ages of 65 and 69 and earn more than $13,500 in 1997, your benefit check will decline by $1 for every $3 you earn over that amount.

SOME EARNINGS EXEMPT

•**Some income you receive after retirement is not counted in the retirement-earnings test.** Payments from an employer—such as accumulated vacation or sick pay… bonuses…severance pay…and deferred compensation—cause confusion for the recipient and the Social Security system. The key question to determine whether such payments are subject to the earnings test is *when the services were performed*…not when payments are received.

The Social Security Administration will generally assume that payments are earned when they are received—unless information is provided to the contrary.

During the application process, explain that these payments were earned in a year prior to retirement. Sometimes, a written explanation from you will be sufficient. In other cases, further explanation or documentation from your employer may be required.

WORKERS AND STAY-AT-HOMES

•**Working spouses are not viewed the same as stay-at-home spouses in terms of benefits.** There is a misconception that a woman who has worked for many years outside of the home loses out because the most a couple can receive is the husband's benefit plus 50% of that benefit for the wife.

That is only true if the wife *never* worked outside the home. If the wife had substantial earnings, she can receive a higher benefit on her own earnings record independent of her husband's benefit.

If the husband and wife were both maximum earners under Social Security, then she can receive the maximum benefit on her earnings record…and her husband can receive the maximum benefit on his.

This year, the top benefit at age 65 is $1,326 a month. So a working husband and working wife who are due the maximum benefits would receive a total of $2,652. If, by contrast, the wife had never worked, her benefit would be equal to half her husband's. The most this couple could collect is $1,989.

DELAYING PAYS

•**People who delay receiving benefits will get more credit on their Social Security payments.** Right now, if you wait beyond age 65 to begin receiving your retirement benefits, you earn delayed-retirement credits.

This means that each Social Security check you collect when you eventually retire will be larger than it would have been if you started collecting at the normal retirement age of 65.

For people born in the years 1931 or 1932, the credit is 5% for each year that benefits are delayed beyond the normal retirement age up to age 70. The credit rises gradually after that until it reaches 8% for people born in 1943 or later.

TOUGHER ON BOOMERS

● **Baby boomers will have to work longer before they qualify for full benefits.** As a result of legislation passed years ago, the normal retirement age will gradually be increased.

Currently, the normal retirement age is 65. But for people born in 1938, it is 65 years and two months. The threshold will gradually increase for people born after that until it reaches 67 for people born after 1959.

Key: That means you must wait longer to collect your full benefits. As long as you are fully insured (approximately 10 years of work covered by Social Security), however, you will still be able to collect reduced benefits as early as the first full month in which you are 62 years old.

Currently, the benefits you receive at age 62 are reduced by 20%. When the retirement-age threshold rises to 66 (for those born in the years 1943 to 1954), the reduction for early retirement at age 62 will be 25%. And when the retirement age rises to 67, that reduction will be 30%.

MEDICARE AND SOCIAL SECURITY

● **Even though the normal retirement age will increase**, the age to qualify for Medicare is scheduled to remain at 65. Medicare is the program that pays hospital costs and medical insurance for the elderly.

Medicare becomes available to you in the month in which you turn 65, whether you are retired or still working.

Currently, you automatically apply for Medicare when you apply for Social Security benefits.

When the normal retirement age becomes 67, you will probably have to apply for Medicare separately once you reach 65, just the way you must do now if you plan to work past that age.

J. Robert Treanor, manager of the Social Security division of William M. Mercer, Inc., an employee-benefits consulting firm, 1166 Avenue of the Americas, New York 10036. He is coauthor of the *1997 Mercer Guide to Social Security & Medicare.* William M. Mercer, Inc.

Collect Social Security While You Work

To receive Social Security while continuing to work, apply for benefits to begin in January of the year you become eligible. *You could save thousands of dollars…*

If you are under age 65, you lose one dollar of Social Security benefits for every two dollars of wages you earn above the legal limit (which is $8,640 for those under age 65 and $13,500 for those age 65 and older in 1997).

But an application for reduced benefits (before age 65) is not retroactive. So—if you apply for Social Security checks in August, you'll have only five months of checks to count against an entire year's worth of earnings, so you'll lose a greater percentage of your benefits.

Solution: Apply to get checks starting in January and you'll have a year's worth of benefits to count against a year of earnings. *Result:* You'll get to keep more of your Social Security —up to $7,000 more, although in most cases the difference will be less.

J. Robert Treanor, manager of the Social Security division of William M. Mercer, Inc., an employee-benefits consulting firm, 1166 Avenue of the Americas, New York 10036. He is coauthor of the *1997 Mercer Guide to Social Security & Medicare.* William M. Mercer, Inc.

Social Security Loophole

Starting at age 62, a divorced woman who was married for at least 10 years may be eligible for benefits based on her ex-husband's earnings—if she hasn't remarried and is not eligible for a higher benefit on her own. A divorced *man* can collect benefits under the same rule from his ex-wife if she worked in a higher-paying job.

Also: Divorced-spouse benefits do not reduce Social Security paid to the ex-spouse. Nor does the individual have to be receiving Social Security—as long as he/she is eligible to collect.

J. Robert Treanor, manager of the Social Security division of William M. Mercer, Inc., an employee-benefits consulting firm, 1166 Avenue of the Americas, New York 10036. He is coauthor of the *1997 Mercer Guide to Social Security & Medicare.* William M. Mercer, Inc.

For a Safer and Happier Future

Verify your Social Security record every three years to be sure you are getting credit for all of your earnings.

A benefits estimate is available by contacting the Social Security Administration, 800-234-5772, and requesting Form 7004—*Request for Earnings and Benefit Estimate Statement.*

Important: Verify that the information on the form about prior-year earnings is correct. If it is not, notify Social Security immediately.

Keys to Understanding Social Security Benefits by Thomas Dickens, PhD, CPA, professor of accounting at Clemson University. Barron's.

Social Security Trap

Social Security earnings records are incorrect for one of 10 people, says a study by Congress's General Accounting Office.

Mistakes range from minor—such as a typo in a name or Social Security number…to major —such as an omission of earnings from the record with a resulting reduction of benefits.

Even a minor error can complicate collection of benefits—and it is your responsibility to check your records and document mistakes. Don't wait more than three years to check your earnings—after that amount of time, it is not required that the error be corrected.

How to do it: Call the Social Security Administration at 800-772-1213, and request Form SSA-7004, *Request for Earnings and Benefit Estimate Statement.*

Barbara Weltman, an elder law attorney practicing in Millwood, NY.

11

Enjoying Your Leisure

How to Have the Time Of Your Life—Free

Diane Warner

You don't always have to spend a ton of money to have a good time. Even a cruise aboard a luxury ocean liner can be free if you know how to go about it...

•Seminars. Cruise lines are always looking for people to give speeches or seminars for the other passengers on board. If you qualify, a mere three lectures may get you aboard the ship of your dreams for an entire week without putting a dent in your bank account. Hot topics nowadays include time management, relaxation techniques, investing and other subjects that are related to retirement.

Phone the cruise lines requesting information or just write a letter, enclosing a résumé highlighting your field of expertise. Bon Voyage!

•Group leader. Another method to find free travel is to arrange your own group tour. Contact travel agencies and tour companies to see if they will accommodate you, providing you can guarantee them an agreed upon number of people for the tour. Then, sign up your friends and relatives to join in all the fun.

•Exchange club. If you can afford the transportation to get to your desired destination, but the lodging is too expensive—look at home exchange clubs. Some cater specifically to one group, like teachers for example.

•Local attractions. If travel isn't your cup of tea, there's still a whole lot to do—and you barely even have to crack open your wallet. Read your local newspaper and check for free events like concerts or festivals. And remember, even the toniest of museums often have at least one day with free admission.

•Hobbies. Biking, dancing or crafts can all be inexpensive—and you may even have the necessary equipment lying around the house. If you always wanted to act when you were younger, get involved with a local theater group.

●**Politics.** It won't cost you anything to get involved as a volunteer for a political campaign. And who knows, it may even save you money if the right candidate gets elected.

Diane Warner, author of *How to Have a Great Retirement on a Limited Budget*. Writer's Digest Books.

How to Get Tickets To Any Event Anytime, Anywhere

Mark Zwartynski
Mark Andrew & Associates Marketing Communications

When the sign reads, "Sold Out," don't believe it. Shrewd ticket shoppers know that you can get into concerts, plays and sporting events even when tickets aren't available through regular channels.

In fact, there is almost no event in the country that is closed to someone who knows the ropes and is persistent.

TONIGHT'S TICKETS

The less time you have to work on getting tickets for a sold-out event, the harder it is. But don't give up, even if the event is only a few hours off.

●**Plays and concerts.** Phone the theater or go to the box office. Ask the salesperson to tell you when ticket returns come in from people who have house seats. These are the blocks of tickets that performers and members of theater management automatically receive. Tickets they don't use generally go on sale to the public a few hours before curtain time.

If there are no returns for performances at the time you call, ask when chances are best for getting returned house tickets. *Alternatives...*

●**If standing-room-only tickets are available, consider taking them.** You can often move into the seats of the no-shows, particularly if you tip an usher.

●**Contact a ticket broker.** There are many resellers of tickets who are listed in the

Yellow Pages. Expect to pay at least 20% above the box office price, more if the show is a hit. Ask the broker for a receipt that lists the exact seat location and date of the show. Don't deal with a broker who won't give you one.

●**Call your friends.** You may have a friend or two connected with the entertainment business. Many of these people enjoy impressing others by getting tickets for sought-after shows.

●**Sporting events.** Many of the same ticket-finding tactics that work for stage plays also work for sporting events. But as a rule, it's harder to get a last-minute ticket to a sold-out sporting event. *Best bets:*

●**Call someone you know.** A friend, or a friend of a friend, may have contacts with sponsors, players or management of the arena. If you strike out there, try to contact someone who works for an affiliate station of a TV network. Networks are a particularly rich source of tickets.

●**Phone the box office.** Ask which companies have promotions with the game. Restaurants near the stadium, for example, often have dinner-and-ticket specials. Contact the restaurant or other companies with promotional tie-ins, and ask how to get tickets.

●**Use a broker.** They can be expensive, but prices nearly always drop as the hour of the event gets closer.

●**Talk with concierges at hotels.** Check with hotels in the city where the event is being held. Concierges usually have tickets or know where to get them. Like most other people, concierges often enjoy favors in return.

Warning: Beware of scalpers. It's chancy to buy from them, especially since new technology makes it easy to counterfeit tickets.

FUTURE PERFORMANCES

If you've had trouble getting tickets in the past and want to make sure that this rarely, if ever, happens again...

●**Cultivate a wide range of people in the entertainment business.** These include employees of theaters, concert halls, radio stations, music stores, sports arenas, ticketing services and the media, especially people who work for network affiliates, who can often be helpful in getting tickets to out-of-town games.

Example: If you live in Cincinnati and want a ticket to the US Open in New York, get to know people at the local CBS affiliate station. They *always* have access to tickets.

Newspaper and television reporters are useful to know because they're frequently offered tickets they don't use. Members of labor unions who work at these venues are also potential ticket sources.

●**Contribute to sponsoring organizations.** That automatically makes it easier to get tickets, especially for concerts, ballets and other subsidized events. But it can give you an even bigger edge.

Example: By going to concerts once or twice as a supporter, you're in a much better position to meet major patrons and musicians. These people can often get you tickets for *other* local events where they have clout.

●**Get to know people who work for major sponsors.** Banks often sponsor sporting events and concerts. If you already use a bank that does, cultivate the local manager. One of his perks is distributing tickets to customers he likes. If you don't use a sponsoring bank, consider opening an account at one that does.

Similarly, executives and employees of advertisers are usually in a position to get tickets. You also have opportunities to meet executives of sponsoring companies and advertisers through activities of chambers of commerce or other local business groups.

●**Swap services for tickets.** A company you've worked for may be able to offer a service to a ticketed event.

Examples: A printing company that can bid on the playbill contract. A restaurant that can supply food to stagehands and the cast.

●**Join a booster club for the local team.** Phone the team's public relations department to get information about the booster club.

●**Make friends with city officials or work on a local political campaign.** The mayor's office, police chief and officials of the convention bureau have access to tickets to nearly every event staged in their city. Politicians enjoy doling them out to their supporters.

Mark Zwartynski, former vice president of business operations for the Milwaukee Admirals hockey team, and currently president and CEO of Mark Andrew & Associates Marketing Communications. He is coauthor, with Dale Ratermann, of *Two on the Aisle: How to Get Tickets to Any Event, Anytime, Anywhere.* Masters Press.

How to See the Concerts And Shows that You Want to See Without Paying Scalpers' Prices

Angie Diehl-Jacobs
MJP, Inc.

You don't have to spend a fortune or be buddies with an industry VIP to get great tickets to great shows and concerts. *Here's how to avoid paying scalpers' prices...*

●**Call out-of-town ticket centers.** Your calls will likely go through more quickly, since phone lines in cities other than where the concert is to be held won't be as tied up the moment tickets for an event go on sale.

In the ticket business, "subregions" are often linked to a larger region's ticket database, so your selection is the same as the person calling from the town of the event. Tickets on phone orders are typically mailed to you, so leave yourself enough time.

Example: If you're trying to get seats to a performance in Los Angeles, call the ticket company's phone line in San Diego, Las Vegas or even Phoenix.

Helpful: Call the ticket center before the on-sale date and ask whether it will have tickets on sale in the outer markets and which ones (they vary each time).

●**Go to a ticket center with the smallest lines.** Some ticket centers do massive business, while others have hardly anyone waiting.

Helpful: A few days before your selected event goes on sale, stop by your local ticket center outlet. Ask a seasoned employee how many people are anticipated for that event's initial lineup.

Ask how long a line they've had for similar shows. Then ask if there's another store or outlet in their chain that may be less busy for that event.

Example: One record store may get long lines for country artists but few people for rock or pop.

Double-check that the store's ticket counter will be open at the designated sale time. Some stores may open their doors but not their ticket counters at that hour. Always stop by or call in advance to ask someone who knows—the ticket manager or store manager.

●**Go to the box office of the arena or theater an hour before show time.** Frequently, tickets that were on hold for VIPs, celebrities and industry executives aren't claimed by curtain time.

The remainder of unused tickets are returned to the box office for sale at the last minute. Unpaid COD or "will-call" tickets may also be released just after show time begins.

Be calm and clear when dealing with box office personnel. Many patrons turn into absolute maniacs at box office windows and are turned down.

If you're remotely pleasant and a genuine fan, you might get great seats—but you may miss a few bars of the opening act.

●**Buy season tickets.** While prices like $1,500 to $3,000 a seat may seem high for 25 or 30 shows per season, it's a lot cheaper if you take on partners.

Combine funds with a few friends or co-workers, then split up the shows on the schedule. The perks for season ticket holders are advance mailings and notifications, discount offers and more.

At some arenas, season ticket holders even have the option of reserving additional tickets before they go on sale to the general public.

Other arenas offer preferred patrons exclusive parking, hospitality privileges or parties as part of the season ticket package.

●**Buy group tickets** if you're only interested in one event.

Helpful: Call the arena or theater, and ask to speak to the group sales or sponsorship director as far in advance of the ticket sale as possible.

Some arenas consider 20 tickets a "group sale." If you represent a number of people at your company, school or organization who would like to buy tickets to a single event, you may be able to place your order ahead of time, get a group discount or both.

You'll have to play collection agent and gather the funds, but it may well be worth the effort to see your favorite performer in a decent seat for a face-value ticket and a nominal service charge.

Angie Diehl-Jacobs, vice president of MJP, Inc., an Encino, CA–based tour and concert promotion company for many of entertainment's top acts. She was previously head of marketing for one of California's largest music retailers, which operates ticket centers in many locations.

How to Get Stars' Autographs

Bill Miller
Autograph Collector Magazine

Collecting celebrity autographs is a great hobby—if your timing and the tone of your requests are appropriate.

Here's how to improve your odds of getting the signatures you want…

●**Hang out where the celebrities hang out.** If you are visiting New York or Los Angeles, you can wait outside movie premieres, Broadway openings or trendy hotels and clubs. You can find these places by looking in popular guidebooks and local magazines.

When you see a celebrity in person, there's a right and a wrong way to ask for an autograph.

Helpful: If you are asking the celebrity to sign a glossy photo, be sure to have a Sharpie brand marking pen. It writes smoothly, and the ink dries immediately.

Expect to be ignored or rudely dismissed if you approach celebrities while they are eating or when they are with their families. Most celebrities are very protective of their downtime and their children.

●**Write to your favorite celebrities.** This is a far easier way to get an autograph, though the signatures frequently have little value since it is impossible to verify who actually signed the celebrity's name. Some celebrities, however, do sign their own names—Muhammad Ali, Lauren Bacall and Janet Leigh, among others.

Helpful: Boost your odds by sending a thoughtfully written letter and including a photo for them to sign, a self-addressed, stamped envelope and two pieces of cardboard to protect the photo.

To reach a celebrity: Call the public relations department of the movie studio, TV network or record company for which the celebrity works, and ask for the address of his/her manager or agent.

Bill Miller, publisher of *Autograph Collector Magazine,* 510-A S. Corona Mall, Corona, CA 91719. The magazine lists hundreds of current addresses of celebrities—or their managers' and agents' offices.

Free Movie Posters

Ask your video store whether the old posters are given away when new ones come in. Sometimes stores will reserve special ones for you by putting your name on the back while they're still being displayed.

Lisa Reid, editor of *PurseStrings,* 36 Camino Cielo, Santa Fe 87501.

Smarter Gambling

Avoid slot machines—50% of the money dropped in goes to the casino.

Better bets: Roulette (only 25%)…baccarat (18%)…craps (15%)…blackjack (14%).

Also: Don't accept free drinks from the casino if you're playing games that require you to have a clear head—particularly poker or blackjack.

The New Gambler's Bible by Arthur S. Reber, PhD, a research scientist and psychologist in Brooklyn, NY. Crown.

Winning Strategies from America's #1 Poker Player

Ken Flaton

For the past 20 years, I have made my living at casino and tournament poker tables. I used to be an accountant, but playing poker was so lucrative for me that it is now a full-time job. I play 200 to 250 days a year and earn big winnings, year after year.

Although the stakes in my games are much higher than the average player's, there are strategies that can help improve anyone's game.

SMART RULES

●**Don't play too many hands.** People who lose frequently don't know when to fold their hands. If you don't have a good chance to win a particular hand based on the cards that have already appeared, you shouldn't be playing it.

●**If you're playing badly or losing**, stop and walk around. When things are going badly, it's hard to play your best. Collect your thoughts…figure out why you're losing…and then go back to your winning discipline.

●**Be willing to accept a loss.** Sometimes you're going to lose. That's the way it goes. The goal is to avoid losing more money by trying desperately to come out ahead. That's a sucker's strategy.

I've seen very good players turn a moderate loss into a disaster because they couldn't stand losing.

MY FAVORITE POKER STRATEGIES

●**Always count the cards on the table.** All good players keep precise track of the live cards—ones that have not yet appeared face up on the table and are likely still in the deck.

They assess the odds of the table by knowing that there are 13 cards in every suit and four cards of every type. They also know that as the cards they need appear face up elsewhere on the table, their own odds of winning decline. When the odds of being dealt a winning card are low—*fold.*

Example: If I'm holding four hearts and I'm one heart away from a flush, I'm probably not going to make it if I see six hearts face up around the table. That tells me there are only three hearts left in the deck for me. Bad odds. But if I see only one other heart out there, then eight hearts are left—some of which may be left in the deck. The odds are now almost three times as good that I'll make my flush.

Such analysis should affect your betting and your willingness to stay in a hand.

Similarly, keep track of cards that could improve your *opponents'* hands. If an opponent is showing a seven, eight, nine and a jack, and three 10s have shown, it is unlikely that the person has a straight.

● **Bet aggressively when you have a good hand.** You increase the odds of winning if you take control of the table's psychology. The goal is to make other players worry that you have a powerful hand. By betting aggressively, you will cause some players to fold hands that may have been better than yours. And—you may also scare off those players who could have improved their hands on the next draw and beaten you.

A player who just calls opponents' hands without raising is cultivating a losing style. People will figure out that when that person raises, it's a sure sign he/she has a great hand.

Important: Though I don't believe in *slow-playing*—refusing to raise even though my hand is likely the winner—there are exceptions.

Example: If I'm holding four of a kind, I won't raise. Sometimes your only chance to win a decent pot is to keep quiet.

● **Always think about your opponents' cards.** If you avoid speculating on the cards your opponents hold, you won't be a winning player. In fact, it's often more important to think about what they have than to figure out how to play your own cards.

Helpful: Constantly assess the relative value of your hand compared with those of your opponents. Study their face-up cards, and try to figure out from the betting patterns and their mannerisms what they might logically have.

Your so-called "good" hand is only truly good if it is better than your opponents' hands.

Example I: If an opponent who is a conservative player starts betting when he has an ace showing, there's a good chance he has a pair of aces.

Example II: A pair of kings can be a terrible hand if you're playing against a pair of aces. A pair of eights isn't much to be proud of, but if you've figured out that your opponent has a pair of sevens, it is all you need to win.

Also, you should always be prepared to fold a strong hand—a straight, flush or a full house—when you're convinced your opponent has something better.

● **Beware of playing above your level.** I'm a great believer in the old poker adage—*If you*

sit down and don't see a fish at the table, the fish is you.

There are games that are too good for me. Wherever I play at a casino, I usually sit down at the table with the second-biggest stakes.

Reason: The more expensive table always has better players.

● **Don't always fold when you suspect someone has a better hand.**

Example: Let's say that I think my opponent has a pair of kings. I have a pair of sixes and an ace. Well, if I draw another ace or another six, there's a good chance that I'll win the pot. So if a lot of the aces and sixes are "live," I'll probably stay in the hand.

Reason: The player with the kings may catch another pair, but if I get one of my cards I'll still win. If the person with the kings bets and someone else raises, then I may fold. Playing catch-up with more than one person is very dangerous.

● **Stay in the game mentally even when you fold.** I recently saved money by figuring out that the player to my left often raised on bad hands to bluff opponents. Then in a hand where he had an ace showing, he reversed his behavior and didn't raise.

Although I had two kings—a very strong hand—I was wary of my opponent, so I bet as meekly as I could. A good thing, because it turned out the guy had started the hand with three aces. I lost, but it would have been a lot worse had I not figured out his betting style.

Ken Flaton of Henderson, NV, winner of the $500,000 first prize at the 1996 US Poker Championship, held at the Taj Mahal Hotel and Casino, Atlantic City. He has won many other tournaments, including a Seven-Card Stud tournament at the World Series of Poker.

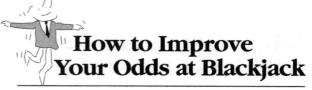

How to Improve Your Odds at Blackjack

Mark Pilarski

Nearly all blackjack players make dumb mistakes consistently. *Result:* Losers! You can significantly improve your blackjack odds by taking the game seriously...

and by following these steps each time you play…

● Use a *perfect* basic strategy. The simplest way to narrow the odds is to play each hand correctly.

When you play perfectly in a game that uses six decks, the house advantage is only a mere six-tenths of 1%.

Even when you have a bad hand, there is always a best move.

Helpful: Get a laminated strategy card* that tells you the best move to make, no matter what your hand and what cards the dealer is showing. Most casinos will even let you look at the instruction card while you play as long as you don't slow down the game.

Example: As uncomfortable as it may feel, always ask for another card when you have cards that total 16 and the dealer has a 7, 8, 9, 10 or ace showing.

● Avoid making the most common mistakes. Even those players who have memorized the strategies on the card can make judgment errors. *Basics…*

● Don't play your hunches. Such deviations from a perfect basic strategy simply lower your odds.

● Follow a set strategy—even when it seems foolhardy. When you have a pair of eights against a dealer's 10, split them—that is, turn them both face up and ask the dealer for two cards face down.

This is hard to do because it looks as if you're inviting defeat twice—instead of just once. While splitting two cards of a kind doesn't mean that you'll win, it does mean that your odds of losing are somewhat lower.

● Always "double down" (bet more) when your chances of winning a hand are greater than the dealer's. Your strategy card has guidelines.

● Alter your betting in selected situations. If you bet the same amount of money hand after hand, the house's slight advantage will be devastating.

*A laminated strategy card can be found in many blackjack books…at many casinos for about $3…or by sending a self-addressed, stamped envelope and $1 to Winners Publishing, 774 Mays Blvd., #10, Incline Village, Nevada 89451.

Better: Raise your bets progressively after you win a hand.

Example: If you bet $2 and win, then bet $4 on the next hand. If you win again, bet $6. Add the amount of your original bet—$2—on each hand. When you lose, return to the minimum bet of $2 and then continue the formula.

● Learn when to leave a table. If you lose three or four hands in a row, leave the game and look for another table. This discipline prevents the casino from grinding you down during a cold streak.

● Play in shifts. If your total stake is $100, divide it into fifths. Go to another table if you lose $20. If you lose another $20—find *another* table. This strategy helps your bankroll last longer and gives you a fresh start at another table—where you won't feel destined to lose.

● Try card counting. You don't have to be a professional to do a rudimentary count in a game that uses only one or two decks. (In the more common six-deck games, the effort probably isn't worth it.)

Example: If a lot of low cards (2, 3, 4, 5 and 6) have already appeared, that gives the players an advantage, since higher cards are likely to follow. When this occurs, consider raising your bets. Conversely, when many aces and 10s have already appeared, the dealer's edge increases.

Mark Pilarski, former professional card dealer and casino pit boss who writes a syndicated casino gaming column for 40 newspapers nationwide. He is the creator of a series of audiotapes called *Hooked on Winning.* Winners Publishing.

Hot New Casino Game: "Let It Ride"

Best way to play *Let It Ride*, the hot casino game right now—avoid the side bet. In *Let It Ride*, the dealer gives three cards to each player and takes two. Players open with three equal bets. After looking at their cards, they may take back one bet and keep playing or let all bets ride. The dealer then reveals one card —and players may take back another bet…or let it ride. If the player's three cards and dealer's two make at least a pair of 10s, the player wins. Payouts are based on how good the combined player-dealer hand is. The casino's edge is only about 3% on the initial bets.

Catch: A $1 side bet offers big prizes if a player receives a straight or royal flush. The house's edge on that bet is a huge 55%—avoid it.

Frank Scoblete, gaming expert and publisher of *Chance and Circumstance,* Box 610, Lynbrook, NY 11563.

Casino Gambling Rules to Play by

Never start gambling without setting a target for how much winnings it would take you to walk away satisfied...and a limit for the losses you will tolerate before quitting.

Caution: The longer you stay at a casino table, the greater the risk you will walk away a loser. Although you may have a lucky streak, the laws of probability will catch up with you. Quit while you're ahead.

Marvin Karlins, PhD, a psychologist and professor of business management at the University of South Florida.

Casino Rip-Off

Casino ads touting big slot machine payoffs are often misleading. Ads that shout "highest payback" and "98% return" usually fail to mention that not all machines in the casino will pay back those amounts.

Reality: Often only one or two machines—in a casino with as many as 1,500—are that liberal.

Tip-off: Look for the words *up to* in the ads.

Strategy: Tip the person who makes change for you a few dollars and he/she may point you to the best machines.

Donald Currier, editor of *Las Vegas Insider,* Box 29274, Las Vegas 89126.

Gambling Secrets— More For You, Less for Casinos

Olaf Vancura, PhD
Harvard-Smithsonian Center for Astrophysics

If you want to keep more of your winnings at the casinos, it helps to understand how they take your money.

Though you can't change the odds on a particular bet, you can make the smartest wagers and avoid the many losing bets that casinos offer.

WINNERS' RULES

●**Don't drink and gamble.** The casino knows that the more free drinks you accept, the more likely it is that you'll eventually surrender all of your stake.

Exception: The only time you should have a drink in front of you is when you're counting cards in blackjack and trying to avoid detection.

Ordering another drink—even though you haven't touched a drop—can help convince casino personnel that you're a tourist on a spree rather than someone who is keeping mental track of the cards that have appeared.

●**Know the rules of each game and the ideal playing strategy.** It doesn't take long, for example, to master a perfect blackjack strategy.

●**Don't place faith in "streaks" or systems.** Statistically speaking, there is no way to take advantage of them. Every roll of the dice is an independent event, absolutely unaffected by what happened before.

Casino employees, however, may encourage you to believe in luck and hot streaks in an attempt to increase your betting. No one has yet found a system—other than counting cards and making the wisest bets—that works in a casino.

●**Don't get caught up in the excitement.** Beware of casinos that spread the word of a player's big win. Odds are the story is true, but the casino is announcing the news so you'll loosen up your play and take greater risks. They want to make back from you what they just lost to the other guy.

●Don't ever bet more than you intended to lose. Your loss limit must be inviolate.

HOW CASINOS TAKE YOUR MONEY

●High-payout slot machines. You'll often see signs in casinos trumpeting the fact that slot machines that take higher-denomination coins offer a "97.4% payout." Technically, this is true. Machines that take a dollar *or more* frequently return 97.4% of each dollar to bettors —a return that is substantially higher than the slot machines that just take quarters.

But this improved return is essentially an illusion. What really matters more to average gamblers is how much they will lose with each pull of the handle, given the machine's denomination and expected return.

Example: Play $5 each time and, on average, you'll lose 13 cents per pull. Stick to the quarter slots, though, and your loss per pull will be about one or two cents—which means that your stake will last about 10 times longer.

You can't make money staking out a machine that hasn't paid a jackpot in a long time. Although the total payout is predetermined, the frequency of payouts is absolutely random.

●Blackjack. It's important not to be distracted by the bad play of others. The way they play has no effect on the odds. Don't ever place an "insurance bet," which is actually a side bet and does not insure anything.

Better bet: The "surrender bet," which allows you to give up half your bet before the hand is over. This is a wise bet when you have a total of 16 and the dealer has a 9, 10 or ace showing—or when you have a 15 and the dealer has a 10 showing. The odds are great that you're going to go over 21 if you take a card—or that you'll lose by keeping what you have.

●Poker. The players at the table may look like tourists, but many aren't. Some play full-time, and they're very good. The higher the stakes, the higher the percentage of professionals at the table.

●Baccarat. The dealer or other baccarat players may encourage you to track the play of the cards and develop a betting system, but this is a wasted effort. Because of the structure of the game, card counting does not work when you are playing baccarat, nor does any betting system.

Better: To maximize returns, always bet on the banker. Even though a bet on the banker pays only 95 cents for every dollar that you have wagered, the odds are slightly better than a bet on the player.

Warning: Never bet on a tie. The house edge here is high—14.4%. For example, on average, each time you bet $100, you can expect to get back only $85.60.

●Craps. The casino increases its craps take by encouraging players to make bad bets. The stickman who controls the dice at the craps table may tell you the "field bet" has more winning numbers than losing ones. This is true, but losing numbers occur with greater frequency, turning the odds against you. The house edge on this bet is 5.56%.

Solution: Stick to only the best bets when you are playing craps. These include the "don't pass" bet, when the house edge is just 1.36%. The house edge is just 1.41% on the "pass" bet. You can also take some "free odds" on these two wagers.

●Cash-advance machines. Some casinos have cash machines right at the gaming tables. *Why you should avoid them...*

●You are probably already putting more cash at risk than you had originally intended to—which is a potentially disastrous situation.

●You are paying a lot for the privilege. For example, on an advance of $1,001, many casinos will charge you $66—a 6.6% fee. That's on top of the standard 2% credit card cash-advance fee ($20.02) and the interest that starts accumulating the second that you take the cash advance. So you end up 8.6% behind —and you haven't even made a bet yet.

Olaf Vancura, PhD, astrophysicist at the Harvard-Smithsonian Center for Astrophysics, Cambridge, MA. He is a consultant to casinos and teaches casino gambling at Tufts University, Medford, MA. Dr. Vancura is author of *Smart Casino Gambling: How to Win More and Lose Less.* Index Publishing.

Lotteries...Lotteries... Lotteries

Ron Jones
Professor Jones, Inc.

While it's true that you can't change the odds in lotteries and other similar games of chance, with a little effort, you can put yourself in a much better position to win.

To get the edge, you need to know two facts of which most lottery players aren't aware...

●**The numbers that come up in lotteries, Lotto and Power Ball** aren't as random as the operators would have you think.

●**All games aren't equal.** Lotteries in some states offer vastly better odds than games elsewhere.

By finding the best games and making the most of winning patterns, you can improve your odds as much as a hundredfold over players who pick tough games and employ no strategies.

Winning strategies for the country's most popular games...

INSTANT GAMES

The odds on scratch-and-win and similar instant games are so long and the prizes so small that it's best to avoid them altogether.

Some states actually sell $1 tickets with the promise that you have a one-in-10 chance of winning $5. While those odds might sound good at first, they actually mean that you have almost no chance of winning a substantial amount of money and only a minimal chance of breaking even.

Strategy: Don't play instant games unless the prize is at least $10,000. And even then, don't buy more than a few tickets.

LOTTERIES

Despite the hoopla about "random" drawings, there's probably no commercial game of chance in the world where the selection of winners is truly random.

Reason: Just as no pair of dice is precisely even and balanced, the *slightest* imperfection in lottery machinery also produces a bias.

Example: Many states determine winners by forcing air into a bin containing balls numbered from zero to nine. The balls that make it into tubes at the top of the bin become the winning numbers.

To make the system completely random, each ball would have to be identical, almost molecule for molecule. The bin and the air shaft would also have to be precision-designed and tested for years before anyone could be sure that the mechanism didn't favor some types of balls over others.

Obviously, it's impractical for any state to attempt this degree of randomness. *How to exploit the bias:*

●**Keep track of the frequency with which each of the balls**, typically 10 in number, comes up as a winner. Because of the system's bias, for example, five and eight may win more often than other numbers.

To collect information on lottery draws, either read the results in daily papers or ask your state's lottery commission for past results. Commissions are nearly always happy to supply them.

Helpful: Computer software that tracks data and identifies biased numbers. It's widely advertised in lottery and gaming publications, which are often on sale at stores where lottery tickets are sold.

Don't track data more than two years old. *Reason:* Earlier biases in the lottery mechanism may not be present today.

●**In addition to keeping track of the frequency**, also track balls that show up as winners in specific tubes or other devices used to catch the balls. This is *positional analysis.*

In the first tube, for instance, four and six may be frequent winners. In the second tube, you might detect a bias for two and nine, and so on.

●**Play combinations of numbers that are most likely to be winners according to your positional analysis.**

Shrewd business: To raise your odds even higher, play lotteries in states and other jurisdictions where the number of players is the lowest and jackpots are the highest. This information is also available from lottery commissions.

Hedge your bets: In addition to playing the positionally frequent numbers, also make one bet on the *least* likely numbers to come up.

There's no mathematical rationale for the hedge, but it can give you peace of mind in covering more possibilities. And it could prove to be the winning tactic if the lottery commission suddenly decides to use new equipment with a new set of untracked biases.

LOTTO

In the typical lotto game, known as "6/49," six balls are chosen from a total of 49, and the odds of winning are one in nearly 14 million.

Positional analysis is again the best strategy. But it can pay to consider two variations of this tactic...

●**Associated numbers.** The nature of biases causes some numbers to appear frequently before and after others. In some state lottos, for example, "18" may frequently be preceded by "12" and followed by "31."

●**Overdue biased numbers.** Track the positional bias just as you would for a lottery. You may discover, for example, that "23" has been the most frequent winner over the past 18 months. But if it hasn't come up in the last six weeks, "23" could be one of the numbers to bet.

There may not be a mathematical rationale for the choice, but many experienced lotto players believe it's valid.

POWER BALL

This is essentially a variation on "6/49" lotto. In Power Ball, however, the sixth number is drawn from its own separate pool of 49 balls. That means the odds of winning are less than one in 105 million.

Use the positional frequency strategy in Power Ball, if you choose.

But since the number of biased combinations can be so large, it's often impractical (and expensive) to play all possible numbers that have proved to be frequent winners.

Experienced lottery players often solve the problem by using what's known as the Dimitrov Wheel. It's a mathematical formula for spreading biased numbers around in the most efficient way.

Example: If there are three biased numbers for each of the six positions in Power Ball,

you'd have to buy thousands of tickets in order to cover all combinations.

The Dimitrov Wheel, however, tells you how to pick the 10 or so combinations that let you maximize the odds. The formula is available in many lottery publications and is built into most lottery software. For more information, call Professor Jones, Inc., 800-553-2256.

And, don't pick "unpopular" numbers on the theory that, if you win, you won't have to share the prize with other winners. If you're lucky enough to win $50 million, would it really matter if you shared the prize? The important thing is to pick the right number.

Ron Jones, a mathematical analyst of lottery systems, and author of Winning Lotto/Lottery for Everyday Players. *Cardoza Publishing. He is president of Professor Jones, Inc., developers of computer programs for lottery players, 1940 W. State St., Boise, ID 83702.*

How to Have More Fun On Your Day at the Races And Win More Money...Or Lose Less

Len Ragozin
Len Friedman

Taking a cue from gambling casinos, racetracks have mellowed during the past few years—without sacrificing any excitement.

Even someone without knowledge of horses and betting can have fun. Easier-to-use information now makes picking horses more understandable and accessible to almost everyone. *Here's what you need to know at the track...*

THE BEST SEATS

Race-goers prefer seats that let them see the entire race from start to finish. That means the top floor of the track in the middle of the stretch toward the finish line...or any seat in a restaurant that is laid out for track viewing.

On an average racing day, to get seated in the restaurant before too many races go by, you will have to slip $5 to the maitre d'—even when the restaurant looks empty. A bigger tip will get you a better-placed table. When a high-stakes race is run, it may take $100 or more.

At many tracks, it is standard practice for ushers to let people who tip at least $10—or more if you are in a group—use boxes they know will be unoccupied by the box owners that day.

FUN INFORMATION

Casual visitors to the track need not burden themselves with trying to decipher the vast array of statistics and horse-performance data in *The Daily Racing Form*—the newspaper of racing fans. You will only confuse yourself.

Instead, have fun by soaking up the atmosphere and studying the general sources of information…

• **The track's program** is available for about $2 from the stands. Most programs at the major racetracks include some past-performance information, such as how each horse did in its last three or four races. It also includes advice on each race from the track handicapper.

Example: The horse may not have liked wet tracks in recent efforts.

• **Closed-circuit television** can be viewed from many seats at the track…at your table in the restaurant at most tracks…or at a casino's horse-betting room. The on-air track handicapper gives analysis on each race about 10 to 15 minutes before it starts. Don't take too seriously the standard phrases used to describe the conditions of various horses—*raring to go …sparkling…prancing.* That's mostly hype.

• **The track's televised report** features information from trainers about the horses that have never run—or that have not run for some time. It gives breeding information, such as whether the horse comes from a line that does well racing on grass or has a record of winning races. The comments can be interesting.

• **Tout sheets** cost about $1 and are available at every track. They offer three or four picks for each race and some capsule comment, such as *Catches them in the stretch… sharp first-timer.*

• **The paddock area** allows you to take a closer look at the horses.

PICKING HORSES

Even for a casual day at the races, the racing and betting action gets more interesting if you make an effort to get a handle on…

…the ability of each horse in a race.

…whether a horse's more recent races are better than its showing some months earlier.

Helpful: Andy Beyer's speed ratings in *The Daily Racing Form* can be your first step toward making such analyses. The past-performance chart for each horse lists its last 10 races. Next to each race is the Beyer speed rating—the higher the number, the better the horse's effort in that particular race.

A more advanced source of ratings that are ideal for casual bettors are the 6" x 9" slips of paper known as *The Sheets.* They are sold at the track and cost about $25. The sheets feature graphed data that show the horse's history and help even novice racetrack visitors to spot trends.

PLACING YOUR BETS

Allow yourself at least 10 minutes before the start of each race to place your bet.

Strategy: Jot down on your program what your bet or bets are going to be before you get to the window. If you pause and act bewildered at the window, you'll be harassed by those in line behind you who fear being shut out of betting on the race.

What to do: The universal way to call out your bet at any track or casino window…

• **Race number.**

• **Amount of the bet.**

• **Type of bet,** *such as:*
  ☐ **Win,** for a horse to come in first.
  ☐ **Place,** to come in second or first.
  ☐ **Show,** third, second or first.
  ☐ **Exacta**—two horses to come in first and second in that order.
  ☐ **Quinella**—two in either order.
  ☐ **Trifecta**—horses that finish first, second, third in that order.
  ☐ **Trifecta Box**—six bets for horses that finish one, two, three in any order.
  ☐ **Exacta Box**—two bets for any two of your horses coming in first and second.
  ☐ **Daily Double**—the winners of two successive races.

•**Number of the horse on the program**—not the name of the horse or the post position.

WOW—YOU'VE WON

If you have a winning ticket on a race, you have two choices between races—to pocket your money or to use it toward a bet on the next race.

Beware: You'll inevitably feel rushed… and, if you are not careful, you might wind up walking away from the cashier with less money than you should. Track cashiers around the country have a tradition of counting out money in an odd way.

Example: Say you hand in a ticket that pays $38. The cashier will swiftly count out a five-dollar bill and three singles. And pause. Then go back to the drawer, deliver a $10 bill—and pause again. A surprising number of eager bettors will grab the cash after one of these pauses and rush away.

Simple defense: Ask the cashier whether it's all there. Then count your money—and re-confirm the amount with the cashier.

Len Ragozin, founder and owner of *Ragozin Data Sheets,* a publisher of horse-racing data, 56 E. 11 St., New York 10003…and Len Friedman, part-owner and manager of New Top Stable in New York, one of the top thoroughbred stables in the US.

Hobbies Can Be More than Just Fun… Turn Yours into Tax Deductions

James A. Cox
Ernst & Young, LLP

You have no doubt picked your hobbies for the pleasure they bring—but they'll be even more enjoyable if you use them to cut your taxes.

Even casual hobbies can provide tax savings. And if you have a serious hobby, with just a little extra thinking you may be able to obtain significant deductions that you can claim against your outside, nonhobby income. *Here's how:*

RULES

Income earned from hobbies is fully taxable, just like all other income.

Expenses are deductible as well—but the extent to which deductions are allowed depends on whether you engage in the activity merely for recreational reasons…or with a *profit motive,* regardless of whether you actually make a profit.

•**Casual hobbies.** When there's no profit motive behind a hobby, expenses can be deducted to the extent that the hobby produces taxable income.

So if you will receive income from a hobby —perhaps from the sale of a collectible or of something you created such as a painting or a sculpture—you will want to have a record of hobby expenses to deduct against the income. *Examples:*

•**If you own collectibles**, the annual costs of maintaining, storing and insuring them are deductible against the income earned from their sale.

•**If you breed animals**, the annual costs of feeding and caring for them can be deducted against the income from their sale.

•**Gains and losses.** A gain realized on a collectible that has been held for more than one year is a long-term capital gain and is taxable at a top rate of only 28%—compared with ordinary rates as high as 39.6%.

Losses on sales of collectibles are deductible against gains on similar collectibles—and only against such gains. They are not deductible against other capital gains or ordinary income.

Thus, when you sell a collectible at a gain, it may be a good idea to "clean up" your collection by selling other items in the same year that have gone down in value. That way you utilize losses and shelter gains from tax.

Important: Be sure to keep a record of your tax costs from collectibles—what you paid for them, plus any amounts you may have paid to improve them.

If you make the common mistake of failing to keep records of costs, the entire sale price of an item may be deemed a taxable gain—and you will be unable to claim any loss deductions because you won't be able to prove them.

If you receive a collectible by...

•*Gift*, your tax basis in the item is the same as that of the donor. Be sure to get documentation of it.

•*Inheritance*, the basis is "stepped up" to market value—a tax break as it eliminates gains tax on appreciation to date.

This tax break can be worth a lot when it attaches to big-ticket items that are passed down through the family—such as antiques, artworks, rare books and so on—so get an appraisal for such items as soon as they are inherited.

•**Deduction limit.** Deductions from a hobby can't exceed hobby income. They are counted among miscellaneous expenses, which are deductible if the total exceeds 2% of your Adjusted Gross Income (AGI).

TAX SHELTER

If you have a serious hobby, you may become able to claim much larger deductions from it with just a little extra work by qualifying it as a "profit-motivated" activity. That's possible even if you don't actually make a profit.

The payoff is that *all* related expenses then become deductible under normal business-deduction rules, without reference to the 2%-of-AGI limit.

And if the expenses exceed your income from the activity, any excess can be deducted against your income from other sources—such as salary—to shelter it from tax. *Items you can deduct...*

•**Part of your home set aside for exclusive use** as a home office or studio where you conduct your activity.

•**Depreciation and related expenses on a separate structure**—such as a greenhouse — used exclusively in the activity.

•**50% of the cost of activity-related meals and entertainment expenses.**

•**Subscriptions to activity-related publications.**

•**Travel related to the activity.**

•**Operating expenses**—such as telephone bills, the cost of stationery supplies, advertising and so forth.

•**Use of your car** for the activity.

•**Equipment used exclusively in the activity**—a personal computer, cellular phone, fax, furniture, etc. These can be depreciated, and up to $17,500 worth may qualify for an expense deduction.

If the activity produces net income, you'll be eligible to make a deductible Keogh plan retirement contribution of generally 15% of net earnings.

And you may be able to deduct salaries paid to family members whom you employ in your activity.

If you're incurring many of these expenses in the conduct of a serious hobby and not deducting them, the result of demonstrating a profit motive for your activity may be a big bottom-line saving.

PROTECTING DEDUCTIONS

As mentioned above, you do not have to make a profit to show a profit motive for your activity. In fact, you don't even have to expect to make a profit in the near future, since legitimate businesses often incur losses for prolonged periods. But you can expect the IRS to be highly suspicious of a hobbylike activity—such as stamp collecting or dog breeding—that's used to generate large tax deductions. So you should have evidence of your intention to earn a profit. *To document your profit motive:*

•**Keep businesslike books and records**, with a separate bank account for the activity.

•**Register with local authorities** to obtain any necessary permits or licenses.

•**Keep a business diary** that includes a record of your activities relating to your hobby.

•**Draw up a business plan**, and update it in light of financial results and changing circumstances.

•**Consult with recognized professionals** in the field periodically.

•**Have business cards and stationery printed.**

•**If you buy and sell items, advertise and register to make sales by credit card.**

Not one of these items is determinative—but the more businesslike you are in pursuing the activity, the safer it will be if challenged by the IRS.

Choice: If your activity involves collectibles, such as stamps, coins or antiques, you must decide whether to conduct your for-profit activity as an *investor* or a *trader*. An investor buys and holds a collectible hoping to profit in the future, while a trader actively buys and sells looking for short-term profits.

●**An investor gets the benefit of the 28% tax rate on long-term capital gains.** But only $3,000 of net capital losses are deductible annually, and other investment-expense deductions may be limited.

●**A trader must pay the ordinary tax rate on all gains but gets a full deduction for all losses and expenses.**

The courts have ruled that the fact that you enjoy your activity does not disqualify it from being profit-motivated.

WINNING IDEAS

If your activity earns a profit during three out of five years, it is presumed to have a profit motive and loss deductions will be allowed for the loss years.

If your activity initially generates big losses and the IRS challenges it, you can delay the challenge by filing IRS Form 5213, *Election to Postpone Determination as to Whether the Presumption Applies that an Activity Is Engaged in for Profit*. This postpones the final determination of the activity's for-profit status until after you've been in business five years. In the meantime, you can claim loss deductions.

Catch: If your activity fails to qualify as for-profit at the end of the five-year period, you will owe back taxes and penalties.

It is possible, however, to incur losses from a hobbylike activity for many years while retaining for-profit status—and deductions for tax losses. *Examples:*

●**An executive who lived in the city bought a farm** and spent his weekends renovating it. He didn't expect to make a profit from it for at least 10 years, but the court ruled in his favor nonetheless. The court said that his expectation of future profits combined with the hard work he put in justified a current deduction for his costs.

Melvin Nickerson, 700 F2d 402.

●**An artistic housewife admitted that she painted for pleasure.** But she also made a serious effort to sell her paintings at shows and galleries. She was allowed to deduct her painting-related costs.

C. West Churchman, 68 TC 696.

●**A full-time probation officer who was a longtime stamp collector** was able to deduct losses that resulted from his collecting after he registered as a stamp dealer. The tax court ruled in his favor—even though the same court had rejected deductions he had claimed for the same expenses in an earlier year when his behavior indicated he was merely a stamp "hobbyist."

Eugene Feistman, TC Memo 1982-306.

James A. Cox, partner, Ernst & Young, LLP, 555 California St., San Francisco 94104.

How to Get a Better Restaurant Table

Get a better restaurant table—even if you're not a regular, a big tipper or a celebrity.

How: Make your reservation through a hotel concierge, even when you're still at home. Since hotels send restaurants a lot of business, a kind word in your favor from the concierge should help you get a good table.

Advice: Afterward, be sure to send a thank-you and a gratuity to the concierge.

Other strategies: Write for reservations using your business stationery…have your assistant call for a reservation—or, if you don't have one, call as your own assistant.

C. Paul Luongo, restaurant critic, writing in *Travel Smart*, 40 Beechdale Rd., Dobbs Ferry, NY 10522.

On-Line Auctions

On-line auctions can bring bargains within reach of anyone with a computer and Internet connection. Coins, stamps, antiques, computer items, etc., are available on-line.

Latest offerings: Airline tickets. Certain travel agencies and some airlines auction tickets a day or two before flights to anyone willing to make last-minute travel plans. Prices can be as little as 10% of ticket values.

Information: Consult your travel agent.

John Edwards, computer industry analyst and writer on high-tech subjects, 3111 Rte. 38, Ste. 118, Mount Laurel, NJ 08054.

How to Win the Auction Game

Ralph and Terry Kovel

The news that a Honus Wagner baseball card sold for $640,500 reminded us that nearly anyone can get carried away at an auction. *Here's our advice to avoid spending more than you want...*

●**Stay cool during the frenzy.** Auctions are exciting, and when you're in the middle of a bidding war, the adrenaline really starts pumping. It's easy to become extremely competitive.

Important: Don't let the bidding process become personal.

Strategy: Write down the maximum you will spend for each item before the bidding starts—and stick to those amounts.

Example: A good friend who attended the Jackie Onassis auction did just that and decided that she would bid up to $2,000 for Jackie's Tiffany tape measure. And she stuck to her limit—which was a good thing, since the item ultimately went for $48,875.

●**Preview the collection.** A big mistake some people make is buying a piece that is in worse condition than they assumed...or that looks great in the catalog next to terrific items, but when isolated looks rather shabby—or certainly unglamorous.

Best: Read the catalog, and look at the item carefully before the auction. Many auctions have previews several days before the sale. All auctions will allow you to look an hour or two before the bidding begins. Is the item you are considering really as special as you think it is?

●**Find out the exact purchase terms.** Every auction has different rules and expenses that could be costly if you aren't prepared for them. Call for the exact terms before you attend. *Examples:*

●**Some auctioneers won't arrange for shipment of purchases.** Often, you are required to remove your purchases from the premises within 24 hours.

●**Know the buyer's premium**, which you'll have to pay in addition to the final price. The buyer's premium acts as a commission and is usually 10% to 15% of the final purchase price. Some auction houses have slightly higher buyer's premiums if you pay by credit card. At Sotheby's, the premium per item is 15% for the first $50,000...and 10% thereafter.

Important: The highest price that you are willing to spend on any item should also include the buyer's premium.

●**At many auctions, you can't bid unless your credit is approved.** Be sure to ask in advance what you must do to establish credit. Often, a credit card is sufficient. At other times, the auctioneer may need a statement from your bank or may want to speak to your banker.

●**Attend a few auctions as a spectator.** Ideally, you should attend at least one auction for practice.

Strategy: Write down the prices that people pay. Try to sense the buying patterns. Who is buying the silver jewelry? Are the sale prices much higher than the estimates? Which buyers seem to have unlimited resources?

This is also a good opportunity to familiarize yourself with the action at an auction.

Example: If four matching chairs are being sold, and you're bidding on a single piece, a $100 final sale price usually means that the four chairs cost $400—plus the buyer's premium.

●**Involve an expert if the item you want is valuable.** If you plan to buy anything expensive—art, jewelry, furniture, etc.—do so only if you have an expert examine the piece first to determine its value.

Some people hire freelance experts to attend the auctions, examine the items and buy the works for them. The standard commission for doing your bidding is 10% of your final bid price or a flat fee. To find a professional auction bidder, contact dealer-specialists who sell the same types of items.

●**Measure your doorway and ceiling heights.** It pays to make sure that what you want to buy will fit through the door of your house and in the room in which it will sit… and that it will match your decor.

We know many people who have purchased items only to find that they did not fit the spaces for which they were intended.

Others couldn't even get these items into the elevators of their apartment buildings or through the front doors of their homes.

Better: Bring all relevant measurement information with you to the auction preview. If there is a catalog, the dimensions of items will be listed. Unlike department stores, merchandise you buy at auction can't be returned the next day.

Ralph and Terry Kovel, who are among the country's top experts in buying and pricing collectibles. They publish Kovels on Antiques and Collectibles, *22000 Shaker Blvd., Shaker Heights, OH 44122, and are the authors of several books, including* Kovels' Quick Tips: 799 Helpful Hints on How to Care for Your Collectibles. *Crown.*

Better Golf

Learn to control the tension that can ruin your golf game by thinking self-enhancing, affirming thoughts rather than negative or undermining thoughts. To gain the proper grip on your club, hold the club too tightly—then consciously loosen your grip until you're holding it with optimal tension. Before swinging, take a deep breath through your nose and then blow out through your mouth to release tension.

Golf: Steps to Success by DeDe Owens, EdD, director of golf instruction at the Cog Hill Golf & Country Club, Lemont, IL. Human Kinetics Publishers.

Mild Ales

Mild ales have less alcohol than normal beer, but more beer taste than nonalcoholic beers. Mild ales contain about 3% alcohol.

Regular beer contains nearly 5%. Labels do not always point the way to less alcohol. Light beer is usually lower in calories but not much lower in alcohol content. Dark-colored beers may have stronger flavor than regular beers but not necessarily more alcohol.

Nick Funnell, head brewer at Great American Restaurants, Centreville, VA.

How to Play and Win the Contest Game

Helen Hadsell

Luck has little to do with the success of veteran contest winners. But if it's not luck, what is it?

In order to win a contest, you can't just fill out an entry form, put it in an envelope, paste a stamp on it and cast your fate to the post office. You'll wind up like all the other contest losers, lamenting that you never win anything.

The way to win: All consistent contest winners rely on the principles listed below in order to win repeatedly…

●**Follow the rules of the contest exactly.** If you and your spouse are supposed to visit a car dealership to pick up an entry form, make sure you both go.

If the entrant is supposed to be over age 18, don't put your young grandchild's name on the entry form. If the form calls for a child's signature, don't forge his/her name. Print when asked to print. Don't use script. Winning candidates are screened by contest officials prior to granting the prize. One tiny mistake and you're out.

●**Enter early and often.** Stagger your entry forms over the period before the contest closing date. This will enable you to get your entry into more than one mailbag. Each canvas mail sack full of entries is numbered, say, one to 100. Then 100 slips are placed in a drum. A blindfolded judge picks a single slip corresponding to a numbered mail sack, reaches into that sack and draws a winner. This system is repeated—picking a sack number from the drum and then picking a winner from that sack—until all the winners are selected.

• **Use entry form substitutes.** Many sweepstakes allow substitutes for official entry blanks and proofs of purchase. Read the fine print. And note the "closing date." If you must use official entry forms and can't find any, write to the sponsoring company and ask for 10. Include a self-addressed, stamped envelope.

• **Use a #10 envelope** (4⅛" x 9½") to mail entries that aren't self-mailers. A letter-sized envelope is easier for a blindfolded judge to grab than a smaller envelope, and not so big that it might be rejected as not within the contest guidelines.

• **Enter local contests.** National contests attract millions of entries and you have a great deal of competition. Local radio, TV and newspapers carry promotions for contests in your area. Watch for displays in local stores. Use the same system for entering local contests as for national contests.

• **Enter "second-chance" sweepstakes, too.** If you receive notification that you haven't won the grand prize, but are still in the running for other prizes, continue to follow the rules and participate. Usually, second-chance sweepstakes offer many more prizes, and your chances of winning are even better.

• **Subscribe to *The Contest Newsletter*.** There are three versions of this newsletter...

• The regular monthly.

• The deluxe monthly, with a larger variety of contests.

• The weekly *CNL Quickie*, with instant information about contests.

Helen Hadsell, author of *Contesting: The Name It and Claim It Game*. Top of the Mountain Publishing.

12

Estate Planning

How to Keep Peace In Your Family

Stanley Hagendorf

Through the years, I've seen hundreds of arguments erupt among even the most loving siblings over the estates of their parents. In nearly every case, such fights could have been avoided had their parents anticipated the problems.

Here are the most common family squabbles —and what can be done to ensure a peaceful transition of assets...

Problem: One child is wealthier than the other. I call this the rich-kid/poor-kid syndrome. The problem is how to divide the family assets when one child has more money than another.

Challenge: Take the case of parents with two daughters—one is a successful lawyer and the other is a struggling artist. If the parents decide to ignore the differences in their daughters' financial situations and divide everything evenly, the artist might not have enough money to send her children to college.

But if they give the artist more than they give the lawyer, the lawyer or her spouse may complain that the parents have cheated her out of her birthright. Typically, the lawyer's argument would be that it is not her fault that her sister chose a low-paying occupation.

Solution I: Explain that you would like to leave the less-fortunate child with financial assets, but ask the wealthier child if there is any family asset that he/she especially wants. Or ask if there is any method of inheritance, such as a trust, to save income or estate taxes. Sometimes the wealthier child is content with inheriting that particular asset or a particular method of inheritance in exchange for less of an inheritance.

Solution II: If the child of modest means has children, consider making gifts to the grandchildren to help fund their college educations. Grandparents could also set up trusts for their

209

grandchildren and make regular transfers from their accounts into the trusts.

Solution III: Parents can take out an insurance policy with the proceeds paid to an educational trust for the children of the less-wealthy child.

Problem: A house must be divided among heirs. Nasty battles often occur on issues of ownership or sale of a house. Not only is a home an estate's largest asset, but there is often sentimental value attached.

Solution I: If possible, while parents are still alive, they can raise the issue with their children of who gets the house so they can reach an acceptable agreement. They can draw up a will in accordance with the agreement and limit the likelihood of fights among the kids.

In situations in which only one child wants the family house but doesn't have enough money to buy out his siblings, you can leave the house to that child—and have the rest of the family divide the remaining assets. Of course, this depends on the fair-market value of the house and the remaining assets.

Or you could put the house into a trust and require that the child who wants to live in it after your death pay rent to the trust. The other children are the beneficiaries of the trust and the rental income. The child could also buy the house from the trust, and the sale proceeds be divided among the other children.

Solution II: If reaching an agreement is impossible, the best way to resolve prolonged wrangles over family real estate is to stipulate in the will that the property must be sold within a set period of time and the proceeds divided between the children.

Problem: Family vacation house. The biggest challenge that arises in the case of a second home in a vacation area is that all the heirs usually want to use the home during peak seasons.

Sometimes, one child wants to own the house and buy out his siblings. But disputes often erupt over fair-market value of the property, since most children who are not interested in buying the house think it is worth more than the appraisal.

Solution: If possible, while alive try to state by agreement which child will get the house

during which time of year—or which child can buy the house. This would be offset by an allocation of other assets to the other children.

Problem: Many heirs want the same family heirlooms, art or jewelry. Sometimes these items have emotional value, regardless of whether they have great financial value. Most of the time, however, the issue is money.

Solution I: If children cannot agree on how to divide up these items, one technique is to allow each child to make one choice (first choice by lot) and then to rotate turns until everything at issue is distributed. Specify this process in your will, but don't list the assets by item. Specifying valuable items in a will could cause valuation problems in the event of an audit.

Solution II: If the children are unable to do this, another approach is to state that all the disputed items will be sold within four to six months after probate and that the proceeds of the sale will then be equally distributed among the children.

Problem: The wrong child is named executor. Parents should share with all heirs their decision as to who will serve as their estate's executor. This will keep the announcement from being a big—and in some cases unwelcome—surprise. It also allows the matter to be discussed among the children to determine who feels most qualified to take on the task.

Solution: Usually it makes sense to name the most financially astute child as executor. That's because an executor is held to legal standards of behavior.

If the other children suspect the executor of being unfair, they could seek a court hearing. If they are not "at war" with each other, you can use coexecutors.

Important: By law, an executor is entitled to be paid for his time for handling the affairs of the estate, though some children decline to be compensated and many parents make this a condition of the will.

Fees can vary widely. They are often figured as a percentage of the estate and range between 2% and 5%.

It is not necessary to name a lawyer as executor. Doing so can dramatically increase the fees.

Many lawyers charge $200 to $300 an hour to settle an estate and also may use paralegals that charge up to half of the same hourly fee.

Problem: A wealthy parent marries a new spouse with kids. The fear here among heirs from the first marriage is that all the assets will pass to the parent's new spouse—or to that spouse's children.

Solution: If you are remarried and want to protect your children from your first marriage, establish a living trust. You can fund it during your lifetime or at your death using a "pour over" from your will.

The trust pays the income to your spouse after your death during your spouse's life. Upon the spouse's death, the trust can either pass the assets to the children of your first marriage—or be divided among the children of both marriages. As an added benefit, this type of trust can be eligible for a marital deduction, which would reduce or eliminate federal estate tax.

Important: If there is animosity among the children and a will contest is a possibility, I prefer the concept of using a trust during your lifetime.

When a trust operates smoothly during your lifetime, the arrangement is harder to overturn after you're gone. Furthermore, property in a trust does not have to go through the probate process, the way property in an estate must.

If the parties want a prenuptial arrangement, I also prefer such a trust along with a prenuptial agreement that sets forth how the surviving second spouse is to be provided for.

Reason: Trusts are more difficult to overturn in most states than prenuptial agreements, which are technically contracts that may be attacked on the grounds of fraud, nondisclosure of all assets or undue influence.

Stanley Hagendorf, an estate and tax attorney in private practice with offices in Florida (6501 Central Ave., St. Petersburg 33710) and New York (609 Fifth Ave., New York 10017). He is a former professor of law in the estate planning program at the University of Miami law school and author of professional books on various aspects of estate taxes and business acquisitions.

What a Will Can And Can't Do

A will *can't* legally disinherit your spouse. However, in most states, you can disinherit your children. *Also:* You can't leave anyone anything you own jointly…and you can't make bequests contrary to sound social policy.

Example: You can't leave money to your daughter on the condition that she divorce her husband. Such a bequest won't hold up in court.

From Cradle to College (And Everything In Between) by Neale S. Godfrey, Mountain Lakes, NJ. Harper-Business.

The Legal Documents Every Adult Needs Now

A will to let you specify how your estate will be divided and your family cared for.

● **A durable power of attorney** that authorizes a trusted person to make financial decisions on your behalf should you become incapacitated.

● **A living will** giving details of whether you want life-prolonging medical care should you have a terminal condition and be unable to communicate your wishes.

● **A health care power of attorney** that, coupled with a living will, authorizes someone to make all of your health care decisions—not just for life-or-death matters—should you be unable to.

● **A financial inventory** listing all of the important financial information—account numbers, addresses, etc.—that your family may need in an emergency.

Martin Shenkman, CPA, an estate attorney in New York and New Jersey and author of The Complete Book of Trusts. John Wiley & Sons.

What You Must Know About Living Wills

Timothy McCall, MD

With today's advanced technology, physicians are often better at keeping people alive than at curing them. For certain individuals, a chance at longer life is worth any price. But someone who has lived a full life may not want technology to stretch that life a few weeks longer—especially if those weeks will be spent on a ventilator.

If you're feeling well now, it's natural to avoid thinking about—much less planning for—the sort of medical care you'd like doctors to provide you near the end of your life. But disaster can strike without warning. If you fail to make your wishes known now, you may never get the chance.

Miracles do occur. Some people whose condition seems hopeless do recover. But in my experience—as a physician *and* as a health-care consumer—such miracles usually occur early in the course of an illness. Pulling out all the technological stops in hopes of producing such a miracle often makes it impossible for the person to die peacefully.

Sixty years ago, most Americans died at home. Today, the overwhelming majority die in hospitals. Death at home affords privacy, dignity and the opportunity for closeness with loved ones. All of this is simply not possible in the hospital. Home health-care services such as visiting nurses can help the family cope with caring for a dying relative.

How can you have your preferences regarding life-sustaining treatment known? *There are three key strategies:*

●**Discuss your feelings with your physician, family and friends.** The more detailed the discussion, the better. Talk about your goals. Do you want to live as long as possible no matter what? Are you more interested in being comfortable? Do you want aggressive medical intervention only when you have a decent chance at a meaningful survival? What is "meaningful" to you?

●**Write a living will.** You might specify what treatments you would desire if you were comatose, terminally ill or irreversibly demented. Be sure to give copies of your living will to your doctor and family members. That way, it will be available when you need it.

●**Appoint a health-care proxy.** This is someone you entrust with making decisions for you should you become incapacitated. (If you regain your faculties, of course, control of your medical care reverts to you.) To fully prepare your proxy, be sure to discuss your goals and feelings explicitly.

The smartest approach may be the combination of all three—talking things over, preparing a living will *and* appointing a health-care proxy. By leaving written instructions, you lessen the burden on your proxy. If the doctors try to ignore the dictates of your living will—unfortunately, an all-too-common event—your proxy can call them on it.

All 50 states allow some form of "advance directive." Unfortunately, the rules and even the terminology vary. To learn your state's requirements, or for more information about living wills, contact Choice in Dying, 200 Varick St., New York 10014. 800-989-9455. http://www.choices.org.

Several weeks before he died, my father was hospitalized. Despite treatment, his condition only worsened. He developed painful bedsores. He hated the food. We could only visit a few hours a day.

Fortunately, he had prepared a living will. In accordance with his wishes, when it became clear that further medical intervention would be futile, we brought him home. He spent the last two weeks of his life on a hospital bed we had set up. He died peacefully, holding my mother's hand.

Timothy McCall, MD, an internist practicing in the Boston area, and author of *Examining Your Doctor: A Patient's Guide to Avoiding Harmful Medical Care.* Citadel Press. Dr. McCall hosts the *Examining Your Doctor Forum* on America Online, featuring weekly columns and regular online chats. *Keyword:* dr.mccall.

Simplest Estate Planning Move

A life insurance trust removes insurance proceeds from your estate—where they would be subject to high taxes. Life insurance payouts are not subject to income taxes but are considered part of a person's estate. Estates are taxed at very high rates after an exemption amount ($625,000 in 1998). This will rise to $1 million by 2006.

To protect your heirs: Create an irrevocable trust to own the policy. Contribute to the trust annually to pay the premiums. Generally these payments are counted among the $10,000 gifts you can make to individuals each year. But be sure you really want to leave the proceeds to your beneficiaries—once the trust is established, you cannot change its terms or the beneficiaries.

Kevin Flatley, director of estate planning at the Bank of Boston.

Living Trusts

L iving trusts do not save taxes as compared to a will. Any tax planning a living trust can provide can be done more simply, cheaper and easier in a will. Living trusts transfer stocks, property and other items to the trust for use by the beneficiary—upon whose death they are disbursed as the trust instructs. This process bypasses probate. Probate can be costly and time-consuming when complex estates are involved.

Helpful: Have a lawyer and a financial adviser help you consolidate and simplify your investments and other assets to minimize probate and other transfer costs. Be sure to draft a will in any case because anything not listed in the trust must also be distributed, either by "pouring" into the trust or under the instructions in the will.

Martin Shenkman, CPA, an estate attorney in New York and New Jersey and author of *The Complete Book of Trusts.* John Wiley & Sons.

Downside to Joint Ownership: Higher Estate Taxes

A nyone can leave an exemption amount ($625,000 in 1998, increasing to $1 million by 2006) to beneficiaries other than a spouse. Over this amount, estate taxes start at 37%. Congress is currently considering raising this limit.

One solution: A bypass trust. Upon the death of a spouse, the exemption amount goes into a bypass trust that is earmarked for a spouse, children and/or other heirs. The trust money is available to the surviving spouse while he/she lives…then it passes to the heirs estate tax free. *Result:* Each spouse passes on the exemption amount tax free, for a total of $2 million by 2006.

Problem: By law, property that is jointly owned passes to the joint owner and cannot fund a bypass trust, so it is better planning when major assets are owned by individual spouses. *More information:* Consult your tax adviser.

Martin Shenkman, CPA, an estate attorney in New York and New Jersey and author of *The Complete Book of Trusts.* John Wiley & Sons.

Nursing Home Trap

I f you co-own a mutual fund—or other securities that are registered in joint names—with someone who needs to go into a nursing home, Medicaid will treat the institutionalized person's share of the fund as belonging to the patient and require that his/her share be spent before Medicaid eligibility kicks in.

Better: Do not put an elderly person's name on securities or real estate, since you could end up losing half of the investments.

A different rule applies to joint bank accounts. These are presumed to be wholly owned by the Medicaid applicant unless the "healthy" owner can prove otherwise.

Alexander Bove, Jr., a tax and estate lawyer located in Boston, and author of *The Medicaid Planning Handbook.* Little, Brown & Co.

Prepaid-Funeral Traps

Ask if the price of the funeral is guaranteed —some contracts contain inflation clauses that increase the bill for your heirs. Find out what happens if you want to change the contract or get out of it—or decide on cremation instead of burial. Make sure any contract moves with you if you relocate.

Better than prepayment: Set aside money for your funeral in an interest-bearing account or insurance policy.

The Beardstown Ladies' Guide to Smart Spending for Big Savings by The Beardstown Ladies' Investment Club, Beardstown, IL. Hyperion.

Today's Estate Planning Statistics

Affluent Americans are not taking the steps necessary to plan their estates. Of those who say they have planned their estates (76%) —fewer than half have appointed a durable power of attorney (46%)...prepared a living will (43%)...purchased long-term-care insurance (38%)...or established trusts (35%). Only about half (48%) of affluent Americans have sought financial-planning advice about their adult children. Even fewer (41%) have sought advice about aging parents.

Survey of 752 Americans ages 40 to 64 conducted by Roper Starch Worldwide for Massachusetts Financial Services (MFS).

Never Own Your Own Safe-Deposit Box

Immediately upon your death, any safe-deposit box that you own will be *sealed*. Your will, insurance policies and any other vital documents that are kept in the box will be unavailable until authorities review the box contents for legal and tax purposes.

Best: Your box should be owned by a trusted family member or friend, or by your business. Or keep important documents such as your will at the office of your lawyer, accountant or other professional adviser.

Robert C. Carlson, editor of *Tax-Wise Money*, 1217 St. Paul St., Baltimore 21202.

13

Very, Very Personal

The Healing Power Of Good Sex

Paul Pearsall, PhD
Henry Ford Community College

Sex involves more than procreation—or recreation. As countless studies have shown, an intimate, sexually satisfying relationship reduces the risk of heart disease...depression...migraine...premenstrual syndrome...and arthritis. It also boosts the immune system.

But sex is genuinely healing *only* if it transcends the mechanical, self-pleasure variety promoted by sex experts.

Indeed, the central goal of sexual healing should not be orgasm—but *connection with your partner.*

PHYSIOLOGY OF HEALING

Healing sex brings a marked decline in bloodstream levels of *adrenaline* and *cortisol.*

These stress hormones provoke anxiety and kill immune system cells.

In a recent study, women who were happily married had higher levels of natural killer cells and helper T cells than those in unhappy unions.

Healing sex is also a potent antidote for social isolation, which has been linked to serious illness and premature death.

A Yale study of 194 heart patients found that those without a spouse at home were *twice* as likely to die prematurely as those with a spouse.

HEALING SEX IS RARE

Most couples never experience sexual healing—because they're too quick to give up on their relationship. It takes at least *four years* to achieve the intimacy needed for sexual healing. Most couples split after only three years.

Why do so many couples split? Lack of intimacy. Intimacy doesn't just happen. You *make* it happen by treating your partner with care and genuine affection...and by taking the time to really connect, both in casual conversation and via sex.

215

Three factors are central to a sexually healing relationship…

•**Commitment.** Affairs and on-again-off-again sexual relationships are not healing—because the two people never form a meaningful bond.

•**Consideration.** The bond between a couple must extend beyond the bedroom. Each partner must continually express tenderness and caring toward the other—by smiling… touching…being polite…giving compliments …and showing respect.

•**Honesty.** There must be no secrets within the relationship—only total connection and total confidence.

HOW TO FORGE A SEXUALLY HEALING RELATIONSHIP

•**Spend time together.** For at least five minutes a day, sit or lie together—just the two of you. Cuddle. Talk. Let your bodies synchronize.

•**Listen more, talk less.** Ironically, good relationships involve little talk. Partners communicate via their own private language—subtle body movements, gestures, expressions and a sense of connection that arises only between lovers who grow ever closer as a result of sharing crises.

•**Do something special for your partner.** If you spend your days apart, call periodically during the day and say something like, "Honey, I've been thinking about you. I can't wait to see you."

If necessary, set an alarm clock to go off periodically to remind you to place the call.

You come to feel love by behaving lovingly, so even the simplest acts of connection can translate to intense sexual feelings.

•**Have sex only when it feels "right."** Trust your senses. If you rely on your "sex sense" for a month, you'll soon see that when you do have sex, it is more fulfilling and sensual.

•**Seduce your partner.** Instead of dressing up in a sexy costume—as sex therapists often recommend—use "brain power."

Send your partner mental "messages" all day long. At night, lie still in bed and send him/her more "sex waves." You'll be surprised at how seductive your own brain can be.

•**Fantasize about your partner.** Put on some sensual music and lie in bed with your eyes closed. Use your brain—not a vibrator or your hand—and envision yourself making love to your partner.

You may become aroused—even experience orgasm—but mental sex can be surprisingly fulfilling even if you don't.

50-MINUTE SEXUAL FITNESS PLAN

My sexual fitness plan—which you can add to your weekly exercise regimen—contains three components…

1. Shared laughter. Twenty seconds of laughter produces the same cardiovascular benefits as three minutes of aerobic exercise, recent studies indicate.

Studies also indicate that a good laugh strengthens the immune system by lowering cortisol levels and raising endorphin levels. And—couples who laugh together become closer and more in tune with one another.

2. Shared crying. Watching a good tear-jerker enhances intimacy—and sometimes leads to sexual arousal. Tears, which contain stress hormones and other chemicals, may be nature's way of washing toxins out of the body.

3. Couple "erotorobics." The following suggested sexual exercises may seem strange, but they increase your ability to respond to intimate physical contact…

•**Simulated sex.** Go through the motions of intercourse—with your clothes on.

•**Genital massage.** This stimulates blood flow in that area.

•**Dancing to erotic music.** Use the muscles you would if you were having intercourse.

•**Flirting.** Arch your back, sway your hips and stick out your chest. And practice sexual gazing and sexual smiling. Both can make you feel more sensuous.

Paul Pearsall, PhD, professor of psychology at Henry Ford Community College, Dearborn, MI, and former director of education at the Kinsey Institute at Indiana University, Bloomington. He is author of A Healing Intimacy *(Crown) and* The Pleasure Prescription *(Hunter House).*

Sensual Massage

Start a sensual massage by putting oil on your hands and applying it to your partner with broad, easy strokes. Be very gentle at first, then feel through your fingers where to press harder. Keep your fingers relaxed. Use your whole palm and fingers for the massage. Keep strokes reliable and rhythmic, so the massage feels like a continuous sequence even though you move from one body part to another.

A Lover's Guide to Massage by Victoria Day, massage therapist and registered midwife, Bristol, England. Ward Lock, distributed by Sterling Publishing Co.

Intimate Secrets

Kiss the inside of your partner's wrist to feel his/her pulse and warm your lips. Brush your lips lightly against his...take his face in your hands...put your lips on his...and press gently while looking into his eyes. Kiss lightly and playfully for several minutes before closing your eyes and kissing with passion.

Sexsational Secrets: Exotic Advice Your Mother Never Gave You by Susan Crain Bakos, author of several books on relationships and intimacy. St. Martin's Press.

Eminent Sex Therapist Reveals Her Secret Weapon Against Sexual Problems

Barbara Bartlik, MD
New York Hospital–Cornell Medical Center

For most of us, erotica has long been taboo—an embarrassing vice. But as leading sex therapists have found, a new generation of "tasteful" videos and literature can be a powerful ally for couples struggling with sexual problems...or seeking to enrich their sexual relationship.

Even couples who find ordinary "porn" offensive often find that they enjoy—and benefit from—the new, sensitive erotica.

These materials—featuring interesting plots and caring, realistic relationships—are designed to excite *and* educate. They have proven helpful in resolving several common sexual problems...

SEXUAL ENNUI

The most obvious use of erotica is to spice up sex for couples who have fallen into a rut.

The pioneering sex therapist Helen Singer Kaplan, MD, coined the term "hot monogamy" to describe couples who seek sexual adventure *within* marriage. This is done by using erotic toys, sexy lingerie, play-acting, reading and viewing erotica together.

PERFORMANCE ANXIETY

Old-style porn focuses exclusively on the sex act, emphasizing sexual prowess and anatomies of improbable proportions. That can exacerbate feelings of inadequacy in men (and women), contributing to impotence and performance anxiety.

Several recent videos depict ordinary-looking people enjoying sex in the context of their broader lives. This gives viewers a more realistic standard against which to compare themselves, helping them overcome fears of inadequacy.

Some erotica depicts couples expressing passion *without* progressing to intercourse. Learning about noncoital ways to satisfy each other can remove pressure, rebuild confidence and curb anxiety—lessening performance concerns.

POOR COMMUNICATION

Many individuals find it hard to ask for what they want in bed—oral sex, anal stimulation, etc. They're simply unassertive...or they fear their partner will feel put down.

Erotica provides ways around this problem. One partner can say to the other, "Let's try what they did" or, "I'd love it if we could do that."

In some videos, such as those in the *Femme* series (described on the next page), partners are shown giving each other suggestions and feedback in a sensitive, lighthearted way. Watching these "role models" can make talking about sex more comfortable.

SEXUAL INHIBITION

Even in our sexually liberated age, many adults come from restrictive upbringings that taught them sex is dirty and good people don't enjoy it. Many of these people never learned effective ways to give and receive sexual pleasure.

Erotica demonstrates a variety of ways to enhance foreplay and intercourse. And newer, plot-oriented tapes show people of all ages and from many walks of life enjoying sex. This can help viewers feel more comfortable with their own sexuality.

RELATIONSHIP CONFLICT

Pent-up anger or other conflicts with a partner can lead to loss of desire. This initiates a downward spiral in the relationship, since unsatisfying sex can lead to even more frustration.

To halt this spiral, couples must confront these conflicts directly—via honest conversation and perhaps counseling.

While couples are working out their difficulties, erotica can help reignite sexual interest, strengthening the bond between them.

LACK OF FOCUS

Some individuals have trouble focusing on their partners and find that they are unable to reach orgasm.

Typically, they're distracted by work pressures, concerns about body image or privacy, etc.

Erotica compensates for these distractions by "turning up the volume" of sexual excitement.

PROBLEMS THAT DON'T RESPOND TO EROTICA

Erotica is not helpful for…

…*premature ejaculation.* Men with this problem need to focus on their own physical sensations, not images of others.

…*sexual aversion.* For this problem, in which sex is extremely anxiety-provoking or distasteful, the partner or partners need to be exposed gradually to sexual activity.

…*some individuals with a history of sexual abuse.*

Even minor problems sometimes require professional sex therapy. If the problem doesn't get better, seek professional guidance.

Helpful resource: American Association of Sex Educators, Counselors and Therapists, 319-895-8407.

WHERE TO GET EROTICA

Rent erotic videos at a neighborhood video store…or watch cable television. Showtime has interesting erotica, including the series "Red Shoe Diaries."

Or browse through the classics of erotic literature in a bookstore's "sexuality" section. I recommend Anaïs Nin's *A Spy in the House of Love*…Henry Miller's *Tropic of Cancer*…and D. H. Lawrence's *Lady Chatterley's Lover*.

If privacy is essential, consider using one of the following mail-order companies…

●**Critic's Choice Video**, 800-544-9852. Carries a selection of erotic videos, including the *Playboy* and *Playgirl* series.

●**Femme Distribution**, 800-456-5683. This video production company, started by former adult film star Candida Royale, features "female-friendly" erotic videos.

●**Sinclair Institute**, 800-955-0888. Carries the Better Sex Video series, featuring realistic couples in tasteful settings.

Barbara Bartlik, MD, psychiatrist and medical sex therapist with the human sexuality program at New York Hospital–Cornell Medical Center, New York. She studied with the late Dr. Helen Singer Kaplan, the renowned sex therapist, and was an associate in Dr. Kaplan's practice.

Men Want More Foreplay Than Most Women Realize

Most men over age 35 say they prefer foreplay to intercourse—and that intercourse and orgasm become less satisfying as they get older.

Possible reason: Increased stress and responsibilities make it more difficult to "let go" completely.

David Quadagno, PhD, professor of biology at Florida State University, Tallahassee.

Get in Sync

Synchronize your sexual desire with your partner's by finding out what is knocking you out of sync—an overcrowded schedule, pent-up resentments, concerns about your attractiveness or your partner's—or anything else. Make decisions that will allow you to plan when to get together.

Examples: Go to bed earlier or later…or take turns setting up lovemaking sessions, so each of you gets a chance to do it your way.

Al Cooper, PhD, clinical director of the San Jose Marital and Sexuality Centre, San Jose, CA, writing online in *Self-Help & Psychology,* http://cybertowers.com/selfhelp.

Lovemaking Is More Than Sex

Limiting lovemaking to sexual times puts tremendous pressure on sex lives and misidentifies the type of connection that true lovers want. The physical connection of sex is only a part of true lovers' intimacy.

Better: Seek real moments of love with your partner—moments to feel your love fully and rejoice in your relationship. Really making love means stirring up the feelings that constantly flow between you.

Real Moments for Lovers by Barbara DeAngelis, PhD, a specialist in human relations and personal growth in Los Angeles. Delacorte Press.

To Say No to Sex Gently

Start by telling your partner why you are not in the mood. Assure him/her you find him desirable and he is not the reason for your lack of desire. Consider nonsexual intimacy instead —snuggling, doing some activity together—so you can still be close without being sexual… and set a date to make love in the near future.

Example: On the weekend, if you are too tired during the week. If your lack of desire is caused by a relationship problem, say so and try to work it out. Talk at a neutral time and place—not in bed.

Shirley Zussman, EdD, a sex therapist in New York, and editor of *Sex Over Forty,* Box 1600, Chapel Hill, NC 27515.

Premature Ejaculation Help

Premature ejaculation is the most common male sexual problem. Most cases can be easily fixed through a start–stop technique in which a man becomes more aware of his own arousal pattern and learns to change his technique.

More information: Consult with your internist or urologist.

Janet Lever, PhD, associate professor of sociology at California State University, Los Angeles, and Pepper Schwartz, PhD, professor of sociology at the University of Washington, Seattle.

Always Check Your Medicine

If your sexual desire is low, check your prescription medications. Antidepressants, anti-anxiety medications and antihypertensives often affect desire. If you are unsure whether a medicine may be causing loss of desire, ask your pharmacist or doctor whether this is a reported side effect. If it is, speak with your doctor about changing medications. Medicines affect different people in different ways—often a different medicine for the same condition will be less likely to inhibit desire.

Marlene Maheu, PhD, a San Diego psychologist who works with people experiencing sexual difficulties, writing online in *Self-Help & Psychology,* http://cyber-towers.com/selfhelp.

Drug Holidays Help Sex Life

About 40% of people taking antidepressants lose interest in sex or find they cannot reach orgasm. Many have found they can reverse the effect for the weekend by discontinuing their medication after taking it Thursday morning, and resuming doses at noon Sunday. Ask your doctor if this drug-holiday approach might work for you.

Anthony Rothschild, MD, a psychiatrist at McLean Hospital, Belmont, MA 02178.

Sex Rarely Causes Heart Attacks

Sex rarely causes heart attacks—even in those who have already had one. A recent study found that the risk of heart attack from sexual activity is only about two in one million. This compares with one in one million if the person did not engage in sexual activity during the prior hour. Heart patients who exercise regularly—meaning they simply walked briskly up a slight hill for 30 minutes a day—had no increased risk from sexual activity.

James E. Muller, MD, associate professor of medicine at Harvard Medical School, Boston. His study of 858 men and women who survived heart attacks was published in The Journal of the American Medical Association, *515 N. State St., Chicago 60610.*

Headaches and Sex

Headaches associated with sex afflict about 3% of women occasionally.

Usual cause: Muscle strain of the neck and shoulders or rapid blood pressure increases from hormonal surges.

Self-defense: Stay in shape—sex requires stamina…take your time—extending foreplay lets hormone levels and heart rate rise gradually, not

surge…change positions—certain positions cause more muscle strain and exertion than others.

Fred Freitag, DO, associate director of the Diamond Headache Clinic, Chicago.

Teens and Sex

To help teens go slow about sex, get them involved in sports or other absorbing activities—busy kids are more self-confident and less likely to buckle to peer pressure. Have a loving environment at home—teens who feel loved are less likely to crave love elsewhere. Chaperone teens by driving them places and picking them up—limiting chances for them to be alone together.

Tom Greening, PhD, professor of psychology at the Saybrook Institute, San Francisco, and editor of the Journal of Humanistic Psychology.

Dating Basics for Seniors

Judy Kuriansky, PhD

Assuming you're single, you never have to retire from dating! Dating enriches life. It keeps singles active and interested in exploring new avenues of fun and growth.

Flirting is a positive experience. It's fun and it makes you *feel* good. Attracting the attention of someone interesting reminds you how interesting *you* are.

JOYS OF DATING

Retirement can bring the freedom to be more socially active than ever. Most major family responsibilities have been taken care of.

You can use your money as you wish and choose vacation spots that may not have been possible over the years. You can stay up late and sleep in. You can travel whenever and wherever you want, taking advantage of airfare wars, off-season bargain hotel prices and extended stays.

Many women feel sexy after menopause because they've stopped worrying about birth control. *Caution:* Protection against sexually transmitted diseases is essential at any age.

BENEFIT FROM TODAY'S OPEN SOCIETY

American society has lightened up. Women can call men on the telephone, introduce themselves at parties or bars and invite men out. These days, women should take the initiative as much as men.

Anyone can submit ads to the "personals" columns of magazines and newspapers. Be discriminating—place your ad thoughtfully, keeping in mind who reads the publication.

Once upon a time, waiters at fancy restaurants handed women menus without prices. Women now often expect to pay their way. But if you and a date both feel more comfortable preserving the social customs of a former era, go right ahead. Always discuss who treats, to avoid confusion or upset.

WHERE TO MEET PEOPLE

You could meet someone while waiting for the train, riding the elevator, walking through the park. But *going somewhere* greatly increases your chances.

Networking is effective not only in business dealings but also for dating. Tell your friends that you're "looking." Say yes to "fix-ups" and blind dates.

Accept invitations to parties you aren't eager to attend. In groups, stand or sit alone *some* of the time. You'll be more approachable.

Seek out places where like-minded people congregate. Routinely study local papers and community bulletin boards for upcoming events. Become more active in groups in religious or community centers.

Subscribe to newsletters featuring low-cost trips for older singles. Get on mailing lists for anything that might bring you and someone special together.

Don't discount the supermarket and Laundromat. Two hearts can beat as one while discussing pasta recipes or folding towels.

PURSUE DATES AND YOUR INTERESTS AT THE SAME TIME

Get involved in an activity you already like to do. Enjoy sports? Participate in (or cheer on) a team sport that attracts the gender and age range you would like to date.

Hit some balls at a golf range every weekend and have lunch in the snack bar.

Sign up for tennis lessons or doubles.

Join a spa or health bar. Or become an active member of the local "Y"—usually inexpensive, with many offerings.

Take dancing lessons. You don't have to sign up as a couple. Ask other singles to dance at weddings.

Art and music mavens may find mates at a local concert series, music store, art supply shop or museum exhibit.

Theater lovers flock to backstage tours...theater trips...lectures on drama...panel discussions by famous actors.

Go on group hikes—whether up a mountain or around and around a mall. Join clubs that feature programs on wine, food, day-tripping or socializing.

The health-minded may want to investigate health clubs, retreats or local health-food stores. Ask an attractive fellow shopper for recipe tips. Invite him/her out for dinner.

If spiritual exploration is your thing, go to holistic health expos, encounter group meetings or weekend retreats.

Heavy-duty readers throng to coffeehouses, super-bookstores with enticing reading nooks and cafés, little neighborhood bookshops where people gather. Read your own poetry at an open-mike session...or attend readings and talks by authors. Stick around for the discussion. Ask that nice-looking person in the corner whether he enjoyed the evening. Being a presenter makes others come to you.

Wherever you go, start sending out vibes that you are happy, open and available. Now, *that's* attractive.

IF YOU'RE SELF-CONSCIOUS ABOUT YOUR LOOKS

Body image can be a big issue as we get older, especially in our overwhelmingly youth-oriented society. Face your fears and try to overcome them. Stay fit and appreciate who you are—inside *and* outside.

Afraid to get into a sexual relationship? There's no rush—wait until you're ready, if ever. You can always date. If you become close to someone, and sex seems like the next step, share your fears. But don't let your fears keep you at home.

IF YOUR CHILDREN OR OTHERS OBJECT

Some children may be uncomfortable with your dating "at your age." Such concerns represent fear of loss of your attention and a generational role reversal. Notice how their reactions to your dating can be the same as your reactions were to their dating.

Explore their feelings. Perhaps negativity about your dating is more a reflection of their own lives than a response to yours. Say you're glad they care about your happiness and you'll make sure anyone you date treats you well. You might even reassure them that you'll never change your will, if that might be an issue (and if you know you won't).

Old friends may have trouble seeing you in a dating role, especially after years of widowhood. Couples you knew as a married person may feel awkward, while other widows and widowers may feel left out and jealous. Don't let their disappointment distract you. Bond with them and encourage them to date, too. Double dates can be fun at any age—and may make you more comfortable about dating as you get back into the swing of things.

CULTIVATE TOLERANCE IN YOURSELF

Dating requires compromises, from where to eat and what movie to see to more complicated issues of money, time and personal space.

Older people tend to get set in their ways and find it harder to make compromises. Maybe you have a fixed bedtime or feel anxious about going far away on a trip.

Without abandoning your priorities, remain flexible and open to suggestion. You'll meet more people that way—whether down the street or in Tahiti. Occasionally go off *your* beaten path. You won't fall over the edge— you know yourself too well by now.

On the other hand, getting older may have made you more tolerant of other people's idiosyncrasies. A woman who insists, at 30, that she'd "never go out with a bald guy with a pouchy tummy" may have different values at age 60.

Dating success depends upon your attitude toward aging. Those who don't adjust well become fearful of *many* things in life, including dating. Those who do, enjoy their lives and may even find a wonderful love.

Judy Kuriansky, PhD, a clinical psychologist and sex therapist in private practice in New York. On her nationally syndicated radio show, "LovePhones," she answers callers' questions about love, relationships and sex. She is author of *The Complete Idiot's Guide to Dating*. Macmillan General Reference.

The Romance Coach Tells How to Add Romance to Your Life

Gregory J. P. Godek

Learn to say "I love you" in different languages. *Examples: Te amo*/Spanish… *S'agapo*/Greek…*Je t'aime*/French…*Aloha I'a Au Oe*/Hawaiian…*Ich liebe dich*/German… *Thaim i'ngra leat*/Gaelic…*Aishiteru*/Japanese …*Ani ohev otakh*/Hebrew…*Ti amo*/Italian… *Jag alskar dig*/Swedish…*Wo ai ni*/Chinese…*Ya tebya lublya*/Russian.

• **Write "I love you"** in soap on the bathroom mirror.

• **Hide love notes in unexpected places.** *Examples:* Carefully open, then reseal product packages…stick inside a fortune cookie… freeze notes into an ice cube…hide them among a bouquet of flowers.

• **Instead of breakfast in bed**—have dinner in bed.

• **Create a public signal or gesture that only your partner knows.** This will allow you to let your partner—but no one else—know that you're in the mood for love. *Examples:* Say, "I think I left the oven on."

• **Make a list of "The 100 Reasons Why I Fell in Love with You."** Too difficult? List 50.

• **Give your partner a book of "Romance Coupons."** *Coupons can be good for:* One candlelit dinner…a weekend getaway…a $100 lingerie shopping spree…flowers, etc.

● **Celebrate your 10,000-day anniversary.** That's about 27 years, four months and 25 days, give or take a few Leap Days.

● **Wash your partner's hair.**

● **Play tourist in your own hometown for a weekend.** Stay at a romantic hotel, visit the tourist sites, have dinner at a great restaurant you've never been to before.

● **Try "All-Day Foreplay."** *How it works:* Plan in the morning to make love that night. Call each other all day long with "reminders," ideas and suggestive suggestions.

● **Go to a drive-in movie**—and sit in the back seat.

Gregory J.P. Godek, America's self-proclaimed Romance Coach and author of *1001 Ways to be Romantic.* Casablanca Press.

Marriage Improvement Made Easy

Harville Hendrix, PhD
Institute for Imago Relationship Therapy

A *conscious* marriage is one that takes work. But too many couples stop working on their relationships and stop growing as a couple. I have counseled couples in their 40s and couples in their 80s.

What I have learned: It's never too late to get love right.

Relationships go through cycles, and you may find that you are at a point in your lives as a couple where you need to make a more conscious effort at loving each other. There are many reasons a new cycle in a relationship begins. It may be retirement or when the last child leaves home—which changes your identity as a couple.

Positive changes you can make to achieve lasting love...

● **Exchange gifts.** I am not talking about giving ties and necklaces. Instead, I am suggesting that you target a specific need of your partner's and give a gift to satisfy that need.

Example: The need for pampering after a long, hard day at work. Once you have identified the need, give a gift such as a foot massage or a cup of tea without being asked. Make sure the gift is unconditional—that you ask for nothing in return.

Mistake: If you let me watch TV in peace, I'll take the kids to the park on Saturday. The result is a *quid pro quo* marriage where each good turn has a price tag.

● **Learn to listen three ways.** Good communication is actually a three-step process...

First: Mirror what you have heard. *You think I didn't pick up your dry cleaning because I was angry.*

Next: Validate what you have heard. *I can see why you might think that, given my past behavior.*

Third: Empathize. *It must feel awful to think you live with an angry, vindictive person.*

By communicating this way, you defuse potential power struggles and learn to listen without becoming angry.

● **Do not run away.** In an unconscious relationship, couples look for the nearest exit. The exit may be major (divorce, addiction)...or minor (TV, work, staying up later than your partner).

In a conscious relationship there are *no exits.* Couples must put their feelings into words and address problems rather than ignore them.

● **Never criticize.** Criticism is a form of abuse. Perhaps you have a specific need. Rather than nag, ask your spouse to make a change.

Example: You don't want to serve lunch to your recently retired husband.

Mistake: You complain, *You're such a creature of habit. You act as if you've never been in a kitchen before.*

Better: Replace criticism with a behavior change request: *I need to know that my day is free, that I don't have to be home at lunchtime. I need your support on this.* You know you're asking your partner for something that he can't easily give, or he would have done so already. Acknowledging how hard it will be for your partner to support you means your partner will be more likely to make the effort.

● **Make an appointment for anger.** In a conscious relationship, you never accuse your partner. Instead you say, *Can I have some time with you? I'm feeling angry.* By setting a special time to talk, you avoid heated arguments. Anger is contained, not discharged. Sometimes, the talk that follows can be so good that the issue dissolves.

●**Expect romantic love to die out.** Even couples who have been married for years and years may still mourn the loss of romantic love. Romance is a wonderful launching pad but real love is the place you want to reach. Problems occur when characteristics that you once found attractive later annoy you.

The independent nature you fell in love with years ago may now be perceived as simply inattentive.

A fun-loving personality may come to be seen as self-indulgent.

Couples need to know that romantic love is *supposed* to end, so that they can begin to work on a conscious relationship.

At first, there will be power struggles as you work through the issues that you have brought with you to the marriage from childhood. Some couples remain in those power struggles throughout their married life. Once you realize that romantic love is not the goal and make a conscious effort to live with and love this other person, the road to real love will become easier to follow.

●**Practice good maintenance.** In long-term relationships, it can be easy to slip out of a conscious relationship. Maintenance is important. Spend quality time together—listening, talking and sharing.

Harville Hendrix, PhD, author of Keeping the Love You Find *(Pocket Books) and* Getting the Love You Want *(HarperCollins). He is founder and president of the Institute for Imago Relationship Therapy, Winter Park, FL.*

 **Surprising Marriage Booster**

Spend some personal time *apart* from your spouse, pursuing your own activities or interests. Having different experiences to share makes the time you spend together more exciting and fulfilling.

Also: It gives you time to focus on your own needs…and can intensify your desire to be together.

Berit Ingersoll-Dayton, PhD, associate professor of social work at the University of Michigan, Ann Arbor, who studied 24 long-married couples.

How to Prevent Marriage Burnout

Michele Weiner-Davis

If your marriage is approaching the burnout stage, you can still do something about it—if you act soon enough.

Here are the warning signs of a troubled marriage—and how to reverse negative patterns and restore the love you once felt toward one another.

WARNING SIGNS

●**Chronic resentment.** When unhappy couples argue, they make up on the surface, but angry feelings linger.

●**Lack of humor.** Happy couples laugh a lot. They're able to see the ridiculousness in tense situations and defuse them. Unhappy couples reserve laughter for everyone but their mates.

●**Change in the way you interact.** For one unhappy couple, a sign of impending burnout might be that they're arguing more often—or more angrily—than normal.

For another couple, the fact that they never argue when they used to discuss everything intensely might be a sign of marriage burnout.

●**Cynicism.** In a healthy marriage, spouses give one another the benefit of the doubt.

Examples: If one person comes home late without calling first, the other might think, *Traffic must have been terrible.* In a burned-out marriage, when one spouse brings the other flowers, the person receiving them will likely suspect the other of feeling guilty about something.

STOPPING MARRIAGE BURNOUT

●**Make the relationship a priority.** It's easy to let marriage take a back seat to work, kids, hobbies or community obligations. Couples grow comfortable in marriage and automatically assume a spouse will always be there. Many busy people nurture their marriages only after they take care of everything else, which is a mistake.

Allotting prime time for your marriage must not be an afterthought. Pencil appointments into your date book if that's what it takes to meet your spouse for lunch or dinner during the week.

●**Don't hide your feelings.** For some couples, keeping anger to themselves or resorting to snide comments seems less threatening than coming right out and clearly saying what is bothering them.

Partners aren't mind readers—and disappointment is inevitable if feelings aren't discussed openly.

However, it is also essential to choose your battles and avoid making issues out of *every* irritant.

●**Share positive experiences.** When spouses drift apart, it may seem impossible to come up with things they will enjoy doing together.

Exercise: Think back to a time when you both felt more passion, energy and involvement. Ask yourself what you enjoyed doing together in those days.

Start by doing some of those things again. Don't feel you have to make a big production out of the event. In fact, an expensive vacation to Paris to relive good times is probably less productive over the long run than rediscovering simple, everyday pleasures.

Examples: A couple I know took walks after dinner. Another hired a sitter and just went for drives together. Getting out of the house helped them relate to one another like adults in love rather than parents struggling to control their children.

Don't get discouraged if your spouse doesn't immediately get excited about the idea. He/she may not believe you are sincere—or may not want to snap out of a funk right away. Expect some resistance, but persist in a calm, friendly way.

Or simply surprise your spouse with theater or sports tickets for a weekend when you both are available. Once you're out together, both your personalities will change.

●**Behave as if positive change has already occurred.** Many couples try to put their relationships back on track, only to have the efforts derailed shortly afterward.

A major reason for such false starts is that the person who initiates the change feels rejected and becomes even angrier.

Repairing a frayed marriage has a better chance of success if the person who makes the first move behaves as if the change has already taken place—no matter how his/her spouse responds.

This strategy is easier than you might think. I suggest to couples that they simply start doing the things they would do if the other person had already made the changes they are hoping for.

Example: One woman I know was upset because her husband was spending most of his free time with his friends and neglecting her and their child. I asked her, *What did he do in the days when he was more attentive?* She replied that he used to pay her more compliments, tell her he loved her and make a point of spending time with her.

Then I asked, *How were you different when he was like that?* She remembered all the things she used to do for her husband that she had stopped doing as her resentment grew. They included waking up early so they could have breakfast together, dropping love notes in his lunch and initiating sex.

I asked her to try to act from that day on as if he were that same old nice guy and to do all the pampering things she used to do for him.

Within days, he had become more attentive …and over time his attitude improved even more.

●**Don't keep score.** If you expect every gesture of yours to be met with an equivalent gesture from your partner, you will put the relationship in a straitjacket.

There is never an excuse for dysfunctional behavior—physical or emotional abuse. But the ability to get along with a partner is largely based on deciding to make it happen—and renewing that decision daily.

Michele Weiner-Davis, MSW, a marriage and family therapist in private practice in Woodstock, IL. She is author of *Change Your Life and Everyone In It* and *Divorce Busting: A Step-by-Step Approach to Making Your Marriage Loving Again*. Fireside. Her home-study audio-cassette course, *Keeping Love Alive*, is available by calling 800-664-2435.

Wiser Marital Fights

Complain, but don't criticize. Attacking or blaming your partner only results in defensiveness.

●**Accept your spouse's influence in your life.** In good marriages, both men and women freely give and receive influence from one another.

●**Learn how to put a stop to conflict.** *One way:* Use *repair statements* like "I'm feeling sad" or "Let's start all over again."

●**Take a *time-out* to calm down.** Stop the argument and retreat to somewhere else in the house for 20 minutes to think things through—or simply to clear your mind.

●**De-escalate conflicts.** Do anything possible to stop the argument. *Suggestions:* Injecting a little humor into the situation…planting a wet kiss on your partner's cheek.

John Gottman, PhD, professor of psychology and family/marriage specialist at the University of Washington, Seattle.

Anger Is as Natural as Love

Painful feelings toward parents are normal—and should not interfere with one's love for them. Accommodating the love *and* anger of the parent-child relationship makes it possible to have intimate adult relationships that include feelings ranging from anger to dependency…without feeling a threat to your sense of self. For true intimacy, we must learn that love and anger are part of deep dependent relationships.

The Soul's Companion: Connecting with the Soul Through Daily Meditations by Tian Dayton, PhD, a therapist in private practice in New York. Health Communications.

Simple Ways to Improve Your Mood

Surround yourself with family and friends who have a positive attitude.

●**Don't stop learning** because you think you know it all.

●**Believe in your dreams.**

●**Know what it takes to make you happy.**

●**Reward yourself**—just because you deserve it.

●**Remember to celebrate victories**, no matter how small.

●**Enjoy your life**…be fully aware each waking moment.

●**Give more often** than you're expected to.

●**Set goals** that inspire you to improve continuously.

●**Don't be too busy to have fun.**

●**Attach positive values to each task.**

●**Act like a success** even when you don't feel like one.

●**Don't expect always to be right.**

●**Realize that there's always something positive you can do.**

●**Spend quiet time alone.**

●**Ensure that your innermost beliefs support**, enhance and further your goals.

●**Never do anything to jeopardize or sacrifice your health.**

●**Register for a self-improvement class.**

●**Don't measure success by dollars.**

●**Write down good ideas** the moment you think of them.

●**Give your very best…always.**

●**Believe in yourself.**

●**Accept life as it is**, then try to make it better.

●**Develop a winning attitude.**

•**Be creative**…your creativity is the place where no one else has been before.

Ella Patterson, founder of Knowledge Concepts Educational Systems, a Cedar Hill, TX, motivational company, and author of *1001 Reasons to Think Positive: Special Insights to Achieve a Better Attitude Toward Life.* Fireside Books.

Relaxation Response Basics

To reduce stress…pain…anger…and anxiety, turn inward. Meditate…focus on your senses—not your everyday thoughts.

•*Choose a word*, sound, prayer or phrase on which to focus…sit in a quiet, comfortable place…breathe slowly and deeply…relax your muscles…repeat your focus silently to yourself as you exhale. As your mind starts drifting, acknowledge it—and return to your repetition.

Recommended: 10 to 20 minutes, twice a day.

Herbert Benson, MD, president of the Mind/Body Medical Institute at Harvard Medical School, Boston, and author of *Timeless Healing* (Scribner) and *The Relaxation Response* (Avon).

Best Time for Conception

A woman's ability to conceive ends after the day she ovulates. Conception is most likely when a woman has intercourse on the day she is ovulating or during the five days preceding that day. Having intercourse every day or every other day during this period maximizes the woman's chance of conceiving.

Study of 221 women, led by Allen Wilcox, MD, PhD, chief of epidemiology at the National Institute of Environmental Health Sciences, Research Triangle, NC.

Vaginal Douching Danger

After 12 months of trying to conceive, about 90% of women who had never douched became pregnant—compared with only 73% of the women who douched more than once a week.

Also: Douching may increase risk of pelvic inflammatory disease and other infections by spreading germs to the upper reaches of the uterus and fallopian tubes.

Donna Day Baird, PhD, epidemiologist at the National Institute of Environmental Health Sciences, Research Triangle Park, NC.

Importance of Calcium During Pregnancy

Calcium during pregnancy reduces risk of high blood pressure and potential death. Women who consumed 1,500 mgs of calcium daily—the equivalent of four servings of dairy products—had a 70% reduction in the incidence of high blood pressure. Cases of pre-eclampsia—a condition that includes retaining fluid, high blood pressure and kidney dysfunction and that can lead to serious problems—dropped by 62%.

Gordon Guyatt, MD, professor of medicine, clinical epidemiology and biostatistics at McMaster University, Hamilton, Ontario. He led a meta-analysis on studies including 2,459 pregnant women.

Vitamin A Can Cause Birth Defects

Among pregnant women who took more than 10,000 units of vitamin A supplements daily, one in 57 gave birth to a baby with a birth defect attributable to the vitamin. Defects were most closely linked to vitamin A taken before the seventh week of pregnancy.

Important: Discuss proper dosage with your doctor. Most women planning to become pregnant should limit vitamin A to 8,000 units a day or less.

Kenneth Rothman, DrPH, professor of public health in the section of preventive medicine and epidemiology at Boston University School of Medicine. His study of more than 22,000 pregnant women was published in *The New England Journal of Medicine*.

Safety of Birth Control Pills

Birth control pills are safe for the vast majority of women, despite continuing concerns about their risks. They are one of the most effective contraceptives, with a failure rate of about 3%...compared with about 12% for condoms. Low-dose pills—the most common form used today—raise blood clot risk in some users only very slightly. And birth control pills significantly reduce the risk of pelvic inflammatory disease, ectopic pregnancies, ovarian cysts and endometrial and ovarian cancers.

Suzanne Delbanco, MPH, MPP, program officer for reproductive health programs at the Kaiser Family Foundation, Menlo Park, CA.

The Pill May Increase Desire

Women using one type of birth-control pill, called a *triphasic* pill, reported more sexual desire and satisfaction than women using *monophasic* types.

Possible reason: Triphasic pills vary the level of the hormone *progestin*, which is associated with decreased sexual desire, during a woman's monthly cycle. Monophasic pills give a constant dose of estrogen and progestin for 21 days each month. Research suggests that ovarian hormone production may be suppressed less by triphasic pills.

Norma McCoy, PhD, professor of psychology at San Francisco State University. Her study included more than 150 women who use birth-control pills.

Diaphragms Increase Cystitis Risk

Women using diaphragms with spermicides for birth control change their bodies' internal environments in ways that allow the bacteria that cause cystitis to flourish. The more frequent the sex, the higher the risk.

If you have frequent bladder infections: Consider a different form of birth control.

Study of almost 800 sexually active women by researchers at the University of Washington School of Medicine, Seattle, published in *The New England Journal of Medicine.*

Female Sterilization Can Fail

One sterilized woman out of 50 may become pregnant during a 10-year time period.

At highest risk: Women sterilized before age 28...those sterilized in a procedure that plugs the fallopian tubes by burning them with an electric current.

Ten-year study of more than 10,000 women, led by Bert Peterson, MD, chief of women's health and fertility at the Centers for Disease Control and Prevention, Atlanta.

Safer than Reverse Vasectomies

Men who have had vasectomies but now want children no longer need to have the surgery for vasectomy reversal. Instead, a small amount of sperm-containing tissue can be removed using local anesthesia—a procedure that takes only about a minute in the doctor's office, compared with about three hours in the operating room for a vasectomy reversal. The sperm is then injected into the wife's eggs through in vitro fertilization. About 500,000 men a year have vasectomies, and 1% to 2% have them reversed—a percentage that is increasing.

Harry Fisch, MD, director of the Male Reproductive Center at Columbia-Presbyterian Medical Center, 944 Park Ave., New York 10028.

New Treatments for Male Impotence

J. Francois Eid, MD
New York Hospital–Cornell Medical Center

Male impotence—or *erectile dysfunction*, as doctors prefer to call it—is one of the most common untreated medical disorders in the world.

In the US, as many as 20 million men may have problems getting or maintaining an erection.

The disorder's prevalence increases with age. Only 5% of 40-year-olds experience erectile dysfunction. The rate among 70-year-olds is somewhere between 15% and 30%.

Of the men affected, however, only one out of 20 seeks medical help. That's unfortunate for two reasons…

●**Consistent loss of erection is not normal at any age**—and can actually be a symptom of an illness.

●**With many effective treatments now available and more on the way**, erectile dysfunction can almost always be treated successfully.

More than 80% of all dysfunction can be traced to a physical (organic) cause—usually an inability to keep blood trapped in the penis after it becomes erect.

A much smaller percentage of cases is psychological in origin. These patients tend to be younger and usually report no erection at all with a partner, though they may be able to become erect when they're alone—watching an erotic movie, for example. (When the dysfunction is physical, the patient will usually have at least a partial erection.)

TREATING ERECTILE DYSFUNCTION

While its incidence is highest among older men, difficulty maintaining an erection is not a normal part of aging. A healthy male with a willing partner can expect to have one or two usable erections a week well into his 80s.

An occasional loss of erection is nothing to worry about. But if it happens consistently, see a physician who's very experienced at treating erectile dysfunction—either an internist specializing in erectile dysfunction (i.e., it makes up at least half of his/her practice) or a urologist.

Main difference: Only a urologist can surgically implant a prosthesis.

WHAT TO EXPECT

The first thing the doctor should do is take a medical history, including all psychological and sexual aspects of the dysfunction.

He should also give you a full physical checkup to identify any underlying illness that might be present. Difficulty in getting or maintaining an erection is often a predictor of vascular problems elsewhere in the body, including heart disease. *Other factors that can affect your erection include:*

●**High cholesterol.**

●**Cigarette smoking** (which constricts the blood vessels leading to the penis).

●**Excessive alcohol intake.**

●**Diabetes** (as many as 60% of diabetic men may have erection problems at some point).

●**Certain prescription drugs**, particularly blood pressure and cardiovascular medications, and some tranquilizers and antidepressants.

●**Radiation therapy.**

●**Pelvic surgery.**

●**Stroke or neurological disease**, including Parkinson's, Alzheimer's and multiple sclerosis.

Addressing these underlying causes can often solve the problem. If the dysfunction is psychological, you'll probably be referred to a certified sex therapist. If the problem turns out to be a simple issue of communication with your partner, a therapist could help you resolve it relatively quickly.

When the dysfunction involves more deeply ingrained issues—for example, inhibition or performance anxiety related to upbringing, religion and social background—it tends to be more difficult and time consuming to treat.

IT'S ALL IN YOUR MUSCLES

Most chronic erection problems aren't in a man's head, however, but in his muscle cells. Ninety percent of physical dysfunction occurs because the penis loses flexibility and elasticity over time, until its ability to trap and store blood becomes impaired. No matter how much blood flows into the penis, it leaks back out.

This happens because the muscle cells in your penis become thinner with age, while their supporting network of collagen (connective tissue) is no longer renewed as quickly as when you were younger, and becomes less elastic. As a result, the muscles in your penis are unable to fully relax—which is necessary for them to keep blood trapped in the penis.

FIVE TREATMENTS

Five types of treatment are now used to combat erectile dysfunction. Your choice of therapy should come only after discussing each option in detail with your doctor, and with your wife or sexual partner.

For a good outcome, it's vital to treat erectile dysfunction as a couple's problem, and include your mate in all aspects of the treatment. In fact, I believe a supportive partner is the most important factor in regaining a full, healthy sex life.

●**Oral medications.** The antidepressant drug Trazodone, taken daily, has been found to prolong erections in many patients. It usually takes about six weeks to notice any improvement. Another, newer drug called Viagra is still being tested in clinical trials, but it holds great promise, since it works specifically on the penile tissue, enhancing the metabolic activity of the penile muscle cells. Look for it to be on the market within the next couple of years. Yohimbine (a vasodilator made from the bark of the Central African yohimbé tree), another popular oral medication, is worthless, in my opinion.

●**Topical cream.** MUSE (Medicated Urethral System for Erection), which contains a prostaglandin cream that's applied into the opening of the urethra just before intercourse, has also produced good results in many patients. This cream is a vasodilator, meaning that it causes blood vessels to widen—encouraging blood flow into the penis. Like Viagra, this method has yet to be formally approved by the FDA for use in erectile dysfunction.

●**Injection therapy.** This is the newest form of treatment to emerge over the past 20 years, and is now considered the most effective. A drug is injected at the base of the penis 20 minutes before intercourse, using a very small hypodermic needle. Like creams, the drug works by dilating the blood vessels. The result is usually a very natural, high-quality erection.

This therapy first came into use in the 1980s, with the injection of choice being a mixture of the drugs *papaverine* and *phentolamine*. The injections have some side effects, however, including scarring from repeated injections, and sometimes a painfully prolonged erection (solved by reducing the dosage).

A new injectable drug has just become available, however, which can be self-administered at home. It is *prostaglandin E_1* (Alprostadil), a substance that occurs naturally in penile tissue. Tests show that scarring from prostaglandin E1 injections is minimal (occurring in only 1% of cases)—and the satisfaction rate is very high. This is currently the only FDA-approved method for penile injection.

Eight out of 10 men tested reported a usable erection and satisfactory intercourse. It also appears to work well for some cases of psychological dysfunction.

●**Vacuum device.** This is the least invasive method of all, involving no medication or surgery. A tube is placed over the end of the penis and the device is then activated, creating a vacuum that encourages blood to flow in, creating an erection. A rubber ring is then snapped over the base of the penis.

While the success rate is very high with vacuum devices, only one-third of the men who buy them end up using them. *The complaints:* It's too cumbersome, while the erection that results can be a bit painful and is usually not quite as hard as normal. Try the device first in your doctor's office, with the salesman present as well. *Cost:* $400 to $500.

●**Prosthetic device.** If injections, pills and creams don't do the job, you may want to think about having a prosthetic device implanted surgically through a small incision between the testicles. This has become a safe procedure, with an infection rate of less than 0.3%, and can be done using local anesthetic.

The most popular device is an inflatable prosthesis, which includes a fluid reservoir and a small pump, which the patient activates to become erect. The prosthesis doesn't interfere with normal sensation or ejaculation. After implantation, the patient can't even feel it—or see it—and often his partner can't tell it's there. However, once the prosthesis option has been selected by a patient, there's no turning back —injection therapy or the vacuum device will no longer be appropriate. Fortunately, the prosthetic device group of patients has an extremely high satisfaction rate.

J. Francois Eid, MD, assistant professor of urology and director of the Sexual Function Center at New York Hospital–Cornell Medical Center, New York.

Surviving Breast Cancer...How One Gynecologist Saved Herself

Barbara Joseph, MD

In April 1991, 36-year-old Barbara Joseph, MD, was nursing her eight-week-old son when she felt a lump in her left breast. Days later, the 36-year-old obstetrician-gynecologist was diagnosed with advanced (Stage III) breast cancer.

At first Dr. Joseph was gripped by panic. But she knew that this was only the beginning of her journey...so she took a deep breath and started to investigate her treatment options.

Ultimately, Dr. Joseph underwent selected conventional treatment, including surgery and chemotherapy. But she gives equal credit for her recovery to her use of holistic medical strategies.

Recently, Dr. Joseph talked with us about how women should respond to a diagnosis of breast cancer...

● **Don't rush into treatment.** By the time a tumor is big enough to be seen on a mammogram, odds are it's been forming for six to eight years. Breast cancer in general is not an emergency situation.

When I was diagnosed, part of me wanted to start treatment the next day. But you need not act the next day—or even the next week. Better to spend a few days or weeks considering all your options.

● **Find the right doctor.** Your diagnosis may have been made by your gynecologist or internist. But when it comes to breast surgery, you'll want a *surgeon*—perhaps one who specializes in treatment of the breast.

You may also need to consult a *medical oncologist* (a cancer specialist who administers chemotherapy)...and/or a *radiation oncologist* (who administers radiation therapy).

The doctor's credentials are important, but they aren't the only thing to consider.

You must feel comfortable with the treatment plan recommended by the doctor...and with the doctor's ability to communicate and listen.

Is he/she compassionate? Do you have rapport with him/her? Will he/she support you in your treatment decisions—even if they're not all conventional ones?

Do not just jump into the first treatment suggested. *Always* get a second opinion.

● **Learn as much as you can about breast cancer.** Talk to your doctors and read everything you can get your hands on.

In addition to my own book (see below), I recommend *Dr. Susan Love's Breast Book* and *Breast Cancer: What You Should Know (But May Not Be Told) About Prevention, Diagnosis and Treatment* by Steve Austin, ND, and Cathy Hitchcock.

Another source of up-to-date information is the Y-Me National Breast Cancer Organization (800-221-2141).

● **Consider breast-sparing surgery.** We now know that *lumpectomy* (removal of just the lump) plus radiation is just as effective as *mastectomy* (removal of the entire breast).

Yet lumpectomy isn't always possible.

If the tumor lies in the center of the breast, for example, mastectomy may be better.

These are also matters you should research —and discuss with your surgeon.

● **Do *not* leave the treatment decision up to your doctor.** You may be overwhelmed by all your options, but ultimately it's you who must decide.

Taking charge of the decision process empowers you emotionally—and physically. A study by Dr. Steven Greer showed that breast cancer patients who exhibited a fighting spirit were twice as likely to be alive 15 years later than those who felt hopeless.

●**Rethink your lifestyle.** Although it's hard to prove, I am convinced that cancer is the body's response to a host of insults that it's been subjected to over the years.

That includes dietary fat and pesticide residues in food...air and water pollution...psychological stress...and repressed anger.

Unless you take steps to eliminate these things, your cancer is likely to recur.

Up to 60% of all cancers in women are related to diet. A woman who eats traditional American fare ingests huge amounts of carcinogens—pesticides, preservatives and other additives as well as cancer-causing partially hydrogenated oils.

Women's breasts are particularly sensitive to these toxins. That's because many toxins are soluble in body fat—and breast tissue is composed of a large percentage of fat.

Since my diagnosis, I've chosen to eat only organic foods (grown without pesticides). My diet also incorporates some of the principles I learned through my study of *macrobiotics*. It consists largely of grains, plant-based proteins and sea vegetables (kelp, nori, etc.) and is free of dairy products.

I also eat lots of soy—miso, tofu and tempeh. These foods contain phytochemicals that are breast-protective.

●**Join a support group.** I believe that repressed anger and other negative emotions disrupt the healing process.

Individual and/or group therapy can help you develop the emotional strength you need to stop investing your energy in old resentments—so that you can move on and live in the present.

The evidence for this is compelling. In one study, conducted by David Spiegel, MD, of Stanford University, women with Stage IV breast cancer who attended weekly group therapy sessions survived *twice* as long as those who didn't attend—even though both groups received the same medical treatment.

To find a support group in your area, contact the Cancer Care Counseling Line (800-813-4673) or the Y-Me National Breast Cancer Organization. Or simply network with other breast cancer patients. Women heal by nurturing one another, and support groups foster this process.

●**Take nutritional supplements.** Foods are the best source of cancer-fighting nutrients. But certain supplements can make a crucial difference—especially if chemotherapy has left you too weak to eat properly.

Ask your doctor (or a nutritionist) about taking...

●**Daily multivitamin/multimineral.**

●**Antioxidants.** Each day, I take beta-carotene and vitamins C and E.

●**Flaxseed oil.** Each day, I add one to two tablespoons of a product called Udo's Choice. It provides essential fatty acids.

Barbara Joseph, MD, an obstetrician and gynecologist in private practice in Stamford, CT. She is author of My Healing from Breast Cancer: A Physician's Personal Story of Recovery and Transformation. *Keats Publishing.*

Have Breast Lumps Checked Immediately

Catching cancer early greatly improves the chance of a cure—often through lumpectomy rather than breast removal. Eight out of 10 breast lumps turn out to be benign—but a biopsy is often needed to be sure.

JoAnn E. Manson, MD, codirector of women's health at Brigham & Women's Hospital, Harvard Medical School, Boston.

Pap Smears Are Not Always Accurate

A Pap test correctly identifies abnormalities in a woman's cervix in 70% to 95% of cases. It misses cancer rarely—less than 1% of the time.

To increase accuracy: Have the test annually, even after you reach menopause or have a hysterectomy. Have it done midway between menstrual periods to make it easier to read.

Also: Avoid sexual intercourse, douching and use of vaginal products for 48 hours before the test.

Rebecca Johnson, MD, head of pathology and clinical laboratories at Berkshire Medical Center, Pittsfield, MA.

 # Lowering Estrogen Risk

R isk from estrogen is lowered by combining the hormone estrogen with another, *progestin.* Menopausal women who take only estrogen increase their chances of developing cancer of the uterus. But hormone-replacement therapy that includes estrogen and progestin does not increase uterine cancer risk.

Howard Judd, MD, professor of obstetrics and gynecology at the University of California at Los Angeles School of Medicine. His three-year study of almost 600 postmenopausal women was published in *The Journal of the American Medical Association,* 515 N. State St., Chicago 60610.

Powder and Ovarian Cancer

W omen who use powder in the vaginal area right after bathing increase their risk of ovarian cancer by 60%. Women using powder deodorant sprays have a 90% increased risk.

Reason: Unknown.

Self-defense: Avoid these products.

Linda Cook, PhD, epidemiologist at the Fred Hutchinson Cancer Research Center, Seattle. She led a study of 313 women with ovarian cancer and 422 without it.

How to Ease Menstrual Cramps

E ase menstrual cramps by avoiding certain foods that can make the cramping worse. Dairy products, fats, salt, alcohol, sugar and caffeine can all make cramping more severe.

Menstrual Cramps Self-Help Book by Susan Lark, MD, authority on women's health care in private practice in Los Altos, CA. Celestial Arts.

Yeast Infection Relief

Y ogurt relieves recurrent yeast infections. In a recent study, women who ate five ounces of yogurt daily containing live bacteria lactobacillus acidophilus had two-thirds fewer cases of recurrent vaginosis as before. This is the first study to demonstrate such positive effects from yogurt containing live cultures.

Theory: Bacteria in the yogurt are believed to protect against infection either by maintaining an acidic environment in the vagina or by producing compounds such as hydrogen peroxide that kill bad bacteria.

Study of 46 women with recurrent vaginosis by Eliezer Shalev at Central Emek Hospital, Afula, Israel, published in *Archives of Family Medicine,* 3400 Spruce St., Philadelphia, PA 19104.

Hysterectomies Have Value

D espite widespread reports of their being performed unnecessarily, hysterectomies sometimes have value. The hysterectomy rate dropped from 8.6 per 1,000 women in 1975 to 5.6 per 1,000 women in 1992. But the procedure can still be the treatment of choice for uterine fibroid tumors, endometriosis and other conditions. Avoiding hysterectomy can lead to years of debilitating pain in women whose conditions are best treated with the operation.

Bottom line: If your doctor recommends a hysterectomy, get additional opinions and information—do not simply dismiss the idea.

Robert Barbieri, MD, gynecologist and head of the department of obstetrics and gynecology at Brigham & Women's Hospital, Harvard Medical School, Boston.

Cervix-Sparing Hysterectomy

In a new alternative to ordinary hysterectomy, only the top of the uterus is removed. *Supracervical* hysterectomy has been used to treat fibroid tumors, pelvic pain, persistent bleeding and endometriosis. It's less likely than ordinary hysterectomy to injure the bowel and/ or bladder...or to cause vaginal prolapse (a shift in the position of the vagina), sexual dysfunction or the "sense of loss" that is common following ordinary hysterectomy.

Ernst G. Bartsich, MD, associate attending obstetrician and gynecologist at New York Hospital–Cornell Medical Center, New York.

Soy Eases Menopause Symptoms

Women who eat moderate amounts (20 grams/day) of soy protein suffer less severe hot flashes.

Possible explanation: Soy contains plant estrogens that are similar to the hormone produced in the human body. *Also:* Women who ate soy had a 10% drop in total cholesterol levels, as well as an 11% decline in LDL ("bad") cholesterol—and no decline in HDL ("good") cholesterol.

Sources of soy: Soy tofu...soy-based milk ...soy burgers, other products containing soy and as a powdered nutritional supplement.

Gregory Burke, MD, professor and vice chairman of Public Health Sciences at the Bowman Gray School of Medicine at Wake Forest University, Winston-Salem, NC, who led a study of 43 menopausal women.

Menopause and Heart Disease

The older a woman is at menopause, the less likely she is to die from heart disease—the leading cause of death in women. Recent studies show that the risk declines by about 2% for every year that menopause is delayed.

Other risk reducers: Cutting out cigarettes —smokers go through menopause earlier...regular exercise...maintaining a healthy weight. A low-fat diet and estrogen therapy after menopause—especially menopause caused by hysterectomy at a young age—may also reduce risk.

JoAnn Manson, MD, codirector of women's health at Brigham & Women's Hospital, Harvard Medical School, Boston.

Before Your PSA Test

Men about to take a PSA prostate test should refrain from sexual intercourse for 48 hours before the test. The test, which measures the levels of *prostate-specific antigen*, a substance produced in the prostate, is used as an indicator of prostate cancer. Researchers have found that the level of PSA shoots up temporarily by about 40% following intercourse, which could result in the patient being sent for an unnecessary, expensive and painful prostate biopsy.

Joseph E. Oesterling, MD, chairman of urology at the University of Michigan School of Medicine, Ann Arbor.

Embarrassment Can Be Fatal

Don't allow embarrassment prevents you from going to a doctor for a prostate or colorectal exam. Twenty percent of men surveyed said embarrassment might stop them from talking about prostate or colorectal problems.

Troubling: Early diagnosis is crucial to stopping the diseases. The five-year survival rate for early stage colon cancer is 88%...for rectal cancer, 80%...prostate cancer, 85%.

Helpful: Women's encouragement. Women who regularly have Pap smears and mammograms can help encourage their partners to go to the doctor to have possible problems checked.

Robert Bahnson, MD, chief of urology at the Arthur G. James Cancer Hospital and Research Institute at Ohio State University, Columbus.

Reducing the Side Effects Of Prostate Surgery

Side effects of prostate surgery—incontinence and impotence—can be reduced if the procedure is performed by a qualified surgeon. In one study of 593 men, 92% had complete urinary control after surgery and only two had stress incontinence serious enough to warrant placement of an artificial sphincter. Potency is preserved in 91% of men 50 years of age or younger...75% of men 50 to 60 years of age...58% of men 60 to 70 years of age... 25% of men 70 years of age or older.

Patrick Walsh, MD, urologist-in-chief and director of the department of urology at Johns Hopkins University School of Medicine, Baltimore, and author of *The Prostate: A Guide for Men and the Women Who Love Them.* Johns Hopkins University Press.

Prostate News

Surgery is extremely successful in treating early prostate cancer. A study of nearly 2,700 men between ages 48 and 79 with early prostate cancer who had their prostate glands removed surgically between 1970 and 1993 found that those with the least aggressive form of tumor had a 94% chance of surviving 10 years.

Those with *moderately aggressive* tumors had an 80% 10-year survival rate, while the comparable rate for men with the *most aggressive* tumors was 77%.

Researchers believe that in more recent years, the success rate has become even higher.

However, because surgery sometimes results in impotence and urinary incontinence, physicians say that for elderly men with slow-growing cancer, it may be better simply to wait and see how the cancer develops before deciding to operate.

Glenn S. Gerber, MD, assistant professor of urology at the University of Chicago Medical School.

Domineering Men Die Sooner

Men who exhibited such vocal characteristics as attempting to interrupt conversations and making quick responses were 60% more likely to die sooner than men who spoke quietly and were more laid back.

Theory: Socially dominating men need to be in control at all times. This increases levels of stress hormones in the blood, which can, over time, damage the heart and immune system.

Michael Babyak, PhD, researcher at Duke University Medical Center, Durham, NC, who conducted a study of 750 men over 22 years.

Looking Thinner: Advice for Men

Don't buy something too small and expect to hide your weight...or something too big and think you will look thinner. Men's clothes must fit right.

Vests: Wear only long, squared-off vests to disguise your weight—avoid body-hugging sweater vests.

Pants: Avoid cuffs if you are short or have short legs. If you are big in the rear, choose pants without pockets and jackets with built-up shoulders.

Shirts: Tuck shirts in to create a more slimming vertical line.

Colors and fabrics: Wear muted prints and textures. Avoid lightweight fabrics that don't hang well.

Susan Dresner, New York–based wardrobe and management consultant and author of *Shopping on the Inside Track* (available at most libraries).

Psychotherapy and Managed-Care Coverage

All visits to a therapist following the first one must be authorized in advance by your insurance company—so check the details of coverage before you start.

Including: Maximum number of sessions covered (usually 30 or fewer in a calendar year) …copayments and deductibles…and which therapists are part of the program.

To get more of your sessions paid for: Make sure your therapist knows of any medical problems connected with your emotional state —for example, a heart condition and stress. If there are family issues, ask whether counseling is covered for your family as a group in addition to your individual sessions.

Barry Lubetkin, PhD, director of the Institute for Behavior Therapy, 137 E. 36 St., New York 10016.

Incontinence Self-Defense

Give yourself plenty of time to empty your bladder completely…limit fluid intake, particularly alcohol and coffee, for a few hours before bedtime…help stretch your bladder by increasing the intervals between urination…

strengthen the muscles that squeeze the bladder outlet shut by practicing Kegel exercises.

How: Contract the pelvic floor muscles for five seconds, then release for five seconds. Repeat 12 contractions eight times a day. For women with "stress incontinence" (incontinence triggered by coughing, sneezing, straining or even simply standing up), try Kegel exercises with specially designed vaginal weights and cross your legs before coughing or sneezing.

Kristene E. Whitmore, MD, clinical associate professor of urology at the University of Pennsylvania, Philadelphia.

The Benefit of High Heels

High heels can relieve heel and arch pain, often experienced by women after pregnancy or weight gain. High heels take pressure off those painful areas and move it to the ball of the foot.

Helpful: Wear heels of different heights at different times of the day to stretch muscles and tendons. The highest heel should be two-and-a-half inches tall. Also, avoid pointed heels.

Suzanne Levine, DO, clinical adjunct podiatrist at New York Hospital–Cornell Medical Center, New York.

Simple Pimple Treatment

At night, put toothpaste—a drying agent — on the pimple. Any type of toothpaste will work—gels included. The next day, apply ice to reduce swelling. Apply warm compresses on the pimple to reduce redness.

Jerome Z. Litt, MD, dermatologist in private practice, Pepper Pike, OH.

14

Nutrition, Fitness And Exercise

Biochemist's Dream Diet Improves Health, Lowers Weight

Barry Sears, PhD
Eicotech Corporation

More than 10 studies have been conducted that suggest that a high insulin level is a primary risk factor in heart disease.

Excess insulin affects hormones that cause blood platelets to clot and clog arteries. No one has discovered a drug that will lower insulin levels. Only food can control its production. So I set out to create a diet that would not only stabilize my own insulin levels and prolong my life but would help others as well.

The result? At age 49, after eight years of following my eating plan, I have the heart of a 25-year-old, according to my doctors. What's more, I dropped 30 pounds in the process and

have kept the weight off. And—my body fat is at a percentage (15%) that is considered ideal for me.

CUT BACK ON CARBOHYDRATES

US guidelines recommend that people eat a diet composed of about 70% carbohydrates, only 15% protein and 15% fat. But Americans haven't slimmed down as a result. Instead, most have *stuffed* themselves on complex carbohydrates, such as bread, potatoes and grains, and fattened up at epidemic proportions.

This type of carbohydrate-loading increases insulin levels in the blood, which in turn builds body fat. When insulin levels are high, the body cannot effectively burn stored fat.

My plan calls for a diet that derives 30% of its calories from protein, 40% from carbohydrates and 30% from fat. This balance ensures that insulin levels remain in an acceptable *zone*—not too much and not too little, since you need a certain amount of insulin to maintain good health.

237

STEPS TO TAKE

My diet's eating plan is based on protein needs rather than total caloric needs. Once you determine how much protein you should consume, you can add a reasonable amount of "good" carbohydrates and beneficial fats for health and weight control. *Strategies...*

●**Concentrate on protein.** Although the US government advises adults to consume about 56 grams of protein daily, that is based on the needs of a 154-pound, sedentary male who has 23% body fat. Protein requirements can vary dramatically from person to person. How much you need depends on your height, weight, percentage of body fat and level of physical activity.

Examples: A six-foot, 185-pound man who exercises aerobically for 30 minutes a day and has 15% body fat needs about 120 grams of protein daily to maintain his muscle mass. A physically active 125-pound woman who is five-feet, five inches tall with 22% body fat requires about 70 grams of protein a day.

The higher your body fat and the lower your physical activity, the less protein you need. *Note:* There are about 15 to 25 grams of protein per three ounces of cooked meat, poultry or fish.

Calculating your body fat is complex. Speak with your doctor, or see the appropriate tables in my book, *The Zone.*

●**Fill up on "good" carbohydrates.** All carbohydrates are not necessarily equal. High-density carbohydrates found in grains, pasta, bread, cereal, rice and potatoes enter the bloodstream too quickly, boosting insulin levels.

Low-density carbohydrates—like many vegetables and fruits—enter the bloodstream more slowly, so insulin levels don't shoot up.

The key is to limit your intake of high-density carbohydrates.

Example: Have two cups of steamed vegetables plus only one-quarter cup of pasta rather than a huge plate of pasta.

●**Add some "good" fat to your diet.** Fat has gotten a bad rap. Saturated fats—found in red meats, egg yolks, whole milk products and butter—have been linked to heart disease and various cancers, so they should be restricted.

Monounsaturated fats—found in olive oil, macadamia and pistachio nuts, almonds, cashews and avocados—not only enhance health but also slow the rate at which carbohydrates enter the bloodstream, thereby lowering insulin levels. The same is true of fish oil, the best source of which is fish like salmon.

Every meal and snack should contain some monounsaturated fat.

●**Eat three meals and two snacks a day.** Just be sure all meals and snacks contain protein, carbohydrate and fat. Never eat carbohydrates alone. They will cause your insulin levels to skyrocket.

An ideal dinner might consist of four ounces of roasted, skinless chicken breast, fish or white-meat turkey surrounded by three cups of steamed, herb-seasoned vegetables.

You'll need to add a little monounsaturated fat to top off the meal, so drizzle one-third teaspoon olive oil over the vegetables or dress them with a tablespoon of slivered almonds.

●**Limit alcohol and caffeine.** Beer, wine and hard liquor have the same effect on insulin levels as carbohydrates. Also, limit intake of caloric beverages such as juice and soda.

If you plan to have a drink with dinner, cut back on your allotted food carbohydrates.

Example: Instead of three cups of steamed vegetables at dinner, have only one-and-a-half cups.

If you drink alcohol, always team it with a protein "chaser," like a piece of low-fat cheese. Protein stimulates production of a hormone that reduces insulin levels. Caffeine in coffee, tea and colas also stimulates insulin production.

Switch to decaffeinated coffee and tea. If you must have coffee, have it with a healthy breakfast with the right amount of protein, carbohydrates and fats.

●**Exercise daily.** Aside from burning calories and toning the body, aerobic exercise, such as walking, swimming, biking and working out on a treadmill, lowers insulin levels.

Don't follow your workout with a low-fat, carbohydrate-rich bagel that will cause insulin to soar. If you're ravenous after exercising, have a snack 30 to 40 minutes before your workout to prevent post-exercise carbohydrate cravings.

Healthy snack choice: An ounce of turkey breast and a piece of fresh fruit.

Barry Sears, PhD, a biochemist who has conducted nutritional research at several major universities. He is president of Eicotech Corporation, a biotechnology company in Marblehead, MA. He is author of the best-seller *The Zone: A Dietary Road Map.* HarperCollins.

Ask for a Doggy Bag Before You Begin Eating Instead of Afterward

Simply have the waiter divide your meal in half and pack half of it for you to take home. This reduces restaurant portions to a manageable size and prevents you from nibbling food left on the plate even when you are no longer hungry.

Your Health, 5401 NW Broken Sound Blvd., Boca Raton, FL 33487.

There Is a Way to Control Your Weight Long Term

Jack Trimpey, LCSW
Rational Recovery

Everyone who is overweight has a good excuse—a slow metabolism that refuses to burn calories…a faulty internal regulator that keeps you hungry…depression or boredom.

With few exceptions, there's only one reason for being overweight—*eating too much.* And only one reason why people overeat—a seeming inability to resist physical cravings for food with lots of fat and calories.

Does this explanation sound hard-hearted? It's really hard-*headed*…and the basis for rational, effective weight control—an approach with which *anyone can eat less food…forever.*

WHERE FATNESS COMES FROM

If you've tried unsuccessfully to lose weight and keep it off, you already know what foods are fattening. You've tried lots of diets.

Diets are great. But they're not enough. To learn self-control, you also have to know where your desire to eat rich, fattening foods comes from.

The human brain has two parts. At the top is the neocortex, the *thinking brain* that produces words and makes decisions.

But below that is the midbrain, which generates strong, compelling appetites for the necessities of life—*food, sex and safety.* It's hard-wired for survival by pursuing pleasure—some call it the party center!

The midbrain produces your hunger for food, *but it can't make you eat.* By itself, appetite can't move so much as your little finger. Overeating happens when the drive from your midbrain is translated into thoughts (*I want that sundae…I need it…I'm going to have it*) and actions by the neocortex. It requires a conscious *decision*—every time. And the decision maker is you.

The hungers of the midbrain are powerful indeed, but the thinking brain is stronger! Instead of carrying out its orders, the neocortex can *inhibit* the appetites of the midbrain.

No matter how compulsively you eat, your neocortex inhibits your midbrain's appetites much of the time. The secret of weight control is recognizing the voice of the midbrain—and learning to resist it.

YOUR INNER ANIMAL

We call it the *Feast Beast*…the midbrain-born thoughts, feelings that lead you to eat unwisely.

When you hear a voice within that says, *It's hours before dinner, but I'm hungry! Why should I suffer? A dish of ice cream won't hurt*—that's your Feast Beast. When you feel unhappy and you know that a big dinner will make you feel better, those are the feelings of the beast.

We hear lots of inner voices, including the rational one that tells us that it's healthier to lose excess weight. But the Feast Beast has a primitive power. And it's *always* hungry.

●**It argues subtly:** *Have a little more… you can skip breakfast tomorrow.*

●**It plays on your fears:** *If you don't give*

yourself a treat, you'll be so depressed you won't get any work done.

● **It whines and pleads:** *I've had such a hard day. Nobody's nice to me…I've got to be nice to myself!*

There's no real beast, of course…the voice comes from your own brain. But it's most helpful to think of this part of you as alien… and your *enemy*. Once you learn to identify the call of the wild thing within, you can face it down. Like any animal, it obeys authority.

Saying *that's not me*…is the biggest step you can take toward true self-control.

Clue: When it's *convincing* you to overeat, your Feast Beast often uses the third person: *You deserve a treat…why should you suffer?… You can go back on your diet tomorrow.*

Impatient and seductive, it switches to *we… Let's get some ice cream! What are we waiting for?*

When commands to overeat come in the form of *I*…translate them into *It*. *I can't stand this empty feeling* becomes *It can't stand being hungry.*

SLAYING THE BEAST

To overcome your Feast Beast, you need a rational plan for eating correctly. I call it *TAPS* because it means "good-bye" to the beast…

● **Time.** Your Feast Beast will tell you that any time is time to eat. But your rational brain knows that regular mealtimes are the only correct times. Three modest, well-balanced meals are all you need, and your body will adapt quickly to this schedule.

● **Amount.** From a rational point of view, you just need modest portions to sustain energy and provide proper nutrition—no more than four ounces of meat…vegetables…a portion of whole-wheat pasta. Your Feast Beast will cry for seconds. *You don't need them.*

● **Place.** Your Feast Beast is ready to gorge anywhere. You know, rationally, that the correct place to eat is at a table. Not in the street, in the car or standing at the refrigerator.

● **Stuff.** The right stuff to eat is a balanced diet of nutritious food. Your Feast Beast will scream for ice cream, cake, candy and other calorie-packed snacks. Tell it *no.*

Important: Eat like a human being. Wolfing down your food means the beast is in control.

To break this momentum, follow the rules of etiquette—sit up straight…finish one mouthful before taking another…carry on a conversation…pause between courses.

HUNGER

If you follow this rational eating plan, you'll lose weight…and keep it off. But you will be hungry. A key anti-Feast Beast strategy is learning to think differently about hunger.

Learn to recognize hunger as a mere physical sensation. And to *cultivate*, not fight, hunger.

It's true that hunger is a hollow, empty, restless feeling…not terribly pleasant. But it won't hurt you. *And there's no way to lose an ounce without experiencing a good deal of it at first.* Soon your Feast Beast will get the message. Accept the feeling of emptiness without complaint—and use hunger. Hunger is the sign of successful weight control.

When you feel hungry, your Feast Beast will whine and roar…

● **We have to fill that empty feeling…** *we have to eat—right now!*

But your rational mind can see hunger differently…

● **Here's the feeling I've been working all day to get…** *it means I'm losing weight. I don't want to ruin it by eating potato chips.*

Some people learn to tame the Feast Beast better in the company of like-minded people. Rational Recovery for Fatness groups have formed around the country. The main idea is *education*, rather than emotional support.

To find out about groups in your area, or for help in organizing one on your own, call 916-621-2667.

Jack Trimpey, LCSW, cofounder of Rational Recovery, an approach for overcoming alcohol and drug dependence. He is coauthor of Taming the Feast Beast: How to Recognize the Voice of Fatness and End Your Struggle with Food Forever. *Dell.*

Weight-Loss Health Trap

Women who become too thin can endanger their well-being.

Reason: Women who go to extremes to eliminate fat from their bodies often go too far. Researchers have found that in healthy women, body fat should be between 16% and 26% of total weight—with the ideal being about 20%.

Quick way to see if weight is in healthy range: Use the hip-to-waist ratio. Pass a tape measure around your body, and cross the navel. Jot down the result. Then pass the tape around your buttocks to measure your hips. Divide the waist measurement by the hip measurement. If the result is below 0.85, you are in good shape. If it is higher than 1.0, you are heavy and need to lose weight.

Stephen Gullo, PhD, president of the Institute for Health and Weight Sciences, New York, which offers one-on-one coaching to retrain eating habits and attitudes toward food. He is author of *Thin Tastes Better.* Dell.

Diet Doctors' Weight-Loss Secrets

Mary Dan Eades, MD
Stephen Gullo, PhD
John McDougall, MD

The secret to looking and feeling younger than your years is following a nutritious diet and exercising regularly. But there are many different strategies for battling everyday temptation and staying slim—so we asked three top diet doctors how they do it…

MARY DAN EADES, MD

My diet is focused on getting the correct balance of foods so that metabolic hormones, particularly insulin, help the body use nutrients as they should. As a result, I consume moderate amounts of protein and fat, and I'm selective about the carbohydrates I eat.

Today, at age 43, I weigh 135 pounds and stand 5'5" tall—with less than 24% body fat.

•**I eat adequate amounts of protein.** Although protein has gotten a bad reputation lately because it can be high in fat, it is the most essential food that the body needs to survive. I eat at least 10 to 12 ounces of protein each day when I am trying to lose or maintain my weight.

I get the protein in the form of lean red meat, fish, poultry, low-fat cheese, eggs and tofu. By eating protein in correct proportion to other dietary components, I am able to burn the incoming fat as fuel for energy rather than store it—as would be the case if I were eating a lot of protein-rich foods and not enough of the other types.

•**I select my carbohydrates carefully.** I keep my carbohydrate intake to a minimum—about 60 to 80 grams daily because of their adverse impact on insulin—especially starchier sources and refined carbohydrates. I primarily get those carbohydrates from a wide variety of fruits and vegetables that pack a big vitamin punch.

•**I take a daily multivitamin supplement** to ensure I'm getting all of the nutrients I might otherwise miss.

•**I exercise regularly.** I practice kung fu—a high-impact aerobic and resistance training regimen—four times a week for one hour. Or, if I can't get to kung fu class, I run and work out with weights.

STEPHEN GULLO, PHD

Living a very busy lifestyle surrounded by fine foods, I frequently find myself tempted to overeat. Obesity runs in my family, and I have the same weight-control problems as my patients. If I'm not careful about what I eat, I can easily add eight to 10 pounds to my 5'11", 168-pound frame. I'm especially prone to weight gain around the abdomen. And that is particularly unhealthful.

Pizza is my downfall. Just one slice can cause me to experience continuing cravings for more pizza, bread and other flour products for weeks. To cap my craving for pizza, I try to minimize my trigger-food problem by "boxing it in"…

…limiting the quantity I eat.

…controlling how often I eat it.

…avoiding all the locations at which I usually am inclined to eat this particular food.

If self-control doesn't work, I "box it out"—temporarily banish pizza from my diet. It's hard at first, but eventually I stop craving the food. If I find myself thinking about it, I use diversion. Some activity that diverts the mind usually turns off the craving almost instantly.

To avoid temptation, I follow a few guidelines...

●**Shop carefully at the supermarket**, since that's where most weight problems begin. I avoid shopping in the late afternoon or right after work, when blood sugar plummets and we're prone to impulsive food purchases. Before I put any product in my shopping cart, I ask myself, *Is this a food I have a history of abusing?* If it is, I put it back on the shelf.

●**When traveling**, I don't accept hotel mini-bar keys. I also ask the maid not to leave cookies or candy on my pillow. Availability creates craving.

●**Never show up at a restaurant hungry.** It is easy to attack the bread basket. Instead, I eat sugar-free Jell-O, nonfat yogurt, nonfat soup or fruit before dining out. Sometimes before a meal I have cold tomato juice, which is a natural appetite suppressant.

●**Exercise regularly.** I jog or put in time on the new "strength trainer" NordicTrack for 45 minutes two to three times a week and do additional strength training. This helps me burn 10% to 15% more calories than I would normally.

●**Take supplements.** I believe in the importance of vitamins and antioxidants. Every day, I take vitamin E (400 IU), vitamin C (500 mg in the morning and 500 mg at night), folate (400 mg), selenium (100 mg) and a baby aspirin.

●**Use cognitive-switching techniques.** This involves replacing negative food thoughts with healthy ones.

Example: Instead of saying, *I'll have just one slice of pizza* (which is not true to my history with this particular food), I tell myself that the craving I'm feeling is only temporary...the desire will pass...and that as much as I want a slice of pizza at that instant, I want to be healthy and in control of my life.

JOHN MCDOUGALL, MD

At age 22, I weighed 220 pounds and stood 6'1" tall. Today, I'm 49 and I weigh 175 pounds. I'm a vegetarian who relies on the starch-based diet followed by the people from China, Japan and the Middle East.

In these cultures, people have lower levels of obesity, heart disease, breast cancer and other health problems than do those who follow the typical high-fat American diet. *Here's what I do...*

●**I eat minimal amounts of protein and fat.** As a vegetarian, I don't eat meat, fish, poultry or dairy products. I believe they lead to medical problems. I get all the protein I need from vegetable sources. I also avoid vegetable oils, margarine and shortenings as well as refined and simple sugars.

●**I eat mostly carbohydrates.** My diet consists largely of whole grains (such as breads, pasta and rice)...root vegetables (potatoes, sweet potatoes, yams, turnips, parsnips)...beans, peas and lentils...and green and yellow vegetables. I can eat these foods until I've satisfied my hunger. I eat *limited* amounts of fruits (because they can be high in sugar and calories) and limited amounts of low-fat dressings and sauces.

●**I don't take vitamin supplements** because I get all the nutrients I need from my diet. While I don't eat dairy products, I get sufficient calcium from potatoes, rice, corn and other vegetables that contain the mineral.

●**I exercise moderately.** Luckily, my low-fat diet doesn't call for intensive activity to maintain my weight. I try to be physically active in my routine. I downhill ski in winter and swim, windsurf and walk in summer. I also work out with weights with a personal trainer one hour each week year-round... although I wish I had time to do more.

Mary Dan Eades, MD, an internist specializing in weight loss and metabolic medicine. She is in private practice, with her husband, Michael Eades, MD, in Little Rock, AR. They are authors of *Protein Power.* Bantam Books.

Stephen Gullo, PhD, president of the Institute for Health and Weight Sciences, New York, which offers one-on-one coaching to retrain eating habits and attitudes toward food. He is author of *Thin Tastes Better.* Dell.

John McDougall, MD, founder and director of The McDougall Program at St. Helena Hospital, Deer Park, CA. He is author of several books, including *The McDougall Program for a Healthy Heart.* Dutton.

Easy Ways to Eat Less Fat

Blot the grease on the top of pizza with a napkin. That will get rid of at least one teaspoon of fat.

- **Leave the last half-inch** of take-out Chinese food in the container so that you'll eat less sauce.

- **Make mashed potatoes with buttermilk** —or skim milk and butter-flavored seasoning—instead of using butter and whole milk.

- **Sauté meat and vegetables in fruit juice** or Worcestershire sauce instead of oil.

- **Do not drink alcohol** on an empty stomach. Alcohol increases food cravings and can trigger a high-calorie binge.

Men's Health, 33 E. Minor St., Emmaus, PA 18098.

Healthy Snack Combinations that Taste Like the Real Thing

Evening refrigerator raids lead to hard-to-lose pounds—unless you reach for more nutritious alternatives. *Here are my favorite snacks when I crave something sinful...*

When you crave: Apple pie (330 calories).

Eat this instead: Baked apple on a fat-free waffle. *Calories:* 180.

When you crave: Cake and ice cream (370 calories).

Eat this instead: 1 fat-free waffle with ½ cup of sorbet or frozen yogurt. *Calories:* 160.

When you crave: Nachos (140 calories).

Eat this instead: Homemade sweet potato chips (sliced thin and microwaved for two to three minutes) with melted fat-free cheese and spices. *Calories:* 80 (½ medium potato with spices).

When you crave: Pretzels (110 calories) or potato chips (160 calories).

Eat this instead: Carrots and celery sticks. *Calories:* 75 (one carrot, two to three celery stalks).

When you crave: Pizza (350 calories).

Eat this instead: Rice cakes with nonfat mozzarella cheese and chopped tomato. *Calories:* 120 (one rice cake, ½ tomato, one ounce fat-free cheese).

Stephen Gullo, PhD, president of the Institute for Health and Weight Sciences, New York, which offers one-on-one coaching to retrain eating habits and attitudes toward food. He is author of *Thin Tastes Better*. Dell.

Fat-Free Food Traps

Be cautious if the label shows more than 11 grams of refined *sugar* per serving...some novel foods, such as soy-based frozen entrées, contain healthy soy oil and may be high in fiber, but watch the sodium level.

Good for you: Products with more than five grams of fiber per serving.

Franca Alphin, RD, LDN, nutrition director at Duke University Diet and Fitness Center, Durham, NC.

No-Fat Food Can Still Make You Fat if You Eat Too Much of It

A calorie is a calorie, whether it comes from fat or carbohydrates. If you eat more calories than you are able to burn, the body stores the extra calories as fat.

Bottom line: Low-fat or no-fat foods are better for the body than their high-fat equivalents—but should still be eaten in moderation.

Voight Precision Training for Body & Mind by Karen Voight, founder of Voight Fitness and Dance Center, Los Angeles. Hyperion.

Late-Night Snack Trap

Don't go to bed too hungry or too full. Sleepers can awaken from hunger pangs, stomach distention or discomfort.

If you do snack, stay away from: Spicy foods—salsa, chili, curry, etc.—which can cause heartburn...oily foods, which are difficult to digest.

Best bedtime snacks: Small portions of food that you find easy to digest. Some scientific studies suggest that foods may even help you fall asleep faster and stay asleep longer.

Gary Zammit, PhD, director of the Sleep Disorders Institute, St. Luke's/Roosevelt Hospital Center, New York.

Dining-Out Health Trap

Portion sizes that are served at restaurants are often huge—and you are consuming two or three times more than is generally considered to be one serving.

Result: You get more calories, fat and sodium than you think when you eat outside your home.

Example: A restaurant muffin can equal two official servings of muffin...a small movie-theater popcorn contains seven cups—more than twice the official serving size.

Self-defense: Plan to share restaurant food or take half of your meal home.

Jayne Hurley, senior nutritionist for *Nutrition Action Healthletter*, 1875 Connecticut Ave. NW, Washington, DC 20009.

Alcohol and Weight Gain

Drinkers tend to eat more, not less, when they consume alcohol with meals—contrary to the belief that consuming alcohol cuts food intake.

Reality: The body does not recognize the calories from alcohol or compensate by cutting other intake. Instead, the extra calories of alcohol add to the already excessive calories of the food, making weight gain more likely.

Angelo Tremblay, PhD, professor of nutrition and physiology at Laval University, Ste.-Foy, Quebec, Canada, who led a study of more than 700 people.

Nonfat Cheeses Should Melt as Well as Full-Fat Ones

Finely shredded *nonfat* cheeses should melt almost as well as full-fat ones...or you can use processed nonfat cheeses that are specifically made to melt.

Caution: Processed cheeses tend to be high in salt—check labels carefully.

Secrets of Fat-Free Cooking by Sandra Woodruff, RD, a nutrition consultant in Tallahassee, FL. Avery Publishing Group.

Jack LaLanne's Fitness Magic

Jack LaLanne

Life is all about survival of the fittest. And you have to be in shape for that! Run a personal fitness check. Do you get enough rest? Eat the right foods? Have a hobby that relieves stress? Exercise to accumulate reserves of energy that will be like money in the bank for the day you need it?

The only way to increase your strength, energy and vitality is to stress your body beyond what it's accustomed to doing.

People up to 95 years old have *doubled* their strength and endurance in a short time with weight-training programs.

A 90-year-old person can't lift a weight as heavy as a 21-year-old person can. But each can work to their own capacity...and get results.

People rationalize about not exercising. Their main excuse—*I don't have the time.* Would you sell your arm for $100 or your leg for $1 million? No, because your most priceless possession is your body. Shouldn't you spend a little time keeping it in good shape?

How you look is a billboard of the way you regard yourself. As you become fitter, and look and feel better, your self-esteem will rise...a good first step for improving your sex life as well.

If you're afraid you'll have a heart attack—be aware that the people who have heart attacks are the ones who *don't* exercise.

MAKE GOOD USE OF COMMERCIALS

When a commercial interrupts a TV show, don't get a snack—exercise instead. *Here's an easy one:*

● **Get up/get down.** Lower yourself gently to the floor and lie on your back. Stand up. Repeat slowly...then quickly. Practice until you can do it fast 15 times in a row. Invite your children or grandchildren to join in.

MAGIC FIVES

I devised these five simple exercises to trim and firm every part of the body. You can do Magic Fives almost anywhere. Your only gym equipment is a straight-backed chair and one or two books.

Start by doing each exercise slowly to a count of 10. Build stamina by exercising a little more vigorously each time, four or five times a week. Consider watching yourself in a mirror to see how well you're doing. Visualize yourself as you want to look. Breathe deeply to bring oxygen to your bloodstream and burn fat.

1. Swings. These work many muscles simultaneously. Hold a light book between your hands. Place your feet a shoulder width apart. Bend your knees slightly.

Bend over at the waist. Breathing out, slowly swing the book down between your legs, trying to touch an imaginary wall behind you. Breathing in, swing the book back up again over your head. Keep your arms straight and try to touch the imaginary wall immediately behind you with the book.

2. Knees to chest. Excellent for the waistline, hip flexibility, abdominal muscles and lower back.

Sit at the very edge of a straight, hard chair. Holding both sides of the seat to keep your balance, lean back until your shoulders touch the back of the chair. Draw both knees as close to your chest as you can (or lift one knee at a time until you can lift both at once). When you become advanced, hold a book between your knees.

Lower your legs. Then make pedaling motions, pretending you're riding a bicycle.

Progress from short movements to large ones. With each rotation, extend your leg down close to the floor before continuing.

For variation, do these exercises while lying on your back on the floor or on your bed.

3. Leg lunges. For sagging hips and flabby thighs.

Stand to one side of a chair. Hold on to the back of it. With your right leg, lunge forward as if you were fencing. Bring it back. Repeat with your left leg. As you get stronger, bend your knee more and step farther out. Keep your upper body erect throughout.

4. Leg extensions to the back. Tremendous for your back muscles all the way down from your neck to the bottoms of your feet. Firms the buttocks.

Facing a chair, bend at the waist and hold both sides of the seat. Keep your arms straight and back away from the chair until you feel comfortable.

Slowly lift your right leg backward as high as possible while pointing your toes, looking up, breathing in and tensing your hips tightly. You can bend your left knee a bit. As you lower your leg, breathe out...put your chin on your chest...and round your back, tensing your abdominal muscles. Repeat with your other leg.

5. Two-way punches. These cardiovascular exercises work most of the upper body muscles. They'll burn calories and trim your waistline.

● **Forward punches.** Helpful for your arms, shoulders, upper back and chest. Stand with your feet a shoulder width apart. Bend your knees a bit. Visualize a punching bag in front of you and punch it hard with one hand at a time. Imagine that your elbow is hitting a wall behind you as it comes back. Increase the pace.

● **Overhead punches.** Works the backs of your arms, the sides of your waist and your calves. Improves your posture. Clench your fists, stand erect and punch your right arm overhead, pretending you're trying to hit the ceiling. Rise up on your toes as you go. Drop the opposite elbow down as low as you can. Alternate arms. Do this exercise rapidly.

● **Combination punches.** Assume the position for forward punches. Pull your waist in and punch forward rapidly, hitting your elbows against an imaginary wall behind you. Quickly switch to an overhead punch. As each arm comes down, push your elbow down as low as you can. The faster you punch, the more calories you'll burn. When you become more advanced, hold a book in each hand for extra resistance.

TRIM UPPER-ARM MUSCLES

The muscle on the back of the upper arm typically gets flabby as people age. That is because the triceps are not used very often. *To tone that muscle:*

- **Do overhead punches** (described above).

- **Push a weight**, such as a small barbell, above your head.

- **Stand with your back to the wall and your arms down**, with your palms against the wall. Push yourself away from the wall and back again. *Bonus:* You'll exercise the backs of your shoulders and improve your posture.

TAKE RESPONSIBILITY

At 81, I spend at least one hour a day lifting weights…and another hour swimming. Can't you find 20 minutes a few times a week to keep yourself in shape?

Caution: Always check with your doctor before starting an exercise regimen.

Jack LaLanne, who opened his first gym in 1936 and has promoted physical culture for 65 years. He is author of six books, including *Revitalize Your Life After 50: Improve Your Looks, Your Health and Your Sex Life.* Hastings House Book Publishers.

Why Good Muscles Are So Very Important And…Best Exercises for Building Them

Ralph S. Paffenbarger, Jr., MD
Stanford University School of Medicine

Ever notice how many people—even those who consider themselves physically fit—seem to develop thin, stick-like arms and legs as they age?

By age 85, the average person loses 45% of the muscle mass he/she had at age 30. As these people grow weaker, their risk of suffering a debilitating fall rises.

Good news: Muscle loss is not an inevitable consequence of aging. In most cases, it's simply the result of disuse.

When it comes to maintaining muscle strength, many people fall victim to three mistakes…

- ***Mistake #1:*** **Thinking that keeping weight off is all that counts.** They think that if they weigh as much as they did in college, they're fit. And they're *wrong*.

At age 21, we're mostly muscle and bone. By age 50, much of our earlier muscle mass has been replaced by fat—even if our weight remains constant.

- ***Mistake #2:*** **Focusing solely on aerobic conditioning**. Walking, running, bicycling and swimming can give you a strong heart and lungs. But you need upper-body strength to carry groceries, play with the kids, enjoy a game of tennis, etc. And that's something aerobic exercises cannot give you.

- ***Mistake #3:*** **Assuming that strength will diminish with age.** We all lose *some* strength as we grow older—even trained athletes. But most adults lose far more than they need to—because they become sedentary.

WHAT'S THE REMEDY?

Advertisements would have you believe that the answer lies with "power" bars and high-protein nutritional drinks. Not so. The real key to strong muscles is strength training (weight lifting).

Though it's often considered a young person's pursuit, weight lifting brings benefits to all ages.

As part of a landmark study by Maria A. Fiatarone, MD, of Tufts University's Jean Mayer USDA Human Nutrition Research Center on Aging, a group of men and women ages 86 to 96 began a program of daily weight lifting.

After eight weeks, average strength in the group had risen a remarkable 174%.

In another study, Dr. Fiatarone worked with nursing home residents, all over age 70.

After 10 weeks, all had more than doubled their strength. Four switched from walkers to canes.

Another Tufts researcher put a group of women in their 60s on a twice-weekly strength-training regimen. A year later, their muscle strength had increased from 35% to 76%.

Bonus: Because muscle burns more calories than fat, the average woman in the study ended up burning an additional 442 calories a week.

You certainly shouldn't wait until you reach your 60s to start strength training. The earlier you begin—and the more muscle you build—the less likely you are to become frail in old age.

REGULAR WORKOUTS ARE KEY

Exercising once in a blue moon will just make you sore—without doing much to build strength. I urge you to work out at least one day a week—and preferably three days. Be sure to include a day of rest between workouts.

Here are six easy strength-building exercises. You can do them at the gym…or in your home. All you'll need is a set of two-pound ankle weights and a pair of two-pound dumbbells.

● **Abdominals.** Lie on your back with knees bent and feet flat on the floor. Reaching forward with your hands toward your knees, lift your head from the floor until you assume a sitting position or as far as you can go. Let yourself back down slowly.

● **Thighs.** Don your ankle weights and sit on a chair. Slowly lift your right leg out in front of you. When your leg is fully extended, pause for a breath or two. Let it back down slowly. Keep your back straight. Now do the left leg.

● **Hamstrings.** Keep your ankle weights on. Stand and hold the back of a chair for balance. Slowly lift your right foot, moving your heel toward your buttocks. Hold for a breath or two, then lower slowly. Repeat with your left foot.

● **Chest.** With a dumbbell in each hand, lie face-up on the floor. Hold the dumbbells against your chest, palms facing your feet. Now raise them slowly until both arms are extended straight up. Hold briefly. Make sure the small of your back is flat against the floor. Lower your arms slowly.

● **Biceps.** Sit on a chair with a dumbbell in your right hand and your right elbow supported on your thigh. Lean slightly forward and support yourself with your left hand on your left thigh. Start with your right arm extended down, then slowly curl the dumbbell up toward your chest. At the top, hold briefly. Then slowly lower the weight. Repeat with your left arm.

● **Triceps.** Sit on the edge of a chair with a dumbbell in your right hand. Begin by holding your right arm straight overhead, so that your elbow is by your ear. Slowly lower your arm behind your head. Then straighten it—slowly —until it's straight up again. Keep your elbow by your ear throughout.

After completing each exercise, rest a minute or two before starting the next one. After two weeks (or as soon as you feel able), try doing a second set of all six exercises. After a couple more weeks, add a third set.

Important: Move on to heavier weights only when you can complete three sets of at least 10 repetitions for each exercise.

Ralph S. Paffenbarger, Jr., MD, professor of epidemiology at Stanford University School of Medicine, Palo Alto, CA, and a senior reviewer of the 1996 *Surgeon General's Report on Physical Activity and Health.* Dr. Paffenbarger, who has run the Boston Marathon 22 times since turning 45 in 1967, is coauthor of *LifeFit: An Effective Exercise Program for Optimal Health and Longer Life.* Human Kinetics.

The Best Exercise Machine

The best exercise machine may be the old-fashioned treadmill. A new study shows that treadmill workouts burn more calories than workouts involving the same amount of exertion on any of the five other most popular exercise machines—including stair steppers and cross-country skiing machines.

Kerry J. Stewart, EdD, associate professor of medicine and director of Cardiac Rehabilitation and Prevention at Johns Hopkins Bayview Medical Center, 4940 Eastern Ave., Baltimore 21224.

Fitness Guru Radu Tells How to Create The Perfect Abdomen

Radu Teodorescu
Radu's Physical Culture

Many people think that the key to strong abdominal muscles is doing lots of abdominal crunches...or working out with one of those "ab machines" now advertised on TV.

Crunches and ab machines *do* give you a flatter abdomen. But what you really want is an abdomen that's flat *and functional*—one that's capable of holding the organs in place, stabilizing the spine, permitting the body to bend, twist, etc.

That's something you simply cannot get with crunches and ab machines alone.

The solution? Make sure you exercise all four abdominal muscle groups—the rectus abdominis...the obliques...the transversus...and the quadratus. The way to do that is to incorporate these nine simple exercises into your regular workout.*

Caution: If you experience pain while doing any of these exercises, stop immediately. Consult a doctor.

TORSO TWISTS

Stand with feet slightly more than shoulder-width apart, holding a broomstick behind your neck. Twist from side to side, keeping your hips facing forward. Start with 10 repetitions. Go up to 25 reps as you grow fitter. Or, time yourself as you do twists for one to three minutes.

KNEE-TO-ELBOW

Stand with your hands behind your neck. Lower your left elbow to your right knee as you bring the knee up toward the elbow.

Return to starting position, then repeat with your right elbow and left knee. Move as fluidly

---

*In addition to a flat stomach, your fitness goals should be strength, speed, endurance, flexibility, balance and coordination. The best way to achieve these goals is via aerobic conditioning...strength training...stretching... and—often overlooked—participation in group or individual sports.

as possible. Alternate sides till you've done 10 to 25 reps per side.

SIDE BENDS

Holding a five- to 10-pound dumbbell in your left hand, stand with knees slightly bent, feet apart and your right arm behind your neck. Bend to the right, bringing your right elbow toward the floor.

Return to your starting position. Then switch the dumbbell to your right hand and repeat, bending to the left. Alternate sides till you've done 10 to 25 reps on each side.

SIT-UPS

Lie on your back with knees bent and feet flat on the floor. Sit up slowly, bringing first your head, then your neck and then each vertebra off the floor. Imagine that you're "peeling" your back off the floor, like a piece of tape.

As you reach a sitting position, bring both arms forward, stretching them past your shins.

Reverse the process, slowly lowering yourself to the floor. Do 10 to 25 reps.

Caution: Do not do sit-ups if you have back trouble.

CRUNCHES

Lie on your back with knees bent and feet flat on the floor. Place both hands behind your head, elbows out. Press your lower back against the floor by tightening your abdominals and curling your pelvis toward the ceiling.

Keeping your lower back against the floor, lift your head and shoulders about three inches off the floor. Keep your eyes focused on the ceiling and your elbows back. Then lower to the starting position. Repeat 25 times.

Once you've got the hang of it, add a little "twist." Maintaining your position, do 10 to 25 crunches in which you lead the "lift" with your left shoulder (twisting to the right), then switch and lead with your right.

KNEELING ARM AND LEG LIFT

Kneel with your head held so that your neck is aligned with your spine. Lift your right arm and extend it in front of you, as you lift your left leg and extend it behind you.

Tighten your abdominals. Hold this position for a count of three, lifting your leg and arm as high as you can without arching your back.

Return to the kneeling position. Repeat on the opposite side. Alternate till you've done 10 to 25 reps on each side.

SITTING "V" HOLD

Sit comfortably on the floor with your torso erect, shoulders relaxed and arms straight out to either side. Keeping your knees slightly bent, lift both knees as high as you can. Hold for 10 to 20 seconds. (Put your hands on the floor behind you for support, if necessary.)

As you become fitter, try this exercise with your legs held straight.

JACKKNIVES

Lie on your back with arms at your sides, hands clenched. Bend your knees slightly, keeping your feet together and your heels touching the floor.

Slowly sit up, bringing your knees to your chest. Let your arms extend as far forward as necessary.

Return slowly to starting position, keeping your abdominals contracted. Do 10 to 25 reps.

Caution: Avoid this exercise if you have back trouble.

ARM AND LEG LIFTS

Lie on your stomach with legs straight and arms extended overhead.

Raise your right leg and left arm off the floor at the same time, then lower them.

Do 10 to 25 reps with the same leg and arm. Then switch sides and repeat with your left leg and right arm.

Caution: Avoid this exercise if you have back trouble.

Radu Teodorescu, founder of Radu's Physical Culture, an exercise studio in New York and East Hampton, NY. He is author of *Radu's Simply Fit: Enjoy the Workout of Your Life with America's Leading Fitness Coach.* Cader Books.

Walking and Strokes

Even light exercise sharply reduces risk of stroke. A study of 906 people found that those who walked 20 minutes a day three times a week were almost 60% less likely to suffer a stroke than couch potatoes.

Other light forms of exercise, including gardening and golf, produced similar benefits. Stroke risk was cut by more than 60% for study participants who engaged in more strenuous activities like swimming, hiking, tennis and bicycle riding.

Ralph L. Sacco, MD, director of the Northern Manhattan Stroke Study at Columbia–Presbyterian Medical Center, New York.

All About Nutritional Drinks

Nutritional drinks claim to be meals in a can —but they are really no more than snack substitutes. A can contains up to 350 calories— and may even contain as much as 13 grams of fat. These drinks are a better snack than a bag of chips and a sugared soda, but they are not as good as a carton of yogurt, a piece of fruit or a multigrain roll. And the drinks are not meal substitutes, despite what some of their labels say—they don't contain fiber and various nutrients needed for a balanced diet.

Elizabeth Ward, MS, RD, a registered dietitian with the American Dietetic Association, Chicago.

Morning Exercise

Exercise as soon as you wake up for a feeling of accomplishment throughout the day. Put the clock across the room so you have to get out of bed to shut it off. Set out your workout clothes next to the clock before going to bed. Work out to energizing music.

Alternative: Get up and shower—before the workout—to get your body going. Warm up thoroughly, then start the session more slowly than you would a later day session.

Men's Fitness, 21100 Erwin St., Woodland Hills, CA 91367.

Exercise and Sleeping

Exercise makes sleeping easier. Adults who had a "moderate" amount of trouble falling asleep and/or getting enough sleep reported improvements after four months of regular exercise.

Regimen: Four one-hour weekly sessions of low-impact aerobics such as brisk walking or stationary cycling. Those who exercised fell asleep in half the time—in 11.5 minutes on average—and slept almost one hour longer than non-exercisers. Differences between the two groups became apparent after 16 weeks— suggesting that regular long-term exercise brings sleep-time benefits.

Abby King, PhD, assistant professor of health research, policy and medicine at Stanford University School of Medicine, Palo Alto, CA.

Case Against Vitamins

The case *against* taking vitamins grows. In fresh foods, vitamins exist in shelf-stable and shelf-unstable forms, naturally balanced against each other.

Problem: Only the shelf-stable forms are put in supplements, so there is no natural balance. Recent projects show that loading up on only one form of a nutrient often is not beneficial—and can be harmful...possibly triggering heart disease, cancer and liver and kidney disease. Supplements don't provide the many other needed micronutrients present in food.

Best: Eat your nutrients—at least five servings of fruits and vegetables a day. (One serving equals one piece of large fruit or about one-half cup of vegetables or berries.)

Victor Herbert, MD, JD, professor of medicine at Mount Sinai School of Medicine and the Bronx VA Medical Center, both in New York. He is coauthor of *The Vitamin Pushers: How the "Health Food" Industry Is Selling America a Bill of Goods.* Prometheus Press.

The Power of Vitamin D

Vitamin D fights the most common form of arthritis—*osteoarthritis*, a painful, degenerative joint disease. People with low blood levels of vitamin D and low-to-moderate intake of vitamin D are three times as likely to have their osteoarthritis worsen than are people with high blood levels and intake.

Good sources of vitamin D: Egg yolks, fortified dairy products, fortified margarine, fortified cereal. The body also makes vitamin D from sunlight, but this capability declines with age.

Timothy McAlindon, MD, MPH, assistant professor of medicine at Boston University, who led a study of 556 men and women with osteoarthritis, ages 60 to 80 years, published in *Annals of Internal Medicine.*

Fresh Vegetables Are Best

Fresh, frozen or canned vegetables all have the same amount of fiber. Canned vegetables have the most sodium...fresh have the least. Frozen and fresh vegetables are equal in vitamins, but the vitamins in canned vegetables are largely in the water—which is usually thrown away. Canned vegetables are usually cheapest...fresh, most expensive.

To retain the most nutrients: Buy fresh vegetables, and cook them for as short a time and with as little water as possible.

Joanne Slavin, RD, professor of food science and nutrition at the University of Minnesota, St. Paul.

Gourmet Coffee Trap

Some gourmet coffees are loaded with calories and fat. Many are made with so much cream, syrup and chocolate that they can have more fat and calories than traditional desserts.

Example: A large cafe mocha with whipped cream from Starbucks contains 500 calories and 40 grams of fat—more than twice the calories and fat of a half cup of Häagen-Dazs super-premium ice cream. Mocha beverages usually have the most calories, with latte not far behind.

Better: Cappuccino without whipped cream. *Best:* Made with skim milk.

The Tufts University Guide to Total Nutrition by Stanley Gershoff, PhD, dean emeritus at Tufts University School of Nutrition, Medford, MA. HarperCollins.

Coffee Danger

Drinking unfiltered coffee may raise your blood cholesterol level. When Dutch researchers measured cholesterol levels of people who switched to unfiltered coffee brewed in French-press plunger coffee pots, they found that they rose by up to 20 points compared with those who stayed with filtered coffee. Scientists theorize that the jump was caused by two compounds that are trapped by coffee filters and have been shown to raise cholesterol levels and affect the function of the liver, which metabolizes cholesterol.

Michael J. Klag, MD, associate professor at Johns Hopkins University School of Medicine, Baltimore.

Bright Colors Increase Appetite

That is why so many restaurants and fast-food places are decorated in orange, yellow or red.

Self-defense for dieters: Surround yourself with darker colors that suppress appetite.

Examples: Use a tablecloth that is dark green, dark blue or warm brown. Paint the kitchen a light neutral color with small touches of the colors of fresh fruits and vegetables—which are invigorating, but not stimulating to the appetite.

Maria Simonson, PhD, ScD, director of the Health, Weight, and Stress Clinic at Johns Hopkins Medical Institutions, Baltimore.

Garlic Linked to Lower Cholesterol in Men

When otherwise healthy men who had high cholesterol took garlic supplements for six months, their cholesterol levels dropped 5% or more. The supplements contained seven grams of aged garlic—equivalent to 10 to 15 grams of cooked garlic or two cloves of fresh garlic.

Possible explanation: Garlic reduces LDL ("bad") cholesterol, although it has no effect on HDL ("good") cholesterol.

Manfred Steiner, MD, PhD, professor of medicine at the East Carolina University School of Medicine, whose study was published in the *American Journal of Clinical Nutrition.*

The Whole Truth About Dietary Fat

Richard N. Podell, MD
University of Medicine and Dentistry of New Jersey– Robert Wood Johnson Medical School

If you've been reading up on dietary fat, you know the news is full of conflicting advice.

●**For years all fats were considered bad for the heart.** Now researchers say fish oil is good for the heart.

●**Nutritionists told us to cut fat intake to 30% of calories.** Then some argued that 10% was better.

●**Polyunsaturated oil was considered healthful**—until some researchers said monounsaturated fat was better.

●**For years, margarine was considered a healthful alternative to butter.** Now some say to avoid margarine, because it contains dangerous trans fatty acids.

To cut through the confusion about fats...

●**Is fat all bad?** Absolutely not. Consumed in small quantities, fat isn't only good—it's *essential.* Essential dietary fat maintains body heat…controls blood sugar levels…and keeps cell membranes functioning properly.

Fats are also needed to make *prostaglandins*, compounds that regulate myriad biological activities throughout the body.

A fat-deficient diet leads to fatigue, skin rashes, hair loss and increased susceptibility to infection. But we're talking about *very* small quantities of fat—no more than two teaspoons of vegetable oil a day for most people.

Sadly, most Americans eat far more than that —getting about 40% of calories from fat. Excess dietary fat raises cholesterol levels, upping the risk of heart attack…and promotes cancer.

Dietary fat also tends to *make* you fat. Gram for gram, it packs more than twice as many calories as carbohydrates or protein.

Obesity has been linked to breast and colon cancer, gall bladder disease, diabetes, high blood pressure and other ills.

●**How much fat should I eat?** If you have heart disease, no more than 10% of your daily caloric intake should come from fat. If you're healthy, you can probably get away with 25% to 30%.

To stay within the 30% guideline, you *don't* have to carry a calculator and compute the fat percentage of everything you eat.

All you must do is eat meat sparingly…drink skim or 1% fat milk…use no more than one teaspoon of vegetable oil in cooking and on your salad…avoid junk food…and stick to sorbets, low-fat or nonfat yogurt and fruit for dessert. Focus your diet mostly on vegetables, fruits, legumes and fish.

●**Which type of fat is least harmful?** Unsaturated fat—the kind that's liquid at room temperature. Good sources of unsaturated fat include vegetable oils (except coconut oil, palm oil or other tropical oils)…tofu and other soy products…nuts and seeds…and cod, mackerel, herring, tuna and other cold-water fish.

Avoid saturated fats. They're the ones that are solid at room temperature. Sources of saturated fat include butter, tallow and other animal fats and tropical oils such as coconut.

●**Which is safer—polyunsaturated or monounsaturated fat?** Safflower oil, corn oil and other polyunsaturated oils have the desirable effect of reducing bloodstream levels of LDL (bad) cholesterol. But they also lower HDL (good) cholesterol.

Olive oil, canola oil and other monounsaturated fats cut LDL levels without lowering HDL. For this reason, many nutritionists prefer monounsaturated fats to polyunsaturated fats.

People who eat a traditional Greek or Italian diet—in which as many as one-third of calories come from olive oil—have *extremely* low rates of heart disease. We don't yet know whether that's because olive oil has a protective effect…or simply that these people consume almost no *saturated* fat.

Another problem with polyunsaturated fats is that they go rancid (oxidize) more quickly than monounsaturated fats. It's possible that consuming oxidized fat may contribute to the body's production of *free radicals*—renegade molecules implicated in ailments ranging from diabetes to heart disease.

To avoid rancidity, store cooking oil away from heat and light. And don't overheat oil, which can cause it to oxidize. Stay away from fast-food french fries and other fried foods. These foods are often cooked in old, overheated fat.

●**Should I take extra "doses" of olive oil?** I wouldn't advise that. But I urge you to pick monounsaturated oil over more harmful types of fat.

●**What are trans fatty acids?** They're unsaturated fats that have been chemically altered to make them solid and spreadable at room temperature (a process known as *hydrogenation*). Margarine is a partially hydrogenated form of corn oil.

Like saturated fats, trans fats tend to raise levels of LDL cholesterol. For this reason a respected minority of nutritionists—myself included—believe that you're better off preparing food with small amounts of butter than with margarine.

●**How about omega-3 fatty acids?** Found primarily in cold-water fish (and in smaller concentrations in soy products, flaxseed oil and walnut oil), omega-3 fatty acids are thought to protect against heart attack and stroke.

What's the evidence for this contention? Incidence of heart disease is much lower among people who eat traditional Eskimo or Japanese diets (which include lots of fish) rather than typical American fare.

Some nutritionists believe it's the *ratio* of omega-3 fatty acids to other fats that's important. Preliminary evidence suggests that too much fat from vegetable sources causes the body to produce an excess of "inflammatory" prostaglandins, raising the risk of arthritis and other inflammatory diseases.

I believe that adding fish oil to the diet helps keep inflammatory and anti-inflammatory prostaglandins in balance.

This is a controversial theory, but it seems prudent to eat fish one to three times a week.

●**Are fat supplements a good idea?** Most people get all the fat they need from the foods they eat.

But people with heart disease, diabetes, Crohn's disease and certain other chronic ailments appear to benefit from certain fat supplements.

I sometimes prescribe fish oil capsules—rich in omega-3 fatty acids—for patients at risk for heart disease. But most people are better off *eating* fish, so I do so only after a blood test shows low levels of omega-3 fatty acids.

Richard N. Podell, MD, clinical professor of family medicine at the University of Medicine and Dentistry of New Jersey–Robert Wood Johnson Medical School, New Brunswick. He is in private practice in internal medicine and nutrition in New Providence, NJ and is author of *Patient Power*. Fireside.

Much Younger Looking Skin in 15 Minutes a Day

Rachel Perry
Rachel Perry, Inc.

You can actually reverse the aging process of your face. How? By using good quality facial cleansers and scrubs along with a few simple isometric facial exercises and self-massage. It takes only 15 minutes a day—and those minutes can be in the shower. My regimen works for men and women.

The general idea is to speed up the process of removing and replacing dead facial skin tissue. It's the dead tissue that leaves the skin tired and muddy looking.

Men don't get those fine lines above the upper lip that many women get because most men shave daily, automatically epidermabrading or exfoliating—i.e., removing dead skin tissue.

CLEANSE AND SCRUB

Daily cleansing and scrubbing is the key to removing dead skin cells.

For a *cleanser*, use either a creamy cleanser or foaming facial cleansing gel. Look for a spreadable consistency. A cleanser should not soak into your skin too easily. The cleanser removes oil and dirt.

A *scrub**—which is used for an abrasive scrub-massage—should have as many natural ingredients as possible. The word "scrub" or "cleanser" should be clearly marked on the container you buy.

For a scrub, I find that two ingredients—sea kelp and sea salt—have the necessary abrasive action, are antibacterial and give a smooth, refined texture to the skin. If you can't find a product with these ingredients, buy them in bulk and add ¼ teaspoon each of sea salt and sea kelp for each ounce of purchased product.

When you use a scrub, dampen your fingers first with water—the additional moisture gives the scrub more spreadability. Always look for products that are pH-balanced.

Caution: Use the scrub gently at first, until you get used to its abrasive action. You don't want to overdo it and leave red patches, or worse, break blood vessels in your face.

You'll also want a supply of small, rough, white cotton terry-cloth towels. Hand towels are a good size.

NOW, THE EXERCISE

It's a good idea to do these exercises whenever you apply cleanser and facial scrub.

*Facial scrubs made from natural ingredients are available in varying degrees of abrasiveness and can be found in your local health food store or the health food section of your supermarket.

Women may also want to do them whenever they apply moisturizer, night cream or even makeup base. This allows your fingers to move smoothly over your face.

Men might find it easiest to do them in the shower. Once you learn the exercises, they will quickly become automatic. After all, you work out to keep your body in good shape. You exercise your arms, legs, abdomen—why not exercise your face?

THE ETERNAL "O"

This exercise firms up the mouth, cheeks, nose and eye area.

First, form a large oval "O" with your mouth, pulling your upper lip downward over your teeth. Smile slightly, but don't move your mouth from the "O"-shape.

At the same time, squeeze your eyelids shut. The purpose of this phase is to stretch the skin tightly across your face, so you can massage it without worrying about damaging the elasticity of your skin.

The massage: Holding the "O" position with your eyes closed, use the fingertips of each hand to trace a complete circle around each eye.

●**Starting from the corners, move over the eyebrows**, then under the eyes (including the upper cheeks), for a complete circle.

●**Do this quickly, a minimum of 10 times.** Eventually, you work up to 50 times or more.

Nose: Next, massage your nose with downward strokes, five times.

Mouth: Then massage in a full circle around your mouth, five times in one direction, five in the other.

Forehead: Finally, put your fingertips at the bridge of your nose, and massage upward and outward over your forehead to your hairline, using five to 10 long strokes.

THE FIRMING SMILE

Now, for the bottom half of your face, to help prevent jowls and a double chin…

●**Roll your lips inward over your upper and lower teeth**, leaving a space of about ½ inch between your lips.

●**Smile as widely as you can**—with your *lower* jaw only.

●**Holding the exercise position**, and using your fingertips, massage the entire lower part of your face in small outward circular motions.

●**Start at the tip of your chin**, move up to your ears and then back down again, to a slow count of 10. With practice, work up to 20.

THE NECK REJUVENATOR

To keep your neck muscles firm, and your neck tissue smooth and supple…

●**Place your thumb under your chin**, and curl your tongue back in your throat until you feel the muscle directly under your chin protrude.

●**Now you can take your thumb away**— but continue to keep your tongue curled back.

●**Next, with your chin pointing upward, stretch your neck as far to the left as possible**, to a slow count of 10.

●**Repeat, rotating to the right.** At the same time, massage upward from the base of the neck with the fingertips of both hands, in long, vigorous upward strokes, up to the jawbone.

THE UPPER-LIP SMOOTHER AND AROUND-THE-MOUTH STRENGTHENER

To prevent those upper-lip lines, smooth the furrows that run from the corners of the mouth to the chin, strengthen the muscles around the mouth and firm the lips…

●**Press your lips together in a straight line**, smiling slightly.

●**Using the index fingers of both hands**, massage in tiny outward circular motions around the mouth, to a slow count of 10.

●**Squeeze your lips together harder and harder**, until you feel a tingling sensation.

●**Then immediately make a small "O" with your mouth**, to a slow count of 10.

●**Pucker harder and harder while massaging in tiny outward circular motions around the mouth**, to a slow count of 10. Release.

Do this exercise with the massage at least twice a day. And also do it whenever you can without the massage—while driving, cooking, cleaning, reading. It's a truly portable exercise.

Rachel Perry, founder and chief executive of Rachel Perry, Inc., a natural skin care and makeup company based in Chatsworth, CA. She is author of *Reverse the Aging Process of Your Face: A Simple Technique That Works*. Avery Publishing Group.

The Easy Route To Vegetarianism

Virginia Messina, MPH, RD
Mark Messina, PhD

If you have been thinking about going vegetarian, you may worry that doing so will disrupt your family's lifestyle.

In fact, the switch-over can be accomplished more easily than you might imagine. Big changes in shopping or meal planning generally *aren't* necessary.

Twelve million Americans now follow a vegetarian diet, according to a recent Gallup poll. *Key benefits:*

●**Vegetarians eat less fat than meat eaters** (30% vs. 36%)…and much less (25% vs. 50%) saturated fat.

●**Vegetarians eat two to four times more fiber than nonvegetarians.** Fiber helps prevent heart disease and colon cancer, among other ailments.

●**Vegetarian diets provide more disease-fighting antioxidants than nonvegetarian diets.** Vegetarians consume twice as much vitamin E and carotenoids and 50% more vitamin C.

●**Vegetarians eat more phytochemicals** —disease-preventing compounds found in plants.

●**Vegetarians are less likely to eat excess protein than nonvegetarians**. Too much protein can cause osteoporosis and kidney disease. Despite what many people believe, vegetarians generally do get enough protein in their diets.

●**Vegetarian men are 50% less likely to die of heart disease than meat eaters**. That's been shown again and again by studies in the US, Great Britain, Holland, Norway, Germany and Japan.

●**Lacto-ovo vegetarians have cholesterol readings 10% to 20% below those of meat eaters.**

●**Vegetarians are less likely to die of cancer** (especially malignancies of the colon and lung). One study found vegetarians' risk to be half that of meat eaters.

●**Vegetarian men are 50% less likely to develop adult-onset diabetes than nonvegetarians.**

THE NINE-STEP PLAN

If you've spent a lifetime eating a meat-and-potatoes diet, you might choose to move toward vegetarianism gradually.

Ultimately, you may decide to become a *lacto-ovo* vegetarian—meaning you continue to eat eggs and dairy products. Or you may even become a *vegan* (pronounced VEE-gan) —meaning you don't eat any animal products.

But *any* move you make toward eating more unprocessed plant foods—and less meat —will be beneficial to your health.

This simple nine-step plan will help you make the transition…

1. Go meatless at dinner three nights a week. Build the dinners around three vegetarian dishes that your family already knows and enjoys.

Examples: Macaroni and cheese…tomato soup with bread and salad…spaghetti with tomato sauce…vegetable or split-pea soup…vegetable chow mein…cheese pizza…bean burritos with rice…stuffed shells or manicotti…quiche…eggplant Parmesan…stir-fried vegetables.

2. Add three *more* meatless dinners to your weekly schedule. One way to do this is to make small changes to favorite recipes that contain meat.

Example I: Replace the ground beef in chili with beans and/or *textured vegetable protein* (TVP). TVP is also a delicious meat substitute in tacos, sloppy joes, soups and stews.

Example II: Substitute tofu for meat in a stew or stir-fry. Or—make stroganoff using chunks of tofu that have been frozen, then defrosted and marinated in soy sauce.

Caution: Buy packaged tofu only. Tofu displayed in open bins of water can be contaminated with bacteria.

3. Find three new vegetarian meals you enjoy. By now you're up to six vegetarian meals a week. To add a few more, peruse vegetarian cookbooks. Try out recipes until you find three that you enjoy and are comfortable preparing.

Once you have nine vegetarian meals to choose from, you can declare *all* your family's dinners meatless, if you wish. As time passes, you'll find yourself expanding and refining your repertoire of meatless meals.

4. Go meatless at lunchtime. If you tend to eat out, look for restaurants that serve pasta primavera, vegetable soups, baked potatoes... or have well-stocked salad bars.

For brown-bag lunches, try a sandwich of vegetarian paté, egg salad or another vegetarian spread. If a stove or microwave is available, heat up a veggie burger or tofu hot dog... a vegetarian entrée...or leftovers from dinner.

5. Focus on breakfast. If you like a hearty breakfast, substitute banana pancakes, French toast or hot cereal for bacon or sausage.

On the run? Grab a low-fat bran muffin and jam...peanut butter on toast...or make a breakfast shake by blending fruit, soy milk and soft tofu.

6. Experiment with new foods. A good vegetarian cookbook may inspire you to try some recipes with ingredients that might be unfamiliar to you—tahini, rice milk, sea vegetables, etc.

Make a trip to a local natural foods store or food co-op. Buy a few items that look interesting, and give them a try.

7. Experiment with egg-less dishes. Diced tofu makes a great substitute for hard-boiled or scrambled eggs.

When baking, replace eggs with a mixture of ground flax seed and water (three tablespoons of flax seed in ½ cup of water equals two eggs) ...or with soy flour (one tablespoon mixed with a tablespoon of water equals one egg).

8. Explore plant sources of calcium. If you plan to eliminate milk products, be sure to get three servings a day of calcium-rich plant foods.

Examples: Almonds, broccoli, leafy green vegetables, figs, soy milk, tofu, beans.

Vegans should be sure to consume cereals and other foods fortified with vitamin B-12.

9. Read labels. If you want to follow a vegan diet, practice reading labels at the grocery store until you can spot "hidden" animal ingredients —lard, whey, gelatin, honey, dried milk and egg whites. Eventually you'll have a shopping list of foods that meet your guidelines.

MEDITERRANEAN CHICKPEAS

This easy-to-make dish will satisfy even the hungriest eaters, including those who cannot imagine life without meat...

2 medium onions, chopped

3 cloves garlic, minced

1 tablespoon olive oil

3 cups cooked or canned chickpeas

1 10-ounce package of frozen chopped spinach, defrosted

1 28-ounce can crushed tomatoes

1 cup chopped fresh tomato

1 teaspoon crushed red pepper flakes

1 teaspoon dried oregano

Juice of two lemons

Salt and pepper

In a large saucepan, sauté the onions and garlic in olive oil until the onions are tender.

Add the chickpeas, spinach, tomatoes, pepper flakes and oregano.

Cover. Simmer for 30 minutes.

Add lemon juice, salt and pepper before serving.

Serves eight.

Virginia Messina, MPH, RD, a registered dietitian who specializes in vegetarian nutrition, and her husband, nutritionist Mark Messina, PhD. Based in Port Townsend, WA, they are authors of *The Vegetarian Way: Total Health for You and Your Family.* Crown.

Drink Up!

To drink your recommended 64 ounces of water each day...

• **Drink a glass as soon as you wake up**—to replenish fluids lost during sleep.

• **Have a glass of water before any meal** or snack to help control your appetite.

• **Buy a 64-ounce container** and fill it every day—then keep it near you, on your desk at work or the kitchen table at home, so you can see how much you are drinking.

• **To have chilled water all day**—freeze a *partially* filled plastic bottle overnight, then top it off with more water in the morning.

Food and You by the editors of *Prevention* Magazine Health Books. Rodale.

Surprising Calorie-Burner

Sipping ice water. Whenever you drink something cold, your body raises your metabolism to keep your body temperature from falling. That process burns calories—eight 16-ounce glasses of ice water will burn an extra 200 calories per day.

Harold Bloomfield, MD, a psychiatrist in private practice in Del Mar, CA, and coauthor of *The Power of 5*. Rodale.

Power Eating... Foods to Make You More Productive

Judith Wurtman, PhD
Massachusetts Institute of Technology

Whether you're an early bird or a night owl, you can maintain a high level of energy *all day* by eating the right foods at the right times.

HOW POWER EATING WORKS

Protein foods, such as meats, fish, poultry, dairy products, beans and eggs, contain the amino acid *tyrosine*. This stimulates the brain to produce *norepinephrine* and *dopamine*, two alertness chemicals. When eaten alone or with carbohydrates, such as breads, cereal products, fruits and vegetables, protein foods boost mental alertness and energy.

Never *start* a meal with a carbohydrate if you plan to work after the meal, because it may trigger drowsiness.

Reason: Carbohydrates contain the amino acid *tryptophan*, which triggers production of *serotonin*, a calming chemical.

FOODS THAT ENERGIZE

All low-fat protein foods produce quick mood-modifying and energy-boosting results. For most people, three to four ounces of the following work well...

Low-fat, low-carbohydrate foods, such as shellfish, fish, chicken (without the skin), veal, extra-lean beef, beans and legumes. *Also good:* Low-fat cottage cheese, yogurt, milk or tofu.

WHAT TO EAT WHEN

The body's "biological clock" plays a big part in how food energizes us. This clock causes us to feel the most energetic and the least stressed during the first six hours after awakening.

From then on, our energy level slowly decreases until the end of the day—usually within one hour of normal bedtime—when we shut down mentally.

The key to maintaining high performance levels is to eat foods that are energizing when your biological rhythms are beginning to slow down. *Meal guidelines:*

• **Breakfast: A nutritious breakfast or a snack before noon keeps you from overeating at lunchtime.** For maximum results, eat within three hours of awakening.

Best: A breakfast rich in protein foods, high in vitamins and minerals and low in fat.

Example: One piece of fresh fruit sliced (or one-half to three-quarters cup of berries) mixed into eight ounces of plain yogurt...a bran muffin with one or two teaspoonfuls of jelly or diet margarine...one cup of coffee (black or with skim milk).

• **Lunch: Your midday meal will either sustain your morning alertness or accelerate the drop in your energy level.**

Best for you: A high-protein, low-fat, alcohol-free meal.

Examples: Three to five ounces of meat, poultry, seafood or fish...or eight ounces of low-fat yogurt or cottage cheese...*or* two ounces of low-fat cheese, such as mozzarella, ricotta or feta ...*or* two eggs. *In addition:* One piece of sliced fruit (or one-half to three-quarters cup of berries) and two slices of whole-grain bread.

Myth: Pasta at lunch increases your mental and physical energy.

Reality: Athletes load up on pasta before a prolonged endurance event because it contains the carbohydrate *glycogen,* which fuels the muscles...*not* the brain.

•*Dinner:* **Your evening meal comes at a time when your biological rhythms are telling your body to shut down.** To stay alert for evening projects, eat high-protein, low-carbohydrate foods.

Example: Four to five ounces of skinned, boneless, broiled chicken...one cup stir-fried mixed vegetables (broccoli, water chestnuts, onions, etc.)...three-quarters cup of steamed rice and one fresh orange. Never begin with a carbohydrate—breads, crackers, deep-fried vegetables, etc.

Caffeine alert: Your brain cells are most sensitive to caffeine first thing in the morning. *Recommended:* Limit your daily intake to one or two cups of coffee or tea when you get up (the effects will last up to six hours) and another cup in the middle of the afternoon.

Important: Avoid caffeine after 4:30 pm if it keeps you awake at night. However, if you have to work late or are fighting jet lag, a cup of coffee with dinner may keep you going a little longer.

PREPERFORMANCE EATING

The foods you eat before giving a speech, presentation or other public performance can make or break it...

•**Never perform on an empty stomach.**

•**Eat sparingly**—if possible, two hours before your performance.

•**Choose low-calorie, low-fat foods.**

•**Drink enough coffee or tea to maintain your body's usual level of caffeine** during your performance. *Caution:* If you rarely drink coffee or tea, don't start now. It will only make you more nervous.

•**Drink little or no alcohol**...and do not drink any alcohol in the three hours before your presentation.

Judith Wurtman, PhD, a research scientist in the department of brain and cognitive science at the Massachusetts Institute of Technology, Cambridge. She is author of *The Serotonin Solution* (Ballantine) and *Managing Your Mind and Mood Through Food* (Rawson Associates).

Very, Very Smart Education

Education for Parents From the Nation's *Teacher of the Year*

Mary Beth Blegen
Worthington Senior High School

As a teacher for nearly three decades and the mother of three grown children, I know only too well that learning begins at home.

But I've also found that too much parental pressure—*and* too much help—can be counterproductive to classroom learning.

How then can parents raise better students? In my experience, the most successful students are children who have discovered their own voices—*their sense of self.*

I often spot these children within the first few days of a new school year.

• **They quickly establish an honest connection with their teachers.** They are responsive to the teachers and are comfortable in the classroom.

• **They are good listeners**, able to concentrate and open to new ideas.

• **They work well with other students.** They know how and when to help others...and when to ask for help for themselves.

• **Most basic of all, they are confident enough in themselves to have opinions and defend them.** Confident high school students can discuss *why* they believe what they do about subjects. This is what we refer to as *critical thinking*, the most prized skill for any modern student—a skill that parents begin nurturing long before their children enter kindergarten.

THE POWER OF READING

A parent's role starts from the first days of a child's life, with cuddling and talking to the baby.

Before long, you graduate to reading aloud —the single most important thing you can do to help your child develop language skills,

259

vocabulary and grasp of sentence structure. The more often you read aloud—and the more advanced the books are—the easier it becomes for your child to understand complex ideas.

Many parents halt this practice too early. They have a second baby...or professional demands make them too tired...or they assume the child is getting enough reading at preschool.

It is best to continue reading to children through age 10 or 11. Nothing can replace the intimacy or pure fun of the bedtime story... and children who are the best readers are those who think reading is fun.

Helpful: Read regularly to your children in the evening. In my experience, parents who find their children are resistant can call them from the office in the afternoon and talk excitedly about how much fun it will be to read that night. There's something about the phone that works well as a presell tool.

Or you can simply take your kids to a large bookstore or the library on the weekends for an hour or two. Larger bookstores are ideal places to read to kids—and to let them find books they would like to read themselves. Children are inspired when they see other kids of all ages reading.

After you read to kids in the evening, allow them a half-hour in bed with their lights on to read to themselves.

ENCOURAGE CONVERSATION

People learn by sounding out their ideas in front of others. When children feel comfortable in dialogue and in hearing their own voices, their confidence spills over into the classrooms.

Example: In my house, at suppertime, my husband and I would make a conscious effort not to talk about subjects that excluded the kids. We called our table talk "open" conversations. We encouraged the kids to talk about the issues on their minds and events in their days. We would take care to affirm their contributions by responding, *Yes, I've wondered about that myself...*or, *That's a really good idea.*

At bedtime, my children and I would discuss their days in more detail. I would ask them collectively whether they experienced anything that day that made them sad...and about the things that had made them happy.

I would just let them talk—and I would listen, without any judgmental comments. I would suggest solutions, allowing them to develop their decision-making skills.

As with reading, listening cannot start too early. Four-year-olds have sharp antennae. They can sense if their parents are distracted, busy or frustrated. They can tell whether they can trust you with *everything*—not just the nice things you want to hear but also the troubles, hurts and mistakes that every child makes.

Established early on, this relationship will prove invaluable during adolescence. Teenagers who trust their parents will feel more comfortable openly discussing alcohol, drugs or sex at home. And their performance in school will be less likely to be derailed by some secret crisis.

HELPING WITH HOMEWORK

Homework is often a major source of conflict between parents and children.

On the one hand, it is important for students to accept responsibility for their own work. They must be taught that their parents are there to *help* them—not to do the work for them...or stand over them until the work is finished.

On the other hand, a child who is struggling has a legitimate need for a parent's help and reassurance.

Parents who stress the importance of homework often link it to other issues—a perceived need to make the honor roll or to succeed in rigorous "gifted" classes. The problem is that children often do not appreciate the same "prizes" for hard work that parents do, and they become discouraged as parents become increasingly disappointed.

Better: Parents need to step back and ask themselves, *How much of this is for our child—and how much for our own gratification?*

We tend to see our children as reflections of ourselves, rather than individuals in their own right. It's easy for a parent's ego to get in the way.

Helpful: Ask your children a simple question: *What do you want?* Find out what they would like to achieve and why. At the same time, keep instilling in them the value of learning and reading.

When children choose not to do their work, parents need to explain that they will have to accept the consequences of bad grades and other disappointments, such as less time for movies, friends and other pastimes that are allowed only after schoolwork is done.

In any case, remember that your relationship with your child is more important than the homework. When children know that their parents are always in their corner, they are far more likely to succeed in school—and everywhere else.

GO PLACES WITH THE KIDS

Every trip a child takes is an education, but a child learns best when he/she is not asked to do too much.

Example: If you go on an outing to a museum, concentrate on a few pieces of art—and then go have an ice-cream cone.

Family trips don't have to be long or ambitious. You don't have to "conquer" the zoo. The benefit comes from talking, laughing and simply being together.

The same applies to a trip to the hardware store…or to a lake.

When children have good times with their parents, they develop a spirit of adventure—a quality no good student can be without.

Mary Beth Blegen, 1996 National Teacher of the Year, who teaches English, history, humanities, writing and English as a second language at Worthington Senior High School, Worthington, MN.

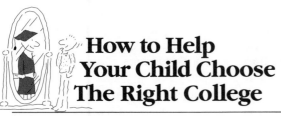

How to Help Your Child Choose The Right College

Deborah Rankin

Helping your high school student select a college is a difficult process, as parents of any college freshman will readily acknowledge.

Here's what I learned this spring as I helped our son choose a college…

•**Start the selection process early.** It takes much longer than you would expect to complete each step of the college-selection process.

Fortunately we began talking about colleges with our son in January of his junior year in high school. To help him be more selective about the 35 or so schools he wanted to consider, we insisted that he read about each of them in a guidebook.*

It took him about a month to work his way through the books and college videotapes borrowed from the high school guidance department before narrowing his list down to 20 schools.

A good deadline is the end of February, so you have enough time to accomplish the other steps.

•**Break the wish list into three categories.** Once your child produces a list of 20 schools, it is time to narrow them even further.

We spent five to six weeks weighing his chances based on his grades, activities and Preliminary Scholastic Assessment Test scores. You can get each school's standards from a college guidebook—or from your child's high school guidance office.

By early March, we had the final list narrowed down to nine schools. They ranged in size, location and prestige. *We broke this list into three categories…*

•**At the top were four highly competitive schools** that our son had a slight chance of getting into.

•**At the next level were three less competitive schools.** He had a good—but not certain —chance of being admitted.

•**We had two schools to which he would have almost no trouble getting accepted.**

•**Determine which schools you're going to visit.** Once you have your final list, visit as many schools as possible before your child applies.

In general, the ideal time to visit college campuses is from March through late April of your child's junior year. The next best time is in the fall of his/her senior year.

*The guidebook we found most helpful was *Fiske Guide to Colleges* by Edward Fiske. Times Books.

• **Spread out your visits.** Some people visit 10 or 12 schools in a week, stopping at two a day. Such a schedule is grueling and can leave you and your children overloaded with information—and confused.

Helpful: We visited one school per day in order to give our son a chance to attend classes, eat with other students—and talk to them—and observe college life.

• **Try to arrange an overnight stay in a dorm.** This is the single best way for your child to get a real taste of what it is like to attend a college. He will sleep in the dorm, eat meals with other students and attend classes with them.

To arrange one of these overnight visits, contact the school's admissions office at least three weeks prior to your planned visit.

• **Have your child ask students what they don't like about the school.** Everyone is glad to share what they like about a school, but it can be even more helpful to find out about the trouble spots.

Example: At one college, our son learned that it was almost impossible for many freshmen to get into the classes they wanted. The former director of admissions had accepted too many applicants the year before, causing overcrowding of classes and facilities.

• **Read copies of the student newspaper.** This is where you will find all the news the college doesn't want to get around. You can pick up copies on campus. Usually what you learn is not an all-important factor in your final decision, just information you should know if your child is accepted and decides to go.

• **Trust your child's gut feelings.** If your child hates a certain school after spending a day on campus, chances are that things won't improve after he spends an entire semester there—and after you've paid for the semester's tuition, room and board. So don't push your child to attend a school he hates.

Deborah Rankin, one of the country's best-known business writers, based in Portland, OR, and author of *Investing On Your Own: A Commonsense Way to Make Your Money Grow.* Consumer Reports Books.

How to Help a Child Get Into an Ivy League School

Bill Paul
Princeton University

Getting your child into an Ivy League school can be a huge challenge. Great grades and SAT scores are seldom enough—since virtually all applicants to these top-notch schools will have great grades and great SAT scores.

But there are ways to improve your child's odds during high school. *First you must avoid the big mistakes...*

Mistake: Having your child take too many advanced-placement courses. These are the high school courses that earn college credits. But when all of a student's classes are difficult, he/she will spend the majority of his time merely keeping up in those tough areas, allowing those subjects in which he might excel to suffer.

Better: Choose challenging classes only in your child's area of greatest skill—and hold the number to three or four per year. It's better to be the best at a few things than simply good at everything.

Helpful: A few classes at a local college after school or on weekends. A community college will do...the Ivy League schools will see that your child pushed himself beyond what was expected.

These college courses should be part of the regular curriculum and not summer programs designed especially for ambitious high schoolers. There is nothing wrong with those programs, but Ivy League admissions officers usually view these summer programs as merely résumé builders.

Mistake: Thinking that grades are the *only* things that count. Parents of high schoolers often encourage their children to spend more time on their homework and less time on other activities. Those efforts can be misguided. Grades are important. But the difference between a 3.8 and a 4.0 grade point average means much less to an Ivy League admissions officer than whether the applicant is a special individual with outstanding skills and talents.

Better: Encourage outside interests—even seemingly nonacademic ones. Gently push children to do what *they* want...not what *you* think they should do.

Example: If that interest is in playing the saxophone, buy earplugs and put up with the racket. If he starts his own band or sets a deal to record a CD, it might be time well spent when it comes to getting into a top school.

Mistake: Expecting club memberships to win admission. Even reaching the level of club president or team captain won't help your child stand out among Ivy League applicants.

Better: Encourage your child to *start* a new group or activity, such as a chamber orchestra. This will get the student noticed.

Mistake: Relying heavily upon SAT prep courses. Prep courses might raise your child's scores. But if that achievement is out of line with the rest of his academic record, admissions officers will wonder why he didn't perform to that level in his classes.

AN EXTRA EDGE

•**Have your child keep a journal.** Nearly all Ivy League application essays are simply a variation on the same theme, *Tell us something about yourself.* By getting into the habit of keeping a journal early on, your child will develop an ability to write about himself that isn't self-conscious.

The essays that get noticed are those that are natural. The student should be himself and write about things that are important to him.

•**Start Ivy League visits in your child's sophomore year.** Use those early trips to select your child's favorite schools. He should return to his favorites during his junior year and really get to know the campuses. That will help him decide at which schools he would be happiest.

If possible, schedule a meeting with a professor in the student's area of expertise—even if it is not his intended major.

If your child makes a favorable impression, the professor may put in a good word with the admissions department. These sorts of recommendations typically carry considerable weight.

WHEN APPLYING

•**Have a set of letters of recommendation sent.** Include letters from a variety of people with whom your child has had close contact, such as a scout leader, an employer or a coach.

The letters can be as long as necessary to get their points across, as long as they are interesting and prove that the child is a good candidate. *Also:* Request that they be *handwritten.*

Important: Ask each letter writer to write about a specific incident or topic that would be a good reflection of the child. Try to have each letter writer tell a different story about aspects of his characteristics or personality to illustrate the quality he is highlighting.

•**Send supporting materials along with the application.** If your child is an athlete, send a video of his highlights. Or you can send a term paper of which your child is particularly proud.

These are often forwarded to the relevant academic department at the college. A good review from a professor can be a big boost to an applicant's chances.

•**Be wary of professional college counselors.** They tend to homogenize college applications, making them bland and less interesting. In addition, they even may try to choose the colleges for the child. A professional college counselor would not know the child and his school environment as well as an in-school counselor would.

Ivy League admissions departments can spot a counselor's hand on an essay a mile away. Moreover, you risk alienating your child's high school guidance counselor—which is never a good idea.

High school guidance counselors, however, should be proactive to help the child develop individual skills or take extra classes.

Example: In one case, a high school guidance counselor even visited a college with the student and his parents in order to help the student get accepted for an accelerated course.

Bill Paul, an alumni interviewer for Princeton University and founder and publisher of *Earth Preservers*, an environmental newspaper for elementary, middle and junior high school students to help develop project skills, Box 6, Westfield, NJ 07091. He is author of *Getting In: Inside the College Admission Process.* Addison Wesley.

When Not to Go to An Ivy League School

Ivy League and other elite colleges are not always the most appropriate choice—even for top students. Elite (highly selective) schools have an abundance of academically superior applicants and award financial aid based entirely on financial need. But many less-selective schools lure top students with lucrative merit-based scholarships. These schools often have honors-rated programs in specific fields in which good students can shine more than they would in the elite schools. This option saves money and maximizes the opportunity of admittance to a top graduate or professional school.

Arthur Mullaney, a high school guidance director and president of College Impressions, which leads college tours for high school students, Box 665, Canton, MA 02021.

 # College Acceptance Is Conditional

Even if a college does not directly say so, it expects a high school senior to continue performing at the same level throughout his/her senior year as he did in the first half of the year—the most recent grades available for determining college admissions. A significant senior slump can lead a college to rethink its admissions offer.

Destination: College by Frank Burnett, EdD, president of Education Now, educational consultants, Box 2832, Springfield, VA 22152.

Careful Planning Cuts College Costs

Kalman Chany
Campus Consultants

Tuition at most colleges this year is up 6% over last year…and financial pressures are mounting on universities to boost tuition in the future.

If you plan right, you can cut your tuition bill. *Here is what I'm currently recommending…*

●**Plan ahead.** One key factor that financial aid offices consider is your income for the year beginning January 1 of your child's junior year in high school.

Aid-boosting strategy: Minimize discretionary income for this period. Sell stocks or bonds that will produce capital gains in the year *before* January 1 of your child's junior year. Self-employed individuals can also reduce income by increasing deductible expenses, such as a computer or other business-related purchases. Avoid IRA and pension withdrawals, if possible.

●**File financial aid forms on time.** Deadlines vary. Some financial aid forms must be returned by December of your child's senior year, and others are due sooner for applicants looking for early decisions.

There is no advantage to being too early—in fact, it could reduce your financial aid offer since the school will sense your strong interest. But being late can also be costly. If you miss the deadline, there will be less available financial aid than the amount you probably deserve.

●**Map out your financial aid negotiation strategy.** Don't passively accept a financial aid package that falls short of what you had expected to be offered. You have nothing to lose—a college's decision to accept your child cannot be reversed simply because you request a better deal.

Begin negotiating during the second week of April of your child's senior year in high school. Any sooner and the school may sense your child is desperate to go there and be less willing to give you a good financial aid package. That's why early decision applicants typically receive smaller financial aid packages.

●**Avoid out-of-state universities.** They're not the bargains they used to be—and their financial aid packages are usually smaller.

Example: It now costs an out-of-state resident an extra $10,000 per year to attend the University of Vermont.

In addition, most states have tightened their residency requirements for tuition purposes.

●**Don't be proud when it comes to student loans.** Student loans are among the best deals you can get.

Example I: The Perkins loan is awarded based on your economic need. No interest is charged to the student while he/she is in school.

Example II: The Stafford loan comes in two versions. If you can demonstrate need, you can get the subsidized version, which is interest-free while the student is in school. If you can't show need, you can still get the loan—but interest will be charged while the student is in school.

Make sure you apply on time for student loans. To qualify for student loans and other types of aid, you must complete the Free Application for Federal Student Aid (FAFSA). Information and paperwork are available through college financial aid offices.

Kalman Chany, president of Campus Consultants, a fee-only company that counsels families on college financing, 1202 Lexington Ave., New York 10028. He is author of *The Princeton Review Student Advantage Guide to Paying for College*. Random House.

Less-Expensive Student Loans

Find a bank that sells its loans to the Student Loan Marketing Association (Sallie Mae). All government-guaranteed student loans are made at the same rate of interest. However, Sallie Mae rewards prompt payers. If you make the first 24 monthly payments on time, they rebate all but $250 of the loan origination fee. If you pay 48 months on time, they reduce the interest rate by two percentage points for the remaining payment period. If you authorize them to debit your savings or checking account, they immediately take 0.25 off the interest rate.

To find a local bank that sells loans to Sallie Mae: Call 800-891-1387.

Kalman Chany, president of Campus Consultants, a fee-only company that counsels families on college financing, 1202 Lexington Ave., New York 10028. He is author of *The Princeton Review Student Advantage Guide to Paying for College*. Random House.

Better Way to Save for College

Save for college through an ordinary mutual fund in the parent's name, not the child's. Although this does not give you any tax benefits, it saves legal fees of about $1,500 to set up a trust that might or might not produce significant tax savings. Also, money in your name reduces college-aid eligibility by less than money in your child's name.

Example: If you save $50,000 in your child's name, a college counts 35% of the amount—$17,500—as available to pay its costs. If you save the same $50,000 in your own name, the college counts only 5.65%, or $2,825.

Kalman Chany, president of Campus Consultants, a fee-only company that counsels families on college financing, 1202 Lexington Ave., New York 10028. He is author of *The Princeton Review Student Advantage Guide to Paying for College*. Random House.

Proven Ways to Boost SAT Scores

The SAT scholastic assessment test is a race against the clock. Students only have three hours to complete the math and English tests, so maximizing the score is largely about good time management. *Here are a few practical ways to put time on your side...*

●**Take advantage of the multiple-choice format** by looking at each question's answers before studying the question itself.

Example: In some math problems, you can find the correct answer by plugging each choice into the problem to see which one works. This is sometimes faster than solving the problem from scratch. If you have time during the test, this is also a good way to double-check your answers.

●**Don't fill in the oval immediately after answering each multiple-choice question.** That wastes time. Instead, write the answers next to the questions in the test booklet. Then fill in the ovals on the answer sheet before you move on to the next page.

This strategy will keep you focused on the test and minimize going back and forth between the booklet and the answer sheet.

● **Don't leave an oval blank if you're even a "little sure" of the answer.** Blank answers don't add anything to your score, while you're penalized only one-quarter point for each wrong answer.

In most questions, you should be able to eliminate at least one or two obviously wrong answer choices. Once you've narrowed the field to two or three choices, the odds of guessing right increase dramatically. One right answer can make up for four wrong ones.

Only leave a blank if you really don't have the slightest clue as to how to answer the question.

Colin Rizzio, graduate of Contoocook Valley Regional High School, Peterborough, NH, whose discovery of a mistake in the math portion of the SAT last fall was reported on the front page of The New York Times. Mr. Rizzio scored a 790 out of 800 on the math portion of the SAT.

SAT Trap

Taking the test over and over again. Colleges look unfavorably at applicants who take the SATs more than three times. Taking them repeatedly is unlikely to improve scores significantly. The only way for students to change their scores substantially is to change how they take the test. SAT preparation courses —or sessions with tutors who know how the tests really work—will point out areas where improvement is needed.

Common mistakes: Lingering over difficult question instead of tackling easy ones...trying to answer every single question...not understanding what the questions are really asking.

Adam Robinson, New York–based education consultant and cofounder of the Princeton Review, a national program that helps students prepare for standardized tests. He is author of several books on education, including What Smart Students Know: Maximum Grades, Optimum Learning, Minimum Time. Crown.

Multiple School Transfers Hurt Students

Elementary school students who change schools four or more times during the first six years of school are one year behind by sixth grade. Students who switch schools because of dissatisfaction usually end up in situations similar to the ones they left.

Study of Chicago public elementary schools by David Kerbow, PhD, researcher at The Center for School Improvement at the University of Chicago.

MBA Programs

Executive MBA programs enroll mid-level to senior managers with at least five to 10 years of experience. In addition to a degree, the programs give students a wide range of new contacts. Both teachers and fellow students are likely to be high-level managers. Both full- and part-time programs are offered...lasting from 18 months to two years. *Tuition:* $30,000 and up. *More information:* Contact universities in your area to find out about local programs.

The Washington Post.

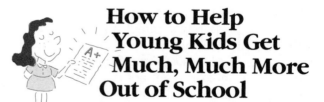

How to Help Young Kids Get Much, Much More Out of School

Lawrence Kutner, PhD

Busy parents want their children to do well in school. Unfortunately, many parents run out of energy. Here are strategies for today's parents to help their children get more out of school...

● **Get to know your child's teachers.** Meet with teachers at least twice a semester, even if there are no problems to discuss. Only showing up when there are problems may cause the teacher to focus just on these issues and reflect only on the difficulties.

Helpful: Talk about the child's strengths, and share information about his/her behavior at home.

Example: If your eight-year-old writes stories at home, tell the teacher about it.

●**Invite teachers to your home.** This practice was common in the 1950s and 1960s, but today we feel we're too busy or are intimidated by the prospect.

Reality: It is often easier to have an adult conversation with a teacher on your own turf. Don't worry about doing anything big, such as dinner. You're probably better off with coffee and dessert. Part of your conversation should be in front of your child...and part in private.

Ask the teacher for his observations of your child. Talk about how you can stay in touch and involved. Only then should you raise any concerns. By having the teacher to your house for just one hour in the evening or on the weekend, you show your child in a dramatic way that you and the teacher are a team.

●**Let homework time be social.** Every parent has been told that kids need to study at clean desks in quiet, closed rooms with no disturbances, but this is not always ideal. Banishing children to their rooms to complete assignments can feel like punishment. They then attempt to rush through homework so that they can return to civilization and human companionship.

Better: Let young children work at the kitchen table or in a room with others around—as long as there are no major distractions. Refer to this period as *study time*, not *homework time*. If children finish their homework early, encourage them to read for the remaining time.

●**Combat frustration by talking about your own struggles.** When children become frustrated with schoolwork, they get upset. Then they are inclined to quit what they're working on and move on to something else.

Spot the signs of frustration—an adamant refusal to continue working on something...an unwillingness to talk about why...and statements of disgust with their own performance or skills.

Helpful: Coax the child back to the difficult project/assignment by sharing a story of how you struggled when you were young. Explain how you worked through it. Gently encourage him to try again, providing hints to help him reach the solution. His sense of accomplishment will help build the self-confidence necessary to succeed the next time.

Important: Playing games that involve learning will make schoolwork more fun. Games like *Scrabble* are great to play with kids as young as seven. Not only will it help develop their spelling abilities, it also develops logic and math skills when children keep score.

●**Ask children to teach you what they are learning.** By having a child show you a math trick or a science fact, you encourage two important developmental skills at once.

You are becoming a participant in the homework, which makes the child more excited about it...and you are helping him demonstrate important information, which means the information is more likely to be remembered.

●**Ask specific questions.** The more you know about your child's daily life, the more involved you can be and the more help you'll be able to offer. Unfortunately, children rarely fill you in on the important events in their days.

Mistake: Asking, *How was your day?* can confuse children, especially young ones. They don't know where to begin or how to organize their answers.

Better: Ask, *Did you play kickball again today?... What did you learn in math today?...* or *What funny thing happened today?* Questions like these require specific answers and are easier for children to consider.

Lawrence Kutner, PhD, a clinical psychologist in Lafayette, CA. He is author of several parenting books, including *Your School-Age Child.* William Morrow.

How Good a Job Does Your Child's School Do?

Adam Robinson
Princeton Review

Even public and private schools with the best facilities and reputations can fail to educate your children properly.

Here are the telltale signs that your child's school isn't doing its job—and what you can do about it…

Beware: **Your child gets good grades in school but low marks on standardized tests.** Wonderful report cards do not automatically mean the school is educating your child.

Because of rampant grade inflation, the average grade today is between B and B+, compared with C a generation ago.

> ***Example:*** A teacher may be inflating report card grades to keep students and parents happy and quiet.

Though standardized tests have many limitations, they can indicate the general *accuracy* of report cards. Your child can take standardized tests as early as first grade.

What to do: Compare your child's scores and percentile rankings on standardized tests with report card grades. If there are big differences consistently between grades and test scores, set up a meeting with the teacher, a school official or, if you think the teacher might be defensive, both. Ask for an explanation of the discrepancy.

• **If the grades are higher than standardized test scores**, it could be because of grade inflation or poor test-taking skills. Do not, however, accept the cliché excuse, *Your child is bright…he just doesn't test well.*

• **If report card grades are lower**, your child may have a motivation problem in the classroom—possibly caused by the teacher.

Beware: **Your child is given "busy work" as homework.** Children learn more when homework demands written expressions of ideas. If your child is given drills, you may want to observe a class or two to make sure the school day does not also involve mindless busy work. If so, you should bring your concerns to the school administration.

Beware: **Homework is given a letter grade but no teacher comments.** If teachers do not routinely provide comments on your child's tests and papers, ask for those comments. Evaluate the quality of teacher comments. Even first- or second-grade students can be helped with the appropriate feedback.

Beware: **Your child's tests are not challenging.** Parents must examine *how* their children are tested since grades don't necessarily reflect aptitude and intelligence.

If most of your children's tests are multiple choice or true/false, they are not being fully challenged. Speak with the teachers, and request more involved tests such as essay responses or other complex, creative challenges.

Adam Robinson, New York–based education consultant and cofounder of the Princeton Review, a national program that helps students prepare for standardized tests. He is author of several books on education, including *What Smart Students Know: Maximum Grades, Optimum Learning, Minimum Time.* Crown.

Children Behave Differently when Parents Visit Preschool

When parents visit a preschool their children behave differently—spending more time with the parent and less time with classmates. When the children do play with other kids, the type of play may be less complex than the type observed on days when no parent is in school. Children are also more likely to whine, cry and throw tantrums when a parent is present.

Bottom line: It can be worthwhile to take a day off from work and volunteer at your child's preschool, but do not judge the school by your child's behavior that day.

Study of 27 three- and four-year-olds, led by Ellen Smith, MA, and Carollee Howes, PhD, researchers at the Graduate School of Education and Information Studies at the University of California, Los Angeles.

16

Consumer Savvy

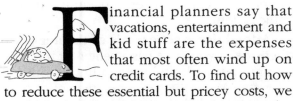

How Three of the Country's Toughest Tightwads Avoid Overspending on Fun

Diane Rosener, Mary Hunt, Jonni McCoy

Financial planners say that vacations, entertainment and kid stuff are the expenses that most often wind up on credit cards. To find out how to reduce these essential but pricey costs, we spoke with three of the country's biggest tightwads for their penny-pinching secrets...

DIANE ROSENER ON VACATIONS

• **Ask for perks and discounts.** The cost of airfare, car rentals and hotels can turn a simple family trip into a debt you could be paying off for the rest of the year.

Reduce those costs by asking for deals and perks—you'll be surprised at what you can get.

• **Airfares.** If you buy plane tickets that the airline reduces a few weeks later, ask to get the difference refunded on your credit card. Recently, my family saved almost $400 on a trip to England when the airline cut its fares.

Ask your travel agent to keep up with any price reductions and alert you right away. That way, you won't spend hours on the phone with the airline.

• **Car rentals.** Some rental car companies will let you park your car free of charge at the airport while you're on vacation if you'll be renting from them when you get to your destination. You might save more than $100 in parking costs during a one-week vacation.

And—some rental companies run free shuttles from the airport to your hotel. That can save from $10 to $60 in taxicab fares each way.

• **Hotels.** Most hotels offer free breakfasts, shuttles, tickets to theme parks, etc. Some hotels let children stay free. Often, these specials aren't advertised, so you have to ask or negotiate for them.

Example: When we recently stayed at a hotel in Kansas City, we asked for—and received

269

—two-for-one tickets to a local amusement park. We saved $60 just on that discount alone.

●**Call the Chamber of Commerce or tourist board** in the town that you'll be visiting a few weeks before you arrive. Often, they'll send you two-for-one coupons for local attractions, hotels and car rentals.

●**Be a group coordinator.** If you're traveling with a group, make all arrangements with the airline. Tell them you are coordinating a group vacation to get reduced fares.

Aim: To get travel agents' benefits, you need to coordinate a group of at least 10 travelers.

Example: My friend coordinated a ski trip to Vail, Colorado, for 25 people. She did all the bookings herself and asked the airline if they could give her a deal for the effort. *Result:* She got a free plane ticket for bringing such a large group on its flight.

●**Rent "efficiencies," rooms with refrigerators, microwave ovens and coffeemakers.** This makes sense especially if you're traveling with a large family on a long vacation.

You'll save big bucks on meals even if you cook only a few meals instead of eating at restaurants the entire time. Many hotel chains have installed stoves and other means of cooking in their rooms.

●**Don't buy excessive rental car insurance.** Car rental companies offer a plethora of insurance options, such as collision-damage waivers and loss-of-use insurance, which covers damages if you wreck your rental car. You may be pressured to purchase these options, even though you might not need them.

Find out if your auto insurance or credit card company covers your car rental. Often you'll find you don't need to purchase options such as collision-damage waivers, which cover the majority of any repair bills you might incur. That can save you 30% or more each day you rent a car.

MARY HUNT ON ENTERTAINMENT

●**The early bird gets the discount.** Instead of dinner and a movie, think matinee and dinner. The typical dinner for two and tickets to a first-run flick cost an average of $40. You can easily cut your expense in half by catching an afternoon matinee and then an early-bird dinner—even at an upscale restaurant.

●**Become tourists in your own city and state.** Call your state's department of tourism to get all the tourist information it has for your area.

You'll be surprised at all the great free or low-cost activities available in your own backyard.

Example: On weekends, my family and I go to beaches, craft fairs or free museum events. My favorite is "Bagels and Bach"—the museum serves free bagels and plays classical music.

●**Spend time with your family.** Take up a hobby that the entire family can enjoy cheaply —such as camping or biking. Or have theme nights at your home.

Example: We have "Christmas in July" night, where we rent holiday movies and make eggnog.

Neighborhood activities are fun and cheap as well. Organize a roving wine and cheese party where each neighbor buys one bottle of wine and one type of cheese.

It's a lot cheaper than buying wine and cheese at an expensive restaurant—and you get to know your neighbors in the process.

Example: Many communities also have clubs that are very inexpensive to join. It's a cheap way to meet new people, and you might even get in shape.

●**Go to free admission days at museums and zoos.** Many museums and zoos that usually charge admission are free one day each month. Often, this occurs on Wednesday or Thursday evenings when museum and zoo traffic is slow.

●**Attend dress rehearsals of theater productions.** If your area has a center for the performing arts, ask about attending the dress rehearsal. Many theater companies offer free or near-free admission for the dress rehearsal —and the performance is just as good as the actual show.

JONNI MCCOY ON KIDS' EXPENSES

●**Shop at resale stores as much as possible.** Resale stores sell first-quality children's clothes at 50% to 60% off what you would pay at a department store. And—these stores don't accept clothes unless they're in exceptional shape.

Example: I recently found a brand-new Laura Ashley dress for my daughter that was only $19 at my local resale store. I would have paid at least twice as much if I bought the same dress at a department store.

These stores typically are well stocked with clothing for kids age 10 and younger. If your kids are older, you'll have better luck waiting for sales or going to outlet stores.

● **Make your own cookies and snacks.** I won't pay lots of money at grocery stores for treats that I can make myself and save up to 75%. There are plenty of snacks that don't have to be purchased at the store.

Example: I make my own candy canes, marshmallows, lollipops and peanut butter cups for pennies. It costs me 25 cents to make 24 ice pops. And my snack-making only takes an hour or two a week.

● **Take advantage of family rates and group discounts.** My kids love amusement parks and aquariums. We organize large groups to get the lowest possible admission prices. School groups get the best deals, but any large group will reduce the price.

Example: I recently organized a 40-person trip to Marine World Africa USA. We got in for $7.50 per person instead of the usual $20 admission. And at the Monterey Bay Aquarium, our group of 30 people got in for only $8 per family, instead of the usual $14 per person.

Diane Rosener, editor of *A Penny Saved*, 8205 Avens Circle, Colorado Springs 80920...Mary Hunt, editor of *Cheapskate Monthly*, Box 2135, Paramount, CA 90723...Jonni McCoy, mother of two children in San Jose, CA, and author of *Miserly Moms: Living on One Income in a Two Income Economy*. Full Quart Press.

How to Save $3,000 a Year On Groceries

Phil Lempert

The key to cutting your grocery bills in today's super-competitive marketplace is to think *value*...not just *price*. Surefire ways to get the most from your shopping excursions, in every aisle, every time you shop...

GET TO KNOW YOUR SUPERMARKET

Value is a balance of four factors—quality, price, selection and service. Supermarket customers visit, on average, two different supermarkets a week and several different stores each month in search of the best value. But— 53% of shoppers say they dislike supermarket shopping...and 14% downright *hate* it.

My aim: To help you get the best value from your supermarket *and* help you have more fun grocery shopping...

● **Choose one store as your regular supermarket.** With more than 35,000 products on most supermarket shelves, there's no reason to keep switching supermarkets.

● **Look for the best preferred shopper program—*and save $300*.** You can easily save $300 a year or more by consistently taking advantage of your supermarket's preferred shopper program—the computer-age version of S&H Green Stamps. So when choosing your supermarket, it pays to look for the best program.

There are a few types, and they may be offered alone or in combination...

● **Frequent shopper programs** issue a membership card or number that is used to electronically track the products you purchase. You accumulate points that can be redeemed for discounts, dollar awards or free products. The better programs offer bonus points on specific products or departments.

Example: If you never buy from the supermarket bakery, you may be offered bonus points on baked goods as an incentive to get you to try that department.

Caution: Be sure to ask how the supermarket uses the information it collects, and how it protects members' privacy.

● **Front-end electronic marketing programs** are similar to frequent shopper programs, but members are rewarded based on the amount they spend. Such programs are often one part of a broader preferred shopper program, rather than a stand-alone benefit.

● **Purchase-triggered coupon programs**, also called purchase-activated coupon programs, issue coupons at the checkout register that are good for future purchases at that particular store. The coupons are "triggered" by the purchases you have just made. These programs do not keep track of your personal shopping habits.

Example: If you just bought Brand X peanut butter, you may receive a coupon for Brand Y peanut butter or a larger size of Brand X…or a jar of jelly.

● **Instant electronic discounts** are also called "paperless coupons." Customers who use their membership cards at the checkout register automatically receive discounts on products that have been identified in mailers or by signs on the shelves. Some supermarkets also offer customers discounts at neighboring businesses, entries in contests and other electronic rewards.

● **Meet the store manager and/or customer service manager.** Be sure to tell him/her that you are a long-time regular customer, and mention what you like about the store—as well as suggest improvements. *Ask the following questions…*

● **What are the best times to shop here?** The worst?

● **What are your biggest sale items?**

● **What day do your weekly sales begin?**

● **Can I get an advance copy of your newspaper and circular ads and a schedule of in-store sales**, product samplings and promotional events?

● **How do I join your frequent shopper program**, and if there is a fee, will you waive it? (Usually the answer is yes.)

● **Finally, ask to be introduced to the various department managers.** That way, they will recognize you as a shopper looking for bargains and the freshest products.

● **Get to know the staff in the store—***and save $100.* Exchanging friendly greetings with the people who work where you shop will always make your supermarket visits more enjoyable—and can save you $100 a year or more. Introduce yourself to the cashiers and to the people in the produce section, deli, bakery and other departments—*and tell them you are interested in sales and special offers.*

Once they know you, the supermarket staff will point out new products, special promotions or sales. They will direct you to in-store coupons, newspaper or circular coupons and rebate offers.

UNDERSTANDING MARKETING EFFORTS— AND TRICKS

● **Use coupons—***and save $300.* If you use just 10 manufacturer's coupons a week, at an average of about 60 cents each, you'll save more than $300 a year.

● **Buy store brands—***and save $2,000.* Switching to your supermarket's "private label" or "store brand" is one of the best ways to save money with no loss of quality.

In most cases, when you compare the ingredients list of "store-brand" products to those of the national brands, you will find that the quality is equal, if not superior, to the name-brand product. Often, store brands are made by the same manufacturers as national brands. You'll have to try store-brand products to see if they are to your taste.

If you currently spend $135 to $140 a week on groceries, you can expect to save *more than $2,000 a year* by switching to store-brand products.

● **Outsmart supermarket display techniques.** Don't fall for these common supermarket display tricks…

● **Placing the highest-priced items at eye level.**

● **Piling up end-of-aisle displays with products that are close to their expiration date**, but are not necessarily on sale.

● **Grouping products to provoke impulse buying**, like chips, dips and soft drinks.

● **Making attractive arrangements of delicious precut fruits** or salad items that are far more expensive than the unsliced versions.

● **Creating an "international" cheese table** or deli display when the same prepackaged products are available in the dairy case for much less.

● **Placing staple items**, such as milk, in the back of the store, forcing you to walk past the rest of the merchandise.

Strategy: If you need just a gallon of milk, avoid temptation by walking down an aisle stocked with items you never buy, such as auto-mobile supplies, pet food, school supplies.

●**Stick to your list—*and save $300*.** Finally, the supermarket shopper's *must*—always shop with a list and control your impulse buys for an easy saving of $300 a year.

I limit myself to three impulse purchases per shopping trip, but otherwise stick carefully to my list. This strategy guarantees that I always have fun while I'm shopping—but I never exceed my budget.

Phil Lempert, food industry expert and inveterate supermarket shopper. He is author of Phil Lempert's Supermarket Shopping and Value Guide. *Contemporary Books.*

Ways to Cut Your Spending in Half

Sid Kirchheimer

Buy a three-year-old car and save 50%. By the time a car is three years old, it should be worth about half the original price and will have been driven between 45,000 and 60,000 miles. Most three-year-old cars should be good for another 60,000 or so miles—or 120,000 miles if it's a particularly well-made car, such as a Mercedes or Volvo.

CLOTHING/OTHER

●**Shop from the middle of the catalog and save 40%.** Clearance items are usually pictured there. Look for them on non-glossy paper, sometimes on the flip side of the order form.

●**Buy a reconditioned watch and save 50%.** A high quality watch that has been cleaned and reconditioned by an expert jeweler is as good as new—and may even come with a warranty.

FOOD

●**Buy meat against the season and save 15% to 20%.** Buy roasts, traditionally a winter cut of meat, in the summer when prices are lower...buy porterhouse and New York strip steaks, popular on the grill, in winter. Eat immediately, or freeze purchases until it's the "proper" season.

●**Keep a supermarket price book and save 50%.** In a notebook, record the average price of grocery items you buy regularly.

You'll soon learn which store has the best prices on which items, and when to "stock up."

●**Have dessert at home and save 20%.** In many restaurants, desserts carry the highest markup on the menu. When you do dine out, save room for dessert and save money by eating it at home.

HOME

●**Put your water heater on a timer and save 35%.** Set the timer to turn off at night and then turn it back on shortly before you wake up in the morning. Set it to turn off after you leave for work, and to turn on later in the afternoon.

●**Buy a two-head VCR and save $150.** The only advantage of a four-head model is that it gives a clearer picture when the tape is paused or run in slow motion, a feature that's rarely used.

INSURANCE

●**Revalue your car's worth and save 40%.** Once the car loan is paid off, consider reducing collision coverage. If, in the very worst case, an older car is totaled, the insurance company will reimburse you only for its market value—which may be even less than the cost of your collision premium.

●**Don't insure your lot and save 20% to 50%.** Even if your home is destroyed by fire, hurricane, earthquake or other disaster, the value of the land won't change. And the insurance company will reimburse you only for the value of the house, not the land.

MEDICAL

●**Save your doctor insurance hassles and save 50%.** Many doctors will cut their rates by as much as half if you agree to pay up front and file the insurance claim yourself.

TRAVEL

●**"Read" the motel parking lot and save 20%.** The fewer cars in the lot, the better your chances of negotiating a lower room rate.

Sid Kirchheimer, coeditor of Cut Your Spending in Half, Without Settling for Less! *Rodale Press.*

Everyone Loves A Bargain...

Eric W. Gershman

Men's quality shirts at half price. Why pay high prices for the private-label men's shirts stocked by the better department stores when you can order them directly from Paul Fredrick's Menstyle Catalog for less? Paul Fredrick offers a wide selection of affordably priced dress shirts and neckwear. *Free catalog:* 800-247-1417.

●**Cosmetics and perfume—up to 90% below retail.** Beauty Boutique offers brand-name makeup and perfume from Oscar de la Renta, Giorgio, Lancôme, Estee Lauder, Maybelline and others at deep discount. *Free catalog:* Beauty Boutique, Box 94520, 6836 Engle Rd., Cleveland 44101...or call 216-826-1712.

●**Free skiing in Colorado.** The Crested Butte Mountain Resort has some of the best black-diamond slopes in the Rockies. *Downside:* It's a 4½-hour drive from Denver. But to offset the inconvenience, it periodically offers free lift tickets which usually cost $44 a day.

Added bonus: Free ski lessons for first timers—a $46 value. Ride the Alpine Express from the airport, and you'll pick up a discount booklet for area restaurants and shops. *For information:* 800-SKI-FREE.

Alternatives: Call other favorite ski resorts for their off-season spring rates—about 40% off, plus promotional discounts.

●**Free attractions in Washington, DC.** Washington, DC, has about 50 attractions you can visit for no charge, and they're all listed in a free booklet available from the DC Convention and Visitors Association. *To order:* 202-289-7000.

Or call the office of your US representative to receive free passes to the House and Senate galleries...and a free VIP tour of the White House that bypasses the long waiting lines.

If you're planning to bring your grandchildren, be sure to mention you'll be traveling with children—there are other freebies offered for kids.

●**Free meals at great restaurants.** Restaurant and Hotel Services reimburses their secret "shoppers" for restaurant meals and bar tabs for two at restaurants ranging from such chains as T.G.I. Friday's to more expensive establishments. In return, shoppers must write a detailed evaluation of their restaurant experience. Checks range from $20 to $120. Those who do their jobs well may be promoted to making secret reports on hotels.

For a shopper's application: Call 703-591-6729 and leave your name and address.

●**Free meals...and free goods...and free services.** Shop and Check runs a similar "secret shopper" evaluation service for retailers, eyewear stores, gas stations, fast-food chains and restaurants. *To apply:* Field Personnel, 7616 Perimeter Ctr. ENE, Atlanta 30346.

●**Airfares at up to 70% off.** Airline coupon brokers routinely save customers 50% to 70% on business or first-class fares by matching travelers who want to sell discounted or frequent-flier certificates with buyers. The coupons are good for one year, and travelers can make date changes with no penalties.

Example: A recent first-class fare from the East Coast to Australia was about $8,500 during peak season, and $2,900 round-trip year-round from a better broker. While brokering tickets is against airline regulations, it is not illegal. One of the most reputable brokers, International Air Coupon Exchange, guarantees its tickets. 800-558-0053.

●**Super deal on airfares for seniors.** Continental Airlines offers Freedom Certificate Booklets to anyone over age 62. The booklets contain eight one-way tickets to anywhere in the continental US for $999. That's about $125 per one-way trip. The booklet is good for one year. 800-441-1135.

●**Free fire extinguishers or first-aid kits.** If you schedule an appointment during Fire Prevention Week in October, Amerispec, a national home inspection company, hands out free fire extinguishers. Summer customers receive free first-aid kits. 800-909-8090.

●**Free cellular phones.** If you are ready to sign up with a cellular phone service, check around for one that offers a free telephone to get you started. The business has become so competitive that great deals abound. You can always change services later if you so choose.

●**Free garden mulch.** Every January, contact the services in your area that chip Christmas trees. *Example:* Many city parks set up giveaway piles—bring heavy-duty garbage bags and help yourself.

●**Free do-it-yourself classes.** The Home Depot sponsors free clinics in its stores nationwide on a broad range of topics—woodworking, building a deck or fence, laying tile, installing a water heater, ceiling fan or home security system *and more.* The company also offers free professional consulting, including computer assisted design (3-D remodeling plan) for your kitchen or bathroom. Then save on the cost of carpenters, plumbers or electricians by doing it yourself.

●**Free herb seed sampler.** Receive a five-packet herb sampler, instructions on herb-growing, recipes and a catalog. *To order:* Send your name, address and $1 for postage and handling to Le Jardin du Gourmet, Box 75-GD, St. Johnsbury Center, VT 05863.

●**Flower bulbs at less than half price.** Order early for the fall planting season and Breck's will send you bulbs shipped directly from Holland for up to 55% off retail, plus a dozen or more free tulip bulbs for orders of $30 and up. They'll even throw in a free book on bulbs. 800-722-9069.

●**Coffee discount.** Receive coupons worth up to $1 off the price of Brothers Gourmet Coffee, as well as copies of their newsletter, *Café Gourmet,* which includes interesting and educational facts about coffee. Call 800-284-5776.

●**Deep discounts on golf and tennis equipment.** Buy brand-name equipment or get price quotes by calling 800-933-7777. Las Vegas Discount Golf & Tennis, 4405 Paradise Rd., Las Vegas 89109.

●**Wine by mail for 45% below retail.** The Gold Medal Wine Club offers premium wines at a 45% discount. 800-266-8888.

You can also order from a fine selection of discounted wines through Topline Wine and Spirits. *Free catalog:* 4718 San Fernando Rd., Glendale, California 91204, 818-500-9670.

●**Save 65% on china and crystal.** Order china and crystal by mail for up to 65% off from discounters who handle Waterford, Lenox, Royal Doulton, Gorham, Christian Dior, Mikasa and more. *Free catalogs:* The China Warehouse, 800-321-3212…Ross-Simons, 800-556-7376.

●**Industrial work clothes.** For casual wear, clothing made for work is sturdy, durable and far less costly than designer brands. For a wide selection of jackets, shirts, aprons, shoes and boots, thermal undergarments and more, try Wear Guard. The company discounts up to 30%—and does monograms and logos! *Free catalog:* 800-388-3300.

Eric W. Gershman, author of *400 Steals Beyond Belief.* Financial Answers Network, Inc.

Discounts After Purchasing

If you return to the same store soon after your purchase and see your product selling for a better price, make sure to let the store know. Some stores will reimburse the difference.

Consumer's Best, 4033 44 Ave. S., Minneapolis 55406.

How to Shop by Phone For Big Bargains on Almost Anything

Sue Goldstein

Catalog shopping can save you time and money. Here are my favorite places to shop over the phone that offer discounts on name brands…

APPLIANCES

●**EBA Wholesale** offers dozens of products from more than 50 top-name manufacturers, including General Electric, KitchenAid, Maytag, Panasonic, Sharp and Westinghouse…and at up to 60% off list price. *Free catalog.*

EBA Wholesale, 800-380-2378.

BED/BATH

●**Harris Levy Inc.** can save you up to 60% on better domestic and imported sheets, blankets and towels. Brands include Crown Crafts, Fieldcrest, Palais Royal and Wamsutta. Also tablecloths, down comforters and pillows.

Harris Levy Inc., 212-226-3102.

COSMETICS

●**Beauty Boutique** sells products from top-name makers such as Almay, Aziza, Charles of the Ritz, Coty, Elizabeth Arden, Jovan, L'Oreal, Max Factor, Maybelline, Revlon and others at up to 90% off retail prices. Besides having all the cosmetics basics—lipsticks, powders, polishes—the catalog offers designer fragrances, grooming aids, costume jewelry and vitamins. *Free catalog.*

Beauty Boutique, 216-826-3008.

COMPUTERS

●**Scala-Mathis Auction** allows you to bid on-line or to call its sister company, Comm-Public, toll free to save 50% to 80% on new and reconditioned computers and components. Available items include ink-jet printers, color scanners, voice/fax/data modems, monitors, keyboards, laptops and memory, etc.

Scala-Mathis Auction, 800-595-1498.

LUGGAGE AND LEATHER

●**Jobson's Luggage Warehouse.** Save 30% to 60% on major brands of luggage—American Tourister, Atlantic, Boyt, Briggs & Reilly, Delsey, French, Hartmann, Lucas, Samsonite, Skyway (Ventura) and Zero Halliburton, among others. The company also sells business cases, attachés, small leather goods, desk and travel accessories and fine pens. *Free catalog.*

Jobson's Luggage Warehouse, 212-355-6846.

MATTRESSES

●**T.F. Howard Bedding Factory.** Save 30% to 40% on standard and custom European and domestic designs. *Also available:* Antique bed frames and unusual shaped mattresses. To get a price quote, call in the dimensions and describe your mattress comfort specifications.

T.F. Howard Bedding Factory, 800-987-2818.

MEDICAL EQUIPMENT

●**Homecare Medical.** Items include seat lifts, scooters, power wheelchairs, adjustable and hospital beds, blood-pressure monitors, blood-glucose monitors and physician scales at discounts of 40%. *Example:* The most popular ultralight wheelchair—The Breezy—retails for $995 but is available here for $597. *Free catalog and delivery.*

Homecare Medical, 214-696-2525.

PET SUPPLIES

●**Mail Order Pet Shop** lets you save 40% to 75% off retail prices on everything for your pet. Free catalog for supplies for aquariums…dogs and cats…birds…small animals…and reptiles. Every order, regardless of size, is subject to a processing charge—but no shipping charges are assessed.

Mail Order Pet Shop, 800-366-7387.

PRESCRIPTION DRUGS

●**Medi-Mail** is one of the country's largest mail-service pharmacies. They provide substantial savings on vitamins, prescription drugs and over-the-counter pain relievers. Doctors' prescriptions are verified and filled within 48 hours. You can receive a 90-day supply within one week.

Medi-Mail, 800-331-1458.

Sue Goldstein, publisher of *The Underground Shopper* and author of more than 60 books on bargain hunting, including *Great Buys by Mail and Phone* (available in most libraries).

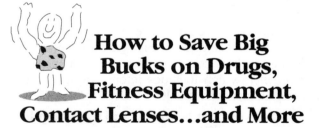

How to Save Big Bucks on Drugs, Fitness Equipment, Contact Lenses…and More

Prudence McCullough

Mail-order guru Prudence McCullough gave us her favorite sources for saving big money on…

MEDICATIONS*

●**Action Mail Order Drug Company.** A reliable source for discount prescription drugs.

*If you order drugs, vitamins, herbal remedies, etc., by mail, be sure to alert your doctor.

Action Mail Order Drug Company, Box 787, Waterville, ME 04903. 800-452-1976.

●**Medi-Mail.** Discounts on prescription and over-the-counter drugs, nutritional supplements, beauty products, etc.

Medi-Mail, Box 98520, Las Vegas, NV 89193-8520. 800-793-4726. Or contact them at http://www.mednetmpc.com. *Free catalog.*

NUTRITIONAL SUPPLEMENTS

●**Freeda Vitamins.** This company makes its own line of nutritional supplements—all free of sugar, starch, sulfites, gluten, pesticides and artificial flavorings. They even sell *kosher* vitamins. Freeda vitamins and minerals cost up to 40% less than competing brands.

Freeda Vitamins, 36 E. 41 St., New York 10017-6203. 800-777-3737 or 212-685-4980. *Fax:* 212-685-7297. *Free catalog.*

●**PIA Discount Vitamins.** At least 20% off brand-name vitamins and herbal remedies, including those made by Twin Lab, Kyolic, Nature's Way and Bach.

PIA Discount Vitamins, 708 Saw Mill River Rd., Ardsley, NY 10502. 800-662-8144. *Fax:* 914-693-3557. *Free catalog.*

MEDICAL SUPPLIES

●**Bruce Medical Supply.** Assistive devices for people with arthritis, diabetes, repetitive stress injury and other ailments. Save up to 60% on some products, although others are not discounted.

Bruce Medical Supply, Department 10754, 411 Waverly Oaks Rd., Waltham, MA 02154. 800-225-8446. *Fax:* 617-894-9519. *Free catalog.*

●**Support Plus.** Save 15% to 30% on support hosiery, back and joint supports and other therapeutic apparel. The company stocks a variety of comfortable (though not orthopedic) shoes and slippers…and some home nursing products.

Support Plus, 99 West St., Box 500, Medfield, MA 02052. 800-229-2910. *Fax:* 508-359-0139. *Free catalog.*

CORRECTIVE LENSES**

●**Contact Lens Replacement Center.** Save up to 50% on soft, hard and gas-permeable

**Mail-order is no substitute for in-person appointments with an eye doctor—for periodic eye exams and, in the case of contact lenses, proper fitting. Mail-order may be appropriate for replacement contact lenses and for eyeglass prescriptions less than one year old.

contact lenses (including toric, aphakic and bifocal lenses). Discounts are also available on name-brand sunglasses.

Contact Lens Replacement Center, Box 1489, Melville, NY 11747. 800-779-2654. *Fax:* 516-643-4009. For a free price list, send a stamped, self-addressed envelope.

●**General Lens Corporation.** Save as much as 75% on contact lenses from Bausch & Lomb, CooperVision and other major manufacturers. GLC members ($25 for two years) save an additional 30%.

General Lens Corporation, 14350 NE 6th Ave., North Miami, FL 33161-2907. 800-934-5665. *Fax:* 800-285-5367. http://www.igc.net/~glc. *Free catalog.*

●**Prism Optical.** Up to 70% off on contact lenses and 30% to 50% off on prescription eyeglasses. Frames by Christian Dior, Armani, Anne Klein, Ray-Ban and others. Bifocal and trifocal lenses are available, as are ultrathin polycarbonate lenses, tinted lenses and scratch-resistant lenses.

Prism Optical, 10992 NW 7th Ave., North Miami, FL 33168. 305-754-5894. *Fax:* 305-754-7352. *Catalog:* $2, but it is credited toward any purchase.

FITNESS GEAR

●**Better Health Fitness.** Up to 20% off stationary cycles, treadmills, free weights, mats, etc. The staff can provide guidance in gym layout.

Better Health Fitness, 5302 New Utrecht Ave., Brooklyn, NY 11219. 718-436-4693 or 718-436-4801. *Fax:* 718-854-3381. Price quotes available by phone or letter (send a stamped, self-addressed envelope).

●**Creative Health Products.** Save up to 30% on exercise bikes, blood pressure monitors, body-fat calipers, heart-rate monitors and other products.

Creative Health Products, 5148 Saddle Ridge Rd., Plymouth, MI 48170. 800-742-4478. *Fax:* 313-996-4650. *Free catalog.*

●**Holabird Sports.** Though the emphasis is on equipment and clothing for racquet sports, Holabird also carries most major brands of footwear for running, walking, basketball, cross-training and hiking (including hard-to-find sizes). Discounts of up to 40%.

Holabird Sports, 9220 Pulaski Hwy., Baltimore 21220. 410-687-6400. *Fax:* 410-687-7311. Free brochure.

Prudence McCullough, a consumer advocate based in Brooklyn, NY. She is editor of *The Wholesale-By-Mail Catalog 1997*. HarperCollins.

Wow! Free Drugs!

Get free prescription drugs from your doctor's nurse. Doctors receive many free samples of prescription drugs from drug companies and are happy to give them away.

Best: Ask the nurse in your doctor's office—often the doctor does not handle them personally.

Bonus: Doctors receive free samples of other medical-related products as well—educational books and videos, thermometers, diapers, bibs, etc. Ask the nurse about these items as well.

Cheapskate Monthly, Box 2135, Paramount, CA 90723.

Effective Ways to Get Out of Debt

Cancel overdraft protection for your checking account—it makes it too easy to write checks for more money than you have. To get out of credit card debt quickly, pay at least double the minimum payment every month.

To hold down debt: Create a budget category for major items instead of buying them on credit. Plan in advance for purchasing cars or durable goods with cash. Make a plan for everything your family wants to buy, rank items by priority and save for the top item first …then the next…and so on.

Your Complete Guide to Money Happiness by Henry Brock, CPA, head of the American Financial Resource Center, a fee-based financial consulting firm in Salt Lake City. Legacy Publishing.

Lower Your Electric Bill

Save on your electricity bill by requesting a *time of use* (TOU) billing plan from your utility. With a TOU plan you pay more during peak demand hours, and get a discount for electricity used in off hours. This lets you cut your electricity bill significantly by running your dishwasher, dryer and other appliances at night or on weekends.

Note: TOU plans vary state to state and season to season.

Rick Doble, editor of *$avvy Discount$ Newsletter*, 195 Old Nassau Rd., Box 96, Smyrna, NC 28579.

Energy-Saver Air Conditioners May Not Save Any Energy—or Money

A switch labeled *energy saver* or *money saver* usually just shuts off a window unit's fan. This may save a little money by shutting the fan down briefly—but the room air is not circulated as well, which could make the compressor come on more often.

More effective and less expensive: Simply run a unit at a slightly higher thermostat setting.

D. Stephen Elder, Roanoke, VA-based home inspector.

Air Conditioner Efficiency

Reduce air conditioner use by preparing oven-cooked meals during the coolest part of the day. When you're ready to eat, reheat the meal in a microwave or toaster oven.

Rochelle LaMotte McDonald, author of *How to Pinch a Penny Till It Screams*. Avery Publishing Group.

Lower Your Thermostat

You can save 3% on home energy costs for every degree you lower your thermostat over a 24-hour period.

Example: A programmable thermostat that lowers the temperature from 70 degrees to 61 degrees for eight hours each night saves about 9% on your energy bill.

Melodie Moore, editor of *Skinflint News*, Box 818, Palm Harbor, FL 34682.

Save Money on Heating

Save money on heating by checking your home's exterior walls for cold-air infiltration. Install insulating pads under the outlet covers on exterior walls—especially if they face the north or west…caulk the gap between the baseboard and the floor, particularly above unheated basements or garages.

D. Stephen Elder, Roanoke, VA-based home inspector.

Get Your Utility Deposit Refund

Ask your utility company to return the deposit you made when you first moved into your home or apartment. After a year or so of on-time payments, most utilities will refund such deposits—*usually with interest.*

Kiplinger's Personal Finance Magazine, 1729 H St. NW, Washington, DC 20006.

Cut Water Bill

Cut water bill costs by as much as 20%—while saving up to 200 gallons of water—per month by storing it in gallon jugs in the refrigerator instead of running the tap each time you need water.

Sid Kirchheimer, coeditor of Cut Your Spending in Half, Without Settling for Less! *Rodale Press.*

Use Appliances at Night

Most power companies charge lower electricity rates at night. Even if your power company doesn't do this, you'll still reduce air conditioning costs if you run your dishwasher, dryer, oven and other heat-generating appliances at night, when it's cooler.

Lucy H. Hedrick, time management consultant and author of 365 Ways to Save Money. *Hearst Books.*

Better Appliance Buying

Clothes dryers: Basic models work well—fancy features usually aren't needed. Gas units cost a little more to buy but much less to operate.

●**Dishwashers:** Higher-priced washers generally clean better—unless the higher price is caused by lots of cycles and little-used features.

●**Ovens:** Self-cleaning ovens are more expensive but also more energy efficient.

●**Ranges:** Like clothes dryers, gas stoves cost more to buy than electric ones but less to operate.

●**Refrigerators:** Top-freezer models are often cheaper and more energy-efficient than side-by-side models.

●**Washing machines:** The standard wash cycles are regular, permanent press and delicate. Other cycles are unlikely to be used and drive up the cost.

Betty Sinnock, a founder of The Beardstown Ladies Investment Club, Beardstown, IL, and contributor to The Beardstown Ladies' Guide to Smart Spending for Big Savings. *Hyperion.*

Don't Fall for Extended Warranties

Service contracts waste money unless you plan to use a product heavily. If you take care of most equipment on which the contracts —also called *extended warranties*—are offered, you will need few or no repairs. Service contract costs over an appliance's life span are four to seven times as high as repair costs predicted by industry-wide standards.

Retailers push the contracts because they are enormously profitable for them. If a product is so unreliable that you need a service contract, buy a different product.

Mike McClintock, home columnist, The Washington Post.

Insider's Secret of Finding the Best Mortgage Deal

Create a simple chart that tracks the total cost of each loan.

Strategy: Keep various loan deals straight when shopping for a mortgage by dividing a sheet of paper into columns. To the right of each mortgage offer, insert the up-front fees (for credit check, appraisal, etc.)…total interest cost for the first five years (the average stay in a home)…and all closing costs (including points). The best deal will have the lowest total amount. Call at least six lenders to widen your choices.

Robert Heady, publisher of Bank Rate Monitor's 100 Highest Yields, *Box 088888, North Palm Beach, FL 33408.*

Home-Insurance Claims

Before filing, get a repair estimate from a local contractor so that you'll have a true cost guideline when the adjuster arrives. If the insurance company makes a much lower bid, insist that repairs be made with materials that are the same as or equivalent to what existed before the damage.

Also: If the damage is so severe that you must make some immediate repairs, take photos first—then make only *temporary* repairs before the adjuster arrives.

Robert Hunter, director of insurance for the Consumer Federation of America, 1424 16 St. NW, Washington, DC 20036.

Travel Money Saver

The best airfare bargains are available through airline consolidators. Consolidators sell airline tickets at prices often well below the lowest published fares.

Snags: There may be restrictions on tickets, such as on the ability to change or cancel flights. Different consolidators specialize in dif-ferent kinds of flights and in working with particular airlines.

Best: Have your travel agent book tickets through a consolidator for you.

Ed Perkins, editor of Consumer Reports Travel Letter, *101 Truman Ave., Yonkers, NY 10703.*

Save on Airfares

Change days and hours of travel to save significantly on airfares. Major airlines often offer discounts for flights leaving on Tuesday, Wednesday or Thursday, which are traditionally light travel days. And airlines also discount flights at specific hours in head-to-head battles with competitors.

Example: One airline charged $800 for a roundtrip from Miami to Los Angeles…except between 5 pm and 6 pm, when a competitor had a $300 fare. During that hour, the higher-priced airline matched the cut-rate fare.

Money, Rockefeller Center, New York 10020.

Airline Tickets Are Like Cash, So Protect Them

If you lose an airline ticket, you are not going to get on the plane easily without it, *or* get a quick refund.

Trap: Someone else can use or cash in the ticket. *Typical:* To make your flight you'll have to buy *another* ticket. Then, if no one uses the lost ticket, the airline will refund the cost to you in about six months. When you do buy a regular ticket, record its number to speed up processing if it is lost.

Alternatives: Fly "ticketless" airlines such as Northwest, Southwest and United—all you will need is a picture identification.

Maggie Simmons, editor in chief of Travel Holiday, *1633 Broadway, New York 10019.*

Keep Track of Frequent-Flier Miles

Carefully monitor how and when your frequent flier miles are added to your account—especially those earned from program *partners* such as hotels, car rental agencies and florists. Quite often, frequent flier miles are lost due to bookkeeping errors and are not credited to program accounts.

Self-defense: Always confirm that your program account is being credited *before* you check out of the hotel, drive away in the rental car, etc.

Randy Petersen, editor of *InsideFlyer*, 4715-C Town Center Dr., Colorado Springs 80916. He is author of *The Official Frequent Flyer Guidebook*. AirPress.

Frequent-Flier Hassles Can Be Avoided

Randy Petersen

Last year, the airlines' frequent-flier programs awarded more than 13 million free tickets. Only four years ago, they gave away 6 million.

But while frequent-flier miles are easier to come by in the air and on the ground, the programs are becoming more complicated and more difficult to enjoy.

Here are the biggest frequent-flier program hassles—and how to keep from being disappointed...

Trap: Your frequent-flier miles expire. To be eligible for a free ticket on nearly any airline, you generally need 25,000 miles in its program. Yet travelers often miss free flying opportunities because their airlines' miles have expired before they could be used.

Example: American Airlines, Northwest and United require you to use your miles within three years of the time they were acquired.

While business travelers may not have to worry about expiration dates, since they are constantly earning miles, "infrequent" frequent fliers have trouble accumulating enough miles within a set period to earn a free ticket.

Solution: Try to stick with airlines whose miles do not expire.

Example: Continental, TWA and USAir do not require you to redeem your miles within a set period.

Trap: You've got the miles—but there are no available seats. When you "buy" a free ticket with 25,000 miles, you are actually buying a *discount* ticket. All discount tickets—whether paid for or awarded through frequent-flier programs—are capacity controlled, meaning the airline only makes a set number available on each flight. Unless such seats are available when you make your reservation, you may be out of luck.

Solution I: If you really want to leave on a particular date and you have many miles in your account, consider forking over more than 25,000 miles. On many airlines, if you trade 40,000 miles, "standard fare" seats become available to you.

Solution II: To improve your chances of getting a seat for 25,000 miles, make reservations as far in advance as possible—from three to six months before you plan on traveling.

Trap: The day on which you want to travel is a "blackout" date. On heavy travel days, airlines will not allow you to use 25,000 frequent-flier miles to purchase a discount ticket. Blackout dates vary by airline.

Strategy: Instead of planning your vacation and then trying to make airline reservations, establish a range of dates on which you are willing to depart and return and see what dates are available for an award ticket.

Again, you can always pay a premium in miles to get around a blackout date. Most airlines will charge you at least 40,000 miles for a domestic coach ticket and 70,000 miles for international flights.

Trap: Free tickets aren't always completely free. More than 30% of so-called free tickets have additional fees for services such as express mail delivery or electronic ticketing.

These fees must come out of your pocket and cannot be paid in miles. What's more, there is sometimes a cash charge if you want to change an award ticket.

Examples: American Airlines charges $50 if you want to change a ticket purchased with frequent-flier miles. And Delta and Northwest Airlines each charge $35 if you cancel a trip or change your itinerary.

Plan ahead: Avoid changing your travel plans once you've reserved an award ticket. If you've purchased the tickets months in advance, you probably don't need them sent to you via an expensive overnight package service.

Trap: Your earned miles weren't added to your account. As frequent-flier programs become more complex, the ways in which you can earn miles other than by flying are increasing.

Unfortunately, these programs may not always credit you for the miles you deserve. Even experienced travelers have found credit for a car rental, hotel room or other such bonus program missing from their frequent-flier account balances.

Solution: Keep track of the miles you've earned in a "mileage checkbook." Whenever you earn miles through a partnership program, log the amount into your book. Also, make copies of any receipts for purchases that earned you miles, and keep them in a separate folder.

When your monthly frequent-flier statement arrives, compare the amount of miles you've earned to the amount you have been credited. If there's a discrepancy, submit the copies of your receipts as evidence and ask to be credited for the missing miles.

Trap: You have plenty of miles—but the airline no longer serves your destination. Many people who save their frequent-flier miles for a once-in-a-lifetime vacation have been disappointed to find that their airline dropped service to that destination.

Example: Continental and Northwest Airlines recently stopped flying to Australia.

Frequent-flier program partners also change frequently. If you are saving miles for a flight on a partner airline or to an exotic location, there's no guarantee your airline will offer that service in the future.

Solution: It's better to use the miles you have now, rather than save them for the long term. But if you've already been saving for a specific destination on an airline whose miles do

not expire, you could continue to save—since there is the possibility that the airline will bring in another partner or reinstate service to that destination.

Example: Anyone disappointed when Continental stopped flying to Australia can now get there again, thanks to a new partnership with Malaysia Airlines.

Randy Petersen, editor of InsideFlyer, *4715-C Town Center Dr., Colorado Springs 80916. He is author of* The Official Frequent Flyer Guidebook. *AirPress.*

Car Rental Savvy

To cut car rental costs, ask about special deals when you call the toll-free numbers.

For example: Airline tie-ins…special rates if you use a particular credit card…group rates for organizations to which you belong. Ask about drop-off charges for one-way rentals—different companies charge different amounts.

Collision damage waiver: Don't pay extra for this if it is covered by your personal auto insurance or credit card.

Herbert J. Teison, publisher of Travel Smart, *40 Beechdale Rd., Dobbs Ferry, NY 10522.*

 # Hotel Penalty Self-Defense

Ask about *checkout penalties* when making hotel reservations—and when checking in.

Most hotels charge only for the nights you stay, even if you leave earlier than planned. But some have started to charge penalties for early departures—claiming they may have turned away other guests because they expected your room to be occupied. If you think your plans may change during a trip, avoid hotels that have early departure penalties.

Ed Perkins, editor of Consumer Reports Travel Letter, *101 Truman Ave., Yonkers, NY 10703.*

Better Film Buying

Decide what you will be shooting, and pick an ISO or ASA accordingly. These typically range from 25 to 1600. The higher the number, the faster the film—meaning less light is needed to take pictures. For shooting in sun, ISO/ASA 100 or lower is best…for overcast outdoor shooting or an indoor event with a flash, choose ISO/ASA 200…for dim light outdoors or indoors, use at least ISO/ASA 400. For shooting an event like a dinner party without using a flash, choose ISO/ASA 800 or 1600.

Charles Hagen, photography columnist for *The New York Times.*

Great Clothes… Best Shopping in New York City

Susan Dresner

While bargains on clothing can be found throughout Manhattan, the best-kept secrets in New York are the values found downtown—from Wall Street north to SoHo. Expect savings of 30% or more compared with prices at mainstream department stores. *Here are my favorite spots…*

WALL STREET AREA

●**Century 21** department store concentrates on name-brand designer apparel.

Examples: For women, designer lingerie can be had for a fraction of the cost at uptown stores. A Missoni mohair coat was found for $450 here versus $1,600 on Madison Avenue. High-end men's Italian suits by Armani, Barbera and Zegna are also discounted from uptown department store prices.

Shop during off-peak hours, from 10:30 am to noon and 3 pm to before 5 pm. There are no fitting rooms, so be sure of your size.

22 Cortlandt St., 212-227-9092.

LOWER EAST SIDE

●**Giselle Sportswear** offers a diversified collection of women's designer sportswear from the US, Germany and Italy.

Examples: During periodic sales, silk blouses go for less than $80…pants for less than $100…and jackets for less than $150. Fitting rooms are comfortable, and good fashion advice is offered by polite salespeople. Shipping is available.

143 Orchard St., 212-673-1900.

●**Jodamo International** specializes in European men's suits, outerwear, shirts and knits. Brands include Burberry, Missoni, Valentino, Versace, Zanetti…and Johnston Murphy shoes.

321 Grand St., 212-219-1039.

●**Orchard Bootery** stocks high-fashion footwear with European sizes—ideal for women with wider feet.

179 Orchard St., 212-966-0688.

Important: Call before you shop. Most stores in this area close around 4 pm on Friday and are closed all day Saturday. They are open on Sunday.

SOHO

●**Palma.** Retro styles with contemporary flair are designed and made in the shop. They are customized to fit different bodies and tastes. Coordinated jackets, skirts, pants, blouses, evening wear and accessories for men and women are priced reasonably. Seasonal sales.

Example: A sumptuous suit you'll never see on anyone else could be had for less than $500.

521 Broome St., 212-966-1722. Closed Mondays.

●**Paracelso** is a Middle East bazaar packed with all types of caftans, gypsy prints, embroidered vests and practical separates for larger women. Prices are usually less than $100.

414 W. Broadway, 212-966-4232. Open daily, 12:30 to 6:30 pm.

Susan Dresner, wardrobe and management consultant in New York specializing in alternative sources to get value for your money. She is author of *Shopping on the Inside Track.* Peregrine Smith.

Better Catalog Shopping

Many of the best deals in catalog shopping are not advertised, so always ask *before* ordering if the item you want is on sale.

Also: Ask the company if it will refund the difference if the item goes on sale within 30 days. Ask for unadvertised discounts, such as ones for new or repeat customers. Read information on shipping charges and return policies carefully. Always pay with a credit card in case of a later dispute.

Elysa Lazar of Lazar Media Group Inc., and coauthor of *Elysa Lazar's Shop by Mail*. Lazar Media Group.

Replace Children's Clothes for Free

Sears offers a nationwide guarantee program that replaces clothes bought at their stores or through their catalogs that wear out before a child outgrows them. The replacement would be for the same style, size and color originally purchased.

Cut Your Clothing Bills in Half by Rhonda Barfield, mother of four in St. Charles, MO. Lilac Publishing.

Which Is the Best Cellular Phone For Your Needs?

Andy Pargh

A working parent needs a phone to keep in touch with kids, spouse and office, usually during business hours. They will probably use it more than expected.

Favorite phone: **Ericsson AF738.** Lightweight. It offers nine one-button speed dials to quickly call the school, babysitter, doctor, etc. About 90 minutes of talk time. $100.* 972-583-0000.

Best service plan: One that offers ample monthly talk time, as well as call waiting. *Typical cost:* $80/month, including 240 minutes of talk time, plus 30 cents for each additional minute.

*Manufacturer's suggested retail prices. Phones are often discounted heavily or free with a signed service contract by cellular providers. Service plans may vary across the country and pricing is approximate.

Purpose: **Business traveler:** Often on the road and on the phone. Needs a lot of airtime, not only on weekdays but also during evenings and weekends.

Favorite phone: **Motorola Star TAC.** The world's smallest and lightest cell phone (3.1 ounces). Up to four hours of talk time. Has headset earpiece for hands-free operation. $1,000. 800-331-6456.

Best service plan: One with a lot of included airtime, plus features such as call forwarding, call transfer, conference calling and voice mail. Cellular paging option. *Typical cost:* About $195/month, plus 25 cents/minute and $2.50/month for paging service.

Purpose: **Emergency user.** Wants to have a phone only in case of an emergency.

Favorite phone: **SOS Phone.** Can make outgoing calls but can't receive them. The keypad has only three buttons. Calls are routed to an SOS operator who can connect you with up to 10 preprogrammed numbers you choose. $100. 800-767-3141.

Best service plan: Service is included with the phone. *Cost:* $8/month, plus $1.95/minute for calls made from the phone. 911 calls are free.

Purpose: **Self-employed.** Needs a versatile phone and a plan with limited free talk time and paging capability.

Favorite phone: **Nokia 2160.** Analog/digital phone that searches for the network system that can best handle your call. Includes voice mail with one-touch message retrieval...pager mode with text reception...up to 210 minutes of talk time. $200. 800-666-5553.

Best service plan: One with limited free airtime, and a paging service. *Typical cost:* $50/month, including 130 minutes of airtime, plus 45 cents/minute for each additional minute, $2.50/month for cellular voice mail and $15/month for paging.

Purpose: **Grandparent.** A light user. Needs a phone that's very easy to operate.

Favorite phone: **Motorola Teltak 250.** No-frills phone with large keys, easy-to-read display and nine-number speed dials for storing doctor, children, grandchildren and 911 info. *Talk time:* 45 to 180 minutes. $100. 800-331-6456.

Best service plan: Look for the cheapest plan available, even if it comes with little or no free talk time. *Also available:* Plans that allow one to two calls per day. *Typical cost:* $40/month, including 60 minutes of talk time, plus 45 cents/minute for each additional minute, and $2/month for a service like Mr. Rescue.

Purpose: Teen/babysitter. Has to stay in touch with parents after school, at night and on weekends. Will also use the phone to chat with friends.

Favorite phone: Mitsubishi AH-129. Low-cost, entry-level model that has easy-to-read display. Up to 2.5 hours of talk time...security features prevent the phone from being overused. $100. 706-654-9500.

Best service plan: Simple start-up plan with average airtime rates, plus free night and weekend calling. Also add a roadside assistance service like Mr. Rescue. *Cost:* About $37.95/month, including free night, weekend and holiday calling, plus 49 cents/minute for peak calls and $2/month for roadside assistance.

Andy Pargh, an independent product reviewer who writes *"The Gadget Guru,"* a syndicated newspaper column. He is also a contributing correspondent to the NBC *Today* show.

Better Deals on Cellular Phones

More companies are now offering monthly plans that don't require long-term contracts—and with rates nearly as good as contract rates. This allows you to choose a provider without being concerned that its rates will drop dramatically while you are stuck with a one- to two-year contract at higher prices. If you already have a contract, try to renegotiate—some companies will lower your costs to keep your business.

Robert Rosenberg, president of Insight Research, a telecommunications research firm, Livingston, NJ.

Caller ID Technology

Caller ID technology is now available in most states. Some caller ID units enable you to block others from knowing your phone number when you initiate a call—a benefit if you don't want to be telemarketed.

Cost: About $5 to $12 per month, plus the price of a unit—which ranges from free to about $150. Some older units may not work with the new features of your local telephone company's caller ID services. *More information:* Check with your phone company.

Neil Sachnoff, president of Telecom Clinic, 4402 Stonehedge Rd., Edison, NJ 08820.

Telephone Slamming Self-Defense

To beat telephone slamming—the scam in which your long-distance carrier is changed without your consent—ask your local telephone company to put a freeze on your "Primary Interexchange Carrier" (PIC) service.

Helpful: Call 700-555-4141 (toll-free) for a message giving the name of your current carrier. Check your long-distance bill every month to be sure the logo of the carrier of your choice is still there.

Trap: Mailings that look like contest entries and promise prizes or low rates. If you sign the entry form, you may be agreeing to change your long-distance carrier.

Bob Spangler, deputy chief of the enforcement division, FCC Common Carrier Bureau, Washington, DC.

How to Get the Best Deal on a PC

For the best deal on a PC, consider buying a refurbished machine. Computer technology is advancing so fast that last year's state-of-the-art models are often available at a fraction of their original price—offering all the computer power most families need for word processing, E-mail, games, tax preparation and more. Computers generally become available at half price just six months after manufacturers stop making them.

How to buy: Dealers of refurbished computers are listed in the Yellow Pages...or you can mail-order from firms such as Boston Computer Exchange (617-542-4414), Compu-D International in Van Nuys, California (818-787-3282) and American Computer Exchange in Atlanta (800-786-0717).

Patricia Robison, president of Computing Independence, 402 W. 20 St., New York 10011.

Bagged Cereal Costs Less Than Boxed Cereal

Recently introduced *Quaker Bagged Cereals* cost about $2 per bag compared with brand-name boxes, which can cost up to $4 or $5 per box for the same amount of cereal.

Woman's Day, 1633 Broadway, New York 10019.

Health Club Moneysavers

Try out the club before you join—most offer several free visits or short, low-cost trial memberships...join with a group of five or so friends to save up to 35%...pay a year's dues in advance to save up to 20%...ask about new-member perks, such as a free session with a personal trainer.

Also: If you need to take a long-term break for travel or other reasons, ask the club to freeze your membership and start it up again on your return. Then you won't have to pay for the time you're not using it.

Mary Monroe, communications director of the International Association of Fitness Professionals, San Diego.

Health Club Discount

If you live near your alma mater, you may be able to use the health center for very little cost. Many universities have special programs.

$avvy Discount$ Newsletter, 195 Old Nassau Rd., Box 96, Smyrna, NC 28579.

Low-Cost Pest Control

To eliminate ants, wash cabinets, floors and counters with equal parts of vinegar and water. For mosquito repellent, rub your skin with apple cider vinegar or citronella oil, available in hardware stores. Leave an open bottle of pennyroyal or citronella oil in rooms that attract mosquitoes.

Dean King, coauthor of *The Penny Pincher's Almanac: The Handbook for Modern Frugality*. Simon & Schuster.

Complaint Letters That Get Results

Keep your letter short. Type it instead of writing it by hand.

●**Document your problem with names**, dates and copies of receipts or bills.

●**Ask for a specific amount of money or other compensation.**

To get someone to accept responsibility: Address your letter to the chairman or a top executive—you can get a name by calling the company.

Follow-up: Call the recipient of the letter 10 days after you mail it.

Send This Jerk the Bedbug Letter by John Bear, PhD, an educational consultant in El Cerrito, CA. Ten Speed Press.

Car Dealer Trap

Don't let a car dealer copy your driver's license when you're negotiating for a car. The dealer will use it to get your credit report and find out how good a credit risk you are …and—if many of your payments have been late—you may not get the best financing deal.

Also: Each credit inquiry stays in your file. If you subsequently want a bank loan, you can be turned down if too many inquiries show up.

Self-defense: Offer to *show* the salesperson your license—but don't let it be copied.

David Solomon, editor of *Nutz & Boltz®*, Box 123, Butler, MD 21023.

Beware of College Credit Cards

College credit cards may start a spending and debt habit that can last a lifetime. Banks bombard college students with credit cards, trying to develop loyalty. Spending limits usually start at $500, but rise rapidly as cards are used. *Result:* Many students graduate with huge debt from their education and credit card use. Some have already ruined their credit ratings.

Self-defense: Teach precollege students about responsible use of credit cards. Paying bills on time could mean the difference between obtaining future credit and/or loans…and not.

Ruth Susswein, executive director of Bankcard Holders of America, 524 Branch Dr., Salem, VA 24153.

Overseas Credit Card Cushion

Before going abroad, consider overpaying your credit card bill by at least $500 to $1,000. This should provide a cushion so you don't exceed your limit—and will cut down on finance charges if you miss a payment.

The Frugal Globetrotter: Your Guide to World Adventure Bargains by Bruce Northam, a New Yorker who leads seminars on budget travel and has circled the globe five times. Fulcrum Publishing.

Successful Garage Sales

Attract attention to your garage sale with conspicuous roadside signs. *Especially attractive:* Paper plates with crepe-paper streamers attached.

50 Ways to Make the Most Money Having a Garage Sale by Cindy Skrzynecki, garage sale professional. CMS Publishing.

Buy Gasoline Early In the Morning

You'll get up to 5% more gas in the summer if you fill your tank before the hot sun has expanded the gas in the service station's fuel tanks.

Lee and Barbara Simmons, authors of *Penny Pinching: How to Lower Your Everyday Expenses Without Lowering Your Standard of Living.* Bantam Books.

Surprising Uses For Dental Floss

There are more uses for dental floss than just cleaning your teeth.

- **Tie poultry for cooking.**
- **Sew buttons on heavy coats.**
- **Repair mesh playpens.**
- **Hang pictures.**
- **Restring necklaces**, or let kids have some for bead-stringing play.
- **Remove cookies from a cookie sheet by sliding floss under them.**
- **Repair umbrellas.**
- **Cut cakes or cheese.**
- **Use instead of twist ties on microwave cooking bags.**

Vicki Lansky, author of *Another Use For…101 Common Household Items.* The Book Peddlers.

How to Seal Cans

Seal used paint cans more securely by first cleaning the groove along the top edge of the paint can. Next, lay a sheet of plastic food wrap over the top. Close the lid, and gently tap it into place with a hammer. The lid will be sealed tightly to keep paint from drying out, yet will pop right off the next time you're ready to paint.

The Family Handyman, 7900 International Dr., Minneapolis 55425.

Better Vegetable Storage

Keep fruits and vegetables fresh longer by putting a dry sponge in the crisper bin. The sponge absorbs the excess moisture that causes spoilage—for about 39¢, as compared with more expensive "vegetable crisper bags."

Martha M. Bullen and Darcie Sanders, authors of *Never Throw Out a Banana Again.* Crown Trade Paperbacks.

Keep Cut Flowers Fresher

Keep cut flowers fresher longer by either using the commercial preservatives sold by florists or brewing up a homemade batch yourself.

Mix: One pint warm water...one pint lemonade or a lemon-lime soft drink. Make enough to cover the lower three to four inches of the stem.

How it works: The sugar in the mixture supplies energy to the flowers...the citric acid helps preserve them.

Bonnie Wodin, owner of Golden Yarrow Landscaping Design, a garden consulting firm, Box 61, Heath, MA 01346.

Beware of Under-Karating

One-third of the gold jewelry being sold in the US is "under-karated."

Common example: A 10k piece is marked as 14k, and is priced at more than twice its worth.

Self-defense: Make sure the piece bears a manufacturer's trademark as well as a karat mark. Buy only from reputable jewelers, and ask for a detailed, descriptive receipt. Check with a jewelry appraiser if you wish to have a piece tested for gold content. Demand your money back if you find a piece has been under-karated.

Dorothy Leeds, author of *Smart Questions for Savvy Shoppers.* HarperCollins.

Moisturizer Secret

Plain old petroleum jelly is as good a moisturizer as much more expensive dry-skin products. And contrary to popular belief, petroleum jelly does not just sit on top of the skin. It penetrates the surface to help replace natural oils.

Ruby Ghadially, MD, assistant professor of dermatology at Veterans Administration Medical Center, 4150 Clement St., San Francisco 94121.

17

Your Car

How to Win the New-Car Game

Bob Elliston
Automotive Consumer Information Service Inc.

Buying or leasing a new car is an intimidating experience for most people. It's even becoming harder to determine if you're getting a fair deal or being taken for a ride.

In order to make a sound decision, you need to know that there are a number of tricks many salespeople employ to make as much on a deal as possible. *Their favorites—and self-defense strategies...*

TRICK #1: THE TENT SALE

Dealers often put up tents on their lots, hire some clowns and advertise big sales. At these events, salespeople will push to get you to buy a car on the spot. They'll quote you what seems to be a reasonable price and say, *This price is only good today because we're having a sale.*

The intent: To get you to make a quick decision.

Beware: The balloons, clowns and hoopla are there to break down your resistance and create the sense that there will never be another deal like this one.

Reality: There is almost no deal today that won't be there tomorrow. For anyone buying a car, every day is a sale day. So...always take some time to think about any deal when negotiating for a car.

Helpful: Wait to purchase a new car until the end of the month, when dealers are interested in moving inventory, not just making big profits. At this time of the month, they want to make their monthly sales numbers look better.

TRICK #2: THE PRICE FEELER

Salespeople want to know how much you are willing to spend on a car, and they have a variety of methods to get that information out of you. The most common tactic is to ask—*If I could get you out the door for $259 a month, could we write up a deal today?*

Sounds great—until you realize that the salesperson is structuring the deal around an 84-month finance program instead of the more typical 48-month loan. Once you give him/her your price, he has the negotiating advantage.

Defense: When the salesperson asks you how much you want to spend, counter by saying, *Before we talk about price, I would like to see if the car meets my needs.*

You should never reveal how much you are willing to pay. Once a salesperson knows how much money you have in your pocket, the negotiation has already begun—on his terms.

TRICK #3: THE TRADE-IN PLOY

The salesperson will want to know how much money you expect to get for your trade-in. His objective is to find out if you have any idea what your car is really worth. He wants to see if you have *underestimated* the value of the trade-in—and if there is an opportunity to get it at a rock-bottom price.

The salesperson might quote a number that is well below the car's actual worth, causing you to blurt out what you think the value of the car is.

Once you've done that, the salesperson has gained another negotiating advantage.

Defense: First, look up the wholesale value of your car in an automotive magazine, such as *Edmund's Used Car Price Guide,* or in an industry publication, such as *The Kelley Blue Book.* Both can be found at the library. Then, find out what your car is worth in the local market by asking for prices from two or three dealers. Also review classified ads for cars like yours. These national and regional prices will give you a better idea of how much you deserve for your trade-in.

TRICK #4: THE FACTORY INVOICE

Some car dealerships will offer their cars at $100 over the factory invoice. They'll even show you the invoice to prove it.

But what they won't show you is the factory-to-dealer incentive on those cars, which can be as high as $3,000 and represents a hidden profit for the dealers.

Strategy: Do your homework by checking *Automotive News.* You can find copies in most libraries. If its "Incentive Watch" confirms that there is factory money behind the car, use that fact in your negotiation.

TRICK #5: THE BUMP

After you and the salesperson have negotiated a price, he/she will say he has to check it with the sales manager.

He will probably come back and announce, *We're so close. If you could come up just a little. All I need is a buck a day.* If you budge once, he may try to get a few pennies a day more before settling the deal.

Keep in mind that those pennies will add up fast. A bump of 75 cents a day over a four-year finance period can amount to $1,095.

Strategies: Hold your ground. Say once and only once that you have made your last offer. Then start to leave. If he wants to sell the car, he won't let you go.

Another tactic is to write down your final offer and your phone number, hand the paper to the salesperson and tell him to give you a call when he can meet your price.

TRICK #6: THE F&I PERSON

After you have agreed on a price, you will be introduced to the Finance and Insurance (F&I) person.

His job is to sell you the *back end* of the deal, which is composed of dealer financing, special insurance, rust coating, paint protection and many other extras.

While you may think your negotiating is over, the F&I person's main objective is to squeeze more money out of you. In many cases, the dealership makes more money on the back end of the deal than on the car itself.

Consider the dealer financing if it is offered at a low rate, but pass on other back-end car options. Many salespeople will dangle options such as paint- and rust-protection programs, which seem inexpensive and tempting but can add up.

Better: If you intend to keep the car, an extended warranty may be worthwhile.

Bob Elliston, president of Automotive Consumer Information Service Inc., New York. He is author of *What Car Dealers Won't Tell You: The Insider's Guide to Buying or Leasing a New or Used Car.* Plume.

Fixed Car Pricing

No-haggle car pricing is fading. It was popularized by General Motors's Saturn division, which still uses it. But other dealers are finding that fixed prices turn off customers—who apparently believe they are not getting the best possible price unless they haggle.

Result: Of the 22,000 US car dealerships, only about 1,000 new-car dealerships have one-price strategies today—down from 2,000 in 1994.

W. James Bragg, CEO of Fighting Chance, a fee-based pricing information service for new-car buyers, Long Beach, CA.

Better Test-Drives

Before starting the car, make sure it is the exact version you want to buy—same engine, suspension, wheels, tires, transmission and seats…check for ease of access….examine all features to see if they add to comfort or detract from it.

While driving: Choose roads on which you want to drive—not ones the salesperson recommends…test highway acceleration, steering ease and braking…drive on a bumpy road to check out the suspension and to listen for noises.

David Solomon, a certified master automobile technician and editor of *Nutz & Boltz*®, an automotive newsletter, Box 123, Butler, MD 21023. He is author of *Nutz & Boltz® Automotive Survival Guide.*

Taking Delivery

Take delivery of a car in daylight rather than at night. Paint imperfections may not show up in artificial light.

When checking it over: Look for dents, scratches and acid blotches in paint…cracked headlight or taillight lenses…imperfections in window glass…paint irregularities or discolorations. Check for signs of paint on chrome or rubber trim—the original factory paints leave none of this overspraying. Open and shut everything, looking for badly fitting doors, windows or hood. Borrow a hose and test for watertightness. Turn the car on, and let it idle over a dry spot to check for engine leaks.

David Solomon, a certified master automobile technician and editor of *Nutz & Boltz*®, an automotive newsletter, Box 123, Butler, MD 21023. He is author of *Nutz & Boltz® Automotive Survival Guide.*

Car Dealer Tricks

Car dealer tricks add costs for trusting customers. *Avoid service contracts and extended warranties*—repairs rarely exceed the contract cost.

If leasing: The "capitalized cost"—used to calculate the lease—is often higher than the sticker price. Bargain for a lower one.

To find out what a car cost the dealer: Call Consumer Reports New Car Price Service (800-933-5555, $12 for one car…$10 each additional car).

Barbara Berger Opotowsky, president of the Better Business Bureau of Metropolitan New York.

When to Finance a Car

Finance a car instead of paying cash when auto-loan rates are lower than your expected investment returns. If you expect a four-year investment return after taxes of 7%—a reasonable rate for the stock market—and car loans are being offered at 5%, it makes sense to finance the car over four years. But if car loan rates are 9%, paying cash is a better deal.

Art Spinella, vice president of CNW Marketing/Research, which provides auto buying and leasing data to corporate clients, Box 744, Bandon, OR 97411.

The Better Way to Buy a Used Car

David Solomon

Buying a used car instead of a new one can be a terrific savings if you know what you're doing.

Here's how to avoid the major used-car traps and come out ahead...

●**Be specific about what you want.** Many people who buy used cars fail to first define for themselves exactly what they're looking for. Instead, they simply search for a car that meets their budget.

The problem with this strategy is that most people wind up settling for a car they don't really want.

Better: Before you shop for a used car, write down the price range you have in mind...the size of the car you are comfortable driving...the maximum age of the car...the options you are looking for...and, of course, the car's make.

Then consult the classified listings to see if the price you had in mind is in the ballpark. Otherwise, you could wind up wasting your time chasing a deal you'll never find.

It's also important to jot down your shopping priorities. If price is your overriding concern and you have a month or so to shop, you can save as much as 25% off the prices charged by used-car dealerships by buying from a private owner who advertises in the classified ads—after you have the car you are considering inspected.

But if you need a car quickly, you are better off shopping at a used-car dealer, where you can wrap up a deal on the spot. Most dealerships offer warranties on their used cars, which can provide you with *some* peace of mind.

Examples: Used-car superstores such as CarMax and AutoNation are popping up around the country, primarily in large metropolitan areas. If you live within striking distance of one, it's probably your best time-saver.

Like traditional used-car dealers, superstores offer warranties and can help with the paperwork and financing. But the superstores' larger selections and no-negotiation policies speed up the car-buying process.

In general, the superstores will be slightly more expensive than a dealership, because they're not willing to reduce their asking prices.

●**Research the local used-car market.** If you do decide to buy a car from a previous owner through a classified ad, spend at least a week scanning the used-car classifieds for cars that meet the criteria you outlined. This exercise will help you know a good deal when you see one.

When you find a car, play dumb and ask the seller direct questions. You're more than likely to get telling answers. *Here are a few good questions and ideal answers...*

●**"How was the car used—for local or highway driving?"** Also ask whether it was driven by an adult or a teenager. Highway miles and experienced drivers can take less out of a car.

●**"Are you the original owner?"** The fewer the owners, the better.

●**"Are there any liens on the vehicle?"** Ask if the title is clear. It will have a bank's name on it if it is not.

●**"What's wrong with the car?"** If the seller says it's in great shape, ask why it's being sold. If the scenario sounds fishy, move on.

●**"Has the car ever been in an accident?"** When you take the car to a mechanic, he should be able to tell when he checks underneath the car.

●**"Do you have the car's service receipts? Can I see them?"** It is unrealistic to expect receipts for everything, but you can also check with the dealer where the car is serviced to see if records exist.

●**Walk away from any car if the seller won't let you have the vehicle professionally inspected.** An inspection costs from $50 to $100 and provides a basic sense of the car's health...and gives you peace of mind that you won't be stuck with a lemon.

Having emissions tested is also important. Take the car to a dealer who sells that specific make. If you are purchasing the car from a dealer, bring it to another dealer of the same type of car.

A good mechanic can find $1,000 worth of legitimate repairs in a good used car. Certain parts might be worn and near the end of their life, or preventive maintenance might be overdue.

With a mechanic's written report and repair cost estimates, you can often talk a seller down to a better price.

Best: Take the vehicle to the local dealership of the model in question. Most will do a used-car check, including an emissions test—for $75 to $100.

Naturally, you'll only want to take this step with vehicles that seem like real prospects. Otherwise, the inspection costs can add up.

● **Be wary of odometer fraud and "curbstoners."** Unfortunately, used-car buyers can fall victim to fraud.

Here are two of the biggest scams today...

● **Odometers that have been rolled back.** Rollbacks are difficult to detect—which is why they are so common.

Example: The National Highway Traffic Safety Administration estimates that more than half of the used cars that were leased, used as rentals or were fleet cars have had their odometers rolled back.

Fortunately, there are ways to improve your odds of spotting such deception.

Helpful: When you test-drive the car, make sure the odometer moves correctly. Also look for service stickers inside the door or under the hood, where odometer readings are written down during periodic inspections. If they are missing, ask the owner why.

Check to see whether the mileage and dates listed on these service records make sense when compared with the odometer's current reading. *Look for two indicators of odometer tampering:* That services took place at mileage readings that haven't yet been reached, and that services that took place some time ago were at odometer readings near the current figure.

If you can't find any relevant mileage number—or any of these stickers appear altered—it's a bad sign.

Dealers who have serviced the car should have warranty or emissions-testing documents to back up the numbers.

If the car is supposed to have low miles, check for undue wear to the driver's seat or wear on steering wheel equipment, suspension and rubber parts.

● **"Curbstoners."** When unscrupulous dealerships come across a salvaged car or a trade-in that's in such bad shape that it won't even survive a three-day warranty, they sometimes try to sell it through a "curbstoner"—someone who lists a used car in the classified ads without acknowledging his connection with the dealership.

By selling the car this way, the dealership has no warranty to worry about—since individual sellers of used cars don't offer them. Vehicles sold through curbstoners typically are the worst of all used cars.

Reason: Their flaws have been professionally hidden, and the cars often appear to be in immaculate condition...at least superficially.

Steps to take to avoid such sellers...

● **Be wary if there's more than one vehicle in the classifieds** under the seller's telephone number. At the very least, ask the seller how he came to have more than one car for sale.

● **Be suspicious if the seller's name or address does not match the name and address on the car's title**—and don't fall for the line "I'm selling the car for a relative who has moved away."

David Solomon, a certified master automobile technician and editor of *Nutz & Boltz®*, an automotive newsletter, Box 123, Butler, MD 21023. He is author of *Nutz & Boltz® Automotive Survival Guide.*

Car Leasing Is Growing Faster and Faster... And Trickier and Trickier

Remar Sutton

More than one-third of all people who shop for a new car wind up leasing instead of financing or paying cash.

Yet leasing a car isn't as simple as it seems. Many people who lease overlook big problems, causing them to pay more than they should or to lease the wrong car for their needs.

Here are the latest car-leasing traps and how to avoid them...

Trap: Falling for tricky ad claims. Many new car-leasing ads are similar to the classic bait-and-switch. *Reasons...*

● **Many advertised terms apply to cars that you would not actually want to lease.** These cars may not have the options you desire, such as power seats. Or the dealership may not have any of the advertised vehicles available when you arrive.

Example: Recently, 14 states filed lawsuits charging one carmaker with unfair and deceptive advertising practices. The carmaker promoted "zero down" leases that actually required $1,000 to lease the vehicles.

Your Car

• **The dealer says that the advertised deal is good only for those people who have excellent credit records.** If a late payment on a credit card bill turns up in your history, you may be disqualified from the deal.

• **Those ultra-low advertised monthly payments of $149 or $199 often come with annual limits** of 10,000 miles. Most drivers exceed this limit—and then must pay high penalties.

Solution: Make sure the lease is based on how many miles you actually plan to drive—plus a cushion of 10%. Be sure to ask yourself whether you expect your driving habits to stay the same over the term of the lease. If not, adjust the miles accordingly.

Trap: Negotiating for the wrong vehicle. Most people are aware that it is smart to negotiate the purchase price of a car first and only later tell the dealer that you want to lease rather than buy. But this plan doesn't work if you lease the wrong vehicle.

Example: You'll get a bad deal if you are talked into an expensive options package that you didn't want in the first place...or a car that has been sitting on the dealer's lot for a long time.

There are two reasons not to lease a car that has been aging on the lot...

• **There may be something wrong with the car.**

• **The value of the car declines faster when you lease late in the model year.** As soon as the model year changes, the car will depreciate significantly. That is a problem if you plan to buy the car later and then sell it.

Helpful: Find out when the dealer took delivery of the car by checking the sticker on the car window. The bill date tells you when the vehicle was built. The dealer probably received it two months later.

To find out when the model year began, ask the dealer when the next model will reach the lot. If you don't get a straight answer—or you get an answer that doesn't seem to make sense—call the car manufacturer for the information. Ideally, you want to lease the newest car you can find with only the options that you want.

Trap: Negotiating the wrong price and getting a bad deal. A lot of dealers will let you nego-

tiate a good purchase price—and then gladly agree to the price when you say you want to lease rather than buy.

Reason: The price that you negotiated is not the price on which a lease is based.

Instead, determine the capitalized cost of the vehicle—which includes all taxes, fees, service contracts and costs to insure it. Then compare the capitalized figure with those of several other dealers who sell the same make of car.

To do this effectively, ask several different car dealers to give you an unsigned contract that spells out the lease terms so that you can comparison shop.

Such a request is not unrealistic. Approximately half of all dealers that you approach will do this for you.*

Trap: Failing to make sure that the amount you received for your trade-in is built into your lease agreement. Not all dealers are above-board when it comes time to deduct from the lease the amount they've credited you for trading in your present car.

In fact, many dealers refuse to disclose the trade-in allowance because they want to increase their profit by keeping the money from your trade-in, rather than giving it to you. Such a practice is not uncommon.

Example: Recently, the Florida attorney general recouped thousands of dollars for consumers bilked this way.

Solution: Insist on knowing the exact trade-in value of your car so you can comparison shop.

How to determine the trade-in allowance: The *net trade-in allowance* line on the contract equals the trade-in value of the vehicle less the amount still owed on it. So you have to know that amount to determine if you're getting a good deal—and then make sure it is listed as a separate item on your lease.

*For more information on how to get a great lease, consult The Reality Checklist for Auto Leasing. It is available from Reality Checklist, Box 7648, Atlanta 30357. Include a self-addressed, stamped, business-sized envelope. Or consult the Internet at gopher.essential.org.

Remar Sutton, an automotive consultant and consumer advocate who has served as an expert witness on automotive matters for the attorneys general of several states. For the past 11 years, he has directed a study of the selling and leasing techniques used by car dealers. He is author of *Don't Get Taken Every Time: The Insider's Guide to Buying or Leasing Your Next Car or Truck.* Penguin.

294

Car-Leasing Trap

The residual value in your lease contract could be less than the car's actual value. Research your car's value at the end of a lease. Figure out the difference between the price you could get if you sold it yourself—and the residual value. If your car is worth more than the lease says, you can buy it, line up a buyer and resell for a quick profit—or negotiate the difference into a new lease.

W. James Bragg, CEO of Fighting Chance, a fee-based pricing information service for new-car buyers, Long Beach, CA.

What to Do When Your Car Lease Is Up

At the end of a car lease, it makes sense to buy "your" car if you like it and its market price is about the same as the residual value established when the lease began. You will then have a good used car whose quirks you already know. Buying the car and reselling it makes sense only if the street value of the car is significantly higher than its residual value. Check used-car guides and classified ads to find out.

Kurt Allen Weiss, former car salesman in New Jersey and author of Have I Got a Deal for You? *Career Press.*

How to Help Your Car Last...and Last...and Last

David Solomon

To avoid having to buy or lease a new car, take good care of the one you own. And save money on unnecessary repairs by doing some simple preventive maintenance.

MOST IMPORTANT
●**Change the oil and the filter at least every 5,000 miles**—or every three months—which-

ever comes first. Motor oil quickly becomes contaminated by dirt and combustion by-products. All oil filters do a satisfactory job, but they are not overwhelmingly effective at screening out by-products after thousands of miles.

Synthetic oil is better than petroleum oil. Use the grade recommended in your owner's manual.

My favorite brand: Redline, 800-624-7958.

Important: Never have the oil changed without changing the filter as well. Otherwise, the dirty filter element will not filter the new oil.

Best: A dealer-supplied filter or a national brand such as Champion, Hastings or Purolater.

●**Have your radiator flushed and refilled every two years**—or every 25,000 miles—whichever comes first. Most radiators become clogged with sediment and mineral deposits that must be power-rinsed by your mechanic.

Best: Schedule the flushing for late autumn, so you'll end up with a fresh fill-up of antifreeze for the winter. Or use a long-life coolant such as DexCool, which lasts five years.

Essential: When having your radiator flushed, ask your mechanic to remove the thermostat, a step that is often overlooked. Otherwise, only the radiator will be flushed—and not the engine block. The old thermostat should then be replaced.

Pay strict attention to the maintenance schedule in your owner's manual. Make sure that the dealer or mechanic who does the work actually performs the recommended services—air and fuel filter changes, tire rotations, spark plug replacement, etc.

●**Have an engine block heater installed** if you live where temperatures drop below 32°F for weeks at a time. Starting a freezing cold engine can cause tremendous wear and tear.

A block heater will substantially extend your engine's life. The heater is a small, simple electric unit that is attached to the engine and plugged into an electrical socket overnight. Heaters typically cost around $25 to $50.

The heater will keep the engine's coolant warm, which results in rapid, more effective lubrication throughout the engine and easier starting.

Better way: Have the heater installed when you buy the car. Or have your mechanic install it now. It is not an aftermarket accessory that is clamped to the engine. Each manufacturer makes one appropriate for its vehicles. The dealer must remove a freeze plug from the engine block and replace it with the block heater.

●**Exercise your parking brake and antilock braking system.** If you always leave your car in "park" and never apply the handbrake or emergency brake, the cables could rust and lock, leaving you without an emergency brake when you need it. Similarly, you could drive for years without ever needing your Antilock Braking System (ABS) to make a panic stop, in which case the ABS valves and line could collect sludge and become inoperative.

Strategy: Once a month, on a safe, empty road or in a parking lot, apply the brakes hard enough to force the braking system to cycle. This exercise will ensure that fresh brake fluid flushes the system.

Helpful: Pick a rainy day and an empty parking lot to perform the test, so you don't have to brake so vigorously to skid the tires.

●**Have the timing belt replaced every 60,000 to 100,000 miles.** Don't try to change it yourself. The timing belt is inside the engine and not immediately visible or easily reached. It should be replaced by a mechanic. *Cost:* Usually $250 to $300.

Every car has a different mileage cutoff point at which its timing belt must be replaced. Check your owner's manual or call your dealer for the correct information.

Danger: If a timing belt is neglected and breaks, the engine will stop and costly engine damage could result.

●**Use only the correct gasoline type for your car.** Check the owner's manual. Paying extra for premium gas if your engine is designed for regular is a waste of money. An engine can only use the octane for which it is tuned.

Worse, premium gasoline can actually decrease engine performance. The average car can't vaporize many lower-volatility premiums and simply pushes the unburned gas out the exhaust, increasing emissions and leading to poor combustion, stalling and hesitation.

Beware: Don't overfill your gas tank. When a self-service pump's automatic shutoff mechan-

ism first clicks off, stop filling. Overfueling saturates the evaporative emissions canister—a device that is intended to trap gas fumes from the tank before they pollute the atmosphere. It can cost $100 to replace.

●**Use only brushless car washes.** Commercial car washes that use spinning brushes or cloth miters damage your car's paint.

During the winter, when the roads are saturated with rust-creating salt, a useful resource is a commercial do-it-yourself car wash that uses a high-pressure, warm-water spray wand. Once a week is adequate, but—of course—avoid doing the task on bitter cold days.

Concentrate on the underside and wheel wells of the car rather than the superficial cosmetics, to power-rinse away metal-eating salt deposits trapped in crannies and crevices under the car.

David Solomon, a certified master automobile technician and editor of *Nutz & Boltz*®, an automotive newsletter, Box 123, Butler, MD 21023. He is author of *Nutz & Boltz*® *Automotive Survival Guide.*

Car Care Traps

Changing the oil is the most neglected routine car service.

Car owners also often fail to take care of cooling and emissions systems and wheel alignment.

Routine maintenance of these systems—including oil changes at intervals specified in the owner's manual—can make a car last longer, with far less chance of major repair bills for severe engine damage.

Donna Wagner, director of operations and spokesperson for the Car Care Council, 1 Grande Lake Dr., Port Clinton, OH 43452.

Most Cars Do Not Need High-Octane Gasoline

Despite the ads, premium gas doesn't provide more power, improve engine performance, reduce wear or increase mileage. Octane is simply a measure of how quickly fuel burns.

Different engines are designed to run on different octane fuel.

Helpful: Fine-tune your engine by trying different grades. Check the owner's manual to see what the manufacturer recommends for your car. If it says 87 octane, that's what you should buy.

Savings: Up to 17 cents per gallon.

North Jersey Traveler, 418 Hamburg Tpke., Wayne, NJ 07470.

Car Service Trap

Never have your car extensively serviced immediately before you go on an out-of-town road trip.

It might seem logical to have your car carefully prepped for a major drive, but if a newly replaced or serviced component is going to fail, it will probably do so during the first several hundred miles of driving.

You're better off "breaking in" the part by driving those miles near your house over several days.

David Solomon, a certified master automobile technician and editor of *Nutz & Boltz®,* an automotive newsletter, Box 123, Butler, MD 21023. He is author of *Nutz & Boltz® Automotive Survival Guide.*

Do Your Own Inspection

Inspect your car yourself before taking it for a state safety inspection. Check tires, and replace severely worn ones. Make sure exterior lights, turn signals and brake lights work. Check high beams and emergency flashers. Be sure windshield wipers work properly and are not worn. Test the horn. Be sure the parking brake works smoothly. Check the muffler and exhaust system for rust and looseness. Test shocks and struts by stepping outside and bouncing the front end of the car until it goes up and down—it should only bounce once.

Eric Peters, automotive reporter for *The Washington Times,* writing in *Consumers' Research Magazine,* 800 Maryland Ave. NE, Washington, DC 20002.

Good Bumpers... Bad Bumpers... Big Difference

Brian O'Neill
Insurance Institute for Highway Safety

When shopping for a new car, most people rarely consider the effectiveness of the car's bumper when making a decision.

Yet bumper performance is one of the factors that insurance providers use to set rates.

What we found out about bumpers...

LESS PROTECTION

We put almost two dozen 1996 vehicles through four crash tests at 5 mph. The difference in performance between two different types of bumpers are enormous.

Example: The damage suffered by the car with the most resistant bumper—the midsized Honda Accord—was $6,740 less than that suffered by the worst vehicles—the Isuzu Rodeo and Honda Passport sport utility vehicles.

Sadly, bumper quality has declined over the past 15 years, reducing the number of cars that have even respectable bumpers.

Reason: In 1981, the government relaxed its standards in an attempt to give Detroit a break. Back then, bumpers were required to withstand 5-mph crashes (with no body or bumper damage). Now the standard is only 2.5 mph—and bumper damage (but not body damage) is allowed.

This means that today even a fairly gentle bump can cause $1,000 to $3,500 in damage if you own a car with bumpers that can't withstand a 2.5-mph fender bender.

In comparison, if you have a car with one of the best bumpers, the damage caused by the same crash might be just $600 to $800.

CRASH-TEST SURPRISES

When trying to determine the quality of a car's bumper, don't go by appearances. They can be misleading. Bumper quality has nothing to do with how heavy a bumper looks or the price of the car.

THE BEST BUMPERS

Here's what it cost to repair 1996 midsized four-door cars after four crashes at only 5 mph:

Honda Accord/*$1,433*
Toyota Camry/*$2,328*
Saab 900/*$1,734*
Volkswagen Passat/*$2,390*
Chevrolet Cavalier/*$1,795*
Chevrolet Lumina/*$2,629*
Subaru Legacy/*$1,966*
Ford Taurus/*$2,814*
Mazda Millenia/*$2,031*
Mitsubishi Galant/*$3,121*
Volvo 850/*$2,131*
Ford Contour/*$3,188*
Chrysler Cirrus/*$2,276*
Nissan Maxima/*$3,605*

THE WORST BUMPERS

All sport utility vehicles performed worse than passenger cars:

Chevrolet Blazer and GMC Jimmy/*$4,168*
Ford Explorer/*$5,639*
Jeep Grand Cherokee/*$5,763*
Land Rover Discovery/*$6,555*
Toyota 4Runner/*$7,147*
Isuzu Rodeo and Honda Passport/*$8,173*

Brian O'Neill, president of the Insurance Institute for Highway Safety, a research organization funded by automobile insurance companies to search for ways to reduce human and property losses in automobile accidents. Its complete bumper-test report is available by writing to 1005 N. Glebe Rd., Arlington, VA 22201.

Parking Lot Self-Defense

About 20% of all low-speed urban-area auto accidents occur in parking lots.

Reduce risk by: Driving slowly and defensively in parking lots, anticipating that pedestrians or exiting cars may appear unexpectedly...Not parking alongside trucks—they block your vision, and other drivers' views of you...

Not parking at the end of rows or aisles, where your car is exposed and more likely to be hit... Not parking next to beat-up cars—they don't get that way by themselves.

George Hensel, president of California Driving School Inc., 111 W. Pomona Blvd., Monterey Park, CA 91754.

Better Remote Car Locks

Thieves can record the radio signal you send from your car's remote key lock to your vehicle...then play back the signal after you leave to unlock your car. New security systems use infrared transmitters—instead of radio frequencies—making them much more difficult to steal because the signal can't be recorded.

Also: The engine will not start without the correct code. The new security system is available on some 1997 BMW, Mercedes and other luxury models.

Kim Hazelbaker, senior vice president of the Highway Loss Data Institute, Arlington, VA.

Air Bag Self-Defense

Sit back. Raise the seat and lower the steering wheel so you are at least 10 inches from the wheel and can still reach the pedals. If necessary, consider pedal extenders that clamp onto pedals. *Cost:* $125 to $165. *More information:* National Mobility Equipment Dealers Association, 800-833-0424.

Also important: Wear seat belts and shoulder belts at all times. They keep you in position, away from the deploying air bag.

Susan Ferguson, vice president of research at the Insurance Institute for Highway Safety, 1005 N. Glebe Rd. Arlington, VA 22201.

18

Self-Defense

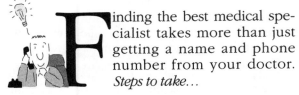

Questions to Ask When Your Doctor Recommends a Specialist

Charles Inlander
The People's Medical Society

Finding the best medical specialist takes more than just getting a name and phone number from your doctor. *Steps to take...*

● **First ask your doctor why you are being referred to this particular specialist.**

Trap: Referrals are often professional courtesies. This may mean that a fellow colleague isn't likely to contradict your doctor's recommendations or that you may not be getting the name of the best person to confirm a diagnosis or treat your condition.

Important: Find out if your doctor knows the specialist's success rate in treating your problem. This is basic information that your doctor should know about the doctor to whom he is referring you.

● **Ask your doctor for a list of all the likely medical causes of your condition before you seek another opinion.** Similar symptoms can exist for different problems. Find out from your doctor the most likely causes of your problem ...and the most remote causes. This information will help you when you seek another opinion.

Example: Hearing loss can indicate that you have damage to the eardrum—or a brain tumor. But the specialists who can diagnose and treat these conditions are in different fields. One is an ear, nose and throat specialist...and the other one is a neurologist or a neurosurgeon.

You can save yourself a lot of time and money by learning—and prioritizing—all your options before you shop around.

● **Once you have a diagnosis, find out how many times the specialist has treated your kind of problem within the last year.** Volume is critical, although the ideal volume depends on the problem being treated. For common problems, such as heart surgery, a specialist

299

should treat hundreds of people a year. For rarer conditions, 10 to 20 cases is acceptable.

If the specialist's office is reluctant to share this information, consider seeking treatment elsewhere.

• **Get the name of a specialist who can give you a second opinion.** Up to 80% of second opinions on *treatments* don't agree with the first. Twenty percent of second opinions disagree with *diagnosis*. That's why it's important to seek several opinions.

If you have trouble finding someone, call the national headquarters of that specialty's association for a few names.

If you live in a rural or suburban area that doesn't have a concentration of specialists with the breadth of experience you need, it's worth it to get in the car or on a plane and go somewhere that does.

• **Find out if there are other treatment options.** Get a treatment plan from each doctor whom you see for an opinion. Then phone a prominent medical school in your state and ask to speak to the person who chairs the department under which your problem falls—for example, the orthopedic surgery department if surgery has been recommended for a knee injury. He/she may be willing to tell you about recent medical advances in the field. You can also do your own research through a local medical school library or an on-line medical database.

Charles Inlander, president of The People's Medical Society, a consumer health advocacy organization, 462 Walnut St., Allentown, PA 18102. He is author of *Take This Book to the Hospital With You: A Consumer's Guide to Surviving Your Hospital Stay.* People's Medical Society.

Prescription Self-Defense

Mistakes on prescriptions are made *17 million* times a year. *To ensure that you don't take the wrong medication…*

When your doctor prescribes a drug, have him/her write down—on a separate piece of paper from the prescription—the exact name of the drug…dosage…number of times a day you should take it…and any side effects you should call to his attention. When you fill the prescription, compare the label with the doctor's note—and talk with your doctor about any discrepancies.

Caution: Mail-order or managed-care companies sometimes substitute drugs. Get your doctor's approval before you take a substitute.

Let your doctor know about *all* medications you use regularly—including over-the-counter drugs.

Charles Inlander, president of The People's Medical Society, a consumer health advocacy organization, 462 Walnut St., Allentown, PA 18102. He is author of *Take This Book to the Hospital With You: A Consumer's Guide to Surviving Your Hospital Stay.* People's Medical Society.

Donating Blood to Yourself

Donating blood to yourself prior to surgery is the best way to avoid the small risk of getting a disease through a transfusion. Called *autologous blood donation*, it involves donating one unit of blood every three or four days. Each donation takes between one and two hours, and blood can be stored up to 42 days before surgery. The amount of blood needed varies by type of surgery.

Examples: Primary hip surgery may require only two units of blood, while revision hip surgery usually requires four or more.

Joseph C. McCarthy, MD, associate professor of orthopaedic surgery at Tufts University, Boston, and attending staff orthopaedic surgeon at New England Baptist Hospital, Boston.

Safer than Seldane

The popular anti-allergy medication has caused at least 40 cases of serious heart-rhythm abnormalities, mainly when taken with the antibiotic erythromycin or certain other drugs. Consult your physician about alternatives such as Claritin, Zyrtec or Allegra—which are *not* associated with heart-rhythm abnormalities.

Andrea Apter, MD, cochair of the pharmaco-therapeutics committee of the American Academy of Allergy, Asthma and Immunology and associate professor of medicine at the University of Connecticut Health Center, Farmington.

Carbon Monoxide Self-Defense

Carbon monoxide (CO) detectors are a must for any home with a furnace or appliance that uses oil, gas, wood or coal...or where cars are parked in an attached garage. Poisonous CO gas produced by incomplete combustion of any of these fuels is colorless, odorless and tasteless...and kills several hundred people every year. The CO detector should be installed near the bedrooms. Also consider for children's play areas. *Cost:* About $30.

If the CO alarm sounds: Open the windows and doors. If anyone feels faint or ill, leave the house immediately—early symptoms of CO poisoning may include headache, nausea and fatigue. Then have your appliances checked to find the source of carbon monoxide.

Rose Ann Soloway, RN, MSEd, administrator of the American Association of Poison Control Centers, 3201 New Mexico Ave. NW, Ste. 310, Washington, DC 20016.

Training Kids To Be Safe

Safety matters most—more than being polite or avoiding embarrassment. Communicating this to your children can be crucial to keeping them safe. Train them to yell deeply and loudly if anyone ever tries to grab them.

Raising Safe Kids in an Unsafe World by Jan Wagner, founder of SAFE-T-CHILD, Austin, TX. Avon Books.

Milk Danger

Milk plays a role in pregnancy-related high blood pressure (preeclampsia).

Recent study: High blood pressure was common in pregnant women who drank less than one glass of whole milk a day...and in those who drank three or more glasses a day. It was rare in women who drank one or two glasses a day.

Theory: The condition is triggered by extra fat from too much milk...and by low calcium from not enough.

Self-defense: Pregnant women should have one or two glasses of skim milk a day.

Barbara E. Richardson, assistant professor of epidemiology at Texas A&M University, College Station. Her study of 9,291 women was published in the *American Journal of Epidemiology*, 2007 E. Monument St., Baltimore 21205.

Household Injuries

The average home has many potential problem zones for children.

Frequent injuries include falls down stairs... off beds...out of windows...and banging into sharp furniture corners. *General prevention:*

●**Install gates at tops of stairways.**

●**Carpet stairs to prevent slipping.**

●**Place guards on windows and rails on children's beds.**

●**Buy doorknobs that don't lock**, so kids can't accidentally lock themselves in a bedroom or bathroom.

●**Place bumpers on objects with sharp-edged corners.**

Jill Baren, MD, assistant professor of surgery/emergency medicine and pediatrics at Yale University School of Medicine. She is a contributor to the book *Now I Know Better: Kids Tell Kids About Safety.* The Millbrook Press.

Automatic Garage Door Hazard

Openers designed to make the door reverse direction if it hits a solid object may not reverse when coming down on a child. *Result:* Between 1974 and 1995, at least 85 children died or suffered permanent brain damage from garage doors that didn't reverse. Since 1993, federal standards have been improved to address this problem, but most doors in operation are older.

Self-defense: Test your door frequently with a large unopened roll of paper towels—if the door doesn't reverse, consult the manual or service person to see if the door can be adjusted. If an automatic door opener cannot be adjusted, it should be replaced.

Other safeguards: Locate the garage door button out of the reach of children—at least six feet off the ground...keep remote controls away from children...do not run under the closing door...and wait for the garage door to close completely before leaving the premises.

Robert L. Kriel, MD, pediatric neurologist at Hennepin County Medical Center, Minneapolis.

Bicycle Theft Self-Defense

Always take basic security measures, such as locking your bike and parking it only in safe, secure places...brand the bike with a security number—such as a driver's license number—that is stamped or scratched onto the bike frame.

Avoid: Stickers with identification numbers —they can be easily removed.

Best: Kryptonite brand locks—believed by many law-enforcement officials to be the best available—has introduced a new three-foot chain lock (called *The New York Chain*) that the company claims is tougher by far but costs about $104 and weighs about six pounds.

Alternative: Even a cheap, $10 to $20 lock may deter most thieves.

David Cope, co-owner of Buzz's Cycle Shop, Old Greenwich, CT.

Bike Helmets Prevent Injuries—Even in *Big* Collisions

New study: Wearing a helmet reduces the risk of head injury by 69%...the risk of severe brain injury by 74%...and the risk of eye, ear, nose and forehead injuries by 65%. Helmets are important for all age groups.

Diane Thompson, epidemiologist at the Harborview Injury Prevention and Research Center, Seattle, who led a study of more than 3,000 cyclists treated for injuries at seven hospitals.

New Bike Helmet Makes Cycling Safer

Developed for mountain bikers, the new design helps keep the helmet in place, especially while the rider is going downhill or if he/she is thrown in an accident.

Secret: A strap that fits above the nape of the neck and locks into a plastic disk. The strap must be worn along with the traditional chin strap. Now available from most major helmet manufacturers. *Cost:* $30 to $130.

Ken Alder, owner of Cycle Dynamics, 12 Riversville Rd., Greenwich, CT 06831.

Iron Danger

Although iron is essential for normal, healthy cells, too much can raise risk of cancer. And in patients who already have the disease it can cause tumors to grow faster. In one study, hepatitis B patients who had high levels of serum ferritin (iron) had a 50% higher risk for liver cancer.

Self-defense: Ask your doctor to check your ferritin level at your next checkup.

Hie-Won L. Hann, MD, professor of medicine at Jefferson Medical College, Philadelphia.

Pesticide Danger

Children eat a less diversified diet than adults. So any contaminant in foods eaten by children is likely to become more concentrated in their bodies than it would in adults.

Since children's bodies are smaller and they eat more food per unit of body weight because they are growing, they could end up with much higher levels of exposure.

Example: Kids consume more fruit juice and mashed vegetables than adults do—risking higher exposure to fungicides.

Self-defense: Wash fresh fruits and vegetables before serving them. Pesticides may be encased in wax and often can be removed only by peeling. If you can scrape wax off with your nail, peel the food.

John Wargo, PhD, associate professor of forestry, political science and environmental studies at Yale University, New Haven, CT, and author of *Our Children's Toxic Legacy.* Yale University Press.

Lyme Disease Warning

To guard against Lyme disease: *Stay on the trail* when hiking in wooded areas. Ticks live in low bushes and tall grass. *Tick-proof your yard* by clearing brush and leaves and making sure woodpiles are in sunny areas. *Wear protective clothing* when outdoors. Light-colored long-sleeved shirts and long pants tucked into boots or socks will help you spot ticks before they bite. *Use a tick repellent* containing *DEET* or *permethrin.*

J. Stephen Dumler, MD, associate professor of pathology at Johns Hopkins Medical Institutions, Baltimore.

Vitamin C Danger

Chewable forms of vitamin C (ascorbic acid) may be bad for your teeth. Breath mints, chewing gum, etc., fortified with C are now being sold as easy ways to get your daily dose of this key nutrient.

Danger: Repeated exposure to any acid—including ascorbic acid—can corrode your tooth enamel.

Most damaging: Habitual use of products containing more than 500 mg of C per piece.

Sheldon Nadler, DMD, a dentist in private practice in New York City.

Osteoporosis Drug Danger

The new osteoporosis drug *alendronate* (Fosamax) can trigger severe throat irritation (esophagitis). Taken incorrectly, it causes difficulty swallowing or a burning or squeezing sensation in the throat, as well as chest pain.

Self-defense: Take alendronate first thing in the morning, with at least six ounces of water. Remain standing or sitting for at least 30 minutes and until after your first meal of the day. Do *not* take alendronate while lying down or if you have a preexisting ailment of the esophagus.

Piet C. de Groen, MD, consultant in gastroenterology and internal medicine at the Mayo Clinic, Rochester, MN. His study of 1,213 people, published in *The New England Journal of Medicine,* 10 Shattuck St., Boston 02115, revealed adverse effects from taking alendronate.

Tap Water Danger

Contact lens wearers should avoid cleaning their lenses with tap water—especially when abroad. Water can harbor an amoeba that causes *keratitis,* a rare but potentially blinding eye infection.

Symptoms: Eye pain…sensitivity to light…swelling…corneal sores.

Self-defense: Follow proper disinfection procedures.

Thomas J. Byers, PhD, professor emeritus of molecular genetics at Ohio State University, Columbus.

Top Security Expert Tells How to Keep Burglars Away

Robert Bonifas
Alarm Detection Systems, Inc.

When I am called to a client's home, I first help identify the factors that make the home vulnerable to burglars. *Prime targets...*

●**Modest homes in affluent neighborhoods.** Thieves will see your house as an easy mark, since you're less likely to have the proper security system installed.

●**Homes with signs of wealth.** Kids who fix their $800 bicycles in the yard and a caterer who delivers family meals twice a week are tip-offs.

●**People with subscriptions to collectibles magazines** attract thieves who check mailboxes for such publications.

●**Bankers, jewelers and other people** whose jobs require them to deal directly with cash or valuables.

●**Current managers at companies that have downsized.** Your home can be vulnerable to theft, sabotage and other crimes if your company is undergoing major labor changes.

●**Anyone who has just won a bitter lawsuit** against someone who is seething with revenge.

PROTECTING YOUR HOME

●**Door locks.** Many home owners rush out to buy fancy electronic devices but overlook the importance of great door locks. Heavy-duty locks can be highly effective because about 60% of break-ins occur through doors.

My favorite: Medeco. The locks are nearly impossible to pick and the keys are hard to copy. *Cost:* About $130 each, installed.

●**Door and motion detectors.** These systems detect intruders, setting off an alarm on the premises and alerting the police or a private security agency.

My favorite brands: Ademco Security Detection Systems...and Fire Burglary Instruments (F.B.I.). *Cost:* One motion detector and sensors on two or three doors typically run $500 to $700 plus about $25 a month for monitoring.

Important: Before buying a system that triggers a police response, ask the vendor to let you speak with other home owners who have it.

●**Window sensors.** If you have many ground floor windows, install alarms on the windows themselves. *My favorite brand:* International Electronics Inc. *Cost:* $60 to $120 per window.

Also, take a list of the electronic devices you're considering to your local police station for opinions. They won't make specific recommendations, but they'll tell you about any brands or vendors with which they've had trouble.

Robert Bonifas, president of Alarm Detection Systems Inc., a security consultant and supplier in Aurora, IL. He is a past president of the Central Station Alarm Association, a group in Bethesda, MD, that monitors security industry standards.

How to Stay Safe in this Crazy, Crazy World

Louis R. Mizell, Jr.

More than 4,000 Americans 55 years of age and older become crime victims in their homes every day.

Criminals target older people, expecting them to be less able to protect themselves and more likely to be poor witnesses.

Eighty percent of these crimes could be prevented if seniors learned more about criminal tactics and took a few simple steps to improve security. Here are the facts about some of the most prevalent crimes and how to avoid them...

HOME SECURITY

The idea that criminals will not enter an occupied house is a dangerous myth. Using force or trickery, crooks enter the homes of more than 500,000 people each year with at least one family member inside. Most of these crimes would not occur if people took the following precautions...

●**Don't open the door** unless you know who is on the other side. Every year, 15,000 seniors are victimized by the "push in" tactic when the criminal forces his/her way in. If you do not know the person, use a peephole and talk through the closed door.

Be aware that a determined criminal can push hard enough on a partially opened door to rip off most door chains that have not been professionally installed.

●**Don't trust people** just because they look respectable.

Example: In Miami, three little girls (one 10-year-old and two 14-year-olds) knocked at the doors of older people and melted their hearts with bright eyes and sweet smiles. After they were let in, one would slip into the bedroom and take cash and jewelry, while the other two distracted the victim. Before they were arrested, they had robbed 26 senior citizens.

●**Be wary of impostors.** More than 230,000 crimes per year are committed by criminals impersonating plumbers, gas and water inspectors, police officers, etc. Check the credentials of everyone who comes to your door *before* you open it. If you feel suspicious, call the organization he claims sent him.

●**Lock your door whenever you leave your home**, even if it's just to take out the garbage…bring in the groceries…get the mail. Of the 3.2 million home invasions, 800,000 were the result of an unlocked door or window.

●**Keep your keys secure.** Someone who has your door keys has 24-hour access to your home, your family, your property and, of course, you.

●**Do not give your keys to anyone**…workers…home-care attendants…realtors…unless you know you can trust them and all their relatives and friends who may also gain access to your keys. Three hundred thousand crimes are committed by criminals who surreptitiously obtain our keys.

●**Don't keep your car ignition key** on the same key ring with your house keys.

●**Don't leave your garage-door opener** in your unlocked car.

CAR-JACKING AND DRIVEWAY CRIMES

In today's mobile world, criminals have learned a variety of ways to exploit vulnerable people in and out of their cars. Driveway crime is rampant.

Example: A top Exxon executive was kidnapped from his 200-foot-long driveway on his estate in northern New Jersey.

Do not drop your guard when you get to your driveway. Check the rear-view mirror as you approach your home and as you drive onto your driveway. If someone is following, keep your doors locked and circle the block. If they are still behind, drive to the closest police station.

If you see anyone suspicious by your house, keep your doors locked and blow the horn. If an unfamiliar vehicle is in your driveway, get a description, take down the license plate number and call the local police department from a neighbor's house before you go home. Keep your car doors locked and your engine running until you are certain there are no suspicious characters around.

Be aware of common ruses used by criminals to get you out of your car. *Two of the most common include:*

●**Bump and rob.** The criminal crashes into the victim's rear bumper…and robs her (victims are usually older women) when she gets out to inspect the damage.

●**Good Samaritan.** The criminal approaches his victim and points out that she has a flat tire (for which the crook is responsible). He then offers the victim a ride, and either robs or assaults her.

ATMS AND PAY TELEPHONES

Automatic Teller Machines (ATMs) and pay telephones provide *many* opportunities for criminals. At least 27,000 crimes, including kidnapping, murder, rape, car theft and robbery occur at pay phones each year. *To maximize security…*

●**Use machines and telephones** that are in public view and well lit.

●**Take along a companion** who can watch you from inside your locked car. If you do not have a car, have him stand 10 or 15 feet away to deter criminals.

●**Do not leave your car unlocked or the keys in the ignition** if you must go alone.

- **Face the street when using the telephone.**
- **Do your business quickly.**
- **Do not make withdrawals or deposits at the same place or time every day.**
- **Keep your PIN confidential.**
- **Be aware of your surroundings** and watch to see if you are being followed.

WISDOM

However safe you try to make your home, it will never be as secure as a bank. Do not keep large amounts of cash in your house. Word gets around.

Since 1989, 3,400 seniors have each had more than *$15,000* in cash stolen from their homes. In 200 cases, the amount exceeded *$100,000*.

Louis R. Mizell, Jr., an expert on criminal tactics and author of *Street Sense for Seniors*. The Putnam Berkley Publishing Group.

Protect Your Valuables While You're Away

Robert Bynum
Paula R. Mazuski

Before you go on a trip prepare a "house book"—and make arrangements with a "key contact person."

The best key contact person is someone who lives in sight of your home who is likely to notice anything unusual. You may have arranged to have your mail held by the post office so that no one will notice it piling up, but flyers and free shopper papers can still be deposited on your doorstep. Your key contact person can promptly remove these, as well as receive packages.

Do *not* leave a note to deliverers on the door for all to see.

Your house book gives the key contact person any information needed to deal with the security of your home.

Example: The book should list any deliveries you are expecting.

Your book should also explain how your alarm system and/or automatically timed light system works. *Other information you should include...*

- **Where in the house you have left an inventory of your valuables.** (For privacy's sake you will probably not want to list the inventory directly in your house book.)
- **Your travel itinerary**, including telephone numbers where you can be reached. In addition, plan to phone your key contact person periodically.
- **Garbage pickup schedule** and instructions on how to store garbage containers.
- **How to contact the police.**

HOW TO PREPARE THE HOUSE FOR YOUR ABSENCE

- **Leave shades and blinds partially open** to give the house an occupied look. *Added benefit:* Neighbors and police can check inside.
- **Leave your car locked and in the driveway**—close enough to the garage doors to prevent them from being opened.
- **Thorny plants near the house**—holly, pyracanthus, roses—discourage prowlers.
- **Don't block windows with plantings.**

Robert Bynum, coauthor, with Paula R. Mazuski, of *Manston's Before You Leave on Your Vacation: How to Protect Your Home, Valuables, Pets and Plants from Theft and Neglect*. Travel Keys.

How I Protect My Privacy

Diane Terry
Trans Union

Armed with a few simple facts about you —such as your name and your Social Security number—criminals can open fraudulent accounts and may even get their hands on your savings.

My company, Trans Union, helps 1,400 fraud victims a *day* with such problems. That's up from only around 10 a day four years ago. *What to do:*

- **Keep your wallet thin.** The sad fact is that wallets get stolen. And—you'll give thieves less to work with if they try to open new accounts in your name. I never carry more than three credit cards.

Important: Limit carrying cards or papers with your Social Security number on it. That includes any insurance company or credit union account information that uses your Social Security number as an account number. In many cases, carrying your medical or health identification card is unavoidable.

● **Don't leave outgoing mail in an unsecured mailbox.** If you use a residential mailbox with the little red flag, you are asking for trouble. Some criminals steal the mail. Others open the envelopes, copy down your personal information, then reseal and send them.

In such cases you wouldn't even know there has been a problem until it's too late. I take my mail to a local official mailbox.

Additionally, you may want to buy a mailbox with a slot and key lock that prevents thieves from stealing your just-delivered mail.

● **Tear up personal documents before you throw them out.** This isn't paranoia—there are criminals who specialize in picking through trash looking for insurance statements, investment reports and even unsolicited credit card applications. Those documents often include your Social Security number and personal account numbers, which are the basis of these sorts of fraud. In addition, use a black marker to cross out the numbers before tearing up the documents.

● **Pay attention to your mail patterns.** I know how much mail on average I receive every day. If I went one day without mail, I would phone the local post office to make sure there wasn't a problem making deliveries that day.

● **Don't give out any personal information over the phone.** This includes your Social Security number, credit card number and even your address—*unless you initiated the call.*

Before I give a credit card number to a telemarketer, I get its phone number, hang up, check the number with the phone company and call the person back. If the phone number is not listed, I do not take a chance by trusting the telemarketer.

Another option is to request that information be sent to you in the mail.

Be wary of all calls that sound "funny." The caller might claim to be from your credit card company checking up on a possible scam...or

from a police group requesting credit card donations.

● **Review your bills as soon as they arrive.** If you see something unfamiliar, such as a charge you didn't make or a bill from a credit card you don't own, iron out the problem immediately.

It might be a simple mistake. But if it's criminal activity, the problem will become worse the longer you wait.

Diane Terry, director of fraud victim assistance at Trans Union, one of the nation's largest credit-rating agencies, Box 6790, Fullerton, CA 92634.

Protect Your Social Security Number

Someone who knows your Social Security number (SSN) can more easily access your credit history, medical records and other private information.

To keep your SSN private: Do not give it out unless you absolutely must. Your bank and some government agencies may have legitimate needs...but be very cautious when giving it to others. If you do give it out, make sure you are dealing with a reputable organization.

Warning: The most common form of identification one is asked to show is a driver's license, which often displays one's SSN. In most states, you can request that the Motor Vehicle Department issue you another ID number instead.

David Banisar, policy analyst with the Electronic Privacy Information Center, an advocacy group in Washington, DC.

Keep Personal Secrets Out of Cyberspace

If something is so private that you would not want it to be printed in your local newspaper, don't disclose it on the Web.

Travel plans: Armed with only your name and home town, a hacker could uncover your street address...and your home could be burglarized while you're away.

Health facts: You may become the target of unscrupulous insurance salespeople and medical quacks.

Personal financial information: Hackers can cause a wide array of financial mayhem with surprisingly little information—a bank branch and your mother's maiden name, for instance.

Employer's name: Would you want a hacker contacting your boss?

John Edwards, computer industry analyst in Mount Laurel, NJ.

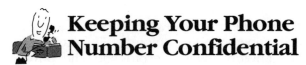

Keeping Your Phone Number Confidential

For caller ID self-defense (where available), dial *67 (1167 on rotary phones) before dialing the number you are calling...or ask your phone company to install a *line blocking* service to block Caller ID. Neither of these tactics will work when you dial an 800 or a 900 number.

For privacy on 800 and 900 calls: Use a calling card or prepaid phone card...or make an operator-assisted call.

Cheapest way to keep your number confidential: List it under another name.

John Featherman, editor of *Privacy Newsletter*, Box 8206, Philadelphia 19101.

Telephone Solicitation Trap

Think twice before giving to charity in response to a telephone solicitation. Commercial telemarketers who solicit on behalf of charities often keep 40% to 80% of the money they raise to cover their own expenses. This can be true even when solicitations are made

in the name of major, reputable charities. When responding to a phone solicitation, get information in writing *first*—a good telemarketer will comply with your request—and *always* make your check out to the full name of the charity, *not* to a middleman.

Jim Bausch, president of the National Charities Information Bureau, 19 Union Square W., New York 10003.

Unauthorized Long-Distance Service Switching Trap

Beware of unauthorized switching of your company's long-distance service from one provider to another. It's called "slamming." Complaints of slamming are widespread and rising—up 400% in 1995 from the level reported in 1993.

Common ploys: A call to an employee asking simply if the company wants to save money on its long-distance or 800-number phone bill. An affirmative response is deemed to be "authorization" to switch to that carrier. Or a deceptive, high-pressure sales call may push an unauthorized employee into accepting a "great" deal.

Defenses: Make one employee responsible for dealing with all phone providers, and have all inquiries about phone service go to that person. Check the phone bill each month to be sure the provider hasn't changed.

Shirley Rooker, president of Call For Action, a consumer mediation service in Washington, DC.

Prepaid Calling Cards

Prepaid calling cards can be a convenience, but they are also a burgeoning area for rip-offs.

Biggest complaints: The cards do not work ...or the user is charged a higher rate than advertised.

When selecting a card: Know the rate per minute and expiration date...make sure the secret Personal Identification Number (PIN) is covered to be certain the card has not been used...buy cards in small denominations. Useful resource—*Buying Time: The Facts About Prepaid Phone Cards*, available free from BBB Publications, 257 Park Ave. S., New York 10010. Include a self-addressed, stamped, business-sized envelope.

Barbara Berger Opotowsky, president of the Better Business Bureau of Metropolitan New York.

Best Bet: Cellular Phone

A cellular phone is your best access to any emergency help you may need while you're in your car. A cellular phone provides instant access to the universal 911 emergency number. And—it also provides a simple way to call a friend, tow service or family member in case you need help on or off the highway. That makes cellular phones much better than the *911-only* phones that are now being sold. If you discipline yourself to use the phone only for emergencies, you will pay only the minimal cost of a basic plan.

To be even safer: Also have a CB radio. While not as convenient as a car phone, a CB radio usually works in areas where a car phone won't due to satellite interference.

David Solomon, certified master auto technician and editor of *Nutz & Boltz®*, Box 123, Butler, MD 21023.

Back Up Your Wallet

Create a "wallet file"—photocopies of items that are kept in your wallet. If your wallet is lost or stolen, you will always have backup. Be sure to update the file regularly.

James Scalone, *Bottom Line/Personal* subscriber, San Diego.

Disaster Preparation

If you know that a severe storm is approaching your area, listen to the TV or radio. If local officials advise you to leave the area, do so immediately. Fill up your car's gas tank—a bad storm can cause a power outage that makes it impossible for service stations to pump fuel.

Before the storm hits: Take in lightweight patio furniture and other outdoor objects that could be thrown around by high winds. Park your car in a garage, if possible. Have a disaster supply kit packed and ready to use.

Afterward: Notify your insurance agent as soon as possible. Keep all receipts for any temporary emergency repairs that you must do. Do not do any permanent repairs until an insurance adjuster approves them...and do not throw away damaged items until the adjuster sees them. For more information, contact your local Red Cross chapter.

Stacy Smith, spokesperson for the American Red Cross, Washington, DC.

Accident-Free Moving

Better to pack plates on edge rather than flat. Wrap each one separately in newspaper or bubble wrap—*and cushion the bottom of cartons, too. Also:* Tape a pillow over your TV screen to prevent damage...tie sofa beds closed so they won't open up unexpectedly.

The Family Handyman Helpful Hints: Quick and Easy Solutions, Timesaving Tips, Tricks of the Trade. Reader's Digest.

Home Inspector Self-Defense

Only a few states license home inspectors, so prospective buyers should be very careful when checking out references.

Look for: An independent inspector, preferably one with experience in building or appraisals...who carries "errors and omissions" insurance...and is a member of the American Society of Home Inspectors (call 800-743-2744 to confirm).

Caution: Never hire an inspector who also does repairs—he/she has an incentive to find things wrong.

David Schechner, real estate attorney with Schechner & Targan, 80 Main St., West Orange, NJ 07052.

Be Wary of Part-Time Life Insurance Agents

Your chance of getting full and accurate information is greater with a full-time agent.

Better: Make sure the agent you choose is a chartered life underwriter (CLU)—a certification held by about 30% of US agents.

Even better: A CLU who is also a chartered financial consultant (CFC), which means he/she has passed the same test as authorized financial planners.

Self-defense: Your state insurance commissioner's office—every state has one—can tell you if complaints have been filed against a particular agent. *Also:* Call a no-load company, such as Ameritus (800-237-2197) or USAA (800-531-8319), for at least one quote.

Robert Hunter, director of insurance for the Consumer Federation of America, 1424 16 St. NW, Washington, DC 20036.

Check Lawyers' Bills... Carefully

Lawyers' bill padding can significantly increase costs—even when fees have been negotiated. Typical extras include charges for photocopies, faxes, word processing, secretarial time, meals and more. The American Bar Association says lawyers should charge actual costs—but some lawyers interpret that to mean a photocopy includes part of the salary of the machine operator and copier maintenance charges.

Self-defense: Speak up when hiring a lawyer—then check bills carefully.

Gary Greenfield, president of Litigation Cost Management, a legal-fee consulting firm in Oakland, CA.

Winning in Small-Claims Court

Ralph Warner

Was your security deposit not returned when you moved? Were your clothes damaged by the dry cleaner? Did your neighbor's dog bite your child or grandchild?

In these and other situations, you can take legal action that is swift and inexpensive. Take your case to small-claims court. By following some simple steps, you can recover your loss without the help of a lawyer.

Limit: Depending on the jurisdiction, the size of your claim in small-claims court can run from $1,000 to as high as $15,000.

•Determine if the effort will be worth it. Even if your claim is valid, don't waste your time on someone who has no assets or income against which you can collect.

You will probably be able to collect if the defendant—the party you are suing—has a job or a bank account. Wages can be garnished if necessary to pay off judgments.

Pensions, welfare, Social Security benefits and unemployment compensation cannot be garnished. If you are suing a small business, look for a cash register from which a sheriff or marshall can collect an award. The sheriff will take the cash.

Mistake: Do not assume that someone with a fancy car will be able to pay. State laws exempt $500 to $2,000 of equity in a car. Given the fact that most people borrow heavily to buy a car, there may not be sufficient equity to satisfy a judgment.

Also decide whether the hours you will spend on the case are worth your time. A $200 property loss may require 10 to 20 hours to collect.

•Send a demand letter to the person who wronged you. Some states require this be done before you go to court. In many cases, the letter alone brings results.

In the letter, spell out the problem and the amount of money you are seeking. Be businesslike. Insults are counterproductive.

●**Make sure you have a claim.** Whether you have a breach of contract, a case of negligence resulting in minor injury to you or your property, a breach of warranty or some other problem, you can state your claim in court papers in ordinary language.

Do some legal research about your claim if it is more complicated. The court clerk may also be of some help.

Be sure to file your claim within the time allowed by law. This time varies with the type of claim, but you are covered in any event if you file within one year of the incident.

Pitfall: If you want to sue a municipality or state, you must first file a "notice of claim" with the government, usually within six months of the event. You cannot sue the federal government or any of its agencies in small-claims court.

Helpful: Get a copy of the procedural rules from your local small-claims court. These will explain not only when you must file, but the maximum amount for which you can sue and what papers are needed.

If your loss is more than the limit allowed in your local court, consider waiving the excess loss.

Example: If your loss is $3,400 but the small-claims court limit is $3,000, ask for only $3,000. Forgoing the excess will surely be less than it would cost you to go to regular court with the assistance of an attorney.

Be sure to sue the right party or parties…

Example: If you are injured by another car, sue both the driver and the registered owner.

●**Evaluate your claim.** Put a dollar value on your loss. Be realistic. For instance, if you are owed money, include not only the principal but also the unpaid interest on the loan. Do not ask for too much because it will only make you look foolish. But do not minimize your loss either.

●**Gather evidence.** As appropriate, take pictures of the scene, the object damaged. Or, try to back up your story in other ways.

Also ask any witnesses to participate. The key is to back up your oral presentation with evidence. Otherwise it could come down to just your word against the other party's.

Example: You might clip out the ad that you answered that offered a warranty.

●**Find a coach to help you practice.** Remember that your "day" in court is a matter of *minutes*. You must be prepared to state your case clearly and not leave out important details. Practice with a coach to hone your skills. The coach may be able to poke holes in your story and help you improve your presentation.

●**Try to settle your claim.** Take every opportunity to reach a compromise with the defendant. Your demand letter is one opportunity.

You can also make an *offer in compromise—* a written letter offering to take less than your full loss in order to resolve the problem. If your offer is not accepted, you are not bound by your lower dollar amount. Say you are out $500 but offer to accept $350 to avoid going to court. If your offer is rejected, you can still sue for $500.

Mediation is another opportunity for settlement. The growing trend is toward mediation in place of litigation. Maine even *requires* mediation before a case can be heard in court. With mediation, no decision is imposed. Instead, the parties simply agree to work out their differences.

Mediation is especially helpful in situations where you will be forced to continue dealing with the defendants (neighbors, relatives) since there are no clear winners or losers in the process.

●**Tell it to the judge.** If all else fails and you must go to court, be sure to state what your case is about in concise terms. Include information on who, what, where, when and why.

Example: Tell the judge that your car was damaged by a collision with the defendant. The accident was caused by the defendant's running a red light on April 1, 1996, at the corner of Main St. and Park Dr. The damage to your car was $900.

Helpful: Write on an index card the four or five points you must include.

Be sure to bring papers and evidence to back up your claim. Hand them to the judge's clerk at the appropriate time. You can learn this by watching other cases or by asking the clerk before court is in session.

Mistake: Do not get angry with your opponent or the judge. Yelling or calling the other party a liar will only hurt your case.

Helpful: Ask the court to award you the costs you incurred—the court filing fee, the cost of serving papers on the defendant, subpoenaed witness fees and the cost of getting documents.

Ralph Warner, attorney and author of *Everybody's Guide to Small Claims Court*. Nolo Press.

Hotel Safety

Instead of keeping your valuables in your hotel room, put them in the hotel's safe—but check first to see whether the hotel's liability is enough to cover your valuables.

What to keep in the safe: Jewelry, cameras and traveler's checks you don't need. Also, personal and travel documents—even exposed film—should be kept in the safe. Keep cash with you in a wallet worn around your neck or waist at all times, not in the hotel safe. *Bottom line*: If you don't need something, leave it at home.

Herbert J. Teison, publisher of *Travel Smart*, 40 Beechdale Rd., Dobbs Ferry, NY 10522.

Domestic Terrorism

Terrorism by domestic groups in the US will *not* increase significantly in the near future. However, terrorism by foreign groups (especially religiously motivated terrorists) remains a threat here and abroad. The chances of becoming a victim of terrorism are minuscule.

But take precautions just in case: Luggage tags should only include your *business* address and phone number—*no names* (frequent-flier programs may issue numbered medallions in place of tags)...join airline clubs—use their waiting rooms instead of sitting in open areas ...don't check luggage.

Warning: As security at obvious targets—such as embassies and army bases—grows tighter, other targets become more attractive. *Helpful resource:* The US State Department's Overseas Citizens Services (202-647-5225).

Benjamin Weiner, president of Probe International, which provides major corporations with evaluations of political developments that could lead to instability and violence, 1492 High Ridge Rd., Stamford, CT 06903.

Laptop Travel Alert

Laptop hustlers often work at airport security stations. While you put your laptop on the conveyor belt, two crooks get in front of you in line. After the first crook passes through the metal detector, the second crook sets off the alarm, stalling the line—and you—while the first crook runs off with your laptop.

Self-defense: Keep an eye on your laptop as it emerges from the X-ray machine. Call for help if you see a stranger grab it. Currently, security personnel will not do hand inspections of laptops.

Consumer Reports Travel Letter, 101 Truman Ave., Yonkers, NY 10703.

Downsizing Self-Defense

Keep your debt to a minimum, even if you have finished putting your children through college and are now tempted to splurge. Maintain hands-on skills—a downsized manager may be unable to find another management position but might find one in his/her original line of work.

Essential: Computer literacy—in a post-layoff job, a manager can't expect to have a staff.

Kiplinger's Retire & Thrive by Robert Otterbourg, a retired journalist in Durham, NC. Times Books.

Tighten Voice Mail Security

Delete the personal identification numbers (PINs) of employees who leave the firm... change all PINs periodically...review reports of voice mail usage to find suspicious patterns ...conduct an "awareness program" to impress employees with the need to protect their PINs and be alert to security concerns.

Warning example: A salesman who left a company for a competitor used his old PIN to enter his former employer's voice mail system, obtain key information about its clients and harass former coworkers. Ultimately, he was arrested by the FBI and charged with 29 criminal counts.

Bill Zalud, editor of *Security*, Box 5080, Des Plaines, IL 60017.

ADA Scams Are On the Rise

Con artists identify themselves as inspectors of Americans with Disabilities Act violations...claim to find problems in businesses... then charge $400 to $1,000 per item to advise companies how to avoid legal action. One firm sold an allegedly skid-resistant chemical to make floors safer for wheelchair users—but the ADA does not require skid-resistant floors.

Self-defense: Carefully check the credentials of any person or company claiming to be a consultant on ADA issues.

Susan Wells, editor of *Research Recommendations*, 1101 King St., Alexandria, VA 22314.

Simple Winter Driving Defense

Use cat litter for traction during winter driving. Carry a heavy bag of clay-based litter in your trunk for extra weight to help keep the vehicle stable. If you are stuck in snow or ice, clear around your drive wheels, pour kitty litter in front of the tires in the direction you want to go, then drive away slowly.

Bonus: Clay does not contribute to corrosion.

Charles Butler, director of driver safety services for the American Automobile Association, Heathrow, FL.

How to Check for Uneven Tire Wear

Uneven tire wear often is easier to spot with your fingers than with your eyes.

Helpful: Run hands from side to side and up and down the tread. Uneven wear could indicate misalignment or loose chassis parts.

Important: Beware of pieces of steel belting or metal embedded in the tire that could cut your hand.

Car Care Council, 1 Grande Lake Dr., Port Clinton, OH 43524.

Beware of Curbstoners

Curbstoners are people who work secretly for car dealerships to unload cars with serious defects. Cars are sold through classified ads, as if they were private-party sales. Prices are very low. When you call, you are told the owner is not available but you can still see the car. The seller meets you at an address different from the address on the title...gives vague answers to questions about the vehicle's history...and comes up with excuses to stop you from taking it to your mechanic.

Self-defense: Never buy a used car whose price seems too good to be true. And never buy without letting your mechanic inspect the car.

David Solomon, certified master auto technician and editor of *Nutz & Boltz*®, Box 123, Butler, MD 21023.

Burn Prevention

Burns are a leading cause of pediatric injuries. *Prevention:*

- **Install latches on appliances** that prevent kids from turning on appliances.
- **Place the microwave out of children's reach.**
- **Don't let kids push stove or oven buttons.**
- **Keep appliances unplugged.**
- **Use a thermometer to be certain that bathwater is below 120°F.**
- **Store household products that can cause burns to skin**—such as furniture polish and silver cleaner—safely.

Treatment: Apply cool compresses—not ice—to a heat burn. Flush chemical burns with water. Seek medical attention if a burn is very large or blisters emerge...particularly if burns occur on the face or hands.

Harry Lubell, MD, director of pediatrics at Phelps Memorial Hospital Center, Sleepy Hollow, NY.

How to Tell when The Sun Is Dangerous

Joseph Bark, MD

Here are little-known facts about the summer sun and ways to protect yourself:

- **Shadow's length and sharpness.** If your shadow is shorter than you are—or there is no shadow—the sun is overhead and at its most powerful strength.

The same is true about the sun's intensity when your shadow—or the shade made by trees and other objects—is very sharp, deep and dark.

- **Altitude.** The higher you are in elevation, the thinner the ozone layer and atmosphere, and less protection against the sun's ultraviolet (UV) rays.
- **Sand/grass traps.** They reflect nearly 100% of the sun's rays. If you're at the beach or on a lawn when the sun is overhead, you get double the radiation.
- **Color.** The deeper the color blue of the sky, the less of a barrier there is between you and the sun's rays.

Protecting yourself:

- **Always wear the highest SPF sunscreen possible**—at least SPF 15—and be sure the sunscreen is waterproof.

Helpful: Men—use sunscreen in place of aftershave lotion. Women—use cosmetics that contain sunscreen.

- **Wear a hat with a wide brim made from a tightly woven fabric** that won't let much light pass through. Avoid baseball caps and sun visors...they don't protect the sides or back of the neck.
- **Wear large sunglasses** that fit close to your eyes and the bridge of your nose. Sunglasses stop you from squinting, protect against wrinkle formation and prevent cataracts and other eye disorders.

Caution: Avoid the small, John Lennon-style sunglasses. The dark lenses cause corneas to dilate, so they are exposed to light that slips in around the glasses. Instead, wear sunglasses at least as large as the eye's orbit—the hollow "cave" that houses the eyeball.

Joseph Bark, MD, a dermatologist in private practice in Lexington, KY. He is author of *Your Skin: An Owner's Guide.* Prentice-Hall.

19

Technology 1998

How Not to Lose Computer Data

Brian J. Croft
John Edwards

As most people in the business world know by now, losing data stored on computers isn't just an inconvenience. The loss can stymie important projects, expose the company to legal problems or, in some cases, erase years of painstaking work.

Fortunately, preventing the loss of computer files—or recovering them after a mishap—does not necessarily require a lot of money. Some peace of mind can be achieved by the least technically minded businesspeople. *Essential loss-prevention steps...*

•**Duplicate all important data.** Many backup systems are on the market, most in the $300 to $2,000 range. What's most important isn't the type of system a company buys—but how regularly it is used.

Important: Put one person in charge of managing the process to ensure that all computer users back up their files.

If the job is left to individual employees, some of them are bound to fail, if only because they forget under the pressure of work.

In the case of irreplaceable data, backups should be made several times daily. With less important information, weekly or semiweekly backup is adequate.

Serious mistake: Putting blind faith in a backup system, only to discover that it hasn't worked properly for the past several weeks or months.

To make sure the backup system is accurately duplicating data, instruct the person in charge to test the system at least once a month. Tests should also be made immediately if the backup system has been recently installed or modified.

It is also prudent to store duplicated computer files off-site. *Reasons...*

●**If a fire or other type of accident destroys the company's computers,** backup files will be safe.

●**When backup files contain proprietary information,** it can be risky to leave them in the main office area.

●**Maintain hardware—and software—fastidiously.** Since files are often lost because of mechanical problems with the computers themselves, it is critical to give the machines constant, thorough maintenance. As a rule, go by the recommendations of the manufacturer or the company's computer consultant.

Give priority to maintenance of computers that store especially important files, such as financial data or customer records, as opposed to computers used for word processing of non-sensitive correspondence.

Very helpful: Instruct employees to report computer malfunctions as soon as they occur and if the problem is accompanied by a mechanical sound, to turn off their machine immediately. Computers that operate improperly can damage data, and if use continues, damage can be irreparable.

Serious symptom: Persistent clicking sound when the hard drive is in use. It can signal what technicians call a "head crash," which is a malfunction of the hard drive itself. Left unchecked, a head crash can permanently erase large chunks of data.

Also—instruct employees not to ignore an error code when it appears on their computer screen. These are red flags that may signal problems with hardware, software or an attempted application. Unless employees are technical experts, they can't distinguish between codes that indicate a minor problem and those that signal impending loss of data.

Challenge: Employees often learn just enough of a program to do a few tasks but aren't skilled enough to avoid the occasional loss of files. The only solution is to make sure computer users are up to speed on the specific software they are using.

Essential: Install anti-virus programs to screen out lines of harmful computer code that malicious programmers try to inflict on unwary users. Make sure the anti-virus software is regularly updated so it is able to detect new viruses. Most major anti-virus software vendors offer a subscription-based update service. Effective anti-virus programs can cost less than $100, and many are included in packages of other software.

It's important that all computers are equipped with these programs because in most offices disks are routinely traded among machines.

Also install surge protectors on all computers. These inexpensive devices (typically $15 to $50 each) help protect the machines against sudden peaks in electrical current, which can damage or destroy data. More sophisticated protection should be considered for servers.

●**Set up effective recovery systems.** It's natural to panic when a computer file is lost. Most users can take some comfort in the fact that today's technology can often recover all or part of it.

For minor problems, consider using one of the commercially available data-recovery programs, most of which cost less than $150.

Examples: Norton Utilities and Central Point's PC Tools. *Alternative:* Call a professional data-recovery service. These services can be found in the Yellow Pages under "computers." It usually pays to call in a professional whenever…

●**The company doesn't have its own data-recovery software.**

●**The software is installed, but you don't feel confident that an employee can run it.**

●**The loss has occurred on a hard drive of a computer that's been physically damaged.**

Typical cost…about $100 to $200 to recover data from a minimally damaged floppy disk to $20,000 to recover files from a large computer network.

Caution: Since files are likely to contain sensitive information, use care in choosing an outside data-recovery service. And, consider asking the data-recovery company to sign a confidentiality agreement that holds it legally responsible in case its employees leak or misuse the data that they're seeking to recover.

Brian J. Croft, communication consultant for Towers Perrin, 175 Bloor St. E., Toronto M4W 3T6, Canada, and John Edwards, a high-technology consultant based in Mount Laurel, NJ.

Kids... Computers... And Educational Software

Mark Estren, PhD

The selection of educational software for children is growing rapidly. Here's just a sampling of programs for today's computer-savvy kids.

READING

●**Reader Rabbit's Interactive Reading Journey 1** (ages 3 to 6). Kids journey to 20 different lands, each focusing on a different letter of the alphabet or sound. Then they answer questions about the information they've read along the way. $99.*

The Learning Co., 800-227-5609.

●**Reader Rabbit's Reading Development Libraries** (ages 5 to 9) feature stories told from three different points of view. These games help kids learn how plots work. Four reading levels. $30 each.

The Learning Co., 800-227-5609.

●**Sierra's School House/English** (ages 8 to 12). A friendly alien named Adi runs a multiple-choice quiz show on vocabulary...reading comprehension...proofreading...more. Excellent graphics, animations and video clips. Interactive learning games are accessible as a reward for good quiz performance. Two-CD set. $30 each. Windows only.

Sierra On-Line, 800-757-7707.

WRITING

●**The Amazing Writing Machine** (ages 6 to 12) helps kids express their thoughts by creating stories or adding to prewritten ones. Hundreds of layouts feature different places to insert text and graphics. $29.

Broderbund Software, 800-521-6263.

●**Creative Writer II** (ages 8 and up) offers

*Prices are approximate retail. Discounts are widely available. All software is available in Windows/Macintosh CD-ROMs, unless otherwise noted.

hundreds of "story starters"—fun or unusual phrases and illustrations to help a child get a story started. Includes 30 fonts, 35 music themes, 2,000 pieces of clip art and Internet web page project. $35. Windows only.

Microsoft, 800-426-9400.

ARITHMETIC

●**James Discovers Math** (ages 3 to 6) teaches counting, shape and pattern recognition, measurement and estimation skills. Software uses playful graphics—such as candles singing a parody of an operatic quintet, then burning out when through. $29.

Broderbund Software, 800-521-6263.

●**Mega Math Blaster** (ages 6 to 12). Robots, spaceships, aliens, digitized speech and excellent music and graphics combine to teach everything from basic addition and subtraction to fractions. Numerous levels. $45 each.

Davidson & Associates, 800-545-7677.

●**Mighty Math** (ages 5 to 14). Cartoon characters teach hard-to-understand concepts using easy analogies. *Examples:* Fireworks help explain fractions...bumper cars explain algebraic sets. Kids can do activities in question-and-answer mode or at their own pace. Five levels, from addition to geometry. $40 each.

Edmark, 800-691-2985.

SCIENCE

●**The Magic School Bus** (ages 6 to 10). A bus and a wildly dressed teacher named Ms. Frizzle help kids explore the age of dinosaurs, the earth, the ocean, the human body or outer space. Based on the Scholastic book series by Joanna Cole. $45 each. Dinosaurs, earth and solar system available for Windows only.

Microsoft, 800-426-9400.

●**Volcanoes: Life on the Edge** (ages 8 to adult). Four multimedia documentaries explain volcanoes and why they erupt. Volcanic eruptions from Mount Vesuvius to Mount Pinatubo are discussed in detail—with photos, maps and animations. $45.

Corbis, 800-246-2065.

Mark Estren, PhD, former editor and publisher of *High Technology Business* magazine. He writes a weekly column about children's software for *Parent Weekly*, Fairfax County, VA.

Limit Kids' Time On-Line

To limit kids' time on-line, you should keep the computer where you can see it and watch what they are doing.

Helpful: Software called *Time's Up*, which automatically bumps kids off-line when they reach a preset time limit.

More information: Fresh Software, 800-846-3787. CD-ROM/$29.95...floppy/$19.95.

Mark Estren, PhD, former editor and publisher of *High Technology Business*, who writes a weekly column about children's software for *Parent Weekly*, Fairfax County, VA.

Lessen Wrist Injury When Using Computers

Tilt keyboards slightly away to minimize wrist bending during computer use and lessen the chance of repetitive-motion injury. People bend wrists less on keyboards that slope 12° away from them. This angle makes it easier to maintain safe posture when keeping keyboards at the recommended level—about one inch above legs at the keyboard's lowest point.

Solution: Use a tiltdown keyboard tray for optimal positioning. Proformix offers one (800-973-2739. *Cost:* $179 to $250). Other keyboard trays can get you close to optimal position.

Alan Hedge, PhD, ergonomics professor at Cornell University, Ithaca, NY.

Getting Quick Callbacks

To get a call returned quickly, send an E-mail message and a fax saying that you urgently need to talk. In many offices, those messages go right to the person's desk—and are responded to before phone messages.

Harry Newton, publisher of *Teleconnect*, a magazine for specialists in telecommunications information services, 12 W. 21 St., New York 10010.

20

Natural Healing Basics

What I Keep in My Medicine Cabinet

Adriane Fugh-Berman, MD

As a holistic physician, I'm often asked what I keep in my medicine cabinet. In some ways my medicine cabinet probably looks a lot like yours—and like most other doctors'. It's stocked with aspirin, adhesive bandages and hydrogen peroxide.

Unlike my mainstream colleagues, I also keep six natural remedies on hand, all of which are available at health-food stores…

•**Activated charcoal.** It's very effective against painful intestinal gas and diarrhea. Two capsules every 30 to 60 minutes as needed will do the trick—though it will also turn your stool black. Don't be alarmed.

Watch out—activated charcoal can interfere with the absorption of other medications. Don't take any other drug within one hour of taking activated charcoal.

By the way, diarrhea should be left *untreated* for the first 12 hours. Your body is trying to rid itself of toxins or disease-causing bacteria. Let the flushing process do its job.

•**Aloe vera.** Great for sunburn, minor burns, scratches, scrapes and shallow cuts. Aloe doesn't kill germs—you still have to clean wounds with plenty of water followed by hydrogen peroxide—but it's remarkably effective at promoting skin healing.

Although you can buy commercially prepared aloe vera gel at the drugstore, it's preferable to keep an aloe vera houseplant. That way, you're assured of freshness *and* purity—things you're not sure of with commercially prepared aloe gels. Simply break off an inch or two of a leaf, slit it open and apply the gel-like sap to the injured area.

•**Arnica.** For sprains and strains, apply ice to the area for 10 minutes. Then apply an arnica cream. Arnica is also great for bumps,

319

bruises and swelling. Do not use arnica on broken skin. It'll heal faster if it's left uncovered.

● **Echinacea.** This immune system booster is good to have on hand when you're coming down with the sniffles or flu-like symptoms.

One-half to one dropperful of tincture or two capsules three or four times a day may prevent you from developing a full-blown viral infection—or shorten the duration of cold or flu. The sooner it's started, the more effective it is.

I also recommend a day or two of Echinacea after being exposed to someone who is sick.

Avoid Echinacea if you have lupus or another autoimmune disease. And take it for no more than 10 days. Longer than that, and it loses its effectiveness.

● **Ginger.** Fresh gingerroot—sold in the produce section of your supermarket—is an excellent remedy for stomach upset, heartburn and nausea.

I usually make ginger tea by peeling and dicing a knuckle-sized piece of gingerroot, covering it with boiling water and then steeping for five minutes. If you prefer, you can simply swallow a piece of candied ginger or a ginger bonbon.

● **Vitamin E oil.** There's no evidence to support the belief that vitamin E applied to the skin prevents scarring. However, vitamin E oil is great for chapped lips or dry skin. It's especially soothing for the painful cracks that some people get on their hands or feet during cold weather.

Many people buy vitamin E-enriched lotions. But these don't contain much vitamin E. Other people buy pure vitamin E in capsule form and then stick pins in the capsules to extract the oil—not very convenient. I recommend buying a small bottle of vitamin E oil.

Rub the oil in well. If you're using it for cracked fingertips or heels, slather it on before bed and put cotton gloves or socks on. That will protect your sheets while helping the oil soak into your skin.

Adriane Fugh-Berman, MD, a Washington, DC-based medical researcher who specializes in women's health and alternative medicine. She is author of Alternative Medicine: What Works. *Odonian Press.*

Miracle Mineral

Selenium may help protect the body against heart disease *and* cancer.

A study of 2,600 people in Finland found that the rates of both those diseases dropped by 60% as blood selenium levels rose from 60 to 103 micrograms per liter. The best sources of the mineral are seafoods, grains, muscle meats and Brazil nuts.

However, *don't* use selenium supplements—it's easy to take too much, which is *dangerous*.

Li Li, MD, PhD at the Division of Cancer Prevention and Control at the National Cancer Institute, Bethesda, MD.

Should You Be Taking Blue-Green Algae?

Adriane Fugh-Berman, MD

Nutritional supplements containing blue-green algae have become quite popular lately. Consumers seem to believe the claims being made about these pills—that they prevent fatigue, promote weight loss, repair aching joints and even boost memory.

Are these claims true? Should you add blue-green algae to your vitamin regimen? Not so fast. *Let's examine these claims one by one...*

Claim: **Blue-green algae is a concentrated nutritional source.** Blue-green algae does contain protein, vitamins and minerals. Ounce for ounce, it's more nutritious than, say, broccoli. But does it really make sense to compare an ounce of broccoli to an ounce of blue-green algae? Absolutely not.

Three large stalks of broccoli weigh about four ounces, or 112 g. One capsule of blue-green algae contains about 1 g. If you were to eat 112 capsules instead of four ounces of broccoli, you might come out ahead nutritionally. But that's not very appetizing. And given the high cost of blue-green algae capsules, that would be prohibitively expensive.

Claim: **Blue-green algae repairs skin, muscles and joints.** If a nutritional deficiency is causing problems with your skin, muscles or joints, supplying the missing nutrient could be helpful. But nutritional deficiencies are very rare in the US.

***Claim:* Blue-green algae is a powerful memory-booster.** There is no evidence for this claim.

The herb *Ginkgo biloba* seems to help memory problems by boosting blood flow to small vessels, including those supplying the brain. Take two capsules or a dropperful of ginkgo extract twice a day.

***Claim:* Blue-green algae is an "energizer."** Anything that you believe will boost your energy probably will. There's no need to waste your money on blue-green algae.

***Claim:* Blue-green algae promotes weight loss.** There is simply no evidence for this claim.

So much for these outrageous claims. But that's only half the story.

According to John McPartland, DO, an osteopathic physician and botanist in Middlebury, Vermont, the euphoria that some people report after consuming blue-green algae may not be their imagination. Some toxins found in algae are chemically related to cocaine—but even more dangerous. It may be the damaging effect these nerve toxins have on the brain cells that produces euphoria.

Animals sometimes die after developing a "fatal attraction" to clumps of blue-green algae that wash onto beaches.

Some strains of the blue-green alga *Aphanizomenon flos-aquae* contain a liver toxin stronger than cyanide. It has been responsible for killing fish, wildlife and pets.

If you must eat algae, at least eat a nontoxic version. According to McPartland, one type of blue-green algae, Spirulina, is less likely to contain dangerous toxins.

One more reason to stay away from blue-green algae: Bacterial contamination of algae supplements is common. That's because algae thrive in sewage. Not only can the bacteria that hitchhike on algae make you sick, but algae may concentrate pollutants sucked up from the muck they grow in.

Adriane Fugh-Berman, MD, a Washington, DC-based medical researcher who specializes in women's health and alternative medicine. She is author of Alternative Medicine: What Works. Odonian Press.

Blue-Green Algae And Cancer

Blue-green algae reduces risk of mouth cancer. After one year of consuming a daily dose of the blue-green alga *spirulina*, 45% of those with whitish precancerous patches in the mouth (oral leukoplakia) experienced total regression. Spirulina, a low-cost source of beta-carotene and related carotenoids, is sold in health-food stores.

Padmanabhan P. Nair, PhD, research scientist, Human Nutrition Center of the US Department of Agriculture, Beltsville, MD. His study was reported in Food & Nutrition Research Briefs, 6303 Ivy Ln., 4th Floor, Greenbelt, MD 20770.

The Super-Powerful Antioxidant

James F. Balch, MD

Antioxidants have gotten lots of press lately—and rightly so. These amazing compounds "mop up" *free radicals,* disease-causing molecules produced within the body.

The best-known antioxidants are vitamins C and E and beta-carotene. But a compound called *proanthocyanidin* appears to be many times more potent.

Proanthocyanidin is found in red grapes, red wine and grape juice. But the best source is grape seed extract, which is sold at most health food stores.

As countless studies conducted in Europe over the past 20 years have shown, grape seed extract prevents hardening of the arteries (arteriosclerosis)...stabilizes blood sugar, helping to control diabetes...blocks the retinal disease macular degeneration...and speeds wound healing.

Grape seed extract also boosts the immune system. After taking it for six months, a recurring skin cancer on my face disappeared. I can't prove it, but I'm convinced that the grape seed extract was responsible.

For my patients interested in using grape seed extract as a general health-protective measure, I recommend taking 50 mg with food once daily.

For those taking it to treat heart disease or another existing condition—or to speed healing from surgery—I usually recommend 300 mg daily. That's 150 mg with breakfast and another 150 mg with supper.

Grape seed extract is safe, with no known side effects. It costs only 25 cents to 50 cents a day. Take it only under medical supervision.

James F. Balch, MD, a surgeon and health counselor in private practice in Greenfield, IN. He is coauthor of Prescription for Nutritional Healing. Avery.

DHEA: The Latest Miracle Pill?

Adriane Fugh-Berman, MD

In recent months, an adrenal hormone called dehydroepiandrosterone (DHEA) has been touted as a miracle drug capable of preventing heart disease and cancer, boosting libido—and more.

If you've heard the hype and have been thinking of taking this nonprescription supplement, I urge you to be very, very wary. Hormones are powerful substances that affect many organs. Short term, DHEA supplementation can cause acne, hirsutism (hairiness) in women, mood swings, insomnia and fatigue. Long-term effects are unknown, but it's possible that the hormone could damage the ovaries, uterus, prostate and/or liver.

Remember the lesson of estrogen: In the 1960s, it was hailed as a sort of fountain of youth for all women. In the 1970s it was found to increase uterine cancer. Estrogen is a "mixed bag"—beneficial in some ways, harmful in others.

There is intriguing evidence that DHEA helps prevent cancer in rats and heart disease in rabbits. But the situation with humans remains unclear and can be confusing.

Recent research suggests a link between high levels of DHEA and lower levels of heart disease in men. In one study, 49 men who had had heart attacks before age 56 were found to have lower levels of DHEA than 49 age-matched controls.

For women, the situation may be reversed. High levels of DHEA seem to be associated with a *greater* risk of heart disease. And while premenopausal breast cancer patients seem to have abnormally low levels of DHEA, postmenopausal breast cancer patients seem to have higher-than-normal levels of DHEA.

The truth is that researchers really don't know whether DHEA levels cause disease...if disease is a result of DHEA levels...or if DHEA levels are unrelated to human illness. Nor do they know whether taking DHEA pills is of any benefit to people whose DHEA levels are low.

A small uncontrolled study of 10 patients with lupus, a common autoimmune disease, found that three to six months of DHEA therapy diminished symptoms. Other recent studies suggest that DHEA supplementation boosts the immune system and the effectiveness of both vaccinations and chemotherapy.

Based on what I know now, I would not recommend DHEA supplementation for everyone. However, if someone with adult-onset diabetes or lupus is found to have low DHEA levels, there is a good case for trying DHEA supplements (5 to 25 mg a day in the morning).

Likewise, men with a history of heart disease may want to ask their doctors about supplementation at similar dosages.

The bottom line? DHEA should be regarded not as a dietary supplement but as a potent drug. (I believe it should be available only with a prescription.) Many of the effects noted by those who have taken DHEA—increased energy and libido, for example—could be the result of the placebo effect.

And even if DHEA boosts longevity in rats, that does not mean it has the same effect on humans. Without a good placebo-controlled trial, claims of these effects can't be taken seriously. More studies are needed.

Adriane Fugh-Berman, MD, a Washington, DC-based medical researcher who specializes in women's health and alternative medicine. She is author of Alternative Medicine: What Works. Odonian Press.

Chinese Medicine Works Very Well on Americans, Too

James S. Gordon, MD
Georgetown University School of Medicine

There's little doubt that Americans enjoy the most technologically advanced medical care in the world. Still, there's much we can learn from the Chinese system of medicine.

Scientific studies of China's ancient healing system are just beginning, and more are needed. But a growing body of research suggests that acupuncture, herbal remedies and other components of Chinese medicine do provide relief for many common ailments—even when Western medicine has failed.

Chinese medicine is helpful for everything from asthma and arthritis to migraines and menstrual cramps. It can help cure alcoholism and other addictions...and helps alleviate nausea and other side effects of cancer chemotherapy.

WHAT IS CHINESE MEDICINE

The Chinese system of medicine is hard for Westerners to accept—or even grasp. More than a collection of exotic treatments, it's a unique way of looking at the world and the body.

The language Chinese physicians use to describe symptoms, diagnoses and physical processes is the language of the natural world. It uses terms like *earth, metal* and *fire* instead of the technical jargon familiar to Western physicians and their patients.

Whereas Western medicine focuses on specific disease entities and diagnostic categories, the Chinese system views the body as both expressing and fueled by a basic animating force called *qi* (pronounced *chee*).

This vital energy circulates constantly through *meridians*—lines along the body on which the acupuncture points lie. Chinese medical therapies are concerned with restoring the balance of qi.

Everything taking place in the organs and elsewhere in the body is considered to be interconnected to the individual's psychology, the time of day, season of the year—indeed, to *all* phenomena in the natural world.

The diagnostic techniques Chinese doctors use are alien to Western physicians. *They include...*

● **Identifying imbalances in the body** by observing the patient's face and voice. For example, dark circles under the eyes might indicate a kidney ailment long before lab tests reveal it.

● **Touching and listening to the belly.**

● **Observing not just one pulse**, but 12 different pulse points along the wrist.

● **Noticing the appearance**, texture and moistness of the tongue. A trembling tongue might suggest that qi is depleted.

ACUPUNCTURE

Acupuncture has proved helpful for a variety of ailments—irritable bowel syndrome... migraines...hot flashes...addictions. It can even serve as anesthetic during surgery.

The Chinese maintain that acupuncture redistributes the flow of qi, thereby affecting the activity of organs.

In Western terms, acupuncture induces the body to release natural anti-inflammatory substances and painkilling opiates.

To find a qualified acupuncturist in your area, ask your doctor or your friends for a referral. If your state requires licensing to practice acupuncture (about half of all states do), call the state medical board to make sure the person you're considering is licensed.

HERBAL REMEDIES

The Chinese use herbs...gold and other minerals...and animal products (such as dried fish, bile and bones) to restore balance to the body.

Example I: Ginseng eases stress, boosts immune function and enhances mood.

Example II: Certain mushrooms, including *shiitake,* strengthen the immune system.

Don't start taking massive doses of an herbal remedy just because you've read about it. That can cause dangerous—perhaps fatal—side effects.

Chinese herbalists use *tiny* doses of many herbs. This strategy ensures maximum benefit while minimizing side effects.

If your doctor, acupuncturist or chiropractor is unable to recommend an herbalist, visit the nearest Asian-American neighborhood. The neighborhood pharmacist may be able to suggest someone. Many states require licensing of herbal therapists.

TAI CHI AND QI GONG

Tai chi (pronounced *tie chee*) consists of a series of smoothly connected postures. There are many different "forms," or sequences, of these movements.

Performed with rapidity, tai chi is a martial art. Done slowly and contemplatively, however, it increases energy, flexibility and mental clarity.

Tai chi instruction is offered at recreation centers, YMCAs, YWCAs and health clubs.

Qi gong (pronounced *chee gong*) is an integrated system of movement, breathing and visualization. It involves fewer movements than tai chi…and greater use of imagery.

In addition to its calming effects, qi gong seems to lower blood pressure…enhance immune function…and ease breathing in asthmatics.

Many Chinese medicine practitioners are trained in qi gong, as are a growing number of Westerners.

FOR MORE INFORMATION

●**American Foundation of Traditional Chinese Medicine**, 505 Beach St., San Francisco 94133. 415-776-0502.

●**American Association of Oriental Medicine**, 433 Front St., Catasauqua, Pennsylvania 18032. 610-266-1433.

●**American Academy of Medical Acupuncture**, 5820 Wilshire Blvd., Ste. 500, Los Angeles 90036. 800-521-2262.

●**Herb Research Foundation**, 1007 Pearl St., Ste. 200, Boulder, Colorado 80302. 800-748-2617.

James Gordon, MD, clinical professor of psychiatry and family medicine at Georgetown University School of Medicine and director of The Center for Mind–Body Medicine both in Washington, DC. He is author of *Manifesto for a New Medicine: Your Guide to Healing Partnerships and the Wise Use of Alternative Therapies*. Addison Wesley.

Fewer Pills… Fewer Bills: How to Make the Most of Alternative Medicine

James Gordon, MD
Georgetown University School of Medicine

Alternative treatments aren't so alternative anymore. Patients trying to conquer chronic pain or disease push for more thoughtful, caring ways to complement today's managed health care system.

Last year, more than 40% of Americans used alternative or nonconventional therapies —including meditation, acupuncture and herbalism.

The US government is now funding studies of various alternative therapies to determine their effectiveness and safety. Even major insurers are starting to cover certain alternative treatments.

Here are four of the most effective alternative therapies—and how to get your doctor to help you find a good practitioner…

MIND-BODY THERAPIES

Meditation and relaxation therapies, biofeedback, self-hypnosis and imagery training are useful in treating or preventing stress… high blood pressure…chronic pain…gastrointestinal disorders, such as irritable bowel syndrome…skin problems…and arthritis.

Mind-body therapies have also been shown to alleviate debilitating symptoms of cancer as well as to decrease the frequency and intensity of seizures in epileptics.

These therapies make you part of the solution. They say, *You can have a profound effect on your health. You don't have to rely solely on pills or a doctor to make you feel better.*

Although there are many books that provide instruction for these therapies, you may want to start by working with an expert, such as a psychotherapist, who can teach you self-hypnosis…or with a relaxation therapist who can help you learn meditation techniques.

More information about mind–body therapies: The Center for Mind–Body Medicine, 202-966-7338.

FOODS AND HEALTH

We are profoundly affected by what we eat and drink. Certain foods make us feel good...others undermine our sense of well-being and can severely damage our health.

Overdosing on caffeinated beverages can trigger agitation, depression or fatigue. And—caffeine can raise your blood pressure and heart rate.

Diets high in sugar have been linked to flares in inflammatory conditions like arthritis and more frequent asthma attacks in children. A low-fat, high-fiber diet seems to reduce risk of cardiovascular disease, certain cancers and other ailments. *Examples...*

● **Cruciferous vegetables like broccoli**, cabbage and brussels sprouts contain substances that may help prevent cancer.

● **Olive oil may boost good cholesterol** and lower bad cholesterol.

● **Onions can be used to combat lung problems.** They clear mucus from the lungs and bronchi and are useful in treating colds, bronchitis and asthma.

● **Three or four cloves of garlic a day**, eaten raw or slightly sautéed, may lower cholesterol and blood pressure.

Consult an MD who is knowledgeable about nutrition and herbal medicine, or seek a licensed nutritionist, registered dietitian or licensed naturopathic physician.

More information: The American Dietetic Association, 800-366-1655...American Association of Naturopathic Physicians (for brochures and referrals, write to 2366 Eastlake Ave. E., Ste. 322, Seattle 98102).

HERBS AND HEALTH

Herbs contain ingredients that have specific pharmacological effects. In Chinese medicine, herbs are used in combinations to improve the functioning of various organs. Herbal therapies are used to alleviate a wide range of ailments, from allergies to migraines. *Examples:*

● **The herb chamomile can relax you before bedtime and ease you into sleep.**

● **Peppermint improves digestion.** You can take enteric-coated capsules if you are prone to heartburn.

Herbs often take longer to work than traditional Western medicines. I advise my patients to take only the dosages prescribed by a physician or an herbalist or what is directed on the bottle label...and to expect health improvements over a period of weeks or months—not days.

Caution: Stop taking any herbal preparation if it does not help the condition you are trying to treat...or if you experience any unpleasant side effects, such as gastrointestinal discomfort, nausea, etc.

More information: The American Herbalists Guild, 303-423-8800.

ACUPUNCTURE

In acupuncture, tiny needles are inserted at various points on your body that affect the body's systems.

Acupuncture treatments have been shown to be effective in treating addictions to alcohol and drugs, depression, asthma, chronic pain and menstrual cramps. Pain relief and a sense of well-being often occur right after a treatment.

Important: If you consult an acupuncturist, find one who uses disposable needles.

More information: The American Academy of Medical Acupuncture, 800-521-2262...American Association of Oriental Medicine, 610-266-1433.

FINDING A PRACTITIONER

Don't be surprised if your physician discourages you from seeking an alternative therapy. Most doctors in the US have little or no knowledge of alternative medicine.

If your doctor maintains that a particular therapy doesn't work or that it is a waste of money, ask him/her to explain *why*. Chances are he will say, *It isn't taught in medical school, and the studies haven't been done to prove its effectiveness.* But 20 years ago, heart bypass surgery—among many other procedures—was not taught in medical schools.

The medical community is just beginning to take a cautious, but serious, look at alternative therapies and the potential benefits...and many major medical centers are creating mind–body clinics that offer alternative treatments.

If your doctor has some knowledge of various alternative therapies, he may be able to recommend a good therapist. If not, there are other ways to locate qualified helpers...

●**Ask friends for referrals.** It's likely that several people you know have seen alternative practitioners and will be able to evaluate a particular therapist's effectiveness.

●**Look for therapists** who are licensed by your state to practice a particular therapy.

●**If possible, consult an MD or DO** (doctor of osteopathy), nurse practitioner or physician's assistant who uses alternative therapies in his practice or who is knowledgeable about a range of therapies and who can refer you to a qualified practitioner.

●**If you decide to see a practitioner who specializes in alternative therapies**—such as acupuncture, nutrition or chiropractic—consider one who works with an MD or DO.

●**Beware of practitioners who say they can heal all your ills** or claim that if you sign up for a *series* of treatments you'll be cured.

●**Also avoid practitioners who tell you to stop going to MDs altogether** or that you should discontinue certain medications (like blood pressure drugs) without first recommending appropriate tests or a "safety" check by your MD.

James Gordon, MD, clinical professor of psychiatry and family medicine at Georgetown University School of Medicine and director of The Center for Mind–Body Medicine both in Washington, DC. He is author of *Manifesto for a New Medicine: Your Guide to Healing Partnerships and the Wise Use of Alternative Therapies.* Addison Wesley.

Alternative Medicine Self-Defense

If an alternative-medicine practitioner recommends a particular treatment, be sure to ask him/her detailed questions. Be suspicious if a practitioner refuses to work with your regular doctor.

To find out more about a recommended therapy: Consult such organizations as...

●**American Cancer Society** (800-227-2345).

●**Arthritis Foundation** (call 800-283-7800 for your local chapter).

●**Consumer Health Information Research Institute** (816-228-4595).

Also: Write for two free publications from the FDA—*Choosing Medical Treatments* (Item 549D)...and *Unproven Medical Treatments Lure Elderly* (Item 560D).

To order, send your name, address and item number(s) to Consumer Information Center, Pueblo, Colorado 81009.

William Jarvis, PhD, president of the National Council Against Health Fraud, Box 1276, Loma Linda, CA 92354.

Healing with Music

Just as basic first-aid items are good for treating minor physical ailments, certain types of music are good for healing the mind.

Recently, psychotherapist Carol A. Bush, author of *Healing Imagery & Music* (Rudra Press), told me that certain pieces help you "work through" difficult emotions—if you close your eyes and pay close attention to any images that the music evokes.

The piece should match your mood. Anger might call for blaring horns and pounding drums, grief for mournful strings. A piece that one person finds healing might be useless for another—it's a matter of taste.

Here are the compositions Bush finds most useful...

●*Velvet Dreams*, by Daniel Kobialka. Classical pieces done in modern style. Good when you're *weary*.

●*Swan of Tuonela*, by Sibelius. Intense, minor key music that's great when you're feeling *sad*.

●*Piano Concerto No. 2*, by Brahms. It's good when you're *angry*.

●*The Emperor Concerto*, by Beethoven. Inspirational when you're *pessimistic*. The version by Stephen Bishop Kovacevich is beautiful.

●*Prelude and Fugue in B Minor*, by Bach. Great for stopping *obsessive thoughts*.

For more information, contact the National Association for Music Therapy, 301-589-3300.

My Favorite Healing Teas

Adriane Fugh-Berman, MD

A good hot cup of tea has long been a tradition in many parts of the world. But drinking tea—whether herbal or "regular"—is far more than a ritual. It's now clear that teas have medicinal value.

Here are some of my favorite healing teas. All are prepared the same way—pour boiling water over a teaspoon of the herb in a mug, then cover and steep for five minutes.

Sweetener may be added, but it won't be necessary to disguise the taste. I've chosen only good-tasting herbs for this list...

Even ordinary tea—made from the evergreen shrub *Camellia sinensis*—may be good preventive medicine. While Americans and Europeans prefer *"black"* tea, Asians drink more *green* and *oolong* tea. It's all made from the same plant, but green tea is unfermented, oolong is partially fermented and black teas are fully fermented.

Green tea is rich in *flavonoids*, a family of antioxidants—also found in fruits, vegetables and wine—that helps prevent heart disease. Several studies have found that men who consume a lot of flavonoids have fewer heart attacks.

Because the processing needed to make black tea destroys most of the flavonoids, green tea is more beneficial. Green tea may also reduce the risk of gastrointestinal cancer.

Black and green teas also contain *tannin*, a compound that makes an effective remedy for diarrhea. In fact, tannin is an important part of the BRAT diet (**B**ananas, **R**ice, **A**pplesauce and **T**ea) prescribed for kids with diarrhea.

Roasted *rice* "tea"—or water boiled in the bottom of a pot used to cook rice—is a helpful Chinese home remedy for diarrhea.

Ginger tea is another Chinese remedy for nausea. Peel and dice a knuckle-sized piece of *fresh* ginger, then prepare as above. It's particularly tasty when sweetened with brown sugar.

Ginger tea is also a soothing drink for morning sickness, indigestion, stomach flu and many other stomach complaints.

Peppermint tea is good for stomach or intestinal cramps. In some individuals, it is helpful against heartburn—though it worsens the problem in others. That's because the muscle-relaxing effect of mint can loosen the muscular ring surrounding the esophagus at the point where it meets the stomach, making it easier for gastric acid to rise into the throat.

A better tea for stomach or intestinal cramps is made from *catnip* (another type of mint). Do *not* steal it from your cat. Most pet-store catnip is brown and old—and *not* very potent. Pick some up at a health-food store. Even dried, it should be green. Your cat will like it better, too!

Insomnia or anxiety can be controlled with several teas, including those made with *chamomile* or with *tilia* (limeflower). Tilia tea is a popular medicine in Spanish-speaking communities. Try a Latino grocery store if you cannot find it elsewhere.

Not everyone will like the taste of a tea made from *hops*, but others—especially beer drinkers—find the slightly bitter taste pleasant. Either way, hops tea is helpful in dealing with insomnia.

Chrysanthemum tea makes a delicious diuretic—good for bloating or mild hypertension. Available in stores catering to Asians, it's traditionally served with lumps of rock candy. These dissolve slowly in the cup, lasting for several refills.

Adriane Fugh-Berman, MD, a Washington, DC-based medical researcher who specializes in women's health and alternative medicine. She is author of Alternative Medicine: What Works. *Odonian Press.*

Natural Painstoppers

Norman D. Ford

Pain researchers now believe that at least 70% of all chronic pain is aggravated—even caused—by psychological stress. That includes neck, shoulder and back pain, most headaches, as well as painful conditions like ulcers, irritable bowel syndrome and rheumatoid arthritis.

Specialists have found that by addressing pain *mentally*, you can control or even stop it. *Here's how...*

TAKE A BRISK WALK

Walking briskly for 35 minutes or more, at a pace that elevates both your pulse and respiration, releases natural opiates in your brain called endorphins. These tiny molecules bind to the brain's pain receptors, blocking pain for hours.

Equally effective: Pedaling a stationary bike at a brisk pace.

CULTIVATE POSITIVE BELIEFS

Every pain has an emotional component, and it's always negative. Negative feelings such as fear, resentment, anger, hostility, guilt, envy, anxiety, frustration or disappointment all trigger your body's emergency "fight or flight" response. This reaction causes increased muscle tension, hyperventilation and suppression of the immune system.

Negative feelings are caused by negative beliefs. If you can replace these with positive beliefs, you'll move from fear-based thinking to love-based thinking, which triggers positive, relaxing emotions. *How to cultivate positive beliefs...*

●**Practice forgiveness.** Refusing to forgive someone for a perceived injustice has led to more chronic pain than any other single cause. Condemning someone else hurts you by keeping you focused on negative, angry thoughts based in the past, preventing you from relaxing in the present moment.

●**Pinpoint negative thoughts.** When you feel tense or upset, ask yourself what you were just thinking about. Were you judging, attacking or criticizing? Feeling resentful, anxious or insecure? Blaming others? Become aware of what underlying negative belief is giving rise to your negative thoughts.

●**Write down your positive beliefs as affirmations.** Substitute unconditional acceptance of others, for worry, resentment and envy.

Examples: "I see only the best in everyone, including myself"..."I let go of any resentment I feel about past events"..."I refuse to feel guilty about past mistakes."

Read through your affirmations whenever you feel under stress.

PRACTICE DEEP RELAXATION

We can only feel intense pain when our brain waves are in the beta range (14 or more waves per second). By shifting your brain into the calming alpha range (seven to 14 waves per second) and consciously releasing muscle tension, you can achieve a state of deep, pain-free relaxation.

Here's a two-part technique for achieving the alpha state...

●**Deep breathing.** Sit with your back straight and your hands in your lap. Inhale to a count of four (one count per second), filling your abdomen, then middle chest and finally your upper chest. Hold your breath for a count of four, then exhale slowly, taking all the time you want (four seconds minimum). As you exhale, smile (to relax your face muscles) and visualize tension flowing out of any muscle that feels tense. Repeat.

●**Release tension.** Lie on your back on a rug, couch or bed with a pillow under your head. Continue deep breathing. As you do, tense each muscle group in turn for six seconds, then release it. Start with your face. Move on to your neck and shoulders, chest, each arm (clench the fist and raise the arm a few inches, then drop it), each leg, the buttocks and, finally, the abdomen and back.

Finish by taking six deep, slow breaths. As you inhale, visualize sunshine flowing in through the soles of your feet and spreading through your body. As you exhale, visualize tension flowing out through your soles.

USE THERAPEUTIC IMAGERY

This technique, also called creative visualization, involves making clear mental pictures of your goal to be pain free, and reinforcing these pictures with silent, verbal suggestions. The process floods your brain with the message, overwhelming the "pain gate" at the top of your spine—the conduit through which pain impulses must pass in order to be sensed by the brain—and preventing pain impulses from reaching the brain. *Examples:*

●**Select a color and an object that seem to best suit the pain you're feeling** (e.g., imagine your headache is an orange hammer). Then choose a "pain relief" color and object that seem the most incompatible with your pain color and pain object (e.g., relief would be a bright pink pillow).

•Do the relaxation exercises described above. Once you've relaxed, focus briefly on the painful area. Visualize your pain object at the most painful point, and your pain color suffusing the painful area.

•Next, "see" your pain-relief object in your hand, radiating warmth, and visualize the object and your hand suffused with your pain-relief color. Reinforce the image with mental phrases such as, "I feel cheerful, optimistic and confident. I know my pain object and color are weak, and can be easily overwhelmed."

•Now picture your pain-relief object next to your pain object, at the point of pain, and picture your pain-relief color flowing into the area. Silently repeat the phrase, "My pain-relief color has replaced the pain color. I feel better already."

•Finally, visualize the pain object melting away and disappearing, along with the pain color. Reinforce with phrases such as, "The pain color and pain object have vanished. I feel wonderfully relaxed, and am completely liberated from pain."

TRY BIOFEEDBACK

One of the best ways to relieve migraines and tension headaches, biofeedback dilates your blood vessels, preventing the constriction of scalp arteries that triggers most headaches.

•After doing the relaxation exercises, go directly into the following imagery: Picture a pleasant, restful scene of yourself lying in the warm sun on a tropical beach. Imagine the sounds, feelings and smells, as well.

•Next, concentrate on your hands and fingers, and silently repeat these or similar phrases: "Warmth is flowing into my hands"…"My hands and fingers feel heavy, warm and relaxed"…"My hands and fingers are tingling with warmth."

•Within a few minutes, the fingers of one or both hands will begin to tingle—an indication of blood vessel dilation. As soon as you detect tingling in one hand, mentally magnify the feeling, then use your imagination to transfer it to your other hand. Silently repeat, "My hands are heavy and tingling with warmth"…

"The tingling is very strong"…"I feel calm and relaxed."

Norman D. Ford, a Texas-based health writer and exponent of a natural lifestyle of health, nutrition and fitness. He is author of a dozen health books, including *Painstoppers—The Magic of All-Natural Pain Relief.* Simon & Schuster.

Simple Ways to Prevent Pain

Try not to use your shoulder as a phone rest. At least shift from shoulder to shoulder while talking.

•Always sit up straight to avoid straining back muscles.

•Avoid heavy loads. Learn the right way to lift heavy objects when you must carry them.

•Do not read while lying down—the position stresses neck ligaments.

•Try a softer pillow—feathers are better for your neck than foam.

•Tell your doctor if any pain lasts more than 10 days.

Laura Flawn, MD, orthopedic surgeon and spine specialist practicing in Austin, TX.

Belly Breathing

James Gordon, MD
Georgetown University School of Medicine

Imagine a remedy that's effective for nearly anything that ails you. It doesn't come from your doctor or pharmacist. And it's free and available anytime.

What is this remarkable remedy? *Your breathing.*

Most of us have a bad habit of breathing shallowly, bringing air only into the upper parts of our lungs. This limits the amount of oxygen that gets into the bloodstream, starving our cells of much-needed oxygen.

A simple deep-breathing technique called *belly breathing* saturates the bloodstream with oxygen while speeding removal of carbon dioxide and other waste products.

Belly breathing twice a day for 15 minutes lowers blood pressure...relieves headache, stomachache, arthritis and other forms of pain-...alleviates allergies...improves mood... and boosts memory and concentration. It even seems to boost female fertility.

Two years ago, a high-powered lawyer came to me with crippling arthritis in his hands. I taught him how to belly breathe, and after a single session his hands, which had become claw-like, began to relax and open up.

HOW TO BELLY BREATHE

Lie on your back. Place both hands on your abdomen. Inhale deeply, until your hands begin to rise. Then slowly exhale as you watch and feel your hands fall.

Once you've mastered belly breathing while lying down, you can use the technique while sitting or even standing.

James Gordon, MD, clinical professor of psychiatry and family medicine at Georgetown University School of Medicine and director of The Center for Mind–Body Medicine both in Washington, DC. He is author of Manifesto for a New Medicine: Your Guide to Healing Partnerships and the Wise Use of Alternative Therapies. Addison Wesley.

Pain-Busting Diet

Norman D. Ford

The typical American diet, high in animal products, actually intensifies pain. *The reason:* It contains too many different types of protein, which block your body's absorption of tryptophan—the raw material used by the brain to make serotonin, the "feel-good" neurotransmitter.

To maximize tryptophan intake: Eat as little meat and poultry as you can. *The best sources of tryptophan:* Nonfat yogurt or cottage cheese, skimmed buttermilk, bananas and avocados. Stick to grains, fruits and vegetables for the rest of your diet.

Foods high in fat or sugar lower your pain threshold. Avoid them.

Other "gremlin" foods: Processed meat, bacon, coffee and caffeinated soft drinks, chocolate, liver and other organ meats, peanut butter, pickled or marinated foods, smoked fish or meat, foods containing the flavor enhancer MSG, beer and wine (especially champagne and red wines).

Should you take nutritional supplements? Studies have shown that many chronic pain sufferers have deficiencies of vitamins A, B-complex, C, D and E, as well as calcium, magnesium and zinc—perhaps because pain increases the body's metabolism of these nutrients. For this reason, I think it's prudent to take a daily multivitamin/mineral supplement.

Norman D. Ford, a Texas-based health writer and exponent of a natural lifestyle of health, nutrition and fitness. He is author of a dozen health books, including Painstoppers—The Magic of All-Natural Pain Relief. Simon & Schuster.

Acupressure: How to Use It to Relieve Common Ailments

Michael Reed Gach
Acupressure Institute of America

Many minor maladies can be relieved quickly and safely via the ancient Chinese technique of acupressure.*

Like the related technique of acupuncture, acupressure promotes healing by stimulating the *meridian points.* Those are areas of high electrical conductivity on the surface of the skin. Instead of needles, however, acupressure uses pressure from fingers and hands.

Few studies have been done on acupressure. But several studies on *acupuncture* suggest that stimulating the meridians...

- **Reduces muscular tension.**
- **Relieves pain.** It does so by stimulating the brain to release morphine-like natural painkillers called *endorphins.*

*Consult a doctor before attempting to self-treat any illness via acupressure. If you have high blood pressure, chronic back pain or another serious condition, don't press deeply or rub vigorously...and don't press on the abdomen.

●**Boosts circulation.** Greater blood flow brings nutrients to the organs and hastens excretion of toxins.

BASIC PRINCIPLES

Place your fingers, thumbs or knuckles on the chosen point. Press firmly—but not so hard as to cause pain—for one to three minutes. Then release. Breathe slowly and deeply throughout.

BACK PAIN

Put your hands on your waist, with fingers to the front of your body and thumbs in back.

Feel for the rope-like muscles about two inches on either side of the spine. Press the outer edges of these muscles with the thumbs, aiming the pressure toward the spine.

Caution: If your back pain is severe or stems from disk problems or acute injury, use care in attempting acupressure self-treatment. Discuss the matter with a holistic doctor knowledgeable about alternative therapies.

THE COMMON COLD

Place your middle fingers beside the nostrils and your index fingers next to them, at the base of the cheekbone directly below the eye.

Press upward to relieve sinus pain and congestion.

HEADACHE

With one hand, press the hollow in the back of your head at the base of the skull.

At the same time, use the thumb and forefinger of the other hand to press into the upper hollows of the eye sockets, on either side of the bridge of the nose where it meets the eyebrow ridge.

CONSTIPATION

Lie on your back with knees bent. Locate the spot three finger widths below your navel.

Using all your fingertips, press downward toward the lower vertebrae, breathing deeply.

This exercise relieves constipation and gas. Done regularly, it will prevent constipation.

MENSTRUAL PAIN

Lie face down, with your arms underneath your body. Place each fist against your groin, on the crease where the front of the torso meets the thigh. Stimulate this spot by slowly raising one leg at a time straight behind you.

INSOMNIA

Lie on your back. Place two tennis balls between your shoulder blades and spine, at about the level of the heart.

Helpful: Wrap up the tennis balls in a sock to keep them from rolling away.

With both knees bent, roll around on the balls so that they press into the area between your shoulder blades.

NAUSEA

The wrist bands that are widely sold to relieve motion sickness work by pressing two spots on the inside of the forearm.

To stimulate these spots yourself, use your thumb to press the center of the forearm, three finger widths from the wrist crease. Then press the spot two finger widths from the crease. Repeat on the other arm.

HICCUPS

Place your fingers in the indentation behind each earlobe, and press gently.

WRIST PAIN

Performed daily, the following acupressure treatment will ease pain and inflammation stemming from carpal tunnel syndrome and/or tendinitis.

Using the opposite (nonpainful) hand, stimulate two spots two-and-one-half finger widths from the wrist crease—one in the center of the outer forearm, the other in the center of the inner forearm. Press these points simultaneously by using the thumb on one point and the fingers on the other.

If stimulating these points hurts the hand applying the pressure—a common problem for people with tendinitis—press using the knuckles instead of the fingers.

Michael Reed Gach, founder and director of the Acupressure Institute of America, 1533 Shattuck Ave., Berkeley, CA 94709. He is author of Acupressure's Potent Points. *Bantam.*

The Alternative Approach To Headaches

Adriane Fugh-Berman, MD

If you gobble painkillers to control recurrent headaches, you may be contributing to your problem. Those who take aspirin, ibuprofen or naproxen on a regular basis run the risk of stomach irritation, ulcers or kidney problems. And if you stop taking painkillers after a long period of dependency, you're likely to find yourself suffering "rebound" headaches.

In many cases, the proper treatment for headache pain is not more medicine—but less. Chronic headaches can often be eliminated simply by learning to avoid the things that trigger them. Common headache triggers include psychological stress...allergies...eyestrain...oral contraceptives, nitroglycerine pills and blood pressure drugs...and certain foods.

Migraineurs, in particular, often get relief by cutting out caffeine...alcohol...the flavor enhancer *monosodium glutamate* (MSG)...and *tyramine*, an amino acid found chiefly in aged cheese, wine and chocolates.

Since trigger foods vary from person to person, it's a good idea to keep a detailed food and headache diary. Jot down all the foods you eat and the time of onset and duration of headaches you experience, and you may be able to pinpoint dietary factors in your headaches.

If you grind your teeth at night—ask your bed partner—have your dentist fit you with a plastic mouth guard. Wearing the guard at night will relieve pressure on your teeth and jaw.

What about herbal remedies? A relative of the chrysanthemum flower called *feverfew* (Tanacetum parthenium) helps prevent migraines—but not tension headaches. Ask your doctor about taking one capsule of dried leaves a day, or a fresh leaf, or a half-dropperful of tincture. Or simply take a capsule every hour at the first sign of a migraine. Feverfew capsules are available at health-food stores.

Biofeedback is effective for both tension-type headaches and migraines, although the setup for each type differs markedly...

●**Tension headache.** Biofeedback for this common form of headache—caused by muscular tension in the head and neck—involves placing electrodes on the skin above the affected muscles. The level of muscular tension is translated into aural or visual signals.

By learning to control the rate of beeps or images on a computer screen, you learn to relax the affected muscle. After a while you no longer need the guidance of the machine to get the desired effect.

●**Migraine.** Since migraines are caused by dilated blood vessels in the head, they are best treated by diverting blood flow away from the head to other parts of the body.

With the help of temperature sensors attached to the hands, you learn to warm your hands. (Warmth is achieved by increased blood flow. When blood flow to the hands is increased, blood flow to the head is reduced.) Again, once the technique is learned, the machines aren't needed.

If you cannot find a biofeedback practitioner in your area, sitting in a hot bath with an ice pack on your head should offer some relief. Doing so constricts blood vessels in the head while dilating blood vessels elsewhere.

For severe migraines, ask your doctor about the injectable drug *sumatriptan* (Imitrex). But because this drug can cause potentially deadly heart rhythm disturbances, it must be used very, very carefully.

Take your first dose in the presence of your doctor. If there are no problems, you can be taught how to self-administer the injection.

Adriane Fugh-Berman, MD, a Washington, DC-based medical researcher who specializes in women's health and alternative medicine. She is author of Alternative Medicine: What Works. *Odonian Press.*

Light Therapy to Beat Heart Disease... Insomnia... Depression...and More

George Brainard, PhD
Thomas Jefferson Medical College

Touted as a quick fix for everything from insomnia to low sex drive, melatonin has fast become one of the biggest-selling nutritional supplements in US history.

For some individuals, however, the problem is not having too *little* melatonin—but too *much*. As a result, many people may be "overdosing" on this hormone.

MELATONIN AND DAYLIGHT

Melatonin is a natural hormone produced by the pineal gland, a pea-sized gland located at the center of the brain.

Melatonin synthesis is governed by *circadian rhythms*—the daily cycles of light and darkness to which each of us is exposed.

During exposure to sunshine or another bright light, the pineal gland stops making melatonin. That makes you alert.

In dim light or darkness in the evening, melatonin production soars. That's why we tend to get sleepy at night.

Problem: For many individuals, this melatonin production cycle has been disrupted. That's because so much of our time is spent indoors, under *artificial* light.

DISTURBED RHYTHMS

If you're not exposed to enough bright light each day, circadian rhythms may fall out of whack. This phenomenon is called *circadian rhythm desynchronization.*

Circadian desynchronization can also be caused by taking melatonin supplements...by jet lag...or by working odd hours.

Heart disease is twice as prevalent among night-shift workers as among those who work a normal nine-to-five shift.

In addition to heart disease, circadian disruption has been linked to...

- Insomnia and other sleep disturbances.
- Gastrointestinal problems.
- Persistent drowsiness or fatigue.
- Poor job performance.
- Menstrual irregularities.

Light deprivation is also associated with a serious form of depression called *seasonal affective disorder* (SAD).

Psychiatrists now believe that SAD affects 10 million Americans (particularly during fall and winter, when time spent outdoors is at a minimum). Another 25 million are thought to have a milder, "subsyndromal" version of SAD called SSAD.

Recently, there have been hints that light deprivation may also be a factor in other disorders. Breast cancer, for instance, is far less prevalent near the equator—where the sun is brightest—than it is farther north or south. And breast cancer rates in the northern US are up to twice as high as rates in the South.

THE MODERN LIFESTYLE

Humans evolved to spend a great deal of time outdoors—and that meant *lots* of exposure to sunlight.

The electric light changed all that. Now our bodies are exposed mostly to artificial light... and most artificial light is far too dim to induce the pineal gland to stop making melatonin.

To stop making melatonin, the body needs about 2,500 lux (10 lux roughly equals the light shed by one candle).

Outside on a sunny day, light can reach 100,000 lux. By contrast, indoor lighting ranges from only 100 to 800 lux.

Implication: You may be working all day in light that's bright enough to see by—yet still be in "biological darkness" as far as your pineal gland is concerned.

THE NATURAL SOLUTION

Should you be worried about light deprivation? If you feel healthy, probably not. But if you are experiencing mood changes, fatigue, insomnia or daytime drowsiness, light deprivation might be an issue.

Simple solution: Get more natural sunlight. I urge my patients to take a 30-minute stroll outdoors each morning before work. Walking at lunch is good, too.

While indoors during the day, try to sit near a window in a well-lighted room.

BRIGHT LIGHT TREATMENT

Light deprivation can also be remedied with daily exposure to special artificial light (brighter than typical indoor lighting).

Typically, 30 minutes to two hours a day of "light therapy" are needed to counteract light deprivation. *Especially beneficial:* Exposure to bright light early in the morning, during the transition from sleeping to waking.

Various artificial light sources are now available. At present, most use white light—although other colors are under study.

•**Light boxes** consist of an array of fluorescent bulbs that collectively give off about 2,500 lux. The individual sits in front of the panel, about three feet away.

•**Work stations** are units angled overhead and placed closer to the eyes than a light box. They produce about 10,000 lux. They are comparable to light boxes in terms of effectiveness.

•**Light visors** are worn like a hat, with light shining onto the face. These devices permit mobility during light therapy.

•**Dawn simulators** slowly increase the light in your bedroom as you wake up. Several studies have shown this approach to be effective in relieving SAD.

For a list of light box manufacturers and treatment centers, contact the Society for Light Treatment and Biological Rhythms, 10200 W. 44 Ave., Ste. 304, Wheat Ridge, Colorado 80033.

George Brainard, PhD, professor of neurology and director of the Light Research Program at Thomas Jefferson Medical College in Philadelphia. He is a consultant for NASA and the National Institutes of Health on the behavioral aspects and therapeutic effects of light.

Hypnosis Helps Keep Lost Weight Off

A recent analysis of several weight-loss studies compared the results when only weight-loss methods were used and when they were used in conjunction with hypnosis. *Result:*

Those receiving hypnosis lost an average of 15 pounds, while those who didn't receive hypnosis lost only six. *Also:* The hypnotism group kept the pounds off for two years following the therapy, suggesting that the effectiveness of hypnotherapy may increase over time.

To find a reputable hypnotist: Contact the Society for Clinical and Experimental Hypnosis, 3905 Vicennes Rd., Ste. 304, Indianapolis 46268...or the American Society of Clinical Hypnosis, 2200 E. Devon Ave., Ste. 291, Des Plaines, Illinois 60018-4534.

Irving Kirsch, PhD, professor of psychology at the University of Connecticut, Storrs, who analyzed studies comparing obesity treatments.

Two Herbs that Calm the Colon

David Edelberg, MD
Northwestern University School of Medicine

If you're plagued by diarrhea, cramping and intestinal gas, you may have irritable bowel syndrome (IBS).

What causes IBS? Emotional stress is often involved...as are certain foods—typically dairy products, bananas, citrus fruits, eggs and grains.

Whatever its cause, IBS can be controlled with two herbs...

Peppermint relaxes smooth muscle surrounding the large intestine, curbing spasms.

During flare-ups of IBS, I tell my patients to take *enteric-coated* peppermint oil—one or two capsules three times a day between meals. If this dosage causes a burning sensation during bowel movements, lower the dose.

St. John's Wort eases anxiety by acting as a mild tranquilizer and antidepressant. It lowers levels of the brain chemical *monoamine oxidase* (MAO). High levels of MAO have been linked to depression.

The usual approach to reducing MAO levels is to take an MAO inhibitor such as Marplan, Nardil or Parnate. But foods that contain *tyramine*, including aged cheese, bananas and pepperoni, can interact with MAO inhibitors—*perhaps lethally.*

There are *no* dietary restrictions with St. John's Wort (though it can make fair-skinned individuals sensitive to sunlight). Take one capsule twice a day with meals.

Both herbs are available at health-food stores. *Cost:* About $15 for 60 peppermint capsules...$10 for 60 St. John's Wort capsules. *Mail-order source:* Arrowroot Standard Direct (800-234-8879).

David Edelberg, MD, clinical instructor at Northwestern University School of Medicine and chief of holistic and preventive medicine at Grant Hospital, both in Chicago. He is also chairman and medical director of American Holistic Centers, a group of clinics offering physician-supervised alternative medical care.

Dandelion...
The Healthful Weed

Peter Gail, PhD
Goosefoot Acres Center for Resourceful Living

The bane of gardeners, dandelions are also an herbalist's dream. Dandelions contain vitamins (more beta-carotene than carrots), minerals and dietary fiber. Eating the leaves (greens), flowers and roots can help control diabetes and high blood pressure... improve the liver's ability to cleanse the blood of impurities...and heal acne and other skin disorders.

A *coffee substitute* made of dandelions has even been shown to lower serum cholesterol. Wash dandelion roots thoroughly, then dry and cut into one-inch pieces. Roast in a 250-degree oven until they smell like coffee—usually about four hours—then grind in a coffee grinder. Steep one teaspoon in eight ounces of boiling water for five minutes.

One of the best ways to eat dandelions is in a *dandelion pizza sandwich.* Top toasted bread with pizza sauce, chopped dandelion greens and low-fat cheese. Broil until the cheese melts.

Do not pick dandelions within 75 feet of a roadway or building or from a lawn or field sprayed with chemicals.

If you'd rather not pick your own dandelions, fresh dandelion greens and commercially prepared coffee substitutes are widely available.

A roasted dandelion beverage called *Dandy-Blend* is sold at health-food stores. Call 800-697-4858 to locate a store near you.

A range of dandelion products is available from Frontier Cooperative Herbs (800-786-1388).

Peter Gail, PhD, former professor of botany at Cleveland State University, OH, and director of Goosefoot Acres Center for Resourceful Living, Box 18016, Cleveland, OH 44118. He is author of *The Dandelion Celebration: A Guide to Unexpected Cuisine.* Goosefoot Acres Press.

Dr. Larry Dossey Tells How to Reap the Healing Benefits of Prayer

Larry Dossey, MD

The role of prayer in human health has long been a taboo subject for medical researchers. Those who tried to study prayer were usually dismissed by their colleagues as crackpots—or religious zealots.

But a growing body of evidence now demonstrates that prayer and other "nonrational" activities do, indeed, affect human health.

More than 150 controlled studies have examined prayer's effects on everything from lab bacteria to humans. In approximately two-thirds of these studies, prayer did have a positive effect...

●**AIDS.** In a study conducted by San Francisco psychiatrist Dr. Elisabeth Targ, 10 AIDS patients were prayed for by community volunteers, while 10 similar patients were not prayed for. Neither patient nor doctor knew who was being prayed for.

After several months, four of the unprayed-for patients had died. No one in the prayed-for group had died. The study is now being expanded to include a larger pool of participants.

●**Heart disease.** In a study published in 1988, Dr. Randolph Byrd of the University of California at San Francisco studied the effect of prayer on 393 heart patients. In addition to the conventional medical care given to all patients in the study, half were prayed for.

The prayed-for patients had a lower death rate and required less medication than the others.

None of the prayed-for patients were placed on a ventilator. Twelve patients in the unprayed-for group were.

In another study examining the effect of prayer on heart disease, Dr. Thomas Oxman of Dartmouth Medical School studied rates of survival and complications among more than 200 bypass patients. Religious faith prior to surgery was the strongest predictor of a good postoperative course.

●**Microbial studies.** Several studies have shown that bacteria and fungi grow faster when they are prayed for. Other studies have looked at the effect of prayer on the healing rate of surgical wounds in rats. Prayed-for rats heal faster.

All told, more than 250 studies suggest a link between spirituality and health.

People who adhere to some religion—which one isn't important—live longer and show a lower incidence of almost every major disease than nonreligious people.

WHY DOES PRAYER WORK

Skeptics argue that prayer is nothing more than an elaborate placebo—that it works because the patient *expects* it to work.

Yet most studies have involved *intercessory* prayer, in which neither the patients nor the doctor knew who was being prayed for. That suggests that something else is at work.

Even if the power of suggestion *does* play a role, shouldn't we be grateful for its effect? Shouldn't we use whatever means possible to harness it?

Some people claim that prayer's effectiveness is proof of the existence of God. Of course, that proposition cannot be proved or disproved. But reputable scientists have come up with hypotheses that are compelling even to many religious skeptics.

Physicists have shown that if two subatomic particles have been in contact and are then separated, a change in one brings an immediate, identical change in the other. That's true even if the particles are separated by a great distance.

Nobel laureate Brian Josephson of Cambridge University argues that such "nonlocal" phenomena explain human phenomena such as mental telepathy… and perhaps prayer.

In addition to trying to explain *why* prayer works, I believe that we should accept the evidence that it *does* work…and test its effectiveness by trying prayer in our own lives.

HOW TO PRAY

Some people view prayer as complicated or intimidating…and fear they might not be doing it *right*. In fact, there is no "right" way to pray.

Prayer need not involve words—the Trappist monk Thomas Merton said, "I pray by breathing." Nor does prayer necessarily require belief in God. Buddhists don't believe in God, yet devout Buddhists twirl prayer wheels all day. Even many agnostics pray on a regular basis, according to one survey.

Exactly what is prayer? One simple definition is *heartfelt communication with the Absolute.* Your conception of the Absolute might be God, Allah, Buddha, cosmic consciousness, the life force, the power of love—anything that engenders in you a sense of universal order, beauty or majesty.

Prayer has also been described not as something you *do* but as an *attitude* of prayerfulness—a feeling of genuineness, empathy and caring that reminds you of the interconnectedness of all creation.

If you aren't used to praying, you might start by saying a silent grace at your evening meal. Then you might try making specific requests in your prayer.

If making specific requests makes you feel foolish or arrogant, consider adopting a *nondirected* prayer strategy—asking simply, "May the best outcome happen in this situation" or "May thy will be done."

Even if you feel ambivalent about prayer, that need not stop you from praying. Accounts of the lives of the saints are full of instances in which these devout people felt like spiritual failures.

Larry Dossey, MD, former chief of staff of Humana Medical City Dallas and former cochair of the Panel on Mind/Body Interventions in the Office of Alternative Medicine at the National Institutes of Health, Bethesda, MD. Now an internist practicing in Santa Fe, NM, he is author of *Prayer Is Good Medicine.* Harper San Francisco. He is executive editor of the peer-reviewed journal *Alternative Therapies in Health and Medicine,* 101 Columbia, Aliso Viejo, CA 92656.

Index